SOUTH

M000163822

Cadogan Books plc
London House, Parkgate Road, London SW11 4NQ, UK

Distributed in North America by
The Globe Pequot Press
6 Business Park Road, PO Box 833, Old Saybrook,
Connecticut 06475–0833

Copyright © Rupert Isaacson 1995
Illustrations © Polly Loxton 1995

Book and cover design by Animage
Cover illustrations by Animage
Maps © Cadogan Guides, drawn by Thames Cartographic Ltd

Series Editors: Rachel Fielding and Vicki Ingle

Editing: Katy Martin-Doyle, Rachel Fielding, Emma Johnson, Mary Monteith
Proofreading: Anne Greenshields
DTP: Jacqueline Lewin
Indexing: Dorothy Frame
Production: Rupert Wheeler Book Production Services

A catalogue record for this book is available from the British Library
US Library of Congress Cataloging-in-Publication-Data available

ISBN 0–94–7754–71–7

Output by Bookworm Ltd, Manchester
Printed and bound in Finland by Werner Söderström Oy on Kymexcote

Typeset in Weidemann and entirely produced on Apple Macintosh with QuarkXpress,
Photoshop, Freehand and Word software

The author and publishers have made every effort to ensure the accuracy of the information in this book at the time of going to press. However, they cannot accept any
responsibility for any loss, injury or inconvenience resulting from the use of information
contained in this guide.

Please help us keep this guide up to date

We have done our best to ensure that the information in this guide is correct at the
time of going to press. But places and facilities are constantly changing, and standards
and prices in hotels and restaurants fluctuate. We would be delighted to receive any
comments concerning existing entries or omissions. Significant contri-
butions will be acknowledged in the next edition, and authors of
the best letters will receive a copy of the Cadogan Guide of
their choice.

About the Author

Rupert Isaacson is of southern African parentage and has trekked and travelled around South Africa and its neighbouring countries on foot, on horseback, hitching and driving. He has also travelled extensively throughout Europe, the USA and Canada, Africa and Eastern Europe as a freelance journalist for wildlife and conservation magazines. The illustrations for this guide have been provided by Rupert's mother, South African-born artist and sculptor Polly Loxton.

Acknowledgments

I cannot thank Art Bijl enough for lending me the laptop computer and for being so understanding about its theft. Of the many people who helped me on my travels particular thanks go to Wendy Pickstone for renting me the excellent vehicle; to Deborah, Loshini and Billie, Claudine and James for initiating me into Cape Town and to Bruce for fixing my computer; to the Metelekamps for putting up with me in Knysna; to Nikki and Co. for the 'Maritzburg stay'; to the Durban policemen who took me fishing in Kosi Bay; to his excellency Tutor Ndamase for helping me in Transkei as well as Kirk and Ben in Port St. Johns; to Johnny at Semonkong—thanks for the stay and the good horses; also to Rod de Vletter at Phopayane in Swaziland, and Darron for organizing the stay at Mkhaya; to Russel Suchet at Sani Lodge—a mine of information—and Wayne Hansen at Okonjma in Namibia, Nad and Ginger at Etosha, Udo and John at Ngepi, Penny in 'Maritzburg.

Special thanks also to Grant for being a good friend and getting me started on the guitar, to my publisher, Rachel Fielding, at Cadogan for giving me the chance and then allowing me to inflate the book to the present monster—thanks also to everyone else at Cadogan for putting up with me through the long summer and in particular to Emma Johnson for putting up with my continual changes and typos; to Katy Martin-Doyle for pulling the book around; to Jo Beall for the invaluable history lesson and to Mary Monteith for the helpful reading list and for making me get it right; to Gordon Maclean for kindly sharing his knowledge of South African birds; to Tommy P. for help on the Eastern Transvaal and Northern Cape; to my parents—to my mother for the pictures that make the book *lekker* and to my father for support, cash, proof reading, everything. Lastly, love always to Michelle.

To my parents,
Polly and Laurence

Contents

Maps

It was warming up after a freezing dawn. The sun was at its most benign, asserting itself gently over the cool air. Up here in Orange Free State's eastern highlands the day would grow warm, but not skull-shatteringly hot.

Introduction

The night's frost was melting off the grasslands which were slowly turning from summer green to autumn gold—for in South Africa it is the grass that changes colour in autumn, not the leaves of the trees. The road, a thin ribbon of yellow ochre, stretched away to the great flat-topped mountain with the sheer sides, on whose cliffs and ledges lived eagles and baboons.

A group of schoolchildren, tiny against the unbounded landscape, were walking barefoot on the road. Girls in gymslips and neat white shirts, boys in shorts, their thin brown legs dark against the yellow road, walking in a halo of fine golden dust in the fresh and waking morning. As they approached, so too did the sound of their singing. They clapped a rhythm, over which one small girl carried the main, high tune and the others backed her with instinctive harmonies. Singing like adults. You could get drunk on this highveld air, pure as spring water, cleansing the brain. The singing was the morning's only sound.

South Africa is known to most Westerners only through clichés of fear and disgust, the legacy of 20 years' media coverage of the worst aspects of white rule, officially known as *apartheid*. Brutality, violence, the injustice of white privilege and black suffering—all these were true, but were only a part of the story. The wide emptinesses of its impossibly beautiful landscapes, the gaiety of day-to-day life, the deep forest hush and the chattering of colourful birds, the twitching, fidgeting herds of antelope forever on the watch for predators, the peace of the empty coasts—these were also true, and remain so.

Few travellers are prepared for the country's immense diversity. There is a dramatic sense of scale—those mountains over there go on for hundreds of kilometres, not mere scores. That man walking by the side of the road may be walking for two days to reach his destination. Climates range from sub-alpine to sub-tropical, from desert to year-round rainfall. The flora, which incorporates the Cape Floral Kingdom—one of only six such zones on the planet—has over 5000 plant species found nowhere else in the world. Mammals include lion, leopard, elephant, buffalo, both kinds of African rhino, zebra, giraffe, wildebeest, and antelope varying in size from that of a horse to a small dog. Several hundred species of bird, including some of the world's most spectacular raptors, inhabit the forests and plains, and the catalogue of reptiles and invertebrates has still not been fully documented.

There is indigenous architecture, from graceful 18th-century Cape Dutch mansions to traditional rondavels and even houses built from tin cans or Coke bottles in the squatter camps on the outskirts of the cities. As a clue to the complexity of South Africa's human mosaic, the country has eight official languages, and local culture embraces the strong rural traditions of spirit diviners and traditional healers as well as the high-tech computerized world of Johannesburg business. In short, South Africa is a place of exceptional human and natural energy.

To travel here is to step continually from one world into another. Yet there is nothing frenetic or traumatic about this, even though the transitions in landscape and human or animal life can be startlingly abrupt. Underlying the country's well-documented strife and conflicts there is a slower pace, a greater appreciation of natural beauty and community life, than the endless pictures of violence shown in the Western media would suggest.

This may seem paradoxical, but that is just the point: South Africa is a place where the paradox is king, where conflict can exist side-by-side with a deep, almost hedonistic languor, or, more importantly, where the medieval oppression of a police state can produce an emergent enlightened democracy in the face of overwhelming odds to the contrary. Yet despite its surface Westernization, South Africa is still deeply rural, with vast stretches of wild country that have barely changed in a millennium. To savour the place, the traveller must change down a gear or two and move more slowly, notice the smell of earth, dung and wood smoke, enjoy the transition from subtle morning to hard midday and to soft evening light, not get fussed by cattle on the highway, sit and wait in the wild places for the game to come down to drink; for this is Africa, and it will not be rushed.

Guide to the Guide

Since the democratic elections of April 1994, South Africa's regional boundaries have been redrawn, erasing both the arbitrary land-partitioning of the colonial surveyors, and the racial boundaries laid out by apartheid—in particular the artificial 'tribal homelands', which have now ceased to exist. The inevitable changing of names in the aftermath of immense political upheaval is a slow process and one which is still continuing. We have tried to include the most up-to-date information wherever possible.

The chapter headings of this guide follow the new provinces, beginning in Cape Town, at the southwest corner of the lush **Western Cape Province**, heading north to the vast, arid **Northern Cape Province**, east to the mountainous **Eastern Cape Province** and **Kwa-Zulu Natal**, then up to the highveld of the **Orange Free State** (whose boundaries have not changed), on to the independent countries of **Lesotho** and **Swaziland** and finally into the newly partitioned provinces of the old Transvaal—**Gauteng** (PWV: Johannesburg,

Pretoria and surrounds), the game-rich bushveld and mountain country of the **Eastern Transvaal** and **Northern Transvaal** and the dry expanse of the **Northwest Province**.

Within the chapters, the guide follows the more traditional regional names by which South Africans know their country: for example, the Western Cape is divided into Cape Town and Peninsula, the Winelands, Overberg, West Coast, and Garden Route/Little Karoo. Similarly, the Northern Cape is divided into the Great Karoo, Namaqualand, Bushmanland and West Griqualand. This makes life easier for the traveller as almost all available tourist literature corresponds to these regional names. Again, to avoid confusion, some of the former 'homelands' boundaries have been included on the guide's regional maps, though only because they are still marked on South Africa's road maps.

All sections of the guide begin with a general introduction, a history, then a detailed look at what to see, followed by activities, where to stay, eating out, and entertainment (where appropriate). The guide is designed to cover the needs of travellers on all budgets. All places to eat and stay are divided into categories of expensive, moderate and cheap (*see* p.19), and all levels of transport are covered, from hiring your own 4x4 to hitch-hiking.

At the end of the guide, a chapter on southern African countries that adjoin South Africa's northern borders gives practical details, travelling highlights and selected accommodation.

To help the reader recognise what is on offer, various icons are used throughout the book.

 A **hiker** stands for activities—principally hiking/walking, but often riding, fishing, scuba diving, watersports, even ballooning, whatever the area has to offer.

 A **chameleon**, a sacred animal to many South Africans, often regarded as having occult properties, denotes a story or legend.

An **aloe** denotes a national or provincial park or nature reserve where flora is the main attraction.

A **bunch of grapes** denotes an area known for the quality of its wine.

A **forest tree** denotes a state forest or forested area.

Crafts indicate 'Shopping' sections and in particular good places to buy South African crafts.

A **springbok** denotes a national or provincial park, a nature reserve or game park, where wildlife is the main attraction.

A **porch** marks 'Where to Stay sections': country hotels, game lodges, B&Bs, backpackers' hostels, campsites.

 An area known for its architecture is marked by a **Cape Dutch house.**

 A **cooking pot** marks 'Eating Out' sections: good restaurants for all budgets.

Bushveld—Big Game Country: Umfolozi/Hluhluwe, Phinda, Mkuze, Tembe and Ndumo and Itala reserves in Zululand. The Transvaal lowveld—including Kruger National Park (Eastern Transvaal), The Baobab Plains of Messina (Northern Transvaal), Waterberg (especially Lapalala Wilderness, Northern Transvaal), Pilanesberg National Park (Northwest Province), Eastern Cape's Fish River Bush (east of Grahamstown—especially good are the Andries Vosloo Kudu Reserve, Double Drift Reserve and Shamwari). Swaziland lowveld—especially Mkhaya and Hlane reserves.

Coasts: Boulders (eastern Cape Peninsula—swimming with penguins), Noordehoek (western side of the Cape Peninsula: white sand, freezing water, few people), Smitswinkel Bay (eastern side of the Cape Peninsula: cliffside path leading down to warm, sheltered swimming cove), Mkambati and Coffee Bay (both on the Transkei Wild Coast: at Mkambati, waterfalls plunge over a cliff into the sea and the coastal bush is full of game; at Coffee Bay is the spectacular Hole-in-the-Wall rock formation) Hamburg (in the former Ciskei 'homeland', one of the most relaxed places on earth), Tities Bay and St Helena Bay (Cape West Coast: rocks, seals and old fisherman's cottages), De Hoop and Arniston (on the Overberg coast: De Hoop is wild coastline, zebras sometimes wander along the beach; Arniston is an old fishing village of thatch and lime cottages and prehistoric caves.

Deserts and Semi-Deserts: Namaqualand's Flowering Desert (a carpet of daisies and other flowers after the rains in mid–late September) and the Richtersveld (blasted mountains, kokerboom and halfmens succulent trees, euphorbias and the wide Orange River, sparse springbok and gemsbok populations), The Kalahari Gemsbok National Park, (dry grassland, red sand dunes and camel-thorn trees supporting huge herds of game and large predators) Augrabies Falls National Park (Karoo-scrub and sandveld supporting reasonable game populations, surrounding the thunderous falls), Rolfontein, (in the Bo-Karoo—arid but dry-vegetated Karoo landscape as it was before sheep farming, supporting large game populations, including rhino and cheetah).

Fishing: **Deep Sea**—Natal and Zululand coasts; **Sea**—Eastern Cape (especially Transkei), Garden Route coasts, Kosi Bay (northern Zululand); **Trout**—Natal Midlands, Cape, Transvaal Drakensberg and Lesotho; **Black Bass**—Garden Route.

Fynbos: De Hoop Nature Reserve (Overberg), Fernkloof Nature Reserve (Overberg), Cedarberg (Western Cape), Table Mountain, (Cape Town), Montagu Mountain Nature Reserve (Winelands, Breede River Valley), Featherbed Nature Reserve (Knysna, Garden Route), Hottentots Holland Nature Reserve (Winelands), Baviaanskloof (Little Karoo/Eastern Cape border).

Hiking: Too much choice to mention here—*see* Practical A–Z.

Mountains: The Drakensberg—Cape, Natal and Transvaal (high, wild, grassland, protea woodland and the best air in the world), The Cedarberg (rock formations and San paintings), Outeniqua/ Tsitsikamma (fynbos upland and hardwood forest), Winterberg (game and emptiness), Malutis and Thaba Putsoa (in Lesotho: peaks above 3000m, no tar roads, access by horse or foot), Amatolas (Eastern Cape: dense forest, flowers and waterfalls), Swartberg and Eastern Little Karoo (fynbos, leopards and deep gorges), the Orange Free State's Eastern Highlands (rolling grasslands, rock outcrops, San paintings), Soutpansberg (game-rich forests and fast-flowing streams above the hot bushveld of Northern Transvaal). Hiking trails run through all areas.

Tended Landscapes: The Cape Winelands vineyards and orchards beneath high mountains. The Garden Route—the green dairy-farming land between Knysna and Nature's Valley—alternate forest and emerald pastures fronting the Indian Ocean. The Natal Midlands—the rolling foothills of the Drakensberg provide lush grazing for racehorses and pure-bred cattle.

Scuba Diving: Sodwana Bay Marine National Park (Zululand)

Trail Riding: Equus (in the Waterberg, Northern Transvaal), Lesotho, Knysna Forest and Cedarberg (through Horse Trail Safaris, Cape Town).

Twitching: Knysna Forest nature reserves, Tsitsikamma National Park and Wilderness National Park (waterfowl, louries, wood hoepoes, sunbirds, fish eagles, jackal buzzard), Kruger National Park, Eastern Transvaal and Ndumo Game Reserve, Zululand (rollers, trogons, louries, secretary birds, chanting goshawks, bateleur, martial and crested eagles, drongos, bee eaters, paradise flycatchers vultures, goliath herons, storks), Kalahari, (bateleur eagle, kori bustard, ostrich, ground hornbill, sociable weavers), Northern Transvaal (sunbirds, rollers, bishop birds, crimson-breasted shrikes, most large raptors and hornbills), Winelands Mountains (sugarbirds, black eagles, egrets, mousebirds, hadeda ibis, pied kingfisher, bulbuls, guinea fowl) West Coast (jackass penguin, lesser flamingo, Cape gannet, sacred ibis and large numbers of resident and migrant waders).

Waterfalls: Hogsback (Eastern Cape), Lisbon and MacMac (Eastern Transvaal), Karkloof (Natal Midlands), Harold Porter, Nature Reserve (Overberg coast), Rainbow Gorge, Mkambati (Natal Drakensberg), Semonkong (Lesotho).

Wetlands: St Lucia (vast lake and coastal forest system in southern Zululand supporting much game, but avoid the resort at the south end of the lake), Kosi Bay and Lake Sibaya (in Tsongaland, or northern Zululand—more remote coastal forest, raffia palms, fishing owls and vultures that live on palm nuts), Wilderness National Park and Goukamma Nature Reserve (Garden Route—wooded islands in freshwater lagoons, incredible birdwatching, swimming, fishing), Nylsvlei Nature Reserve (Northern Transvaal—birdwatching and marsh woodland).

Whale Watching: Eastern Cape Peninsula beaches and Overberg Coast (especially Hermanus and De Hoop). Season from October to January.

Architecture: Cape Dutch: Central Cape Town, Constantia, Stellenbosch, Paarl, Tulbagh, Swellendam, Graaff-Reinet, the Moravian Mission Stations of the Western Cape; **Georgian British Colonial**: Grahamstown, Salem and Bathurst, in the Eastern Cape; **Victorian wrought-iron fronts**: Central Pietermartizburg, Long Street and Adderley Street in Cape Town, The 'Feather Palaces' surrounding Oudtshoorn; **Edwardian**: Union Buildings, Pretoria, Groot Schuur and the University campus, Cape Town. **Art Deco**: Greenmarket Square and St George's Mall, Cape Town, Central Johannesburg.

Caves: Kalk Bay (eastern Cape Peninsula, you need a local guide), the Echo Caves and Sudwala Caves of the Eastern Transvaal and Sterkfontein/Taung (Northwest Province—where the remains of *australopithecus africanus* were found).

Crafts: Operation Hunger, Mbabane and Manzini markets, Thohoyandou potteries and wood-carving workshops, Venda, BaSotho Hat, Sodwana Bay market, Clocolan and Lesotho weaveries, Knysna furniture and weaving factories.

Eccentricities: Nieu Bethesda, Eastern Karoo (the Owl House with its semi-occult sculptures); Calvinia Museum, Western Karoo (includes a stuffed sheep that survived wild in the local mountains and a cake tin struck by lightning); Williston Corbelled Houses, Western Karoo (beehive-shaped stone roundhouses built by early Boer settlers); Oom Martin Vogel, Aliwal North, Eastern Cape (a talented horse trainer and farmer); Happy Valley, Port Elizabeth (attractive pleasure park of 1950s high kitsch); Prince Albert Museum, Western Karoo (includes children's school exercise books from the 1930s laid out to read); Red Ox Monument, Riebeeck Wes in the Swartland, Western Cape (a statue to a particularly hardworking bovid); Wayside Lodge Farm, Northern Transvaal (a castle made of bottles, a Buddhist temple and a Polynesian village).

Music: Rustler's Valley and Splashy Fen music festivals, OFS and Natal Midlands, respectively; the Ruby in the Dust and Ruby 2, Cape Town; the Tandoor, Timewarp and the Roxy Rhythm Bar, Johannesburg,; the Moon Hotel, the Rift and Jam & Sons, Durban.

Restaurants: Ralph's (Stellenbosch), Gramadoelas (Johannesburg), Leipoldts (Johannesburg), Piekenaar's Pass (Citrusdal) De Rust Guest House (Williston), Ramola's (Cape Town), Brass Bell (Kalk Bay), Forest Hall, Hunter's Country House and Hog's Hollow (near Plettenberg Bay), O' Pescador (near Knysna), White Mischief (Pietermaritzburg), The Colony Club and Api Taki, (Durban).

Sacred Sites and Sights: Thathe Vondo Forest and Lake Fundudzi, and the Domba Dance (Venda, Northern Transvaal) , Ncwala Ceremony (Swaziland), Pirie Forest Caves (Amatolas, Eastern Cape).

San Rock Art: Denorben (Eastern Cape Drakensberg), Blyde River Canyon (Eastern Transvaal Drakensberg), Christiana (ancient rock engravings—Northwest Province), Cedarberg Mountains (Western Cape), Natal Drakensberg.

Where to Stay: The Vineyard (Cape Town, expensive), Hout Bay Forest, Cottages (western Cape Peninsula, moderate), Rustler's Valley (Orange Free State, all budgets), Phophanyane (Swaziland, expensive/moderate), Joel House (Johannesburg, expensive), Sani Lodge (Natal Drakensberg, cheap), Ganzvlei Cottage (Knysna, Garden route, expensive/moderate), Forest Hall, (east of Plettenberg Bay, expensive), Kosi Bay Cabins (northern Zululand, expensive/moderate), Old Joe's Kaia (Eastern Transvaal, expensive), Game Valley (Natal Midlands, expensive/moderate), Buzzard Mountain (Northern Transvaal, moderate), Port St John's Backpackers (cheap), Nuwerust Guest Farm (Cedarberg, moderate), Verlorenvlei (expensive/moderate), Trackers, near Blyde River, Eastern Transvaal (moderate/cheap), Semonkong Lodge, (Lesotho, all budgets).

Wine Estates: Paddagang, in Tulbagh, Boshendal, La Couronne and Haute Provence, near Franschoek, Simonsig, Delaire and Blaauwklippen, near Stellenbosch.

Travel

Getting There

Most visitors travel to South Africa by air. Direct flights from London are the cheapest, but it is possible to fly from mainland Europe at a slightly higher price. Fares from North America reflect those of standard main carrier economy flights from London, as do flights from Australia and New Zealand. Flight times from Britain are between 12 and 13 hours.

Bucket-shop deals are certainly the cheapest way to go, as long as you do not mind the inevitable restrictions that apply to such deals. London reputedly has the best value bucket-shop tickets. A more interesting way to go, however for those with the money and the time, is by overland truck across Africa, or by a self-drive safari from southern Africa. Both options are detailed below.

Travelling with an organized tour takes care of the hassle of organizing flights and accommodation. The only problem is that you are also organized during your stay in South Africa—this is both frustrating and unnecessary—the country is condusive to independent travel and, unless on a special interest tour, it is more rewarding to float around freely.

Getting There from the UK

By Air

main carriers

British Airways, ✆ (0345) 222 747, flies from London Heathrow to Johannesburg, Cape Town, and Durban. Regular economy return (1 year, fully flexible) is roughly £1200. Flights (min 2 weeks, max 3 months) range from £625 low season to £940 high season.

Air Zimbabwe, ✆ (0171) 491 0009, offers the same price for an open-ended year return, also from Heathrow and flying via Harare.

South African Airways, ✆ (0171) 312 5000, offers a 6-month return for about £680, with a slight reduction if you fly on a Tuesday or Wednesday, and a further reduction to about £600 between 19th April and 1st June. Return dates must be set on purchase. Flights are from Heathrow to Johannesburg, Cape Town and Durban.

Air Namibia, ✆ (0181) 543 2122 is the cheapest and most flexible, offering a year's open return from Heathrow to Johannesburg and Cape Town for under £600 (unless you fly over Christmas, when the fare shoots up to £700).

Olympic Airways, ✆ (0171) 409 3400 flies from Heathrow to Johannesburg via Athens. The flights range from £380 to £470. The return must be booked, but can be changed without a penalty

As a last resort, you could try **Alitalia**, ✆ (0171) 494 2092 and **El Al**, ✆ (0171) 437 9277. Neither are cheap (return fares vary between £700 and £1000 for 6-month returns) and go via Rome and Tel Aviv respectively. Return dates have to be booked on purchase. London bucket-shops have the cheapest deals for return fares of up to a year.

charter flights

Try **STA Travel** ✆ (0171) 937 9962/9971/9921 or **Trailfinders** ✆ (0171) 938 3366/3939. Otherwise scour the pages of *Time Out* and *TNT* magazine for the latest deals.

Encounter Overland, ✆ (0171) 370 6951 organizes truck journeys from London down through the Western Sahara, through west and east Africa and finally to Cape Town over about 26 weeks at a cost of about £4500. Alternatively, you can fly to Nairobi in Kenya and travel by truck to Cape Town over 10 weeks at a cost of about £2300.

Truck Africa, ✆ (0171) 731 6142 offer a cheaper deal—a 5–7 month trip down through Africa to Johannesburg for about £1500, while **Economic Expeditions** ✆ (0181) 995 7707 offer the same trip for about £100 less.

Safari Drive, ✆ (0171) 622 3891 will hire out fully equipped 4x4 vehicles from the neighbouring countries of South Africa at a cost of about £250 a week. Split between several people, this works out to be very good value and means that you can travel by the most remote, wild routes away from main roads. This highly experienced company will set out an itinerary, provide a driver, book accommodation, or make any other arrangements, just as you wish.

Getting There from Mainland Europe

By Air

Lufthansa: Frankfurt to Cape Town and Johannesburg. A 3-month return costs about £800, and a youth fare costs about £600. Fares rise over Christmas.

Air France: Paris to Cape Town and Johannesburg. An open return for one year costs around £1200, while a 3 month return with fixed dates costs about one third less.

Iberia Airlines: Cape Town and Johannesburg via London (2 separate flights), but it is not cheap—a 6 month return costs about £1000 and dates must be set on purchase.

Alitalia: Rome to Cape Town and Johannesburg and offers a 6-month return at about £1200. Return dates are flexible.

Getting There from North America

By Air

USA

South African Airways, ✆ (212) 418 3700 offer 4 flights a week from New York to Johannesburg and twice a week from Miami to Cape Town and Johannesburg. A 3-month (fixed) return about $2000 plus tax at peak season (December 15th–Jan 14th or June, July and August). An off-peak 3-month fixed return is about $1900 plus tax. A lower return fare (for one month) is offered at about $1800 peak and $1500 low season with fixed dates and a 15 day advance purchase. A 6-month return (open) is $2500 plus tax at peak season and about $2400 low season. All these flights are direct.

Taxes out of New York are roughly $40.

Continental Airlines, ✆ (718) 565 1100 offer a 3-month return to Johannesburg via London (not direct) for about $2500. Prices go down between mid-January and June1st.

Canada

Air Canada, ✆ (514) 393 3333 offers flights from Montreal to South Africa changing flights in London. A 3-month return fare (fixed) to Johannesburg costs about $CAN 2460 or $CAN 2800 from Cape Town. A 6-month return fare (open) costs about $CAN 3200 from Johannesburg and about $CAN 500 from Cape Town. Again, in both the USA and Canada, cheaper deals can be had through flight agents.

Getting There from Australia and New Zealand

By Air

Quantas Air, ✆ Sydney 957 0111 or ✆ Auckland 357 8900, offer a 6 month return from Sydney to Johannesburg for about $AUS 2499 and a 3 month return from Auckland to Johannesburg (via Sydney) for about $NZ 3700 (pex). For a return of 3 months or more you can only buy a full price ticket—about $NZ 7900. The only other cheaper way is to buy 2 separate tickets, 1 from Auckland to Sydney and 1 from Sydney to Johannesburg (prices vary with length of stay). Again, cheaper deals can also be found through flight agents.

Passports, Visas and Customs Formalities

Travellers from the United Kingdom and Ireland do not require a visa to enter South Africa but other nationalities do. They can be obtained free-of-charge from a South African embassy or high commission. Allow several weeks for it to process. Do not try to obtain a visa upon arrival as you will become involved in a long wrangle and may be turned back. (The South African bureaucracy is fearsome and not to be trifled with.)

You need a valid passport for travelling within South Africa, partly for ID, partly because you need to produce a passport to enter Lesotho and Swaziland.

South Africa's customs allowance is 400 cigarettes, 250g of tobacco and 50 cigars per person. You may bring in 1 litre of spirits, 2 litres of wine, 50ml of perfume and 250ml of eau de toilette. This is meagre, but prices for booze and smokes in South Africa are so low, and the quality so good, that there is no need to import. An airport tax of R20 is charged when you leave the country, although it can often be included in the price of the ticket.

Specialist Tour Operators in the UK

Wildlife: Cazenove & Lloyd Safaris ✆ (0171) 376 3726, Guerba ✆ (01373) 826611, Wild Africa Safaris ✆ (01372) 362288, Art of Travel ✆ (0171) 738 2038, African Journeys ✆ (01704) 20463, Wildlife Worldwide ✆ (0181) 667 9260, Naturetrek ✆ (01962) 733 051, SAR Travel,✆ (0171) 287 1133.

Botany: Temple World ✆ (0181) 940 4114.

Exploring & Trekking: Worldwide Journeys and Expeditions ✆ (0171) 381 8638). Also, contact the above numbers (under Wildlife) as many offer trekking alternatives to their more traditional safaris.

Agriculture & Forestry: Agricultural Travel Bureau ✆ (01636) 705 612.

Riding, Fishing, Hunting, Walking, Wine tours and Safaris: Abercrombie & Kent ✆ (0171) 730 9600, Grenadier Travel ✆ (01206) 549 585.

Sports: Specialized Tours ✆ (01789) 720501, Sport Abroad ✆ (01483) 225 000, Gullivers Sports Travel ✆ (01684) 293 175, Mike Burton Sports Travel ✆ (01452) 419 666.

Geology, Fossils & Ancient Sites: Temple World ✆ (0181) 940 4114.

Specialist Tour Operators in the USA

Wildlife: Boabab Safaris ✆ (800) 545 8653, Discover Tours ✆ (800) 545 8653, Safariplan ✆ (800) 358 8530, Safariworld ✆ (800) 366 0505, Born Free Safaris ✆ (800) 372 3274, Park East Tours ✆ (800) 223 6078, Safari Consultants ✆ (800) 762 4027, Safari Centre ✆ (800) 223 6046, Sue's Safaris ✆ (800) 541 2011, Wilderness Travel ✆ (800) 368 2794, Travel Beyond ✆ (800) 823 9063, Interworld African Safaris ✆ (800) 751 7960, New Horizons Safaris ✆ (800) 323 8020.

Hunting: Abercrombie & Kent ✆ (800) 323 7308.

Golf: Huddy's Golf Tours ✆ (800) 525 2230, Sun Golf Tours ✆ (800) 486 8770.

Scuba Diving: Rothschild Travel Consultants ✆ (800) 359 0747.

Getting Around

Transport to and from the Airports

South Africa's three international airports, Jan Smuts (Johannesburg/Pretoria), D. F. Malan (Cape Town) and Louis Botha Airport (Durban) all run half-hourly bus services to and from Johannesburg/Pretoria, Cape Town, and Durban respectively. Services run from 5am until 10pm. Taxis can be picked up from the drop-off points.

Airlines in South Africa

Flying within South Africa is expensive and rather defeats the object of going—to see the country. However, if you are in a hurry, the internal air service is very good. Travellers intending to fly internally can buy an **African Explorer** ticket for about R900 (£180) for up to 1 month's unlimited travel on all South African Airways internal flights (with the proviso that no sector can be covered twice in the same direction). These can be booked from the UK by calling SAA, ✆ (0171) 312 5001.

Other internal airlines are: Airlink, Flitestar, Comair, Letaba Airways, Metavia Airways, National Airlines, Regional Air and Transkei Airways.

Internal flight routes run as follows:

Cape Town to: Alexander Bay, Bloemfontein, Durban, East London, George, Kimberley, Johannesburg, Kleinzee, Port Elizabeth, Springbok, Upington and Walvis Bay. Call D.F. Malan Airport on ✆ (021) 934 0444 for flight details.

Johannesburg to: Bloemfontein, Cape Town, Durban, East London, George, Hoedspruit, Kimberley, Mmbabatho, Nelspruit, Phalaborwa, Pietermaritzburg, Pietresburg, Port Elizabeth, Richard's Bay, Skukuza (Kruger National Park), Sun City, Tzaneen, Umtata, Upington. Call Jan Smuts Airport domestic terminal on ✆ (0171) 975 9963 or Lanseria Domestic Airport on ✆ (011) 659 2750 for flight details.

Durban to: Cape Town, East London, George, Johannesburg, Nelspruit, Port Elizabeth, Richards Bay, Umtata. Call Louis Botha Airport on ✆ (031) 426 156 for flight details.

Bloemfontein to: Cape Town, Durban, East London, George, Johannesburg, Kimberley, Port Elizabeth, Upington. Call Bloemfontein Airport on ✆ (051) 481 812/473 811 for flight details.

Port Elizabeth to: Bloemfontein, Cape Town, Durban, East London, George, Johannesburg, Umtata. Call Port Elizabeth Airport on ✆ (041) 344 444 for details.

East London to: Bloemfontein, Cape Town, Durban, George, Johannesburg, Port Elizabeth, Umtata. Call East London Airport on ✆ (0431) 445 299 for flight details.

By Car

Travelling by car is by far the best way to get around South Africa. The country has always been geared towards the independent traveller—whether it was by ox-wagon, horse or cart. As a result, car hire is comparatively cheap (especially if you split the cost between several people) if you avoid the main companies—Avis, Hertz and Budget, which have offices in all major towns, as well as at the international airports—and seek out the smaller local companies. These are listed in the 'Getting Around' sections of this guide. However, if arriving in Johannesburg, Cape Town or Durban, here are the companies offering the cheapest deals.

Johannesburg: try U-Drive, ✆ 331 3735, Tempest, ✆ 397 1850, Dolphin, ✆ 885 1122, or the slightly more expensive Imperial, ✆ 337 2300

Cape Town: try Peninsula Car Hire, ✆ 591 0155, or Dolphin, ✆ 439 9696.

Durban: try Forest Drive Rent-a-Car, ✆ 582 8433 (or ✆ 423 547 after hours), Master Rent, ✆ 561 1296 or Maharani Car Hire, ✆ 370 211.

By Train

Interpax (used to be called Spoornet until 1994) is the official name for South Africa's railways. However, many people in South Africa do not know the railways by either name, and if asking for directions it is best to ask simply for the station or the train. The passenger services central information line is in Johannesburg ✆ (011) 774 4469.

South Africa's railways are not what they once were. Many of the smaller regional tracks have been closed or converted to goods services only. However, the mainline routes are still efficient and good value, with first and second class carriages having fold-down bunks and third class having no frills. Several steam-train narrow-gauge lines still operate, offering fun for the railway enthusiast, these are: The **Union Line** (offering a number of routes through different areas of the country, taking up to 2 weeks and making side trips into

Namibia and Zimbabwe, ✆ (011) 773
9238), the **Outeniqua Tchoe-
Choo** (Western Cape,
Garden Route,
✆ (0441) 738 202),
the **Neerail Line** (Eastern
Cape, Drakensberg ✆ (0551)
41362), and the **Shamwari Express** (from
Pretoria to Shamwari Game Reserve in the Eastern Cape
✆ (041) 31 1127), the **Banana Express** (Kwa-Zulu/Natal,
Southern Natal, ✆ (03931) 76443/22322) and the **Pride of
Africa** luxury
line from
Pretoria to
Cape Town
(*see* below).
For further infor-
mation on these lines, *see* the
'Activities' sections of the relevant chapters.
There are also some less regular steam services.
These are: the **Umgeni Steam Train**, ✆ (031) 764 5313 (once a month from Durban
to Botha's Hill), the **Magaliesberg Express**, ✆ (011) 888 1154 (once a month from
Jo'burg to Magaliesberg), the **Ostrich Express**, ✆ (0443) 223 540 (weekends between
Oudtshoorn and Calitzdorp) and the **Midmar Steam Railway**, ✆ (0332) 305 390 (week-
ends between Pietermaritzburg and Midmar Historic Village near Howick).

The luxury **Blue Train** from Cape Town to Johannesburg/Pretoria, ✆ (011) 773 7631
and the **Rovos/Pride of Africa** (a steam-train) from Pretoria to Cape Town and to the
Eastern Transvaal right up to Dar-es-Salaam in Tanzania), ✆ (011) 323 6052, both also
offering trips to the Victoria Falls and 5-star VIP treatment for those who can afford it.

A Note About Rail Fares

Train travel is more expensive than bus. Here is an example of fares at the time of writing.
A first class return fare for Johannesburg–Cape Town cost approx £140 per person and a
second-class return for the same route, approx £100 per person. A couple sharing a two-
person compartment (known as a coupe) for the same return fare cost £110 first class,
proving to be the best value fare. Tourists get a 25% discount on first class fares.

Similarly for a Johannesburg–Durban return ticket, the price at the time of writing was
approx £75 per person first class, £50 return second class and, again the best value deal
was a two-person coupe (for couples only) which cost £55 per person.

The coupe deal applies to all long-distance journeys.

Train Timetable

Destination	Frequency (Hrs/Mins)	Journey Time	Service
Johannesburg–Cape Town	Daily	25:25	**Trans-Karoo** express
Cape Town–Johannesburg	Daily	24:40	
Johannesburg–Durban	Daily	13:30	**Trans-Natal** express
Durban–Johannesburg	Daily	13:14	
Cape Town–Durban	Monday	6:55	**Trans-Orange** express
Durban–Cape Town	Thursday	36:45	
Johannesburg–East London	Daily	20:45	**Amatola** express
East London–Johannesburg	Daily	21:00	
Johannesburg–Port Elizabeth	Tues/Thur/Sun	20:25	**Algoa** express
Port Elizabeth–Johannesburg	Mon/Wed/Fri	20:30	
Johannesburg–Mossel Bay	Thursday	27:41	
Mossel Bay–Johannesburg	Saturday	26:53	
Johannesburg–Komatipoort	Daily	12:29	**Komati** express
Komatipoort–Johannesburg	Daily	12:09	
Kimberley–Pretoria	Daily ex Sat	11:24	
Pretoria–Kimberley	Daily ex Sat	11:25	
Johannesburg–Bulawayo	Tuesday	24:50	
Bulawayo–Johannesburg	Thursday	24:05	
Johannesburg–Harare	Friday	24:55	**Limpopo** express
Harare–Johannesburg	Sunday	25:02	

There is also the daily Marula Express which runs between Johannesburg and Louis Trichardt (and back) via Potgietersrus and Pietersburg.

By Bus

Buses are by far the most efficient means of affordable public transport in South Africa. But remember: **always book your ticket 24 hours in advance**. The bus companies insist on this, and jumping on at the last minute, or buying a ticket on the day, is, irritatingly, not allowed. Listed below are the main national services and their operators. Local office and telephone numbers are listed in this guide with the bus stations in the main cities.

There are six main bus companies offering a long distance service between all major South African towns and points in-between. These range from the relatively luxurious **Trans-Lux**, **Greyhound** and **InterCape Mainliner** companies, to the more basic, but cheaper, **Transtate**. All have offices in the bus stations of South Africa's cities (except for Transtate, *see* below). Central information numbers are listed here. Between the Western and Eastern Cape and Natal, runs another large bus company, **Garden Route InterCity** (*see* below).

Transstate operates the densest and cheapest network of bus services. You may safely assume that most small regional towns may be reached by Transstate. The company used to be for blacks only, and because of black reliance on public transport offers a more comprehensive service than the other bus companies, running services into the former 'homelands', and into Lesotho and Swaziland as well as into the more remote areas of South Africa. Be aware that for this reason, in most big towns, Transstate bus stops are usually at a slightly different location from the main bus stations, but you can get directions for the Transstate bus stops from the main bus stations. Central information lines are Johannesburg ✆ (011) 774 3333/31031, Cape Town ✆ (021) 218 6185, Durban ✆ (031) 361 762, Bloemfontein ✆ (051) 408 2262, and Port Elizabeth ✆ (041) 552 585.

InterCape Mainliner links the main towns of the Western, Northern and Eastern Cape with those of the Orange Free State and Transvaal and to Durban. Services also run between Cape Town and Windhoek in Namibia. Central information, Grahamstown ✆ (0461) 934 4400.

Greyhound links the country's cities; Cape Town, Port Elizabeth, Grahamstown, East London, Durban, Pietrmaritzburg, Bloemfontein, Kimberley, Upington, Johannesburg and Pretoria along the main highways, with stops at main towns in-between. Central information, Johannesburg ✆ (011) 403 6463.

TransLux is part of the same company as Transstate, but is, as the name suggests more luxurious and runs only between the main cities. Services are also provided up to Harare in Zimbabwe and Windhoek in Namibia. Central information, Cape Town ✆ (021) 218 3871.

Garden Route Intercity links Cape Town and Port Elizabeth via the N2 with stops at all large towns along the route. Central information, George ✆ (0441) 707993.

By Black Taxi

Black taxis (which are not black) are minibuses that ply both within towns and on long-haul jouerneys. Almost every town in the country, no matter how small, can be reached by black taxi, and they are cheaper (and sometimes faster) than buses. However, there are three potential problems in using this mode of transport: a high accident rate, mugging at the taxi ranks in towns (and where they stop in townships) and overcrowding. It would be irresponsible for this guide to recommend that anyone travel by black taxi except on well-known routes within towns. Female travellers using them for long-haul journeys may well get into trouble. They are for the adventurous only. If you want to be assured of safety, leave them alone.

For those who do want to travel by black taxi, within towns, they ply the municipal bus routes (i.e. along the main roads, stopping at bus stops), while each town has a taxi rank from which long-haul journeys leave. Ask at the local Publicity Association for directions. If you are determined to travel long distance, it is better to take a bus or train out of the city first, so as to avoid the first leg of the journey through the townships. The same goes for arriving in a city—better to get off at an outlying town and catch a train or bus in. At the time of writing fares were roughly R10 per 100km.

Hitch-hiking is also risky, but many travellers do it. As with black taxis, it is better to get beyond the township zone if hitching out of cities. On main routes, lifts can be a long time coming, as people drive fast and, on the whole have become a little scared of hitchers. Display your backpack and always carry a sign and you should get a lift eventually.

In between small towns, your chances of getting lifts are much higher, especially from local farm traffic. The only problem is that this traffic *is* local, so travelling a long distance can only be done in fits and starts. However, for getting from small towns into nature reserves and state forests, hitching can be the best way to go, if you have no transport.

A way around having to hitch for local lifts is to visit the local Publicity Association. Especially in the smaller towns, the people working there will tend to know many farmers, game rangers, foresters and other such useful people in the region. It is always worth asking if a lift can be arranged through the Publicity Association, even if you have to wait a little. South Africans are generally friendly and happy to help, and such requests usually meet with a sympathetic response.

Tour Groups

For those who cannot afford a car, getting into game reserves and remote areas can be a problem, as even the Transtate buses and black taxis limit you to towns. A way around this is to book a trip through a tour group. For game reserves this will mean sitting in the vehicle and being driven around by the guide, which can be annoying, but better than not going in at all. However, many tour groups offer packages for guided hiking, riding, canoeing and other activities that get you out into the bush, and generally involve seeing game—in some places even big game. These are listed in this guide under the 'Sports and Activities' heading of the **Practical A–Z** chapter (*see* p.26), and, where appropriate, under the 'Getting Around' and 'Activities' sections of the regional chapters.

Any company listed with a major town number will organize your transport into and out of the area you wish to visit, while companies listed with local numbers require you to reach them independently. If you ask for a pick-up from the nearest town reachable by public transport, they are often happy to oblige.

Practical A–Z

Beaches

South Africa has thousands of kilometres of coastline, most of which meet the sea in long, sandy beaches. Those on the West Coast have cold water, from the South Atlantic's Benguela Current which drifts up from the Antarctic. Those on the south and east coasts front the warm Indian Ocean, whose sub-tropical Aghulas Current supports a brightly coloured universe of marine life.

In winter (April–Sept), the West Coast beaches and the Indian Ocean beaches near Cape Town are too cold for swimming, but during the blistering summer months they provide blessed relief from the heat. From the Eastern Cape up to northern Natal, the beaches are warm enough for swimming all year.

Choosing where to go can be a problem—some stretches of coastline have been heavily developed, others have hardly been touched since the first Europeans sailed by in the late 15th century. Here is a pick of where to go and where to avoid.

Undeveloped coastline with good swimming and vehicle access can be found at: the West Coast, especially in the West Coast National Park and Eland's Bay; Smitswinkelbaai, Noordehoek, Rooi Els and Gordon's Bay near Cape Town; Arniston, De Mond and De Hoop in the Overberg; Buffalo Bay, Nature's Valley and Oyster Bay in the Garden Route; Kenton-on-Sea, Kariega and Morgan's Bay in the Eastern Cape; Hamburg in the former Ciskei; the Wild Coast in Transkei; and Umlalazi, St Lucia, Sodwana Bay and Kosi Bay in Natal. Avoid the developed resort beaches of Port Elizabeth, East London and the Natal coast from Port Edward up to Stanger. For slightly developed but still unspoilt beaches try: Camp's Bay and Boulders near Cape Town; Hermanus and Arniston in the Overberg; Still bay, Wilderness and Plettenberg Bay in the Garden Route; Port Alfred and Kidd's Beach in the Eastern Cape; Port St John's in Transkei; and Sheffield Beach, Ginigindlovu and Mtunzini in Natal.

Any developed beach will have public toilets, usually a shower, and places to eat and drink. A few in the undeveloped category will have facilities nearby, but on the whole you should bring your own supplies. Hazards when swimming away from main resorts are bad currents and sometimes sharks. Currents are worst on the West Coast and there are sharks in the Indian Ocean. These only become a danger if you swim far out, although there have been recent attacks on swimmers. Avoid swimming near river-mouths when the tide is changing.

For fishing, diving, windsurfing and other watersports, *see* under 'Sports' below.

Cafés That Aren't

An irritating aspect of travelling in South Africa is the apparent profusion of cafés in small towns. After a long, hot journey your eye will continually be caught by the word 'CAFE' printed in large letters on the side of a building, and you will think 'Ah yes, just what I need'. But a café in South Africa is almost never a café—it is a small supermarket or general store where you can get anything but a cup of coffee and a bite to eat (unless you buy instant coffee and a loaf of bread). Equally confusing and frustrating is being directed to a 'café' when you want to buy groceries.

One word of warning, however; in smart Cape Town and Johannesburg shopping malls a café *does* mean somewhere to sit down and have a cup of coffee. So do not go to these places to buy groceries.

Calendar of Events

Coon Carnival: Despite its politically incorrect name, this New Year's parade of music and street partying is staged by Cape Town's 'coloureds' for themselves, and can be riotous fun. The floats start from the Gardens area and end up at Green Point stadium. Contact CapTour ✆ (021) 418 5214 for more details.

Grahamstown Festival: South Africa's answer to the Edinburgh Festival—theatre, art, cabaret, performance art and music and a festively cultured atmosphere for two weeks every July at Grahamstown in the Eastern Cape. Contact the Grahamstown Publicity Association, ✆ (0461) 23241 for this year's dates.

Ncwala Festival and Umhlanga Dance: The Ncwala is Swaziland's sacred festival to the harvest and the monarchy—a moveable feast which usually occurs at th end of December or beginning of January. The Umhlanga is the annual dance of the Swazi unmarried maidens which takes place every August/September.(*See* also 'Swazi Culture', p.468). Contact Swaziland Tourism for details, ✆ (09268) 42531.

Manzini Trade Fair: Also in Swaziland, an agricultural fair held every August/September and worth visiting for the exhilarating *sibhaca* team dancing. (*see* 'Swazi Culture').

Domba Dance: The dance in honour of the Python God held every year between September and December in the Venda country of the Northern Transvaal (*see* 'Venda Culture' p.583). Contact Venda Tourism, ✆ (0159) 41577 for details.

Mampoer Festival: A great event in the Boer culture of the Western Transvaal—celebrating the devastating home-made peach brandy made by the local farmers. Expect some serious drunkenness and bonhomie. Held in the town of Zeerust in the Northwest Province near the border with Bostwana. Contact Brits Publicity Association for this year's dates, ✆ (01215) 9111.

Splashy Fen and Rustler's Valley Music Festivals: These two Woodstockian events held every April/May provide a showcase for the best of South Africa's incredibly diverse musical talent, ranging from township jive to hard rock, and all points in between. Splashy Fen is held on a farm just outside Underberg in the Natal Midlands, near the Drakensberg foothills. Rustler's Valley is held at the Rustler's Valley farm in the Witteberg mountains in the eastern highlands of the Orange Free State. Both locations are stunningly beautiful. Ring Frik at Rustler's Valley for exact dates, ✆ (0563) 3939.

Stellenbosch Wine Festival: Famous booze-up for the Cape's smart society, Stellenbosch's students and serious connoisseurs, held every October/November in the elegant Winelands town of Stellenbosch. Contact the Stellenbosch Publicity Association for this year's dates, ✆ (021) 8833584.

Roughly speaking, South Africa can be divided into two climatic zones—of winter rains (from the Garden Route west to the Atlantic) and of summer rains (from the Garden Route east). In general, the countryside everywhere is at its prettiest and the climate at its most temperate just after the wet season. In the west this will be from September to December, and in the east from March to June. Highlights of the post-rainy season in the west are the coastal and desert wildflowers of the West Coast and Namaqualand, and the fynbos flowers of the mountain heaths. In the east after the rains, the Transvaal lowveld and Zululand game reserves are full of animals with their young.

Winters in the west can be cold. Around Cape Town, you will need a jacket and jumper during the day, although in the Great Karoo a T-shirt is sufficient. However both areas experience bitter nights and snowfalls are not uncommon on the highest ground. Winters in the east are much milder, and characterized more by dryness than by cold. Here the coasts are still warm enough for swimming. The exception to this is the highveld, where winter days can be chilly and nights frosty. Again, mountains are colder with snow on the highest tops.

Summers everywhere are baking—dry in the west and on the highveld, but progressively more humid through the Eastern Cape, lowland Natal and the Transvaal lowveld. Avoid Durban, Zululand and the Eastern Transvaal in high summer. If hiking, riding or trekking in any region through the summer, remember always to wear a hat and to carry at least two litres of water per person. Mean temperatures are listed in the table below, but remember this is only a mean—heatwaves can send temperature soaring way above what is officially listed.

Long-term travellers to South Africa can avoid the extremes of climate by making an anti-clockwise circle over about six months, west–east, beginning at Cape Town in September and travelling through the hotter east until December, then heading into the highveld for the hottest months. Finally it is worth avoiding the school holidays when everywhere is packed.

Average maximum temperatures in degrees Celsius

	Jan	Feb	Mar	Apr	May	June	July	Aug	Sep	Oct	Nov	Dec
Cape Town	26.5	27.1	25.8	23.0	19.9	18.5	17.2	18.1	19.1	21.5	24.0	25.5
Pretoria	28.8	28.1	26.8	25.1	22.5	20.2	19.1	22.7	25.7	28.3	28.1	28.7
Johannesburg	26.3	25.6	24.3	22.1	19.1	16.5	16.4	19.8	22.8	25.0	25.3	26.1
Port Elizabeth	25.4	25.5	24.6	22.8	21.9	20.1	19.5	19.9	20.1	20.9	22.4	24.0
East London	25.2	25.6	24.7	23.5	22.6	20.9	21.0	21.3	21.4	21.6	22.8	24.0
Durban	27.2	275	26.9	25.6	24.1	22.5	22.0	22.4	22.9	23.6	24.9	26.2
Bloemfontein	29.8	28.3	26.3	22.8	19.0	16.6	16.4	19.6	22.8	25.8	27.5	29.2
Kimberley	32.5	31.0	28.4	25.3	21.2	18.6	18.5	21.8	24.6	28.3	29.9	31.7
Kruger	31.4	30.6	30.1	28.6	27.0	25.0	25.0	26.0	28.5	29.0	30.0	30.0

Dagga

Dagga (marijuana) is so widely available in South Africa that the traveller is almost bound to come across it at some point. Although its use is better tolerated here than in the West, it is an illegal substance and the tolerance does not extend to high-profile use (i.e. smoking openly in public, or taking it across 'homeland' or international borders). If you do try it, remember that African marijuana tends to be much stronger than in the West and first-timers should exercise some restraint, especially if the dagga comes from Swaziland or Transkei. Certainly you should not drive after smoking it, nor go anywhere where you need your wits about you (bus stations, taxi ranks, city centres, etc.).

Independent travellers, especially backpackers, who go into Transkei, Lesotho or Swaziland, will generally be offered dagga for sale, rather than just by other users. Be careful—the police in these areas and the South African regions surrounding them look out for hippy types who may be going in to buy. Also, be aware that many people regard whites who smoke as drop-outs worthy of little respect. Finally, if anyone offers you 'buttons' or mandrax, refuse. This is a plant extract from India that some smokers mix with dagga to produce a sledgehammer effect. It is extremely bad for the health and reduces most people to a numb, twitching wreck within seconds.

Electricity

The voltage in South Africa is 220/230 volts AC, except for in Pretoria, where it is 250 volts AC. Buy a three-point round-pin adapter for any electrical appliances you may bring.

Embassies and Consulates

International

Australia	Embassy: Pretoria, ✆ (012) 325 4315/24.
Botswana	Embassy: Pretoria, ✆ (012) 342 4670.
Canada	Embassy: Pretoria, ✆ (012) 324 3970.
France	Embassy: Pretoria, ✆ (012) 435 5564/5.
	Consulates: Johannesburg, ✆ (011) 331 3468;
	Cape Town; ✆ (021) 215 617; Durban, ✆ (031) 62214;
	Port Elizabeth, ✆ (041) 532 070/544 610;
	East London. ✆ (0431) 20483/24463.
Germany	Embassy: Pretoria, ✆ (012) 344 3854/5/6/7/8/9.
	Consulates: Johannesburg, ✆ (011) 725 1519;
	Cape Town, ✆ (021) 242 410; Durban, ✆ (031) 305 5677;
	Port Elizabeth, ✆ (041) 545 572.
Ireland	Consulate: Johannesburg, ✆ (011) 836 5869.
Italy	Embassy: Pretoria, ✆ (012) 435 541/2/3/4.
	Consulates: Johannesburg, ✆ (011) 728 1392/3 738 1309;
	Cape Town, ✆ (021) 241 256/7/8; Durban, ✆ (031) 301 4107/8
Lesotho	Consulate: Johannesburg, ✆ (011) 290 751.

Netherlands	Embassy: Pretoria, ✆ (011) 344 3910/5.
	Consulates: Cape Town, ✆ (021) 215 660/1/2/3;
	Durban, ✆ (031) 304 1770.
Namibia	Embassy: Pretoria, ✆ (012) 342 3520.
New Zealand	Embassy: Harare, ✆ (026) 34 75922 is the nearest.
Spain	Embassy: Pretoria, ✆ (012) 344 3875/6/7.
	Consulate: Cape Town, ✆ (021) 251 468.
Swaziland	Consulate: Johannesburg, ✆ (011) 299 776/7/8.
U K	Embassy: Pretoria, ✆ (012) 433 121.
	Consulates: Johannesburg, ✆ (011) 3378940/4;
	Cape Town, ✆ (021) 253 670; Durban, ✆ (031) 305 3041;
	Port Elizabeth, ✆ (041) 552 423; East London, ✆ (0431) 25521.

United States of America Embassy: Pretoria, ✆ (012) 284 266.
Consulates: Johannesburg, ✆ (011) 331 1681/3;
Cape Town, ✆ (021) 214 283; Durban, ✆ (031) 304 4734.

| Zimbabwe | Consulate: Johannesburg, ✆ (011) 838 2156/7/9. |

Former Homelands National Offices

Bophutatswana:	Pretoria, ✆ (012) 436 001/4/5/6; Johannesburg, ✆ (011) 331 6020; Klerksdorp, ✆ (018) 641 1247/8; Vryburg, ✆ (01451) 4702/4793; Welkom, ✆ (0171) 29600/29961; Bloemfontein, ✆ (051) 303 589; Kimberley, ✆ (0531) 21288/9.
Ciskei:	Pretoria, ✆ (012) 343 2334/5/6/7; Johannesburg, ✆ (011) 3393497/8; Cape Town, ✆ (021) 2150303/1; Bloemfontein, ✆ (051) 30491/303 604; Port Elizabeth, ✆ (041) 515 696; Durban, ✆ (031) 307 4572/4/5.
Transkei:	Pretoria, ✆ (012) 215 626/7/8; Johannesburg, ✆ (011) 331 5935; Durban, ✆ (031) 65748; Port Elizabeth, ✆ (041) 542 224/5; Bloemfontein, ✆ (051) 75654; Cape Town, ✆ (021) 217 582/3, 217 579; East London, ✆ (0431) 22446.
Venda:	Pretoria, ✆ (012) 344 3950/1/2/3; Johannesburg, ✆ (011) 834 3462/36; Pietersburg, ✆ (01521) 75117/8/9.

Food and Drink

Cape cuisine

Unbeknownst to most people, South Africa has its own cuisine, known as Cape cooking. A mixture of Malay, Dutch, French and German influence, the cuisine has evolved over the last 300 years and focuses on spicy variations of European dishes. (*See* p.76.)

seafood

Seafood is cheap and plentiful in South Africa, and the country is a paradise for seafood addicts. Both shellfish and line fish are easy to get hold of, whether fresh off the boat (if you are on the coast), or in restaurants. Although most shellfish are common, South African specialities are crayfish (clawless lobster) and perlamon, or abalone (mother of pearl). For distinctively South African line fish, try kingclip, snoek, red roman, cob or snapper.

venison and game

Ostrich meat is served in almost every Cape and Little Karoo restaurant, as are guinea-fowl (a much tastier bird than chicken). For venison, try the smaller antelope, whose meat is tender and aromatic from browsing on veld herbs: springbok, duiker and, reedbuck are the best. Some of the larger antelope provide good meat if hung: kudu and gemsbok steaks in a wild mushroom or fruit sauce is often on restaurant menus during the winter months. Fresh trout is common in Natal and the Eastern Transvaal. Delicacies such as crocodile tail (delicious—like a more delicate version of lobster), giraffe (very lean) and occasionally even fried marula grubs can be found at the more expensive city restaurants.

red meat: braais, Karoo mutton and poitjies

Beef and mutton are the staples of most white South African diets, many visitors are taken aback by the level of red meat consumption. The *braaivleis,* shortened to *braii,* is a weekly ritual among many white South Africans—a barbecue in which quantities of meat, sausage and beer are consumed, along with a few token vegetables like baked squash and aubergine.

While you may not want to eat as much red meat as those around you, do not leave South Africa without having tried the superb Karoo mutton, whose distinct flavour comes from the succulent semi-desert plants and herbs on which the sheep feed. Karoo mutton has very little fat and is more tender then European lamb. A variation on the *braaivleis* is the *poitjiekos* (pronounced poikykos), a Boer traditional feast in which meat, beans, squash and whatever else the cook wants are layered in a black cast-iron cooking pot (the *poitjie*) covered in water and left to cook over several hours until the water has boiled away and all the levels have been cooked. The concentration of flavours is mouth-watering, and as usual, the meal is accompanied religiously by beer drinking.

biltong and boerevors

South Africa's wind dried meats, or *biltong*, look highly inedible, coming in blackened strips that resemble an odd hybrid of leather and wood (unless you buy it ready-shredded in a supermarket). But the tough outside usually belies a moist, often still red inside that remains juicy for months. *Biltong* can be made from most meats, but the best is undoubtably from game, especially kudu and springbok. Your best bet is to ask at small town butchers for their current varieties. The only problem with *biltong* is that it can be expensive—a tragedy, as the stuff is supremely moreish. If you can find any cured with black peppercorns, buy large amounts, or you will run out and suffer withdrawal.

Less universally loved is the long, coiled *boerevors* sausage. The quality of this general-purpose protein can vary from the sublime to the inedible. Again, buy from small town butchers, many of whom stuff the meat with African veld herbs. Some *boerevors* is made with a thin strip of cheese running through the centre, which melts with cooking and adds a richer quality to the meat.

South Africa is strangely lacking in good local cheeses—strange for a country with a thriving dairy industry. Most cheese tends to be mass-produced and over-priced. However, this is slowly changing, and many local farms now sell their own cheese. The countryside around Stellenbosch, Franschoek and Paarl in the Cape Winelands now produces some very good cow's and goat's milk cheeses. Ask at the local publicity offices for directions to the farms. Otherwise, it is worth asking around when you are in a farming district—there will generally be somebody making cheese in an on-site dairy, and you may discover something wonderful.

fruit and vegetables

Fruit and vegetables are often ignored by the meat-mad South Africans. But the country is one of the world's major producers of citrus and soft fruit as well as exotic vegetables. The orchards of the Cape produce vast quantities of peaches, nectarines, apricots, eating grapes, apples, oranges and pears, all of which can be bought cheaply from the many farm stalls on the country roads. From the Eastern Cape through Natal and lowveld Transvaal, sub-tropical fruits like guava, mango, pawpaw, banana and avocado grow wild and are offered (very cheaply) for sale by women and children at most roadsides. A delicacy of the usually arid Karoo is the fruit of the prickly pear, which tastes somewhere between pineapple and pomegranate, but is sweet and does not dessicate the mouth. Ask in small town stores in the Karoo during the summer months. Watermelon and honeydews are available everywhere. Fruit preserves—jams, chutneys and bottled slices—can be bought at most craft shops and farm stalls all over the country. Around the Cape, these tend to be spicy, with a sweet and sour edge. Devotees claim that the best preserves come from the Breede River Valley in the Cape Winelands.

South Africa is one of the few countries where fresh asparagus can be grown year-round and, again, farm stalls (mostly in Natal and the Orange Free State) often sell it by the road. Butternut squash (delicious when cooked with butter and cinnamon), small star squash, courgettes, marrows and, of course, the omnipresent *mealie* (maize) form the staple vegetables of the South African diet. A vegetarian dish popular among blacks, but almost universally snubbed by whites, is *samp*, a tasty mish-mash of maize and beans that can keep you going for weeks. This can be bought from street stalls in most towns (often near the taxi ranks) for very little money. Mushrooms are always expensive, and do not thrive in South Africa's dry soils and climate, and which, apart from a few wild species in the temperate hardwood forests (*see* below) generally have to be artificially raised.

veldkos

An Afrikaans word meaning, literally, 'field cooking', *veldkos* stands for all edible produce of the wild African veld. For the initiated, this represents a universe of edible delicacies, such as Kalahari desert melons, desert truffles and a vast array of wild fruits. But for the novice the obvious choices are few: easy to identify are monkey oranges—large round fruits in a hard skin that grow on trees in Natal and the lowveld. It is best to get a field guide to edible plants (*see* **Further Reading**).

breads, pastries and puddings

These are another Boer speciality. Around the Cape, the home-baked breads are among the best baked anywhere. Try the poppyseed and sesame-seed sprinkled wagon wheels— large, round white loaves usually sold hot from the oven—or the dense, almost oily, wholemeal loaves with sunflower seeds. Almost anywhere in the country you can buy Boer pastries. The most common is the *koeksister*, a very sweet small cake rolled in a spiral shape. Fruit tarts, cheesecakes and *melktaart* are standard desserts and, in general, are of very high quality. Home-made biscuits can usually be bought from the little craft shops found in country towns.

foreign cuisine

The massive influx of Indians to South Africa from the 1860s to the 1920s brought a wealth of Indian cuisine—usually southern Indian and Sri Lankan. Durban's better Indian restaurants are rated as among the best in the world, while Cape Town and Johannesburg also have some superb Indian eateries. Less good is South Africa's Chinese food, which tends to be very bland to suit the Western palate. South Africa's many Portuguese restaurants, mostly owned by refugees from Mozambique and Angola, are much better. Specialities are deep-fried calamari steaks and chicken *peri-peri* (fried chicken in a hot, hot sauce).

Apart from these, most European cuisine is represented in South African towns. Good Greek and Italian restaurants are always easy to find in the larger towns, while in the cities you can find superb French *cordon bleu. See* 'Eating Out' sections for details.

cheap and fast food

Despite its huge choice of indigenous food, South Africa can be a hard place to find a good meal when you do not have time for a full sit-down affair in a restaurant. Most light meals are catered for by take-away shops, which can generally be found in even the smallest of towns, and which invariably serve deep-fried food or toasted sandwiches (for some reason, usually billed as 'toasted treats'). However, look for Indian-owned take-aways, and you will generally find good *bhajees* and *samosas*. In Natal, the general Indian influence has spread to all fast-food joints, resulting in a peculiarly South African phenomenon, the Bunny Chow. These are quarter, half or three-quarter (depending on the price) loaves of bread, hollowed out and filled with vegetable curry, making a meal that is its own plate. Bunny Chows are normally filling, tasty, very cheap and prevent the budget traveller from overdosing on fried food. For the cheapest eating out (i.e. not cooking for yourself), try the many take-aways you will find in even the smallest town, many of which cater mainly to black Africans, and where you can generally fill up for around R10 or less.

Prices

expensive	over R75 per head with wine.
moderate	R50–R75 per head with wine though if you choose wisely many restaurants in this category will feed you for less.
cheap:	under R50 per head with wine. Many cheap restaurants charge close to R30 per head with wine

wine

One of the world's major producers of red, white and fortified wines, South Africa is heaven to the traveller who likes to drink well for little money. A history, guide to the varieties and suggestions on wine-buying are included in the Cape Winelands chapter (*see* p.135). Suffice it to say here that South Africa's staple red is the good old Cabernet Sauvignon, while for the white, Chardonnay is the most widely successful. Table wines are produced in the Winelands region north and east of Cape Town, along the Orange River in the Northern Cape, and in some parts of the Little Karoo. Ports and sherries are mainly produced in the Breede River Valley and Little Karoo. *See* p.136–7 for more detailed information on Cape Wine.

beer

Most South African beer is mass-produced and of rather poor quality, despite the fact that hops are widely grown in the Cape. The two main producers are Castle and Lion. Both manufacturers produce a light-coloured, gassy lager that quickly fills the belly and the bladder and comes in at a standard 5 per cent alcohol. There is one decent beer, however, brewed in the Garden Route town of Knysna (called Bosuns Bitter). Many Cape pubs, and some in the main cities, serve Bosuns on tap. If none is available, and you fancy a change from Castle and Lion, try the Castle Milk Stout, a palatable, strong (usually about 6 per cent alcohol) brew that comes in bottle and tins. African home-produced beer is worth drinking. Often made from maize or sorghum, it is generally sold at country road stores in the Transvaal and Zululand. However, strains vary with the locality and you should (discreetly) ask where to buy the best at local bars.

spirits

The best Cape brandies command high prices the world over, but the cheap stuff can easily double as a sweet paint-stripper. Top of the cheap brands is Klipdift which, served with Coke, is an Afrikaner staple at *braais.* Anyone attending such an evening will be sure to know the full effects of a hot-sun hangover next day, usually after waking where they fell. A home-made spirit common on farms is *witblitz* or 'white lightning', which can be made from anything and takes your head off in true home-brew style. Another hard-hitting Afrikaner speciality is *mampoer*, a clear peach brandy or schnapps that is famed for its debilitating qualities. Those interested should attend the annual *mampoer* festival in Zeerust in the Marico district of the Northern Province.

fruit juices and soft drinks

Far more healthy, and just as good as South Africa's alcohols, are its fruit juices. South Africa has two main brands, Liquifruit and Ceres—both produced in the valley of Ceres in the Cape Winelands. Exotic juices such as apricot, mango, banana, strawberry, peach, and guava vie with the more traditional citrus varieties.

Home-made soft drinks are Afrikaner specialities, most easily found in small stores in small Karoo towns. Home-made ginger beer, lemonade and prickly pear fruit juice make the long, hot driving rewarding.

While South Africa produces Indian teas on plantations in the Eastern Transvaal, the country has two indigenous bush 'teas' that lack both tannin and caffeine, yet are more robust and tastier than most herb teas. The best-known of these is *rooibos* (meaning 'red bush' tea), which comes from a Cape mountain shrub. The town of Clanwilliam in the Cedarberg region of the Western Cape is famous for producing *rooibos*, and teabags of it can be bought in almost any shop. According to taste, *rooibos* can be served with milk, black with sugar, or with sweet fortified wine. Slightly sweeter is honeybush tea, also made from a Cape shrub. Not as dark as *rooibos*, honeybush should be brewed strong and taken black with sugar.

coffee

South Africa produces some coffee, but mostly imports it from Zimbabwe and Malawi and it is not hard to find good coffee in shops and the better city cafés. However, in small towns, and often in people's houses, good coffee is harder to track down. For some reason, many South Africans prefer cheap chicory coffee to the real thing, and take it very milky and weak with plenty of sugar. In small coffee shops, be sure to ask for your coffee brewed strong. Having said this, there are some decent instant coffees, such as Nescafé, on sale.

Geography

South Africa rises from a low-lying coast to a high central plateau via a series of mountain ranges. In general, the land gets drier as it rises, with the coastal mountains being forested and the inland plateaux turning to dry bushveld or grassland—the exception to this is the arid Cape West Coast. The series of main mountain ranges dividing the inland from the coastal zones is known as the **Great Escarpment**, and can be traced on a map as a giant U-shape from the far northwest down to the temperate southern Cape coast, eastward through the arid Great Karoo to the greener Eastern Cape and Natal and finally northeast up into Swaziland and the East and Northern Transvaal. The Great Escarpment is divided into several different ranges connected by high passes, and behind the highest section, the Natal Drakensberg, lies the remote Kingdom of Lesotho, where rise most of South Africa's perennial rivers. East of the Great Escarpment falls the **lowveld**, a sub-tropical bushveld and forest zone that continues into Mozambique via the low Lebombo mountains. West and north of the Transvaal section of the Great Escaprment lies the **highveld**, an upland plateau of wide grasslands, extending west towards the Kalahari region of the Northern Cape, through the drier grasslands of the Orange Free State into the arid Great Karoo.

Health and Insurance

Health

South Africa has a remarkably antiseptic climate, owing to the high elevation and dry air of much of the country. Only in the foetid, sub-tropical lowveld and on the Natal coast do the more typically African health problems occur. Both areas are highly **malarial**, and should not be visited without a course of tablets started at least four days before going in. **Bilharzia**—a debilitating parasite that punctures its way around the intestines—is also a problem in the rivers and lakes of these regions. The disease does not usually manifest itself until a few weeks after the parasite has entered, and symptoms are a general torpor and loss of energy with, eventually, blood in the urine. However, bilharzia is easily cured with a course of pills available from chemists in South Africa and in the West. Another parasitic problem can be **tick-bite fever**, which is like a more intense but shorter-lived version of glandular fever. This can be avoided by checking yourself for ticks after a foray into the bush and removing any you find—if you do contract it, you simply have to rest until it works its way out of your system. More serious problems are **hepatitis**, which can be avoided by vaccination and washing fruit or vegetables before eating, and **HIV/AIDS**. Although South Africa has a far lower incidence of the latter two diseases than most African countries, the risks are still clear, and appropriate precautions should be taken.

As for **vaccinations**, doctors recommend that you get shots against polio, tetanus, hepatitus, typhoid, cholera and yellow fever, though the latter three are only necessary if you intend travelling further up into Africa, or if spending time in the poorest squatter camps (for example as a voluntary or health worker). **Tap water** is safe everywhere.

Other dangers to avoid are **sun-stroke** and **dehydration** when hiking (always wear a hat and carry at least two litres of water per person) and **fatigue** from long-distance driving (the drives are always longer than you think). Danger from animals is minimal—you will seldom be close enough to big game for it to chomp you, and snakes tend to avoid people. Exceptions are the highly toxic puff and berg adders, which sometimes sun themselves on roadsides and walking trails. Spitting cobras may also sometimes sit on a trail. There are more toxic snakes, but unless you find and deliberately disturb one it is rare to be bitten. Keep a look out, and if you see one, back off and give it a wide berth. Always hike in pairs, so that if someone does get bitten, another may run for help. There is usually a grace period of a few hours during which you can find serum without terminal damage to tissue.

Insurance

One of the best deals is through **Endsleigh Insurance** ℰ (0171) 436 4451/930 8343, which offers specialized South African cover of up to a year, including travel within other southern African countries. The policy has two options—one for physical cover only (including most sports) and one extending to belongings. It is worth insuring your baggage as certain areas, notably Johannesburg, the Transkei and any of the larger cities, are known for theft. Other comprehensive cover can be found in ascending price scale through **Trailfinders** ℰ (0171) 938 3939, **Jardines** ℰ (061) 228 3742 or **American Express** ℰ (0444) 239 900. If you plan to do any specialized sports, such as scuba-diving, white-water rafting, microlighting or parascending, check whether or not you need additional cover. If going on an organized tour or safari that includes insurance, it is still as well to have your own cover for any time you spend in the country away from the tour company.

Money and Banks

Currency and Exhange Rates

The South African currency is the *rand*: 100 cents = 1 *rand*.

The great thing about South Africa for most western travellers is the exchange rate. Although not cheap by African standards, the country nonetheless offers you a chance to multiply by four or five times the amount of sterling you bring in (make the appropriate adjustment for dollars or deutschmarks) as a rand buys in South Africa only a little less than what a pound buys in Britain, and the exchange rate is generally around five *rand* to the pound, two to three rand for a US dollar and deutschmark. When exchanging, always keep your receipts, which must be produced if you change your last rands on departure.

The favourable exchange rates make available a wide range of possibilities for more specialized travel, sports and safaris, even for budget travellers. If you have an enthusiasm, such as scuba-diving, riding or simply staying in good hotels and eating well, you will be able to afford it in South Africa. Changing money on the black market is not really an option in South Africa, and does not exist as in neighbouring Zimbabwe and Mozambique. However, you may be asked to exchange money privately by people you stay with. This is illegal, but the choice is yours.

Banks

Foreign currency can only be (officially) exchanged at banks and the opening hours are archaic—between 9 and 3.30 only, with an hour off for lunch in the small town branches. Only in large towns will you find a branch open on Saturdays (usually from 8–11). Opening a bank account is a hassle too, as no South African bank will allow someone with a foreign address to have a cheque book or cashpoint card. Worse, they will insist that you queue at the enquiries desk and fill out several forms before you can draw from a teller. Irritating, but useful if you want to budget yourself, as the prospect of a trip to the bank to get more money after a blow-out does not appeal, when you know you will have to queue for at least an hour.

traveller's cheques and credit cards

The obvious way around this is through traveller's cheques (which can be exchanged at any bank and at some hotels and travel agents) and credit cards. However, as regards the latter be warned: most petrol stations, many smaller places to stay and some of the accommodation in nature reserves do not accept plastic, and you should always have at least R200 in cash on you to cover emergencies. If travelling outside South Africa, US dollars are accepted in many hotels in Zimbabwe and Zambia while *deutschmarks* are accepted in some hotels and guest farms in Namibia. The most widely accepted credit cards are: Visa, American Express, Diners Club and Mastercard.

National Parks, Nature Reserves and State Forests

South Africa's conserved areas are mostly governed by three state bodies: the National Parks Board, the Provincial Parks Board and the Ministry of Agriculture and Forestry. All charge an entrance fee, but the rules regarding each are slightly different, and it is helpful to have an idea of the bureaucracy before going in.

The **National Parks' Board** administers 12 parks with tourist facilities, and is busy establishing several others. Compared to the provincial nature reserves and game reserves, prices for entrance fees, accommodation, camping and facilities such as hiking or riding trails tend to be slightly more expensive. Trails must also be booked in advance, either by telephoning the park direct (local numbers are listed where appropriate in this guide) or by telephoning the National Parks' Board in Pretoria © (012) 343 1991. Some trails, like the 5-day, guided big game hikes in the Kruger, are very popular and must be booked several months in advance. Others, like the Springbok Trail in the Karoo National Park, can be booked with only a few days' notice.

All national parks have a shop where you can buy (overpriced) supplies—though do not rely on being able to find non-essentials such as camera film—and most have a restaurant. The Kruger even has village-sized camps with bank machines, post offices, supermarkets and several restaurants. Most national parks have petrol stations, but always fill up before you go in. Entrance gates shut at sunset and open at dawn.

The **Provincial Parks and Nature Reserves** have a head office in each province and/or former 'homeland'.These reserves are often larger than the national parks (except for the vast Kruger National Park) and in some cases cover entire mountain ranges (these are usually called Conservation Areas or Wilderness Areas). Some, like the reserves of Zululand and the Northern Transvaal, harbour big game. Others, like those of the Western Cape, are better known for their flora and landscape, yet still support significant wildlife populations. Entrance fees, accommodation and hiking/riding facilities are cheaper than in the national parks, and in general do not need to be booked more than a week in advance (accommodation and camping in the smaller, or more remote reserves can usually be had just by showing up). The exceptions are the reserves of Zululand, whose facilities get booked up in holiday periods (December/January). To book accommodation or other facilities, telephone the reserve direct (numbers listed in 'Activities' or 'Where to Stay' in each section). Most reserves close their gates at sunset, so arrive before 6pm. Larger reserves have shops and sometimes petrol, but you cannot always rely on this. Accommodation is always self-catering.

State Forests are usually in mountain areas and offer hiking trails with refuge huts or campsites. Other accommodation, petrol and supply stores are not offered. Trails sometimes have to be booked in advance (telephone numbers of state forests with hiking trails are listed in this guide), but often you can simply show up, as state forest trails are seldom fully booked. Fees for hiking and overnight huts/camping are cheaper.

National/Public Holidays

January 1	New Year's Day
April 6	Founder's Day
End March/beginning April	Good Friday
April 4	Family Day
May 1	Worker's Day
Early-mid May	Ascension Day

May 31	Republic Day
December 16	Day of Conciliation
December 25	Christmas Day
December 26	Day of Goodwill

Opening Hours

Pubs: 10am–2am daily.

Government Office Hours: 8.30am–4.30pm Mon–Fri. Many places shut for lunch between 1pm and 2pm and may not be open weekends. To be safe, always allow for tracking down tourist information on a weekday.

Liquor Stores (known as 'Bottle Stores'): 9am–6pm. Always remember to stock up on liquor before the evening. You cannot buy booze on Sundays, except in a bar.

Museums: These generally stick to business hours (8 or 9am–4 or 5pm), but there are usually variations of half an hour to an hour for each museum. Also, all but the largest close for lunch, usually between 1 and 2pm (again with minor variations), so always plan to go mid-morning or mid-afternoon. Most museums have a small entry charge of R2–R5.

Safety

cities and townships

Despite the high level of political violence, it is mainly confined to the townships of the larger cities, and the traveller will not encounter it. Crime, however, is high. Break-ins to houses are often bloody affairs, so if staying with friends make sure you double-lock all doors and windows. Mugging is a problem in downtown Johannesburg by day (by night you should not go in at all), Transkei and to a lesser extent Cape Town by night. Stay out of the townships altogether unless on a guided tour or with local residents—poverty and racial hatred make the townships a bad place to be white and alone.

hitch-hiking and black taxis

Many people will tell you never to hitch or take a black taxi. While there have been horror stories about both (attacks with hitching, high-speed crashes with black taxis), it is only fair to point out that many people continue to use both forms of transport. The risks are there, but with hitching, the number of violent incidents tends to go up and down according to the local political situation, so ask young people and youth hostel keepers for the latest information before setting out. Mugging can be a problem at the taxi-ranks for black taxis in large towns—and anyone using them for a long-haul journey should not pick them up or asked to be dropped off until outside the city, as they pass through the townships on their way in and out. As for the crashes, these are real enough at any time. Drink-driving and drivers falling asleep are the usual causes. The choice is yours.

Although conspicuous consumption of Western goods is very much a part of life for the wealthy South Africans, tourist shopping is most rewarding if confined to things African.

African crafts

There is a large range of exquisite South African crafts for sale—the most notable being South Sotho woollen rugs woven with geometric designs, Zulu bead jewellery, Xhosa woodwork and basket weaving and Venda totemic carving. These are by no means the only crafts on offer, and there is a certain amount of overlap between regions, but these can serve as a pointer. Widely available from curio shops in most cities, most African crafts are best bought from markets and workshops in the indigenous region (listed where appropriate throughout the guide). If you cannot get into the back-country, try the Operation Hunger shops in Cape Town and Johannesburg, the craft shop at the Cape Town National Art Gallery or at Durban and Johannesburg's flea markets.

Crafts such as leatherwork, printed textiles and silver and goldsmithing can be bought from independent craftspeople at any of the larger city flea markets such as Greenmarket Square in Cape Town and Bruma Lake in Johannesburg, as well as smaller markets in tourist towns like Knysna on the the Cape south coast (which is also known for furniture-making from the local hardwoods) and Grahamstown in the Eastern Cape.

precious and semi-precious stones

Semi-precious stones such as tiger's eye, amethyst, agates, malachite and a host of others are cheap in South Africa, and some very good jewellery can be found in Johannesburg's Smal Street Mall and Market Square flea market, Cape Town's Waterfront shopping arcades as well as at the better city curio shops. Gold and diamonds are also cheaper in South Africa than just about anywhere else, and addicts of costly baubles should trawl Johannesburg's jewellery shops for bargains.

traditional curios

Traditional curios such as animal skins (worked and plain), antelope horn products, stuffed animals and the like are sold at curio shops in all the big cities, as well as at the shops attached to the National Parks. Some of these, such as spotted cat skins (from culled animals), may not be exported, and all skins require a veterinary stamp for legal exporting. Make sure the curio-seller knows you are intending to take the product out of the country, so that you will not buy something that will later be confiscated.

Sports and Activities

South Africa has an outdoor climate and a largely unspoiled landscape. Sports of all kinds are popular and widely practised.

Hiking

There are few countries with better facilities for wilderness hiking. Most of South Africa's national parks, nature reserves, state forests and conservation areas have marked hiking trails of one to several days in length, with overnight huts provided containing a toilet, fresh water, firewood and (usually) cooking implements. Hikes are always booked in advance by telephone. Most are described area by area in the guide, but for general orientation here is a list of what is on offer.

coastal hiking

The best areas are: The Otter Trail of the Garden Route's Tsitsikamma National Park, the Transkei's Wild Coast Trail, and the hiking trails of St Lucia Nature Reserve and Cape Vidal State Forest in Natal.

forest hiking

South Africa's unique hardwood forests can be explored by marked trails in the Diepwalle State Forest and the Tsitsikamma National Park in the Garden Route, in the Hogsback, Katberg and Pirie forests of the former Ciskei, in the Kosi Bay nature reserve of northern Natal and in the Soutpansberg mountains of the Northern Transvaal.

hiking with game

Guided hikes through 'Big Five' country with an armed game ranger are offered in the Kruger National Park and adjacent private game reserves in the Eastern Transvaal, Umfolozi Game Reserve and Phinda Private Game Reserve in Natal. Guided hikes with large, but less dangerous game (including white rhino) can be organized at Mkuzi and Itala Game Reserves in Natal, Tsolwana and Double Drift Reserves in the former Ciskei, the Lapalala Wilderness Area in the Northern Transvaal and Tuissen die Rivieren Game Farm in the southwest Orange Free State. Although you won't see big game, there are hiking trails in Eastern Karoo's Mountain Zebra National Park and the Western Karoo's Karoo National Park offer close encounters with antelope and zebra. Both trails close during the hot summer.

mountain hiking

The best areas are: Natal, Eastern Cape and Eastern Transvaal Drakensberg, the south-western Cape ranges near Cape Town, the Cedarberg of the West Coast, the Swartberg and Baviaanskloofberg of the Little Karoo, the Tsitsikamma mountains of the Garden Route, the Amatola Mountains of the Eastern Cape, the Belelesberg of northwest Natal, western Swaziland and the Soutpansbergof the Northern Transvaal.

Riding

Although there is no shortage of private riding stables near most towns, and the larger country hotels generally offer riding, South Africa offers some really spectacular long-distance trails on good horses. Again, details are listed with the appropriate region, but here is a rough guide.

Equus Horse Trails, ✆ (011) 788 3923, in the Lapalala Wilderness Area of the Northern Transvaal, guide riders for several days through bushveld with sightings of large game. **Benghoil Horse Trails,** ✆ (04562) 2203, lead trail-rides deep into the mountains near Cathcart in the Eastern Cape. **Giant's Castle** and **Rugged Glen Nature Reserve**, in the Natal Drakensberg both offer rides of up to several days into the mountains, ✆ (0331) 471 961, while **Jacana Trails** (based in Pretoria, ✆ (012) 346 3550) offer trips into the mountains of Zululand around the town of Melmoth. Lesotho's **Government Pony Project**, **Malealea Lodge** and **Semonkong Lodge** will guide you and a pack mule into the high, remote valleys of Lesotho where machines cannot go, and where villages resemble those of the medieval Scottish Highlands (*see* **Lesotho** chapter for details). **Bokpoort,** ✆ (058) 261 181, and **Rustler's Valley Guest Farm,** ✆ (051) 923 939, in the Eastern Highlands of the Orange Free State offer superb day-trails into the Witteberg on well-schooled horses. **Horse Trail Safaris** (based in Cape Town, ✆ (021) 734 936) offer trips of up to five days into the forests near Knysna in the Garden Route, into the Cedarberg Mountains north of Cape Town, and up the beaches of the barren West Coast.

Many smaller guest farms can arrange riding, and those interested should always ask at the local hotel or publicity office, where something can generally be arranged. Always look in the 'Activities' sections of this guide, where individual riding schools will be listed.

Drag-hunting can be arranged near Cape Town through the Cape Hunt Club, and near Johannesburg through the Rand Hunt Club (contact CapTour and the Johannesburg Publicity Association for details). The hunt season is from May to September. **Polo** is also popular, particularly among the farmers of Natal and the Orange Free State. Ask at the local hotel for the local club. Also, in Afrikaans areas, a form of Dutch high-school dressage riding called ***Boereperd*** ('farmer's horse') still thrives. Horses are trained to five gaits and individual farmer/trainers will often allow competent visitors to ride their beautifully schooled beasts. Again, ask at the local hotel bar or publicity association for who's in the area.

Other Sports

ballooning

Balloon safaris over the veld can be arranged through **Lindbergh Lodge** in the Western Transvaal, an upmarket hotel and private game reserve near Wolmaranstad, west of Johannesburg (*see* **Northwest Province**, p.602). You can also go ballooning in the Winelands of the Western Cape near Paarl. Contact the **Paarl Publicity Association** (*see* **Western Cape**,p.149) for details.

camel safaris

Journeys by camel into the back-wilderness of the Orange River country in Bushmanland in the Northern Cape are offered by **Camel Runners**, ✆ (011) 403 2512 a branch of River Runners in Cape Town. Clients have the option of breaking the jouney into different sections by horse or canoe (*see* **Northern Cape**, p.278).

canoeing & white-water rafting

Long canoe trips along the Orange River through Bushmanland and the Richtersveld can be arranged through **River Runners**, ✆ (021) 762 2350, and **Felix Unite**, ✆ (021)762 6935; both have offices in Cape Town and Johannesburg (*see* **Northern Cape**, p.263). Trips down the Breede River northeast of Cape Town are aranged by **Breede River Adventures** in Cape Town, ✆ (021) 461 4537 (*see* **Western Cape**, p.172). Canoeing in the Eastern Transvaal's rapid waters is organized by several guest lodges and hotels, (*see* respective 'Activities' for details). In Natal, white-water rafting through the thunderous Tugela Gorge is arranged via **Kwa-Zukela** in Johannesburg, **Sunwal** and **Felix Unite** in Durban (*see* **Zululand**, p.416).

South Africa's mountains are riddled with caves but there are few that are generally known about and those can only be safely explored with the proper equipment and with experienced party leaders. Those interested should contact the caving clubs at the universities of Cape Town, Witwatersrand (Johannesburg), and Natal (Pietermaritzburg). Less problematic to visit are the **Kalk Bay Caves** just above the fishing village of Kalk Bay on the eastern side of the Cape Peninsula, south of Cape Town. There are no lights to mark the way, but the local publicity office (at Muizenberg) can arrange for a guide with torches.

More publicly accessible cave systems with guided tours are the **Cango Caves** of the Little Karoo, the **Sudwala** and **Echo** of the Eastern Transvaal and the **Sterkfontein Caves** in the Western Transvaal. The Cango Echo and Sudwala systems are famous for their stalactite/stalagmite formations, and the Sterkfontein caves for their pre-human fossil and early remains (*see* respective chapters for details).

climbing

The Cape Mountains and Natal and Eastern Transvaal Drakensberg are famous the world over for their climbing routes. Contact the mountaineering clubs at the universities of Cape Town, Witwatersrand and Natal to join an expedition.

fishing

Sea fishing off South Africa's coasts is very rewarding. A range of line and game fish can be hooked from beach and rock promontory. Much sought after by anglers are the large, hard-fighting snoek, kingclip and kob of the Cape coasts, the large sharks, fierce barracuda and and elusive milk-fish of the Natal Coast, and the deep-sea game species such as marlin and dorado which can be caught anywhere off the Indian Ocean coast. Tackle-hire and boat operators can be contacted through the publicity associations of the larger coastal towns.

Fresh-water fishing: fly-fishing for trout is popular in the the mountains near Cape Town and in the Eastern Cape, Natal, Lesotho and the Eastern Transvaal. The Orange and Vaal rivers offer indigenous coarse fish such as yellowfish and barbael (a South African catfish), while most dams, lakes and some streams harbour bass. Check the 'Activities' sections of all regions for details.

mountain biking

For those who have not brought their own, bikes and guided tours for the Eastern Transvaal mountains and/or recommended independent itineraries can be had via **Excitement Seekers Cycle Tours**, in Johannesburg, ✆ (011) 792 7109.

paragliding

In Cape Town, on the hill called Lion's Head, a paragliding school offers ascents leaving you hovering high over the Eastern Cape Peninsula. Contact **CapTour** in Cape Town, ✆ (021) 418 5214 to arrange a trip, or **Paragliding Africa** in Johannesburg, ✆ (011) 646 9714.

scuba diving

The Kwa-Zulu/Natal coast is reknowned for its coral reefs. **Sodwana Bay** has a permanent school offering courses for beginners and diving safaris for the experienced. Contact **Durban Unlimited** ✆ (031) 304 4934 for the latest prices at Sodwana and the other Natal locations.

skiing

South Africa is the only African country where regular (if poor quality) skiing can be had. Three places have permanent ski-lifts: above the Hex River Pass in the Western Cape, on Ben Macdhui near Rhodes in the Eastern Cape Drakensberg and at Oxbow in the Maluti Mountains of northern Lesotho. Snow deep enough for skiing is by no means to be counted on, but the 'season' is usually in June and July. To arrange skiing at Hex River, contact **CapTour** in Cape Town ✆ 418 5214/5 (*see* **Western Cape**, p.100); for skiing at Rhodes contact the **Rhodes Hotel** ✆ 04542) 21(*see* **Eastern Cape**, p.312); for skiing at Oxbow contact **Oxbow Lodge** in Lesotho (*see* **Lesotho** p.438).

watersports

Windsurfer and jet-ski hire can be arranged at most coastal resorts. Ask for details at the local publicity association.

Telephones

Public phones are cheap and easy to use. You insert your coin (a minimum of 20c) and dial. Unlike in Britain, you get several minutes of chat for your coin, and longer-distance calls are comparatively cheap.

Telephone booths are usually blue (if public) or free-standing with an orange soundproof shell if outside a post office where queues are often long. In big towns, avoid trying to make calls at lunchtime or at knocking-off time in the late afternoon, when it can take an hour for a phone to come free.

Time

South Africa is two hours ahead of GMT, one hour ahead of Europe and seven hours ahead of eastern USA standard time. There are no different time zones within South Africa.

Tourist Offices

South Africa's tourist offices are divided into a confusing number of semi-independent groups for each town. These are usually called **publicity associations**, but sometimes go by other names such as visitor's bureau, publicity office and very occasionally, tourist information. Annoying as this may be, when asking for the local tourist office, just use the words 'tourist information' and most people will know what you mean. Very small towns, such as those in the Karoo, will have tourist information in the town clerk's office, usually referred to as the 'Municipality'. To make matters worse, all tourist offices keep strictly to weekday office hours, usually close between 1 and 2pm for lunch and seldom open at weekends. So you cannot rely on them at odd times of day or in an emergency.

You can greatly simplify the tourist office problem in the Cape by visiting **CapTour** ✆ (021) 418 5214, a tourist office on Adderley Street in Cape Town that deals with all matters pertaining to the Cape. Visitors arriving in Johannesburg can get information for the whole country by visiting the **SaTour Office**, ✆ (011) 970 1669 in the arrivals hall at Jan Smuts International airport. Durban's main tourist information centre, **Durban Unlimited** ✆ (031) 304 4934), is in the Marine Arcade on Gardiner Street.

It is as well to do a bit of research before you go—particularly if you are a budget traveller looking for cheap safari outfitters and for specialist tour-operators. SaTour, the South African Tourist Board, has several offices abroad: **SaTour UK** is at 6 Alt Grove, Wimbledon, London SW19 4DZ ✆ (0181) 944 8080/6646; **SaTour USA** has a western and an eastern office, at 747 Third Avenue, 20th Floor, New York, NY 10017 ✆ (212) 838 8841 and at 9841 Airport Boulevard Suite 1524, Los Angeles CA 90045 ✆ (310) 641 8444; **SaTour Germany** is at D–6 Frankfurt, Alemannia Haus, An der Hauptwache 11, Postfach 60313 ✆ (69) 20656; **SaTour Australia & New Zealand** is at Level 6, 285 Clarence Street, Sydney NSW 2000, ✆ (02) 261 3424; **SaTour Italy** is at Via M Gonzaga 3, Milan 20123 ✆ (2) 869 3847/3856; **SaTour Netherland**s is at Parnassustoren 7E, Locatellikade 1, 1076 AZ Amsterdam ✆ (20) 664 6201; **SaTour Israel** is at Century Towers, 14th Floor, 124 Ibn Gvirol Street, Tel Aviv ✆ (93) 527 2950/2351.

VAT

Travellers can reclaim Value Added Tax on any purchase of over R250 when leaving the country by presenting the goods and receipts to the airport customs upon departure.

Where to Stay

Over the past 15 years, most South Africans have been cut off from the rest of the world by sanctions and a weak currency. The result has been a massive development of internal tourist facilities, including places to stay.

Traditionally, this has been through **chain hotels** aimed at the upper end of the market (South Africans love the word 'upmarket'), but with the recent influx of foreign travellers the market has changed to suit people used to less institutionalized travelling and those looking for bargains. The result has been a growing number of B&Bs and guest farms in the moderate price range, and of youth hostels and budget accommodation in the cheap price range. South Africa is now open to travellers on any budget, even in the remote places.

The best of the top-end, but still personally run accommodation is found through the **private game reserves** of the Transvaal and Natal, and through the old lodges and country hotels (though seldom town hotels, which tend to be scruffy) in the Cape, Orange Free State, Swaziland and Lesotho. All are listed in this guide. Some of the game lodges will also accommodate moderate and cheap budget travellers in separate facilities.

Town and country B&Bs and the chalets and rondavels of the national parks and nature reserves provide very comfortable, though generally self-catering, accommodation for travellers in the moderate price range, and can be brought into the cheap price range if shared between more than two people. All such accommodation usually comes with its own bathroom.

Backpackers' and youth hostels have sprung up everywhere in the last few years, reflecting the increased number of backpackers visiting the country as part of a general Africa tour. These are generally very well-run and offer a choice between dormitory accommodation and double rooms. Bedding is sometimes an extra, however, and you will share bathrooms. The owners of backpackers' hostels are generally good sources of local information, and will sometimes arrange pick-ups for people with no transport. Recently, some of the guest farms of the Drakensberg, Lesotho and the spectacular eastern highlands of the Orange Free State have begun to offer facilities for budget travellers, as have some near the game reserves of the Eastern Transvaal. All are listed in the guide.

Campsites can generally be found in every town and nature reserve—almost always with ablution facilities. Alternatively, you can often camp on farms, with permission from the owner, if you are far from anywhere and need to stop for the night.

Prices

This guide divides places to stay into into four price categories as follows:

luxury/very expensive: over R300 per person per night. In some cases, such as in the Eastern Transvaal private game reserves, prices may be as high as R1500 per person per night.

expensive: between R110 and R300 per person per night. The guide will generally state if a place is at the bottom or top end of this scale.

moderate: between R50 and R110 per person per night. Again, the guide usually states which end of the scale applies

cheap: under R50 per night. In the case of backpackers' dormitory accommodation and parks' board camp sites, expect to pay around R20 per person per night, self-catering. In the case of hiking huts in state forests or nature reserves, expect to pay under R20 per person per night self-catering. Those with cars can usually camp for free in the veld with prior permission from the local farmer/village headman.

Women Travellers

Unless hitching, or walking around bus/train stations and dark streets very late at night, women travellers will generally experience no more hassle for simply being female than in any Western country. However, one tip for lesbian women is important—most outward displays of homosexual affection are taboo with both white and black South Africans. Nude bathing is also not a good idea, unless in a large, mixed party and/or away from the public eye.

South African History

Prehistory to Colonial Times

Anthropologists often refer to Africa as the 'cradle of mankind', a claim based largely on the discovery of the world's earliest fossil hominid remains by Dr Richard Leaky in north-east Africa during the 1950s. Although it seems unlikely that the entire human race sprang from under a rock in northern Kenya, equally early finds from South Africa seem to support the idea of man developing his present form on the African continent. Earlier this century, the fossilized skulls of pre-human primates known as *australopithecus africanus* had been identified at two cave sites—at Sterkfontein in the Western Transvaal and at Taung in the Northern Cape—dating back an estimated one to three million years. These finds were followed by the discovery of skulls of the more advanced *homo erectus* in two other Western Transvaal cave systems—Makapansgat and Swartkrans—near modern Potgietersrus and Krugersdorp respectively. Thought to have lived 80,000–1 million years ago, *homo erectus* was a hunter-gatherer who used co-operative hunting techniques, such as driving game into ambush, and was probably the first hominid to use fire. He was not confined to Africa, but seems to have spread all over Europe and Asia, which indicates a northward drift from 'mankind's cradle'. This may account for the lack of early *homo sapiens* finds in South Africa; few sites have been dated to earlier than 20,000 years ago, and these remains bear similarities to the San (bushman) hunter-gatherers who inhabited much of southern Africa when the first whites arrived in the 15th century, and who still cling on in scattered communities in Botswana and Namibia today. Historians speculate that between 80,000–20,000 years ago people drifted north from southern Africa up to the Sahara, then green and lush. Very early rock paintings similar to those of the South African San found in the mountain ranges of the central Sahara support this view. Others claim that South Africa was populated from 100,000 years ago by the ancestors of the modern San, on the evidence of a few isolated engravings in South Africa and Namibia. What seems likely is that some *homo sapiens* stayed on in South Africa, while others forayed north, only to migrate slowly southward again around 30,000 years ago when the Sahara began to dry out.

Certainly, most of South Africa's late Stone Age finds date from around this period. Scattered across the country are caves painted in San style and strewn with the San's customized tools, such as ostrich-egg water containers. The San lived in small family groups of hunter-gatherers, moving with the timeless cycles of game migration, rain and drought; a lifestyle unchallenged until as late as about 2500 years ago, when the first groups came into contact with black pastoralists migrating down from the north, and acquired livestock. These groups were initially confined to the lush grazing country of northern Botswana, but the practice seems to have drifted south into the Cape within a few centuries, and from this point there is a recognizable division between the livestock-owning San and those who remained hunter/gatherers. The herders began calling themselves Khoi, which is thought to mean simply 'real men'. A certain amount of inter-breeding between the northern groups and the black pastoralists, combined with a milk diet, seems to have increased the stature of the Khoi and given them an appearance slightly distinct from the San, but generally the difference between Khoi and San was merely one of lifestyle.

To confuse matters, South Africa's coastal caves are known to have been inhabited as early as 40,000 years ago by *strandlopers*, non-hunting KhoiSan who lived off shellfish, seabirds and fruits from the coastal bush. When the pastoral Khoi reached the Cape coast about 2000 years ago, some abandoned or lost their stock and joined the *strandlopers*, others kept their livestock and established themselves on the good grazing lands of the coasts, while the San hunter-gatherers retreated to the wilder mountain areas.

Meanwhile, black pastoralists had also migrated south, but on an easterly path to the modern Transvaal. These small groups had iron-working skills and practised rudimentary agriculture and their slow southeastward drift became a mass migration 1000 years later (historians set the date between 1 and 300 AD). Bantu-speaking people (Bantu is a general term for southern Africa's black languages) began to fill the Northern and Western Transvaal. Skilled smiths, with a sophisticated technology of pottery, weaving and house-building, their complex religious and ritual life was based around ancestor worship, animism and, above all cattle. Any San hunters in the way of the new invaders were killed or pushed west into the Cape. By the 15th century, today's Transvaal, Natal except for the Drakensberg, Swaziland, Orange Free State and parts of the Eastern Cape were densely settled with various Bantu-speaking clans, while the Western and Northern Cape was still the range of the San hunters, Khoi herders, and, on the beaches, *strandlopers*.

Such was the picture when the first Portuguese ship rounded the Cape in 1488. Why the Portuguese deemed it necessary to brave the unknown southern Atlantic at a time when it was still thought possible to sail off the edge of the world requires explanation. The search for a sea route to the Indies was not in itself enough reason, as there were existing over-land trade routes east via the Mediterranean. The answer lay in Portugal's vulnerable position with the Spanish House of Castile, which had come to dominate the Iberian Peninsular during the 14th century. From 1383 to 1411 the Portuguese fought to keep the Castilians out of their little country and by the end of the war it became clear that only a powerful trading economy could secure Portugal the necessary foreign support to check Castile. It fell to the Portuguese King Jao (John) I to act.

A great fleet was prepared to attack the Moorish city of Cueta, in modern Morocco, which had grown rich on the gold trade north across the Sahara from West Africa. The gamble paid off—Cueta fell in 1415 and turned out to be far richer than the Portuguese could have hoped. Portugal suddenly found herself mistress of the trans-Saharan gold route from Guinea and the Congo—a wealth of gold that gave credence to an old European legend of a Christian king, called Prester John, who was supposed to live somewhere down in Africa in a kingdom incomparably rich in gold. The legend was partly substantiated when Portuguese explorers reached Christian Ethiopia much later in the century—though there was no sign of any Prester John—and from the 1430s, Portuguese ships searching for both this mythical king and, more practically, for a trade route round to the East, began sailing ever southward along Africa's west coast. In 1488, the explorer Bartholomieu Dias sailed around the Cape of Good Hope and put ashore at modern Mossel Bay, where he attempted to bargain with the local Khoi for cattle. However, the Europeans and the Khoi misunderstood each other's intentions and fighting broke out.

It was not until 1498 that the Portuguese sailed that way again, this time under Vasco da Gama, who also put in at Mossel Bay. He stayed two weeks but, after successfully bartering for cattle, his sailors also fell foul of the locals and after a brief skirmish, da Gama fired a cannon and broke up the party. From then on, the Portuguese traders regarded the South African coast, with its bad currents, frequent storms, and dangerous locals, as not worth the trouble of settling. The Cape's only importance lay in its marking the halfway point from Europe to the East Indies.

During the 16th century other Europeans learned of the route to the Indies and from around 1580, Dutch, English and French captains began rounding the Cape on a regular basis. Some stopped to barter with the Khoi; cattle and sheep were acquired for metals, particularly copper wire, which the Khoi fashioned into fine jewellery. The Khoi/European relationship became friendly and familiar. The white men never stayed, but brought trade, while the bartered livestock and fresh water came as blessed relief to the mariners who had already been at sea for months.

In 1608, to impress the South African natives with European splendour (and no doubt to impress the Europeans with a genuine 'savage'), a Dutch captain took a Khoi man to London and Holland, then returned him to his home on the Cape Peninsula with instructions to set up a regular cattle supply for Dutch ships at Table Bay. And again, in 1631, the Dutch took a Khoi chief (whom they dubbed Harry) to Java, where the newly formed Dutch East India Company was setting up trading stations, and trained him in Dutch and English. Harry was also returned to the Cape, and was persuaded to act as interpreter, post-master and cattle supplier for Dutch and English. Other shipping captains began to use large trees and boulders visible all the way along the Cape coast as 'post offices' where messages for colleagues could be left.

But in 1647 the *Haarlem*, a Dutch ship, was wrecked off Table Bay. The survivors built a makeshift fort and waited for rescue. A timely coincidence—the Dutch East India Company now had an established East Indies trade and was looking for a permanent supply stop for its ships. In 1650 it sent a commission to look into the possibilities of Table Bay. The leader, Jan Van Riebeeck—the ship's doctor on the rescue team that succoured *Haarlem* survivors— saw a chance to advance his career. Despite the Cape's frequent storms and cross-currents, Van Riebeeck waxed enthusiastic about the area's potential. By 1652 he had persuaded his employers to the take same view, and was sent to Table Bay with about 100 men and women to set up the supply station. A strong fort was erected and Cape Town was born.

The Dutch Colonial Era

The Dutch East India Company was formed from a syndicate of powerful merchants from Holland's major towns. They acted with the sanction of their government, but were expected to fund their own adventures. Modelled on the medieval trading oligarchies of the Mediterranean, the Dutch East India Company's success inspired several other northern European powers, especially Britain, to form similar companies, two of which (the London Company of Adventurers, later the Hudson Bay Company, and the British East India Company) were to attain unprecedented commercial power in the northern hemisphere. Commerce, rather than conquest, was their motto. Although such companies all eventually became masters of huge foreign territories, empire-building was never the original idea, for conquest was expensive. The Dutch Cape Colony was thus never meant to extend into the interior.

To this end, the first colonists were expressly forbidden to enslave the locals, trade with them on anything other than Company business, or settle outside the confines of the fort. However, cattle-buying expeditions into Namaqualand in the northwest and the Hottentots' Holland (today's Winelands, *see* p.156) gave the colonists a glimpse of the great sub-continent's potential and from the 1670s settlers began to mark out farms around the Cape Peninsula, despite the protests of the Company. In the 1680s the adventurous governor Simon Van der Stel sent mineral prospecting and cattle-buying expeditions up the West Coast into Namaqualand, and beyond the Hottentots' Holland Mountains, where he founded the colony's second town, Stellenbosch. The same decade saw the arrival of settlers from France (Hugenot refugees) and Germany, who set up extensive European-style wine and dairy farms, and the Dutch Cape Colony was officially extended over the entire Western Cape. Individual trade with the Khoi was finally allowed and land was bought cheaply from the Khoi for iron, brass and copper.

Many traditional histories assert that the Khoi were easily persuaded to work for the Europeans and that they became an underclass by default of a natural fecklessness. But this was not the case. Resistance was often fierce. Many Khoi resented the white men's steady expansion into the hinterland, while others took to raiding both the settlers and the neighbouring Khoi who had grown rich from the cattle trade. From the 1670s the Company found itself having to send troops on regular seasonal campaigns against hostile Cape Khoi. Having committed itself to the colony, the Company was now obliged to uphold it, spending money on a series of inconclusive wars that resulted in a gradual northward and eastward extension of the colony's border—dragging the Company into a reluctant but steady cycle of conquest of the interior. At the same time, the Company began to lose control over its own settlers. Many adopted the Khoi's pastoral lifestyle and set off with wagons and flocks to live as they pleased. This new class of settler became known as 'trekboer' (meaning literally, 'travelling farmer')—a freebooting, independent bunch who grazed their sheep, hunted game and subjugated the local Khoi and San as they wished. By 1700 the trekboers had pushed to the north and east, as far away from European authority as they could.

Smallpox, brought ashore in soiled linen at Cape Town, erupted among the Cape Khoi in 1713. Thereafter, regular epidemics ruled out concerted resistance to the Dutch and, while wars flared between Khoi and settlers until the 1750s, the Khoi rapidly lost their territories.

Still technically forbidden to own Khoi slaves, the trekboers began to force them into servitude. The Company had brought out slaves from Batavia—Dutch Indonesia—and West Africa from the early 1650s to pre-empt the colonists' obvious temptation to enslave the Khoi, but the plan had never really worked. Buying slaves was beyond the means of most colonists and their care involved cost. To the trekboers, far from Company authority, the Khoi seemed a gift from nature; scattered into already feuding tribes, they presented no united front against white settlement and could be subdued with firearms.

South Africa's 18th-century trekboers began to use the Khoi as slaves in all but name, treating them with a careless brutality that became legendary among liberals back in Europe, and setting a precedent for violence from employer to hired hand that persisted to modern times.

By the 1760s the Dutch East India Company could no longer finance its huge and expanding trading empire. Despite several attempts to regularize the colony's frontiers through the establishment of *landdrosts* (magistracies) there simply was not the money to administer the interior. The trekboers pushed east to the Fish River in the Eastern Cape, flagrantly flouting the Company's orders to the contrary. But there they drew up short. They had encountered the Xhosa—a mighty black African nation whose territory extended east from the good grazing lands around the Fish River. At first relations between the Xhosa and trekboers were peaceable enough, but as more and more settlers drifted in, competition for grazing became inevitable. Three centuries of white/black conflict for the land were to follow.

Enter the British: the Frontier Wars

While Holland's maritime fortunes floundered, Britain's were on the rise. The latest of the European powers to pursue territory in the east, by the 1790s Britain required its own refreshment point for ships rounding the Cape. On top of this, she was at war with Bonapartist France, whose powerful navy was anxious to cut Britain off from India—control of the Cape meant control of the shipping route east and Britain could not afford to let the French get there first. In 1796 a British force took Cape Town from the Dutch and annexed the colony. In 1801, thinking the French defeated in Europe, Britain restored the Cape to Holland, but after Bonaparte resumed hostilities in Spain, Britain retook it.

Immediately, the new masters of South Africa found themselves embroiled in war on the eastern frontier between trekboers, Khoi and Xhosa. With no experience of Africa, the British dispatched troops to sort out this three-way struggle and embarked on a series of nine Frontier Wars that were to last almost 100 years (until 1879). First the Boers rebelled against the British, then the Khoi against the Boers, then the Khoi against the British, while the Xhosa periodically invaded the Cape Colony. No sooner had the Boers and Khoi been settled than the British went to war against the Xhosa in earnest. By the mid-1830s the British government was desperate. If the Dutch had found South Africa costly, the British found it ruinous. Not only were the Frontier Wars draining the treasury, but the frontier was not even secure; despite the influx of thousands of English settlers and the constant annexation of more Xhosa land, the eastern and northern frontiers remained dangerously unstable. In 1836 a large number of Eastern Cape Boers, tired of both the British and the continued Xhosa threat, organized themselves into three parties of several thousand, got into their wagons and headed north and east away from European rule, just as their trekboer forebears had done.

The Great Trek and Mfecane

This mass movement to colonize the northeast differed from the trekboer's in its organization and fixed objective. While the trekboer had travelled with just his family and servants, in search of a spot far from anyone else, the Boers of the Great Trek (or 'Voortrekkers' as they became known) set out en masse to conquer a new country for themselves. Pastoral nomadism was no longer a Boer ambition. Under Louis Trichardt, Andries Potgieter and Hans van Rensburg, the first parties crossed the Orange River, the Cape Colony's official northern boundary, into the great unknown. Colonial histories often assert that this great territory was largely empty, owing to a series of massive tribal upheavals caused by the rise of the Zulu empire in modern-day Natal through the 1820s and '30s.

The traditional line is that the Zulus caused a domino effect over thousands of miles—that they forced clans to flee into each others' territories, fighting, moving and gradually depopulating the interior. However, this process, usually referred to as the *Mfecane* (Zulu for 'crushing'), has more recently been refuted as grossly inaccurate. Instead, the violent rise of the Zulu empire is regarded as part of a much wider process of warfare and political upheaval taking place between Natal and the Transvaal and across the highveld to the Orange Free State—various ethnic groups, competing for local control of the expanding ivory and slave trade routes to the Cape and to Delagoa Bay, subjugated their weak neighbours and went to war with their competitors. In the early 1800s, the expanse of country north of the Orange River (today's far Northern Cape, Orange Free State and Transvaal) had been explored and settled by missionaries such as John Campbell, Robert Moffat and David Livingstone ('I presume'). They had encountered a violent, semi-desert world where rival groups of Tswana, Griqua (mixed Khoi and white) and, latterly, Ndebele (a renegade offshoot of the Zulus) competed for control of the trade routes and raided each-other mercilessly.

The Ndebele had invaded TransOrangia (as the highveld was then called), in the early 1830s and the Voortrekkers ran into immediate resistance from them as soon as they entered the 'empty' north. Gathering Tswana and Griqua allies, the Voortrekkers pushed eastwards over the Vaal River, driving the Ndebele before them and causing them to overrun countless other clans. Contemporary accounts of this chaotic time describe how the Voortrekkers, arriving after the Ndebele, found villages abandoned and the surrounding veld strewn with bone shards. On the strength of this, later colonial historians claimed that these areas had been de-populated through genocidal warfare, and that the Voortrekkers' conquest of the north was peaceful. But the truth is that such 'empty' areas had only been abandoned for safer sites in more defensible positions, and the Voortrekker advance was a violent affair made slow by continual resistance from local chiefs.

The Boers experienced a major setback in 1838 when a group of about 2000 Voortrekkers under Gert Maritz and Piet Retief broke away from the highveld parties and set off across the Drakensberg into Natal—the southern extent of the Zulu empire, then ruled by Dingane, half-brother of the legendary chief Shaka. Dingane was quick to realize that the arrival of the Voortrekkers could only mean disaster for his independent kingdom. He invited the leaders to negotiate a land grant, had them killed once they were in his court, then sent warriors to massacre two large Voortrekker parties near the Tugela River. It took the Boers some months to retaliate, but eventually they drove Dingane north where he was killed—probably by the Swazis, whose territory he had consistently raided during his reign. The Boers then put Dingane's brother Mpande on the Zulu throne, and declared their own republic in Natal.

It was to last only five years. The British were close on their heels and annexed Natal in 1843. Through the 1850s the Boer settlers abandoned the territory and trekked north again to join their fellows in the new republics of the Orange Free State and the Transvaal.

While the British began to colonize Natal in earnest and continued to make war on the Xhosa of the neighbouring Eastern Cape, the Voortrekker statelets in the north sank into their own series of wars with the Swazi, Pedi, Sotho and Venda. The Boers managed to hold onto an extensive territory, but were unable to dislodge these established African nations from their best land.

Diamonds, Gold and War between the Whites

In 1870, the British, Griquas and the *burghers* of the Orange Free State came into conflict over Colesberg Kopjie, a small rocky hill west of the Vaal River. The land belonged to the Griquas, but the British took it anyway and paid off the Free Staters to keep the Griqua quiet. The hill in question was full of diamond-bearing rock. Diggers and prospectors were already active in the area and the hill soon became a hole, with hundreds of small claims worked by Tswana from the Orange Free State and Western Transvaal.

Within a few years the hole was surrounded by the booming mine town of Kimberley. The small claims were steadily bought up by larger companies, the biggest of which, De Beers (named after the farmer on whose land the town was built), was run by a charismatic young Englishman called Cecil Rhodes. Britain was overjoyed—it seemed that her costly South African colonies would finally be made to pay. The Free Staters felt robbed by the hated British, and both they and the Transvaalers resented the drift of black labour away from their farms. Caring little for the Boer's laments, the British secured their northern boundary by annexing the South African Republic (SAR) in 1877.

In the late 1870s gold was found near Barberton, in the Transvaal Drakensberg, but under British rule, the local farmers had to sit by and grind their teeth while the revenues from the Barberton rush went into the hands of foreigners. Eventually, in 1881, a small Boer force under General Joubert managed to eject the British troops from the SAR after a battle at Majuba Hill on the Natal border (an incident that later became known as the First Anglo-Boer War) and, embarrassed, but lacking the means to effectively retaliate, the British restored the SAR's independence in 1884. However, the republic remained grindingly poor until a new, massive gold strike was made in 1886 along the 500km Witwatersrand, just south of Pretoria. Excited, the SAR Boers, under their fiercely anti-British president Paul Kruger, realized that this new mineral resource could both enrich their country and buy enough arms to keep the British out forever.

But the SAR government also lacked the money to mine the gold on a large scale. Not without misgiving, they invited De Beers and the other Kimberley mining companies to the Witwatersrand and let them provide the necessary machinery and labour, while levying a tax on mining revenue. This plan worked insofar as the first mines near the new village of Johannesburg were operational by 1887. Black migrant labourers drifted in from all over the country and revenue filled the Transvaal's coffers. However, the mining magnates and businessmen of the new Johannesburg were mostly English-speaking and their loyalties lay with Britain. Cecil Rhodes, in particular, was outspokenly jingoistic and active in Cape politics. Knowing this, president Paul Kruger sought to prevent the magnates threatening his republic by denying the vote to all foreigners, meanwhile using the mining revenues to stockpile weapons from Germany.

By 1890, the mining companies had transformed their financial power into political power—albeit outside the SAR—after Cecil Rhodes, now the richest man in South Africa, became Prime Minister of the Cape. Johannesburg was now the territory's largest town stuffed with foreign businessmen who chafed at being denied the franchise. Rhodes began to stir up the Cape and Johannesburg press against Kruger's government, and the British government, eager to grab the gold mines and to redress their 1881 embarrassment at Majuba, expressed support. In 1895, Rhodes decided to force the issue by financing a coup d'état against Kruger's government in Pretoria. Under one Dr Jameson, an associate of Rhodes, a force of mounted adventurers crossed into the Transvaal from the Cape under cover of dark and rode towards Pretoria. The Jameson Raid, as the affair became known, was hopelessly bungled; the invaders were picked up by a Boer commando and jailed in Pretoria. Rhodes, highly embarrassed, resigned from the Cape Prime Ministership. The British government, although it had not openly supported the raid, came under heavy fire from the European press, whose sympathies lay with the Boers. War was inevitable. The British gave Kruger an ultimatum over the foreigners' franchise but he remained defiant, and in 1899, the Second Anglo-Boer War broke out.

The war lasted three years, costing both sides dear. At first the Boers made use of their newly-bought artillery and rifles to hold the British invasion force at bay for almost a year at the Tugela River in Natal, while also besieging the existing British garrisons in Ladysmith, Mafeking and Kimberley. But once the British had broken the Tugela line and invaded the Orange Free State (with the loss of thousands of soldiers), the Boers broke up into small war parties—*commandos*—using guerrilla tactics against the lumbering British columns. By 1902, 450,000 British soldiers had been sent to South Africa and General Kitchener began burning Boer farms and interning the women and children in concentration camps (where over 20,000 died). The *commandos* finally surrendered, leaving the gold fields in British hands. But Britain had lost over 25,000 men (mostly to disease), dipped alarmingly deep into the national treasury, and etched the already existing hatred for the British deeper in the Boer mind.

Following the surrender at Vereegning in the Transvaal, the Boer generals Louis Botha and Jan Smuts decided to work with the British and negotiated the share of power while keeping South Africa as a British Dominion. In 1910, the Union of South Africa was declared, with Botha as Prime Minister. But the Boer struggle was far from over. In 1914 a renegade Boer group formed a new political wing—the National Party in Bloemfontein—whose objectives were to win back South Africa for the Afrikaners and enforce white rule, which they saw as threatened by British tolerance of the growing black labour movements in the mines and political movements in the Eastern Cape.

A Three-Way Split: Blacks, Brits and Boers: 1879-1948

To understand this rise in black political consciousness, we must look back to the late 1870s, when the military might of the Xhosa, Zulu and Pedi nations had finally been crushed by the British, after the Ninth Frontier War, the Zulu War and the Pedi Campaign (all 1879). Despite their defeats, the Xhosa and Zulu people bounced back during the 1880s and '90s and began to make money from wool, maize and vegetables—to the point where many black communities in the Eastern Cape and Natal were making more than white farmers. Under British colonial law, blacks who owned land had voting rights and the thought of an economically strong black majority alarmed the Cape government into passing the Glen Grey Act in 1894, which restricted the amount of land that black individuals could own.

Despite this, the rising tide of black fortune extended outside of the Cape and Natal—from 1870, the Tswana, Pedi, Swazi, Venda, Sotho and other black nations of the Boer republics began offering themselves for contract work first in the sugar cane fields of Natal, then in the mines of Kimberley and Johannesburg. Under Boer rule, these blacks had been denied the right even to own land, let alone vote, and had suffered repeated Boer raids against their villages to kidnap children to work on farms. But with the advent of migrant work, many black families gained breadwinners who earned hard cash, and who were often given a firearm as part of their pay-off. In the 1880s and '90s, the Pedi, Sotho, Venda and other Transvaal peoples successfully rebelled against the Boers, while the Swazi and BaSotho maintained their independence. During the Second Anglo-Boer War, many Tswana fought for the British. By 1900, South Africa's blacks, despite being generally dispossessed, were beginning to exercise political power.

A small middle class of mission-educated blacks was also emerging, especially in the Eastern Cape and Natal, where the previous generation had suffered crushing military defeats. These men realized that they could best protect their societies through the white man's methods. Men like Alan Soga and J. T. Jabavu, Pixley Seme, Alfred Mangena, George Monstsioa, John Dube and Sol T. Plaatje entered the professions, becoming lawyers and journalists, and began to garner support for black grievances through the publication of native language newspapers and through parliamentary lobbying.

These men were by no means always in agreement. Soga, Seme, Plaatje, Dube and others favoured aggressive (by the standards of the day) politics and in 1903 founded the South African Native National Congress (SANNC), later to become the ANC. Jabavu and his followers favoured more subtlety and began raising funds to create a black university that could compete on equal terms with any white institution. It took some years, but Jabavu eventually garnered enough philanthropic support at home and abroad to inaugurate the University of Fort Hare, at Alice in the Eastern Cape in 1916. Still active today, the university provided a launch-pad for the political careers of many future black freedom fighters. Graduates include Nelson Mandela, Walter Sisulu, the late Oliver Tambo and the president of Zimbabwe, Robert Mugabe.

Parallel with the efforts of the new black middle class, the Indians of Natal and the Transvaal also began forming political cells under the leadership of a young Indian-born lawyer called Gandhi, who had become committed to fighting racism since his first week in South Africa when he was thrown off a train at Pietermaritzburg for refusing to leave a carriage full of whites. Gandhi aimed at elevating Indians to the middle classes through commerce, starting a self-help scheme at Phoenix, just north of Durban in 1906, with finance from prominent Indian businessmen. Preaching passive resistance to acts of government racism, such as the Pass Laws of 1913, Gandhi put Indians on the political map, masterminding strategies such as a protest march from Newcastle to the Transvaal—which, though broken up by baton-wielding police, made it plain that Indians would push for equal rights, no matter how summarily the government dealt with them.

Although black and Indian politics were still far removed from each other, by 1914 concerted political resistance to white rule was well established. This was just as well; if the new British/Boer government was anything but liberal, the emerging Boer Nationalists, under Barry Hertzog, were busy establishing an even more right-wing opposition, and lobbied government to extend the 1913 Pass Laws into an almost total ban on non-white ownership of land—whites were to own 87 per cent of the land space, blacks a mere 13 per cent, all inside set 'reserves', the forerunners of the later 'homelands'.

Hertzog's predominantly rural nationalists found unexpected support among the skilled white workers of the Rand goldfields. The mining magnates had long wanted to break the colour bar between skilled and unskilled labour, knowing that it could reduce costs by putting blacks in skilled jobs. At the same time the companies could solve what had become a chronic labour shortage, as blacks, lacking the incentive of more senior jobs to make them stay on, drifted away from the mines once their contracts were up. But white workers had no intention of competing for jobs with an overwhelming back majority.

Immediately before the First World War, mass strikes involving tens of thousands of white workers broke out across the Witwatersrand, protesting at the mining companies' attempts to break the job/colour bar. But with conscription, most of these white workers went into the army, and black miners, inspired by the success of white strikes in securing wage increases, also staged mass strikes. Distracted by its war effort and the need for increased production, the government and mining companies gave in to a few of the demands (though making a show of force in putting the strikes down).

When the white workers returned from the war and found their jobs once again under threat from cheap black labour, their anger knew no bounds. From 1918 white mineworkers staged a series of violent strikes and riots, which culminated in a General Strike of whites in all industries in 1922. Prime Minister Jan Smuts only restored order to the gold fields after sending in the combined army and air force, but capitulated to the white workers and made the job/colour bar law.

This is one of the sad ironies of South African history. With so much in common, a united front by white and black workers might have brought an early racial equality, and saved the country tens of thousands of deaths throughout the rest of the 20th century. But with working-class whites and blacks competing for jobs, a united front could never happen. From the 1920s the country became increasingly racially divided, and the fear felt by working class whites towards blacks provided the grass-roots support for the later apartheid governments.

The far right opposition was quick to exploit this. In 1918, an organization known as the Afrikaner *broederbond* ('brotherhood') had been set up, with the objective of infiltrating industry and government with educated Afrikaners of Nationalist persuasion.

At the same time, the growing black resistance became increasingly political. In 1923 the SANNC changed its name to the African National Congress (ANC)—later to become almost a household word throughout the world—and in 1928 began working with the South African Communist Party (SACP) to build a white/black workers' movement. Hertzog's Nationalists countered this by forcing the government to make racial segregation compulsory in urban areas, and took advantage of the general world economic depression to ferment more fear among white workers at losing their jobs to blacks. By 1930 even the more moderate whites were moving to the right, and in 1934 Hertzog and Smuts formed the United South African National Party—the iron fist of racism inside a velvet glove—a joint Prime-Ministership with Smuts as the soft-talking front man being pushed ever further to the right by Hertzog and his followers.

In defiance, the ANC and SACP united to urge a general burning of Pass Books, but the government retaliated by summarily taking away the Cape's black franchise, leaving South Africa's blacks with no vote at all. However, the whites were still not united and the Smuts/Hertzog union began to suffer internal splits. In 1939 Hertzog resigned over South Africa's joining the British war effort. The Nationalists reverted to their isolationist, anti-British stance and prepared for a mass attack on the colonial government as South Africa went to war against Germany again. The furthest right wing even formed a Hitlerist society called the *Ossewabrandweg* (Ox-wagon sentinels—referring to the Great Trek) who dodged the draft and beat up South Africans seen in uniform. English and Afrikaans whites were as divided as they had been since the British annexation 150 years before.

Not so the blacks. With the eyes of government for the second time diverted by a World War, the ANC and black trade unions capitalized on their successes of the 1930s. From 1940, a series of bus boycotts brought down the cost of public transport for black workers in Johannesburg's townships. Blacks waiting to be allotted housing rebelled, and began erecting huge squatter camps. The African Mineworker's Union (AMU) was founded in 1941 and the ANC Youth League in 1943. The same year saw the SACP and ANC unite over anti-Pass Law protests and in 1946 the AMU went out on mass strike over segregation and low pay. But with the Second World War over, the government could once again concentrate on home affairs. The strike was crushed by paramilitary police units. In 1948, a general election was called amidst white alarm at the rising strength of black politics, and the ultra-right-wing Nationalists, under Prime Minister D.F. Malan were voted in.

Apartheid and the Rise of Violence: 1948–90

With the arrival of the Nationalist government, any pretence at positive race relations went out of the window. Between 1949 and 1960, mixed marriage, squatting, 'riotous assemblies' (i.e. black demonstrations), even mixed education, were all banned. The Cape 'coloureds' were disenfranchised (despite a national outcry from white liberals), the residents of Johannesburg's lively Sophiatown, the centre of black counter-culture, were forcibly removed to the new township of Soweto, Sophiatown itself was razed and the SACP and ANC suppressed. Of course, there was resistance—in 1952 rioting broke out over the loss of the 'coloured' vote and in 1953 after the Bantu Education Act which denied blacks entry to white universities. A short-lived 'Defiance Campaign' led by the ANC's Youth League under a young lawyer, Nelson Mandela, attempted to thwart racist government policies. But to many blacks, the ANC seemed powerless, especially after the publication of their Freedom Charter in 1955 only led to a huge government crackdown on left-wing political organizations—even on marginal movements such as the liberal white women's organization, the Black Sash, who had protested the ban on the Cape 'coloured' franchise, but these were confined to warnings. Members of the ANC and Communist Party leaders (black and white) were dealt with more harshly—being arrested and tried for treason.

The Treason Trials lasted four years, severely hobbling the liberation struggle. In 1959, militants from the ANC expressed their frustration by forming a new anti-white organization, the Pan African Congress (PAC) under the charismatic Robert Sobukwe. In 1960, the PAC called on all Johannesburg's blacks to burn their Pass Books, deliberately provoking a mass arrest of the entire black workforce—bringing industry to a halt and overloading the police. The plan was welcomed, but at Sharpeville, south of Johannesburg, a vast crowd of demonstrators milling around a police station were fired on and in the panic, the police killed over 200 people. With typical over-reaction the Prime Minister Hendrik Verwoerd, a Dutch-born super-racist, declared a brief state of emergency. Sobukwe was arrested and both the ANC and PAC banned. Oliver Tambo, who was one of the ANC's most senior leaders until his death in 1993, went to London to carry on the liberation struggle from abroad. The government resisted foreign pressure to tone down its racist stance, withdrawing from the Commonwealth in 1961. South Africa's leaders were no longer subject to the British crown, but were heads of state who could do as they pleased. But the struggle had advanced too far to be given up so easily and both organizations went underground, forming military wings. *Umkhonto we Sizwe* (the Spear of the Nation——MK for short), was the ANC wing determined to target government installations and public services, but *Poqo*, the PAC wing, favoured terrorism and several white civilians were killed at locations around the country. To avoid arrest, the MK and *Poqo* based their operations in Communist-backed countries such as Algeria, Angola, Tanzania, Mozambique, and also Ethiopia.

In 1962 Nelson Mandela, chairman of the MK, returned from Ethiopia and met with other MK members at their headquarters on a farm in Rivonia, near Johannesburg. He was picked up in the small town of Cedara and initially sentenced to 5 years for 'inciting African workers to strike and leaving the country without valid travel documents'. But a year later the security forces got wind of the Rivonia meetings, tracked down the farm, found draft documents outlining plans of guerilla warfare and managed to arrest other MK leaders, including Walter Sisulu—today one of the most prominent members of the ANC government. Together with Mandela, they were charged with sabotage and sentenced to life. The ten years following the Rivonia Trial are referred to as the 'silent decade'. Those ANC and PAC leaders who escaped arrest were forced into exile, and the liberation struggle was effectively on ice, as the resistance leaders struggled to organize operations from abroad.

'When I ask you to produce proof, I mean your identity card!'

© David Marais. First published in *The Cape Times*, 24 November, 1959.

The government took advantage of the lull to further enforce apartheid. It began the 'homelands' policy of creating separate states (or 'bantustans') for blacks, stripping them of South African citizenship, and giving them poor, overcrowded, but nominally independent reserves within the country that would still supply the labour market. Between 1960 and 1981, ten of these 'bantustans' were created, complete with repressive, puppet regimes that would act under Pretoria's directives.

The one voice of open dissent in the early 1970s came from a young black medical student called Steve Biko, who was studying in Durban. One of the few multi-racial organizations left in South Africa was the university-based NUSAS, or National Union of South African Students. Biko, despite being isolated on a black campus, became a prominent figure in the organization. He began to publish in its journal criticisms of South Africa's white liberals, who he accused of complacency. His writings were distributed on white and black campuses alike, and his philosophy, which he called Black Consciousness, widely accepted. The basic idea behind the movement was simple enough; blacks should not feel undermined by white supremacy, and should take a conscious pride in their black identity. Whites and blacks should be prepared to share democratic power, wrote Biko, but South Africa was wasting a vast talent pool by denying blacks equality and by fearing a black political majority. Furthermore, he pointed out that the running of apartheid was too expensive to be sustainable for more than a generation, and that all South Africans, white and black, would ultimately suffer the continual drain on the economy.

The Black Consciousness movement sparked a series of demonstrations. Biko was arrested in 1974 and accused of fermenting terrorism. Yet he argued his own case so eloquently in court that he won over many of his jurors and inspired a wave of support in the international press. By far the most sophisticated politician of his time, Biko inspired a deep fear in the government. Taking heart from Biko's stand, the black working class began to find a voice again from 1973 with the Labour Movement. Strikes in Durban spread through the country, protesting not at working conditions or pay, but at apartheid, pure and simple. By 1974/5, the ANC and PAC leaders who had been jailed for 10 years after the Rivonia Trial, completed their terms. On their release they began gathering support from both the Black Consciousness and Labour movements. Neither movement involved violence (except on the part of the police); but this was soon to change.

In 1976, the liberation struggle exploded into action again, and in the last place the government would have expected—among Soweto's schoolchildren. There was no central organization, just a few demonstrations against the compulsory learning of certain subjects in Afrikaans. Riot police called into Soweto were stoned and attacked and hundreds of schoolchildren were shot or jailed. For black youth to act independently of parental authority was unprecedented; traditional South African society is severely hierarchical; the Soweto rising pointed as much to a breakdown of the traditional black societies under ghetto life, as to a precocious political awareness among Soweto's adolescents. Those who escaped arrest fled to ANC camps abroad and the organization gained much new blood to take the freedom struggle into the next decade.

But for the moment, the strength of the government's crackdown on the new rise of black protest was harsher than ever. Police violence against detainees became murderous. The most famous victim was Steve Biko, who died while in police custody in Port Elizabeth in 1977. Tragically his death did not unite the new generation of freedom fighters—far from it. Soweto schoolchildren supporting his Black Consciousness democratic movement and those supporting the more anti-white, hardline PAC policy began to fall out, and sporadic but lethal fighting broke out between the factions.

Meanwhile, the ANC was looking for allies abroad. In 1979 the late Oliver Tambo met with one Mangosotho Buthelezi, a young Zulu nobleman who was head of a Natal-based black organization called Inkhatha. Although formed back in the 1920s Inkhatha had languished in obscurity until taken up by the charismatic young Buthelezi, who had wide Zulu support. The ANC saw Buthelezi and Inkhatha as an opportunity to form an above-ground wing in Natal that could play a vital role in upholding the freedom struggle in Natal. But Buthelezi was not content to be a tool of the ANC. He and Tambo could not reach an agreement—a split that was to have violent consequences later on. In the early 1980s, Buthelezi re-organized Inkhatha into the militant pro-Zulu Inkhatha Freedom Party (IFP) and began to campaign for his own place in the national political arena.

The same period saw a marked increase in general violence in South Africa. Existing ethnic tensions were eagerly promoted by the South African government in the mines, the townships, and even in the surrounding countries as South African troops were deployed to support anti-communist rebel factions in Namibia, Angola and Mozambique. This divide-and-rule policy, honed over the centuries of white colonial rule, caused intense fighting in the Witwatersrand miners' hostels—between Zulu, Xhosa and other 'tribal' groups, advancing the government's claim that only it could control the violence inherent in the African soul. But today it is widely believed that the government security forces (generally referred to as the 'Third Force') were behind much of this fighting, which claimed thousands of lives through the 1980s and early 1990s. This claim seems likely, given the billions of dollars the government spent on its military projects abroad.

By 1986, world condemnation of apartheid was made concrete in the form of international sanctions against the country. Gold prices plummeted and massive disinvestment by foreign companies threatened the financial future of apartheid. The government realized that it would have to make concessions, yet still it clung to the hope that outward reform would be sufficient. Under president P. W. Botha, the more obviously right-wing members of the National Party were expelled and a small number of Indians and 'coloureds' were allowed back into Parliament. The exiled ANC began to court white liberals (mostly academics), from abroad, and set up the United Democratic Front (UDF) to campaign for the release of political prisoners.

However, by now the political violence in the townships had reached fever pitch. From 1986–90, the disputes between Soweto schoolchildren supporting Biko's Black Consciousness and those favouring a hardline anti-white policy, caused an adolescent death-toll that mounted into the thousands. IFP and ANC fighting in Natal townships claimed even more lives. Many black shopkeepers and businessmen claimed that local PAC, IFP and ANC leaders were demanding money from them for their campaigns, threatening those who did not pay, and that businesses forced to support one group were burned out by another. A 'them-and-us' mentality arose, in which anyone publicly denounced as a government informer or sympathizer was liable to be killed by a mob, often by 'necklacing'—a form of public murder in which the victim had a petrol-filled tyre put around his or her neck and was then set alight.

The government took advantage of the black to black fighting, and its attendant atrocities to declare a State of Emergency (i.e. martial law) and sent troops into the townships. Detention without trial, even of white academics supporting the UDF, became common. Many people suspected that the extreme violence in the townships was being fermented by the security forces, and P. W. Botha's 'reforms' were seen to be a sham. However, the extent to which black factional fighting had run out of control was tellingly revealed when Winnie Mandela was implicated in a murder trial in 1989.

The body of a 14 year-old boy named Stompie Mokhetse was found at her house and subsequent investigations alleged that Mrs Mandela was at the centre of a series of beatings and kidnappings, even murders, of Soweto youths opposed to the ANC. Mrs Mandela was charged with hiring thugs, who posed as a 'football club' for boys from broken homes, to carry out the crimes. Graffiti appeared on walls all over South Africa announcing 'Winnie's in the Pooh'—the lighter side of what turned out to be a sinister web of intimidation and violence. She was brought to trial, amid much national and international media shock, having been much fêted through the preceding years for standing by her husband and for helping to make him an international symbol of the wrongs of South Africa. Although Winnie Mandela's case was hardly representative of the ANC's ethics, it severely damaged the party's credibility and exposed cracks in the morality of South Africa's liberation struggle. Although found guilty, Mrs Mandela was not charged—the political climate was too tense. The ANC was quick to distance itself from her, but today she remains a part of the new government.

In 1989 tightened sanctions and a badly failing economy finally prompted the white government to begin the dismantling of apartheid. P. W. Botha was voted out in favour of President F. W. de Klerk and real reforms followed. While the far right of the National Party broke away to form the Conservative Party, and the neo-Nazi AWB gained popularity among many Afrikaans-speaking whites, de Klerk set about repealing some of the apartheid laws, such as segregation, and the ban on mixed marriage and education. By 1990, nursing South Africa's crippled economy, de Klerk persuaded the foreign powers to lift sanctions against his country, by withdrawing the army from Angola and Namibia, unbanning the ANC and PAC and releasing Nelson Mandela from jail. The eyes of the world were on de Klerk as he pledged to work towards a multi-racial society in which the black majority would gain power through democratic election.

Into the Great Unknown

This is a time to heal the old wounds and build a new South Africa.

Nelson Mandela

Mandela's release did not stop the violence. Conflict between the IFP and ANC continued to rage in the Rand and Natal. From 1992 unemployment became acute as the mines, suffering under the ever-dropping gold price, laid off tens of thousands of workers. Violent crime rose accordingly, as did terrorism. For example, during 1993 APLA (formerly *Poqo*), the armed wing of the PAC, launched a series of attacks on white civilians across the country and yet more rioting followed the assassination of the South African Communist Party president Chris Hani by a right-wing fanatic. Political violence finally spilled from the townships into the white city centres and a general fear polarized the racial communities until it seemed that the long-awaited election, set for April 1994, would plunge the country into civil war. This was compounded by Buthelezi and the IFP's refusal to aid the peace talks between the National Party, the ANC and the other political parties. But to everyone's surprise, and great relief, the elections went off with almost no violence at all. It was as if the country had sated itself during the bloody lead-up to the ballot day. The ANC polled 62.6% of the national vote, a percentage which qualified them to hold 252 of the 400 seats in the national assembly, but not quite the two-thirds of the vote which would have allowed them to write a constitution without input from other parties. On 10 May, 1994. Nelson Mandela was inaugurated as South Africa's first black president with a dream to bind the wounds of the country and unite all South Africans.

So what of the future? Does 'The New South Africa' exist and if so, where is it going? For many whites, the first problem is that of Affirmative Action. White-collar jobs have traditionally been reserved for white necks in South Africa, but this is changing fast. Not only are black students suddenly filling the universities, but many companies are adopting a positive discrimination policy for new recruits. The economy has still not recovered from the economic downturn caused by the international sanctions and foreign disinvestment of the final apartheid years. The gold price is at an all-time low, and to cut costs, mines are laying off workers: unemployment is getting worse and crime rising. People are scrambling for local government jobs—a tempting security in the present economic climate—and there is a danger that government itself may become silted up in the process.

The accession of the ANC has brought its attendant problems. Many South Africans fear that there is too great a gulf between the party's senior leaders and the increasingly disaffected black youth—especially as the change in government has not automatically produced economic benefits for the poor. An ideological split in the younger leadership of the ANC—a divide between socialism and communism fostered in different ANC training camps abroad — may also threaten the future of the party. An effective opposition has already established itself in Kwa-Zulu/Natal in the form of the IFP, which now promises to challenge the government on a national level.

However, the prospects are by no means all gloomy. Considering that, for an African police state, a relatively bloodless change from repressive to democratic government is unprecedented, one should not underestimate the enormous will of the South African people as a whole to make their new country work. This is evident, for example, in the retention of many former white, Afrikaans-speaking Nationalist Party MPs as regional directors of agriculture—the whites had taken the land in the past, but had also learnt sustainable techniques of food production, so their expertise is not being thrown away. At the same time, improved education will mean an inevitable alleviation of problems such as over-population, erosion through bad farming and environmental destruction, especially in the former 'homelands', where education and all public services have long been neglected. Foreign investors are trickling back to South Africa and tourism is booming.

Even changes within the army have not caused serious upheaval; for example, following the absorption of the MK into the regular South African army in April 1994, a group of former MK members, dissatisfied with army life, assaulted their commanding officer and marched on the government buildings in Pretoria. President Mandela—himself a founder member of the MK—met them personally, and diffused the situation. Unlike most other African countries, South Africa is not threatened by its armed forces.

Most South Africans feel great relief at having made the change at long last. Travellers who have visited the country more than once report that the fear and tension that built up before the elections has dissipated. South Africans finally have access to one another's cultures. South African sport is back on the international circuit and its rugby and cricket teams seem set to steal some world titles over the next few years. Soccer, traditionally the sport of South Africa's black communities, can also finally enter international competition—and its league teams rival the best in Africa.

South Africa is on the brink of coming of age as a society. Nationalism and racism will continue to flare, but Lesotho and Swaziland, the two independent countries within South Africa's borders, have already demonstrated that a multi-racial society can work, despite the conflicts suffered for 300 years. A democratic government has finally come to power, there is a Bill of Rights, and a reconstruction and development programme that avoids the settling of old racial scores and concentrates on simply reorganizing the country along more just lines. Perhaps the best omen for this is contained within the new national anthem, *Nkosi Sikelel' iAfrica* (God Bless Africa), whose meaning is purely religious. For the first time in its history, South Africa has, at least symbolically, laid politics aside.

People and Culture

A Zulu Sangoma

Most Westerners are familiar with the word *apartheid*, having read about its injustice and racial oppression in their home media. But racial segregation and rule by force exist to a lesser or greater extent in many countries of the world. What attracted Western media attention to South Africa in particular was that its ruling white society resembled the Western model so closely that Western commentators felt a profound discomfort and not a little guilt when looking at South Africa. This was no bad thing: the Western media's incessant condemnation of apartheid did much to push their own governments to impose economic sanctions on South Africa and so hasten the system's demise. But, as many foreign onlookers are now becoming aware, the Western picture of South Africa was over-simplified—the most obvious interpretation of a more complicated web of ethnic and racial tensions permeating all levels of South African society.

Apartheid was inspired by deep fear, felt over a century and a half by the Afrikaans-speaking descendants of the Voortrekkers for those they had conquered by means of horse and gun. At the back of the Boer mind lay the very real fear that one day the conquered, who vastly outnumbered the conquerers, would rise. The only way to prevent this, it seemed, was to keep the conquered under an iron heel from the beginning. In his superb, painful book *My Traitor's Heart* (Bodley Head, 1990), the white South African writer Rian Malan illustrates just how deliberate was this philosphy of oppression: '*Soon, many Afrikaners were calling themselves Doppers, after the little metal caps with which they snuffed out their candles. They called themselves Doppers because they were deliberately and consciously extinguishing the light of the Enlightenment, so that they could do what they had to do in darkness...There are many truths about Afrikaners, but none so powerful and reverberent as this wilful self-blinding.*'

This 19th-century fear is easy to understand. Less easy is the confidence of the 20th-century architects of apartheid, who seemed so sure that they could uphold their system indefinitely, despite the overwhelming numbers and the ever-growing resentment of the oppressed. Alan Paton, in his novel *Cry the Beloved Country* (Charles Scribner, 1948), written in the year of the first apartheid government's accession, sheds some light on this. '*...We shall live from day to day, and put more locks on the doors, and get a fine fierce dog when the fine fierce bitch next door has pups, and hold our handbags more tenaciously... We shall be careful, and knock this off our lives, and that off our lives, and hedge ourselves about with safety and precaution. And our lives will shrink, but they shall be the lives of superior beings... And the conscience will be thrust down....put under a bushel...for a generation that will live by it again, in some day not yet come; and how it will come, and when ...we shall not think about at all.*'

So much for apartheid, which for all its police and soldiers and gold lasted no more than a generation. By no means all South African whites supported the system, and many suffered at its hands, particularly during the repressive State of Emergency of the 1980s, when anyone suspected of having ANC contacts could be detained without trial. However, barring certain individual incidents, white suffering was a drop in the ocean compared to that of South Africa's more than 20 million blacks.

So why did the blacks not rise and smash apartheid with one strike of their collective fist? Many Western journalists could never come to terms with the oppressed majority's apparent inability to offer concerted resistance to apartheid. But the problem was that these journalists, with their Western eyes, were making judgements that, though well-intentioned, were in some ways just as racist as those of apartheid. For referring to 'the blacks' in South Africa is like looking at the West before the Second World War and referring to the different nations collectively as 'the whites'.

Many of South Africa's black nations were and are as culturally removed from each other as, say, the English from the Hungarians. Some had, and still have, histories of warfare and conflict. Some, like the Zulus, suffer from endemic inter-clan fighting within their own nation. Even in the gold mines, where black trade union and labour movements have been active since the First World War, fighting between different groups in the workers' hostels consistently hampered the labour leaders' attempts at industrial action. The mine bosses knew this all too well, and encouraged ethnic conflict from the start by dividing the workers' hostels by 'tribe', knowing that the periodic fighting would keep the workers mistrustful of each other and sabotage any possibility of unity.

The colonial administrators and after them the apartheid leaders applied the same divide-and-rule policy to devastating effect, and tragically many of these ethnic conflicts exacerbated by white rulers continue today—though with the exception of Zulu inter-clan fighting in Kwa-Zulu/Natal's townships ethnic strife has fallen off dramatically since the 1994 elections, and the present ANC leadership is the first to represent South Africa on a pan-ethnic level. However, it will be a long time before South Africa can be said to be one nation.

The racial question does not end with mere black and white—what is the future for South Africa's six million 'coloureds', a racially mixed people descended from the Cape's original Khoi inhabitants, Mozambiquan and Malaysian slaves and European settlers (*see* **South African History**)? A predominantly Afrikaans-speaking people, they also suffered terrible repression under apartheid, yet, not being officially 'black', they are now caught between cultures. And then there are South Africa's more than one million Indians, who were similiarly repressed under apartheid, yet who are also caught between cultures. Apartheid may have ended, but racism remains on all sides, and these people in particular may well suffer from alienation and discrimination in the new South Africa, albeit not by law, unless the national psyche can relax sufficiently to bid a final farewell to the whole issue of race and colour. Perhaps in a generation or two.

Complicating the situation still further is the matter of creed. The Afrikaners, in an attempt to justify their oppressive rule, adopted a stern Calvinist brand of Christianity (the Dutch Reformed Church), which successfully rolled their political and religious creeds into one: South Africa was their promised land, or so their *predikants* (pastors) preached; and by this premise the subjugation of blacks was perceived as a necessary part of the divine scheme for bringing Christianity and 'civilization' to the unenlightened. The fact that the 'enlightenmentees' would be denied the benefits of this 'civilization', and would merely be its drawers of water and hewers of wood, was firmly ignored.

The Voortrekkers claimed that God had demonstrated his sympathy for their cause, by granting them victory over the mighty Zulu empire in 1838 at the Battle of Blood River, when the Boers, installed behind their *laager* or circle of wagons, poured volleys of lead at the charging Zulu *impis* and mowed them down without losing a single man. The day of Blood River was subsequently called the Day of the Vow, after the supposed pact with God that had given the Boers their victory, and was made a day for Afrikaner celebration. Under apartheid it became a public holiday, complete with a thanksgiving service in the massive Voortrekker Monument in Pretoria. It says much for the new government's will to forgive that the public holiday has been kept but the name changed to the Day of Conciliation.

Fortunately for South Africa it was only the Afrikaners who complicated their political creed with an aggressive God. Many blacks under apartheid used religion more positively, holding fast to Christian faith to alleviate their suffering, whether under the apolitical Zionist Church or the more active Anglican and evangelical orders. Some black church leaders did much to advance the freedom struggle, notably Desmond Tutu, Cape Town's first black archbishop, who organized peace marches from Cape Town's cathedral through the 1980s and preached passionately for black unity and an end to violence. In fact, religion has proved to be South Africa's one point of general tolerance. For example, there is almost no religious tension between South Africa's Muslims (there are over a million, both Malay ('coloured') and Indian), Christians and Hindus, and religion has never been an issue even with the white governments. This bodes well. Religious hatreds never die, but racial hatreds can and do diffuse over time.

First World or Third World?

Many visitors to South Africa find the juxtaposition of Western and traditional life confusing. Most of us like being able to classify things and put them into boxes, and South Africa, maddeningly, presents so many different faces that this is impossible. The large cities, with their high-rises, shopping malls, freeways and wealthy suburbs, belie the appalling living conditions of the surrounding shanties and squatter camps. At the same time, the centuries-old traditions of some of the older residential quarters and villages, such as the 18th-century Malay Quarter (or Bo-Kaap) of central Cape Town, and the Moravian Mission Stations of the Western Cape, present a picture of Cape life that seems hardly to have changed since the early 1800s.

The contrasts become more abrupt as you penetrate the interior—for example the medieval world of the Lesotho Highlands, whose people get about almost entirely on horseback, sits just above the rich, westernized farms of the Natal Midlands. In the former 'homelands', you might be confronted with traditional life only marginally removed from the way it was when the first settlers arrived, yet five minutes later drive into a modern, pre-fabricated city complete with industrial areas, government offices and all the regular South African chain stores. Wild bushveld country, whose primeval, game-rich landscape has never been touched by man might sit next to a sophisticated mining operation whose administrators will live in neat little bungalows with garages, and the workers in traditional huts in the bush.

Driving the endless, empty roads of the Northern Cape, you will pass donkey carts and horse-drawn wagons moving across the hot landscape at a fast trot or people simply walking. Stop and offer the person a lift and you will often find that they are making journeys of up to 100km on foot in the hot sun, thinking little of the distance, the time or the hardship. Even in the cities you will glimpse horse wagons, roadside butcheries and people in traditional dress from the highways that speed over the townships and squatter camps to the city centres. Downtown, the markets are alive with the traditional life of the country—stalls and shops selling animal skins, organs and herbs for *muti* (magic and traditional medicine) and sometimes even *inyangas* and *sangomas* (diviners and faith healers) walking the main streets in their costume of office—complete with inflated goat's bladders affixed to the head—amid the besuited hurry of the commuter crowds.

The mix is confusing, but enthralling. Time and again you think you have the measure of the country, only to be shocked or surprised into a total change of view. The South Africans have a way around the problem. They term their country 'Second World'—poised midway between the traditional and the modern, both of which exert an equally strong influence on the people. Cattle and goats unhurriedly crossing a busy highway, tribal rituals attended by office workers, beds in township houses raised on bricks to allow spirits to pass underneath, baboon skulls and hi-fi equipment for sale on the same stall, boys daubed with the white clay of initiation into manhood standing in a queue at a take-away, white farmers consulting a diviner to make rain—such are the pictures of modern South Africa.

People, Culture and Language

While most visitors to South Africa are more than aware of the country's ethnic conflicts (*see* pp.52–3), few are aware of just how many different cultures there are, and from which areas they come. The following is intended as a brief outline.

KhoiSan

These were the Cape's original inhabitants (*see* also **South African History** p.34). By the time the first European settlers showed up in the 17th century, the KhoiSan had divided into three distinct cultures: the cattle-owning Khoi pastoralists, the San hunter-gatherers, and the *strandlopers* (beachcombers) of the the coast, who were non-cattle-owning Khoi reduced to living off shellfish and seabirds.

The Khoi were nicknamed 'Hottentots' by the white settlers after the linguistic clicks of their language, and after the songs of their regular moon-worshipping ceremonies, which early travellers describe as revolving around a regular chant that sounded like 'hottentot' to the Western ear. The Khoi were gradually stripped of their land by conquest, weakened by smallpox, alcohol and venereal disease, and gradually absorbed into a mixed-blood labouring class, known as 'coloured', that today provides the bulk of the poor classes in the Western and Northern Cape. Some of these mixed Khoi/Europeans went north in the 18th-century and established free bands of raiders and cattle-herders, known as Bastaards or Griqua and established large territories near the Orange River in the Northern Cape, even trekking into Natal. However, these too were eventually dispossessed—this time by the British—and under the racial obsessiveness of apartheid were redefined as 'coloureds'—bogus 'ethnologists' classified 11 different degrees of 'coloured' to make sure that none slipped through the 'white' net, however white they might appear. The original Khoi language exists only in poems written down by early missionaries (*see* 'Literature').

As for the San, they were called 'Bushmen' by the Dutch and English, and had every hand in the country— white and black — turned against them during the 19th century. Dutch farmers hunted them for sport, while the Xhosa, Sotho and Zulu peoples also killed the San where they found them. By the 1850s the San had been driven into the remoter Cape and Natal mountain ranges, and then north into the dry Kalahari. The San people still exist, but no longer in South Africa—their few remaining nomad bands now wander the remote wastes of eastern Namibia and western Botswana. The language and culture has survived, but their numbers are few and their future uncertain.

Cape Coloured and Malay

These are the Cape's four million 'coloureds', or descendants of mixed Khoi/European, and in some cases Malay slave blood. Although there is great variation in ancestry and thus outward appearance, the 'coloureds' (a name made up by white racists in the 19th-century, but still unfortunately in general use today) are united in language, being predominantly Afrikaans-speakers. The urban culture of Cape Town's 'coloureds' is jazzy and vibrant, a world away from that of the farm-labourers of the Winelands and Garden Route, or the desert shepherds of the Northern Cape. But the shared experience of racism and language has forged Cape 'coloured' culture into a recognizable whole, and one that is uniquely South African in that it comprises a blend of all the cultures and peoples who have come to the country since 1652.

The Malay culture is specific to Cape Town. Although designated 'coloureds' under apartheid, Cape Malays trace their ancestry to the highly skilled Javanese and Indonesian slaves brought over from Dutch Indonesia (then called Batavia) in the 18th century. A few Malay princes, such as the Sultan of Macassar, were also exiled to the Cape after rebelling against the Dutch, and their tombs, at False Bay, are now Muslim pilgrimage sites. Following the abolition of slavery in the 1830s, many Malays bought properties in an old residential quarter on Signal Hill, just above the city centre—known as the Bo-Kaap, and still a Malay quarter today. Others were forcibly removed to the township of Mitchell's Plain in 1966. But the culture has survived: Muslim mysticism is even practised by some of the *mullahs* and young men who perform a dance called the *Khalifa* that involves the ritual piercing of flesh with blades and walking on hot coals while in trance.

Xhosa

The Eastern Cape province is the heartland of the Xhosa people, who speak a language classified as part of the Nguni group of southern Africa. The Xhosa fought the longest and hardest fight of all against white rule, resisting every inch of settlement and invasion between 1799 and 1879 (The Frontier Wars). These wars of resistance ultimately left them

landless and had a devastating effect on national morale, resulting in a strange mass destruction of most of the nation's cattle and grain in a collective act of despair during the 1850s.
However, the Xhosa bounced back during the 1870s, and were the first black people to
begin effectively fighting the white man at his own game by sending the sons of their
nobility through mission schools and British universities at the end of the 19th century. By
1916, a group of Xhosa professionals founded the country's first black university at Fort
Hare, near Alice in the Eastern Cape, whose graduates have produced some of South
Africa's best-known black freedom fighters, including Nelson Mandela. Traditional life is
still strong in the countryside and the traditional red clay facial cosmetic is still seen among
rural women, as are long smoking pipes. Traditional costume has all-but disappeared, but
adolescent initiation rituals and belief in the occult is still strong in the countryside.
Numerically, the Xhosa are the largest ethnic group after the Zulu. For a more detailed look
at Xhosa culture, *see* p.315.

Zulu

Also part of the Nguni language group, Zulu is spoken by most blacks in Kwa-Zulu/Natal,
and the Zulu nation, which now incorporates other groups in the region, such as the Hlubi
and the Kwa-Zulu/Natal Tsonga, is the largest in the country, and there has been talk of
Kwa-Zulu/Natal seceding from the union to form its own country. Famed for their martial
culture, the Zulus have long fascinated military and social historians, both for the rise of
their early 19th-century empire under Shaka, the first Zulu king, and for Shaka's grandson
Cetshwayo's massive defeat of the British at the battle of Isandlwana in 1879.
Unfortunately, this warrior culture has its nihilistic side, and the townships and farmlands
of Kwa-Zulu/Natal's 'tribal' areas are riven by bloody inter-clan wars whose obscure origins
of past grievances defy the comprehension of anyone not born into the Zulu way of life.
Having said this, Zulu culture is highly creative. Zulu crafts such as basket-weaving and
bead-work jewellery are sold in shops all over the country and are renowned for their
beauty and exquisite detail. For a more detailed look at Zulu culture, *see* p.402.

Swazi

Another Nguni-speaking group are the Swazis, some of whom live within South Africa,
but most of whom live in the small independent kingdom of Swaziland and whose
language, Seswati, is very similar to both Zulu and Xhosa. Although several of southern
Africa's black nations have kings, perhaps no nation reveres its monarchy so much as the
Swazis, whose king has absolute state power within Swaziland. Except for those who now
live within South Africa, the Swazi were never ruled directly by whites, nor did they suffer
the injustices of apartheid. As a result, white/black relations in Swaziland are noticeably
unstrained. Although Swaziland is relatively westernized, rural life is still ruled by tradition, and, more than the Xhosa, the rural Swazi have a reputation for belief in witchcraft
and the occult. For a more detailed look at Swazi culture, *see* p.468.

Pedi

The Pedi are a North Sotho-speaking group who live mostly in the Eastern Transvaal,
north of Swaziland. Traditional rivals of the Swazi until the 1830s, the Pedi then turned

their military attention to the Voortrekkers, after repeated incursions into their territory forced them to war. The Pedi put up a spirited resistence to white settlement and beat off several Boer attacks until the British put them down in 1879 after having annexed the Boers' South African Republic. However, the Pedi were among the first of South Africa's black peoples to see an opportunity for independence in the diamond and gold mines of the Northern Cape and Johannesburg, signing up as contract labourers for fixed periods after which they received a cash payout and a firearm. These they used to great effect in armed insurrection against the Boers in the 1880s and '90s. Since then, the Pedi have remained a largely rural people, from 1972 to 1994, forcibly confined to the 'homeland' of Lebowa.

Ndebele

The Ndebele were originally an offshoot of the Zulus who, under the leadership of the opportunist general Mzilikazi, broke away from Zululand and invaded the highveld in the 1830s, establishing themselves as the dominant military force there. However, their power was challenged by the Voortrekkers who arrived in the highveld in 1836 and immediately went to war against Mzilikazi, pushing him gradually north, and finally forcing his people accross the Limpopo into modern Zimbabwe. South Africa's remaining Ndebele live, for the most part, in modern Gauteng Province (PWV). With a rich material culture, the Ndebele are justly famous for the superb, brightly coloured geometric designs with which they paint their houses, and whose bold primary colours make startling contrasts with the brown highveld grasslands. Traditionally, Ndebele women used to wear their wealth on their bodies, in the form of huge necklaces and arm-rings of beads wrapped around the arms, legs and torso and elongating the neck. Incredibly uncomfortable as this must have been in a hot climate, the practice was widely seen until a few years ago, and even now Ndebele women in a few areas continue the tradition. For a more detailed look at Ndebele culture, *see* p.526.

Tsonga

Also known as the Shangaan, the Tsonga speak their own *bantu* language and inhabit two main areas of South Africa: northern Kwa-Zulu/Natal and the Eastern Transvaal's former homeland of Gazankulu. Part of a much larger nation in Mozambique, the Tsonga maintain a slight cultural distance from the other South African black cultures. Those of northern Zululand have been governed by the Kwa-Zulu administration for over 20 years, but still maintain their language and take no part in Zululand's inter-clan wrangling. The Tsonga of the Eastern Transvaal originally came over the Lubombo mountains from Mozambique to escape the widespread tribal wars that flared in that country during the mid-19th century, but were forcibly resettled by the apartheid government in the fragmented 'homeland' of Gazankulu. For more information about the Gazankulu Tsonga, *see* p.576, and for a look at the Tsongaland territory in northern Kwa-Zulu/Natal, *see* p.414.

Venda

Another group whose language is distinct from the other black language groups of South Africa are the Venda of the Northern Transvaal. Although they represent the smallest black nation within South Africa (approx 550,000 people), the Venda were never conquered by either Boer or Brit, and have lived in their remote country since at least the 12th century. Builders and settlers rather than pastoralists, by the 16th century the Venda had built permanent stone fortresses and towns similar to those of Great Zimbabwe north of the Limpopo River. Protected by the wide river to the north, by the Lebombo mountains to the east and the Soutpansberg to the south, the Venda were able to beat off numerous attacks, both from the neighbouring Pedi and Swazi, as well as Zulu and Ndebele forays and the inevitable attacks by white settlers.

The Venda also have a strong mystic and occult tradition, stronger even than those of the Xhosa and Swazi, and the lakes and rivers of their well-watered forested country all have sacred significance. Totemic wood carving is widely practised, and propitiation ceremonies common—the most spectacular being the annual *Domba* snake dance of the unmarried maidens, who dance to win the favour of the Python God, the deity who controls both the rains and fertility of the people. Less picturesque is the territory's reputation for *muti* murders, or ritual killings to obtain body parts for magical use. While this goes on, to a greater or lesser extent, in all rural areas of South Africa, it has apparently reached something approaching epidemic proportions in Venda over the past 15 years. This does not affect tourists, however, and is contained in secret within the community. For a more detailed look at Venda culture, *see* p.583.

Tswana

Like the Pedi, the Tswana people are a North Sotho-speaking conglomeration of several large clans. Spread over a very wide area, the Tswana are the third most numerous ethnic group in South Africa and live mostly in the Northwest Province and Northern Cape, although other communities are scattered throughout the highveld. The Tswana are thought to have the longest direct chronology of any black nation in South Africa—historians claim about 1000 years. When the apartheid government forced the Tswana people into the 'homeland' of Bophuthatswana in the 1970s, the new Tswana government promptly took advantage of their 'separate' status to open casinos—at the time forbidden in South Africa. Sun City, the first large hotel/casino complex, was such a success that it inspired all the other 'homeland' governments, as well as those of Lesotho and Swaziland, to open similar enterprises. The Tswana have also, to a large extent, kept out of the political violence that dominated South African life over the last 20 years —with the exception of one attempted coup d'état of the Bophuthatswana government by the 'homeland's army in the mid 1980s, and the early 1994 shooting of three AWB men by a Bophuthatswana policeman—and it may well be that, at last unfettered by the restrictions of white rule, the Tswana may become one of the country's dominant economic communities. For a more detailed look at Tswana culture, *see* p.603.

South Sotho

Usually known as the BaSotho, or simply Sotho, the South Sotho language speakers live mostly in and around the kingdom of Lesotho and the Orange Free State. Keepers of cattle, sheep and angora goats, the Sotho are known for their superb wool-weaving, for their houses decorated with painted geometric patterns (similar to those of the Ndebele, but with more muted colours) and, in Lesotho itself, for their hardy, well-trained BaSotho ponies. As a nation, the BaSotho have not existed for very long, being the offspring of various groups of refugees who fled into the area from the 1830s to the 1850s to escape the warfare and raiding in Natal and the highveld and flocked to the mountain fortress of the charismatic South Sotho-speaking chieftain Moshoeshoe. Moshoeshoe forged a nation out of his ever-growing numbers of subjects and fought off continual attacks from the Griqua, Tswana, Ndebele, Boers and Brits. The BaSotho were never conquered and those living in Lesotho itself escaped the apartheid yoke.

However, their most fertile territories were annexed by the Orange Free State in the 19th century, and the independent BaSotho retreated to a narrow arable plain east of the Caledon river and the high mountain country behind. Thus the South Sotho speakers today are culurally divided between those living in the Lesotho and Orange Free State lowlands, and the fiercely independent highlanders, whose horse culture is famed throughout southern Africa, and whose world, though beautiful, suffers one of the harshest climates on the continent. For a more detailed look at BaSotho culture, *see* p.431.

Indian

The areas around Durban have a huge Indian population—both Hindu and Muslim, which combined with smaller populations in and around Johannesburg and Cape Town, numbers an estimated million, of mostly Tamil or Gujarati-speakers. Durban city centre has a very Indian feel, with its huge mosque, bazaars and restaurants (the Indian food in Durban is superb). The Hindu temples are mostly in the old Indian townships some distance from the city centre—one in the Durban suburb of Westville and another in Pretoria's city centre allow tourist visits.

South Africa's Indians almost all trace their ancestry to poor, low-caste labourers brought over from southern India in the 1860s to cut the sugar-cane fields of Natal. Paid criminally low wages, these labourers had nonetheless begun to climb out of pauperdom by the 1900s, having obtained traders' licences. Some went north to Johannesburg, but most stayed in Natal. It was here that the Indians began their long freedom struggle, under the leadership of one Mohandas Gandhi, an Indian-born lawyer who went to South Africa on business in 1893 and stayed until 1914. After being ejected from a train for refusing to leave a whites-only carriage, Gandhi began to weld South Africa's Indians into a political force, founding a self-help business scheme at Phoenix, north of Durban in the late 1890s, an Indian Red Cross during the Boer War of 1899–1902 and a newspaper called *Indian Opinion* in 1903. In 1913, when all non-whites were ordered to carry passes, Gandhi orga-nized a peace march from Newcastle to the Transvaal, which despite being met with police violence, was ultimately successful in having Indians removed from the 'native register'. Under apartheid, Indians were again made to carry pass books, were disenfranchised and made to live in 'townships'. Although by then many were successful businessesmen, they were subjected to racsim on two fronts; whites regarded them as inferior, blacks regarded them as alien. Much of this racism survives today, yet the Indian freedom struggle has never resorted to violence, trusting instead to patience and parliamentary lobbying.

Afrikaner

Of all the white people living in South Africa, only the Afrikaners are truly African, in that many can trace 10 generations of Dutch, German and Huguenot French ancestors in the sub-continent and whose Afrikaans language, though evolved from European Germanic roots, has developed entirely in Africa.

In order to understand the nuances of Afrikaner culture, the meaning of the words 'Afrikaner' and 'Boer', respectively 'African' and 'farmer', need a little clarification. Both have wider implications: 'Afrikaner', while occasionally used as a collective expression referring to all Afrikaans speakers, usually refers to those of the Cape, while 'Boer' generally refers to those of the Orange Free State and Transvaal. 'Afrikaner' often implies a certain liberalism, while 'Boer' implies reaction and racial intolerance. There are reasons for this: the Cape has always had a more liberal tradition than the rest of the country, perhaps because it was never threatened by black military power during the 19th century, and because life there was comparatively prosperous: the great manorial wine-growing estates, Cape Dutch architecture, furniture-making, music and literature and the Afrikaans language all evolved in the Cape—albeit on the back of Khoi and 'coloured' virtual slave labour. The elegance of the Western Cape's Afrikaner lifestyle was enviously noted by that inveterate social commentator Anthony Trollope who, after visiting the Cape in the 1870s, wrote, '*the visitor is tempted to repine because fate did not make him a wine-growing, orange-planting, ostrich-feeding Dutch farmer.*'

The Boer heritage also has its roots in the Western Cape, but has been culturally distinct since the mid 19th century. The word derives from the term 'trekboer', meaning 'travelling farmer', and describes the first white pioneers to wander into the interior with their live-stock during the 18th century. These people represented the poorer side of Cape Afrikaner culture, those who had no land and who stood to inherit nothing. They followedthe rains and the grazing, hunted the plentiful game, traded a little with the indigenous people and, eventually, carved out extensive farms around permanent water sites. In the Northern Cape, the trekboers hunted out and annihilated the San hunters who killed their sheep and cattle in retaliation for the white depredation of game stocks, but in the east they encountered a power that was stronger than their own—the Xhosa nation. At first, they shared grazing land with the Xhosa, but increasing numbers of trekboer settlers soon led to competition and conflict—the Frontier Wars into which the British were drawn from 1799, following their annexation of the Cape. During this period, a vehement racism began to creep into the Boers' (as they were now known) relations with both Khoi and Xhosa— inspired by fear and the need to hate one's adversary.

The Eastern Cape Boers decided to leave the eastern frontier to the British and the Xhosa during the Great Trek of 1836 and headed for the interior, solidifying their racism through incessant wars with the nations of the interior—in which the Boers, or 'Voortrekkers' (meaning 'forward travellers') did not always come off best, despite their superior weaponry. Added to this, only a few Boers really prospered in the new territories—life for most was an incessant struggle against parasites, fever, wild animals, justifiably hostile locals and sometimes British troops. When gold was found in the Transvaal in the 1870s and '80s, few Boers benefited from the mining—most of which was controlled by English-speaking companies from the Cape. A few years later, Britain invaded the Boer republics of the Transvaal and Orange Free State, and in the course of this, the second Anglo-Boer War (1899–1902) many Boers lost their farms and families. In the years of reconstruction, most Boers remained poor, and only gradually managed to penetrate the professional and governmental world, being obstructed all the way by English snobbery and condescension.

Given all this, it becomes easier to understand the ferocious racism and xenophobia that characterized the Boers' 20th-century rise to supremacy via the brutal workings of apartheid. However, their brand of tough survivalism and attendant racism is capable of change—as has been demonstrated by the lack of right-wing reprisals in reaction to the accession of the new ANC government. Hopefully, the Boer/Afrikaner energy and desire to succeed will, in future, be harnessed for the whole country's benefit.

British

There are few areas of South Africa where English is the dominant language. Sizeable English-speaking communities exist in Cape Town, the Garden Route, Johannesburg and the Eastern Transvaal, Swaziland, and over a wide area in Kwa-Zulu/Natal. But in all these places English is still only one language among many. However, since it was a British Colony from 1806 to 1910, and a British Dominion from 1910 to 1948, the *lingua franca* of South Africa's administration was solidly English until the rise of apartheid, and even that aggressively Afrikaans system did not eradicate it from official use. Added to this, the mining companies have always been run by English-speakers.

British South Africans have traditionally presented themselves as liberal and non-racist, and, while this has often been true in spirit, it is by no means a generally accurate picture. It was the British who systematically destroyed the Xhosa nation during the Frontier Wars of 1799–1879, who smashed the Zulu and Pedi kingdoms, and who acted as arbitrary brokers of the independent kingdoms of Swaziland and Lesotho until their independence in the 1960s. The British brought in, and then ostracized, the Indians of Natal, and most of the later British missionaries harangued and condemned the African cultures they had been sent to evangelize. Britain exploited South Africa's human and mineral resources for her own benefit, and used South Africa as a testing-ground for experiments in total war, such as Lord Kitchener's concentration camps, which were responsible for the deaths of tens of thousands of Boer and African women and children between 1900 and 1902.

However, under apartheid, English-speakers often found themselves at odds with the new order. Though they remained the most economically privileged group, their old racism began to fray and most of the country's whites who campaigned for black rights through the 1970s and '80s were English-speaking. This did nothing to improve the old enmity between them and the Afrikaners and Boers, whose slang names for Brits included *sout-piels* (which translates to 'salt dicks', meaning that they had one foot in Britain, the other in South Africa, and their genitals hanging in the sea), and *rooinek*, meaning 'red neck', referring to the British inability to withstand the African sun (and therefore its hard life). Fortunately, in recent years this Boer/Brit division has eased a little and while the communities still lead largely separate social lives, the old hatreds have softened to rivalry.

Towards a Composite Society

Finally, it must be said that although it is worth understanding the complexity of South Africa's ethnic scene, it is easy to overemphasize the differences between the cultures. Perhaps for the first time in the country's history, there is now a conscious movement among South Africans of all races finally to lay down the burden of mutual hostility and misunderstanding and to work towards something new—the chance of becoming a composite society. That such a deliberate movement should be taking place after so many centuries of conflict is exceptional—we are far more used to seeing the negative side of humanity whenever the problems of nationalism, racial difference and in tolerance arise —and South Africa more than anywhere else has come to be seen as a symbol of this negativity. But what the traveller will notice is an almost unbelievable will to forgive and forget among most South Africans that would have been unimaginable even two years ago. Today's South Africans are doing their best to become what they have never really been— South Africans. Nobody expects the transition to be smooth but, as Steve Biko wrote in his last book before his death in police custody in 1977:

> *'We are looking forward to a just and egalatarian society in which colour, creed and race will form no point of reference.'*

Art and Architecture

Architecture

South Africa's indigenous architecture goes back to the early Middle Ages, when the ancestors of today's Venda people migrated south from Zimbabwe into the Northern Transvaal, bringing with them the Zimbabwean tradition of building walled villages and towns of stone. The practice was abandoned after the 17th century, when the Venda monarchy collapsed and the society reverted to a series of chiefdoms, but the ruins of the old capital, Dzata, can still be viewed, and the workmanship, though simple, is beautiful, with the bases of rounded towers and the rough-dressed masonry of the main walls still standing, despite the ruins having been reclaimed by the surrounding forest (*see* **Northern Transvaal**, 'Venda').

 However, South Africa's most famous architecture is known as Cape Dutch, an elegant, simple style of building that began in Cape Town in the 17th century and continued throughout the old Cape Province into the early 19th century. Its most elegant period was between 1790 and 1810, under the collaboration of the architect Louis Thibault and the sculptor Anton Anreith, who built the best-known Cape Dutch structures, Groot Constantia and the Lutheran Church, both of which are in Cape Town (*see* 'Cape Town, Architecture'). Cape Dutch style is immediately recognizable by its distinctive curved roof gables, sitting atop simple whitewashed fronts, with well-proportioned mullioned windows and dark roofs of slate (in the towns) and thatch (in the country). Most houses spread over one storey, and only the very late buildings (or very grand) rise higher. In general, the gable is the only purely decorative feature, and is thought to have been inspired by the Renaissance gables of

Florence, adopted and gothicized. But the Cape gables are often curved in a way that is not seen in Holland or the Low Countries, and this is ascribed to a Batavian (Indonesian-Malay) influence, the Dutch having colonized the East Indies some years before the Cape of Good Hope. Though more deliberate decorations are lacking, the calm and proportion of Cape Dutch style relies on this simplicity. The earliest surviving houses (from around 1710) are usually built in a T-shape, the long part of the letter extending back from the gabled front. From about 1750 a grander H-shape appears, whose gables are sometimes adorned with mouldings or, occasionally, a pediment. At the apex of Cape Dutch style (roughly 1790–1820), a more complex U-shaped house appears, with the space formed by the U generally occupied by a courtyard, sometimes with pillars supporting a railed balcony.

Cape Town and the Cape Peninsula, the Winelands regions and the Overberg (all in the Western Cape) have the highest densities of Cape Dutch architecture, the best examples being the Constantia homesteads, the towns of Stellenbosch and Paarl (and surrounding countryside), Tulbagh, Greyton and McGregor. However, the Northern Cape has some fine set-piece towns, notably Graaff-Reinet in the Eastern Karoo (built 1781) and Colesberg (1814–30). Side by side with this later, aristocratic Cape Dutch building came some beautiful, if very simple vernacular cottages. Many old wine estates' workers' cottages survive from this period, but from a traveller's point of view the best places to see whole surviving villages is the Bo-Kaap (Malay Quarter) of Cape Town, and in the Moravian mission stations of the Western Cape countryside. At the same time, in the Northern Cape, the earliest Boer settlers of the 1800s built beehive huts of layered stone (known as corbelled houses), similar in form to the ancient Celtic brochs of Scotland Ireland and Brittany, and a number survive around the Western Karoo towns of Williston and Carnarvon.

The early British occupation saw some elegant Georgian building, particularly in the settler country of the Eastern Cape. Though not as elegant as the Cape Dutch style, the British Georgian period nonetheless produced some superb buildings whose look will be familiar to British travellers. Some whole towns survive, notably Grahamstown, Salem and Bathurst, between Port Elizabeth and the Fish River. During the Victorian era many buildings of the solid imperial school, went up in all of South Africa's larger towns. But in general this period, though handsome, is not exciting, and is all too familiar to Western travellers. However, in one town, Pietermaritzburg in Natal, the Victorian building achieved a harmony and simplicity of design unusual for the colonial arcitects of the time, who generally built large edifices designed to impress. Pietermaritzburg's residential neighbourhoods, in particular, have some superb houses—almost all in fine red brick, one to three storey high, with filigreed verandahs of white-painted wrought iron extending up the fronts.

This ironwork became a mainstay of Edwardian design and until the 1960s almost all South African towns boasted handsome arcades. But unfortunately the early apartheid governments with their economic boom and aggressive adoption of the Western industrial aesthetic, tore down many of these arcades and replaced them with ghastly concrete and glass lumps. Some good examples do still survive—notably upper Adderley Street and Long Street in Cape Town and Diagonal Street in Johannesburg.

The Edwardian era also produced South Africa's most innovative architect, Sir Herbert Baker. Mostly active in Cape Town, he contrived an ingenious mix of the Cape Dutch with the English vernacular. Baker's most famous work was Groot Schuur in Rondebosch, Cape Town, commissioned by the mining magnate and empire-builder Cecil Rhodes. Now the Cape Town residence of the South African presidents, Groot Schuur was followed in 1910 by the Union Buildings in Pretoria, a terracotta design of Classical style. But, after this, Baker left South Africa to collaborate with Lutyens on the building of New Delhi in India, and the Union Buildings represent the last distinctively South African Western design to appear in the country—although some handsome Art Deco buildings went up in Cape Town and Johannesburg in the 1930s (take a walk around St George's Mall and Greenmarket Square in Cape Town or on Jeppe and Eloff streets in central Johannesburg). Since the Edwardian period, little has appeared that is not merely imitative of Western post-war industrial design.

However, this is to forget that the most distinctive form of South African architecture does not appear in the cities or centres of white culture. Just as South Africa's architecture begins with the black tradition, so does it end. Throughout all the periods listed above, the most common style of building has been the rondavel, or thatched round hut (though many are far larger than mere 'huts') found in almost all rural areas. For simplicity of design and harmony of form, there is nothing to touch the rondavel. It blends with and complements the landscape, rather than attempting to dominate or influence it. Not all black rural housing conforms to the round pattern (tradition has it that the lack of corners is to give malevolent spirits no place inside the house to hide)—the Ndebele, South Sotho and Xhosa often build oblong buildings, painted with complex, exact geometric designs (*see* 'People and Culture' above). But almost all black rural architecture uses an adobe or mud/dung mix, cool in the heat, yet holding the warmth of a fire when it is cold outside. In Zululand, the traditional form of building is a large, round grass hut with a low entrance door, densely woven from reeds so as to be both watertight and windproof. In the Lesotho Highlands, rondavels are often constructed from dry stone with an inner and outer plaster of mud and dung which can withstand the harsh climate for an indefinite period. As yet, the rondavel has not been incorporated into civic architecture. But now that South Africa is finally being ruled by the majority, it may be that vernacular forms of architecture may finally start to appear in the cities and transform the towns' overall feel to something more genuinely African.

Art

South Africa's earliest rock engravings (mostly found near the Vaal River in Northwest Province) have been traced back approximately 1000 years, and much of the San (bushman) rock painting (found at sites all over the country) is around 30,000 years old. Bearing great resemblance to the prehistoric rock paintings of the Ahaggar Mountains of the central Sahara, San art, with its animal and spirit-world motifs, varies from the highly stylized to the incredibly life-like—especially in its depiction of animals. The San tradition of rock art continued until about 1850, when the last known artist was shot by a farmer (the San were hunted like game from the late 18th century—*see* **Western Transvaal**, 'History') in the Drakensberg mountains, the unfortunate man's corpse being found to have a quiver of pigments strapped around the waist. The later San paintings often depict white men on horses with guns and ox-wagons and sometimes show running fights between San and white men, or San and Bantu warriors, who also ruthlessly persecuted the hunter-gatherers. That both black and white South Africans combined to exterminate the San, who raided their livestock as the game was steadily denuded through the 19th-century, was a crime that will never be atoned for, which has deprived the country of one of its oldest, most peaceful and, many would argue, richest culture.

In the early 19th century, white South Africans began to celebrate the landscape and in some cases the people and willdife of what was then regarded as a savage land. However, a few artists portrayed the indigenous people without caricature; some of the early water-colours and drawings by Samuel Daniell (an English artist who visited the Cape between 1801 and 1803) are superbly beautiful, though the landscapes he sets them in resemble more an ideal of classical Europe than an accurate portrayal of South Africa. Daniell also painted some famous pictures of trekboer life. His best paintings (watercolours) are in the Rust-En-Vreugd collection, in Cape Town. Another Englishman, Andrew Smith, who travelled into the highveld in the early 1830s painted an amateurish but highly valuable record of life among the Tswana, KhoiSan, Ndebele and BaSotho before white settlement. These are housed in the Museum Africa collection in Newtown, Johannesburg. Other commentary-style artists of the period include Thomas Baines (particularly good for the Frontier Wars), W. J. Burchell (mainly pictures of the Khoi), Eugene Carsalis and C. D. Bell (again, pictures of life in the highveld and Karoo), also in the Museum Africa collection.

The later 19th century saw a rise of epic landscape painting in oils, the most notable exponent of which was Pierneef, whose bold colours and slightly stylized outlines resemble the real landscapes of South Africa far more than those of the earlier illustrative painters. Pierneef has a museum dedicated to him in Pretoria, though most of his landscapes were of the Cape and Namibia, rather than the Transvaal. Even more stylized was the Cape Town artist Irma Stern, who studied with the German Expressionists in Berlin from 1913 until the First World War. Her work, featuring African landscapes and people, though not well received in conservative South Africa, remained popular in Europe until the 1950s. She made painting expeditions to Swaziland, the Transkei and Zululand, and further up into German Central Africa (Cameroon) and Tanzania. Her house, in Rondebosch, Cape Town, is now a museum, and has a good collection of her work.

More populist in her approach (she used to sell sculptures to sailors docking at Cape Town) was the nun, Sister Helen Vorster, who created an incredibly lifelike collection of scupltural portraits of San, Khoi and Tswana people in the Northern Cape during the 1930s and '40s. Most belong to private collections, but some of her family groups, showing village and family life, are now in the Pretoria Art Museum, and serve as a precious record of a now-vanished culture, the KhoiSan of the region having moved north or been absorbed into the general Cape 'coloured' population soon afterwards, while many of the Tswana were forcibly resettled in reserves by the apartheid government in the 1960s and '70s, resulting in an erosion of much of the original culture.

Helen Martins, another woman artist active through the 1940s to the 1960s, hardly sold or exhibited any of her work, yet is considered by many to be South Africa's most original white artist. A recluse, Martins lived in the tiny Eastern Karoo village of Nieu Bethesda, north of Graaff-Reinet. Many rumours have been circulated about her private life, from suggestions that she worked as a prostitute (unlikely in the lonely Karoo) to ascribing her an almost saintly status. Certainly her work—almost all sculpture, and almost all contained in the back garden of her small house—is often biblical or occult in subject, with prayers to the moon, and, above all, owls, all crafted in, of all mediums, concrete; they crowd into the small outdoor space, creating an atmosphere that is impossible to define. The Owl House, as Martins' home became known, is now open to the public (*see* **Northern Cape** p.253).

With the exception of some sculptors, such as Eric Skotnes, there is little contemporary white South African art to compare with the work of the past. However, in the past 25 years black artists have emerged to lead the art world in South Africa. Township Art, as it is known, became a recognized movement in the late 1930s, but did not achieve outside recognition until the 1960s, just as apartheid was coming into its own. The early artists, like Gerard Sekoto, George Pemba, Selby Mvusi and others, painted and sculpted in a *naif* style that was a blend of traditional craft motifs and depictions of street life—a meeting of the traditional rural and emerging urban black cultures of the time. Their work was mainly realistic, but this gradually changed, with ritual and superstitious subjects being brought in by artists like Eric Ngcobo and Gladys Mgudlandlu in the 1940s and '50s.

Despite the rise of apartheid, growing interest in township artists caused several unofficial art schools to open up—the best-known being on Polly Street in Sophiatown, Johannesburg (which later moved to Soweto after Sophiatown was razed), and in the Lutheran Church at Rorke's Drift in Zululand. A plethora of work emerged from these schools, much of it reflecting the suffering and hardship of black life, and combining urban, mythical, Christian and animal motifs to express a variety of strong emotions. Of note within this movement are Julian Motau, Welcome Koboka, David Mbele, David Mgalo and a host of others. Although some of the work is brutally realistic, much is heavily stylized in its attempt to put across the extreme nature of black South African life in the late 20th century. Sculptors such as Sydney Kumalo, Ezrom Legae, Aubrey Nxumalo and Lucky Sithole have been particularly effective in this. Painters currently in great demand include Louis Maquela (famous for his use of mythological themes) and Winston Saoli. Commercial galleries, especially those of the smart Rosebank and Sandton suburbs of northern Johannesburg, now ask very high prices for township art.

Public collections can be viewed at the Johannesburg, Pretoria and Cape Town art galleries, but the largest and most comprehensive collection is at the University of Fort Hare, near Alice in the former Ciskei (now part of Eastern Cape province).

European-style poetry and prose have thrived here for only 200 years, but the indigenous traditions of KhoiSan and Bantu oral poetry have their roots in prehistory, and their preoccupation with suffering, survival and the surrounding natural beauty has affected all subsequent South African literature, whether black, English or Afrikaans; almost every work containing a similar atmosphere of profound, if unspoken, melancholy combined with passionate love of the landscape and the wild creatures that live there.

South African Poetry: from the San Era to the Present

San and Khoi poetry, transcribed by a handful of 19th-century missionaries and linguists, unveils a picture of South Africa before the primeval order was upset by colonial adventure. In many, the poems are simple, beautiful appeals to the animal spirits to grant success to the hunter. But occasionally there is room for something more abstract. For example, in one San poem, the wind is perceived as a man coming out of his hut and travelling freely with the birds, scattering grasses over the land. A shaman watches their passage and is noticed by the bird, who speaks, saying, '*I am he who arouses the wind.*' How better could one convey the limitless space and power of the South African wild?

Khoi poems use the animal world as an allegory for human life. In one song from the 18th century, a hyena mother laughingly asks her children, as they clamour for food, how she can possibly satisfy them, when every man's hand is set against her? Humour, hardship and the life of a scavenging predator—the Khoi poet might have been singing of his own life on the arid veld. In another Khoi poem, about a zebra stallion, the poet declaims, '*you dappled fly, you of the shadow and light.*' The hunter salutes his prey; for its beauty, for its skill in using its stripes for camouflage—the '*shadow and light*' of its hide merging with that of the bush—and for the swiftness of its flight from danger, dodging the thrown missile, eluding its clumsy hunters who must watch its escape through the dappled shadows of the bushveld.

The Bantu oral tradition concerns itself with ancestor-worship in the form of epic praise poems to their warrior kings. However, allusions to the natural world are again the main themes of these long anthems. In one such, recording the birth of King Moshoeshoe, the leader who forged the BaSotho nation in the early 19th century (*see* **Lesotho** 'History'), the poet talks of the birth pangs echoing through the caves of the surrounding mountains, the antelope taking fright and stampeding on the veld as the young king emerges from the womb shield in hand. '*Halala you Zulus!*' cries the poet, challenging the BaSotho's hereditary rivals, '*We too have a chief today!*' The Zulus themselves have probably produced more praise poems than any other South African nation, echoing their succession of legendary 19th-century warrior kings. Shaka, the first and fiercest of these, is the object of most such poems. Again, the natural world is brought in to provide similes. Shaka is compared to the slippery pebbles on the riverbed of a ford his enemies are trying to cross, to a leopard stalking his prey in the day, to a buffalo turning on the attacking hyena pack and driving them off with his horns.

Not all poetry from the black tradition is taken up with war, and there is a wealth of more reflective work. Among the most beautiful is a poem by Makholotso Makhomo, a Sotho woman poet who began publishing her work in the 1950s. In one long poem called 'When He Spoke to Me of Love' she becomes a young bride fearing that her new-found bliss may slip away: her voice is burned by a fire in her throat. Despite her pride, she cries, silently, for fear that the groom might change his mind and leave, that the village dogs will drive off the cattle of her bride-price. She goes to him as if in prayer. Only when he speaks is she reassured, and finds words: *'my tongue, unstrung, confessed to him'*.

Most of the more recent black poets deal, inevitably, with the sufferings of their people under apartheid. 'Black Mamba Rising', an anthology of worker poets published in 1986, is a good example of the bitterness and anger the system inspired. More considered are the works of Dennis Brutus, a 'coloured' writer born in Zimbabwe in 1924, who spent many years teaching in South Africa before joining the freedom struggle. Brutus was shot by police, survived, but was imprisoned on Robben Island. He is still writing today (though living in the USA), and his poems rank among the most emotive of the apartheid era. In one poem, 'Pray', written while on Robben Island, he looks at his ideals broken by white rule, crying that he and his people *'have splintered our hearts on their marble whiteness'*.

The necessity of moving to the cities for work, and the breakdown of traditional culture, became a theme of black poetry from the late 19th century which continues today, and here the allegories of the natural world begin to disappear. In his poem, 'The Dispossessed', by Modikwe Dibode, the hero leaves wives, children and cattle to go and work in the mines to pay the hut taxes and poll taxes imposed by the British. The family hold back their tears as their man leaves: *'The custom allows no crying.'* He describes the seeming efficiency of the white man: *'He is awake earlier than you, murmuring, "Blooming Kaffir",'* but the hero is worked to the bone under the ground. When he returns home he finds more taxes that cannot be paid. In absence, one wife has disappeared, his son has left for the mines and *'Nothing is left. Take another contract'*.

Finally, the frustration and sense of futility suffered by blacks merely trying to live from day to day under apartheid is summed up in Jabulani Sibaya's peom 'What Do you Want Me to Do?'. As he points out, *'You arrest me when I complain. You kick me like a dog when I do not complain. What do you want me to do?'*

Equally rich is Afrikaans poetry. The earliest 18th-century poems tend to eulogise the natural beauty of the land. Many 19th-century poets, such as Jakob Du Toit (known as 'Totius', a famous campaigner for Afrikaans as an official language), deal with tedious religious themes, but some delve into a strange fatalistic look at suffering—from the elements, from the British, and from themselves—coupled with a fierce love of place. Much of the early 20th-century poetry develops this theme, often beautifully; in 'The Gods Are Mighty' N. P. van Wyk Louw, considers the guilt of his people, and his own place among them: *'I know the final dream of my breed,'* he says, aware of but not condoning his people's lust to conquer and rule the land; to him that is the way of things: *'but blood is manifest, and words are vain'*. More lyrical is C. Louis Leipoldt (also a doctor, traveller and famous gourmet—*see* 'Cape Cuisine'), who sees the whole country as beautiful, but inextricably caught in bloody conflict. In his poem 'The Banded Cobra' the snake emerges from its hole to find that the long-awaited rains have come. But the other animals, gathering around, point out that the ground is not wet with water but with human blood, and the bushes of the countryside are feeding on it. In the late 1940s, Alan Paton, who is better known as a novelist, summed up the extension of this fatalism towards his people's instigation of the apartheid system: '*We are going to set you apart for ever. We mean nothing evil towards you.*'

Some of the most recent Afrikaans work harks back nostalgically to the natural world of the KhoiSan, before it was broken and dipsersed by the ancestors of the writers themselves, before the land became tainted with the conflicts and injustices of its colonial and recent history. Michael Picardie, a contemporary South African poet, mourns the vanished KhoiSan, becoming for a moment the San hunter struggling in the face of white settlement; '*He hunts me*', sings the San of the farmer; '*I am become his animal.*' Then he prophesies the evil that will follow the annihilation of his people; '*My death is the death of the world.*'

English-language poets have taken this nostalgic line right from the beginning. One work from 1812, written by one George Marshall, an early settler at the Cape, eulogises the Khoi lifestyle (although part of the poem expresses disgust for their physical appearance), and allows that they may hold the key to some ancient wisdom that the white man has forgotten: '*He knows no wants but those which instinct gives... He pities us in search of wealth who roam*'. Much of the 19th-century poetry then breaks with any such attempts at understanding the country and its people and deals with adventure, but continues to laud the wild—subduing wild animals and wilder men, digging for gold, fighting and winning—the usual 'Boy's Own' subjects of Victorian imperial verse make the English poetry from this period amusing, but not particularly interesting.

However, this changes in the early 20th century. A good example is Guy Butler, who described the colonial scene with more amibiguity. In his poem 'Surveyor', he becomes the white government man, in starched khaki, trying to fulfil his contract of cutting a road through the bush. He has reached an impasse, as the local chiefs try to block him—'*I called an indaba of headmen and foremen, and sat like Solomon in my canvas chair between them,*' knowing himself to represent '*The invaders, the roadmakers, the breakers of custom.*' He sits as the chiefs wrangle, thinking of girls and malaria and booze until he admits defeat, at which point the chiefs suddenly withdraw their objections, and the road goes through. The surveyor makes no pretence at understanding this, nor the people that surround him. His last comment on the road is, '*The Commies are using it now.*'

Like the contemporary Afrikaans poetry, much of the recent English-language work concerns itself with despair at the modern South Africa and a futile desire for the pure, prehistoric past. Mark Swift writes about a trip to the Natural History Museum in Cape Town, in which there is a life-size display of San life, using realistic models to create a tableau of the country before white men. Here, the themes of suffering and love of the natural world come together clearly. Swift sees the model of the Bushman (San) '*taut behind glass*', and '*stripped to the bone*', exposed for the education and curiosity of modern tourists, his freehold of the land gone, his world collapsed, and his people and the game dispersed and vanished.

South African Prose

South African prose, particularly fiction, is comparatively recent. The earliest work is related literature written by explorers, such as the Portuguese mariner Vasco da Gama (c.1469–1524), and the much later English-speaking visitors of the early 1800s—Lady Anne Barnard, who wrote entertainingly of life at the Cape, Thomas Baines, who travelled the Eastern Cape, and Andrew Smith, one of the first explorers to travel the highveld in the 1830s (just before the Voortrekkers) and who met with the region's warlords—men like Moshoeshoe and Mzilikazi—and saw their world before the Boer conquest. However, South Africa's best novels are 20th-century.

The works of Eugene Marais, an early-20th-century Afrikaans author (also widely regarded as a fine poet), bridge the gap between the early commentaries and fiction, being mostly fanciful but perceptive studies of the natural world. His two most famous, *The Soul of the Ape* and *The Soul of the White Ant,* deal with those eminently South African but hardly eulogised creatures, baboons and termites. He finds all of human life displayed in the behaviour of wild creatures. In this extract, from *The Soul of the White Ant,* Marais talks of the lifelong attachment between the king and queen ants of a termite colony—despite the female's gradually growing far larger than male. Even if the mound is broken open, '*he*' (the termite king) '*clings to her gigantic body and tries to defend it, and if the ruthless attacker so wills, he dies at her side. What a wonderful example of married love and fidelity, which can survive this terrible change of his beloved to a loathsome mass of fat.*'

It seems as if there is irony here. However, the most ironical writer of them all has to be Herman Charles Bosman, another Afrikaans writer, active in the 1930s, whose short stories deal with every aspect of South African life from racism, through war and the occult, to simple love stories and the eternal bickering between Boer families. Again, there is a great love of place, even though the Marico Bushveld of the Western Transvaal, where the stories are set, is one of the driest and least spectacular areas of the country (*see* **Northwest Province,** 'Groot Marico'), and no visitor to South Africa should go without reading Bosman's set of short stories, *Mafeking Road.*

By contrast, the works of Olive Schreiner, though from the same period, lack any irony at all. Her short novel *The Story of an African Farm*, about life in the arid Great Karoo, is a simple romantic tragedy, with some painful passages of religious torment and guilt, but it has somehow won the position of being South Africa's most widely read novel. It is worth reading some of Schreiner's short stories, contained in most anthologies of the country, which deal, again, with hardship—this time for the early Transvaal Boers. Schreiner's grave, near the town of Cradock in the Eastern Karoo, is a mecca for many Afrikaans devotees of early South African fiction. A far different perspective on the dry regions is offered by Laurens van der Post, who published *The Lost World of the Kalahari* in the 1950s. Rather than write about the white struggle to survive, van der Post was concerned with the fate of the country's original inhabitants, the San, and describes a journey into the Kalahari desert of Botswana to find the few groups of San who still survived with their traditional culture intact, looking at what the white man has destroyed.

South African prose came into its own under apartheid. Many writers from this period are now international names, and there is a clear difference between the work of the established white authors and the emerging black writers of the time. The period's best-known novelist is probably Nadine Gordimer, who won the Nobel prize for literature in 1991. Her anti-apartheid novels are famous, particularly *Burger's Daughter*, in which a young woman, born into an established white family, awakens to the injustices of her people's way of life. J. M. Coetzee, a Cape Town author, has also achieved international fame with his stylized novels which act as effective metaphors for apartheid. *Waiting For the Barbarians*, his best-known work, is set in an imaginary country where the governor of an imperial outpost awaits the inevitable destruction of his world and the retribution of those he governs.

André Brink's novel *A Dry White Season* is more direct—a young Afrikaner befriends a black man, only to learn of his death while in police custody. In his attempt to find out what really happened, the young Afrikaner enters Soweto for the first time, and learns something about that other side to his city—an alien world on his doorstep. Johannesburg's black areas are also the setting for Alan Paton's superb story *Cry the Beloved Country*, written in 1948, the very year that the first apartheid government came to power. A Zulu pastor from Natal comes to Johannesburg to find his lost son, who has vanished after going to work on the mines. The world of destroyed African values, of broken culture that the priest encounters illustrates clearly the hugely negative impact of white colonial society on South Africa's traditional world, and the confused, amoral vacuum it left in its wake.

However, undoubtedly the most powerful book about the apartheid era by a white author is *My Traitor's Heart* by Rian Malan. Although the book is not fiction, the sheer power of its delivery—as Malan reconstructs his family history and, their place in creating the system and recounts his experiences of white/black, black/black and white/white violence and atrocity—is almost too much to bear, exactly because the reader knows that none of it is imaginary. Malan's final admission of his own culpability as a white Afrikaner is moving and real. Anyone who wishes to gain a greater understanding of the violent, apparently directionless hatred and violence that consumed the country through the climactic years of apartheid should read this book.

The best-known black writer of the apartheid years was probably Steve Biko. Again, though not a novelist, Biko's writings were so much to the point, so powerfully accurate in their criticisms of both white complacency and black internecine conflict, and moving in their appeals for simple justice and democracy, that they warrant mention at the head of a list of black literature. His best-known work, *I Write What I Like*, shows just how far Biko was prepared to go to put his case. One passage describes the brutalities of police interrogation (of which he had experience)—the internee, beaten and exhausted, is told by the policeman that he will be killed. His only response is '*How long will it take you*'? Biko's bravery was exemplary. He himself was killed in police custody in Port Elizabeth in 1977.

A welcome note of humour (albeit morbid) appears in Lewis Nkosi's work, especially his story *The Prisoner*, in which a white man falls in lust with his black maid, seduces her, and is then blackmailed—mixed sexual intercourse was banned under apatheid. The white man is jailed, and subjected to the routine beatings and tortures usually reserved for black prisoners, and the narrator speaks dispassionately, and with humorous asides, of the victim's surprise and shock at suddenly being on the other side of the fence. Less vindictive are the works of Daniel Kunene. In his collection of short stories *From the Pit of Hell to the Spring of Life* Kunene deals with the dilemma of being black and middle class, of hesitating to commit to the dangers of the freedom struggle. A young black worker deliberates whether to join a strike or try to keep his head down and survive. A black man and wife revisit the black Johannesburg neighbourhood of Sophiatown, razed by bulldozers in the 1950s and its inhabitants forcibly removed to Soweto, with two friends who are a white couple. The problems of mixed-race friendships under apartheid are beautifully underplayed amid the ruins as the four try to reconstruct in their minds the bustling life that has been reduced to mere blocks of rubble.

The apartheid years produced few 'coloured' novelists compared to black. However, Alex La Guma—a Cape Town 'coloured' who became a leading light in the South African Communist Party (SACP) in the 1950s and 60s, and who, after being jailed in 1964, went into exile in England—has emerged as one of the South Africa's best novelists. Cape Town's ghettos provide the scene for *A Walk In The Night*, in which the squalor and poverty is vividly portrayed: '*the massed smells of stagnant water, cooking, rotting vegetables, oil, fish, damp plaster and timber, unwashed curtains, bodies...cheap perfume and incense, spices and half-washed kitchenware, urine, animals and dusty corners became one vast, anonymous odour.*' Amid this world, a young 'coloured' man finds a murdered white man in a back alley, and wonders what to do, knowing that he could be implicated, fearing any brush with the brutush white authority. More recently, Zoe Wicomb, another 'coloured' writer, published *You Can't Get Lost In Cape Town*, the sad story of a young, unattractive 'coloured' woman who leaves her poor family farm in Namaqualand for a scholarship in Cape Town, where she falls in love with, and is made pregnant by, a white student. Again, the daily humiliations of being a second-class citizen are made apparent, while at the same time the author brings alive the fierce gaiety of Cape 'coloured' life.

The authors featured here represent only a fraction of those who make up South African literature, both poetry and prose, and unfortunately there is no room here to go into further depth. However, it is worth speculating for a moment on what changes can be expected from the new era of flux that the country has just entered. A new set of problems now confront this complex country. What writers and works will emerge from this can only be guessed at.

Muti and Medicine

Muti and Traditional Medicine

Muti, meaning magic, is a word that travellers in South Africa will hear continually. Magic in South Africa carries a different meaning from in Europe, where it is confined to the fantastic and the mythical. Magic or *muti*, as it is understood in South Africa, is better described as folk medicine and divining. About 80 per cent of the population regularly consult traditional healers and herbalists (generally referred to as 'witch doctors'), and many Western-trained doctors in the country speak of their knowledge of the curative powers of indigenous roots and herbs with high regard.

The word 'witch-doctor', though widely used, is misleading. The correct appelations are, for a diviner, *inyanga*, and for a herbalist and healer, *sangoma*. The *inyanga* is usually a male office, whose services are psychic and spiritual—he is called in to deal with possession, where bad spirits must be exorcised and bad influences diverted, to look into the future and to talk with ancestor spirits to ask advice. *Sangomas* are usually women and their job is more practical—to treat the sick. Both offices take some years to learn and there are recognised schools that teach the initiates (usually chosen by one already in office) in most eastern parts of the country. Most do not allow outsiders to observe any part of the training process, but there is an exception—the Swazi government *Inyanga* and *Sangoma* Training College at Siteki, where visitors are allowed in by prior arrangement (*see* **Swaziland**, 'Siteki').

So strong are these traditions that they have been one of the few aspects of black culture to fully survive the shift from rural to urban life. Holders of both offices can be seen even on the busiest streets of the big cities, where their services are required more than ever by the rapidly growing black populations. It can come as a shock when walking in one of the westernized city centres to come face to face with an *inyanga* or *sangoma* dressed in the robes of office (including the inflated bladders of sacrificed animals fixed to the hair, worn in long braids), and you will inevitably step aside rather than meet the power of their stare.

Muti shops, where the requisite animal skins, roots, herbs and charms are sold, can be found in almost any town, and to enter one is to step back immediately into old Africa. Some of the items on sale can be gruesome, including the dried organs of animals, dried snakes and lizards and the like, while others are beautiful—spotted genet cat or ochre-coloured lynx skins—and some, like the myriad dried roots or crosses in bottles filled with holy water, frankly baffling. However, the owners of *muti* shops are generally friendly and willing to explain the use of most things on sale, and a visit and chat reveals much about South Africa that you cannot learn from books.

Until the 1960s, such willingness to talk about *muti* was largely unknown, and even now the mysteries surrounding the real practise of *inyanga* and *sangoma* rituals are kept secret. However, in 1966 a Zulu *inyanga* called Credo Mutwa decided to break silence and publish the entire Zulu mythology (which is very similar to that of the Xhosa and Swazi) in a great work (still in print) called *Indaba My Children*. Although this met with much opposition from his colleagues, Mutwa defended his decision, explaining that in his opinion the roots of white opresion of the blacks lay in the whites' total misundertanding of black culture. He sought to try and rectify this by publishing the oral mythologies, followed by several other works of oral history and, finally, novels.

Mutwa had good reason to do this, having lost his fiancée to a police bullet during the Sharpeville shootings in 1960. He pointed out that, from the beginning of colonial history, the white man's ignorance of some fundamental points of belief had brought unnecessary conflict—for example, in *My People*, his book of oral history, he asserts that an undocumented reason for the unceasing resistance of the Xhosas to white settlement during the

Frontier Wars of 1799 to 1879 was the whites' unthinking and endless slaughter of the Eastern Karoo's great springbok herds, which were sacred to the Xhosa people. Such assertions are impossible to verify, but his point was valid, and his books did much to open white eyes to the wealth of culture that lay in the country they had settled. More importantly, they also prompted genuine white interest in *muti* itself, and today there are several white *inyangas* and *sangomas* practising in Natal, with numbers steadily growing.

There is a darker side to *muti*, however. Human sacrifice, or ritual murder to obtain body parts, is still fairly widespread all over southern Africa. In the Venda country of the Northern Transvaal it reached such a pitch a few years ago that an official investigation was called, which cost the jobs of several people in local government (*see* p.585). Human parts are generally needed for rituals designed to intercede with the spirit world for matters of material fortune or warfare. Therefore, areas undergoing rapid urbanization and business development, such as the new cities of the former 'homelands', have been hard hit by *muti* killings in recent years, as have those areas, like Zululand and the townships of the Natal Midlands, where clan-fighting on a large scale still continues. Victims are generally children, and are often chosen with the community's (even the parents') consent, and the matter is generally kept quiet and not investigated by the police unless—as in Venda—it gets out of hand.

This seems a sad development of traditional culture, but a telling one, illustrating how disrupted and eroded traditional life has become over the course of this century. However, it must be stressed that this is only one side of *muti* and that it in no way involves the modern traveller.

Animism and spirituality has formed a strong part of South African life from prehistoric times—the surviving San hunting songs are full of reverence for the spirits of the natural world—and any visitor to the country will not fail to be impressed by the landscape's almost palpable charge. Occult, or at least inexplicable experiences, come to most people who spend any time there.

These can be everyday in nature: for example when the author was in Swaziland, his highly Westernized hostess came down one morning, visibly upset. She had dreamed that night of snakes, and while vacuuming her room had tripped and fallen. When asked why that should be so distressing, she said both were bad omens, not personally, but for someone close. Some hours later, she had a phone call informing her that her niece had been run down by a car. They can also verge on the fantastic: for example in the 1930s, the doctor, poet and gourmet C. Louis Leipoldt records being told of an old labourer on a farm in the Lowveld, who could speak with the dead. Leipoldt was known for his incisive, almost cold intellectual objectivity, and at the time held the position of health inspector of schools in the Eastern Transvaal. It was on one of his rounds in that region that he was introduced to the man, who was almost a derelict, and decided to put him to the test, though the man in question was unwilling and claimed he was too old. Rather flippantly, Leipoldt asked him to raise the Renaissance German alchhemist Theophrastus von Hohenheim (also known as *Paracelsus*), widely regarded as the father of medical chemistry. To Leipoldt's astonishment, after achieving trance, the old man began to talk in high German, described by Leipoldt as

Bobotie

Take 2 onions, 1kg of minced meat (preferably lamb, beef or game), 1 cup of milk, 1 tablespoon of curry powder, ½ teaspoon of pepper, 2 teaspoons of salt, ½ tablespoon of turmeric, 1½ tablespoons of sugar, a generous wodge of butter (and a bit of olive oil for glazing), 1 slice of good white bread, 2 eggs, 1 lemon, ½ cup of raisins (or dried apricots), 3 tablespoons of chutney, 4 bay leaves and 6 almonds, cut into quarters.

Pre-heat your oven to 350°, peel and thinly slice the onions and sauté them lightly in butter and oil for half an hour, then add the mincemeat and fry until slightly cooked. Soak the bread in the milk, squeeze out the milk, and mash the bread. Pop all the ingredients (except the milk, one egg and the bay leaves) into a bowl and mix 'em up, then put the lot into a greased dish. Put the bay leaves into the meat mixture and bake for an hour. Meanwhile, beat the egg into the remaining milk and pour over the meat after half-an-hour. Serve on yellow rice with a piquant chutney and as big a salad as you can make (particularly good with watercress and nasturtium flowers.

If the prospect of cooking your own is too much effort, the following restaurants serve superb Cape cuisine (details listed in the relevant sections of the guide).

Cape Town: **Kaapse Tafel**, on Queen Victoria Street or **Rozenhof**, on Kloof Street.

The Winelands: **Ralph's**, Die Kelder,
Le Pommier and **Doornbosch** in Stellenbosch, or
the **McGregor Haus** and **Old Mill Lodge** in McGregor.

The Overberg: **Wildekrantz Country House**, near Grabouw and
Huis de Villiers, Greyton.

The West Coast: **Plaaskombuis Guest House**, near Eland's Bay,
Vanmeerhof, on Piekenaars Pass, south of Citrusdal,
Reinhold's, in Clanwilliam,

**Garden Route
and Little Karoo:** **Portland Manor**, Plettenburg Bay,
Welgevoden Guest House, near Calitzdorp.

Great Karoo: **De Rust Gasthuis**, Williston.

Johannesburg: **Gramadoela's**, by the Market Theatre, Newtown, and **Leipoldt's** (named after the man himself) in Braamfontein.

Wildlife

Flora

South Africa boasts a wealth of fauna but even this is easily surpassed by its spectacular flora. The world has six known Floral Kingdoms and most of them cover several continents; but one, the Cape Floral Kingdom, is entirely contained within South Africa. The country has over 20,000 plant species—about 10 per cent of the world total—of which several thousand occur in South Africa alone.

The Cape Floral Kingdom is mainly composed of a heathland vegetation locally known as fynbos (Afrikaans for 'fine bush'), many species of which, such as ericas and strelitzias, flower profusely in the spring. The most famous are the weird, prehistoric-looking protea flowers. Some of these grow to become huge. Whole forests of protea trees flourish in the Cape and Drakensberg mountains, and around Cape Town alone there are some 3000 species of fynbos.

Along the Garden Route coast, and in some parts of Natal and Northern and Eastern Transvaal, grow dense temperate rainforests that appear almost European but for the giant ferns, taller than a man, which sprout beneath them, and the weird shapes of some of the trees, most of which, again, are unique to South Africa. Strangest of all are the knobthorn trees whose trunks are covered with formidable wooden spikes. Some species, like the yellow-wood, mature to become giants of over 30m, and can live for over 1000 years.

A throwback to prehistoric times is the cycad, a giant fern that lives on high downland. Found in the Eastern Cape, Natal, Swaziland and the Eastern Transvaal, these plants were so sought-after by gardeners that they began to disappear from the wild, and it is now illegal to disturb them. Readers of the Victorian adventure writer H. Rider Haggard will remember that in his book *She*, about the mythical Rain Queen of Southern Africa, a weird forest is described as surrounding her homeland. This was inspired by the real cycad forest in Lebowa, in the Eastern Transvaal—the only such forest in South Africa—which is sacred to the Pedi nation and is home to a real Rain Queen who sometimes grants an audience to those who ask. The cycad forest is now a nature reserve and can be visited by anyone (*see* **Eastern Transvaal**).

'*What the oak, ash and cypress tree are to Europe, the thorn tree is to South Africa.*'

So wrote the South African novelist Charles Bosman in the 1930s. And he was right: the richest areas of flora do not support the most game. It is in the less spectacular bushveld that most animals live, where the densely packed acacia thorn trees provide a dense thicket of cover within which the game thrives. The bushveld regions of the Eastern Cape, Natal, and the Swaziland and Transvaal lowveld most closely resemble the picture of 'Africa' many travellers have in their minds: an endless plain of flat-topped thorn trees under which animals graze.

Far less spectacular than the other floral regions of South Africa, the bushveld still holds some surprises. Giant wild fig trees, sometimes the size of buildings, grow in the dry river beds, while the even larger, bulbous-trunked baobab trees stand like the frozen children of Daleks and Michelin men on the acacia plains of the Northern Transvaal. In the wetter bushveld areas, the smooth, white-trunked fever tree, named for its association with malaria, grows in dense copses. At night the white trunks shine faintly and appear as ghosts.

Finally, there is the arid zone of Namaqualand and the Kalahari. The strange *halfmens* tree, a giant desert succulent (water-holding plant) named for its human-like form, clings to the heat-blasted, shale hillsides of Namaqualand, occasionally sharing space with the giant aloe tree known as the *kokerboom* or quiver tree—the name a throwback to the days when the San (bushmen) still hunted the dry country, and used the tough bark to make quivers for their arrows. In the Kalahari, golden grass fed by meagre annual rains shimmers between the widely spaced giant camel-thorn trees, creating a natural parkland where antelope graze.

It is the dry region that in fact steals the floral show in South Africa. Once a year, in September, just after the winter rains, the Namaqualand and western Karoo desert-floor erupts into bloom. A carpet of wild daisies, orange, white, yellow and pink, stretches over the veld and smiles in the warm sun. The flowers stay for one glorious month, then shrivel and the land returns to drought.

South Africa can be visited for flora alone, and the traveller cannot help but be enchanted by the contstant diversity. A wealth of literature that almost equals the number of plant species has been written on the subject—it is a good idea to pick up some of the widely available handbooks so as to be able to identify what you see (*see* **Further Reading**).

Fauna

South Africa is home to the 'Big Five' (in reality the Big Six), which are: elephant, buffalo, lion, leopard and white and black rhino. The reserves where all these can be seen together are confined to the Eastern Transvaal and to Zululand. However, apart from lion, the other 'Big Five' species can be found at game reserves throughout the country. Indeed the leopard (the shyest but most common big cat) lives in almost all the South African mountain ranges, regardless of whether or not it is actively conserved there. A pair is even reputed to breed on Table Mountain above Cape Town. As for elephant and rhino, while populations elsewhere across the continent continue to decline under the heavy toll of poaching, in South Africa the species are well protected and are actually on the increase.

Antelope are common everywhere—large species in the nature reserves and hunting ranches; small species in even the most settled farmland. The same goes for the smaller predators such as caracal (or African lynx), serval, genet and civet cats. However some predators have yet to recover from intense persecution of the last hundred years. The hardest-hit have been cheetah and wild dog, both of which are great killers of cattle and sheep. While both species are numerous in the Kruger National Park and in Umfolozi Game Reserve in Natal, elsewhere they are confined to relict populations. However, re-introduction programmes are under way at several locations and it is hoped that these predators will establish stable populations over the next twenty years.

To see dense concentrations of game, head for the bushveld country of the Eastern Cape, Natal and Transvaal, or into the Kalahari. Mountain ranges tend to be more limited in the amount of game you can see, but large herds of eland, blesbok, mountain reedbuck, zebra and grey rhebok will still be seen, plus baboons, and leopard or caracal if you are lucky. The lush indigenous forests that flourish in some of the coastal mountain ranges support the least game, usually only bushbuck, duiker, genet, vervet monkey and baboon, with lynx and leopard as predators. However, the forests above Knysna, in the Western Cape, still support a few shy elephant, survivors of uncontrolled ivory–hunting that wiped out a population of thousands between 1860 and 1920. Even in the dry Karoo, the nature reserves are surprisingly rich in game, and it is worth looking out at night for the rare aard-wolf (an insect–eating relative of the hyena) and for the elusive brown hyena, smaller than its spotted cousin, which feeds on the night rodents and birds of the semi-desert.

In all areas of South Africa the birdlife is profuse and colourful. Again, of the hundreds of indigenous species, many, like the green lourie, the long-tailed sugarbird and the headed ibis (whose harsh call is one of the definitive sounds of South Africa) are unique to the country. Spectacular birds of prey, such as fish eagles, black eagles, crowned eagles, bateleur eagles, goshawks, secretary birds and a host of others, are commonly seen. Strangely, though, vultures, despite their scavenging lifestyle, have been largely shot out and thrive only in the bushveld game reserves and in a few isolated mountain locations.

Reptiles abound. From the dozens of harmless lizard species (one of which, the leguaan or rock monitor, grows to over a metre) to the most venomous of snakes, the veld literally crawls with the creatures. The only problem (for the enthusiast) is that they tend to hear people coming and hide. This is particularly true of snakes. While the bush around you may harbour a huge number of them, you are unlikely to see them except by chance, and even then they will tend to speed off as quickly as possible. The exception is the sluggish puff adder, which sometimes suns itself on mountain paths, and delivers a nasty bite if you tread on it. Be careful climbing trees in the sub-tropical regions: green mamba and boom-slang often hunt birds in the lower branches. Other common poisonous snakes are the deadly black mamba, the Cape cobra and the spitting cobra, or rhinkals. However, it can never be asserted enough that the traveller has little to fear from snakes and is unlikely even to see one.

This is not true of creepy-crawlies. Outsize insects and arachnids are a feature of southern Africa, and the traveller will have to get used to living with large spiders, beetles, crickets, locusts and sometimes scorpions around. The only really hair-raising invertebrates are the yellow baboon-spider (related to the tarantula and as big as your hand), the back–hunting spider (a bit smaller), the scorpion (usually dun–coloured) and the sun-spider or solugifid, which looks like a giant cross between a spider and a scorpion minus the sting and the claws. Of these, the first three are venomous, but not enough to induce more than a fever, while the sun spider is harmless.

In any case, encounters with these big nasties are rare, and can be avoided by shaking out shoes and sleeping bags, zipping up tents,. and not carelessly putting your hand under stones or logs.

On a more positive note, the landscape also abounds with colourful butterflies and beetles, which are encountered far more often than the scary stuff, and it is worth buying a field guide to identify them (*see* **Further Reading**).

Wildlife and Conservation

Xkhoagu, Hunting star, blind with your light the springbok's eyes.

San hunting song.

Since primeval times, South African conservation and the hunting of its wildife have gone hand-in-hand. But the instinctive conservation of the San and Khoi hunters, who left animals alone in certain seasons and never killed more than they needed, meant that neither they nor the pit-trap and spear-hunts of the black cattle herders made much impression on the vast numbers of game that then lived in the country. It was only when gun-bearing Europeans began to penetrate the interior during the 18th and early 19th centuries that mass wildlife slaughter came to South Africa. Although the eastern areas, settled later, remained game-rich, the Western, North and Eastern Cape and Orange Free State were all but stripped of their game in under 100 years.

To give an idea of the original numbers involved, many early travellers in the Karoo reported antelope migrations, particularly of springbok which could take two days to pass a farm. The trekking antelope numbered millions. One Gordon Cumming, travelling the Karoo during the 1840s, reported 'the plains and hillsides, which stretched away on every side, thickly covered, not with herds, but with one vast mass of springboks, as far as the eye could strain, the landscape was alive with them, until they softened down to a dim mass of moving creatures.' (quote from *Plains of the Camdeboo*, Eve Palmer, Collins Cape Town 1966). Along with the springbok came a host of other species and, trailing them, great numbers of predators.

With such an apparent infinitude of wildlife it was small wonder that the early settlers and travellers orgied in killing, whether for sport or to clear the veld for their livestock. But the muskets killed faster than the game could reproduce. By 1850, three species, the Cape lion, the quagga (a kind of zebra) and the bluebuck had vanished, and by the 1870s the Cape interior was all but empty of game. As settlement penetrated Natal and the Transvaal, the game there began to disappear too. It was only at the end of the century that a few far-sighted individuals began pressing the colonial governments to begin conservation of game.

In 1895, President Paul Kruger of the South African Republic (Transvaal) was persuaded to proclaim an area of what later became the Kruger National Park. Around the same time, the British in Natal preserved Umfolozi, the old royal hunting ground of the Zulu kings, and in the 1900 the Pongola Game Reserve (now known as Itala) was set up. These provided a starting point for South Africa's conservation ethic, and began to attract the first non-hunting wildlife–spotting tourists. Poaching remained rife as local farmers asserted their right to hunt, but the efforts of men like James Stevenson-Hamilton, head ranger of the Kruger National Park for over 40 years, began to persuade the government that wildlife preserves could both bring in money through tourism, and also make attractive showpieces for the country's public image.

The conservation movement had begun: between the 1930s and '60s serious attempts were made to rehabilitate South Africa's wildlife. Species like the bontebok, Cape mountain zebra and Eastern Cape elephants, all of which had been on the brink of extinction, were given their own preserves. Several national parks and hundreds of new nature reserves were proclaimed across the country, even in the Karoo, where re-stocking programmes brought back most of the non-dangerous game with unexpected speed.

What is surprising is that most of this positive conservation happened during the most repressive era of apartheid: while the South African government spent millions on restocking the old game ranges and on setting up well co-ordinated armed patrols to prevent the poaching of elephant, rhino and spotted cat, South African soldiers abroad in Namibia, Mozambique and Angola attacked the game in those countries with a will, and the scandal of South African army officers trafficking in illegal ivory from those countries is only beginning to break.

However, at home, through the 1970s and '80s, things got progressively better for game as even the hunter began to work for conservation. Many farmers in the lowveld districts of the Northern and Eastern Transvaal began to look to raising game, after trying for years to raise livestock in the feverish, drought-ridden country. By restocking their farms with game species, many of these farmers found that they could produce meat without veterinary bills, without having to irrigate, and without the veld becoming overgrazed. On top of selling the meat, they could actually charge hunters money to come in and slaughter the meat for them. At long last the gun was working in favour of wildlife—admittedly only because it paid—and through the late 1980s many farmers in the Eastern Cape and the Karoo also restocked their huge farms with wild game. Even traditional livestock farmers have become far more accepting of game on their land in recent years, and many are beginning to restock with antelope for purely aesthetic purposes.

Today, the proclamation of new nature reserves and national parks continues. New national parks have been laid out at Vaalbos, near Kimberley in the Northern Cape, in the Tankwa Karoo area of the Northern Cape (south of Calvinia), in the semi-desert Richtersveld (also in the Northern Cape) and at several other locations. Of these, only the Richtersveld is open to visitors, as major restocking programmes are under way in the others, and the National Parks Board intends to let the vegetation recover (these are old farming areas) before setting up tourist facilities. Meanwhile, a massive new nature reserve in the Northwest Province (part of the former 'homeland' of Bophutatswana) called Madikwe has been restocked with the 'Big Five', and lion have been re-introduced to the Eastern Cape and Shamwari Game Reserve near Grahamstown, as well as extending their present range in Zululand with re-introduction to the new Phinda Game Reserve. Plans are afoot to extend the vast Kruger National Park into neighbouring Mozambique, and to establish similar vast reserves around Weenen in Natal (at present overgrazed farmland) and in Tsongaland.

The curent number of game reserves, nature reserves, national parks, wilderness areas, conservation areas and state forest—all of them subject to strict anti-poaching laws—now exceeds 350, and if you add to this a similar number of game farms—many of which extend to tens of thousands of hectares—a very healthy conservation picture, easily the healthiest on the African continent, begins to emerge. Meanwhile, within these reserves major work is being carried out to re-establish all the indigenous vegetation and take out all exotics. So successful has South Africa's conservation policy been, that today it is one of the few countries in Africa where even rare game species such as elephant, leopard, lion and white rhino are actually expanding, while endangered species such as black rhino and cheetah are stable.

With tourism on the increase in South Africa since the elections, the new government has pledged to keep ploughing money into its wildlife. On top of this, some of the reserves are beginning to pay for their own conservation, either through selling hunting licences to take out game marked for culling, the money from which pays for the special breeds programmes such as rhino and cheetah, or by selling live game to game reserves elsewhere in Africa which have become depleted. For example, the Kruger National Park now has too many elephant and, rather than cull them, has sold and translocated hundreds to reserves in Kenya, Namibia and Zimbabwe. Even black rhino, now breeding a small surplus in the Kruger, have been sold to restock areas of Namibia, and, if this trend continues, South Africa's wildlife can look to a secure future.

Landscapes

Once, when asking directions from a Free State farmer, I asked, 'Is the route beautiful?' He looked at me for a moment, shrugged, and said 'The whole place is beautiful. Have you seen any ugly land since you came here?'

South Africa is a land of intense physical beauty; one of the few things that all South Africans have in common is a shared love for the silence, winds and endless wide spaces of their country. Space and room to breathe: in the red and black, blasted hills and semi-desert plains; in the wide, green farmland valleys; in the high splendour of its ancient mountains, whose peaks, long since levelled to flat plateaux, rise vast and aloof, to hang suspended in mid-sky; in the dense, cathedral forests; in the singing, sub-tropical thickets of the bushveld; in the smooth golden grasslands of the highveld plateaux; in the endless beaches of white sand—space, colours sharpened by the intense southern sun, the whole landscape radiating presence born of heat and harsh light. Ancient and independent of man, even in the stillest midday hour South Africa's landscape feels deeply alive: raw, remote and beyond understanding.

Mountains: in the Cedarberg we climbed to a great cliff whose face was split with fissures that widened to smooth corridors, and gave onto a circle of level grass encircled by a rampart of savagely eroded rock through which the wind whisted and sang like flutes. In the greener heights of the Hottentots' Holland, we spent the night cowering in our tent as a male baboon descended from the wooded kloof above and challenged our scent with barks and shouts. On horseback in the high Malutis of Lesotho, our pack mule bolted down a mountainside so steep that he seemed certain to tumble into the river gorge below. Yet with a skip and a buck he dumped our provisions on the brink and cantered back up to us, arching his neck and snorting to show how clever he was. In the Bankberg of the eastern Karoo we sheltered in a cave as the heavens opened and rain that had been two years in coming transformed the dry mountains into giant, sodden mud-slides. Intent on shelter, a family of mountain zebras skittered by, their thick black stripe doubled now with stripes of running water.

Semi-Deserts: our first night in the Karoo, awed to silence by the level plain whose distant hills turned blue and mauve and disappeared into a night of stars so bright and close and numberless that you imagined they were singing. Next day, in the fearsome heat of Christmas Eve we panted in the shade of thorn trees and traced patterns with a stick around the paw-print of a lynx impressed in sand too hot to touch, the air drowsing to the cooing of doves.

Coasts: night-time with the moon at Cape Columbine, the dry veld inland awash with spring flowers. The rough Atlantic exploded onto the rocks where we sat swaying with tequila sipped from limpet shells and glimpsed the silvered backs of playing seals breaking surface to greet the moon. Further north, with the moon waxing, we walked a wild beach and came upon a young seal beached and heaving with exhaustion; through the long night we sat with it until we realized that it should be left to die alone with the proper, secret dignity of a wild thing. At Noordehoek in the icy, sapphire waters, a mother whale and calf rolled, lazy, in the swell just off the beach, and a lone male splashed his enormous tail far out in the bay. On a moonless night as black as pitch, we cast the round, weighted net into the warm Keiskamma estuary and filled the buckets with writhing prawns. Again by night, on the Wild Coast, walking a forest path above the sighing breakers, we were halted by a delicate scent as pretty as a song—a creeper covered in secret night-flowers, white like ghosts that open only when the last rays have fully gone and await the great grey moths that come to take their pollen. On the wide lagoon at Kosi Bay the silver milkfish took the line and made its run for the open sea, bending the rod double, sending the reel into rattling hysterics and causing the fisherman to leap from the boat into the waist-deep shallows, heedless of the crocodiles and his sarong, which dropped from his body and left him bare to the sunlight, water and the laughter of his friends.

Forests: in the Outeniquas, a woodland green as England under an un-African drizzle—except that the trees soar to a canopy too high for anything but the vervet monkeys that occasionally distract the eye with branches left swinging, dropped twigs and leaping, shadowed forms. Rustlings and crashings in the thickets as animals escape the eye; giant ferns, twice as high as you, create a forest within a forest; above all there is a great calm disturbed only by the knowlege that, somewhere in the woods, elephant are walking, perhaps watching you now.

Atop the Soutpansberg, another drizzle falls on tall, sub-tropical trees that disappear halfway down the mountain, revealing brown bushveld hundreds of metres below, where rain will not fall for another six months; on the sodden forest floor, porcupine quills wet with blood mark a leopard's lost night-time battle; across the track flies a blurred arrow of russet, as a red duiker—shy forest antelope—crosses quicker then the eye can follow. In the dense, impenetrable sand forests of Tsongaland, lithe spotted cattle and their herd-boys follow elephant tracks to hidden clearings whose pasture they share with the forests' beasts. At Hogsback, above the tree-line, we stumble on a herd of aggressive, half-wild cattle by night and have to creep beneath a huge bramble bush, shivering at the thought of giant spiders down the back, as the great horns swish and we quiver, half terrified, half-embarrassed until they go and only the owls remain.

Bushveld: in the dry and golden morning an impala ewe stepped from cover onto the warm dirt road. Such a common sight, an impala, but so beautiful that you must stop and wonder how so elegantly perfect a form should be no more than protein for half the predators of Africa. Another morning, after sleep disturbed by the distant sound of lions—their heaving cough waking us immediately, a primeval memory of danger as clear as yesterday, jutting rudely into our modern psyche, despite the millenia since our ancestors worried about such things as lions—another morning, but this time the yellow bushveld grasses wet with dew and the thorn trees hung with summer green. An incessant chatter of birds, who swing and flit between the thorns in little darts of colour. A hundred yards in front of the tent stands the massive bulk of a rhino, who only snorts and carries on feeding when we get up and light the fire for coffee.

Kalahari: no surface water for hundreds of miles, yet reserves of water below the ground give life to the great camel-thorn trees and shimmering grasses that march between the miles of blood-red dunes. Atop one, using the sandy rim as shade, sprawl a pair of lions, lazy with daylight, drowsing away the hours of heat until night-time and the hunt. Knowing this, the antelope—dainty, liquid-eyed springbok on fragile legs, and great, sturdy gemsbok with horns like lances—stand quietly about, despite the proximity of their persecutors. Taking their cue, we stop around a sand-dune corner from the lions, switch off the engine and listen to the silence. Despite the life around us, nothing stirs. Below the road is a dry river-bed. Breaking all the safety rules, we leave the car and cross the fossil river into Botswana, tense with knowing that the great cats are close, and dance a silent polka under the wide and sunlit heavens.

The Western Cape

*Table Mountain seen
from Blaubergstrand*

'...the most stately thing, the fairest Cape we saw in the whole circumference of the earth...'

Sir Francis Drake, after rounding the Cape of Good Hope in 1580

If the wind is in the north, the flat top of Table Mountain is hidden by a great cloth of white cloud, giving the impression of a giant locomotive frozen in headlong rush to the sea. If the wind is in the west, the clouds pour over the landward slopes in a thick cotton-wool waterfall, a leviathan duvet ten miles long. One of several legends has it that the cloud is smoke from the pipes of the Devil and St Peter, who sit playing cards on the mountain, their hands deciding the fate of the great vibrant city that sprawls below, spilling out across the plain of the Cape Flats towards the far-off wall of the Hottentots' Holland.

The Cape Peninsula, a narrow spine of forest and mountain, runs 75km out into the ocean off Africa's extreme southwest corner, neatly dividing the warmer and cooler ocean currents. Table Mountain and Cape Town form the boundary between the peninsula and the continent behind. The Cape of Good Hope marks the peninsula's southernmost point, terminating at Cape Point in a white-topped swirl of shifting waters.

On the peninsula's east side, the Agulhas current makes for beaches of warm water, overlooking the wide miles of False Bay, along whose distant further shore marches the southern end of the Hottentots' Holland mountains. The west side's beaches are chilled by the Benguela current, up from the Antarctic.

On both sides, small resort and fishing towns cling to the narrow coastal strip between mountain and beach. The Cape of Good Hope itself is now a nature reserve, while the Peninsula's mountains, also divided into several reserves and national forests, culminate in a high massif on the north end of the Peninsula—Devil's Peak and Table Mountain—whose wooded slopes lead down to Cape Town's handsome city centre and the harbour of Table Bay. A smaller upland—the Lion's Head and Rump (the Rump is also known as Signal Hill)—also rises out of the city, joined to the north side of Table Mountain by the Tamboerskloof Pass. Below this lie the wealthy beachside suburbs of Sea Point, Clifton and Camp's Bay.

Inland from Table Mountain, between False Bay and Table Bay, stretch the Cape Flats, a marshy, sandy plain some 60 to 70km across. Cape Town spills into them first as white suburb—the residential areas of Bellville and Parow around the low Tygerberg hills—then as industrial suburb and township, or 'locations' in the old language of apartheid.

Atlantic Ocean

Robben Island

Milnerton

CAPE TOWN

Table Bay

Sea Point

Green Point

Parow

Bellville

Lion's Head

Maitland

Clifton

Woodstock

Pinelands

Observatory

Camps Bay

Univ. of Cape Town

Devil's Peak

Rhodes Memorial

Langa

Table Mtn.

Groot Skuur

Rondebosch

Athlone

Crossroads squatter camp

D.F. Malan

NEWLANDS FOREST

Newlands

Guguletu

Nyanga

CECILIA FOREST

Kirstenbosch Bot. Gdns.

Llandudno

World of Birds

CONSTANTIABERG FOREST

Wynberg

Constantia

Hout Bay

Groot Constantia

Mitchell's Plain

Khayelitsha

TOKAI STATE FOREST

Tokai Homestead

HOUT BAY FOREST RESERVE

SILVERMINE FOREST & NATURE RESERVE

Noordehoek

Sunrise Beach

Muizenberg

False Bay

Kommetjie

Kalk Bay

Fish Hoek

Seal Island

Scarborough

Simon's Town

Boulders

Atlantic Ocean

CAPE OF GOOD HOPE NATURE RESERVE

Smitswinkelbaai

N

Land over 200 metres

10 kms
6 miles

Cape of Good Hope

Cape Peninsula

89

These vary from the relatively prosperous 'coloured' townships of Athlone and Mitchell's Plain, to the poorer, predominantly black townships of Langa, Guguletu, Monwabisi and Khayelitsha. There are desperately impoverished shanty towns, like Crossroads, and many squatter camps, which are now creeping from the Cape Flats to the Peninsula mountains. Townships used to be divided by law into more-or-less exclusively 'coloured' and 'black' areas, and even though apartheid no longer exists, the townships have mostly retained their racial boundaries. Lately, however, there has been greater ethnic movement between the townships, and those who have the money have begun moving into Cape Town proper. Certain areas of the city, such as Maitland and Woodstock, are now at least half 'integrated'.

The north and east of the Cape Flats are still farmed, mostly as market gardens, giving way to vineyards. In the far eastern stretch behind False Bay, some 40km from the city proper, racehorse studs and training stables sit among pine plantations below the slopes of Sir Lowry's Pass. The N1 and N2 highways, which connect Cape Town with the great country beyond the mountains, both cross the Flats, the N2 servicing the D.F. Malan International Airport as it goes.

Possessed of a tangible vitality, Cape Town's collage of human, floral and geographical contrasts seduces most visitors. Capetonians themselves, at whatever economic level, tend to love their city fiercely, regarding it as a place apart from the rest of South Africa. From the busy Art Deco streets and wrought-iron arcades of the old colonial town, you can look up at the deep forest and giant buttresses of rock that cling to the wild face of Table Mountain. Lynx, baboon and small buck still live up there, and even leopard have been reported. The blue ocean is never more than a few minutes away.

At the core of Cape Town life are two distinct but related cultures; the Cape 'coloured' and 'Malay' Islamic, both derived from three centuries' mix of the Cape's original Khoisan, Dutch settler, Malaysian and West African slave blood. Afrikaans and English culture are equally strong among Cape Town's whites. Black African influences (mostly Xhosa) and a small Indian population add spice, giving the city an atmosphere that is part Asian, part African, part European. Street markets, musicians, prostitutes and beggars throng the old city and harbour areas. Neighbourhoods have distinct flavours. Alternate *joie de vivre* and languorous *ennui* best describe the feel of Cape Town.

Climate

Cape Town and the Peninsula are blessed with a 'Mediterranean' climate; a green winter of heavy rains and chill northwest winds, and a largely cloudless, baking summer (though the odd shower does occur). Wind is the love and bane of Capetonians. Winter sea-winds bring coughs and colds. Summer brings the southeasters—violent blustery annoyances that can blow for days at a time. But locals call it the 'Cape Doctor' for its supposedly cleansing property. Certainly, it blows the smog away and takes the edge off a potentially foetid summer.

Flora

Cape Town and the Peninsula are part of the unique Cape Floral Kingdom (one of the world's six Floral Kingdoms). Over 3000 species of fynbos (heath) plants and flowering protea shrubs cover the mountains where exotic tree species have not been planted, with some species specific to the area. The most spectacular of these are the silver trees—largest of the protea family at up to 10m high—whole shimmering woodlands of which grow on Table Mountain and Lion's Head. In spring and early summer, look out for clumps of purple erica, similar to heather; tall watsonias, like a wild iris, in scarlet and rose; fiery flowering aloes, called red-hot pokers; micranthus, whose tiny blue flowers are tinged with red; the bright orange 'flames' flower (endemic to the southern Peninsula), white, blue and purple wood orchids, dry-petalled everlasting flowers, and a host of others, all colourful.

The dense forests which extend along eastern Table Mountain, brushing the edges of many residential neighbourhoods, are almost all composed of introduced pine, oak and gum. Most noticeable from the city are the tall, flat-topped Mediterranean umbrella pines, groves of which dot the slopes around the University of Cape Town campus, and under which eland, wildebeest and zebra graze safely behind a game fence.

Cape Town's wet winter is cheered by tall white arum lilies that grow wherever there is grass. In summer, the city riots with myriad exotic flowers. Most common are bougainvillaea (whole trees of it), purple jacaranda, luxuriant hibiscus, red flowering gum, and clematis—many of the world's most colourful flower species are found in Cape Town's parks and gardens.

History

The Cape's original inhabitants were the San and Khoi peoples (respectively the 'bushman' and 'hottentot' of colonial language). Both were yellow-skinned, athletic people, but with distinct cultures: the San were hunter-gatherer and the Khoi pastoral nomads herding sheep and cattle. Historians dispute the exact date of arrival of animal husbandry to the Cape, but current estimates put the Khoi's move to pastoralism at early in this millennium, following contact with black African pastoralists moving down to the central and eastern Southern Africa from Cameroon and the Sahel. By the time the first Portuguese mariners rounded the Cape in the 1480s, Khoi culture seems to have become dominant on the good grazing lands near the coast. Living off a milk diet, the Khoi had grown taller and stronger than the San and had pushed them further into the interior where grazing was less good. A sub-culture of Khoi clans who had lost or never possessed cattle existed on the Cape beaches, and were christened *strandlopers* (meaning 'beachcombers') by the Dutch. They gleaned their living from the tides and were held in low esteem by livestock-owning Khoi. As with pastoralist cultures elsewhere in Africa, livestock, particularly cattle, were at the centre of social and ritual life. The Khoi trained their cattle for riding and even, by a series of whistles and shouts, to surround, trample and stampede through the enemy in war.

The first documented contact (though there was almost certainly contact before this) between Khoi and Europeans at Table Bay was violent and portentous. Contemporary Portugese chroniclers recorded that in 1510, the viceroy of India was on his way back to Lisbon to retire and receive due honour from the king. He ordered the ships to put in for water at the Cape and to barter for cattle with the local Khoi. The Portuguese took more beasts than were agreed, and the Khoi became aggressive. The outraged Europeans went back to the ships for reinforcements, landed again with about 100 men, drove off more cattle and snatched some children. The Khoi whistled to their cattle to surround the invaders, who had come ashore without armour or guns, thinking the Khoi not worth the trouble. In the ensuing skirmish, most of the Portuguese, including 12 captains and the viceroy himself, were killed, As Noel Mostert wrote in his superb history book *Frontiers* (Pimlico Press, 1992), they had 'Fallen at the hands of those they considered the least of men...victims of their own contempt'.

Over the following 150 years, Europeans and Khoi continued to trade, and sometimes fought, but both peoples seem to have become accustomed to each other. Portuguese, Dutch, English and French ships began stopping for fresh water and food at Table Bay before rounding the Cape and plying the dangerous currents of the south coast towards the Indies, but no European power claimed the Cape for its own until the mid-17th century, when Holland's maritime economy, having survived the chaos of the European religious wars that had collapsed both the Portuguese and Spanish overseas empires, became suddenly dominant. The Dutch had acquired prosperous new colonies in Batavia (modern Indonesia), but their fleet had no permanent stopping point for taking on water and supplies during the long voyages to and from the East Indies.

Dutch ships had traditionally used Lisbon to service their East Indies shipping, but the wars had put paid to that, and the Dutch East India Company was looking for a new servicing point further towards the East. The Cape was not their immediate choice; its storms and cross winds could prevent ships from making landfall for weeks. However, in 1650, a Dutch East India ship was stranded there for some months and the crew survived well, trading with the Khoi and hunting the plentiful game. They managed to get word of their plight back to Europe, and in 1651 a relief force was sent to fetch them home. One of the rescue party was a ship's doctor called Jan Van Riebeeck, who had, in fact, been dismissed from the Company for dishonesty, and was trying to get re-hired. While at the Cape, he made a tentative survey of the its resources. Back in Holland, he urged the East India Company directors to opt for Table Bay, and suggested himself as a possible Governor.

In April 1652, Van Riebeeck returned to the Cape with about a hundred settlers, whose initial enthusiasm very soon waned; elephant, lion and the local inhabitants made walking around dangerous, and limited farming to what could be raised inside a bank-and-ditch barricade. The settlers were under strict orders not to invite trouble by infringing on Khoi land with the plough. Nor were they to enslave the Khoi for labour. Instead, slaves were imported from Batavia (Indonesia) and from West Africa. Many of these died in the cold winters or tried to escape. The surrounding Khoi did brisk trade capturing runaways and returning them for a fee, but the settlers, lacking a vigorous labour-force and unwilling to labour themselves, immediately began to stagnate.

A certain mutual contempt between Khoi and settler had been present from the beginning. The Khoi seem to have regarded the Dutch as weak, for their inability to prosper in the surrounding plenty. For their part, the Calvinist Dutch found many Khoi customs repugnant. For example, the Khoi used to cover their bodies in animal fat, both for adornment and to keep the flies from biting; this stank, and there are many accounts of settlers retching while doing business with the locals. On top of this, the khois' nudity and polygamy inflamed both the religious outrage and libidos of the frustrated settlers.

A dislike of the Khoi, seems to have been the early colonists' only point of agreement. Behind the colony's earthern ramparts resentment smouldered: the Company forced its settlers to service the visiting ships for their livelihoods, but only as company employees shifting company merchandise—they were forbidden to trade their own goods. Fortunes were not being made. Morale among settlers and garrison was low, and the Company's officers only kept discipline via a brutal regime of brutal floggings and hangings. After five or six years, the pressure of settlers trying to evade the authority of the mud and brick fort from which Van Riebeeck governed, finally forced the Company to abandon its initial caution and approve 'Free Burgher' farms outside the colony boundary. Morale improved, but the first land conflict between white settler and native South African had begun.

Once the Dutch moved outside the fort, the Khoi immediately around Cape Town began to be gradually absorbed into dependence on the settlers—as farm employees and suppliers of cattle, despite a series of wars in which the Dutch did not always come off best. Disease, alcohol and firearms were powerful weapons for the Dutch, and the Khoi tribes around Cape Town lost land and herds and in the space of about 30 years, becoming dependent on the settlers for food.

Through the 18th century towns sprang up on the Peninsula and the immediate interior, while Cape Town saw a steady immigration from both Christian Europe and the Muslim East (modern Indonesia and Malaysia). These Asians, brought in as slaves, were often skilled craftsmen. A few aristocratic Indonesians, such as the Rajah of Tambora and Sheik Yussuf of Macassar, who had rebelled against the Dutch East India Company in Indonesia, were exiled in the Cape, but the majority were brought in as skilled slaves (mostly craftsmen) and became the ancestors of today's Cape Malay population.

By the 1780s, the Dutch East India Company was foundering, but the Cape itself was finally prospering, and the 'coloured' and Malay cultures were well established, giving Cape Town a cosmopolitan flavour that surprised many travellers of the time. The white-settlers too, now several generations in, were evolving their own Cape Dutch society, used to acting without governmental control. But their independence was about to be curtailed.

Confident after a century of sporadic but victorious wars with the Dutch, and worried at the rise of Napoleon's navy, the British East India Company found itself in the same position as the Dutch had been 150 years before. Valuable new possessions in the Indies necessitated control of the trade route east. In 1795 Cape Town was taken from the Dutch following the Battle of Muizenberg off the Cape Peninsula, given back for a few years, then annexed again in 1806 after the Battle of Blaauwberg.

The Cape's British Governors tore their hair out trying to keep the Cape Afrikaners under British rule. The most prosperous burghers had little difficulty adapting to the tighter regime, but many poorer Afrikaners simply boarded their wagons and headed even deeper into the interior, involving the British in a series of expensive native wars. Meanwhile, Cape Town's port, servicing all of Europe's cargo and troop-carrying ships to and from the Indies, was thriving, and acquired its name 'Tavern of the Seas'.

Through the 19th century, Cape Town became the centre of sporadic British attempts to unite the rest of the fragmented country under the Union Jack. But despite the inevitable stuffiness of British rule, Cape Town had by now evolved its own atmosphere—a mix of narrow, but educated liberalism among the old Cape Dutch and English, and a unique brand of anarchic, hedonistic survivalism among the Cape's down-trodden 'coloureds'. After the Boer War (1899–1902), the Cape parliament was re-organised along Westminster lines. Blacks had a qualified vote, while 'coloureds' had full male franchise. Cape Town's English colonialism, though racist, could not actively stifle 'coloured' culture.

The Second World War saw the apex of Cape Town's importance as a port—the Suez Canal was closed, and all British troop and merchant shipping had to round the Cape. Simon's Town, on the Peninsula, became a prime British Navy base. Many 'coloureds' joined the Cape Corps, as they had in the Frontier Wars, Boer War and the First World War, (*see* **South African History**) and fought with distinction overseas.

Even following the accession of the Afrikaner Nationalist Party in 1948, geographic and cultural distance from Pretoria meant that Cape Town and its enfranchised 'coloureds' continued their lively isolationist culture for two more decades as apartheid slowly closed in. The 'coloureds' finally lost their vote in the late 1950s, following the Separate Areas Act of 1950. But it was another 16 years before Cape Town's 'coloureds' were subjected to the full, humiliating demonstration of their newly official status as second-class citizens.

In 1966 District Six, the vibrant 18th- and 19th-century residential and commercial centre of Cape Town's 'coloured' culture, was declared a 'white' area. Often described as 'the soul of Cape Town', District Six suffered the expulsion of most of its 55,000 odd inhabitants to a new township called Mitchell's Plain, out on the Cape Flats. Government blustered that the area had become a health hazard, and was to be the figurehead of a benign urban re-planning. Bulldozers razed the quarter. Though the land was prime real estate, developers did not buy it, and the empty patches of grass remain today, green scars between the city centre and the Southern Suburbs. Plans are now afoot to redevelop the site for housing, but so far, nothing has happened.

But through the 1970s and '80s, Cape Town still retained its (much debated) reputation as South Africa's most liberal city. Archbishop Desmond Tutu, Cape Town's first black archbishop, began his long campaign of conscience from St George's Cathedral (which continues today in his appeals to end the factional violence). The University of Cape Town was known as a hotbed of anti-apartheid activity through the 'State of Emergency'. Students and academics were routinely arrested and detained.

Since the dismantling of apartheid began in 1990, Cape Town has changed drastically. More politically violent than before, the city has also seen, over the past 15 years, a huge acceleration in the influx of Xhosa people from the former Transkei and Ciskei 'homelands' to vast squatter camps on the city fringes, which have introduced all the problems of Third World urban poverty. But today's city of two million and rising is still one of the most culturally vivacious and geographically beautiful in the world, and a distinct world apart from the rest of South Africa.

Architecture

The Cape has a rich architectural history. The earliest buildings, of which many still survive (both humble and grand) were constructed in a style now commonly known as Cape Dutch. Their principal feature is a curved gable, which evolved from the Florentine-influenced medieval buildings of Holland, the colony's 'motherland', and from the Asiatic styles seen by the Dutch East Indian settlers in Batavia (Indonesia) and designed and built at the Cape by Indonesian slaves. Walls are usually whitewashed with a tough lime produced from sea-shells. In country areas, the roofs were traditionally thatched, but those in the city were built with flat, slate roofs to guard against fire. Half-doors like those of a stable are common and windows are generally mullioned.

Cape Dutch interiors were also distinctive, with an emphasis on indigenous South African hardwoods. Yellowwood, which casts an airy, golden light, was generally used for ceilings, beamed across with dark, reddish stinkwood. Cape furniture makers also used yellowwood and stinkwood in their work, creating simple, well-proportioned pieces of great beauty often with simple but pleasing inlaid patterns, but also created such a demand for the woods that whole forests were cut down. Today yellowwood and stinkwood are rare and expensive. For a more detailed look at the various forms of Cape Dutch architecture and how they developed, *see* **People and Culture**, 'Art and Architecture'.

During the late 18th and early 19th centuries, Cape Dutch architecture flowered in the work of two European artists, Anton Anreith and Louis Thibault— sculptor and architect respectively—who settled in the Cape at the end of the 18th century and blended their styles with great success. Born in Germany in 1754, Anreith came to South Africa as a soldier in 1777, switched to sculpting and remained in the Cape until his death in 1822. His wood or plaster sculptures in high baroque style can be seen on many of the city's pediments and church pulpits. Louis Thibault, born near Amiens in 1750, studied architecture and military engineering in Paris, and also came to the Cape as a soldier (1783), his regiment having been hired by the Dutch East India Company. He turned architect before the British invaded in 1795. The pair's best-known works are the Lutheran Church, on Strand Street and the wine cellar at Groot Constantia, the Cape's oldest and most opulent wine estate.

More modest, but no less beautiful, is the Bo-Kaap, an area of 18th-century artisans' cottages on the Lion's Head, just above the city centre, which were taken over by Malay ex-slave craftsmen in the 1830s, after Britain abolished slavery in her colonies. The area has a strong Eastern flavour, with the houses painted in bright colours, and the minarets of small mosques peeping above the cottages.

Under the Victorians, Cape Town acquired solid neoclassical and Gothic public buildings, such as the Houses of Parliament and St George's Cathedral, and whole streets of elegant town-houses with distinctive wrought iron balconies, good examples of which still survive in Long Street, Upper Adderley Street and in the Southern Suburbs. The Edwardian era saw some superb work by the architect Sir Herbert Baker, who built Groot Schuur manor house in Rondebosch for the billionaire mining magnate Cecil Rhodes—a building that has since become the Cape Town residence of the South African heads of state. Baker went on to design the Union Buildings in Pretoria before heading off to India to work on the New Delhi project with Sir Edward Lutyens

In the 1930s, with British Imperial prosperity at its height, there was a flurry of building in the Art Deco style in South Africa—Cape Town's St George's Mall and Greenmarket Square are pure Art Deco.

After the Second World War, Cape Town suffered, as did everywhere, from lumpish modern building; the Foreshore and the Business District below Strand Street are unhappy testaments to this, as is the Golden Acre Shopping Mall on Adderley Street, by the train station. However, most of the concrete and glass was concentrated in the compact little business district below Strand Street. If you stay in the upper city centre, you hardly need look at any ugly buildings.

Cape Town

Getting There

by air

International and domestic flights arrive at D. F. Malan Airport, 20km from the city centre on the Cape Flats along the N2 highway. **Car hire** can be arranged at the airport, and a **bus service** to Cape Town's bus station (run by Inter-Cape) leaves every half hour from outside the international terminal. Passenger services and general information ✆ (021) 934 0444

by car

The main highway connections to Cape Town (Kaapstad) are: the N1 northeast to Pretoria, Johannesburg and Bloemfontein via the Winelands and the Great Karoo; the N2 east to Durban via the Garden Route and Eastern Cape; the N7 north to Windhoek in Namibia via Springbok

by bus

Bus services along main highways are run by InterCity Greyhound ✆ (021) 419 2246, Inter-Cape ✆ (021) 934 4400 and TransLux ✆ (021) 405 6209/3333. All buses leave from the central bus station on Adderley Street (*see* below).

by taxi

Black taxis, cheap, fast but more dangerous, run along all the main highways and connect Cape Town with even the smallest towns along them. These also pick up and set down at the Adderley Street bus station.

by rail

Cape Town is linked to most of South Africa's (and southern Africa's) larger towns by rail. Trains are often slow, but the best way to see the landscape. Particularly scenic is the Cape Town–Johannesburg train—24 hours through the Winelands, the Cape mountains and the Great Karoo. All services depart from and arrive at the central train station on Adderley Street once daily. Information ✆ (021) 940 2667/8/9. Reservations ✆ (021) 940 2033. The luxury Blue Train and the 'Pride of Africa', ✆ (021) 218 2672, also leave from Cape Town (*see* '**Travel**, By Train').

Getting Around

For the compact city centre, walking is best. It is hard to get lost in Cape Town with Table Mountain as a landmark. In the city centre, if the mountain is behind you, you are facing east; if it is to your right, you are facing south; to your left, north, and facing west gives you a full-on view of the mountain.

by bus

Buses to the suburbs and residential neighbourhoods leave from Adderley Street and the terminus just behind it. The stop immediately outside the OK Bazaar supermarket services the Gardens, Tamboerskloof, the cable-car station, and the western side of the Peninsula to Hout Bay. The stop opposite, on the other side of Adderley, services Green Point, Clifton and Camps Bay. The main bus terminus, in the Parade, the great open area behind the Golden Acre shopping mall, services the southern suburbs and east side of the Peninsula as far as Simon's Town. Turn south on Strand Street where it joins Adderley and the station is half a block on the right.

by train

Trains servicing the Southern Suburbs and eastern Peninsula as far as Simon's Town leave every half hour from the main train station on lower Adderley Street. Trains running eastwards into the suburbs of the Cape Flats, servicing Maitland, Bellville and Durbanville, also leave every half hour from the main station.

Cape Town

Atlantic

Ocean

Three Anchor
Bay

GREEN POINT

WESTERN BOULEVARD

MAIN

HIGH LEVEL

BEACH

BEACH

MAIN

HIGH LEVEL

HIGH LEVEL

▲ Signal Hill
350

Lion's Rump

SEA POINT

BEACH

BEACH

KLOOF

KLOOF NEK

NEW CHURCH

TAMBOERSKLOOF

VICTORIA

BEACH

KLOOF

▲ Lion's Head
669

KLOOF

Molteno
Reservoir

Clifton
Bay

KLOOF

VICTORIA

CLIFTON

LOWER KLOOF

KLOOF NEK

Cable-car

Table
Mountain

Camps Bay &
Western Peninsula

Table Bay

Granger Bay

Fort
Wynard
New
Somerset
Maritime and
Military Mus.
Cape
Medical
seum
Victoria Basin
WATERFRONT
PORTSWOOD
DOCK
WEST QUAY
FISH QUAY
South African
Fisheries Museum
FORESHORE
ALFRED
MAIN
EASTERN BOULEVARD
DOCK

Duncan Dock

Ben Schoeman
Dock

SOMERSET
STRAND
SHORTMARKET
LOOP
LONG
HANS STRIJDOM
COEN STEYTLER
HEERENGRACHT
TABLE BAY (N1)
D F MALAN
HERTZOG BOULEVARD
MALAY
QUARTER
Greenmarket
Square
WALE
BREE
LOOP
LONG
QUEEN VICTORIA
GOVERNMENT
CHURCH
ST GEORGES
ADDERLEY
LONGMARKET
DARLING
PLEIN
BUITENKANT
ROELAND
Railway
Station
FORESHORE
N 2
N 2
Eastern Peninsula &
Southern Suburbs
The
Parade
Castle
SIR LOWRY
NEW MARKET
SIR LOWRY
VICTORIA
ALBERT
WOODSTOCK
VICTORIA
GARDENS
MILL
JUTLAND
(M3)
DE WAAL
(N2)
EASTERN
BOULEVARD
Woodstock
N 2
M 3
Eastern Peninsula &
Southern Suburbs

Devil's
Peak

N

\\\\ Main nightlife areas

800 metres
800 yards

by taxi

Black taxis follow the main bus routes and pick up and set down at regular bus stops. They are marginally more expensive than buses, but much quicker. They do have a reputation for cowboy driving (crashing), however. Hail them as they pass bus-stops, as the 'conductor' leans out and shouts the destination and stopping points en route.

Ordinary taxis are expensive and should only be used when there is no other option. There are three official taxi ranks; two on Adderley Street and one in Plein Street, just behind the main post office building. Or find a number in the *Yellow Pages*. You can't just hail a taxi on the street.

by car

Avoid the city centre in a car unless you want to sit in idle frustration between short traffic-light hops and in one-way systems. For the rest of the city, two main highways service the residential neighbourhoods and Peninsula: the M5 runs from Sea Point through the city centre towards Muizenberg, along the border of the mountain and the Cape Flats; the M3 runs along the upper slopes, in the same direction. Avoid both highways during rush-hour and be careful at all times: one is often fed into the fast lane, so quick acceleration is necessary. Cape Town drivers are often careless and aggressive. All the international **car hire** agencies have offices at the airport, but Cape Town has some good local rental companies that are cheaper, and who will deliver cars to the airport, bus or train stations if you arrange it in advance. Try Peninsula Car Hire, ✆ 591 0155, Dolphin Car Hire, ✆ 439 9696, at 6 Anchor Bay Road, or Ace Car Hire, ✆ 782 6804/6636.

by cable car

Every visitor should ride the Table Mountain cable car to the summit just once, ✆ 245 148/248 409. Take the Kloofnek bus from outside the OK Bazaar supermarket on Adderley Street. Expect long queues in summer, and no service at all in very bad or windy weather, when it is best to phone before making the journey.

Tourist Information

CapTour, ✆ 418 5214/5, the central tourist office, is in front of the bus and train stations on lower Adderley Street. The office is almost like a museum it has so many displays, and even a little coffee shop. The staff are very helpful and can advise on most areas of the Cape, as well as the city and Peninsula. For tourist information on the rest of South Africa, go to the **SATour** office ✆ 216 274, also in the CapTour building on Adderley Street.

Medical Emergencies: Groot Schuur, ✆ 404 9111, is the largest Cape Town hospital and the best in emergencies. This vast building is in the Mowbray neighbourhood, on Main Road. For ambulances ✆ 101 77.

Central Post Office occupies half a block on the corner of Plein and Adderley Streets.

Despite its easy-going atmosphere, Cape Town's high unemployment and poverty levels make for one of the highest violent crime rates in the world. Admittedly, much of this is confined to the townships, but it does spill into the city and the suburbs too.

Cape Town centre at night can be dangerous, especially near the harbour area (though you are more likely to see drunks fighting than be mugged yourself) and around St George's Mall, which gets deserted after dark. However, in a group you should be fine, if you treat Cape Town as you would any large city where the poverty level is high. Do not go into the townships unless with a local or a tour. Women should not walk alone in the centre at night, nor on the mountain—though attacks are relatively rare, they do happen.

Cape Town Centre

Laid out along an easy-to-follow grid, central Cape Town is small and can be crossed in half an hour of fast walking. However, so much is packed into the centre that at least a couple of days are needed to explore it. Adderley Street runs down the middle from the sea to the Old Company Gardens. Where Strand Street crosses Adderley marks an invisible division of the city centre into two areas; upper and lower.

The lower centre (downhill from Strand) and upper centre (uphill from Strand) have distinct characters. Together, the two halves of Cape Town's centre, dominated at all times by the mountain, make up a pleasant mix of 17th-, 18th- and 19th-century Dutch and English colonial styles, Art Deco (especially in the upper centre), marred only by the inevitable concrete and glass.

Unlike many colonial towns, Cape Town's old buildings are often still in use. Only a few are museums, so there is no museum feeling to the place. Bustling and infectious, the hotch-potch culture that created the city still prevails.

Cape Town City Centre

TABLE BAY BOULEVARD

TABLE BAY BOULEVARD

DOCK

ALFRED

WESTERN BOULEVARD

COEN STEYTLER

HEERENGRACHT

DF MALAN

Nico Malan
Opera House and
Theatre

EASTERN BOULEVARD

HERTZOG BOULEVARD

HANS STRIJDOM

BUSINESS
DISTRICT

SOMERSET

BREE

LONG

Railway Station and
Bus Station

STRAND

SIR LOWRY

Castle

Lutheran
Church

STRAND

Koopmans de
Wet House

LOOP

Sendinggestig
Museum

SHORTMARKET

ADDERLEY

ST GEORGES

Central Post Office

Captour/
SATour

The Parade

DARLING

LONGMARKET

Old Town House

CHURCH

Groote
Kerk

Greenmarket
Square

BUITENGRACHT

MALAY
QUARTER
(BO-KAAP)

St George's
Cathedral

WALE

South African
Library

South African
Cultural History
Museum

Houses of
Parliament

PLEIN

BUITENKANT

Tuynhuys

BREE

LOOP

LONG

QUEEN VICTORIA

Company
Gardens

GOVERNMENT

ROELAND

Rust-en-Vreugd
Museum

BUITENCINGEL

ORANGE

National
Gallery

Jewish Museum and
Great Synagogue

BUITENKANT

JUTLAND

South African
Museum

N

NEW CHURCH

KLOOF

ANNANDALE

MILL

Mount
Nelson

Main nightlife
areas

400 metres
400 yards

The Castle of Good Hope

Open every day 10–4. Guided tours 10, 11,12, 2 & 3.

The Castle of Good Hope, on Darling Street and facing the south side of the Parade, is where colonial South Africa began. The original earth-walled fort of 1652 was expanded in the 1660s to the present massive pentagon. The Castle has never lost its military function; today it is the headquarters of the South African Defence Force's Western Cape Command, and houses the **Maritime and Military Museum**, in what was the old Cape Governor's House. The museum exhibits artefacts from the early days of the colony. The entrance has a beautifully ornate 18th-century pediment, called the Kat balcony, designed by Anreith, (*see* 'Architecture').

The official tour is more fun then you would expect, and the only way into the Castle's interior. A soldier in ceremonial dress leads you from outside the reception/guard room, through the second courtyard to the Dolphin Court—a fountain pool where Lady Anne Barnard, the spirited and highly intelligent wife of the Cape's Secretary to the British Empire, was supposedly spotted bathing nude by sentries and had to be reproved by the Governor. Lady Anne Barnard went to the Cape soon after the first invading force of 1795. Her journals, letters and watercolours provide some of the most vivid, and most irreverent, accounts of early Cape Town (and interior) life. It is worth picking up a copy of her letters (available from any Cape bookshop) which are often hilarious in their descriptions of the pompous colonial characters of the time. While staying here at the Castle, Lady Anne Barnard witnessed the coming of the Cape Town burghers to swear their allegiance to Britain after annexation. Fresh from England and unaware of the already deep-seated independent spirit of the Cape Dutch, she glibly wrote; 'I think many of them seemed very sulky and ill-affected. Their manner seemed to say, "There is no help for it. We must swear, for they are the strongest".'

Once inside the castle, the tour takes you past whipping chambers and cells where people were put to die. In one of these there are deep scratches on the wall, which the guide claims were made by the exposed finger-bones of one of the inmates.

The soldiers' cells—used for less lethal punishment—have two centuries of graffiti carved into the oak doors, including a swastika left by the crew of a German U-Boat that was captured off the Cape coast—the city's only direct involvement in the Second World War. The tour then takes in one of the bastions before ending in an archaeological museum of the earliest colonial artefacts found during restoration work.

Around Buitenkant Street

The area around Buitenkant Street has been known for producing clothing for almost 200 years. Indeed, the street itself is known as **Old Slave Walk** after the Malay slaves who worked the textile factories here before the abolition of slavery in the 1830s.

If approaching Buitenkant Street from the Castle, the first two blocks are taken up (on the left) with 19th century factories, many of them still functioning, and now mostly owned, as well as staffed, by the descendants of Cape Malays. There are many good take-away shops on the ground floors, serving spicy curries, samoosas and fried fish. Halfway up the first block is the **Old Granary**, a very handsome Cape Dutch 18th century building with an Anreith lion and unicorn added to the front after the British Cape annexation in 1806. Now the Ministry of Works, one can only admire the front. On the right side of the street are the backs of Cape Town's red-brick late Victorian government offices, still in use today.

At the junction of Roeland and Buitenkant Streets, the large late Victorian building with an upstairs veranda on the right-hand side is the **Kimberley Hotel**. Even if you don't drink, stop in the public bar. The building is held in trust by the man who owns the liquor store across the road. One of the conditions of inheritance is that nothing, not even the plumbing, can be changed. The result is a gem of an original bar, with nothing kitsch or modern added because nothing but straight repairs have been done to it. The walls are tiled, the ceiling sculpted in plaster, the bar is luxuriant hardwood, all solid and still in use. The place is a hang-out for 'coloureds' and the less racist working-class Afrikaners. If you have time, it's worth getting into conversation with the regulars, who can reveal something of 'coloured' life to the non-Afrikaans speaker.

Rust-en-Vreugd Museum

Open weekdays 9–4, admission free if you use the ticket from the Castle guided tour. Another minute's walk uphill on Buitenkant's north side.

A large white wall with a wrought iron gate conceals a herb garden, behind which stands an 18th-century mansion, now a museum housing a huge collection of historical Cape lithographs, engravings and watercolours (late-18th to mid-19th century). Many of the period illustrations in South African history books come from pictures in this collection. The best is upstairs—especially the grotesque George Cruikshank cartoons from the early 19th century of the first British settlers in the Cape being tricked into ideas of a land of plenty, then being devoured upon arrival by grinning savages. Oddities of colonial life, such as pictures of British cavalry officers fox hunting through Xhosa villages, and heavily stylised paintings of wildlife, hang next to pictures of the now-vanished Khoi tribes who inhabited the Cape when the Europeans first arrived. As a pictorial record of colonial expansion from the Cape colony to the interior, the collection has no equal.

Last stop on the Buitenkant walk is the **Perseverance Tavern**, Cape Town's oldest pub (the present building dates from 1836, but occupies an earlier site). It claims to have the country's oldest grape vine in the courtyard. The Perseverance used to be the first stop for wagoneers entering Cape Town from the rough mountains beyond and the last stop for those leaving town. Its cellar-like interior is a good place to drink and rest before heading back down Buitenkant to **Plein Street**, which runs along the west side of the Parade.

Along here is the old **City Hall**, a pompous building dating from 1905 that is now a concert hall and occasionally used for ceremonial purposes, including Nelson Mandela's first speech to the nation on 9 May 1994. One block further, Plein Street crosses Darling. On the east corner is the huge Art Deco **Central Post Office**, a 1920s edifice. Inside are huge murals romanticizing early Cape colonial life; rather beautiful, if politically unsound.

Around Adderley Street

From Plein, a left turn takes you into upper Adderley Street, a mish-mash of Edwardian colonial and older buildings, in the middle of which is the **Groote Kerk**. This suitably austere building was the first Dutch Reformed Church built in South Africa. Begun in 1678, consecrated in 1704, the original building was burned down in the early 19th century. Only the steeple remains, sadly dwarfed by the squat, ugly main church, rebuilt in 1841. The carved pulpit (an Anreith) was saved from the fire, and adds the only graceful note to an otherwise lumpish landmark.

Further up Adderley on the same (south) side, is the far more attractive **Old Slave Lodge**, which now houses the **South African Cultural History Museum** (*open Mon–Sat 9.30–4.30*). The building started life in the late 17th century as an unofficial brothel (the Dutch East India Company was practical, if discreet, about such matters) using Asian and West African women. The British changed that, turning it (with unconscious irony) into the city's Supreme Court. As with the Old Granary on Buitenkant Street, a lion and unicorn pediment sculpted by Anreith were tacked onto the building's back pediment (on Church Square, which runs behind and parallel to Adderley Street) after the British annexation in 1806.

Today's museum is eclectic and rather eccentric. The first few rooms are not South African at all, but devoted to Egypt, Greece, Rome, India, China and Japan, no doubt for the education of Cape Town's schoolchildren. South Africa only begins upstairs. Highlights include a room devoted to the 'Post Office Stones' under which the Dutch, Portuguese and English sea captains rounding the Cape from the 15th to the 17th centuries left messages for each other. A room devoted to the Frontier Wars between the British and the Xhosa (*see* **Eastern Cape**, 'History') lacks actual artefacts, but gives a concise (if settler-orientated) chronology of this confused and tragic 100 year conflict. Other curiosities include the flag of a Confederate ship from the American Civil War, sunk off Table Bay in the 1860s by a passing Union frigate, and the cobbled courtyard, shaded by oaks, where sits a replica of the tombstone of Jan Van Riebeeck and his wife.

The museum lacks any display of 'indigenous' culture (i.e. San, Khoi, or black African). Instead, an excellent exhibition of these cultures can be found at the South Africa Museum (*see* below), which the curators are trying to have moved to the Cultural Museum; its current absence is an uncomfortable reminder of the apartheid days when South African history and culture were regarded as an almost exclusively white preserve.

After the museum, Adderley Street swings right towards Signal Hill, becoming Wale Street. Continuing in the same direction as Adderley is **Government Avenue**, a shaded pedestrian walk that marks the beginning of the **Company Gardens Area**. **St George's Cathedral** sits at the entrance to the Gardens. A fine piece of neo-Gothic (designed by Sir Herbert Baker in 1848), the timbered ceiling in the choir is particularly lovely. The cathedral came to prominence in the 1980s, following the appointment of Archbishop Desmond Tutu. A beautiful Mass is sung here on the last Sunday of every month.

The Company Gardens

Behind the cathedral are the Company Gardens. Part botanical collection, part park, they started life as the first colony's vegetable patch (1652), when the surrounding country was still off-limits to the settlers, and too full of Khoi livestock and wild game to allow crop-rearing. Once the colony was allowed to expand beyond the original earth rampart, the Company Gardens became ornamental. A pavilion was built in the 1680s (now called the Tuynhuys, and used by the State President as a downtown residence). Rare plants were introduced from Asia and the gardens extended. Today, massive exotic trees shade the walks. Look out for an old pump embedded in an oak tree, having been wrenched from the ground as the tree grew. There is a Victorian Aviary and Tea Garden (and 17th century slave-bell) at the centre, near a statue of the De Beers founder and tireless empire builder Cecil Rhodes (*see* **South African History**) giving what appears to be a Nazi salute.

Government Avenue

On Government Avenue, which runs along the south side of the gardens, are the Victorian neo-classical **Houses of Parliament** (built 1884, expanded 1910). The buildings are not heavy or ponderous, but genuinely handsome. Take a guided tour when Parliament is not sitting (July–Jan/Feb), or buy a ticket for the public gallery when it is (Jan/Feb–June).

Inside, the **Library of Parliament** houses the Mendlssohn Collection; 50,000 reference books on Africa, mainly of interest to academics. The rather uninspiring **Parliamentary Museum** exhibits portraits of South Africa's past statesmen and ceremonial paraphernalia and houses important historical records.

On up Government Avenue to the **Tuynhuys** and its wide lawn, called the Stal Plein. The mounted statue in the centre is of General Louis Botha—first prime minister after the Union in 1910, and one of the last generals to surrender in the Anglo-Boer War. The avenue then opens into a wide piazza. On the left is the **South African National Gallery** (*open Mon 1–5, Tues–Sun 10–5*), a must-see. The gallery is small, but has some very fine modern paintings and sculpture, alongside some indifferent 18th- and 19th-century British paintings. Of particular note is the life-size sculpture 'The Butcher Boys', by Jane Alexander, depicting three youths seated on a bench, horns sprouting from their heads, spines bursting from their backs. The gallery shop sells some of the best examples of indigenous arts and crafts you can buy outside the townships and former 'homelands'.

Next door the **Great Synagogue** (dating from 1905) stands next to the smaller **Jewish Museum**, (*open Tues 2–5, Thur and Sun 10–12.30*), in fact South Africa's oldest synagogue, founded in 1862. From here, the avenue continues uphill from the piazza. On the corner of the two is the **South African Museum** (*open daily 10–5*). The ground floor has a comprehensive display of ethnic South Africa in chronological order, from bushman through to the present black African societies. There are life-size models cast from real people, a little eerie in their life-likeness, and technically correct in dress. More importantly, histories, beliefs and mythologies, ethics and material culture are clearly explained. This display is somewhat out-of-place here: the South African Museum is supposed to be devoted to natural history, but under apartheid, African ethnicity was confined to these zoological, rather than cultural, premises. Today's curators are trying to have the dsiplay moved to the South African Cultural History Museum on Adderley Street.

Upstairs, whales hang from the ceiling as you mount a series of ramps to cases of stuffed animals: South American deer, North American bears, rooms of South African reptiles and fish, and natural curiosities such as the sea bean, a giant palm nut that looks like a leviathan coffee-bean and which occasionally floats from Mozambique to the South African coast. The bean used to be much prized by witch-doctors. The history of printing is displayed next to a large, unlit case of unidentified birds. South African mammals occupy another gallery, while yet another is devoted entirely to Table Mountain's flora and fauna. In short the museum is educational, but exhausting.

Along the last stretch of Government Avenue runs a high, white wall. A gate marked 'Bertram House' leads into a collection of old buildings that is now the University of Cape Town's downtown campus. **Bertram House** itself (*open Tues–Sat 9.30–4.30*) is a museum of furniture and ornaments from the 18th century. Behind this is the **Egyptian Building** (1839), now the sculpture department of the University of Cape Town's Fine Art faculty. Wander in and look at the students' work.

From here, the shaded walk of Government Avenue brings one blinking onto the busy rush of Orange Street. A right turn one block into Queen Victoria Street (which runs parallel with Government Avenue down the north side of the Company Gardens) leads to a cheerless, narrow street with just one point of interest—the **South African Library** (built in 1818) (*open Mon–Fri 9–6, Sat 9–1*). The library contains two famous collections of early Africana: the Grey Collection of rare books and the Von Dessin Collection (dating from 1761). For researching African history and natural history there are few better libraries. It is pleasant just to sniff the scent of old books and take in the high classical interiors. Admission is free and anyone can use the reference books.

Long Street

Long Street, which runs one block north of and parallel to Queen Victoria Street, is one of the city's best walks, having an attractive mixture of colonial wrought-iron arcades, second-hand book shops, antiques, restaurants and general browsing. Start at the top, at the junction with Orange Street, and stroll slowly downhill towards the harbour. Here are the city's old **Turkish Baths** (*open seven days 9.30–8*)—still a pleasant place to steam among the Victorian tiles on a gusty, wet winter day. Then stop for a drink or sandwich in **McGawley's Pub**, an old Cape Town institution complete with dusty hunting trophies and pool tables. Across the road is the **Junk Shop**, selling anything from coins to pinball machines behind a beautiful colonial wrought-iron front.

The rest of the street is a mad jumble of second-hand bookshops (from collectors' first editions to torn paperbacks), old clothes shops, restaurants, pawnbrokers and antique shops. There are also two elegant little mosques dating from the early 19th century. At the lower end of Long Street, near the junction with Castle Street is the head office of the **National Parks Board** (*open weekdays 8–4.45*), useful for booking trails or accommodation in advance, and the **Sendinggestig Museum** (1804) (*open weekdays 9–4*), the first mission church to be built by South Africans. This simple but elegant old church has a yellowwood gallery held up by pillars made from ships' masts. It lost its 'coloured' congregation after the Group Areas Act removed everyone who wasn't white from the city centre (*see* **Cape Town** 'History').

At Castle Street, the next junction, one has reached the end of the upper city centre. From here down, Long Street enters first the dull (and tiny) finance district (concrete buildings), then the red light sleaze (after dark) of the windblown Foreshore. Avoid that part at night.

But that is not quite all. Double back up Long Street to **Shortmarket Street**, and into **Greenmarket Square**. This wide cobbled space is home to a permanent craft market selling clothes, shoes, jewellery and antiques, bounded on three sides by some of Cape Town's grander Art Deco buildings, some of which have terraced cafes. The northwest corner has a heavy, late-Victorian Methodist church, but on the fourth (west) side is the **Old Town House** (*open seven days 10–5, adm free*), a mid 18th-century Dutch building of singular beauty. Once the seat of the old Burgher Senate, it now houses the Michaelis Art Collection of works by Dutch and Flemish Masters, including some Van Dyck portraits. The paintings, on the whole, are not first rate, but some of the drawings on display on the ground floor (depicting 17th-century agricultural life in the Netherlands and the Cape) are very fine. The building is worth visiting just for itself though. Look out for the Dutch tiles painted with 17th-century soldiers around the walls and ornamental brick fireplaces of the side-rooms, the night sky painted above the grand staircase and the dark wood and white plaster ceiling of the upstairs gallery. A wide balcony gives out from here onto the square.

St George's Mall leads down towards the harbour from near Greenmarket Square. An extension of the craft market, it is a pedestrian street, which also contains some fine Art Deco office buildings (the *Cape Argus* newspaper building is one example). These peter out into concrete as the road connects with Strand Street and the lower city centre. **Church Street**, which runs between Queen Victoria and Long Streets, is known for its antique shops and open-air stalls, which sell both South African and European antiques.

Loop Street runs parallel to, and one block north of, Long Street, and has some elegant Cape Dutch buildings still in use as offices. But the area is best known for nightclubs (*see* 'Nightlife'). These vary from student rock'n'roll and techno dance clubs to good live music venues and 'Korean' clubs, discos aimed specifically at sailors, many of whom come from the Far East, hence the name. Many prostitutes—female, male and transvestite—walk Loop Street at night.

The Bo-Kaap

Arguably the most interesting residential area in the city is the Bo-Kaap (meaning 'above-Cape'), a small neighbourhood on the lower slopes of Signal Hill. The heart of Moslem Cape Town runs roughly parallel with Long Street, beginning four blocks to the north. Composed of brightly-painted 18th-century artisan cottages bought by Cape Malay (Dutch Indonesian) slaves freed in the 1830s, the area has been solidly Islamic ever since. There are many small mosques and a little museum, on Wale Street (*open Tues–Sat 9.30–4.30*), shows how Cape Malay home interiors would have looked in the early 19th century. Cape Town's Muslim culture keeps itself to itself, and you are unlikely to get a look inside the present houses unless accompanied by a guide. But Cape Islamic culture, though often hidden, is rich and has some extreme practises. For example, behind the colourful but locked doors of the neighbourhood, young men practise a dance called *Khalifa*, in which they pierce their flesh with knives while in ecstatic trance. The dance is occasionally performed at festivals which outsiders can attend. Generally though, the outward atmosphere in the Bo-Kaap is rather sleepy. The narrow streets make for pleasant afternoon strolling, and there is a superb Cape Malay restaurant, called Biesmiellah, near the museum on Wale Street (*see* 'Eating Out').

The Lower City Centre

This generally refers to everything downhill from the line made by Strand Street where it crosses Adderley, and includes the **Waterfront** harbour complex and the reclaimed land of the **Foreshore**. The Golden Acre Mall, where Adderley and Strand meet, supposedly stands on the site of Jan Van Riebeeck's original fort, built in 1652, and the remains of a 17th-century reservoir is on view behind glass on the basement floor.

Downhill on Adderley from Strand Street, the entire block on the right is occupied by the **Central Train and Bus Station**. On display in the station hall is South Africa's first steam train (imported from Scotland in 1859). In front of the station is a permanent **flea market** selling mostly clothes and imported goods (watches, stereos, etc.), as well as fruit and vegetables. It makes for a lively scene. Next to the train and bus station at the east end of the block, is the **CapTour Tourist Office**. After the stations, Adderley widens into a large traffic circle, in the middle of which are fountains and a statue of Jan Van Riebeeck and wife. This is the beginning of the Foreshore. A right turn at the traffic circle takes you onto Hertzog Boulevard and towards the **Nico Malan Theatre Complex**, comprising an opera house and two theatres, with its own resident theatre, opera and ballet companies, and orchestra.

Strand Street, north of Adderley, has two national monuments, **Koopmans-De Wet House** (1701) (*open Tues–Sat 9.30–4.30*) and the **Lutheran Church** (*open Mon–Fri 8.30–1, 1.30–4.30*). The former, a townhouse, was home to one of the 19th century's principal campaigners for recognition of the Afrikaans language, Maria Koopmans-De Wet. The front of the house is well known for its combination of Anreith's carving and Louis Thibault's design. Inside are early Cape furniture, Chinese porcelain and European ornaments from the 17th and 18th centuries. The Lutheran Church and its neighbouring parsonage, both recently restored, are on the opposite side of Strand Street, uphill from Koopmans-De Wet House The church is simple inside, but the carved pulpit is ornate Anreith, as is the design of the parsonage, behind which is a quiet walled garden where you can escape the rush of the city for a while.

Cape Town's small financial district lies on the opposite side of Strand Street. Mostly an uninteresting collection of tower blocks, this area can be bypassed. Better to walk back to Adderley and the CapTour Office, outside which there is a bus that runs every 15 minutes to the **Waterfront Harbour Complex**.

A lot of media hype surrounded the opening, in 1992, of the 'finished' Waterfront development. The area centres around the original docks, the Victoria and Alfred (not Albert) basins. A mixture of kitsch and history, replete with restaurants, bars, cinemas, a flea market and shops, shops, shops, the Waterfront still harbours many of Cape Town's small trawlers. Seals dive off the inlet called Bertie's Landing. One of the docks (the Robinson Graving dock) still operates for light cargo ships, and most of the handsome old warehouses still stand. Amongst all this thrives a consumer maelstrom. Love it or hate it, you should at least have a look at the Waterfront.

The bus sets you down by the entrance to both the flea market and the Waterfront proper. The flea market (to the right of the entrance) sells some of the best of Cape Town's local crafts. In the Waterfront, you can relax, in the summer months, to live outdoor jazz in a small amphitheatre in the main concourse. The **Marpro Fish Market** is a covered hall where one can wander among aisles of Atlantic and Indian Ocean fish. On the dockside, opposite the market, is **Quay Four**, a gigantic bar, always teeming with drinkers. **The South African Fisheries Museum** (*open Tues–Sun 10–4*) has a computerized marine encyclopaedia that can tell you what a jib-sheet is, or how to catch a snoek. Other attractions are a small aquarium and old fishing and naval artefacts, including three museum-ships, docked in the wharf below.

There are several good (but expensive) seafood restaurants around the Waterfront (*see* 'Eating Out'), including Bertie's Landing, reached by the 'Penny Ferry', a rowing boat costing R1 per person. After wandering the shops (which sell everything from South African wine and curios to Scottish terriers cast in pewter), take one of the various **boat trips** out into Table Bay. A cruise to the aptly named **Seal Island** can be made for R5 per person (takes an hour). Cruises to the notorious ex-prison **Robben Island** cost R70 per person (three hours, price includes cold drinks and snacks). A ride in a catamaran can be had for R30 per person (takes an hour). All boats leave from the dock outside the Victoria and Alfred Hotel.

The Waterfront has two live **jazz bars** (*see* 'Nightlife'), and makes a good place to spend at least one evening. However, unless you have a car, you will have to pick up a taxi home. Make sure you agree the price before you get in.

Table Mountain

In Cape Town, you are constantly aware of Table Mountain. It dominates the city, a massive chunk of wild nature rearing above the crowded streets. Whenever you look up, there it is; cliff, forest, mountainside and cloud.

Table Mountain is not a single entity, but the northern extremity of the Peninsula Mountain chain, joined to them via Devil's Peak, a sharp promontory that dominates the residential neighbourhoods known as the Southern Suburbs. In the city itself, Table Mountain is joined by a saddle pass (Tamboerskloof) to the Lion's Head and Signal Hill.

There are many walks, climbs and trails on Table Mountain's 1086m sandstone bulk—some gentle, some very strenuous. CapTour issues a map of all trails, both on the city side of the mountain and the state forests that grow on the slopes behind Devil's Peak (*see* 'Southern Suburbs').

The traditional way to the summit is by cable-car from the cable station on Kloof Street, a five minute ride. The flat plateau at the top of the mountain, if not obscured by cloud, provides an awesome view clear down the Peninsula to Cape Point, foreshortening the 70-odd kilometre distance to what seems only a few hundred metres. There is a little restaurant, and a prosperous colony of dassies (rock hyraxes) who eat what the tourists drop. The cable car runs from 8am–10pm Dec–April and 8.30–6 May–Nov, weather permitting.

About 350 paths wind from various access points to the summit. More interesting for the tourist, and less strenuous, are the two **Contour Paths** connecting Table Mountain with Constantia, 20km to the south. It is a climb to reach the paths, but once on them it's level walking, and there are hop-off points from the Contour Paths every few kilometres.

Table Mountain has a wilder climate than the city below it. Don't go walking on the upper slopes without a waterproof, good boots and a map. Even on a fine day, the weather can change very quickly and there are fatalities every year from falls and hypothermia, so don't try anything too ambitious unless with someone who knows the mountain.

The Cape Floral Kingdom is well in evidence on the mountain (roughly 3000 species of wildflower and fynbos). There is wildlife too. Rhebok is the largest antelope, though more common are the smaller duiker and grysbok. Baboons are common, as are caracal, though you would be lucky to see one. There are even one or two leopard in the kloofs and inaccessible gullies, whose territorial radii have been marked as far as 100km inland from the mountain. Walkers often spot the exotic Himalayan tahr (an Asian mountain goat), colonies of which have established themselves on the mountain since their escape from the Groot Schuur Paddocks (a fenced nature reserve on the southern part of the mountain) in the 1930s.

Exotic trees are everywhere, mainly bluegum, oak and various pine species. The gum trees are in the process of being slowly removed (killed by having rings cut from their bark), as they have been found to dry out the thin topsoil.

Devil's Peak (also over 1000m) is the sharp point that divides Table Mountain from the rest of the Peninsula chain. You can walk up it from access points in Rondebosch and Newlands Forest (*see* 'Southern Suburbs') or from the Contour Paths. On the lower slopes are the **King's** and **Queen's** blockhouses, small ruined stone forts built after the first British occupation in the early 1800s.

The **Lion's Head** and '**Rump**', officially known as **Signal Hill**, comprise the long upland with a conical peak that rises from the city opposite Table Mountain—to which it is joined by the Tamboeskloof. The walk up the Lion's Head (through shining woods of silver trees), ends with a strenuous pull up the final steep slope with chains bolted into the rock. The

Lion's Head is used by Capetonians as a weather-vane. If there is a little ring of cloud just around the tip of the Head, bad weather is coming.

For practical information on hiking and rock climbing on the Table Mountain and the Peninsula chain, *see* 'Activities'.

The Central Residential Neighbourhoods

The **Gardens District** is a residential neighbourhood to the west (uphill) of the Company Gardens (with which it should not be confused) and extending south in a curving arm. This is an eclectic area, part 'coloured', part Cape Malay, part white yuppie. Entertainment is plentiful. The interestingly named **Labia Cinema** (*see* 'Entertainment') shows good repertory films. The **Fringe Nightclub** (*see* 'Nightlife') also screens films and plays music from township sound to funk to thrash. Gardens also has several of the city's best restaurants, particularly Cape Malay and Cape country (*see* 'Eating Out'). Cape Town's most luxurious hotel, the **Mount Nelson**, offers superb teas with tiered cake dishes of cream cakes and pastries (*see* 'Cafés and Bars').

The Southern Suburbs

The Southern Suburbs are a series of 19th- and early-20th century neighbourhoods extending from the city centre south to the eastern side of the Peninsula, running along the centrally connecting Main Road and joined by rail to Cape Town's central station. The first, **Woodstock**, has traditionally been an area of working class 'coloureds' living in elegant, but run down 19th-century houses. The part of Woodstock furthest from town is being gentrified by white yuppies.

Closest to town is the 'coloured' district, which includes the semi-industrial region, **Salt River**. This is lively by day and night. One of Cape Town's most notorious nightclubs (for gangsters and their molls) is **Odyssey**, on Main Road (*see* 'Nightlife').

Further along is **Observatory**, a hippie neighbourhood favoured by university students. The street which runs parallel to and downhill from Main Road, **Lower Main Road**, has some handsome colonial arcades with good live music bars, cheap restaurants (*see* 'Nightlife' and 'Eating Out'), and general evening fun. Some of Cape Town's best youth hostels are here (*see* 'Accommodation').

Observatory's eastern boundary is formed by the Liesbeeck Parkway (part of the M5 highway), which runs along the **Liesbeeck River**. Despite the rushing traffic, you can walk the riverbank and see kingfishers, darters (river cormorants) and other waterfowl. Just off the Parkway is **Valkenberg Manor** (1770) (*open Mon–Fri 9–5*), a large Dutch homestead that used to farm the area.

On the far side of the river (where Station Road crosses the Parkway) is the **Observatory** that gives the neighbourhood its name. This opens to the public, free of charge, on the first Saturday of every month at 8pm and offers views of the night sky through the large telescope. Ask to be shown the rings of Saturn.

Mowbray, just south of Observatory, is another student area, notable mainly for the massive **Groot Schuur Hospital. Rosebank,** the next south, is a small neighbourhood, worth visiting for the **Irma Stern Museum** on Cecil Road (*open Tues–Sun 10–1 & 2–5*). Irma Stern was a Cape artist active in the early part of the 20th century. The museum comprises her house, studio and a small collection of her work (*see* **People and Culture,** 'Art and Architecture').

Rondebosch is home to the **University of Cape Town,** a beautifully laid-out campus of late 19th-century neoclassical buildings on the mountainside above Main Road and the M3 highway (connected with Main Road by a pedestrian tunnel and stairway). **Mostert's Mill** (*open weekdays 10–5*), built in 1796, sits just below the campus, as does, Cecil Rhodes' old house, **Groot Schuur,** a 17th-century barn that was converted into an opulent mansion for the jingoist billionaire by the architect Sir Herbert Baker in the 1890s. What was good enough for Cecil Rhodes is now good enough for South Africa's state presidents—Groot Schuur has been their main Cape Town residence since Rhodes' death in the 1900s. Behind the house are two smaller residences, the state guest house **Westbrooke,** and the **Woolsack** (now a campus residence) where Rudyard Kipling used to stay as Rhodes' guest when visiting the city.

Next to the university campus, on the city-ward side is the **Rhodes Memorial** (in the style of a Greek Temple) and **Tea Garden,** which give a panoramic view of the city. Around both Memorial and Tea Garden are the **Groot Schuur Paddocks,** shaded by umbrella pines, where fallow deer graze and sensual, white arum lilies grow. One can follow a track uphill from here to the King's Blockhouse and the mountain's Lower Contour Path.

On Main Road, below the University campus, is the **Baxter Theatre and Cinema,** showing repertory drama and films seven days a week (*see* 'Entertainment'). Below Main Road, academics and the wealthier students live next to each other in large houses set in larger gardens.

Newlands, a suburb for the rich (it always has been—Lady Anne Barnard lived here in what is now the Vineyard Hotel), has two museums that warrant a visit, both in the same building. **Josephine's Water Mill** (*open weekdays 10–2*), next to the **International Rugby Stadium,** was built in 1840 and named after the then Queen of Sweden. Unlike Mostert's Mill in Rondebosch, this mill works. The **Newlands Rugby Museum** (*open weekdays 10–4*) occupies the mill's ground floor. A clue to just how much of a religion rugby is among white South Africans, the museum has a varied selection of exhibits from the late-19th century to the present day, many of which have the status of holy relics.

Best of all though, is the magnificent **Newlands Forest.** The entrance (and car park) is a little tricky to reach; you have to cross the M3 highway, but there is a footbridge near the University, on the border with Rondebosch. The world under the pines is deep green. Trails lead up to the Contour Paths between crowding oaks, silver trees (a species of giant protea) and more pines. Hanging above, through the breaks in the trees are the towering cliffs of Devil's Peak. Above the treeline, if you follow the trail to the Upper Contour Path, is a steep series of steps cut into the mountainside, leading up to a pass over Devil's Peak. A few hours in Newlands Forest clears the mind and refreshes the spirit.

Claremont, the next suburb south, is unremarkable except for a rather lovely Victorian park, the **Ardene Gardens** (on Main Road) and the **Cavendish Square Complex** which is another shopping mall that houses a multi-screen cinema (also on Main Road, south of the gardens).

Wynberg, further south along Main Road, has a large public park, behind which is an area of pretty, white-washed 19th-century houses called **Little Chelsea**, home to some good antique shops, and Cape Town's best Indian restaurant, Ramola's (at least, in the author's opinion) (*see* 'Eating Out'). There is also a good craft shop, the **Operation Hunger Showroom**, in the Coates Building, on Maynard Road. This is a non-profit organisation, and the African crafts it sells are first-rate, more authentic than what one sees in the many curio shops around Cape Town.

South from Wynberg, along the foot of the mountain, is **Kenilworth**, whose **Racecourse** is on the M5 road to Muizenberg, and **Plumstead**, a residential neighbourhood. Then comes **Retreat**, also residential, and named after the Dutch army's rout following the Battle of Muizenberg in 1795, when the British chased them through this area back towards the Castle.

Constantia and the Wine Estates

Constantia, uphill from and south of the Southern Suburbs, is a gracious area of mansions set in forest, vineyards, horse paddocks and mountain. Some of the Cape's most famous Dutch homesteads are to be found here.

The area takes its name from South Africa's oldest and most famous wine estate, **Groot Constantia**, ✆ 794 5178. Founded by Simon Van der Stel, Cape Governor in 1685, and run by Hugenot settlers, Groot Constantia's wines were in demand even in Europe throughout the 18th century. The estate has changed hands many times, but has always been the leading one in the colony. Lady Anne Barnard was brought here in 1798, and was treated to the sight of Hottentot (Khoi) slaves treading wine. Ignoring the gracious buildings around her, she instead wrote of the slaves, 'what struck me most was the beautiful, antique forms, perpetually graceful, of the three figures, half naked, dancing in the wine press'.

Now State owned, Groot Constantia is still operational, though not through slavery. Noted for red wine, its vineyards spread away up the hillsides to the forested **Constantiaberg** (part of the transition between Table Mountain and the rugged spine of the Cape Peninsula). The homestead is one of the most handsome (and largest) examples of early Cape Dutch gabled architecture in the country. Inside is a museum (*open weekdays 10–5*), exhibiting Simon Van der Stel's fine furniture, some exquisite antique porcelain, and a history of the estate. In the old stables behind the main house is a second museum (*open weekdays 10–5*), of wagons, carts and carriages. A craft and wine shop in the courtyard in front of the homestead offers free wine tastings. The two-storey wine cellar was designed by 18th-century French architect Louis Thibault, its pediment frieze carved by Anreith (*open by guided tour, on the hour from 10–6*). The vineyards and forest fringes can be wandered at will. Two restaurants—the Tavern (buffet food), and Jonkershuis (Cape cuisine lunches and teas) adjoin the main homestead. If you have the time and energy, the best way to reach Groot Constantia is on foot along the Lower Contour Path on the mountain. Otherwise, take the M3 highway to the Constantia exit and follow the signs for Groot Constantia.

The neighbouring estate of **Klein Constantia** (1796) is also open to the public, though privately owned (*open weekdays 11–3, with tastings weekdays 9–5 & Sat 9–1*). Renowned for its white wines, Klein Constantia's fine homestead is smaller than Groot Constantia's, but less crowded with visitors.

Next door is a third estate, **Buitenverwachting**, a new winery with a well-known restaurant. Its wines have won many awards, and are worth bringing home, as they are hard to find outside South Africa. Klein Constantia and Buitenwerwachting are reached by car as for Groot Constantia.

Alphen, another fine Cape Dutch manor, and now a hotel and restaurant, is an 18th-century estate (also with its own vineyards) that used to belong to a Captain De Waal, a senior officer in the Dutch Company army. Louis Thibault, a military man as well as an architect, witnessed Captain De Waal commanding his troops during the Battle of Muizenberg, and was not impressed. Thibault wrote, 'He was too prudent to expose himself, and kept his distance half-a-mile back from the line of combat, so as to have a good view of the whole adventure.' Whatever its first owners' shortcomings, the estate and homestead are fine, and worth visiting for their own sake—they are on the M42 between Kirstenbosch and Hout Bay. (*See* 'Where to Stay and Eating Out'.)

Kirstenbosch Botanical Gardens (*open seven days 9am–sundown*), just off the M3 between the city and Groot Constantia, display an incredible variety of South African plants; 9000 of the country's 18,000 species, with thousands more exotics. One of the southern boundary points of the original Cape Colony, part of the defensive hedge and earthwork erected by Jan Van Riebeeck's men still runs through Kirstenbosch. The formal gardens and lawns stretch expansively (the total area is 560ha, over 1000 acres) below a steep, wild section of mountain forest cut through with signposted paths. Picnicing in Kirstenbosch is a Cape Town tradition, the manicured beds of exotic flowers and small copses of trees affording a measure of privacy in which to enjoy the peace, the colours and the songbirds that flock to the Gardens in great number. Watch particularly for the iridescent sheen of sunbirds (brightly-coloured relatives of the humming-bird), which suck nectar from the blooms. Landmarks within the Kirstenbosch are **Lady Anne Barnard's Bath**, a natural spring that (according to local historians) was never actually used by Lady Barnard (but never mind) and the **Compton Herbarium**. Kirstenbosch has a unique disabled facility—a **Braille Walk** for the blind that leads along a route of plants selected for their perfumes.

Table Mountain's Forests

Cecilia State Forest, one of Table Mountain's four state forests (and named after Cecil Rhodes), has its entrance on the winding mountain road that continues on uphill from Kirstenbosch and Groot Constantia towards Constantia Nek and Hout Bay. The forest's many trails are clearly marked on the CapTour Table Mountain map. For the fit, a steep uphill path from the forest entrance leads to a small waterfall, with wide views over the Cape Flats and False Bay. The same path leads into **Constantia Nek Forest**, which can also be reached by car along the Hout Bay road on from Cecilia Forest. Predominantly pine, the forest gives way to fynbos as it climbs the mountainside. Baboons and lynx are common here, though the lynx are too shy for any but the very lucky to spot, and the baboons tend to leave hikers alone (you might hear them, though). After a few hours under the trees, cross the road from the forest entrance to the **Constantia Nek Inn**, which has an open-air terrace for teas, and serves meals. Folk bands often play in the evenings (*see* 'Eating Out' and 'Nightlife').

Tokai, the forest suburb south of Constantia, also centres around an old wine estate **Tokai Homestead** (1795), named after a wine-producing region of Hungary. Attributed to Thibault, Tokai is smaller than Groot Constantia, but of great proportional beauty. Take the M3 to the Tokai exit and follow the signs to the homestead, either driving or walking past (you can't go in).

Tokai State Forest begins 500m left of Tokai Homestead. The lower section, on the Cape Flats, is not very interesting—serried ranks of commercial pine plantation. But as the forest climbs the mountainside, it becomes mixed with various deciduous exotics—oaks, chestnuts, maples and flowering gums as well as indigenous species, all planted at the turn of the century as part of an experiment to see which species would be hardy enough for commercial growing in South Africa. Many Capetonians call the upper section of Tokai Forest the 'enchanted woods', and certainly, among the kloofs and frequent mists you could be forgiven for fairy-tale imaginings. There is a cave (Elephant's Eye) and a network of trails (marked on the CapTour Table Mountain map).

Newlands Forest is the closest forest to the city centre, beginning on the mountain slopes above Newlands (*see* 'Southern Suburbs'). Its two entry points accessible from the M3 just south of the University of Cape Town campus. A network of trails lead up to both Contour paths, or up a steep series of natural steps to Devil's Peak.

Cape Peninsula

Getting Around the Cape Peninsula

By car is the easiest. However, trains run out along the east side of the Peninsula as far as Simon's Town from the central station in Cape Town. This is worth taking just for the view, especially the last few kilometres, where the railway runs along the actual sea-shore, and the waves crash directly below the train windows. Black taxis go as far as Muizenberg in the east and Camps Bay in the west. Buses leave the terminus in Cape Town Parade every hour, going around both sides of the Peninsula, though not to Cape Point. Tour buses to the Cape of Good Hope Nature Reserve and Cape Point can be arranged through the CapTour office.

Many people hitch around the Peninsula; there is always a steady stream of traffic, even to the further points like Noordehoek, and picking up hitch-hikers is a fairly well-accepted tradition in Cape Town. Best is to get as far as Muizenberg or Camps Bay by train, bus or taxi, then try your luck from these points. Do be aware that some people have been assaulted and worse this way. Girls should never hitch alone, and even hitching in a pair can be risky.

Eastern Peninsula

Muizenberg

Continuing south from Tokai and Retreat, the M3 splits—left to **Muizenberg** and right over the Silvermine Pass to the western Peninsula. The train through the Southern Suburbs also stops in Muizenberg. At the turn of the century, this was Cape Town's seaside resort for the wealthy. The town was beloved of Cecil Rhodes (who built a seaside house there; Rhodes Cottage) and Rudyard Kipling (who eulogised the 'white sands of Muizenberg' in a poem). Today, though many of the old villas still stand, the town has become rather glitzy and, on weekends and hot days, crowded with thousands of holidaymakers from the city.

The beach is still white sand, but can be over-full. Better is to walk south along the promenade to **St. James Beach** or eastwards around Muizenberg beach, for about a kilometre, as it curves into the warm waters of False Bay and becomes **Sunrise Beach** (*see* p.124).

Muizenberg has some interesting sights. **Rhodes Cottage** (*open Tues–Sun 10–1, 2–5*), on Main Road at the end of town furthest from Cape Town, is a small museum of Cecil Rhodes' personal effects from the last days of his life, following the Anglo-Boer War of 1899–1902 (*see* **South African History**). On the slope behind Rhodes Cottage is **Rust-En-Vrede** (Afrikaans for 'rest-in-peace'), a brick mansion designed for Rhodes by Sir Herbert Baker and Sir Abe Bailey (two prominent English Edwardian architects). The name was perhaps a little fateful, for Rhodes died before the mansion was completed.

The somewhat spectacularly named **Natale Labia Museum**, a satelleite museum of the National Gallery, is on Main Road, in the centre of town (*open Tues–Sun 10–5, but closed during August*). It is named after the Italian Prince Labia (an ambassador to South Africa who married a mining magnate's daughter, and after whom the Labia cinema in the Gardens area of Cape Town is also named), who lived here in the early 20th century. Patrons of the arts, their collection of furniture and paintings is on display.

The Edwardian **Muizenberg Railway Station** on Main Road has been converted into a seafood restaurant and craft market (*market open Sun and public holidays only*).

Kalk Bay

Kalk Bay is the next village south of Muizenberg, along the Peninsula by Main Road and the railway. Not a resort, but a pretty, working fishing village of white-washed cottages and houses crowding down to a small harbour. The word 'kalk' is Afrikaans for lime; in the 19th century the village made a living burning sea-shells to produce lime for whitewash. But fishing has always been the main activity. In the early afternoon, when the boats come in from False Bay, you can buy fresh fish directly from the small concrete jetty in the harbour. There is a cabaret theatre, the **Eauvre the Top Café** (*see* 'Entertainment') and the **Brass Bell**, one of the Cape's most fun restaurant/live music venues, overlooks the sea at Kalk Bay (*see* 'Nightlife' and 'Eating Out'); you should indulge in one of the Brass Bell's obscenely large seafood platters.

Behind Kalk Bay are a line of steep hills, hollowed out underneath by a series of **caves**, often inter-connected. These are blessedly undeveloped, no guides, no entry fee, no artificial lights. One can explore them (safest in a group as it is easy to get lost) by torchlight. The **Fish Hoek Publicity Association** © 782 1162, on Main Road, supplies maps of the caves and can arrange a guide.

Fish Hoek

Fish Hoek is the next town south on the Peninsula, founded by the British Cape Governor, Lord Charles Somerset, in 1818. Predominantly a retirement and holiday-home town cen-tred around a beach, Fish Hoek has little for the tourist. However, it does have the dubious distinction of being the only 'dry' town in South Africa. No alcohol may be bought or sold here at all, an irritating leftover clause from the town's original title deed. At the time of Fish Hoek's founding a British naval base had just been established at Simon's Town, a few kilometres south, and the Cape Governor decreed the no liquor clause to prevent Fish Hoek from becoming a sailor's roistering spot. Since then, no one has seen fit to overturn it. Fish Hoek is reached by the Main Road and by train.

Simon's Town and Around

Simon's Town was founded in 1810 by Lord Charles Somerset as a naval base, taking his cue from the Dutch, who had long been using it as a wintering spot for the fleet, preferring False Bay's calmer waters to the unpredictable squalls of Table Bay. During the Second

World War, Simon's Town became Britain's crucial naval base for the southern hemisphere. The South African Navy is still based here. Even now, there are signs forbidding you to take photos of the base, not that one would want to snap the dull concrete docks behind high wire fences. However, the town itself is very attractive; the Main Street has a grand 19th-century colonial front, complete with wrought iron balconies and arcades. This is the end of the line for the Peninsula railway, and the last few kilometres from Fish Hoek run along the actual ocean shore. Waves break on the rocks only a few feet away from the train window.

Simon's Town's Georgian and Victorian **Main Street** (known locally as the Historical Mile), is lined with antique shops, restaurants and tea shops (*see* 'Eating Out'). **Runciman's Buildings** (1785), on St George's Street are particularly fine and have now been converted into a coffee shop and tea garden, set around with the obligatory curio and gift shops and, unfortunately, twee art galleries.

The **Stempastorie** on Church Street (*open Mon–Sat 9.30–4.30*), originally a Dutch Reform Church parsonage, carries an eccentric display, the story of South Africa's national emblems (its flags, songs, regimental and sporting team devices and so on). This was where the Afrikaans national anthem, Die Stem, was written.

The **Simon's Town Museum** on Court Road (*open Tues–Fri 9–4, Sat 10–1*) is, not surprisingly, dedicated mostly to the Dutch, English and South African navies. The building itself, built in 1777, is stolidly handsome, being the old slave quarters, or less politely, the town's original brothel

The **Martello Tower** (*open Mon–Fri 10–3.45*), displaying the history of the modern South African navy, is in the Naval Dockyard. The British built it on arrival in 1796, after the Battle of Muizenberg, and it claims to be the oldest surviving British building in the country. Also in the Naval Dockyard is the **South African Naval Museum** (*open Mon–Fri 9–4, Sun 10–1*).

A lighter-hearted contrast is the **Warrior Toy Museum** (*open daily 10–4*), on St George's Street: a permanent exhibition of vintage toys, particularly original Dinky Toy cars, boats and trains. Semi-precious stones are processed at a nearby factory called **Topstones** on Dido Valley Road. Their 'scratch-patch' (or reject dump) is a good place to pick up malachite, amethyst, tiger's eye, rose quartz and other beautiful stones at no cost. Many of Cape Town's flea market jewellery-makers get their gems from here.

A 2km walk or drive south leads to **Boulders**, one of the most charming swimming spots in the Cape. A tiny cove with a miniature beach, sheltered by giant rocks, Boulders is both a place to swim and a nature reserve for a resident colony of **jackass penguins**, who gaze at you quizzically from the rocks and will sometimes swim to within a few feet of you, or come and join you on the beach. Neither particularly shy nor forward (they do not come for food), the penguins give the impression of generously sharing their territory with the human visitor. The result is one of the real treasures of the Peninsula. However, you should avoid Boulders at weekends, when it can get a bit crowded, and the penguins retreat to the caves and sea fringes. Another swimming place (with a good restaurant) is **Miller's Point** (*see* 'Eating Out'). Below the restaurant is a pool with only a low wall separating it from the sea, so that the tides wash clean water in and out. Fish and anemones live in the pool.

From Simon's Town, the Main Road becomes a coastal drive along cliffs, climbing gradually up towards the top of the Peninsula. The cliffs drop dizzyingly away from the road on the seaward side, giving an uninterrupted view of the Hottentots' Holland Mountains, 60km away on the other side of False Bay. There are no more towns between here and Cape Point; instead, fynbos and purple-flowering erica (like heather) cling to the slopes on the landward side of the road.

About 7km south of Simon's Town, the road bends around a large cliff buttress to a viewpoint where you can park and look out over the ocean. A small footpath leads down the cliffside from here to **Smitswinkel Bay**, another small cove and sheltered swimming spot. The steep walk down the cliff is not for the vertiginous, but the cove is worth reaching for its isolation. On weekends there are usually a few people down there. On weekdays, seldom anyone.

The Peninsula road continues along the cliff sides for another few kilometres, steadily climbing until it reaches the plateau in the middle of the Peninsula. Here the road forks; west to the other side of the Peninsula, or south (straight on) to **The Cape of Good Hope Nature Reserve** and **Cape Point**.

As it enters the reserve, the road swings inland to the windswept fynbos heath of the Peninsula's end. There is a gate, open sunrise to sunset, that takes your money (R5 per car plus R3 per person) and then you are on the road to Cape Point. Ostriches are a common sight here, but the rest of the reserve's considerable list of fauna (Cape mountain zebra, red hartebeest, white-faced bontebok, rhebok, grysbok, eland and duiker) tend to keep away from the road. It is better to walk one of the reserve trails (marked on the map they give you at the gate) if you want to see game.

What you will certainly see is baboons. They hang around the car park below the hill that climbs up to Cape Point, wanting food. Don't feed them. Several people get bitten every year by baboons that have decided not to wait to be offered food. The man who owns the ice-cream cart outside the car park's refreshment kiosk carries a long metal stick to keep them at bay.

It is a steep climb to Cape Point, but worth it (alternatively there is a bus from the car-park that goes most of the way up). In front of the balustrade, the ground becomes cliff and plunges about 100m into the ocean. Contrary to traditional belief, the Indian and Atlantic Oceans don't actually meet here, but you do see part of the massive meeting of their two currents, the warm Agulhas (Indian Ocean) and cold Benguela (Atlantic). Look out for gulls and cormorants flying to their cliffside nests. The wind picks them up as they approach the wall of rock, accelerating them to what seems certain oblivion. At the last minute they swing back and, miraculously, brake in mid-air, landing on their narrow ledges with ease.

According to legend, a ship called the *Flying Dutchman* has sailed the turbulent ocean around Cape Point since the 17th century. A Dutch East Indiaman captain, Hendrik Van der Decken, frustrated by the notorious cross-winds of the Cape, swore to round the Point even if it took forever. It is still sailing. Many people have claimed to have seen the phantom ship, including King George V, who visited Cape Point while serving in the Royal Navy at Simon's Town.

The reserve has about 40km of wild coastline, including some deserted beaches, excellent for walking. Expect to see some interesting birdlife, for example concave-beaked avocets (a much-coveted sight for British birdwatchers) and black oystercatchers.

From the Cape of Good Hope Reserve the M5 road continues over to the western side of the Peninsula.

The Cape Flats

Most visitors are so busy with Cape Town's centre that they do not see the Cape Flats, where the townships are, except at a distance from the mountain. However, a whole side of Cape Town culture exists in the townships. In the past, there was fairly free social movement between city and township, though a certain risk, legal or otherwise, was always present. But times have changed. In the current tense political climate and rapidly rising crime rate, most townships have become very dangerous, even for those who live there. Unless you know someone in a township, contact **Otherside Tours** ✆ 637 5763 for a knowledgeable guide.

Western Peninsula

Facing the cold Atlantic, the Cape Peninsula's western side begins in the city centre at Green Point, near the Waterfront, and continues around to Cape Point via Sea Point, Camps Bay, Llandudno and Hout Bay. South of Hout Bay, the Western Peninsula is wilder than the eastern and its lonely beaches such as Noordehoek—reckoned by many to be Cape Town's loveliest— are worth making a special trip for.

Green Point

Green Point, the area between Signal Hill and the Waterfront, is best known for its old lighthouse (1824) and sports stadium (on Main Road). The stadium is the end point of the **Coon Carnival New Year Parade**, a procession of floats accompanied by a drunken street party (*see* 'Festivals'). Green Point is mainly passed over by people on their way to the beaches of the Western Peninsula. At night, it is a red light district.

Green Point has three museums, the best being the **Cape Medical Museum** (*open Mon–Fri 9–4, adm free*), inside the New Somerset Hospital on the corner of Beach and Portswood. Cape Town's doctors have long been one of South Africa's most popular unofficial exports to the rest of the world and the displays of medical innovation in the museum help you to see why. Most interesting of all though, is the story of Dr James Barrie, a diminutive and charismatic Scot who came to the Cape in the early 1800s (and performed the colony's first Caesarean operation in 1818). A confidante of the then Cape Governor, Lord Charles Somerset, the time they spent together and the doctor's effeminate figure led to rumours of a homosexual affair. After the doctor's death, it was discovered that Dr Barrie was, in fact, a woman, who had disguised herself through medical school in Edinburgh and through her years in the male-dominated Cape colony.

Sea Point

The next suburb along, Sea Point is a neighbourhood somewhat distinct from the rest of Cape Town. Its stretch of Main Road is one of the liveliest in the city with flagrant displays of glamour from the young suburbanites who live in the houses on the hill above Main Road, and much pleasure-seeking from everybody else. The cafes, bars, clubs and restaurants pulsate with life, especially through the summer (*see* 'Nightlife' and 'Eating Out'). There are few places in Cape Town as good as Sea Point's Main Road for people-watching. However, Sea Point's rocky beach front has been heavily built-up, and is unpleasant for swimming.

Clifton, however, the neighbouring suburb, has a fine beach packed with young narcissists strutting their magnificent bodies up and down the sand. This is entertaining for a while, but tiring for a full afternoon; there is little humour in the place, and the atmosphere is rather forced.

Camps Bay

The beach at Camps Bay is wider, and there is a healthier mix of the beautiful people and others just there to swim. You can watch the surfers out in the bay, and there is a good selection of cafes and restaurants with outdoor terraces fronting the beach. These are mostly chain pizza and burger joints, but the location gives them atmosphere. Camps Bay also has a couple of fine restaurants set back from the beach front, and a good youth hostel set in a Victorian house (*see* 'Eating Out' and 'Where to Stay'). Behind the beach the Cape Peninsula mountains rise in twelve peaks known as the Twelve Apostles. As the beach faces west, Camps Bay is one of the favoured spots for, 'sundowners', a Cape Town tradition of taking a bottle (or bottles) of something and watching the sun set over the ocean. Look out for dassies (rock hyraxes) among the rocks on either side of the bay.

Llandudno is separated from Camps Bay by 15km of mountain road with the standard spectacular Peninsula views. The town itself is far downhill from the Main Road, clustered around a small bay. Picturesque from a distance (though most of the buildings are modern beach-mansions), and a good surfing spot, Llandudno is of little interest as a town. Better to take the road on the left as you turn off the main road to Llandudno, signposted to **Sandy Bay**. This winds for about a kilometre among houses and ends at a little car park. From here, a leisurely two kilometre stroll through fynbos and tunnels of wind-blown trees leads to Sandy Bay. Do not be shocked if a naked man or woman comes walking up the path towards you; Sandy Bay is one of South Africa's few legal nudist beaches. For all that, about half the people there wear swimming costumes, and there is no tension between those that wear and those that don't. Sandy Bay itself is entirely undeveloped, a lovely, natural place to spend an afternoon.

Hout Bay

From Llandudno, another drive along the precipitous cliffs leads to Hout Bay. 'Hout' means wood in Dutch; the early sailors and colonists felled timber here, and the slopes around the town are still densely forested.

Hout Bay is a worthy destination in itself. It has a working fishing fleet, and freshly-caught fish can be bought from the little harbour. On Main Road is an old Dutch homestead, **Kronendal** (1800), now a museum and restaurant (*see* 'Eating Out'). Unfortunately, the harbour has been developed for tourism, but not enough to take the soul out of the place. Mariner's Wharf is a kind of mall full of curio shops with a good, but expensive seafood restaurant (*see* 'Eating Out'). It is pleasant simply to wander around the small harbour, or walk behind it, to Andrews Road, and the **Hout Bay Museum** (*open Tues–Sat 10–12.30, 2–4.30*) which has some good exhibits of the area's early *strandloper* (beachcomber) cultures, settlement sites of which have been found in caves near Hout Bay, the Cape of Good Hope Nature Reserve, and round the Peninsula at Fish Hoek. Fishing and fishermen, naturally, takes up most of the rest of museum.

Just outside Hout Bay is the **World of Birds**, ✆ (021) 790 2730 (*open daily 8.30–6*). It sounds kitsch (and it certainly is a major tourist draw) but the bird park is actually fascinating. Giant aviaries house hundreds of South African birds living naturally in landscaped habitats. An hour in the World of Birds is as informative as a day spent looking at a bird book (though only 450 of the thousand-odd South African species are represented; not all the country's birds can survive in the Cape climate).

From here yet another spectacular cliff-side drive leads on round the Peninsula. Officially known as **Chapman's Peak Drive**, this 10km of cliff sides and look-out points is a riot of wild flowers in spring. But whatever the season, the drive is always breathtaking; wide views of the ocean and sudden, sharp bends.

Noordehoek lies at the end of Chapman's Peak Drive. Many Capetonians say this long, long beach is the most beautiful on the Peninsula. Noordehoek stretches for over 10km of white sand, with seldom more than a few people dotting its wide expanse. The water is cold, and the distance from Cape Town far (about 40km), which helps to keep the crowds away. Neither is there any beach-front town. In the mornings and evenings, riders bring their horses down for exercise on the packed sand at the water's edge. Visitors can rent horses from a nearby stable (*see* 'Activities').

Kommetjie and **Scarborough**, are the two small resort villages between Noordehoek and Cape Point. Both are known surfing spots with a cluster of holiday houses clinging round the small beach. At Scarborough watch out for 'dumper' waves at the north end of the beach. These are waves in a cross-current that dump you on the sea-floor rather than taking you to the shore. From Scarborough, the road winds up between wind-battered farms, along the boundary of the Cape of Good Hope Nature Reserve, until it meets the M5 and drops down to Simon's Town on the east side.

The Peninsula's Central Spine

Much of the Peninsula's central mountain chain is inaccessible by road. However, the **Old Cape Road** does traverse part of it, through **Silvermine Nature Reserve**, which begins south of Tokai and runs over the central mountains above Muizenberg and Kalk Bay. The road goes through the reserve and comes out at Noordehoek. There is an official parking area from where you can walk one of the many trails, easy or strenuous, to viewpoints over Hout Bay, False Bay, Cape Town and Constantia. To get there, take the M3 highway out of Cape Town towards Muizenberg, take the Muizenberg exit, but turn right at the Stop sign, instead of left into Muizenberg. At the next junction, turn left up a steeply climbing road, which takes you to Silvermine. If you have no car, take the train to Kalk Bay and enter via the steep hillside walk called **Jacob's Ladder** (ask for directions at the station).

Alternatively, you can take a guided three-day hike along the whole chain from Table Mountain to Cape Point (*see* 'Activities').

False Bay

Though not a part of Cape Town proper, the waters of False Bay lap the coastline of the eastern Peninsula, the Cape Flats and the southern Hottentots' Holland Mountains. Known for whale sightings in early summer (November and December), False Bay's beaches are less developed than many others in the Cape Town area. To get there, take the M5 (car or taxi) to Muizenberg, but at the traffic circle before Muizenberg, turn left to **Sunrise Beach**. This was designated a 'coloured' beach under apartheid, and this coupled with its proximity to the townships of Mitchell's Plain and Khayletsha, has kept it relatively free from crowds, though locals and shrimp fishermen use it regularly. False Bay, because of its warm current, can be prone to tides of jellyfish called **bluebottles**, usually after high winds (and Sunrise Beach can be *very* windy). These have a very painful sting. Before going in the water, check the tide-line. If a lot of bluebottles have been washed up, take care in the surf. If you see none, then swim with impunity. Fishermen net from the shore on the Muizenberg end of Sunrise Beach, and if you go at about two, you should catch them trawling in—a good time to buy fresh fish.

Following the R310 road (Baden Powell Road) around the beach eventually takes one past **Strandfontein** (a small resort on an extension of Sunrise Beach with a reptile park and pavilion) to a junction with the N2 highway. Continue through two sets of traffic lights and turn right to **Gordon's Bay**, a holiday village made up simply of cottages and a beach. Gordon's Bay and **Rooi Els** (an even smaller village just south) are considered among the best swimming-spots in the Cape. This road follows the coastal feet of the Hottentots' Holland Mountains, all the way around to Cape Hangklip, their southern extension and the easternmost point of False Bay.

Table Bay

Much of the bay is taken up by the docks, but the northern side is worth visiting. You get there via the R27 road through the suburb of **Milnerton**. The main street is quite lively with junk shops and family-run stores, but that's about the extent of it. The next suburbs are Table View and Blauberg. These are uninteresting, but the long cold-water beach that runs in front of them, **Blaubergstrand**, is truly lovely, looking across at Table Mountain on the other side of the bay: a good spot for a photograph, and the one used for most postcards of Table Mountain seen from afar. The annual South African surfing championships are held here in the summer.

Robben Island, the infamous prison where three centuries of African political prisoners were held; from the first Khoi chiefs to fall foul of the Dutch, to the Xhosa kings that fought the British (*see* **Eastern Cape** 'History') and Nelson Mandela, lies about 30km out in the bay. The prison is now unused and has been opened to visitors. Boats charter out to it from the Victoria and Alfred Dock at the Waterfront (*see* p.110). It is rumoured that plans are afoot to develop Robben Island for tourists, but as yet there is no confirmation. The island's austere, arid face seems ill-suited for such frivolity. The boat trips to Robben Island are good for seeing Cape fur seals and large sea-birds (skua and albatross), but the island is nonetheless very bleak, and carries an unmistakable aura of despair.

Festivals

Cape Town is, to some extent, in a permanent state of festivity. The biggest organized festival is the **Coon Carnival New Year Parade**, in the first week of January. This mainly 'coloured' celebration involves a procession of floats which starts in what used to be District Six and proceeds down Main Road to Green Point, where they enter the stadium to be judged.

The Carnival is controversial; the word 'coon' is provocative and whites have traditionally ignored it either for this reason or from a desire to distance themselves from 'coloured' culture, depending on their political orientation. Ironically though, the word 'coon' was adopted by the 'coloureds' themselves as a piece of self-mockery and a subtle jibe at white South Africa. The result is an event that tends to embarrass white Capetonians, but provides entertainment for those who participate in the Carnival.

Shopping

 Crafts, particularly jewellery, clothing and shoes, are something of an institution in Cape Town. The range is wide but usually reflects a blend of African and European styles. The two permanent **craft markets** in Greenmarket Square (and St George's Mall) and the Waterfront sell some of the best, although prices are jacked up for tourists. Rondebosch Library hosts a covered market (on St Andrews Road) on Wednesdays, Fridays and Saturdays. There are monthly craft markets in Constantia and Hout Bay, usually advertised in the back pages of the *Cape Argus*. Prices here are lower, but the quality is as good. A word of warning; if buying a pair of the soft leather boots or shoes that are a speciality of these markets, stick to ones with solid soles; the others are often only glued together and tend to split. More unusual are the Herb Market, on St Andrews Road, Rondebosch every Thursday, and the Botanical Society Market at Kirstenbosch, Constantia, which sells plants and flowers on the second Saturday of every month).

For **African crafts**—jewellery, wall hangings, wire cars and bicycles, and cloths—the craft shop in the National Gallery (next to the Company Gardens on Government Avenue) sells some of the best in the country. Also try the **Operation Hunger Showroom**, on Maynard Road in Wynberg.

Although **antiques** may be difficult to transport home, they are worth looking for. Cape Town's 300 year history and colonial culture brought a lot of valuable objects into the country, both indigenous and imported. The weekend open-air antique stalls on Church Street are worth a look, as are the smarter shops on Long Street. Long Street's **bookshops** are well known for selling first editions cheaper than in the West, and South Africa has many excellent private libraries to stock such shops.

Activities

The mountain and the ocean are irresistible forces in Cape Town, and the city has a strongly outdoor culture, whether it's paddling on a beach, strolling in a forest, or doing the hardcore stuff like rock-climbing or surfing.

beaches

You can escape the city's summer heat by plunging into sparkling ocean within half an hour of any point in town. Bear in mind that beaches on the east side of the Peninsula have warm water, while beaches on the west side are cold. The best of those close to the city are **Camps Bay**, which is busy and friendly, with cold water, white sand and safe swimming, and **Sunrise Beach** on False Bay, between Plumstead and Muizenberg, which is often all but deserted. White sand, warm water, no bad currents, but look out for bluebottle jellyfish. On the eastern Peninsula **Boulders** beach, at Simon's Town, is a tiny, warm-water cove sheltered by huge rocks and inhabited by jackass penguins that you can swim next to. **Noordehoek** beach, in the western Peninsula, is long, lonely and fabulously beautiful, with white sand and water so cold you gasp.

surfing and wind surfing

Unless you have several months to spare, there is not much point in trying to learn to surf—it's a bit like trying to learn a musical instrument in an afternoon. Body-surfing, though, is great fun and can be done by beginners (though you should always stay close to those who know where rocks and currents are). Camps Bay, Llandudno and Muizenberg are good spots. Call CapTour, ✆ 418 5214/5, for details of hire companies for both body surf-boards and wind surfers, as companies tend to come and go by the season.

boat trips

Trips from Hout Bay to Duiker Island, a smelly but interesting Cape fur-seal colony, give non-anglers the chance to see the Peninsula coast from the sea. Drumbeat Charters, ✆ 438 7208/790 4859 charge under R20 for an hour. Also *see* p.110.

sea angling

The Cape Peninsula, like most of South Africa's coastline, offers excellent fishing in largely unpolluted waters which, because of the two ocean currents, are heavy with cold and warm water species. Tackle can be hired from most tackle shops in the Peninsula towns. No permit is required for fish or shellfish; you can cut mussels from the rocks of many beaches at low tide. Oysters, crayfish and abalone can also be taken, but are subject to strict catch quotas (CapTour supplies a leaflet with full details). Everywhere on the coast except Table Bay harbour is open for fishing.

Big game fish abound in the further waters. Marlin (black and blue), three species of tuna, swordfish, doredo and other monster species can be sought via several big-game charter companies such as Big Game Fishing Safaris, ✆ 643 837; Hout Bay Boat Yard, ✆ 790 3619; Bluefin Charters, ✆ 831 756; African Fishing Safaris, ✆ 721 272; Condor Charters, ✆ 470 741; Neptune, ✆ 782 3889.

walking

Table Mountain, Devil's Peak and the State Forests: For those who would rather not hike up Table Mountain on their own, John Macdonnel, ✆ 452 503, will collect you, guide you along the strenuous first recorded route up to the summit, and bring you down by cable car. Alternatively, and for free, join a party of walkers. There are various hiking and walking clubs in Cape Town. The Mountain Club, ✆ 453 412 organizes easy or killer excursions into the mountains around Constantia and Kirstenbosch Gardens.

In the Peninsula: The hiker can roam at will in the Cape of Good Hope Nature Reserve, and stands a good chance of seeing large game; usually red hartebeest, Cape Mountain zebra and bontebok. Guided day walks in Silvermine Nature Reserve and Table Mountain Reserve (over the Twelve Apostles) are offered by Wanderlust Walks, ✆ 438 1948. Alternatively, do it yourself using the CapTour map of the Table Mountain Reserve, or the map of Silvermine's seven trails, available from the reserve office.

Hout Bay has some beautiful walking, both strenuous and easy. The Hout Bay Publicity Association, in the Trading Post on Main Rd, ✆ 790 4053, has a map of the trails. Breeding leopard have been reported near here. You won't see them, but it's nice to know they're around.

A hard, three-day hiking trail from Table Mountain to Cape Point is open through the National Hiking Way Board, 7th Floor, Foretrust Building, Hammerschlag Way, Foreshore, ✆ 402 3093.

bird watching

Table Mountain and the Peninsula reserves offer birding as good as any up-country, with over 300 species recorded. The best spots are Kirstenbosch, Rondevlei Reserve (a small wetland reserve on the Cape Flats near the township of Mitchell's Plain), Rietvlei reserve on the coast north of Milnerton and outside Cape Town's official limits (an important breeding place for wildfowl and sea-birds), the Liesbeeck River in Observatory (sadly marred by the roar of traffic) and the Cape of Good Hope Nature Reserve. Call the Cape Bird Club ✆ 686 6393 for a guide.

riding

Experienced riders can rent horses for guided exploratory one-day rides into the Peninsula Mountains and along the beaches (including Noordehoek) from John

Foster at Horse Trail Safaris, ✆ 734 396. Beginners should try the Downs Riding Centre, ✆ 621 414.

On Sundays from May to October there is a drag-hunt based in Cape Town with whom you can ride to hounds in the nearby countryside after a pre-laid scent (there is no live quarry). Call the hunt secretary ✆ 963 968 about hiring a horse for the day.

Cape Town ✆ (021–)

Where to Stay

luxury

The **Mount Nelson Hotel** on De Waal Drive, just opposite Government Avenue, ✆ 231 000, is British colonial Africa flaunted unashamed. From the high wrought-iron gates, the drive leads through landscaped parkland to the handsome classical pile that is the hotel. Famous for its formality, luxurious suites and cream teas (though not its restaurant), there is really nowhere else to stay in Cape Town, if you can afford it. White liveried waiters and footmen will attempt fulfil your every whim. However, in healthy competition for both age and status is the **President** on the beach front at Sea Point, ✆ 434 0809. Another handsome relic from colonial days is its restaurant, Finch's, which is renowned.

The Cellars on Hohenhort Avenue, Constantia, ✆ 794 2137, though ungraded, qualifies as a luxury hotel. A 19th-century homestead with sumptuously furnished suites, it is not as interesting as the Constantia homestead hotels in the cheaper 'expensive' range (*see* below).

The other five star hotels in the town centre are rather dull modern chain hotels, including no less than three of Sol Kerzner's Southern Sun chain. They are: the **Capetonian Protea** on Heerengragcht, ✆ 211 150; **Cape Sun**, on the corner of Strand Street and St George's Mall, ✆ 238 844; the **De Waal Sun** on De Waal Drive ✆ 451 311; and **Newlands Sun** on Main Rd, Newlands, ✆ 611 105.

expensive

St George's in St George's Mall, ✆ 419 7010, is big, modern and rather dull. More interesting is the **Tulbagh Hotel**, ✆ 215 140, in an early 19th century town house in Tulbagh Square in the upper city centre. Very quiet, even though it's at the heart of things. In Greenmarket Square, one of Cape Town's most atmospheric quarters, is the **Inn On The Square** ✆ 232 040. You pay more for the location than for the quality of the rooms, which are clean, neat and comfortable, but not especially charming. However, you can sit on the terrace and sip coffee while the busy square goes about its business. The **Metropole** on Long St, ✆ 236 363, is comfortingly small and handy for second-hand bookshops. It has a family-run feel, the service is attentive and the rooms very comfortable.

By far the best of the expensive range is the **Vineyard Hotel** on Main St, Newlands, ✆ 642 107. Built at the end of the 18th century and famous for being where Lady Anne Barnard stayed, it is decorated in early Cape style, with stinkwood and yellowwood furniture, crystal and silver. Similar in style is the **Alphen** in Constantia, ✆ 794 5710. Another 18th-century Cape Dutch homestead set under tall oaks and with its own vineyards, the Alphen is opulent, quiet and beautifully furnished. Its superb restaurant specializes in Cape cuisine. On the M42 road between Kirstenbosch and Hout Bay, **Hout Bay Manor**, ✆ 790 4730, is another gracious white homestead set under large oaks. Facing a fountain-court and over-shadowed by Chapman's Peak, Hout Bay Manor is a National Monument. Surprisingly priced on the moderate end of the expensive range, it is a good place from which to explore the Peninsula.

moderate

There is little moderately-priced accommodation in Cape Town. The **Breakwater Lodge** is a large budget hotel on the Victoria and Alfred dock, Waterfront, ✆ 406 1911. Clean, comfortable and good value (under R50 per night). **Rodenburg**, a large, handsome turn of the century house at 8 Myrtle Rd, Rondebosch, ✆ 689 4852, offers B&B (or meals by request) in spacious, comfortable rooms. The place is family-run, and guests can relax in the huge living-room (which has a very large record collection) and enjoy the garden.

More central B&B is offered in a family-run house in the Gardens neighbourhood; **7 Hof Street**, ✆ 244 984. Very straightforward and unpretentious, the nicely-proportioned rooms are comfortably furnished. The **Room With A View**, 51 Upper Cambridge St, ✆ 472 820, is similar.

cheap

For low-budget accommodation in Cape Town, you are spoilt for choice. Most places are youth-hostelish (sharing rooms or dormitories), but some offer very cheap single and double rooms as well. The best known is **74 New Church Street Hostel**, Tamboerskloof, ✆ 234 530 (take the bus from outside the OK Bazaar on Adderley St, or walk up Long Street, turn right then third left and first right again). Choice of dormitories or double rooms, and the use of a swimming pool, laundry, showers, a kitchen and a mail holding service; friendly and helpful. Also in Gardens is the **Albergo**, at 5 Beacham St, ✆ 221 849, which does dormitory rooms, singles and doubles, as is **Oak Lodge**, ✆ 456 182, which only offers dorm bunks. **Shanti Lodge**, ✆ 461 1408, again in Gardens on 17 Princes Street also offeres dorm accommodation only, with a free pick-up from the city centre. On New Church Street, at the mountain end of Buitengracht Street, is the **Zebra Crossing**, ✆ 221 265, offering dorms, singles or doubles, bedding and 24-hour check-in. Also in the town centre is **Long Street Backpackers**, on Long Street, ✆ 230 615. Off Bellevue Road, on Higgo Crescent, is the **Belvidere**, ✆ 231 316/7, which also has dorms and double rooms.

Observatory has several budget places. **Namaste Lodge**, ✆ 448 1879, at 23 Trill Road is an old Victorian house run by travellers for travellers. Free pick-up from the bus/train station (and sometimes airport), bike hire, mail holding, dorms, double rooms and camping are offered. Also on Trill Road the **Holistic Lodge**, at No.16,

℗ 470 481 is clean, bright, and friendly with a pool table and big garden, offering dormitory accommodation only. **Rolling Stones Youth Hostel** is on the upper floor of one of the colonial arcades on Lower Main Rd, opposite Pancho's Mexican Restaurant ℗ 474 834. The front rooms have verandas. Dormitories and double rooms at R20 per person per night. Residents get 15 per cent off meals at Pancho's Mexican and Moghul's Indian restaurants, also on Observatory's Lower Main Road. On Low Street, also in Observatory, is the **Petra Backpackers**, ℗ 471 793.

At Green Point, the **Hip-Hop Traveller's Stop**, ℗ 439 2104 can be found at 11 Vesperdene Road. The Waterfront is close by, you can check-in 24 hours a day and they will arrange a pick-up from the bus and train station in town. An extra attraction is a large swimming pool. Further along the peninsula, at Sea Point, is the **Bunkhouse**, on Antrim Street, ℗ 434 5695. In Camps Bay, is the official YHA Youth Hostel **Stand Alt Youth Hostel**, The Glen, ℗ 438 9037. This is reachable by bus or black taxi from the bus stop on the opposite side of Adderley Street from the OK Bazaar, and has a swimming pool and dormitories. **Muizenberg Youth Hostel**, on 11 Maynard Road, ℗ 788 2301 (take the train to Muizenberg station, then walk along Beach Road to Maynard) gives access to the eastern peninsula. Very basic, but handy for the beach.

The Cape View Hostel in Bloubergstrand on Table Bay, ℗ 562 127, is some way from Cape Town, but has a superb view out over the bay. The hostel runs a free shuttle service from the city centre, and water-skiing can be arranged.

Cape Town ℗ (021–)   ***Eating Out***

Cape Town and the Winelands evolved a distinct cuisine through the 18th century, mixing French, Dutch and Malay cooking. Game, lamb and fish feature strongly. Spicy, but not overly hot, Cape Cuisine uses fruits and curries to create original versions of European food. Some dishes are very simple, like *bobotie* (a kind of curried moussaka). More elaborate are spiced game dishes, using guinea fowl and venison. For more detail on Cape Cuisine *see* p.76.

City Centre

expensive

The **Old Colonial**, Barnett St, Gardens, ℗ 454 909, has two licensed restaurants in elegant early-19th century buildings, serving Cape dishes among a wider menu. **Biesmiellah** ℗ 230 850 on Wale St in the Bo-Kaap, occupies two small front rooms of a cottage dating from the early 1800s. The food is good value, beautifully prepared, very hot and eaten with fingers. No alcohol is allowed. **Rozenhof** ℗ 241 968, on Kloof St in the Gardens area, is a formal place, serving a mixture of Cape, French and house dishes. The service is excellent, and the food very tasty, but the place does feel a bit impersonal.

Trawler's ✆ 419 0249, in the Victoria and Alfred Basin on the Waterfront, is a well-known and lively seafood restaurant housed in a 19th-century pavilion. Apart from traditional shellfish and line-fish (all fresh that day), there are some good Portuguese seafood dishes. Ask for the specials. **The Round House** ✆ 438 7193/2320 in Camp's Bay, is one of Cape Town's snootiest restaurants. Set under tall trees in The Glen (just behind the beach front), this place serves annoyingly small nouvelle cuisine dishes and more substantial cordon bleu. But the food really is good and it is fun to watch the diners, dressed to the nines, behaving as impeccably as the staff.

moderate

Crammed into a small, very beautiful 18th-century house in one of the Gardens' most handsome squares, **Maria's**, ✆ 452 096 (Barnett Street) is very informal and serves some of the best Greek food on offer anywhere—try the salad. Very popular, so booking is advisable. **Christo's**, ✆ 249 250 on Long Street, has a beautiful Art Nouveau front and a simple, spacious interior. It serves a mixture of good pasta and fish dishes. The **Tokyo** restaurant ✆ 236 055, at 31 Long Street, is for sushi lovers. At the expensive end of the moderate range, Tokyo is still cheaper than sushi restaurants in Europe. Run by a Japanese family, the restaurant is traditional—diners sit on the floor. Fun. **The Kaapse Tafel** ✆ 231 651, on Queen Victoria Street in the Gardens, serves goodly portions of Cape country food. Try the *bobotie* or Karoo lamb. Set in a small 18th century house, the restaurant is not licensed but you can take your own wine. Friendly and relaxed.

cheap

Mykonos Souvlaki ✆ 439 2106, on Main Road, Sea Point, serves very good value Greek and Lebanese food. The falafels are really good. Cheerful, crowded and cheap. On the same road is **Stone's** ✆ 439 6747, done up like a strumpet's boudoir and serving pastas, vegetarian dishes and chef's specials to a young crowd. Take your own wine. It can get loud later in the evening.

Southern Suburbs

expensive

Almondbury ✆ 885 789, on Lakeside Drive, is an unpretentious restaurant with a simply furnished interior that has quite a following in the Cape for the excellence of its food. Again, the cooking is not pretentious; traditional Cape, seafood and French dishes served in an informal atmosphere. Ask about the day's specials. **Alphen, Buitenverwachting** and the **Jonkershuis** are three showpiece restaurants in 18th-century manors on old Constantia estates. All are period furnished, formal and very beautiful. Alphen ✆ 794 5011, on the M42 between Kirstenbosch and Hout Bay, is set in forest; Buitenverwachting ✆ 794 3522 is the homestead next to Klein Constantia, and is signposted from the M5. Jonkershuis ✆ 794 6255, on the Groot Constantia estate, is signposted from the same road.

The Woodstock ✆ 477 726, on Essex Street, Woodstock, serves an original menu of Cape, Continental and seafood dishes in cheerful surroundings. The cooking is of the highest quality, and the restaurant is justifiably popular. Booking is advised. Ever good for value, Observatory's Lower Main Road offers **Pancho's** ✆ 74854, a Mexican restaurant with a really beautiful late-19th-century, two-floor interior. Try to get a table upstairs in the covered balcony. The food isn't terrific, but the helpings are big and the prices very reasonable. In a private house in a close just of Lower Main Rd, parallel with and one block south of Trill Road.

Ramola's ✆ 797 0019, at 13 Wolfe Street. in the area of Wynberg known as 'Little Chelsea', is perhaps Cape Town's finest Indian restaurant. Mostly open for lunches, the restaurant serves dinner on varying nights of the week—check by phone. The kitchen is open, so you watch the food being prepared. The dining room is simple but pleasant. Incredibly good value, Ramola's offers the best food at mid-budget prices.

Eastern Peninsula

expensive

The Brass Bell ✆ 885 456 in Kalk Bay, has a great seafood restaurant overlooking the ocean. At the moderate end of expensive, their seafood platter is a challenge even to those with huge appetites. Informal and relaxed, with the ocean breaking on a sea wall about 50m from the windows.

moderate

Restaurant Don Pepe on Main Road, Muizenberg, ✆ 888 459, serves really good Portuguese food. Take your own wine. **Black Marlin** on Main Road, Simon's Town, ✆ 786 1621, serves set menus, with an emphasis on seafood fesh that day, in the front room of a Victorian house. Very friendly. Booking is advised.

Western Peninsula

expensive

Bressay Bank ✆ 790 1140, is on a boat in Hout Bay harbour. Pricey seafood, very good service. Also in Hout Bay is **Kronendal** ✆ 790 1970, a 250 year-old homestead; the dining room is newly renovated and rather suburban. Good Cape cuisine.

moderate

Much more fun is **Camel Rock**, in Scarborough ✆ 801 122. Chef's specials are on the board—mostly seafood. Very relaxed and enjoyable. Take your own wine.

Bars and Cafés

Of the many bars in the city centre, the following is a small selection. **Crow's Nest**, in the **Crow Bar** on lower Loop Street, has a pleasant upstairs veranda from which to watch the city go by. There is also a dance-floor (mostly Top 40) that gets busy at weekends. Almost opposite, on the same street, are the **George** (which caters to a similar crowd) and **Havana,** a little seedier, with strip shows on certain nights. **McGawley's Pub** on Long Street has colonial atmosphere and pool tables, as does the **Kimberley Hotel**, on the corner of Buitenkant and Roeland Streets (though it can get a little rough at night). The **Perseverance Tavern** on Buitenkant Street is interesting for its history (*see* 'City Centre'), but is a little conservative, as is the **Stag's Head** on Hope Street (parallel to Buitenkant, one block north). On Lower Long Street, near Waterkant is **Doo-Me**, a bar catering to a mixed crowd of young pleasure seekers. The Waterfront has several bars: **Quay 4** is the busiest (usually packed to capacity), but you can sit outside by the dock. (*see* 'Live Music' for other bars here.)

In the Southern Suburbs, Observatory's Lower Main Road has several relaxed bars; **Ruby In The Dust** (also a live music venue) has a hippie and racially mixed crowd of musicians and students, as does its sister bar, **Ruby 2**, on Victoria Road, Woodstock. **Heidelberg**, also on Lower Main Road, Observatory, is more hearty— long benches and loud drinkers. **Barrister's** on Main Street, Newlands, is quiet and civilized. On the eastern Peninsula, the **Brass Bell** at Kalk Bay (also a restaurant and live music spot) is friendly, provides complimetary fish & chips (usually on Tuesdays and Thursdays about 7pm) in the bar and has the ocean outside the window. On the western side, **Barrister's** in Hout Bay (same owner as Barrister's bar in Newlands) has jazz on Sundays.

Cafés are harder to find. Despite Cape Town's sunny climate, there is a distinct lack of outdoor terraces on which to sit and have a coffee. However, lower **St George's Mall** has outdoor tables in the middle of the thoroughfare. Sit down at one and a waiter will find you. On the same street is **Square's**, which serves light meals as well, but is rather expensive. **Greenmarket Square** has several cafés. **The Tea Garden**, by the aviary in the Company Gardens, is a peaceful break in the city's rush; sit inside or out. The **Mount Nelson Hotel** on De Waal Drive serves teas of splendour in the most gracious surroundings for surprisingly little. In the Southern Suburbs, Observatory has **Fiddlewoods** (also excellent for breakfasts and light meals), on Trill Road, just off Lower Main Road. The **Rhodes Memorial Tea Garden**, off the M5, is a shaded place of great beauty whose outside terrace overlooks the Cape Flats and False Bay. The cheesecake is fabulous. After a walk in the state forests above Constantia, wander into the **Constantia Nek Restaurant**, which operates as a café in the afternoons.

Entertainment

theatres

The **Nico Malan** on Hertzog Boulevard, Foreshore, ✆ 217 695, has an opera house and two theatres and its own permanent opera, ballet and drama companies. The Cape Town Symphony Orchestra regularly give classical concerts here. The **Baxter** on Main Road, Rondebosch, ✆ 685 7880, is more avant-garde. Fringe theatres include **Café Mozart** on Church Street, with only 25 seats, ✆ 243 774. The **Little Theatre** ✆ 242 340 in Orange Street in the Company Gardens, The **Dock**

Road Theatre ✆ 419 5522 at the Waterfront, the **Herschel** on Main Road in Claremont, The **Masque** on Main Road, Muizenberg ✆ 750 141, the **Eauvre The Top** ✆ 788 3746 (specializing in cabaret) in Kalk Bay, and the **Theatre on the Bay**, ✆ 438 3300 in Camps Bay.

classical music

The **Cape Town Symphony Orchestra**, plays at the **Nico Malan** ✆ 217 695, and at the **City Hall**, ✆ 461 7084, on the Parade. Thursday and Sunday are regular concert days, though the orchestra take a holiday from mid-December to mid-January and for June and half of July. The **Baxter** theatre also has concerts, usually once a month, (✆ 438 9007). The **Old Town House** in Greenmarket Square, ✆ 246 367, has a chamber orchestra. Concerts are irregular, but worth finding out about for the setting alone.

cinema

The best for non-Hollywood movies are the **Labia**, ✆ 245 927, on Orange Street and the **Baxter** ✆ 685 7880 on Main Road, Rondebosch (downstairs from the theatre).

Nightlife

live music

Cape Town's nightlife is notoriously fickle; clubs open and close almost by the month, and the scene is constantly changing. The clubs listed below were active at the time of publishing, but it is possible that some of the venues may have changed by the time you check them out. Ask in local bars for the latest in what's on.

The **Stage**, on Loop Street, in the city centre, has live rock bands several nights a week, usually playing hard rock and metal, but with an increasing number of funkier bands coming on the scene. Try **Ruby In The Dust** (Lower Main Road, Observatory) or **Ruby 2**, on Victoria Road, Salt River, ✆ 476 574 for township music, funk and original rock bands. Upstairs at **Moghul's**, an Indian restaurant on the same road, local rock and folk bands play two or three nights a week. Look out for posters around the city. The **Constantia Nek Restaurant**, opposite the entrance to Constantia Nek State Forest, has live folk bands on Saturday nights. The **Brass Bell** in Kalk Bay (behind the station on Main Road) has blues and rock 'n' roll. **Bertie's Landing** in the Waterfront has live bar bands playing American rock covers for yuppies to get drunk to.

Good jazz is played at the **Green Dolphin** and **Rosie's** at the Waterfront, at the **Fire Escape** on Buitengracht Street and at **Tattler's**, in the Don Hotel, Main Road, Sea Point.

dance clubs

The **Fringe** on Harrington Street in the Gardens neighbourhood (parallel to Buitenkant Street, one block south) plays everything from funk and techno to thrash, depending on the night; mixed crowd, very relaxed. **Crossroads** on

Shortmarket Street in the upper city centre has bands that play a fusion of rap, ethnic sounds and jazz-funk to a relaxed, mixed-race crowd. The **Playground**, on Loop Street rocks to metal and indie sounds. The **Stage**, up Loop Street from the Playground, offers hardcore, metal-funk crossover and grunge on its non-live nights.

There are two **Hardrock Cafés**, one on Main Road, Sea Point, where the beautiful young beach-heads dance and drink, and one on Main Road, Rondebosch, where yuppie students do the same. Both play mainstream dance music. **Odyssey** on Main Road, Salt River (the city end of the Woodstock neighbourhood), plays disco music, and is notorious for being a hang-out of 'coloured' gangs, but actually is pretty relaxed. **Browns** on lower Loop Street, opposite the Crow Bar, is a very similar scene.

Eden on Main Road, Green Point, is almost laughably pretentious. The music is the worst of the Top-40, but the kings and queens of the dance floor really shake their thing.. The **Yellow Door** in Guguletu township (drive or take a cab) plays authentic township jive and rap. This can be a good place to meet township residents on politically neutral territory. However, bear in mind that the volatile social situation in South Africa has made visiting the townships potentially very dangerous. Ask local advice before going in. Do not go as a single girl.

The Winelands

'This is our Holland, the Hottentots' Holland'

The Khoi-chiefs of the Winelands to the first Dutch land speculators in the 1650s.

On either side of the Hottentots' Holland Mountains, some 60km north and east of Cape Town, stretch the Cape Winelands, a region of vineyards and orchards sheltered by tall mountains and watered by cold, fast-flowing rivers. In the wide valleys stand white-washed 18th-century mansions, serene beneath groves of great oaks. The juxtaposition of cultivated charm and rugged mountain wilderness delights the eye, and is reminiscent of the idealized landscapes of old Europe in fairy-tale books.

The Winelands (or Boland, meaning 'upland'), are the home of Cape Dutch architecture (*see* pp.63–4), of well-proportioned manor houses whose distinctive roof-gables owe a little to the medieval Low Countries, and a little to Indonesia (the Dutch having colonized the East before South Africa). Cape Dutch interiors are light and airy, fitted with bright yellow-wood ceilings, rich, red stinkwood floors and simple, handsome furniture. Dating from the 1680s, the oldest Winelands towns, such as Tulbagh, Stellenbosch and Franschoek, are still largely Cape Dutch, while most others have sizeable sections of old buildings. Almost every wine estate has its big Cape Dutch homestead (and small workers' cottages in the same style), many of which are open to tourists.

History

Jan Van Riebeeck's first Cape-grown wine was poured in 1659, seven years after the Cape Colony's founding. Of all the European plants he coaxed from the sandy soil of the Company Gardens outside the colony's fort, the vine was the one that Van Riebeeck wanted most to thrive. 'Praise Be The Lord', he wrote in his diary the day the first bottle of wine was brought to him. Unwittingly, he had found the formula that would make the southwest Cape rich.

Then came the Huguenot settlers in 1688. Their early Cape vineyards pre-date even those near Bordeaux in France, and were laid out when elephant and lion still lived around Table Bay. In the mid 1700s, Governor Simon Van Der Stel harnessed the Huguenots' knowledge to found Groot Constantia, the first Cape wine estate to export wine to Europe. He is thought to have used sweet Muscat grapes from Alexandria, known in South Africa as hanepoort (a name derived from the word '*hanekloot*', which is Dutch for 'testicles'). However, the pious burghers of the Cape quietly neutered the name, changing it to hanepoort, which doesn't mean anything, and by which name the grape is still known.

Hanepoort grapes can be red or white, but these days are generally grown only for eating.

The Cape vineyards developed as settlers established estates out in the valleys of the present Winelands region during the early 19th century, importing the hardy red Cabernet Sauvignon grape which gradually began to dominate the Cape vineyards. This grape is still reckoned to be the best for withstanding the Cape's wet winters and searingly hot summers, producing a full-bodied, mellow claret said to need about seven years' ageing to reach its prime. Many purists still believe that the Bordeaux-like Cabernet Sauvignon is the Cape's 'true' wine, and certainly it is the most successful grape grown near the coast. But these days, it is the Pinotage, a uniquely South African hybrid of Pinot Noir and Cabernet Sauvignon grapes, that is regarded as the Cape's best wine.

Since the mid 1970s greater experimentation has taken place and South Africa now produces and exports over 100 varieties of wine. Recent successes include Merlot (a Bordeaux-like claret), Chardonnay (a white Burgundy grape, said to produce South Africa's finest dry white wine), Sauvignon Blanc (from which some Cape estates have produced vintages that have been compared to the best white wines of the Loire) and Chenin Blanc (a versatile white that can be fruity, sweet or dry depending on the estate).

Also popular in the Winelands is the German Gewurztraminer (a sweetish, spicy white wine), and Weisser Reisling (which varies from off-dry to sweet depending on the age), the French Gamay (a successful Beaujolais now exported from the Cape to California and France) and the smoky, purple Shiraz wines. In the drier, arid regions bordering the Karoo, Muscadels and fortified wines have been winning international awards since the early 1980s.

At harvest time (February and March) the Winelands resemble an Old Master's painting; a wide, green landscape peopled by armies of ragged labourers hand-picking the grapes under tall windbreaks of oak and pine, the ever-present Cape mountains looming behind. Small estates still flourish, partly due to the availability of cheap labour. This means that the corporate producers (such as KWV, the Cape's largest exporter) and the Anglo-American owned estates (such as Boschendal, largest estate in the Franschoek region) are in no danger of dominating and thus dulling the market. In fact, the opposite has been true; the smaller estates' continued success has encouraged the larger producers to follow their example, importing oak barrels from France and ageing their wine for longer to improve the quality.

Buying Cape Wine

Until recently, South Africa's bottling system followed uniform guidelines denoting quality. A blue band on the neck meant a wine of origin (i.e. grapes from a single area), but whose grapes might be from different vineyards and years. A red band confirmed that the year printed on the bottle was the year of harvest. A green band meant that the wine contained at least 75 per cent of the grape variety printed on the label. A red, white and green band was an indication of high quality, and this was reflected in the price. The highest grading a bottle could have was a gold seal, which meant that the wine had been judged superior by a team of experts and could be very expensive. Although bottles are still sold with these bands on the neck, this system is being phased out, as the corporate producers, such as KWV, complained that the market was being prejudiced against good blended wines.

Price is no longer a sure gauge of quality; many of the smaller estates now sell their own wines, often bottled on the premises, and of good years, for as little as R10–R15. The best way to find the wine you like is to ask around, or to explore one or more of the Wine Routes (outlined further on in the chapter) and taste the wines for yourself.

N

Land over 1000 metres

30 kms
20 miles

138

The Different Wineland Regions

The Winelands are divided into several separate regions. The lush, populated **Hottentots' Holland region**, close to Cape Town, includes the graceful Drakenstein Valley and the old towns of Stellenbosch, Franschoek, Paarl and Somerset West. The **Breede River Valley** is a drier, emptier region north of the the Hottentots Holland reached by the N1 highway or the train via two spectacular passes, Du Toit's Kloof and Bain's Kloof. **Ceres** and its environs (the most outlying part of the Winelands) is divided into two, the **Warm Bokkeveld** (lowlands) and **Cold Bokkeveld** (uplands). Finally, the **Hex River Valley** connects the Breede River Valley with the arid Karoo.

Getting Around the Winelands

By train: Stellenbosch and Paarl can be reached by rail from Cape Town, with services running several times per day. Call Paarl's main railway station, ✆ (02211) 236226 for train times.

By bus: Several tour companies offer bus trips into the Winelands, although usually only to the Hottentots' Holland region. These are mostly day trips from Cape Town, but some companies offer longer tours. **Springbok Atlas**, ✆ (021) 654 5448 offers a day-trip around Stellenbosch, Paarl and Franschoek, with a visit to two estates, as well as longer tours into the Breede River Valley and to the beautiful town of Tulbagh. If Springbok Atlas is booked up, call CapTour, ✆ (021) 418 5202 for details of other tour companies operating.

By car: The best way round the Winelands is by car, allowing independent movement around the side-roads and access to the many bed and breakfasts and farms for camping. Good, cheap car hire is available in Cape Town (*see* **Cape Town**, 'Getting Around'). Beware, however; following a Wine Route can obviously involve downing several glasses of wine, and although nobody seems to mind tourists driving from estate to estate in a mildly sozzled state, some of the precarious mountain roads can catch you out. And drinking and driving is still an offence.

Hitch-hiking: Hitching is fairly easy in the Winelands themselves, but thumbing a lift out of Cape Town can be dangerous, as the N1 highway passes through the Cape Flats and their townships. Better to take a train out to Stellenbosch and hitch from there. The same applies to taking black taxis.

Stellenbosch and Surrounding Area

Stellenbosch is the heart of the Winelands. Its fine Cape Dutch buildings and oak-lined streets nestle in a natural bowl beneath jagged, forested mountains, which form part of the vast Hottentots' Holland Nature Reserve. Stellenbosch is known for its restaurants, museums, and as the beginning of the Stellenbosch Wine Route, the most extensive of the Cape's wine routes. It is impossible to wander the beautiful old town and surrounding countryside without catching a sense of the gracious living cultivated here by the Afrikaans wine growers since the early 18th century.

Despite being a solidly conservative town, Stellenbosch has an Afrikaans university which has traditionally been regarded as the centre of Afrikaner liberalism. Some free-thinkers have certainly been produced, but it must be said that Stellenbosch University also produced almost all the National Party Prime Ministers of the apartheid era, and few Stellenbosch academics were outspoken in their criticism of the government.

History

Stellenbosch's name betrays its history. The word can be translated as 'Stel's Bush', after Simon Van der Stel who was Cape governor through the 1670s and who founded Groot Constantia, the country's first wine estate, in the Cape Peninsula. He visited the Stellenbosch area in 1679 and made a semi-permanent camp where the town now stands. In 1680 the first settlers planted oak trees here and built white lime-washed cottages with thatched roofs, which were later expanded into the grander town houses you see today.

It is hard to imagine quiet, gracious Stellenbosch as the frontier town it was through the 1680s. Beyond the encircling mountains stretched Africa. Hunters, adventurers and a few settlers trickled over the mountain passes, returning to Stellenbosch for the annual fair that Van der Stel inaugurated and attended each year. At that time big game roamed where today there are vineyards, orchards and timber plantations.

Tourist Information

Stellenbosch Publicity Association in De Witt House, 30 Plein St, ✆ (021) 8833584/8839633.

The Town of Stellenbosch

The first thing to do is to visit the **Village Museum** (*open Mon–Sat 9.30–5 and Sundays 2–5*), a collection of four early 18th- to mid 19th-century houses on Rynveld Street, set under spreading oaks in the old town centre. The museum gives a good idea of the gradual rise of this wealthy town. Lovingly restored and furnished in the original style (even the gardens are planted with what would have been grown at the time, according to the little guide booklet), the houses range from the humble Schroederhuis (1709), a small pioneer cottage, supposedly the oldest in town, to the magnificent Grosvenor house (dating from 1800, round the corner on Drostdy Street), with two later, Victorian houses showing the contrast between Cape Dutch and British colonial architecture. Allow at least a couple of hours to get around the four houses, which are all within a block of each other. A map and explanatory booklet are supplied at the museum entrance in the Schroederhuis cottage on Rynveld Street.

Also on Rynveld Street is the **Eban Dondes Gallery** (*open Mon–Fri 9–4, Sat 9–5, Sun 2–5*), which displays work by Maggie Loubscher, a Cape artist whose use of vibrant colours in her landscapes and agricultural scene sets her apart from the usual restrained style of Cape landscape painters.

The Kruithuis (*open weekdays 9.30–1, 11.30–5, closed June and July*), the old Dutch East India Company powder magazine (1777) on Bloem Street, houses a small military museum. After the indigenous KhoiSan tribes were pushed out of the area in favour of the vine, bands of dispossessed Khoi bandits and army deserters haunted the local mountains until the mid 19th-century, and the museum charts both early colonial history and some of the later campaigns against the freebooters (*see* p.37).

Bird Street and **Dorp Street** run through the oldest quarter of the town. Bird Street leads past handsome terraces of old Cape Dutch town houses to **Die Braak**, a green on which there used to be military parades. Around Die Braak are some important old buildings, including the beautiful **Rhenish Mission and Parsonage**, a fine Cape Dutch church and small, thatched manor set amid oaks and a miniature formal garden dating from the 1700s. **The Burgher House** (*open weekdays 8.30–4.30*), also overlooking Die Braak, is a good example of later Cape Dutch style and is now a museum devoted to the history of the Dutch East India Company. Built in 1797, it mixes the simple Dutch gabling with modest classical forms. The English colonial days are represented by the **Anglican Church** (St Mary's). Dating from 1852, this is a young building by Stellenbosch standards. At 176 Dorp Street, in an old house, is the **Dorp Street Gallery** (*open Mon–Fri 10–5, Sat 10–1*), which shows work by local Cape artists. Exhibitions change every month, so it is worth popping in to see what is on display, as work can be bought from here.

On Dorp Street, is the old **Krige Homestead**, the house where Isie Smuts, wife of Prime Minister Jan Smuts, was born. This is a private home, but a few doors down is the fine **Libertas Parva** (*open Mon–Fri 9.30–12.45, 2–5*). Built in 1783, this H-shaped manor house contains the small **Rembrandt Van Rhyn Gallery,** showing works by some of the better-known South African artists, including some excellent paintings by Irma Stern. Another small art gallery belonging to Stellenbosch University occupies the old **Lutheran Mission**, built in 1851. One of the mission homesteads, **La Gratitude,** has the eye of God sculpted on its gable, to ensure that you are paying proper attention to the town's architectural details. Lastly, there is the craft shop, **Oom Samie Se Winkel** (meaning 'Uncle Sammy's Shop'), an old trading store that is now a national monument. Among other things, it sells kitsch pioneer memorabilia and rather good biscuits and fruit preserves. A coffee shop attached to the store serves light lunches. (*Both are open 7 days a week until about 6pm*).

The Oude Libertas Centre (on the R310, just south of town) is an open-air amphitheatre used for plays, concerts, dance and the like. On Sunday afternoons in the summer, this place is full of people picnicing and drinking wine. Ask at the Publicity Association for concert listings.

Slightly out of the town centre, next to the railway station, is the **Bergkelder**, meaning 'Mountain Cellar', a series of cellars hollowed out of the sides of 'Parrot Mountain', one of the massifs that rise above Stellenbosch town (*Tours (including wine tastings) Mon–Sat 9–5*). Wine is stored here in huge vats.

Stellenbosch's accomodation is somewhat limited and most of it is expensive. For cheaper accommodation, you have to go out of town (*see* 'Around Stellenbosch').

expensive

The Lanzerac Hotel, on Jonkershoek Rd, ✆ 887 1132, is a late 18th-century manor, beautifully furnished with Cape Dutch yellowwood, saffronwood and stinkwood period furniture, with the obligatory polished yellowwood ceilings and stinkwood floors. There are 32 en suite rooms and a private suite. The restaurant is one of Stellenbosch's best (*see* 'Eating Out'). **Bonne Esperance**, 17 Van Riebeeck St, ✆ 887 0225/6, is a large Victorian bungalow built in high colonial style, with a wrought-iron verandah, corrugated iron roof and a small tower. The 16 rooms are furnished in period, and are all en suite. The dining room is large and airy, and lit by chandeliers.

D'Ouwe Werf ('the Old Farmyard'), 30 Church St, ✆ 887 1608, dates from 1802. An elegant, simple Georgian house, again furnished with antiques. Its 25 rooms are large, with polished brass bedsteads, armchairs and fireplaces. D'Ouwe Werf's vine-shaded courtyard restaurant is open to non-residents (*see* 'Eating Out'). **110 Dorp Street**, ✆ 883 3555 is a Georgian town house restored to include a sauna, steam-bath and jacuzzi. There are three luxurious suites furnished in Victorian style. The **Fynbos Guest House**, ✆ 883 8670/1/2, is a Victorian house on Neethling St with seven en suite rooms done up in expensive chintz complete with hangings above the beds, a pool and garden.

moderate

The **Dorpshuis**, ✆ 883 9881on the corner of Dorp and Weidenhof streets offers B&B in 12 en suite rooms. The house is Victorian, and the rooms are furnished in mock period style. The **Villa Merwe**, 6 Cynaroides St, ✆ 880 1185, is a mock Cape Dutch house in one of Stellenbosch's small suburbs. It offers B&B in 5 en suite rooms, and has a garden.

---

expensive

Ralph's, on Andriga St off Drostdy St, ✆ 883 3532, serves Cape country cuisine and game, with variations on the traditional menus, all cooked by Ralph, the proprietor and chef. Try the thinly sliced kudu meat as a starter, and the springbok with cranberry sauce or the tender ostrich steak to follow. You can drink their wine or take your own. Ralph's has a relaxed formality; the seating is in padded armchairs so comfortable that one could gladly stay all night (and people often do). It is better to book.

The Lanzerac Hotel is an old Cape Dutch mansion on Jonkershoek Road, ✆ 887 1132, incorporating a small art gallery and one of the most renowned wine cellars in the country. Despite the formality of the interior, with its dark, polished wooden ceiling and floor, starched linen table-cloths and subdued lighting, the atmosphere is less severe than one would expect, and the waiters will happily help you through the vast wine list. Cape seafood fresh from the Peninsula is a speciality.

Die Kelder ('The Cellar') is on Dorp Street, ✆ 883 3797, in an old house (1790). A little snootier than the previous two, Die Kelder serves some very good Cape country cooking (particularly good is the succulent Karoo mutton), complemented by fresh home-made breads. **Doornbosch** (the 'Thorn Bush'), on Old Strand Road, ✆ 886 6163, is more cordon bleu than Cape country, despite the Afrikaans name. It is very popular with Capetonians, and like Ralph's restaurant, is comfortable and relaxed. Try any of the poultry dishes and finish with some of the local fruits.

moderate

Le Pommier on New Helshoogte Rd, ✆ 885 1269, serves traditional Cape country in chintzy surroundings. They do an excellent, spicy *bobotie* and the home-made vegetable soups are good to start with. **Cortina** 886 474, an Italian restaurant on Bird Street, serve home-made pasta in a cosy dining room with a big fireplace. There are also separate rooms if you are a large party.

Die Volkskombuis ('The People's Kitchen', though the word 'Volk' implies Afrikaner farming folk, rather than everyone in general) is on Old Strand Rd, ✆ 887 2121. Yet more Cape country cuisine. Try the *bredies*, slightly sweetened mutton and vegetable stews seasoned with unusual spices such as aniseed and cinnamon. **D'Ouwe Werf** ('the Old Farmyard'), on Church St, ✆ 887 1608, has an outside courtyard shaded by a mature vine trellis, making it an idyllic place to eat in summer. An inside dining room with a log fire serves in winter. Again, there are traditional Cape country dishes, mixed with seafood (always fresh) and some French cuisine.

cheap

Decameron, on Plein St, ✆ 883 3331, serves pasta and pizza with no frills. The sauces are thick and garlicky, and the seafood antipasti as fresh as anything from the Mediterranean. **Oom Samie Se Kaffiekammer** is the eatery attached to Oom Samie Se Winkel on Dorp St, ✆ 887 0797. Unfortunately it only does lunches, but good Cape country ones. Try the Vleis Pasties, spicy meat pies with vegetables. **Mama Roma**, off Merriman Ave, ✆ 886 6064, in the modern and none-too-attractive Pick n' Pay centre, makes up for what it lacks in period atmosphere with good, inexpensive pasta.

Being a university town, Stellenbosch has some lively bars, all of which stay open until about 3am. **Die Akker** ('the Acorn'), on Dorp Street plays good rock music and has a less conservative atmosphere than is normal for Stellenbosch. Those students that pretend to hippiedom drink here, as well as the more general pleasure-seekers. **Die Kelder** on Dorp Street, has a cellar pub decorated in Cape Dutch style, that attracts a more mature crowd. **Legends**, on Dorp Street, has irritating mass-produced posters of old Hollywood stars on the walls, but there is a pleasant bar under the rafters of the upper floor, and you can sit outside.

The Stellenbosch Wine Route

Stellenbosch's countryside has the Cape's oldest wine estates (after Groot Constantia near Cape Town) and some of the province's loveliest mountain walking.

The tourist offices in the Cape tend to overplay the Wine Route, which does not follow a logical 'route' at all, but incorporates a collection of estates lying around Stellenbosch. Unless you have days to spare or have come to the Cape specifically to taste wine, it is a waste of time to try and see all the estates, and unless you take a tour bus from Cape Town (*see* 'Activities'), you will need a vehicle to reach them. Each estate offers free wine tastings, and most let you wander the vineyards and, in some cases, look around the homesteads and their gardens. Watch out though; the tastings often come in full glasses and you can be driving drunk before you know it. An afternoon spent at one or two estates is enough to get a feel for them without trying to take in too much, as despite their beauty, most of the estates are very similar. The list that follows should not be considered a comprehensive guide to the Wine Route, but a pick of the bunch (in the author's opinion). A detailed map of the Wine Route is available from Stellenbosch Publicity Association.

Rustenberg estate is over 300 years old, with a beautiful Cape Dutch manor and one of the most famous Cape wine labels. Although it has only produced wines since the 1880s, the estate is known for its reds, particularly its Cabernet Rustenberg Gold and Cinsault-Merlot, both deep, rich clarets. The Pinot Noir 1988 was described by experts as 'lively and fruity', and the dry, white Chardonnay has been called 'charming'.

Libertas is the area's largest producer, and has a fine homestead set in lawns, just one kilometre out of town on the Cape Town road. The Stellenbosch Farmer's Winery (a co-operative) has its cellar here. The Libertas Pinotage, a wine blended from Pinot Noir and Cinsault grapes, and unique to South Africa, is highly rated by wine critics. **Delheim**, a mountain estate on the Simonsberg (one of the mountains that tower above Stellenbosch) is also a famous label. You can get lunch here, exclaim over the superb views, and try the very good Cabernet Sauvignon, which is considered one of the Cape's best-value quality Bordeaux. The Merlot/Cabernet blend is also considered good, as are the Sauvignon Blanc and Chardonnay. Delheim produces a variety of other grapes, including sweet German whites such as Gewurztraminer, as well as Shiraz and Pinotage reds.

Delaire, at the head of the Helshoogte Pass (on the road to Franschoek) has breathtaking views out over the Berg River Valley and the tall Wemmershoek and Simonsberg mountains. Delaire is known for white wines, especially a full-flavoured Chardonnay blend called Barrique, and a light, dry Rhine Reisling. **Spier**, on the Cape Town road, has two superb Cape Country and continental restaurants, where you can end the day with more wine and some food to absorb it. The Pinotage is considered the estate's best wine. **Avontuur**, a young estate (since 1987), on the Somerset West road, is a thoroughbred stud as well as a winery. The reds are best, Avon Rouge is a good, gentle Cabernet. Their full-bodied Merlot has also had good reviews.

Simonsig is famous, and has been in the Malan family for several generations. A large range of reds and whites are grown. The red (Cabernet and Merlot) vintages from 1984–1991 are generally regarded as excellent, as are the Chardonnays made between 1988 and 1991. The estate also produces popular dessert wines. **Blauwklippen** (meaning 'blue rocks') has one of the area's best Cape Dutch homesteads (1789) and sells preserves as well as serving lunches. Like Simonsig, this estate scored high with its 1980s reds, especially its Cabernet Reserve. Zinfandel, a red wine hardly grown in South Africa, has done well here, and is worth trying for its rarity alone.

Scenic Drives

The Wine Route covers most of the countryside around Stellenbosch, but if you want to just drift a little try the **Devon Valley** (off the R310 to Cape Town), a meander among gentle farmlands. Along the way is the **Protea Heights Nature Reserve** (a few kilometres from Stellenbosch, on the northern slopes of the Papegaaiberg. Alternatively, the road to Franschoek takes you through **Helshoogte Pass**, which has scenery you normally would not see unless hiking through the Hottentots' Holland; fynbos uplands, waterfalls and wildflowers. Many of the local farms have roadside stalls, selling most kinds of fruit very cheaply.

There are several interesting stopping points on these drives. The **Van Rhyn Brandy Cellar**, signposted from the R310 to Cape Town, is South Africa's largest brandy distillery. Concerts are sometimes given in the cellars, and tours of distillery itself are available. The **Jean Craig Pottery** is off the R310, along the Devon Valley Rd). Set amid woods and fields, the pottery also offers tours and sells its wares from a small shop. The crockery is good, but the ornaments rather twee.

Activities

 Walking in the Wine Route: The Vineyard Hiking Trail (24kms over one or two days) is a way to explore the estates on foot. There are no steep hills, just a long, pleasant wander amid orchard and vine. The trail starts at Oude Libertas. Permits are available from the the Publicity Association in Stellenbosch.

Walking in the Hottentots' Holland Mountains: The mountains visible from Stellenbosch are mostly part of the huge Hottentots' Holland Nature reserve, whose closest access point to the town is Jonkershoek State Forest, on the Franschoek road. Marked trails lead through timber plantations and across great sweeps of bare hillside, and begin at the Forest Station, as does the Boland Hiking Trail, a two-day hike which crosses the wild heart of the Hottentots' Holland Mountains, with refuge huts every 20 or so kilometres. The required permits are available from the Forestry Department at Jonkershoek. There is some small game: duiker, grysbok, grey rhebok and baboons are most common, while dassies and birds of prey are also in evidence. At night, genet cats and porcupines snuffle about. There are lynx and leopard, but you are unlikely to see them. Plants and their associated bird life are abundant. The mountains are covered with fynbos, which flowers in spring. Proteas and wildflowers are particularly good in the nearby Assegaibosch Nature Reserve, which also has marked walking trails. To get to Assegaibosch, take the road to Jonkershoek State Forest and follow the signs.

Riding: There is no better way to explore the vineyards and mountains than on horseback. **Vineyard Horse Trails** supply good horses for full-and half-day rides on local estates. They also lead more expensive overnight trails up into the mountains; moonlight rides and evening rides with a bottle of champagne at the end. Call Michele on ✆ (021) 981 2480.

Stellenbosch ✆ (021–)

Where to Stay: Around Stellenbosch

expensive

L'Auberge Rozendal, ✆ 887 6854, is a wine farm a few kilometres south of town, near Jonkershoek, that produces a red Bordeaux. The 19th-century house serves as dining room and lounge, while guests stay in a terrace of Victorian single-storey cottages, each with a wrought-iron verandah. There are large oaks in the garden, and views out over the vineyards to the surrounding mountains. All 16 rooms are en suite.

Nassau Guest Farm, Vlottenburg, ✆ 881 3818 about 5km from Stellenbosch on the R310, has old thatched cottages shaded by big oaks. Each cottage has brass bedsteads and a self-contained kitchen. Alternatively, there is a suite in the old farmhouse. Guests can wander the paddocks and vineyards. The owner also has an impressive collection of vintage cars in the outbuildings, and it is worth asking for a ride.

moderate

Wedge Farm B&B, ✆ 883 2826, in Ida's Valley, is an old farmhouse with a solid teak front door, a rose garden and views over the farming valley and forest. After about 5km from Stellenbosch on the Franschoek road, turn left into Lelie St which leads to the farm. **Oak Cottage**, ✆ 855 1818, has three bedrooms (sleeps five) on, of all things, a protea farm. Also on the Franchoek Rd, ten minutes drive up the Helshoogte Pass from Stellenbosch. Self-catering accommodation only, with mountain walks and a swimming pool.

cheap

Joostenberg Guest Farm, ✆ 884 4425, on the Malmsbury Road north of Stellenbosch (the R304), offers very good B&B in an old cottage, but prices are at the top end of the cheap range. **Gasthuis Die Eike,** ✆ 903 1203, a farm about 20km down the Kuilsrivier road (M12), offers a hearty breakfast with room for R66 per person. The owners will organise riding and hiking in the area. This place is well-known to budget travellers.

Paarl

On the north bank of the Berg River, in the Drakenstein Valley, about 30km northeast of Stellenbosch, is Paarl, the second town of the Winelands. Paarl translates to 'Pearl', after the dome-shaped rock on the mountain summit that dominates the town, on which stands the Taal Monument to the Afrikaans language. The old section (through which runs the R45 road, which becomes Main Street) is similar to Stellenbosch, with many Cape Dutch buildings and, in some places, vineyards reaching right down into Main Street from the slopes of Paarl Mountain. **KWV**, the best-known of South African wine labels abroad, has its headquarters on Main Street, in the grand, pedimented building called La Concorde. Across the river from town are the Klein Drakenstein Mountains, a hiking and mountain-driving paradise. Oaks and jacarandas line Main Street, the long road (7km) along which the old town straggles. At the northern end is a small, shabby industrial area, which contrasts sharply with the serenity of the old town.

History

The Berg River Valley was first charted by an explorer, Abraham Gabbema, in 1657, while hunting for game to bring back to Cape Town. Settlers drifted in during the 1680s, displacing the local Khoi and laying out farms, but Paarl itself is a latecomer by Winelands standards. Founded by the Dutch East India Company in 1720 as a base from which people could cross the mountains into the interior, Paarl became the 18th-century centre of Cape wagon-making. The local craftsmen used indigenous hardwoods to build wagons strong enough to survive the rugged treks through the Cape mountains and into the stony semi-deserts beyond.

The fertile Berg River Valley also provided Paarl with a local farming community to service. Orchards and vineyards were planted, grand homesteads built, and today the area around Paarl has wine estates to rival those of Stellenbosch. Along while the Groot Drakenstein Valley (which follows the Berg River towards Franschoek), peach, pear and apricot orchards. However, despite its gentle surroundings, Paarl was one of the fiercest hotbeds of emergent Afrikaner nationalism during the late 19th-century, and it was from here that the movement to have Afrikaans recognized as an official language enjoyed its first successes.

Paarl and the Afrikaans Language

The Winelands have always been staunchly Afrikaner, under both Dutch colonial and British rule. In 1875 Arnoldus Pannevis, a Dutch schoolteacher working in Paarl, became intrigued by the richness of shared culture and language in the Cape; white Afrikaners, Cape Malays, and Khoi people were all speaking a language evolved in the Cape. Pannevis decided to regularize the Afrikaans language. He and some friends formed the Institute of True Afrikaners, and set down a standard grammar and vocabulary. In 1876, they published an Afrikaans newspaper (*The Afrikaans Patriot*) from the house of Gideon Malherbe, an Institute member. The house is now a museum (*see* below).

From then the movement grew until, in 1925, Afrikaans replaced Dutch as the country's second official language after English, and after 1948 it became the major language of politics and business (though English also remained as the joint official language) and a compulsory part of black education—a highly controversial rule that sparked the famous Soweto schoolchildren's risings of 1976 (*see* **Gauteng,**'Johannesburg', p.495). However, this last aspect has been done away with since the 1994 elections, and there are now 11 official languages in South Africa.

In 1975 the rather ugly Taal Monument to the Afrikaans language was unveiled on the mountain above Paarl. Abstract, lumpy shapes symbolize the African and Malay influence, while more elegant arches give thanks to the European for making it all possible. A fountain represents the language's growth, and a soaring pillar represents hope that Afrikaans will continue to develop.

Tourist Information

Paarl Publicity Association is at 215 Main St, ✆ (02211) 24842.

Paarl: Main Street

Most of the sights worth seeing are along the Main Street, which comprises most of the old town. **La Concorde**, the headquarters of KWV, South Africa's biggest exporter of wine, is worth seeing for the imposing classical front. Inside are offices, but round the corner on Kohler Street are the actual **KWV Cellars**, (*open for tours and tastings Mon–Fri 9.30–5*). KWV also run **Laborie**, ✆ 631 001, an estate at the foot of Paarl mountain, whose vineyards come down to Main Street. Laborie's cellar is open by appointment only, although its restaurant can be visited anytime.

Further down Main Street is **Die Oude Pastorie & Strooidakkerk** ('the Old Parsonage and the Thatched Church'; *open Mon–Fri 9–5, Sat 11–4, Sun 2–4*). The Parsonage, next door to the Tower Church on Main Street, now houses a collection of Cape Dutch furniture, silver and assorted Afrikaner and Huguenot antiques. The building dates from 1786. Built on the site of an earlier church, the Strooidakkerk, further down Main Street, is a later Thibault design dating from 1805 (*see* 'Architecture') and is still used for services. A coffee shop serving light meals is attached to the church, and keeps the same opening hours.

Off Main Street, on Pastorie Avenue, is the **Gideon Malherbe House** (*open weekdays 9–5*). The museum occupies the house where the Institute for True Afrikaners used to meet during the 1870s and '80s. The museum is interesting more for its cultural significance than for the exhibits themselves, an example of which is the printing press on which the first Afrikaans newspaper, *The Afrikaner Patriot*, was produced.

Around Paarl

Paarl Mountain Nature Reserve and the Taal Monument, sit just below the pearl-shaped summit of the mountain that gave the town its name. In fact, the summit comprises three separate dome-shaped peaks. The biggest is Brittania Rock, followed by Gordon Rock and Paarl Rock. The first two names seem oddly British for a town and mountain dedicated to Afrikaans and Afrikanerdom, an unwitting monument to the cultural jumble that makes up South Africa. On the lower slopes stands the Taal Monument, while on the rest of the mountain nature takes over in a huge sweep of fynbos, protea, hardwood copses and aloes. There is plenty of bird life. Look out for sugarbirds and black eagles particularly. There are marked trails and good views. To reach the monument and nature reserve, follow the signs from Main Street past the **Mill Stream Wild Flower Garden**, a wash of colour in springtime.

Bonheur Crocodile Farm, on the Franschoek Road just south of town (follow the signs) is a strange thing to find here in the un-African atmosphere of the Winelands. Still, if you have never seen a croc, crocs there are here, more than a thousand of them waiting to become handbags, shoes and exotic items on restaurant menus (crocodile tail has a wild flavour, a little like chewy crayfish). Belts and bags are sold in the farm shop.

The **Nederberg Wine Estate**, about 10km north of Paarl, off the Wellington Road (R303) is one of the best-known vineyards in the Cape, with one of the best-preserved original homesteads, an H-shaped gabled mansion built in 1792. Nederberg produces around 50 wines, mostly reds. Just about all of them are good, and the reds did especially well in the 1980s. The estate has a wine auction every April, which becomes a Cape society booze-up lasting a couple of days. For some reason, Nederburg does not want to be included in the official Paarl Wine Route, but there is nothing to stop the traveller from including it in his or her itinerary.

The Paarl Wine Route

Like the Stellenbosch route, Paarl's wine route follows no logical sequence, but includes estates in all directions from the town, although it has far fewer than the Stellenbosch route. For a comprehensive map and guide booklet, visit the Paarl Tourist Office. In the meantime, here is a pick of the bunch.

The **Paarl Rock Brandy Cellar** is in town on Dromadis Street. Watch brandy being made from grape to spirit, then try some. **Fairview**, south of town on the slopes of Paarl mountain, offers tastings of its own, very good, estate-produced goats' cheese, as well as wines. Fairview's reds (Cabernet, Merlot and Pinotage) did well from 1987–91, as did the dry, white Cardonnays from 1991–3. The estate's full range is wider than this, however, and it is worth asking the staff in the tasting cellar for their recommendations. **Backsberg** estate, on the Stellenbosch road, has won a lot of prizes for both reds and whites. Its Bordeaux blend, Klein Babylonstoren, has been reviewed as 'delicious'. Backsberg has a small wine museum as well as a cellar.

Rhebokskloof ('Reedbuck Gorge'), just north of Paarl Mountain, offers a guided tour in a Land-Cruiser. The range of wines is small, and most of the estate's success has come from its Cabernets. Rhebokskloof has a Cape country restaurant. South of town, **De Leuwen Jagcht** ('The Lion Hunt') has a very handsome Cape Dutch homestead, but the wines have not been particularly celebrated. **Villiera**, on the other hand (on the R101 parallel with the N1 highway towards Cape Town) produces popular white wines, dry and sweet, and has a terraced restaurant serving lunch under great, spreading trees. The Sauvignon Blanc and Rhine Reisling are recommended by wine guides, and the Merlots from the late 1980s and early '90s were described as 'exceptional'.

Paarl ✆ (02211–)   ***Where to Stay and Eating Out***

expensive

Mountain Shadows, ✆ 623 192, is a luxurious guest-farm out of town, set in beautiful surroundings. Basie Maartens, the owner, has done much to gear Paarl up for tourism and is a good source of information about the country in general. Hunting in the local mountains can be arranged.

Roggeland, ✆ 627 501, is an old homestead, also at the expensive end of things, in the Dal Josaphat Valley. The kitchen has a good reputation. You could also try **Bosman's**, another restaurant set in a handsome old homestead, ✆ 632 727, an expensive restaurant that has won several awards for both its gourmet fare and its wine. With less of a Cape menu than a continental one, Bosman's is worth visiting in summer, when you can dine on its outside terrace.

moderate

More moderately-priced accommodation is to be found at **Goedemond**, ✆ 611020/26613, a family-run B&B on Cecilia St in the town centre. **Troubadour**, ✆ 633 556, a French restaurant with a good reputation, is in town on Church Street. Book in advance as it is generally full. **Rhebokskloof Estate**, ✆ 638 606, has a good country restaurant. Take the road about 4km to the village of Agter Paarl. The gates are on the north side of the road.

This is the loveliest part of the Winelands. As you travel the 20km up the Drakenstein Valley to Franschoek, following the swift Berg river, the mountains crowd closer and the cultivated lands become narrower. Orchard and vineyard give way to pasture, and pine forest, from which rocky outcrops jut like turrets. The village of Franschoek sits at the head of the valley, before the road climbs up into the Hottentots' Holland proper and disappears into the mist, over the Franschoek Pass. **Franschoek** itself (the name means 'French Corner') was settled in 1688 by Huguenot rather than Dutch settlers. The site was, in fact, given to the Huguenot refugees as a land grant. Perhaps as a result, Franschoek, though very small, is one of the loveliest villages in the country, a few streets of white-washed buildings, thatched and slated roofs, while the wine estates around the town are perhaps the most graceful in the region.

Despite its small size, the Main Street of Franschoek has plenty for the tourist. Of particular note are **La Patisserie Bakery** (which sells good Boer breads as well as light pastries), the **Pippin Farm Stall**, selling fruit, preserves, honey, dried fruit, cakes and other wholesome goodies, and the **Oude Stallen**, a little period enclave of shops and eateries around a vine-shaded court near the **Huguenot Monument and Museum** (*open Mon–Fri 9–5, Sat 9–1, 2–5, Sun 2–5*) on Lambrecht Street, the road leading up to the Franschoek Pass. A history of the Huguenots in early colonial South Africa is housed in a very grand Cape Dutch homestead, called Saasveld, which was translocated from Cape Town in the 1960s.

The Franschoek Wine Route

A detailed map and guide booklet are available from the Publicity Office at **La Provence Estate**, on the R45 just west of town, or at the **Vignerons Office** on Main Street; here is a selection of the estates on view, ✆ (02212) 3287. **Boschendal** estate is in the Drakenstein Valley between Paarl and Franschoek, set under the flatiron wall of the Groot Drakenstein mountain. The estate is owned by the huge corporation Anglo-American as, indeed, is most of the valley (and sizeable sections of the whole country). These orchards and vineyards were originally aquired by Cecil Rhodes in the 1890s, and bought by the huge corporation after his death. Boschendal is one of the most prestigious wine estates in South Africa. Boschendal dates from 1685, though the present manor is 18th-century, and is open to the public. Estate tours run Mon–Sat, with tastings in the Taphuis—try the Chardonnay. There are also two restaurants open for lunch.

L'Ormarins homestead was built in 1811, although the original estate dates from 1694, and produces a wide selection of wines. Any red from 1984–89, or Chardonnay from 1988–91 is likely to be very good. The Sauvignon Blanc, aged in oak, has been praised for its light, lemony quality. **Bellingham** is another estate high on the prestige list. Founded in 1693, it produced South Africa's first Shiraz, rosé and Premier Grand Cru wines. Recently, however, none of Bellingham's wines seem to have caught the critics' attention, but this does not stop the wines selling. The nearby **La Motte** estate dates from 1709, the manor and cellar from 1752. Hidden in the Wemmershoek mountains on the north side of the Berg river, La Motte has attracted a lot of praise lately. The reds from 1986–91 were described as 'intensely flavoured'.

La Couronne is a stud breeding showjumpers and dressage horses as well as a wine estate; a look around the stables and paddocks is fun. The wines have received no particular attention recently, but it is a beautiful estate to visit. Nearby is **La Bri**, which dates from 1694. A classic H-shaped homestead, it was granted by Cape Governor Simon Van der Stel to one Jaques De Villiers, a Huguenot who founded one of the longest-running family dynasties in South Africa. The current owners (no longer De Villiers) have won various awards for their white wines wine and are involved in developing a vineyard in Britain, that country's largest one, in fact; 100 hectares in Surrey. La Bri's tasting room is a small art gallery showing work by local landscape artists.

Haute Provence sells a wine called Larmes des Anges ('Angel's Tears'), based on a legend wherein angels descended on a French village, tasted the wine, and wept for joy because it was so good.

Activities

 Walking in the mountains: The Franschoek, Wemmershoek and Groot Drakenstein mountains (all part of the Hottentots' Holland chain) loom above Franschoek village and valley. One can disappear into them on foot for hours or days. Most of the trails require permits and map, both available from the Huguenot Museum.

The **Franschoek Pass Trail** starts at the head of the Pass, in the **Mont Rochelle Nature Reserve**, about three kilometres above the village. You are supposed to buy a permit first from the office at the Huguenot Museum, but there is nobody up there to check. The trail winds up through high kloofs, crossing clear, drinkable streams, to reach a small pass with a spectacular view over to the Wemmershoek mountains, whose almost sheer cliffs form a deep valley around the blue Wemmershoek dam. Look out for dassies, baboons, black eagles and klipspringer antelope. You do need to buy a permit for **Wemmershoek Dam**, as there is a man to check at the gate. The dam fills a valley that used to be farmed by a family called Wemmer. It is worth walking the trail around the shore, listening to mountain silence broken only by the occasional barking of baboons on the cliffs. Take a picnic. There are wonderful wild flowers in spring.

The Boland Trail, part of the same two-day trail that begins at Jonkershoek State Forest near Stellenbosch and crosses the Hottentots' Holland to Somerset West, runs through the mountains near Franschoek. Get a map and permit from the Huguenot Museum. There are overnight huts on the trail.

Riding: Verdun Stables, ✆ Rayanne Schafer on (02212) 2635, takes trails out into the mountains and down the valley. **Robertsvlei Stables**, ✆ (02212) 2160, on the Lambrecht Road to the right (away from the Pass) also takes trails.

expensive

Auberge Du Quartier Français, ✆ 2151, on Huguenot St, at the corner of Wilhelmina and Berg Sts, is worth the money. Simple, elegant and not chintzy as many South African country hotels can be, it was voted best country hotel in the Cape in 1992. It has 14 double en suite rooms with fireplaces and period furniture. There is also a courtyard, garden and a pool.

Le Ballon Rouge, ✆ 2651, is another restored Victorian villa, but more intimate than the Auberge. Bed and hearty breakfast. On Dirkie Uys Street (one up from and parallel to Huguenot Street). Just out of town, on the road up to Franschoek Pass, is **La Petite Ferme**, ✆ 3016, a delightful place to stay, if only for the views back down the valley.

moderate

La Cotte Inn, ✆ 2081, on Huguenot Road just before Louis Botha Street, is convivial, with a pub that locals frequent, and offers good B&B in pleasant, simple rooms. **La Merci**, ✆ 41656, offers B&B in en suite rooms on the lovely Bellingham Wine estate. Down the R45 (over the Berg River bridge) towards Paarl. **Vermers Cottage**, ✆ 2354, has bed and breakfast in a tiny cottage on the La Terra de Lucqe Farm (R45 just west of town). **La Provence**, ✆ 2542/2315, offers another opportunity for B&B on one of the old wine estates. This one is in the Jonkerhuis cottage (meaning the house for the eldest son) dating from the 1700s. On the R45 just west of town.

self-catering (moderate/cheap)

The area around Franschoek has a lot of self-catering accomodation in farm cottages that works out to a moderate to cheap price for two or more. Farms are always offering self-contained cottages on a formal or informal basis. **Paradise Cottage**, ✆ 2160, is on Robertsvlei Farm, a right turn on Lemabrecht Street away from the Pass. The farm has marked walking trails and horses for hire, and you can even fish for bass in the dam. **Chamonix Wine Estate**, ✆ 3531, has two 5-bedroomed guest houses. You need several people to bring the cost down, but the estate is lovely, being higher up the valley than most of the others. Above town (follow La Cotte Street uphill from Huguenot Street).

La Verdure, ✆ 3239, a farm cottage overlooking a dam with trout fishing, sleeps four. **Dassenburg**, ✆ 2107, is another farm cottage with mountain and river walks. **La Bri Holiday Farm**, ✆ 3133, has budget dormitory accommodation in pleasant surroundings. Follow Lambrecht Road to the right, away from the Pass.

For such a small place, Franschoek and the Drakenstein Valley have a surprising wealth of choice, albeit mostly of French cusine.

expensive

L'Auberge Du Quartier Français, ✆ 2151, has made a big noise in South African travel and gourmet magazines. And the place is lovely; an old Victorian hotel with tin roof, white walls and wrought-iron pillars on the verandah. It has two restaurants: the **Le Quartier**, very French and voted one of the best in South Africa, and the more informal **Café Français**, where you can have lunch outside and drop jaws over the towering mountains. On Huguenot Road on the corner of Berg Street.

Le Ballon Rouge, ✆ 2651, is in Franschoek, so it must be French. The chef grows his own vegetables and herbs. On Dirkie Uys St, the block before Berg Street.

Chez Michel, ✆ 2671, is the oldest restaurant in the village. Its informal, bistro-type atmosphere, is more fun than the rather self-consciously good French restaurants nearby. **La Maison De Chamonix**, ✆ 2393/2498, is on Main Road, opposite the corner of Uitkyk Street. In case you are missing French cuisine, this place does yet more cordon bleu. But to be fair, this restaurant does some superb Cape country cooking too. For lunch, you can picnic in the garden with one of their buffets. Wonderful views over vineyards.

Boschendal Restaurant, ✆ 42137, in an old homestead on the Boschendal Estate 15km towards Paarl, is formal and rather grand. Very tasty, very large helpings of Cape Huguenot cuisine, which is much the same as Cape country; spicy variations on European dishes. Only open for lunch. As with Le Quartier Français, Boschendal has a more relaxed, cheaper outdoor lunch place, annoyingly called **Le Pique-Nique**, where you can sit outside by ponds and pines.

moderate

Gideon's Pancake House, ✆ 2227, is very reasonably priced, and serves imaginatively-filled pancakes in an informal atmosphere. On Huguenot Road between De La Rey and Bordeaux Streets.

La Vie, ✆ 2101. *Mon Dieu*—French again! A more Mediterranean version this time, in atmosphere as well as menu. Tables outside or in. On Main Road just after La Cotte Street. Closed Mondays. **Dominics**, ✆ 2255, on the corner of Huguenot and Kruger Sreetts, is better for lunch than dinner as the helpings are not enormous. Some good spicy food, though. **La Cotte Inn**, ✆ 2081, is also on Huguenot Street, before Louis Botha Street. The Inn's restaurant, **Lanternhof**, is connected to the bar where many of the locals drink. Consequently, this is a good place to meet people. Hearty fare and reasonable prices.

Polyfyntjies, ✆ 3217, (meaning 'souvenirs' in Afrikaans) is on a farm just west of town on the R45 (the farm's name is **La Terra De Luc**). Eat in a restored farm-house: log fires in winter, garden tables in summer. (*Closed Mondays*). **The Swiss Farm Excelsior Restuarant**, ✆ 2071, is 3.5km out on Lambrecht Road to the right (away from the Pass). There appears to be no particular logic behind the name. Better for lunch or afternoon tea as the views are truly magnificent. Watch the cloud blankets roll over the mountains in between mouthfuls. **La Petite Ferme**, ✆ 3016, is another out-of-town inn. High up the road to the Pass, the views are even more magnificent than at the Swiss Farm Excelsior. Again, go for lunch or tea, unless you are staying there, as it would be a shame to miss the views. The smoked trout is a speciality. Beware: the drive back to town has sharp bends that challenge wine-addled brains.

Somerset West

Tourist Information

Somerset West Publicity Bureau, Victoria Street, Somerset West, ✆ (024) 514 022

Last of the 'oldest towns of the Winelands', Somerset West sits on the southern slopes of the Hottentots' Holland just inland from False Bay and Strand, about 25km from Stellenbosch and Franschoek. Cape Town is only 45km away along the N2 highway.

Somerset West is where the name of the region, 'Hottentots' Holland', was born. The first Dutch adventurers visiting the area found a prosperous tribe of Hottentots (Khoi) flourishing amid well-watered pastures; several mountain rivers meet at this point on their way to the nearby sea. During 'negotiations' with the Dutchmen, the Khoi compared their love of their land with the Dutchmen's love for Holland. However, despite the Khoi's attachment to the region, the beloved land was traded piecemeal with settlers for cattle, beads and iron. The colonists then called the area the 'Hottentots' Holland', reflecting their nostalgia for Europe (remember that in 1657 the Cape Colony had only been going five years and was not flourishing).

Somerset West remained a loose-knit farming community until the British decided to make it a magistracy and named it after Lord Charles Somerset, the then Governor, in 1820. Through the 19th and 20th centuries, Somerset West existed quietly, prospering as a wine town. However, over the last 20 years, the improved road to Cape Town has caused the town to grow into something of a commuter suburb, and the handsome old centre is now surrounded by development.

The countryside towards the mountains is as lovely as anything in the Winelands, and the old town centre has some fine buildings, in particular an **Old Dutch Reformed Church** on Victoria Street, whose Parsonage operates as a small restaurant and coffee shop, and serves light meals. Follow Victoria Street down to the Lord Charles Hotel, turn right at the traffic light, drive for about 2km and take the signpost for **Vergelegen Winery** (*open 7 days 9.30-4*), a superb H-shaped Cape Dutch manor house and wine estate whose homestead sits under two huge camphor trees. Visitors can wander the house, which has a very good library, and a collection of Cape Dutch furniture; the old slave quarters behind are also open. Vergelegen has a small restaurant that serves lunch outside under the trees.

Helderberg Nature Reserve climbs the mountain behind the town and looks out over the sea. The reserve is approximately 400ha, with walks through the fynbos, and is particularly good for proteas and birds. You may spot grey rhebok and duiker, and there is also a small forest of yellowwood, hard pear, stinkwood and various other hardwood trees.

False Bay

Somerset West is only about 8km inland from the sea and the large commuter beach-town of **Strand** lies just to the south. Better to visit is **Gordon's Bay**, on the R44, where the road turns away from the N2 (which climbs up into the Hottentots' Holland via the spectacular **Sir Lowry's Pass**). Gordons Bay is a fishing village and weekend resort (rapidly becoming more resort than village) with good beaches running at the foot of the mountains.

Somerset West (✆ 024–)   ***Where to Stay***

expensive

Ou Pastorie, ✆ 852 2120, 41 Lourens Street, ✆ 51370, has 8 large en suite rooms furnished in mock-Victorian style, with a communal sitting room and fireplace. A few kilometres from town is **Willowbrook**, ✆ 514 152, a Victorian country house with bedrooms that look out onto a parkland garden, through which a fast-flowing river tumbles down from the surrounding mountains. There are 12 en suite rooms and one suite, a beautiful sitting room with french windows looking onto the garden and a conservatory. Turn up Lourensford Rd from Main Rd and then up Morgenster Ave.

At the moderate end of the expensive range is **Straightway Head Guest House**, ✆ 517088/9, along the Parel Vallei Road from Somerset West. This thatched country house has 18 en suite rooms. Tea can be served under the great trees in the garden and there is a choice between B&B or full board.

moderate

Arksey Guest House, ✆ 517 853200, 200 Main Road, Somerset West, offers B&B (with dinner by request) at the upper end of the moderate scale. Accommodation is in an Edwardian bungalow with 12 en suite bedrooms, a small pub attached, a large garden, a log fire in the sitting room and a pleasant, family-run atmosphere. **Keerweder Farm**, ✆ (02231) 90053 (up the R44 towards Stellenbosch), offers B&B in an old farmhouse at the foot of the mountains. Some good hill walks and a pool. **Dove's Den Garden Cottage**, ✆ 552623, offers B&B or self-catering accommodation in a small one-bedroomed cottage (with fireplace, large garden and pool) on a farm.

expensive

Die Oude Pastorie at 41 Lourens Street, © 513710, is a small restaurant serving Cape Country cuisine in a Victorian one-story bungalow with a verandah and tin roof. Fires in winter. **The Lord Charles Hotel** on Victoria Street, © 512970, has a good restaurant (fresh seafood!) on the terrace overlooking the garden.

moderate

Chez Michel, © 516069, is not to be confused with the restaurant of the same name in Franschoek. This one is very pleasant and relaxed (more fresh seafood) on Victoria Street.

The Northwest Winelands

Follow the road north from Paarl (R44) towards Wellington, and the land flattens out to the left, into the vast wheat and vine-growing plain of the Swartland. To the right masses the western edge of the Great Escarpment, of which all the Cape mountains form a part. Far behind the mountains, which retreat, chain after chain, to the north and east, lies the great, dry Cape interior. Along their fringe, as the R44 travels north, cling the last valleys of the Boland.

Wellington

Wellington is a prosperous farming and wine town lying below the Slanghoekberg and Limietberg (meaning 'snake's corner mountains' and 'farthest mountains'). The first 17th century settlers called this area the Limiet Valley ('farthest valley'), as it was about as far as 'civilization' reached. The valley gradually established itself as a fruit-growing region through the 18th and 19th centuries, and even enjoyed a brief boom as a wagon-building town when the Kimberly diamond rush began in the 1870s. Before that, however, Wellington (so named by Cape Governor Sir George Napier in 1840, after the Duke of Wellington) had produced its own 'great man'. Piet Retief, who moved from Wellington to the Eastern Cape in the 1820s, became one of the great heroes of Afrikaner history; the man who emerged as one of the main leaders of the Great Trek of the 1830s (*see* **Zululand,** 'History'). Retief was eventually killed in Natal by the Zulu king Dingane, while negotiating land grants for the trekboers. Dingane's act of deliberate treachery in killing Retief and his party helped to stave off white encroachment into Zululand for another generation, and ensured Retief his status as an Afrikaner martyr.

Wellington was garrisoned during the Anglo–Boer War, after Boer Commandos (mobile fighting units) began campaigning in the Cape. The British (under Lord Kitchener) built 8000 blockhouse forts across the country to help intercept the Commandos. One is just north of Wellington and is open to visitors.

Apart from **Twistniet**, an old homestead on Main Street (the farmhouse of the farm called 'Champagne', on which the original town was laid out), there is little in the town to interest the traveller. Not as beautiful as the southern Winelands towns, Wellington is generally used by tourists as a petrol and food stop on the way to Tulbagh and the Ceres Valley. But north of town, signposted off the R44, stands the **Boer War Blockhouse** (*open weekdays 9–4.30*), now a national monument.

A handsome Cape Dutch wine estate called **Onverwacht**, ✆ (02211) 34315 sits on Addy Road in the outskirts of town, offering tastings and tours Mon–Fri from 9–5. The estate's manor house is a particularly fine example of 18th-century Cape Dutch.

Wellington also has a famous ghost story, at Brakwater, a family farm not far from the town. Around 1880, the owner died, leaving a widow and a daughter. The widow's brother took over, but made life hard for the women, especially for the daughter, who was courting a young man from Wellington. One night, the suitor rode to the farm and met the ghost of the old farmer, who bade him tell the brother-in-law to treat the women better, or he would burn the man alive. He then told the gaping young man to wrap a blanket round his fist. The youth did as he was instructed. The ghost grasped the covered fist, his phantom hands scorching the blanket, and then disappeared. The terrified young man told the brother-in-law what had happened, showing him the blanket and repeating the ghost's words. This was evidence enough for the brother-in-law, who promptly vacated the property. Convenient for the young man and the daughter, perhaps.

Where to Stay

Fisantekuil Guest Farm, ✆ (02211) 64 1184, a fruit and wine farm that offers mountain walks and fishing in the dam (bring your own tackle) and secluded cottages, just off the Paarl/Wellington road, about 5km south of town. Prices are at the cheap end of the moderate scale but you must bring your own food. Walking trails wind off towards the nearby mountains.

Bain's Kloof and the Limietberg Mountains

Bain's Kloof is a spectacular pass road running east/west through the Limietberg east of Wellington (R303) into the Breede River Valley. Built in the 1840s by Andrew Geddes Bain (son of the famous engineer Thomas Bain, who built most of the Cape pass roads), using convict labour, the pass runs through some of the loveliest Cape mountain scenery accessible by road.

At Tweede Tol **camp site** in the Hawequas State Forest, halfway along Bain's Kloof, is the start of a two-day hiking trail over the mountains (with overnight hut) to Du Toit's Kloof. Permits and maps are sold at Tweede Tol. For the less ambitious there is a three-hour circular walk along a watercourse, with good birdlife, small antelope, dassies and fynbos vegetation.

Following the R44 about 40 km north along the escarpment of the Elandskloofberg, the road climbs up into the tortuous Nuwekloof Pass, then drops down into a bright green, narrow valley between tall mountains (the Witsenberg, Winterhoekberg and Saronsberg), where sits the town of Tulbagh, a backwater that has remained almost unchanged in outward appearance since the 18th century.

History

Early in the 18th century a few settlers pulled their wagons over the Nuwekloof Pass and discovered this valley, where the Klein-Berg River (main tributary of the Berg River) has its source. The Khoi and San people both used the valley as a hunting ground. The familiar pattern repeated itself; the indiginous people were hunted out, vineyards planted, homesteads built, and a town sprang up.

Tulbagh has always been a tranquil spot, though it produced the militant Afrikaner Boer War hero, Danie Theron, who led a team of English-speaking scouts in and out of the British lines when the British invaded the Orange Free State in 1900. Theron's end came later that year while single-handedly holding off a British attack on the hill where his small force was camping. Theron sniped at the British with lethal acccuracy while his own men evacuated safely. The British finally stormed the hill, showering it with rifle-fire, but were perplexed to find only one body when they reached the top. It was Theron. His men had escaped without harm.

Tulbagh drifted through the 20th century without much incident until 1969, when a freak earthquake killed nine people and destroyed much of the old town. As the 32 buildings on Church Street constituted the largest concentration of old buildings in South Africa, a massive restoration programme got under way, and today you would never know there had been any damage.

Tourist Information

Tulbagh Publicity Office: the Old Church, Church Street, ✆ (0236) 301 348

The Town

Tulbagh has two main thoroughfares: the R46 is lined with shops and fairly modern buildings (i.e. up to 1950); behind and parallel to the R46 runs **Church Street**, which has barely changed since the 18th century. Two of the houses here are museums, **The Pioneer Museum** (*open Mon–Fri 9–4.30, Sat 10–4, Sun 11–4*), dedicated to early Cape life (including a detailed display of herbs and their medicinal uses), while the **Tulbagh Museum**, (*opening times as for Pioneer Museum*) at 4 Church Street, gives a brief history of colonial Tulbagh, and a photographic record of the restoration that followed the earthquake.

At the eastern end of Church Street is the **Old Church Museum** (*opening times as for Pioneer Museum*). Built in 1743, it is a splendid thatched affair with a gallery, now housing a collection of particularly fine Cape Dutch furniture and period curiosities, including six original paintings by Thomas Bain, the famous pass-builder. Also on Church Street is **The Victorian House** (*opening times as for Pioneer Museum*), home to more antiques.

Tulbagh has a very good vineyard, the **Paddagang Estate**, the gates to which are off Church Street, about a block west of the Old Church. Paddagang has a Cape Country restaurant and produces what the author and his travelling companions thought was one of the best red wines of the Cape. The Paddagang labels are distinctive, always depicting a frog.

About 3km from town, along the Winterhoek road, is the **Old Drostdy,** ✆ (0236) 301 086 (*open Mon–Sat 10–1, 2–4, Sun 2.30–5*), a beautiful building designed in 1804 by the famous Cape Dutch architect Louis Thibault. Sherry from the Tulbagh wineries can be tasted here, and the building houses a collection of Cape Dutch furniture. Also on the premises is Tulbagh's old jail. Visitors can sit in the cells. Next door (about 1km further north) is the **Tulbagh Wine Cellar,** ✆ (0236) 301001 which also offers tastings and tours (*open Mon–Sat, 9–5*).

The Mountains Around Tulbagh

The ranges circling this valley are very wild. To the north, the **Groot Winterhoekberg** sweep off to a great area of jagged wilderness, accessible to fit hikers via the **Groot Winterhoek Forest Station** (take the R44 north of town to Porterville, then take the dirt road east over the Daskup Pass). Choose between three long trails of three to four days each, with abandoned farmhouses to sleep in along the way. Maps and permits from the Forest Station. Particularly rewarding is the hike into Die Hel, a deep, wild gorge and waterfall that drops into a large, cold pool surrounded by cliffs. Black eagles, klipspingers, sunbirds and dassies will be your companions, and you may be watched from afar by leopard and lynx.

Tulbagh (✆ 0236–)   **_Where to Stay_**

moderate

Schalkenbosch, ✆ 300 654, lies under the Witsenberg mountains, 8km north of Tulbagh. The road ends at the farm, which offers self-catering accommodation in luxurious cottages dating from 1792. Spend a night in this peaceful valley if you can.

Tulbagh (✆ 0236–)   **_Eating Out_**

Paddaagang Estate, ✆ 300 242 just off Church Street, offers moderately priced lunches in its Cape Dutch dining room. The **Kirzenlicht Resturant,** ✆ 300 071 in the Tulbagh Hotel is cheaper and offers a continental menu for breakfast, lunch and dinner.

Michell's Pass

To reach tbe Bokkeveld from Tulbagh, drive over the 2031m **Michell's Pass**, which saw its first wagon in 1760. Andrew Geddes Bain built the existing road, naming it after Charles Michell, Surveyor-General of the Cape in 1846. For thirty years, until the building of the Hex River Pass near Worcester (where the N1 highway now goes), Michell's Pass carried most of the country's northward traffic. The transport riders, who took the inland cargoes north by ox-wagon, are commemorated in a museum in Ceres. The **Old Toll House**, where they paid before descending into the town, is now a national monument, craft shop and tea room.

Ceres

Tourist Information

Publicity Association, The Public Library, Voortrekker Street, ✆ (0233) 61287

Ceres lies east of Tulbagh over the Hex River mountains, flush against the Witsenberg mountains, and facing the vast Bokkeveld Valley. The tree-lined Dwars River snakes through town. The town lies in a warm bowl; blindlingly hot in summer, and warm in winter, even when the surrounding mountains are covered in snow.

Ceres is synonymous with fruit and fruit juice; the LiquiFruit and Ceres fruit juices sold all over the country are produced here. A late-comer by Cape standards, it was founded in 1854 to process the fruits of the Bokkeveld Valley, and was named after Ceres, the Roman goddess of fruit.

The town is not beautiful, having been much 'improved' during the 1950s and '60s. However, the **New Belmont Hotel** is a relic of the Victorian age, and has a 7ha **Bird Park** (home to over 200 species) in the grounds. Huge walk-in cages afford the opportunity of being splatted on from above by brilliant-feathered exotics. The hotel grounds run along the Dwars River and make good strolling after a long time in the car. Sundry other animals, such as goats and donkeys, provide distraction.

The **Transport Riders Museum** (*open Mon–Fri 9.30–11, 1–5, Sat 9–12*) celebrates the era of ox-wagons straining over the Cape passes to the Kimberly diamond mines and Rand gold fields. Some very good old photographs show just how tough this was.

The Mountain Fynbos Reserve lies just between town and the Witsenberg Mountains (the entrance is at the end of town, just as the road curves uphill to Michell's Pass). The reserve is full of flowers in spring; there are a number of walking trails and an indigenous nature garden. Take water in summer and avoid walking at midday.

Ceres Valley: the Warm Bokkeveld

The Warm Bokkeveld is the farming area of the valley around Ceres. Some of the Warm Bokkeveld fruit farms can be visited via the **Fruit Route** (map and guide booklet from Ceres Publicity Association). There are only so many fruit farms and processing plants that one can look at. The biggest, **CFG** (Ceres Fruit Growers), has its packing sheds just outside town, where Ceres, LiquiFruit and Fruitree juices are parcelled up. If the thought of industrial-scale fruit-juice packing doesn't appeal, try the **Du Toit Fruit Farm**, further down the R46. You can tour around the military-order farm and watch boxes of fruit travel about on water canals to avoid bruising.

Klondyke Cherry Farm (*open Mon–Sat 9–5*), is more fun. This pick-your-own farm is along the Lakenvlei road, over the low Swaarmond Pass and 18km beyond. Watch out for baboons on the road. Pay R2.50 entry, pick as many cherries as you can, then pay R7 per kilo for them on the way out. They get annoyed if you climb the trees for the good cherries, so wander as deep into the orchard as possible. Be wary of snakes in summer.

The Uplands Above Ceres: The Cold Bokkeveld

The Cold Bokkeveld is a beautiful mountain area alongside the Skurweberg mountains, on the R303 towards Citrusdal. Before climbing, the R303 passes through the unremarkable village of Prince Alfred Hamlet. However, the **Prince Alfred Hotel** is owned by Jos Kahn, chairman of the local Publicity Association, so stopping in for a drink or coffee often yields good local information. After Prince Alfred Hamlet the road rises steeply over the Gydo Pass, with fabulous views back over the Ceres Basin.

Along the road beyond the pass is the farm **Houdenbeck**, scene of a slave revolt in 1825. The owner and some house guests were killed. Next door is **Morester-Houdenbeck**, a farm where you can pick onions or potatoes or just walk around and breathe the clean, cold air. The neighbouring farm, **Sandrivier**, has an old homestead that offers accommodation (*see* 'Where to Stay'), and which has trails for day-hikes in the silent mountains around.

The Ceres Karoo

East of the Cold Bokkeveld mountains is an empty upland plateau, where begins the south-western section of the Great Karoo. This area is semi-desert, quite rich in game, and makes a sharp contrast to the relatively lush scenery of the Winelands. Follow the R303 north until a dirt road turns off east, marked with a brown sign that says **Kagga Kama**. This is one of two private game reserves (the other one is **Sadawa**) in the vast emptiness of the Ceres Karroo. Both reserves offer accommodation (*see* 'Where To Stay').

Kagga Kama has a bizarre tourist attraction; a resettled Bushman (San) family lives on it, although the Ceres Karoo's last original San inhabitants were hunted out in the 1820s.

Apparently the owner of the vast reserve (37,000ha) made a deal a few years ago with some Bushmen who were struggling to survive in the Kalahari: they can hunt and live for free in Kagga Kama, provided they put on dances for the tourists and look picturesque. The brochure for Kagga Kama is full of photographs of young San girls with bare breasts. Still, however one feels about the morals of Kagga Kama, it is certainly an interesting phenomenon.

Ceres ✆ (0233–)

Ceres Town and Valley

expensive

The **New Belmont Hotel**, ✆ 21150, is a 40-room Victorian joint on Porters St. Luxurious inside, the hotel also has a riverside park, with large walk-in cages housing exotic birds.

moderate

The **Herberg Guest House**, ✆ 22325, on Voortrekker St provides bed and breakfast in 20 rooms (some en suite) and seven self-catering chalets. Lunch and dinner are optional. **The Mill and Oaks**, ✆ (0236) 310 860, also offers moderate prices. A country inn on the R43 at the foot of Michell's Pass, it is comfortable and friendly with a pub-restaurant frequented by locals. Finally, there is **Prinshof Farm**, ✆ 22298, a 19th-century farmstead 9km from town on the R46. Accommodation by arrangement only.

cheap

Pine Forest Holiday Resort, ✆ 21170, squeezed between Ceres and the Skurweberg mountains (at the north end of town), has chalets, caravan and camping sites, a pool and close access to the Mountain Fynbos Reserve. There is no booking-in after 10pm.

Cold Bokkeveld & Ceres Karoo

expensive

Kagga Kama Private Game Reserve, ✆ (02211) 638 355, has luxurious thatched huts with fireplaces. The reserve has a wide variety of game, many hiking trails, rock formations, Bushman paintings and real Bushmen, specially imported from the Kalahari. Take the R303 north and then the signposted dirt road east for about an hour. **Sadawa**, ✆ 22483/22512, is another private game reserve in the Ceres Karoo, 65km north of town on the Sutherland road (follow R46 east from town to Hottentotskloof, then north-east on the R356 dirt road). Most plains antelope live in the hills of this vast private reserve (160,000ha). Day and night trails offer good birdwatching, including eagles, owls, bustards and waterfowl. There are also Bushman paintings.

cheap

Houdenbeck Guest Farm ✆ 70748/70636 offers moderately priced B&B in its old farmhouse. Hopefully you won't be troubled by the ghosts of the guests slain there in 1825 when the farm's slaves rebelled. Full board is offered at slightly higher prices. Farm walks, and pick-your own vegetables are also offered.

Sandrivier Guest Farm, ✆ 70757/70748, in the Cold Bokkeveld uplands, on the R303 towards Citrusdal, is very good value. Choose between bed only, bed and breakfast or full board. Hiking trails and bass fishing are offered, and there is snow in winter.

The Breede River Valley

North of the Hottentots' Holland, dividing the lush southwest Cape from the Karoo, runs the broad valley of the Breede. The valley runs west to east, its main centres being Worcester, Montagu, Robertson and McGregor, all handsome towns with much surviving Cape Dutch architecture. Vineyards, orchards and pastures cling to the river. Roadside farm stalls sell fresh fruit, preserves and other goodies. A wild mountain hinterland rises behind, much of which is accessible to the rambler or hiker through various nature reserves (listed below) rich in small game, birdlife and fynbos.

Passage into the valley from the south is limited to two mountain passes, **Du Toit's Kloof** (through which runs the N1 highway) in the Klein Drakenstein mountains north of Paarl, or Bain's Kloof in the Limietberg east of Wellington. Both are spectacular drives, and provide jumping-off points for hiking trails through the surrounding mountains. From Worcester east to Montagu, the Breede River Valley is traversed by the R60. East of Montagu the R60 leaves the valley and enters the Little Karoo, while the Breede River itself swings south-east through a gap in the Langeberg mountains to Swellendam and the Overberg region. Most people enter the valley from Paarl, heading to Worcester via Du Toit's Kloof. Driving up into the pass from Paarl, a sign informs you of two routes; one is a tunnel which cuts 11km off the trip, misses all the scenery and costs R7. Only take this tunnel if driving at night, when the scenery is invisible and the bends dangerous, or you'll miss a superb drive.

Two ghosts are supposed to haunt Du Toit's Kloof. One is a large black car that sometimes appears at night, driving on the wrong side of the road, straight at the oncoming traffic. Several people have reported encounters with this phantom car, shutting their eyes in expectation of the impact, and then finding that the phantom car has disappeared. Apparently the police even chased it once, while looking for a car that matched its description, only to be treated to the same experience. The second ghost is more lethal; a girl hitch-hiker said to cause fatal accidents to those who pick her up. While looking out for her, be careful not to run over baboons, which are very real and sometimes sit in the middle of the road, playing chicken with the traffic.

A hiking trail runs from Du Toit's Kloof to Bain's Kloof, with an overnight hut halfway. Hikers can start from either end, but most people start from Bain's Kloof, as the trail-head is better marked from there (*see* p.159).

(*see* p.159)

Worcester

After Du Toit's Kloof the N1 leads to Worcester, the largest town in the valley, with a wine route to equal that of Stellenbosch. The town centre, built around a huge, bare square, is not so attractive (more 1950s and '60s 'improvements') but a stroll into the residential streets reveals some very handsome early 19th-century houses.

Tourist Information

Publicity Office, 75 Church Street, Worcester, ✆ (0231) 71408

Worcester was founded in 1818, and named after the Marquis of Worcester, elder brother of the then Cape Governor, Lord Charles Somerset. Its function has hardly changed over the years; half wine and agricultural town, half stopping and servicing point for those on the road north.

Worcester has four museums, all of which share the same opening times; daily from 8.30 to 4.30. The largest, and best, is the **Kleinplasie Open Air Museum**, (*open Mon–Sat 9–4.30; Sun 10.30–4.30*), on the main road (R60) at the east end of town, is a museum of of old farm life, occupying the site of two of the smallholdings sold as part of the original town layout. The museum has replicas of farm buildings, a small restaurant and a cellar of local wines and various traditional activities, including Witblitz making (White Lightning distillation), tobacco rolling and corn threshing using horses. The activities change from week to week.

The **Stofberghuis**, (*open Mon–Sat 9–4.30; Sun 10.30–4.30*), built in 1920, houses a history of Worcester. The **Hugo Naudenhuis**, (*open Mon–Sat 9–4.30; Sun 10.30–4.30*) on Russell Street, was the home of Hugo Naude, a landscape painter active in the late 19th century. This rather grand house, built by him in 1900, is now a gallery of his paintings, and those of his contemporaries, and includes a sculpture garden. The **Beckhuis** on Baring Street (*open Mon–Fri 9–1, 2–5; Sat 8.30–4.30; Sun 2–5*), was built in 1841 and is named after Cornelius Beck, who owned a lot of property in the town during the first half of the 19th century. The museum is furnished as a Victorian town house.

The **Karoo Botanical Gardens** make lovely walking. Take the N1 north and follow the signs for about 3kms. The garden is large—154ha; and full of flowers through winter and spring. (*Open daily, sunrise to sunset.*)

The **Pioneer School** in Church Street is a craft shop selling carving, leatherwork and jewellery made by the blind.

The Worcester Wine Route

The Worcester Wine Route consists of 26 wineries dotted along the Breede River Valley. A map and guide booklet can be had from the Publicity Office or from the display wine cellar at the Kleinplasie museum on the east end of town.

The Worcester estates are not as historically interesting as those of the Hottentots' Holland, but there is plenty here for wine buffs. The cellars are mainly co-operatives producing white, dessert and fortified wines—on account of the Breede River Valley's more arid soil and drier climate—though a few reds are produced. Most prestigious is the **Nuy Estate**, which hugs the foothills of the Hex River mountains, a few kilometres east of town. Nuy has won awards for dessert wines, fortified muscadels and for a well-regarded Cape Colombard, a sharp table white that should be drunk soon after bottling.

Botha Wine Estate, ✆ (0234) 740 is 20km from Worcester on the Ceres Road. An elegant Cape Dutch homestead, it offers tastings, but tours by appointment only. Also handsome are **Groot Eiland**, ✆ (0231) 91140 16km from Worcester towards Rawsonville, which offers regular tours and tastings through the week of dry and semi-sweet white wines, a few reds and sweet hanepoort juice, and **Slanghoek,** 30km from town which also produces dry and semi-sweet whites.

Other Worcester estates worth visiting include **De Doorns** and **Louwshoek**. While they are estates of great scenic beauty, they lack the graceful manors and homesteads of the others estates and are pretty well limited to fortified wines and the odd white table wine. For a greater range, you have to travel further east along the Breede River Valley to the town of Roberston (*see* below).

The Hex River Mountains and Valley

Before heading east down the rest of the Breede River Valley, it is worth making a trip north as far as the Hex River Pass, which is the main road and rail route north. The pass is as spectacular as one would expect, but, as is usual with mountains, it is better to get out and walk. Hikers can explore the Hex River mountains most easily by taking the **Jan Du Toit's Kloof Trail** (not to be confused with Du Toit's Kloof in the Klein Drakenstein mountains). The trail starts at **Kluitjieskraal** (pronounced 'Klykieskraal') **Forest Station**, ✆ (0232) 2327, near the small town of Wolsely (west of Worcester on the R43). Maps and permits sold at the forest station. The Hex River Mountains are skiied in winter (one of three regular ski points in South Africa). The ski-club hut is on the Hex River Pass. Trips can be arranged through the Worcester Publicity Office.

Robertson

The next town east of Worcester along the Breede Valley is Robertson. Though not a particularly attractive town, Robertson's surrounding countryside is lovely. The vineyards specialize in fortified wines from muscadel grapes, producing sherry, brandy and jeropico. There are 15 wineries around the town, including the country's largest brandy distillery.

There is also a lot of throroughbred breeding in the area, 14 studs in all, and it's worth taking a detour or two on some of the country roads off the main R60 to enjoy the scenery, particularly along the road to McGregor.

The Robertson Museum on Paul Kruger Street (*open Mon–Fri 9–4.30*) houses the obligatory collection of local Victoriana. The **KWV Brandy Distillery** is huge (130 stills) and lets visitors taste the goods. Attached is the Branewynsdraai pub and a Cape country restaurant.

The Local Wineries

One can visit most of the surrounding farms and estates by arrangement through the **Publicity Association** in the Municipal Buildings on Main Street, ✆ (02351) 3112. Meanwhile, here are few pointers: **Bon Courage** is a superb 18th-century Cape Dutch estate producing well-received dessert wines and a good Chardonnay. **De Wetskloof** had success with Chardonnays from 1987–91, as well as producing dessert wines. The **Graham Beck Winery** makes very dry white wines, while **Van Loveren** specializes in South African rarities such as the Spanish Fernao Pires and the Hungarian Harlesvlu, both whites. **Welvrede** is a new estate, trying its first few Chardonnays and fortified wines, and **Zandvliet** is one of the only wineries producing reds in the Breede River Valley. Its Shiraz is reckoned to be one of the best in the country.

McGregor

To reach McGregor, detour 26km south from the R60 through the Vrolijkheid Nature Reserve to where the little town lies at the foot of the Riversonderend Mountains.

McGregor has been described as the best-preserved 19th century townscape in Cape Province, and many travellers recommend the town as the place to stay while exploring the Breede River Valley. It is an almost completely intact late Georgian village of white-washed cottages clustered round a mill stream, and is certainly the prettiest town in the valley. What was once a backwater for farmers and wine growers is increasingly becoming a holiday-home village, because of the pretty white buildings, shading oaks and surrounding mountains. There is an old mill to stay in, from which you can explore the great stretch of wild mountain rising to the south, and there are almost no 20th century buildings in sight.

The **McGregor Winery** is about 300m north of town on the main road. **Greengables Restaurant and Coffee Shop**, on Voortrekker Street, and the **Pottery**, on Breede Street, are all within a few blocks of each other.

Vrolijkheid Nature Reserve, north of town, is the trail-head of a two-day hike into the southern mountains called the **Boesmanskloof Trail** which winds south over the Riviersonderend Mountains to the small town of Greyton. Vrolijkheid (pronounced 'frolick height') is known for bird-watching. Phone © (02351) 4437 to book.

Montagu

Montagu is the last town of the Breede River Valley winelands before the river turns south east into the Overberg region. The approach is dramatic: a spur of the Langeberg mountains juts abruptly across the valley, causing the road to twist suddenly through the Kogmanskloof canyon, whose walls of folded strata rear 1500m towards the sky. The town is surrounded by the large Montagu Mountain Nature Reserve, of which the encircling mountains form a part. About 3km west of town the R60 passes under a natural rock arch overlooking a large bend in the Breede River: atop the arch is the ruin of an old fort built by the British during the Boer War.

Montagu is a singularly pleasant place, peaceful, with many surviving late Cape Dutch buildings. There are two hot-springs north of town; one is sadly over-developed, the other quiet, and only used by local farmers. The usual juxtaposition of orchard, vineyard, pasture and wild mountain provides the backdrop.

Long Street has a wealth of Cape Dutch houses, barns and cottages, some 14 of which are national monuments. The **Montagu Museum** (*open weekdays 9–4.30*), also on Long Street, concentrates more on the Little Karoo region than on the Breede River Valley (Montagu is roughly the border point between the two). The museum occupies several buildings, one of which is Joubert House, the oldest house in town. The Montagu Museum collects and supplies (by mail or for sale on the premises) fresh herbs, both African and European, and provides information on their nutritional and medicinal uses.

The Something Special Coffee Shop on Bad Street (meaning 'bath street', the road to the hot springs) does fabulous cheesecake and sells local crafts.

Around Montagu

Montagu Hot Springs Spa is 4km north of town, in a deep valley between the Langeberg and the excellently named Waboomsberg (meaning 'Wagon-Tree' mountains, rather than mountains that go WA-BOOM!). Although the back of the spa looks onto a canyon where black eagles, dassies and klipspringers live, the place itself is a monument to 1970s bad taste, complete with concrete mini-golf course, large hotel and all.

Fortunately, there is another hot spring about 4km further north, on a farm called **Baden** (on the right off the R318, about 2km down a dirt road; look out for springbok on the hillside by the road). This spring flows into a small man-made pool. Visitors can only bathe on Sundays, presumably to stop the place from being overrun.

Montagu Mountain Nature Reserve, 2km west of town, is very lovely. There is a hiking hut in a ravine (where live hundreds of dassies), giving access to two long day-walks (one 12km, one 15km) that lead up into the wild kloofs of the Langeberg. The 15km trail is tough but beautiful, climbing almost 1500m, through high valleys that resemble miniature gardens. Several waterfalls are encountered on its home-ward stretch. There is also a 7km hike along a river to the Hot Springs Spa. The river is full of fish, some of whose species are unique to the area. Hikers should see klipspringers, baboons, sunbirds, sugarbirds, black eagles, many dassies and several types of protea. To book the trail, call ✆ (0234) 42471.

North of Montagu

Follow the R318 north past the hot springs and the road leads first to a fertile valley on the north side of the Langeberg called **Die Koo**, where most of South Africa's fruit and vegetables for canning are grown. From there, the road winds through the wild Nouga Hills into the Hex River Valley and the Karoo; an interesting drive if you are heading north to the N1 highway.

Activities

Hiking in the Mountains: The Breede River Valley and its surrounding mountains have excellent hiking trails, details of which are included with the town entries in this section.

Canoeing: The Breede River itself is made accessible through **Breede River Adventures**, based in Cape Town, at 104 Upper Maynard Street, in Vredehoek, in the Gardens neighbourhood ✆ (021) 461 4537. Trips run from two to seven days.

Where to Stay

Worcester

Good, moderately priced accommodation can be found at the **Kerkstraat Herberg Country Lodge**, 27 Church Street, ✆ (0231) 25194. The lodge occupies some old workers' cottages, and is rather luxurious for the price range. The owners let you prepare your own breakfast basket. Along the R60 for about 10 km from Worcester, then turn north on a dirt road about 2km to Nuy. **Oude Schuur Country Cottage**, ✆(0231) 21275 is in the Nuy Valley, down the R60 for about 10km from Worcester, then turn north on a dirt road about 2km to Nuy. Also moderately priced, Oude Schuur is a self-contained old thatched cottage that takes up to six people. Bass fishing and good walking are available at the farm, and you can check out the farm dairy where they make feta cheese. **Nooitgedacht Farm**, ✆ (0231) 21284, (8km down the R60) offers B&B, farm walks, fireplaces and breakfast in bed.

Robertson

Excellent moderate/cheap accommodation is offered by the **Pat Busch Private Nature Reserve** in the Langeberg about 10km north of town, ✆ (02351) 2033. Visitors stay in self-catering chalets with hiking along streams and through fynbos where live small buck and birds.

McGregor

McGregor has the best expensive accomodation in the Breede River Valley. **The Old Mill Lodge**, ✆ (02353) 841, offers pampering in an old mill, with waterwheel and all. Victorian furnishings and large, comfortable beds with the sound of the mill stream tumbling by at night make this a tranquil place to stay. Also expensive is **The McGregor Haus**, ✆ (02353) 925, an old Victorian town house with a restaurant, pub and seven double rooms. At the south end of Mill St, on the corner of Voortrekker and Hoff Streets. **McGregor Country Cottages**, ✆ (02353) 816, offer moderately priced en suite accommodation in a group of self-contained old thatched worker's cottages.

Eating Out

Worcester

moderate

Kleinplasie Farm Museum Restaurant, ✆ (0231)2225/6, is a country restaurant specialising in Cape dishes and Breede River wines. At lunchtime there are old-time farm displays, such as corn threshing with horses on a round stone floor. Also good is **Fairburn's**, ✆ (0231) 24479, on Fairburn Street, which offers good value, filling but unimaginative food. The **Barlinka,** ✆ (0231) 72641 on Stockenstroom Street is slightly more expensive, and has a continental menu.

Robertson

expensive/moderate/cheap

The **Braenewynsdraai Winehouse**, on Kromhout Street ✆ (02351) 3202 serves classic Cape Dutch dishes and a wide range of local wines. You could also try the **Oude Fontein** restaurant, on Reitz Street ✆ (02351) 61417, which offers a slightly cheaper, more standard continental menu, or the **Loer-in Koffiekroeg** ✆ (02351) 2346, on Church Street is a coffee-shop serving light lunches, teas and cakes. In the neighbouring village of Ashton is the **Normandy**, ✆ (0234) 51590, serving very good French dishes at the top end of the moderate scale.

McGregor

expensive

The McGregor Haus, ✆ (02353) 925, in an old Victorian building on the corner of Voortrekker and Hoff Sts, has a good Cape restaurant specializing in Karoo mutton, home-made breads and local fruits.

The Old Mill House Lodge, ✆ (02353) 841, at the end of Mill Sreet on the south end of town, is a good country restaurant in an hotel serving Cape dishes, such as denningvleis (diced, braised mutton sharpened with vinegar and tamarinds) and sosaties (grilled, marinaded meat on a skewer). **Greengables Restuaurant** on Voortrekker St, ✆ (02353) 626, does delicious lunches, such as vleis pasties or trout.

In the nearby hamlet of Bonnievale is a good, traditional Cape country restaurant called **Die Rietdak**, ✆ (02346) 3236.

Montagu

moderate

The Something Special Coffee Shop (on Bad St) does things special for lunch (especially cheesecake).

The Overberg

> *'South Africa is so far off that I cannot hope to be able to excite English readers to visit the Cape colony for the sake of the scenery— though...I cannot imagine that any trip should be more pleasant and serviceable..'*

Travels in South Africa Volume I, Anthony Trollope

South and east of the Hottentots' Holland lies the Overberg, a coastal land of sheep pasture and wheat fields bounded by high, wild mountains. To the west, the high Riviersonderendberg fall to a narrrow coastal plain whose old resort towns give way to wilder and emptier beaches as you travel east. The Overberg coastline is famous for whales and from June to November mothers and calves can be seen rolling in the swell just a few hundred metres offshore. Inland, the farmlands stretch away north to the handsome 18th-century town of Swellendam, behind which the sheer walls of the Langeberg mark the beginning of the great interior.

The Overberg has some fabulous nature reserves, the best being the **Harold Porter Botanical Reserve** and **Kogelberg Nature Reserve**, which protect a large chunk of coastal mountain behind Betty's Bay, **De Hoop Nature Reserve**, a sweep of wild coastline in the east, **Marloth Nature Reserve** and **Boosmansbos Wilderness Area** in the towering Langeberg to the north, and **Bontebok National Park** near Swellendam, founded in the 1960s to protect the then almost extinct bontebok antelope. Lapped by the warm Aghulas current, the Overberg's coast is popular among Capetonians, who escape to the crowded, elegant 19th-century resort town of **Hermanus**, or to the emptier beaches at **Gansbaai**, **Arniston** and **Port Beaufort**. Africa's southernmost point, **Cape Aghulas** (unfortunately a rather ugly resort town), lies on the Overberg coast, 20km below the town of Bredasdorp.

History

The Overberg was one of the first 'interior' regions to be affected by white expansion outside the original Cape colony. At the end of the 17th century, by following the elephant herds that trekked seasonally from the coast to the interior, ivory hunters and explorers had discovered the mountain passes leading from the Cape to the Overberg, whose temperate climate and rich grazing attracted settlers seeking to live outside the control of the Dutch East India Company. By the 1720s, trekboers (nomadic farmers who had adopted the Khoi's patoral lifestyle) were pouring in with their vast sheep herds, much to the dismay of the indigenous Khoi and San people. By the 1740s, there were so many settlers in the region that the San had gone, and almost all of the Khoi were reduced to working on farms that had once been their land. In 1743 the Dutch East India Company decided to regularize the Overberg (i.e. make it taxable), created a town and *landdrost* (magistracy) at Swellendam, and the region became part of the Cape colony.

As Swellendam's administration became more effective through the 18th century, many of the Overberg's more independent-minded settlers trekked east to the present-day Garden Route and Eastern Cape. In fact, the area became something of a corrridor for the Cape's more lawless types to pass through on their way to the wild interior. In the Overberg's mountain ranges, deserters from the Dutch East India Company garrisons, dispossessed Khoi and runaway slaves formed bandit gangs, raiding farms and travellers as the opportunity arose. By the late 18th century, their depredations were forcing many farmers to abandon their properties, and the Dutch Governor-General tried to induce trekboers to settle permanently by offering 200 rix-dollars to any burgher who converted 50ha into freehold property.

In the decades following the Cape Colony's extension to the Fish River in the Eastern Cape (1780), the Overberg began to settle into its present farming landscape. The local garrisons swelled, and the mountain freebooters and bandits drifted to the new lawlessness of the eastern Frontier. Although Xhosa warriors from the Eastern Cape raided into the Overberg a couple of times during the early 19th century Frontier Wars, the region bowed out of South Africa's political theatre and became a prosperous agricultural hinterland for Cape Town. Swellendam evolved into a wealthy regional capital whose burghers serviced both the local farming population, and the steady stream of settlers, traders and hunters journeying to and from the Eastern Cape and, after 1840, Natal.

By 1850, the Overberg's Khoi had virtually ceased to exist as an identifiable group, following the inevitable sexual exploitation of their women by farmers and townsfolk alike. As with Cape Town and the Winelands, the Overberg's indigenous people had therefore been absorbed into both the white economy (as labourers and servants) and population, yet were still referred to as 'Hottentots' or 'coloureds' and treated as an under-class. A few managed to trek north to the (as yet) barely settled reaches of the vast Karoo to merge with the free Griqua (mixed Khoi-Boer) groups living around the Orange River but most lacked the means to do so and stayed on the farms.

Today, little has changed. The Overberg has remained a quiet, predominantly Afrikaans-speaking rural backwater, remote from the turbulent events of South Africa's late 19th- and

20th-century history. Apart from the tourism on the coast, most of the economy still detrives from sheep and grain, and the wild mountain reaches, once the haunt of bandits, are now a hiker's paradise of uninhabited fynbos and forested kloofs. Most travellers still only pass through the Overberg on their way east/west, so its quiet pleasures are known only to the few that take time to explore.

Getting There

By car: There are three ways into the Overberg from Cape Town: over **Sir Lowry's Pass** (on the N2) through the southern end of the Hottentots' Holland Nature Reserve to Grabouw; via the northern Hottentots' Holland from Franschoek in the Winelands via the spectacular **Franschoek Pass** (R45); or along the coast, following the east side of False Bay along the foot of the southernmost Hottentots' Holland Mountains where they jut into the sea at **Cape Hangklip**, around to Betty's Bay (R44). The first and last of these routes are the most beautiful, and if making an excursion into the Overberg from Cape Town, it is worth going in by one route and out by the other.

From the north, the R60 from the Wineland town of Montagu (via the Kogmanskloof Pass), or the R324 from Barrydale in the western Little Karoo (via the Tradouw Pass) provide spectaular drives over the Langeberg. From the east, the N2 from the Garden Route towns of Knysna, George and Mossel Bay runs between the Langeberg and the coast.

By bus: InterCape, Greyhound and Trans-Lux all travel east/west along the N2, and stop at the main towns en-route. From here local transport to nature reserves and/or the coast can usually be arranged by contacting the Publicity Association of the town nearest your destination.

By rail: Trains run from Cape Town to Swellendam via Worcester, taking in the beautiful Hex River Mountains and running along the foot of the Langeberg. From the east, trains from Port Elizabeth to Cape Town take in Swellendam and the other main towns. Again, for local transport, telephone the Publicity Association of the town closest to your final destination.

The Overberg Coast: Betty's Bay to Port Beaufort

The R44 road south from the N2 (just west of Sir Lowry's Pass), between the Hottentots Holland and False Bay, enters the Overberg via Cape Hangklip, a small peak falling into the sea at the southern extremity of the Hottentots' Holland range.

Cape Hangklip was a bandit stronghold (*see* **South African History**) during the late 18th century, but today its **Hangklip Hotel** is a haunt of fishermen, both amateur and professional. It's worth spending an evening in the bar hearing coastal yarns. The clientele can get a little rough, although this tends to be with each other, rather than with strangers.

Betty's Bay, a small settlement of holiday houses strung out along the coast with a single store has a couple of small, safe swimming beaches, but the real attraction is the **Harold Porter Botanical Reserve** set just into the coastal mountains rising behind the bay, and clearly signposted from the R44. The reserve's walking trail follows a deep kloof up a series of waterfalls. In spring the profuse wildflowers are a feast for the eye. Duiker, grysbok, baboon and dassies, as well as the usual invisible leopards live here, and over 60 bird species are recorded. There is no accommodation.

The mountain country behind the Harold Porter Reserve is protected by the 18,000ha **Kogelberg Conservation Area**, ✆ (0225) 4301). The entrance is along the R44 from Betty's Bay, about 2km before the town of Kleinmond. Kogelberg is a typical stretch of wild western Cape mountain fynbos with forest kloofs. Grey rhebok, klipspringer and baboon are common. Leopard are the main predators. Day hiking only is permitted, with one particularly beautiful trail along the course of the Palmiet River. There is no accommodation.

From Betty's Bay the road wanders on beneath the mountains to **Kleinmond**. Another small resort of Capetonian holiday homes, Kleinmond sits on a small lagoon at the mouth of the Palmiet River. There are several camp sites, with safe swimming in the lagoon (though not on the beach, which has a cross-current). **Kleinmond Nature Reserve**, west and north of town, incorporates sea-shore, coastal fynbos and montane fynbos. Five short walking trails cimb into the mountains behind. The entrance is signposted from the R44 west of the village. Kleinmond is a popular fishing spot, but for private anglers. There are no tackle-hire shops until Hermanus.

Between Kleinmond and Hermanus is **Onrus** (meaning 'restless' after the pounding surf). One of the quieter holiday villages, Onrus also has a small lagoon, safe beach and camp site. Another safe beach a few kilometres further east is Sand Bay.

Hermanus and Around

Tourist Information Office: Marine Drive, Hermanus, ✆ (0283) 61040

Hermanus is the largest town on the Overberg coast, named after one Hermanus Pieters, a trekboer who, in the mid-1830s, settled with his flock at a spring near the shore here. His peaceful life as fisherman and grazier became more disturbed each year, as the tiny natural harbour, rich grazing and vast fish-shoals off-shore, attracted more and more settlers. By the end of the 19th century, Hermanus had been discovered by Capetonians. Hotels sprang up around the little town of white lime and thatch cottages. Larger mansions for the wealthy followed. Hermanus has been a resort ever since.

Although the small harbour has been restored as an open-air fishing museum, and despite the town's bustle and life, Hermanus is no longer as attractive as the quieter places further east along the coast that it once resembled. However the mountains and the beaches are worth exploring, and in summer, Hermanus is a good place to spot whales.

The **Old Harbour Museum** on Marine Drive (*open Mon–Fri 9–4, closed 1–2; closed Sun*), displays old fishing boats. There is also an old fisherman's cottage, mostly showing old photographs of the days when the fishing harbour was active. If visiting at the weekend, go to **Lemm's Corner Craft Market**, just off Marine Drive, a good place to pick up crafts, preserves, biscuits and other goodies and open on Saturday mornings.

Walker Bay, just east of town, is where Hermanus' famous beaches begin and is the best vantage point for whale-watching; **Grotto Beach** and **Voelklip Beach** stretch for some miles along the bay. Both have safe swimming and beautiful walking.

A hiking trail runs along **Hermanus Cliffs** west of town, giving spectacular views out over the Indian Ocean. Where Marine Drive meets the foot of the cliffs, is the **Mermaid's Tidal Pool**, in fact a set of clear freshwater pools. Nearby is a monument of four wagon wheels commemorating the first Overberg ox-wagon to creak north over the mountains to join the Great Trek in 1836 (*see* **South African History**). About 3km east of town is **De Mond Lagoon**, a small resort (signposted from the R44) where you can hire canoes, windsurfers, fishing tackle, snorkels etc. There is also good, calm swimming, bird-watching and fishing.

In the mountains just north of Hermanus is **Fernkloof Nature Reserve**. Like most of the southwestern Cape reserves, it comprises a wild stretch of montane fynbos, with indigenous forest lining the kloofs. Hikers may see grey rhebok, duiker, grysbok and klipspringer on the network of walking trails. To reach the reserve, take the 'Mountain Drive' road signposted from the R44 just west of Hermanus.

Under the mountains at the eastern end of Walker Bay are **Die Kelders**, a set of magical undergound pools whose farmer-owner sometimes allows the public in to swim. Ask at the Tourist Information Office in Hermanus to find out if they are open.

Gansbaai

Gansbaai ('Goose Bay'), the next town east of Hermanus, is less of a resort than a fishing village, known by local anglers as one of the best spots for shore fishing. Whale watching from here can also be rewarding, and the village is still fairly unspoilt; with some handsome old lime-and-thatch cottages among the newer buildings. Get down there around 2pm, when the boats are coming in, to buy fresh fish straight from the fishermen (they put in and out from the old harbour at the end of the main road into the village).

On the promontory south of Gansbaai is **Danger Point**, marked by a lighthouse and scene of a famous shipwreck. In 1852, the HMS Birkenhead was carrying about 500 soldiers from Cape Town to the Eastern Cape, to fight in the eighth Frontier War (*see* **Eastern Cape**, 'History'). Also on the ship were about 20 women and children. A storm washed the ship onto the rocks at Danger Point. As it foundered, the crew found that only three of the lifeboats were in working order. Lt. Col. Seton, the officer commanding, called the troops up on deck, drew his sabre and threatened with death any man who crowded the boats where the women and children were gathering. Even as the horses were being put overboard to swim for it, the troops stayed in line, and when the ship went down almost all were drowned or eaten by sharks. The incident was much celebrated in Victorian England as a noble tragedy and tradition has it that the maxim 'women and children first' originated here (though this seems far-fetched, as the soldiers were presumably obeying the maxim when they went to their deaths). There is a memorial to the dead at Danger Point.

Elim

From Gansbaai the coast becomes wilder and less populated. Rough grazing farms come down to the sea. About 8km east of Gansbaai the road forks: one road continues along the coast to **Pearly Beach**, a lonely stretch of pale sand bordered by huge dunes with safe swimming and good walking; the other, a dirt road, heads inland to the old Moravian Mission station of Elim.

Like Wuppertal in the Cedarberg, Elim (built in 1824) is a jewel of early 19th century architecture, left untouched owing to its status as a 'coloured' community—the village was never modernised. The road enters Elim via some common grazing land (watch out for loose horses) to a village that might serve as a film set for a Thomas Hardy novel. The old whitewash and thatch cottages of the village's three streets have suffered no alterations, only loving care or dismal neglect depending on the circumstances of their occupants. Chickens scratch in the street. Kids play. There seem not be any vehicles. At the top of the main street is the large white **Moravian Church** and its **Old Mill**, now restored and a national monument, but seldom open to the public. Very few of the 'public' ever get to Elim. In no way has the place been altered to accommodate tourism.

Around Cape Aghulas

Whether you have followed the coast road, or headed inland to Elim, the next 20km of coastline has no road, and to explore the Overberg coast further you must swing north to the town of Bredasdorp (*see* p.184) and then south again, across the marshy plain of Africa's southern tip to **Cape Aghulas**, the continent's southernmost point. Here, unfortunately, Africa ends unobtrusively, with none of the drama of Cape Point. Worse, man has made it ugly. The holiday resort villages at Struisbaai and Cape Aghulas (the two run into each other) are dull to say the least, with no centre and few permanent residents. There is a lighthouse to look around, but otherwise the only reason to go is to be able to say that you have seen Africa's southernmost point. 'Aghulas' means 'needles' in Portugese, either in warning of the sharp rocks waiting to bite into the bellies of unwary ships, or from the fact that at this point, the needle of a compass points due north—which is the only way out of Aghulas; back to Bredasdorp (20km). However, from here you can make some more rewarding trips.

De Mond Nature Reserve, ✆ (0284) 4217, not to be confused with De Mond resort near Hermanus, is reached from the Bredasdorp/Arniston road (look out for the signpost 11km south of Bredasdorp), this is a hidden stretch of milkwood forest and coastal dunes fronting a wild beach where a small river (safe for swimming) flows into the sea. The birdwatching is superb, especially for pelicans and terns, and there are small buck in the woods. There is no accommodation—a good thing, as this quiet corners would soon be spoiled by too much human presence.

Arniston and Around

Another there-and-back route to the coast, is to **Arniston** (also known as Waenhuiskrans, meaning 'wagon house cliff'). Arniston today offers the tranquility and romance that

Hermanus must have offered many years ago. The old fishermens' cottages still stand; two-roomed, single-storied thatched buildings that are cool in summer and warm in winter. People do holiday here but it seldom gets crowded. There are miles of white sand beach, with some enormous caverns eroded into the low sea-ward cliffs behind. The largest is **Waenhuiskrans Cave**, into part of which flows the sea, but which stays sufficently dry to overnight in, something people have been doing for millennia. Small stone mounds on the beach nearby are the remains of prehistoric fish-traps and shell-middens made by the 'strandlopers' (beach-dwellers) who originally inhabited the caves.

Much newer, from the 19th century to mid-20th, is the **Fishermen's Graveyard** at Arniston. Worth a visit, it has many crudely-cut headstones fashioned by the fisher folk themselves who had no stone-masons to do the job professionally. Most are the graves of 'coloured' fishermen lost at sea, who, because of their traditionally low status, have not been honoured except by their own community. Today, the old fishing village is mostly owned by Capetonians, though a few fishermen still inhabit the farther-flung cottages. Arniston has a camp site, and cottages for rent (*see* 'Where to Stay').

From Arniston, you again have to back-track to Bredasdorp to go further east, but it's worth it, for the road (R319 north, then after 8km take the dirt road east) leads to **De Hoop Nature Reserve** ✆ 02922 700, one of the wildest accessible spots on the Western Cape's south coast.

The reserve, which includes an offshore area, is vast (over 60,000ha) with about 40km of wild beach. Inland is a huge fynbos heathland, a range of hills and a large lake. The reserve supports large mammals, including the rare Cape mountain zebra, eland, bontebok and grey rhebok, as well as smaller antelope and mammals. The Salt River, which flows into the lake, is a good place to spot otters (if you're very quiet and still). Whales are often seen offshore and the reserve harbours 228 recorded bird species. Of the many indigenous fynbos plants, 50 are known to exist only within the reserve. De Hoop has several groups of rondavels and camp sites, so accommodation is not a problem, and it is worth spending a few days here walking the trails or just beach-combing in the wind and silence.

At the far-eastern end of De Hoop Nature Reserve, at **Cape Infanta**, the Breede River flows into the sea. A small resort (again, just a few holiday homes) on the east side of the estuary, Cape Infanta marks the border between the Overberg coast and the Garden Route.

Activities

Walking and Hiking: All of the reserves listed above have good day trails through beach and upland fynbos country. De Hoop Nature Reserve is the only place offering overnight hikes.

Fishing: The Overberg coast is known for its superb sea fishing, both from the shoreline and in the deeps of the warm Aghulas current offshore, where big game fish can be caught. Tackle and boat hire for both kinds of fishing can be arranged through Hermanus Publicity Association (*see* above).

Whale Watching: The Overberg coast is also known for the large numbers of southern right whales that cruise offshore during the summer months. Some swim to within a few hundred metres of the beaches, and can be clearly watched for hours as they roll in the swell. The beaches at Walker Bay, near Hermanus, and De Hoop Nature Reserve are the best sighting spots, though almost any beach or promontory will do.

Where to Stay

expensive

Stanford House ✆ (0283) 300, 20 Victoria Street, in the small village of Stanford (10km east of Hermanus on the R44 around Walker Bay), is a 19th century manor house set just below the mountains. The rooms are done up in colonial style, but without being overblown. The **Marine Hotel** ✆ (0283) 21113, on Marine Drive, Hermanus, is the town's best-known hotel, dating from 1902. Very pricey, but beautifully furnished, it has views out over Walker Bay and serves superb seafood.

moderate

Mountain Drive Guest House ✆ (0283) 24452, 66 Mountain Drive, Hermanus, is a short walk from the old harbour and the bay. Good value B&B (with reductions for kids), Mountain Drive is friendly and informal. **Arniston Seaside Cottages** ✆ (02847) 59772 must be booked at least a day in advance. This will secure an old lime and thatch fisherman's cottage, allowing you to explore the beaches and caverns on the empty coast. Very romantic. Take your own food. **The Arniston Hotel** ✆ (02847) 590 00 is a good bet if you cannot get a cottage. Not as beautiful as the other buildings of Arniston, but a small, friendly place with 23 en suite rooms. **Potbergerhuis Guest House** ✆ (02922) 665 976. This is the author's recommendation. A farmhouse under the Potgeiter Mountain, just outside the eastern edge of De Hoop Nature Reserve, there are ostriches as well as sheep grazing the surrounding fields, horses to ride, endless walking, and the great wild coastline of the nature reserve to explore. Set in the classic high, rolling Overberg landscape, the house is simply but comfortably furnished (sleeps up to 6) and has log fires. You can either bring your own food, arrange B&B, or ask the farmer's wife to cook three meals a day, just as you wish.

cheap

The best value roofed accommodation is at **De Hoop Nature Reserve** ✆ (02922) 782, which has seven sets of rondavels in quiet seclusion. Those by the De Hoopvlei lake have excellent birdwatching. All have comfortable beds and a communal kitchen. These are often booked up in holiday season, but mid-week is usually safe. Phone first. Hermanus has the **Hermanus Youth Hostel**, ✆ (0283) 21772, on Church Street, while **The Diedre Gasthuis**, 38 Du Toit Street, Bredasdorp, is poised inland between Cape Aghulas, Arniston and De Hoop Nature Reserve. It offers simple, straightfoward B&B in a family house.

Should you tire of buying fish direct from the fisherman, almost all the Overberg's coastal restaurants serve seafood. Menus vary little, though the quality is always very high, and what you eat is always fresh from the sea.

expensive

The **Marine Hotel**, Hermanus ✆ (0283) 21112 is well known for seafood of all kinds. The dining room is a little impersonal, but a good place to eat the more exotic big game and deep sea fish as well as the usual seafood repertoire.

moderate

The **Beach House Hotel**, Kleinmond ✆ (02823) 3130 is smart but not too pricey and has a nice Edwardian feel. More seafood. The **Arniston Hotel** ✆ (02847) 59000 serves good fish and is also a good place to meet people, normally Capetonians with cottages in Arniston. Not as beautiful as the older buildings in the village, but relaxed and friendly.

cheap

The **Cape Hangklip Hotel**, Betty's Bay serves more the fish n' chips end of seafood cuisine, but is nonetheless very good, everything being freshly caught. The bar is a regular hang-out for local fishermen. If you get talking, good stories usually follow.

The Overberg: Inland

To enter the Overberg interior from Cape Town, take the spectacular Franschoek Pass (R45) through the northern edge of the Hottentots' Holland Nature Reserve. The winding road drops from the mountains to the Overberg's rolling plain, coming out on the shores of the huge **Theewaterskloof Dam** where the little town of **Villiersdorp** hugs the foot of the wild Riviersonderend Mountains.

Villiersdorp's ugly Main Street hides the pretty houses and gardens behind. Here, a community of artists, exiled from Cape Town, have collaborated to form the **Akkedis Art Route**, a tour covering seven studios around the little town, which you visit to see the artists at work. It makes a pleasant, easy walk after time in a car. The map is available from the **Dagbreek Museum and Restaurant**. The house is late Cape Dutch, decorated in Victorian style. Light meals and coffee are served on the porch, overlooking the garden. The **Overberg Protea Nursey** on Van Riebeeck Street displays just about every wierd sub-species of this extraordinary flower. Some of the open, fleshy forms are almost obscene.

The R43 north of Villiersdorp leads over the Riversonderend range towards Worcester. On the **Elandskloof Pass** is **Bo Radyn**, a farmstead built in 1777. You can look around the farm, or hike from the **Villiersdorp Nature Reserve**. Two circular overnight trails, the **Ratelberg** and **Spitskop**, begin from here. There is also a cultivated wildflower garden and a caravan/camp site. South of Villiersdorp is the orchard town of **Grabouw**. Named by its German founder after a town in his native land, this is the centre of South Africa's apple-growing region. Naturally, Grabouw has an **Apple Museum**, on Main Road, with a display of old implements from local farms. More interesting are the area's mountain passes, and their views. **Sir Lowry's Pass**, on the N2, 20km west of town, looks onto the whole sweep of False Bay, and in the 18th century was a hot-spot for bandit attacks; the viewpoint is still notorious for robberies and you should beware if stopping here. **Houw Hoek Pass**, 20km further east on the N2, winds over fynbos heathland to the **Houw Hoek Inn** which claims to be South Africa's oldest. **Viljoen's Pass**, on the R321 to Franschoek, is quieter and forested at the summit, from where the road takes a deep plunge down to the Palmiet River.

Caledon, a market and spa town about 40km east of Grabouw along the N2, is one of the Overberg's larger towns. Once handsome, the centre has suffered 'improvement' 1950s style, although a few things have survived. **Donkin Square** still has some Georgian houses. The **Holy Trinity Church** on Trinity Street is solidly neo-Gothic, having been designed by Sophia Grey, the energetic wife of Cape Town's Archbishop Grey, who in the 1850s designed and built Anglican churches throughout the colony. The **Caledon Museum** on Krige Street has a collection of Victoriana. The **Old Mill Art Gallery** sells work by local artists, sometimes very good, sometimes not, but worth a look.

Caledon Hot Springs pour into a pool built in the last century. Around it has been built a small, rather smart resort, **De Overberger**, surrounded by forest and mountain and offering tennis and riding, weights and aromatherapy.

For quiet strolling, a wander in the **Caledon Nature Reserve and Wildflower Garden** is hard to beat. A flower show is held here every spring, when the reserve erupts in colour. Either walk in the cultivated garden or wander onto the slopes of the Swartberg mountains and check out the views. About 30km north of Caledon, under the towering Riviersonderend mountains (passing the 4000ft Swartberg peak), are two gems, the villages of Genandendal and Greyton.

Genandendal is a Moravian Mission station dating from the 1830s. Lime and thatch cottages line the narrow street and cluster around the old church. The Cape's surviving Moravian Mission stations (there are others at Elim, Wuppertal, Zoar, Mamre and Stilbaai set up by Protestant missionaries from Moravia, now part of the Czech Republic) are set pieces of 19th-century living, untouched because they are home to 'coloured' families, so no bungalows, or even tarred roads have appeared in these little villages. Genandendal is no exception. All of the Cape's mountain villages must have looked like this 100 years ago.

Greyton, 6km east, is equally pretty, but wealthier and less poignant than Genandendal. Also mostly composed of 19th century white buildings, it is a peaceful farming village. A two-day hiking trail, the **Boesmanskloof Trail**, leads from the **Greyton Nature Reserve** over the Riviersonderend mountains north to McGregor in the Breede River Valley (*see* p.169). The trail winds through uplands where dassies, duiker, baboon, klipspringer and grey rhebok live. Like so many wild areas of the western Cape, the mountains blaze with flowers in the spring. East of Greyton the R406 (a gravel road) follows the Riviersonderend massif for about 30km, before joining the main N2 highway for a last 60km through the sheep and wheat farmlands to **Swellendam**.

Before Swellendam was founded in 1743, the Overberg was a chaotic world of wandering trekboers, Khoi tribes, and freebooting raiding bands composed of deserters from the Company's garrisons, escaped Malay and West African slaves and dispossessed Khoi.

All were gradually drifting east, extending the range of 'settled' land outside the sphere of Company control. The region's few settled farmers were beginning to demand protection. The Company laid out their new town, complete with grand Government buildings, at the foot of the Langeberg, on the banks of the Koornlands River.

The Overberg soon settled down as the lawless element drifted east to the Fish River frontier, and by the early 19th century, Swellendam had become the quiet administrative and agricultural town that it is today. The old town has been lovingly preserved, though today it is a tourist and farming centre, and there is little to suggest its old function as an outpost of European colonial adventure.

Tourist Information

Publicity Association: The Oefeninghuis, Voortrek Street, Swellendam, ✆ (0421) 42770.

The Old Town

The **Drostdy Museum** (*open Mon–Fri 9–5, Sat & Sun 9–4*) is housed in seven old buildings on Swellengrebel Street (map available from the Swellendam Publicity Association). This is a modest piece of classic Cape Dutch civic building, the white walls topped with thatch to take the edge off the grandeur. Built in 1747, it now houses the standard collection of fine Cape Dutch furniture and crafts. Some interesting details are the early paper money minted by the Dutch East India Company during the 18th century and the original watermill, still grinding corn. The flour and bread are sold at a stall in the museum gardens.

The late 19th-century **Dutch Reformed Church** on Voortrek Street, while of less historical importance, dominates the small town's skyline. Far more ornate than is usual for the Calvinist austerity of most of South Africa's Dutch Reformed churches, this one has a bit of everything—Baroque, classical, Gothic. Much simpler in style is the **Oefeninghuis**, which now houses the publicity association. Built in 1838 as a Sunday School (Oefening translates roughly to 'religious exercise') and later used as a school for educating freed slaves, the building also has a semi-permanent exhibition of local art.

Immediately north of town rise the **Langeberg Mountains**, a great dark wall scored deep with tangled forest kloofs of yellowwood and milkwood trees. The stretch of the mountains visible from town are part of the huge **Marloth Nature Reserve** ✆ (0291) 41410. The 5-day **Swellendam Hiking Trail** runs over these heights, with huts at the end of each section. This trail should not be attempted unless you are reasonably fit; summer temperatures can soar on the Langeberg slopes and the gradients can be really punishing. There are several day trails in the reserve though, which, while still steep, are comparatively short. However, it is worth overnighting at one of the Swellendam Trail huts; at night the kloofs are a-dance with fireflies and, in the exhilarating mountain air, you might be tempted to dance with them. Look out for black eagles. There are plenty of pools to swim in and to drink from. The way to the reserve from town is along Andrew White Street, follow the signposts to Swellendam State Forest. The office there will issue permits for whichever walks you wish to do.

There are two scenic drives drive north over the Langeberg into the western end of the Little Karoo. Either follow the R60 for 50km west to Ashton, before driving over the **Kogmanskloof Pass** to Montagu, or head 11km east on the N2 until the juction with the R324. After 14km turn north over the breathtaking **Tradouw Pass** to Barrydale. The English author, Anthony Trollope, crossed this pass in the 1870s while making a tour of South Africa. When the axle on his Cape cart gave way, a young Boer farmer offered to take Trollope's party to the next town. The writer's offer of half-a-crown for the touble raised a smile and the comment…'I might as well take it, but you'd have had the cart all the same without it.' Trollope was continuously impressed by the open-handedness of the Afrikaners. He was also impressed by Tradouw Pass, which he claimed '…beats in sublimity all other South African passes that I saw. I have never seen rocks of a finer colour or twisted about into grander forms…'

On the road to Tradouw Pass is a tiny settlement, **Suurbrak**, originally a mission station founded by the London Mission Society in the mid-19th century. It is still known for its furniture workshops, which produce a kind of chair that is considered unique. Visitors can watch the furniture makers at work, and buy from the workshops at cost price.

Follow the R322 past the turn-off for Tradouw Pass and Barrydale, for about 10km towards Heidelberg, and you reach a signpost for the vast, wild **Boosmansbos Wilderness Area** ✆ (02934) 22412, part of the even larger **Groot Vadersbosch Nature Reserve**, an area of the Langeberg that very few people visit (or even hear of). This is one of the wildest accessible areas in the Western Cape. Larger even than Marloth Reserve, Boosmansbos is a huge expanse of steep montane fynbos, rising to tall peaks. Yellowwood, stinkwood and the rare mountain cypress (one of Southern Africa's few indigenous conifers) thrive in the kloofs, where lives a lot of game, albeit shy. Bushbuck, grey rhebok, duiker, klipspringer and grysbok live on the slopes. Black and martial eagles are common. There are lynx and leopard. It can rain at any time of year here, so it is as well to carry a waterproof whatever the sky looks like. Permits for a two-day hiking trail with overnight huts and various day trails, are available from the Forest Station as you drive in.

South of Swellendam is South Africa's smallest national park, the **Bontebok National Park**, founded in the 1960s to protect this large antelope species, which was then almost extinct. The bontebok are curious-looking animals; a handsome chocolate brown with white bellies and legs and a broad white blaze down the face. They look almost identical to the blesbok, which occurs widely through northern and eastern South Africa. In fact, there is much controversy among zoologists as to whether these two antelope are not, in fact, subspecies of one species, rather than separate cousins. Who knows? They canter in circles and snort and look at you with bovine confidence, exposing their flanks to full view so that it is small wonder that they were shot almost to extinction. However, the park has been very successful, and from the 80-odd individuals left when the Park was founded, there are now thousands scattered through reserves all over the Cape. The park also has grey rhebok (rarely seen anywhere, so grab the chance), zebra, and red haartebeest. Lynx are the only large predators. There is a camp site and self-catering accommodation. Apart from two short walking trails, one of them along the Breede River, visitors are confined to their cars.

Bredasdorp and east of the Breede River

Bredasdorp sits at the head of two there-and-back roads to the coast, one to Cape Aghulas, and one to Arniston. If heading for either coastal spot, it is as well to stop in Bredasdorp for supplies, as they are cheaper here than in the little coastal villages. Founded in 1838, Bredasdorp serves both the coast and the sheep-farming downland hereabouts. A small town, it has a fascinating **Shipwreck Museum** (*open Mon–Thurs, 9–4.45, Fri, 9–3.45, Sat, 9–1, Sun, 11–12.30*). So many ships have foundered on this treacherous coastline that it is hard to keep track of them. Some, like the HMS *Birkenhead* (*see* 'Overberg Coast'), are famous, but most are only known to enthusiasts. The museum charts all the recorded wrecks, a catalogue of human tragedy and vulnerability. Stirring stuff for such a quiet town.

The dirt road east of town leads beyond De Hoop Nature Reserve (*see* 'Overberg Coast'), past the **Potberg Mountain**, to the Breede River, at the point where it becomes estuarine on its way to the ocean. Clinging to the banks is **Malgas**, a collection of smallholdings with an old trading store, unchanged since the 1930s, and a large church. You cross the river here by means of a **pontoon bridge**, hand-operated by two men and the last of its kind still working in South Africa. It is very cheap (R2 when the author went), so tips are appreciated. Follow the dirt road along the western bank of the Breede for 32km towards the coast and you come to **Infanta-on-River**, one of the quietest hidden beaches on the Overberg coast, with great wild camping and beach walking.

The R324 gravel road along the eastern bank of the Breede leads to two more quiet coastal gems; **Port Beaufort** and **Witsand**. Port Beaufort, now a sleepy village, was once a port of some importance: the Breede River is navigable for about 32km upstream from its mouth, and a lot of cargo traffic used the port in the last century. But the only remaining evidence of this is a huge church (the 'Barry Church') where the port's merchants and seamen used to worship. Today Port Beaufort is a tranquil haven much favoured by fishermen. A chat with the locals could secure a fishing trip or water-skiing outing. Witsand is the beach a few kilometres down from Port Beaufort. A bit busier than Port Beaufort (i.e. not very), Witsand has safe beaches. Again, there is camping and good beach walking.

Activities

Walking and Hiking: All of the nature reserves listed above offer good day-hikes. Longer overnight mountain trails are the 5-day **Swellendam Trail** in Marloth Nature Reserve ✆ (0291) 41410, the 2-day **Boosmansbos Trail** in the Boosmansbos Wilderness Area between

Swellendam and Heidelberg ✆ (02962) 1812 and 2-day **Boesmanskloof Trail**
✆ (02353) 621/671 between Greyton and Robertson.

Where to Stay

expensive

Wildenkranz Country House ✆ (02824) 49042, is near Elgin,
in the Grabouw area. Built in 1820, Wildenkranz is an elegant
Cape Dutch building set in pear orchards, with luxurious rooms
furnished in period. The **Houw-Hoek Inn** ✆ (02824) 49646,
Grabouw, is supposedly the oldest licensed inn in South Africa. A charming 2-
storey white building c.1834, it sits on the Houw-Hoek Pass (N2) east of Grabouw.
De Overberger ✆ (0281) 41271, is a small, late-19th-century resort surrounding
Caledon's hot mineral springs. Set in forest, the mountains towering behind, it is a
bit insitutional, though luxuriously so. The **Swellengrebel Hotel**, Swellendam
✆ (0291) 42493, is large, modern, expensive and dull. TVs in every room.

Walkabout, ✆ (021) 262 520, is a bush camp set among milkwood forest on the
banks of the Breede River south of Malgas (continue past Malgas on the
Malgas/Buffeljags dirt road and look out for the signpost on the left). Beautifully
landscaped, the camp has wooden cabins on stilts, or stone-and-thatch cottages and
offers excellent river-rafting in inflatable canoes to ride the local rapids. Forest
hikes, birdwatching and fishing are also offered, as well as excursions to
Swellendam and local nature reserves. Self-catering only.

moderate

Huis De Villiers, 13 Victoria St, Villiersdorp ✆ (0225) 31386 is particularly nice
in winter, with fires, gluwein and a view of the snowy peaks that dominate the
town. There are 5 en suite bedrooms.

The **Post House**, Main Road, Greyton ✆ (02822) 9995 (built 1860) used to be the
village post office. The house is beautiful, with splendid yellowwood ceilings,
although the 14 en suite rooms are a bit chintzy. Locals drink at the attached bar.

cheap

Campsites: Villiersdorp Nature Reserve; Bontebok National Park.
Wild camping: Infanta-on-River

Eating Out

All the establishments listed above have good restaurants in the same
price bracket. Particularly recommended are **Wildenkrantz Country
House** ✆ (02824) 49042, which serves succulent Karoo lamb and
game in season, and the **Houw-Hoek Inn** ✆ (02824) 49646, which
specializes in Cape Country cooking, in particular an excellent spicy bobotie. **Huis
De Villiers**, in Villiersdorp ✆ (0225) 31386 and **The Post House**, Greyton
✆ (02822) 9995 have a more intimate feel, with log fires, small dining rooms and
carefully prepared Cape and French dishes and home-made breads.

There is little that is both good and cheap, with the exception of the **Dagbreek Museum restaurant**, a small Victorian house on the corner of Graaf Street and Union Avenue in Villiersdorp, now a museum. Good food is served on the verandah and there are seldom more than one or two other people, but unfortunately the restaurant is only open for lunch.

The West Coast

Fronting the chill Benguela current, Africa's lonely Atlantic coast stretches north of Cape Town in an almost unbroken beach. The west coast is barren and eerie: the ocean roars incessantly against empty beaches shrouded with mist at morning and evening, and the currents, even close to shore, can be treacherous. Apart from a small area around **Saldanha Bay** and a few fish-processing towns to the north, the coastline itself is largely uninhabited, and accessible via a few villages and nature reserves, the best being the **West Coast National Park**, south of Saldanha, and **Cape Columbine Nature Reserve**, just to the north, which support game species and large populations of seabirds. In spring, the coast-ward scrub is covered with yellow, orange and purple wild flowers. Summers are dry and parched; winters stormy with a brief season of heavy rain. Inland, the country is empty but for scattered farms and hamlets. The few larger towns are generally rather ugly, but are made up for by the romance of the smaller fishing villages of 19th-century thatched cottages, where poor 'coloured' fishermen still live as they have for over a hundred years, netting their living from the harsh Atlantic.

For the first couple of hundred kilometres north of Cape Town, the inland area is a patch-work of coastal fynbos and scrubby farmland. To the

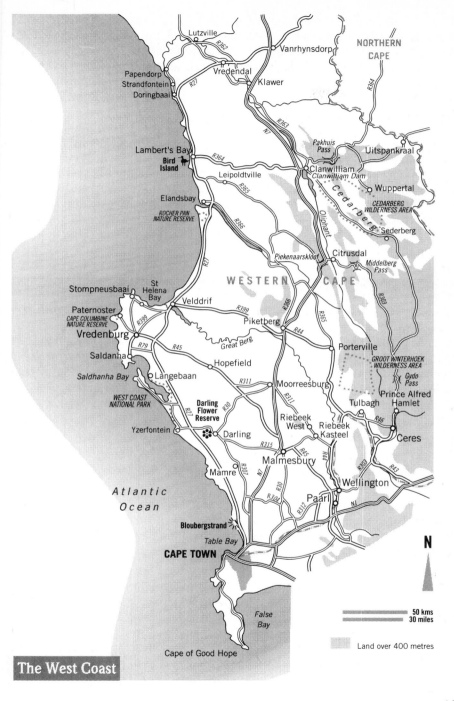

The West Coast

east, the land becomes more fertile, stretching in a vast, wheat-growing plain called the **Swartland** to a wall of high mountains—first the Perdeberg and Kasteelberg, then the wild, jagged **Cedarberg**—the western edge of South Africa's Great Escarpment. Running north–south, parallel with the Cedarberg, is the **Oliphants River Valley**, which winds north through progressively drier wine and orchard country until the river turns to the sea and the Cedarberg merge with the lower Bokkeveld escarpment, some 400km north of Cape Town.

Getting to the West Coast

As always in South Africa, a car is most convenient, although the West Coast can be reached by public transport. **InterCape Mainliners** run a bus service to the main town of Saldanha from the bus station in Cape Town. From there, Black taxis to other towns and villages are generally safe, if recklessly driven. Access to the area's reserves is more difficult, but this can be overcome by hitching. Otherwise ask at the town's Publicity Office if a lift can be arranged with a ranger or a local going that way.

The Coast: Cape Town to the Oliphants River Mouth

The coast road leaves Cape Town via the R27 and the ugly suburbs of Parow, Milnerton and Table View. It is worth stopping at **Blaubergstrand** ('blue mountain beach') by Table View, to admire Table Mountain rising across the bay, the great city spread at its feet. North of Table View, buildings are abruptly replaced by fynbos heath and scrub. Here, unfortunately, the ocean disappears from sight, so put pedal to metal for about 50km, until the R315 crosses the R27. A left turn leads to the coastal village of **Yzerfontein**, while the right leads inland to **Darling**, a quiet, dairy-farming town on the edge of the Swartland (*see* p.202).

Yzerfontein consists of a collection of holiday homes around an old jetty that juts into the sea in picturesque ruin, a caravan park and good surf. And that's about it, except in spring when the wild flowers are out, and the country around the village becomes a bright sea of colour.

Yzerfontein is within spitting distance of the southern-most tip of the **West Coast National Park**, but to gain access to the park you have to drive about 40km north to **Langebaan**, on the eastern shore of the lovely **Saldanha Bay**, a vast expanse of calm water dotted with rocky islands colonized by nesting sea birds (*see* below).

Langebaan is another example of ugly man-made structures rising out of glorious natural beauty, a theme repeated all over South Africa. Perhaps ugly is too strong a word, but it is not an attractive town. Langebaan lies at the mouth of a lagoon (in fact a large inlet of the bay). A resort town of temporary-looking holiday homes frequented mostly by Afrikaans-speaking Capetonians, it has three caravan and camp sites, two bungalow parks and a brand new, expensive self-contained resort called Club Mykonos, apparently modelled on a Greek village. Watersports go on loudly in the lagoon.

West Coast National Park

Follow the signs from Langebaan to the **West Coast National Park** on the south end of town. Near the park entrance is **Langebaan Lodge**, which doubles as park reception and visitors' accommodation. From here, tours set out for the three bird-colony islands in the Bay, which was part of the park and home to Cape gannets, cormorants, jackass penguins and southern black-backed gulls. The park also includes Langebaan Lagoon, and part of Saldanha Bay's west shore, covering 20,000ha in all. An old Cape Dutch thatched homestead, **Geelbeck**, about 5km along the park road from the entrance, is a coffee shop and education centre, and the starting point of several **walking trails**, though these are only open in spring, when the flowers are out, and must be walked with a guide.

As the park road swings up along the west shore of the bay, extensive mud flats come into view. When exposed at low tide, these are covered with wading birds. A superb swimming spot can be reached from the road by a wooden walk-way. Underfoot, the mud changes to sand and the water stays shallow for hundreds of metres out into the bay. About a kilo-metre on from here, the road is blocked by a gate. Passing through, the visitor is in the peninsula end of the national park (actually a separate reserve managed by the national park), where the park's large antelope live.

Eland, zebra, bontebok, black wildebeest and gemsbok, as well as smaller game (the author saw an African wildcat here) thrive on the peninsula. There are also thousands of tortoises and you are likely to see snakes on the road. Eventually you have to turn and come back the way you came, as the park ends abruptly at a fence declaring itself to be the boundary of Defence Force land. Oh, well. There are the grazing antelope to look at, as well as a double sea view to admire (of the open Atlantic to the west and the calmer Saldanha Bay to the east) before heading back out of the national park.

Saldanha

Larger, but no less ugly, than Langebaan, Saldanha is also the gateway to an area of intense natural beauty, the **St Helena Peninsula**. Saldanha, does have an interesting history though. The name Saldanha was originally given by the Portuguese to today's Table Bay to commemorate the visit, in 1503, of Admiral Antonio de Saldanha, who anchored his fleet there on the way round to the Indies. When the Dutch began taking an interest in the Cape during the following century, they transferred the name to present-day Saldanha, even though the admiral of that name had never anchored there.

In the early 17th century, before Holland colonized the Cape, French sailors visited Saldanha Bay regularly, hunting the colonies of seals and sea-birds (both of which have, thankfully, survived to this day). Later, merchant traders began collecting the rich guano from the colonies and shipping it back for sale to farmers in Europe. Such was the demand for this excellent fertiliser that fortunes were made, and the collecting parties sometimes fought each other for possession of the pungent prize; local legend has it that the preserved body of a French victim of a guano skirmish was dug out of the muck on one of the three main bird colonies in the bay during one of the last collecting sprees in the late 19th century. It was shipped back to Europe as a curiosity.

Saldanha Bay was also a pirate refuge during the 18th century, when lawless bands operated from here almost unchallenged: the bay's sea bed is littered with the wrecks of ships that they plundered and sank. Treasure has been recovered from some, one wreck alone yielding about half a million rands' worth of gold. Divers still try their luck under the sheltered bay's calm waters.

Today, the little town has little to suggest such a romantic past. There is a permanent whiff from the fish-processing factory, and a general industrial feel. However, the coast north of Saldanha is heavenly, and dotted with guest farms that offer riding, canoeing and bird-watching (see 'Activities' and 'Where to Stay').

St Helena Bay, Paternoster and Cape Columbine Nature Reserve

Take the R399 north of Saldanha to Vredenburg, a largish farming town, where the road forks: the west fork, a gravel road, leads directly to Paternoster and the Cape Columbine reserve, the R399 continues, bearing east and north, until a westward turn-off onto another gravel road, sign-posted to **St Helena Bay**. This eventually leads back around the coast to Paternoster and Cape Columbine. More interesting than the direct route from Vredenburg, it leads between dusty ploughed fields at the centre of which stand groups of oddly-shaped boulders, heaped together by the area's first farmers. These resemble megaliths, which seem somehow in keeping with the brown emptiness of the coastal fields around them.

Then the road hits the coast. At St Helena Bay, you pass groups of old, white thatched fishermen's cottages and newer, small fish-processing sheds. Out in the bay swim huge shoals of anchovy and pilchard, netted by small trawlers crewed by 'coloured' fishermen. The beaches, unlike those in the sheltered lagoon in the West Coast National Park, are too cold for swimming. The road goes on to **Stompneusbaai**, a slightly larger settlement than any of the hamlets strung along St Helena Bay, and then turns back inland for about 8km before forking west again to the coast at **Paternoster**.

Paternoster is almost untouched, a period piece from the 19th century. 'Coloured' fishermen and their families peer from the open doors of square, lime-washed cottages, living in much the same conditions as their forefathers did. The village is lively—people will be anxious to chat and sell you seafood. However, unless you speak Afrikaans, talking will be problematic and, as for the seafood, never buy crayfish on the street, however tempting the price, as it is strictly illegal and can be a set-up for a spot fine.

However, it is well worth walking around (in the day—at night the locals can be a little rough). It is generally acceptable to take photos, though you should ask first.

On around the coast, the road passes the last manned lighthouse to be built on the South African coast (built in 1936) at Teities Bay, and then enters **Cape Columbine Nature Reserve**. A small ranger's booth spans the road selling entry and camping permits. Inside the reserve, the ocean crashes against wierd volcanic rocks that seem to have been moulded by giants from massive chunks of Plasticine. Seals play offshore. You can hike a 13km trail along the lonely beaches and rock promontories, go fishing or gather shellfish (*see* 'Activities'). The author camped here one memorable night under the moon, and found that the giant limpet shells that litter the beaches, if filled with guava juice and tequila, make a superb natural marguerita.

Farther North: Velddrif, Eland's Bay

The Great Berg River meets the sea at **Velddrif**, a town about 15km east of St Helena Bay. The town is nothing much, though the last few years has seen it develop as a tourist spot for South Africans. The countryside inland, where the river is estuarine, is worth exploring by car, if only for the flocks of flamingoes and pelicans that live on the water.

North of Velddrif the country gets ever drier on the way to Eland's Bay. The ocean retreats again behind a range of low hills and the R27 changes to gravel. At this point, there is a small lagoon to the west of the road, **Rocher Pan Nature Reserve**, clearly signposted from the road. Although it is not possible to camp here, there are some short walking trails around the lagoon, where wading birds and waterfowl congregate in large numbers. There are also small antelope; springbok, duiker and steenbok. Look out for mongooses hunting along the paths.

The road to Eland's Bay passes through a farmyard and runs alongside another freshwater lagoon, or lake, the 25km long **Verlorenvlei**. Watch out for loose livestock. Again, there is often good bird life to be seen here, though to see it you have to get out onto the lake in a boat, which can be arranged at **Verlorenvei Guest Farm**, a 150 year-old homestead, 5km along the lake from Eland's Bay (*see* 'Activities' and 'Where to Stay'). The town itself, so long awaited, is little more than a village, much frequented by surfers ('tube' waves, similar to those off Hawaii, break here) and crayfish divers in summertime. In winter it is rather dead, but it is still rewarding to explore the countryside around Verlorenvlei. North of Eland's Bay, the countryside seems even more deserted. The road passes old ruined farms shaded by tall gum trees, their thatched roofs falling in. It seems unlikely that another town should lie this way, but there is one, in fact the West Coast's largest.

Cape gannets

Lambert's Bay and Beyond

Lambert's Bay announces itself in its own tourist literature as 'the Star of the West Coast'. Whatever that means, it is an interesting and quietly eccentric little town. The crayfish-canning capital of South Africa, it also has an extraordinary colony of Cape gannets, jackass penguins and southern black-backed gulls called **Bird Island**, reached by a causeway leading out from the small harbour. Bird Island is incredible, a churning, squawking morass of seabirds, constantly shifting and shuffling shoulder-to-shoulder as those flying come in to land, and those sitting launch into flight. Don't go near the place with a hangover; the stench brings you to your knees. A concentrated guano reek staggers the brain, augmented by a stomach-turning under-stench of decay; a closer look (handkerchief over mouth and nose) reveals that these sociable birds live atop the corpses of their dead relatives. For the brave, there is a fenced-off walkway leading to a bird-watching tower, giving intimate eye and nose access to the colony. Expect the smell to linger in your hair for a day.

Lambert's Bay has an entertaining **Publicity Office**, ✆ (027) 42088/58, on D.F. Malan Street, behind the old harbour. The man in charge will dress you in a white coat and hat and march you off to the crayfish canning factory. Delights of the tour include the 'spare parts department' where bits of broken crayfish are cobbled together into collective whole, packed and sold to Japan at vast profit.

More ordinary attractions include the **Sandveld Museum** (*open Mon–Fri 9–12 and 2–4, Sat 9–12*), one of South Africa's many museums of spartan pioneer farm life. The prize exhibit is a bible printed in high Dutch and reckoned to be 300 years old. There is also an old horse-driven mill.

Lambert's Bay was also distinguished (when the author visited) by having one of the last bottle stores to practise apartheid, with one side for 'coloureds' and another for whites. The author wandered into the 'wrong' side and was not served until he went into the side for whites. Such throwbacks to the bad old days are now sufficiently rare as to warrant inclusion as curiosities.

North of Lambert's Bay, the country gets even drier, even emptier than before. Trees disappear completely. Low sandveld scrub spreads on either side of the road. Amazingly, there are two small resort villages up here, **Doringbaai** and **Strandfontein**. The beach at Strandfontein is good for swimming; and is often all but deserted. Only swim in the section facing the town, as the cross-currents further up the beach are dangerous. One of the best wild camping spots on the West Coast is accessible by car from here. Follow the dirt road running north along the low sandstone cliffs parallel with the beach for about 3km. It becomes quite bumpy and sandy, so go slow. Eventually you will come out by a large salt pan on the right and dunes on the left. The dunes give excellent shelter. By night, the long beach is pure magic. Don't risk more than a paddle though, as again, the cross-currents are strong.

Just north of Strandfontein the R27 turns inland to follow the Oliphants River back south, under the wall of the high Cedarberg, while a dirt road turns west to the mouth of the river at a cluster of houses called **Papendorp**. Before heading back inland, it is worth having a look at the Oliphants River's sluggish entry to the sea: north of here, there isn't another perennial river flowing into the Atlantic until the Orange River, more than 500km away.

Activities

Walking: The best time to walk is between August and early October when the countryside is ablaze with spring flowers. Marked hiking trails can be found at West Coast National Park (guided walks only). Cape Columbine Nature Reserve north of Saldanha has a 13km hike along the rocky shore. There are usually seals playing in the water and interesting shells to collect. Rocher Pan Nature Reserve, just west of the R27 between Velddrif and Eland's Bay has short trails along the lagoon, where flamingos, pelicans and other waterfowl congregate. You may also see small buck. All the above reserve trails require a permit, issued at the reception offices.

Riding: The open beaches and wide fynbos scrub inland makes the West Coast good riding country. **K'Taaibos Adventures** near Saldanha, ✆ (02281) 44094, offers day rides or 2–5 day treks (beach and inland riding). All levels of ability are catered for. **Horse Trail Safaris** near Lambert's Bay, ✆ (021) 734 936, offers day rides along the beach or trips of several days into the Cedarberg mountains. **Orangevlei Guest Farm**, also near Saldanha, ✆ (02281) 42261 offers 1–3 day rides at all levels. **Oliphantskop Guest Farm**, near Langebaan, ✆ (02287) 22326, offers day rides.

Swimming: Any of the beaches fronting the resort towns of Yzerfontein, Langebaan, Eland's Bay, Doringbaai and Strandfontein are safe. Otherwise do not swim unless guided to a safe spot by a local, as the West Coast cross-currents are dangerous.

Watersports: Langebaan lagoon is a sheltered spot for windsurfing, which can be arranged through Langebaan Lodge, in the West Coast National Park office. Boat trips out to the bird colony islands of Saldanha Bay are also arranged from here.

Canoeing Trips: are sometimes available from Verlorenvlei Guest Farm, near Eland's Bay. The bird-watching is good—for waterfowl, including pelicans and flamingos—and if you trawl a line, you may catch your supper.

Where to Stay

 Although there are various holiday camps and hotels dotted around the West Coast towns, the area's guest farms offer the most attractive settings, the best food, and often the most reasonable prices.

expensive

Oliphantskop, near Langebaan, ✆ (02287) 22326, and **Orangevlei**, near Saldanha, ✆ (02281) 42261, offer similar facilities. Orangevlei, a large farmstead dating from 1832, specializes in riding (beach rides or treks of up to five days into the interior) but also has tennis courts and a pool. Oliphantskop is more modern, has horses for day rides, and offers out-of season rates. Both places provide either B&B or full board and offer Cape country cuisine, and seafood of the highest standard. The **Marine Protea** on Voortrekker Street, Lambert's Bay, ✆ (0627) 3249, will do if neither of the above guest farms have space. It offers the usual bland luxury of the expensive Protea chain, serves very good seafood, especially crayfish.

Langebaan Lodge, run by the West Coast National Park, is over-priced and has horrid orange curtains in the 5 bedrooms, but does overlook the sea and has access to swimming in the lagoon and a pool.

Verlorenvlei Guest House, ✆ (0265) 724, built in 1842 and 5km inland from Eland's Bay, faces the 25km long Verlorenvlei lake. Waterfowl by the thousand live on the lake margins. The homestead has 5 double en suite rooms. At the expensive end of the moderate range, Verlorenvlei offers B&B or full board by request.

Plaaskombuis Guest Farm, near Lambert's Bay, ✆ (0276) 732 326, is a restored, thatched 19th-century farmhouse on Steenbokfontein Farm, 9km south of Lambert's Bay on the R27. The owners are a good source of local information, and can help organize permits and equipment for more complicated activities, such as diving for crayfish or sea fishing. There is good bird life on the farm.

Cashel Bed and Breakfast, ✆ (02245) 475, a Spanish-style house overlooking the tiny old harbour at Yzerfontein, has two double rooms and a self-contained flat that sleeps 6. The beach is right there, all 20km of it, and you can arrange fishing trips with the owners. The **Paternoster Hotel**, ✆ (02285) 703, overlooks the beach near the small fishing village of Paternoster. A little run-down, what recommends it is its location near the old fishing village. Local fishermen drink here, making it a good place to hear tales of the sea.

The only cheap accommodation to be found is camping. However, the West Coast has some beautiful camping spots. **Kliphoek Guest Farm** and **Verlorenvlei Guest Farm** both have water-side camp sites with ablution blocks and good bird life. You can also camp at the **Cape Columbine Nature Reserve** at Tieties Bay, with the ocean roar only metres away. The camp site has an ablution block.

Eating Out

All the guest farms listed above provide Cape country cooking of the highest order for their guests. Otherwise, restaurants are few and far between on the West Coast.

Oliphantskop, near Langebaan, ✆ (02287) 22326, opens its restaurant to non-guests. Try the kingclip, if it is in, or any of the shellfish. The **Marine Protea Hotel**, Lambert's Bay, ✆ (062732) 49, also serves very good seafood, including a well buttered and garlicky crayfish thermidor that leaves you sated and gasping.

The **Kreefhuis**, ✆ (027) 432 2335, on Strand St, Lambert's Bay (just behind the old harbour), also serves seafood fresh that day, with crayfish as the speciality.

The **Strandloper** on the beach at Langebaan does seafood braais (shellfish, plus the catch of the day) in the open air. Bring your own wine and gorge yourself as the waves break on the night-time beach.

Plaaskombuis Guest Farm, near Eland's Bay, ✆ (026732) 326, also opens its kitchen to non-guests. Again, seafood braais are the speciality.

Bosduifklip Farm, ✆ (026732) 661, 4km along the R364 between Lambert's Bay and Clanwilliam, braais seafood, beef, lamb and game (in season) in the open air.

Oddly out of place on the barren West Coast is the **Villa Romano** on Voortrekker St, Lambert's Bay. This Italian restaurant is surprisingly good, especially the seafood antipasti. No need to book.

The Oliphants River Valley and Cedarberg Mountains

The Oliphants River Valley, if followed north to south, winds from dry country to lush. Though by no means South Africa's largest river, the Oliphants is known to support more species of indigenous fish than any other south of the Zambezi. To the north, near its mouth, the river supports a narrow belt of orchard and vineyard, which make a ribbon of vivid green against a dusty backdrop of brown and ochre hills. The Bokkeveld, part of the Great Escarpment, runs along the eastern horizon. The R27, which has led so faithfully up the coast, follows the river only as far as the small town of Lutzville, then breaks away east to the Great Karoo. To keep along the river, follow the R363 south to Vredendal, amid the narrow farms and irrigation channels of this semi-arid region until it joins the N7 highway at **Klawer**. The N7 then heads south, straight as an arrow, through a landscape gradually quickening with vegetation, until the ridge of the Bokkeveldberg retreats further east to become the higher, more jagged Cedarberg range. An interesting parallel route runs on the east side of the river. About 10km south of Klawer, take the sign marked 'Oliphants River Irrigation Scheme'; this is a dirt road, and not for those in a hurry. Both roads follow the river for 52km south to Clanwilliam.

Clanwilliam

Clanwilliam, the gateway to the Cedarberg, has existed since about 1732, though its 'official' status as a magistracy was only granted 1808. The town, which had been predominantly Dutch in population, was deliberately settled with English during the 1820s, which accounts for the town's name—after the Earl of Clanwilliam, the then Cape Governor. Only six of the English settlers persevered in this staunchly Afrikaans region, but the name remained. Today, Clanwilliam is a handsome little town, dominated by the conical peaks of the Cedarberg to the east (unusual in this country of flat-topped mountains) and the massive Clanwilliam dam to the west.

The **Old Prison** (1808) at the eastern end of Main Street, is now the **Publicity Office**, ✆ (027) 482 2024, and houses a small museum of early pioneer life in the Cedarberg (*open Aug–Sept Mon–Fri 8–4.30, Sat–Sun 9–1*). **Visser Street**, which runs behind and parallel with Main Street, has some fine old buildings, including the **Old Magistrate's Court** (also built in 1808), and an old **Dutch Reformed Church** (1864), closely rivalled by an Anglican Church (1866).

Far more picturesque is early 19th-century '**coloured' location**, behind the Old Prison. This small quarter is composed almost entirely of old thatched cottages in various states of repair. This is by far the liveliest part of the small town, and wandering here is generally fine by day (after dark is less advisable, and out of the question for a woman alone). But for the jeans and T-shirts, the scene could be a century ago: ragged children playing in the dusty street between the old thatched cottages, dogs and chickens.

Most of the cottagers work at the **rooibos tea factory** on Main Road, about 100m up from the fork by the Old Prison. The factory was built in 1831, which entitles Clanwilliam to the position of 'the home of rooibos tea' (in the words of its own tourist literature).

The Cedarberg and its rural life has inspired a lot of South African artists. Some of the better local attempts to capture it are for sale in the **Clanwilliam Art Gallery** on Main Road, which advertises itself as 'the only gallery between Paarl and Windhoek' (in Namibia). Be this true or no, it is worth looking in, as some of the work is very good.

Around Clanwilliam

Before entering the high passes of the Cedarberg proper, there are some places to explore in the foothills.

Clanwilliam Dam is a very large expanse of water just southwest of town, the haunt of windsurf and powerboat enthusiasts. There is good angling and bird watching too, though the latter is better further into the hills. If you follow Main Road south towards the dam, you will pass the **Clanwilliam Wildflower Garden**. The flowers are named and labelled, making it easier to recognize them when in the veld. Also dedicated to flora is the **Ramskop Nature Reserve** to the southeast of town and well signposted. The small (54ha) reserve has a mixture of sandveld and fynbos plants; representative of the two vegetation zones that meet around Clanwilliam. A wildflower garden from each vegetation type has been set aside.

Pakhuis Pass, north of town, is a rugged, twisting, beautiful drive (via the R364, a good gravel road) through the northern foothills of the Cedarberg. The road leads over an upland of red boulders, fynbos and lone, weathered trees, including oaks and a few surviving examples of the Cape cedar, the tree that gave the surrounding mountains their name. From the picnic spot halfway up the pass wind some marked walking trails, but you can also wander at will, drinking in the clean air and the wide views. The poet, Louis Leipoldt (also a famous gourmet, *see* **People and Culture**, 'Cape Cuisine' and 'Literature') loved this pass so much that he asked to buried here. His grave is marked by an inscribed stone under a rock overhang on the north side of the pass. Pakhuis was also the involuntary grave of an English soldier killed in a skirmish during General Smuts' raid into the Cape during the Anglo-Boer War (1899–1902).

To the north, the pass descends into the wide the Doring River Valley before climbing away via the Botterkloof Pass towards the town of Calvinia in the endless Karoo. Turning back into the Cedarberg foothills, take the turning on the south side of Pakhuis Pass for **Wuppertal**. If Clanwilliam's 'coloured' quarter is reminiscent of the 19th century, Wuppertal has never left it. A Moravian Mission Station dating from the 1830s, Wuppertal is a jewel barely touched by the technological age, a tiny village of thatched cottages, often snowed up in winter, and subject to all the savage vagaries of the Cape mountains' climate. The villagers produce superb leatherwork, especially shoes (and have done since the 1800s), which can be bought if you show up on a weekday. Wuppertal is on a dead-end road. Unless you plan to continue into the mountains on foot or horse, retrace your tyre tracks to Clanwilliam where you can pick up a road into the main range.

The Cedarberg Mountain Wilderness Area

Rising to over 2000m at Sneeuberg, the highest point, the Cedarberg are spectacularly beautiful. Formed from conical and jagged peaks, rather than the more usual flat-topped massifs so typical of South Africa's mountain ranges, the Cedarberg are full of what appear to be natural rock sculptures: various elemental assaults on the natural sandstone has formed galleries of strange rock shapes on the mountains' higher points.

The entire Cedarberg range is protected as a reserve. A good thing too, as within its 80,000ha are some species of vegetation found nowhere else, including the Cape cedar, one of Africa's few indigenous conifers. The trees, like small, gnarled Scots pines, used to be common here, but the early settlers' axes and fires destroyed all but a few. More modern timber plantations now cloak many of the valleys, but these are not unsightly. The only road into the Cedarberg from Clanwilliam (via Algeria Forest Station) passes through several mature plantations before penetrating the wilder recesses of the range.

Algeria Forest Station, **Kromrivier Farm** and **Dwarsrivier Farm** are the usual jumping-off points for hiking in the Cedarberg, whether for day-trails or hikes of several days (*see* 'Activities'). All issue maps, but overnight hiking permits can only be bought from Algeria.

Dwarsrivier, in particular, is the trail-head of some superb walks. Marked one-day trails lead to spectacular sculpted rock formations such as the **Maltese Cross**, the **Wolfberg Cracks** (which involves a steep scramble up and down) and the **Wolfberg Rock Arch**. For the first two trails, allow four to five hours, but for the Wolfberg Arch, a full day. There is also a shorter trail along the Driehoeks river. This is pure heaven in summer; the river falls over a series of steps, forming still, deep swimming pools accessible from the trail. Hikers should see klipspringer, grey rhebok, mountain reedbuck, duiker, baboon and dassies by the score. Black eagles and sugarbirds are frequently spotted along the trail. Leopard and caracal lynx are quite common, but seldom seen.

South of the Cedarberg and Clanwilliam, the Oliphants River runs broad between banks of white sand to the town of **Citrusdal**, a tiny, sleepy place nestled between the Cedarberg and Citrusdalberg. Citrusdal was founded as recently as 1916 as a fruit-packing station for the local citrus farmers. It is unremarkable, except for its **hot springs**, which are 15km south of town down a dirt road following the Oliphants River.

The hot springs (temperature about 42°C), are one of the least developed in South Africa. They rise on a farm called, unsurprisingly, 'The Baths'. There is a central pool, looking much the same as it did in the 1920s, a set of jacuzzis fed by the spring, well hidden in a wooden shed, and a handsome Victorian stone house (*see* 'Where to Stay'). Several walking trails head off from the farm into the surrounding hills. There are Bushman paintings on some of them. Ask for a map at the office.

The Citrusdal valley is a fruit-growing area, and the town itself is mainly concerned with servicing the farms, but there are one or two points of interest, if you have the time. South Africa's oldest orange tree grows on one of the farms, **Hexrivier**. The tree is about 200 years old and still bearing fruit. It is pleasant just to wander around the orchards. The local **Museum**, on Church Street (*open Mon–Fri 9–4.30*), has exhibits of early settler life in the valley. The **Marmalade Pot Craft Shop** is housed in the same building.

Around Citrusdal, you'll also notice car registration plates with 'CAR' as the first three letters. This is Citrusdal's registration, and a useful reminder if you cannot remember what the machine is called.

There are two ways to drive south out of Citrusdal, both over spectacular mountain passes. The tamer one (tamer in that it's tarred) is **Piekenaarskloof Pass**, the route taken by the N7 highway. Piekenaar means 'pikeman', recalling the 18th-century garrison that guarded the pass against Khoi raiders. A new holiday resort has been built on the crest of the pass. Not too glitzy, it consists of thatched stone cottages built around a large pond where geese cruise to and fro. The central lodge has a 'farm shop' selling local foods and preserves, and a Cape country restaurant (*see* 'Eating Out').

The other mountain route south of Citrusdal is the **Middelberg Pass** towards Ceres (the R303), which becomes a dirt road shortly after leaving town. Be careful on the sharp bends, corrugations and worn patches where our wheels can slip. Stay in low gear and do not attempt the pass if towing a trailer. In spring, the mountainsides are covered with orange daisies, and in winter, the pass is sometimes snowed up. Small, white-washed farmsteads pop up from time to time. Eventually, the road levels onto a high plateau, a green, lonely drive between two sets of matching peaks leading 100km into the Cold Bokkeveld and to the town of Ceres.

Activities

Walking and Hiking: The Cedarberg are among the best hiking ranges in South Africa. Trails of 2 hours to 5 days snake through the passes and over the lower peaks, taking in Bushman paintings, impressive rock formations and wide views out over the range or north to the Karoo. There is abundant wildlife and a great sense of space. **Algeria Forest Station**, ✆ (02682) 3440, **Dwarsrivier Farm**, ✆ (027482) 2825, and **Kromrivier Farm**, ✆ (027482) 2807, are the best places to hike from. Algeria has a system of marked trails and refuge huts for hikes of more than one day, while Dwarsrivier and Kromrivier have day-hikes to the better-known rock formations. **The Baths** farm at the Citrusdal hot springs, ✆ (02662) 3312, has one-day trails to Bushman paintings. **Piekenaar Resort**, 7km south of Citrusdal on the N7 has trails into the Citrusdal mountains, ✆ (02662) 181.

Riding: The most exciting riding is with **Horse Trail Safaris**, ✆ (021) 73496, a Cape Town-based company that offers a 4-day ride into the Cedarberg. The trail covers some tough terrain, and includes visits to Bushman paintings, and camping out with the horses, which are schooled and do not just follow the leader. Booking is essential. **Piekenaar Resort**, ✆ (02262) 181, on the N7 south of Citrusdal, hires horses for one-day rides into the Citrusdal mountains.

Canoeing Trips of 4 days down the Oliphants River are offered by **Felix Unite** of Cape Town, ✆ (021) 461 0033. The route leads through a mixture of wild and farmed country, and you camp on the white sand banks by the river.

Where to Stay

expensive

The **Clanwilliam Hotel**, ✆ (02682) 61/70, a 1930s imitation Cape Dutch building in the town centre, has 17 en suite bedrooms, a pool and an outside tea garden. At the moderate end of the expensive range, the Clanwilliam is rather tasteless, and is best used as a journey breaker before going into the Cedarberg proper. However, there is a very good Cape country restaurant attached.

The Baths ✆ (02662) 3312, is the farm where the Citrusdal Hot Springs rise, about 15km south of the town along a dirt road (signposted from town). Accommodation is in a large Victorian stone-built lodge with views out over the Oliphants River Valley to the Cedarberg. **Piekenaar's Kloof**, ✆ (0662) 181, a new resort built on the crest of Piekenaarskloof Pass on the N7 south of Citrusdal, has been well designed—its stone and thatch cottages huddle into the mountainside as Cape cottages should. They are luxurious inside. The Cape country restaurant is good, and there are hiking trails, horses to ride, a swimming pool and tennis courts.

moderate

Nuwerust Guest Farm, ✆ (02682) 1402, is a handsome old farm lying in a green, lonely valley on the the Cedarberg's southest tip. Getting there involves a spectacular drive: take the road from Clanwilliam to Algeria Forest Station, and, ignoring the turn-offs for Sandrif, Kromrivier and Dwarsrivier, follow the signs for Ceres across the Matjies River. At the sign for Ceres and Wuppertal turn right and continue for about 8km, then look out for the sign to Nuwerust. The farm offers self-catering accommodation (except for breakfast, which is provided), so take your own food and bedding. There are three cottages. The farm is old-fashioned and barely mechanized; a stay here is a step back into old Cape life.

About 13km north of Clanwilliam on the Pakhuis Pass is **Krakatouw**, ✆ (02682) 1222, a mountain farm offering two self-contained thatched cottages. The hikes and walks in the Cedarberg foothills are spectacular.

The Baths self-catering chalets, ✆ (02662) 3312, are a cheaper alternative to the expensive accommodation at the Citrusdal Hot Springs. These are clean, comfortable stone chalets with cooking and bathroom facilities.

Algeria Forest Station, ✆ (02682) 3440, has a camp site and trails leading up to spartan refuge huts (only firewood and water provided), several hour's hike into the mountains. Bear in mind that fires are not allowed and you must take a cooking stove. If Algeria is booked up, a few kilometres further on is **Dwarsrivier Farm**, ✆ (02482) 2825, (turn left at the fork after Algeria), and, beyond that, **Kromrivier Farm**, ✆ (027482) 2807. Both farms have been in the Niewoudt family for over 100 years. In fact, almost all the farms in the Cedarberg are owned by this once pioneering family—look out for the name on farm signs. Kromrivier and Dwarsrivier each have self-catering chalets (cheap if shared between 2 or 3 people), and a camp site with ablution block.

The Baths Camp Site, at the Baths, Citrusdal, ✆ (02662) 3312, are isolated camp sites set under trees near the hot springs.

Hennie Van Zyl's Camp Site, 2 Oewer Street, in Citrusdal, ✆ (02662) 554, offers spots on the Oliphants River, with an ablution block.

Eating Out

expensive

The **Vanmeerhof Restaurant**, ✆ (02662) 181, in the Piekenaarskloof Restort atop Piekenaar's Pass on the N7 just south of Citrusdal, is Cape cooking at its best. Try the bobotie, springbok (in season) and the waterblommetjie (a stew seasoned with watercress flowers and fried onions). Although it is fairly new, it feels older, with stone walls, a thatched roof and beams.

moderate

Reinhold's, ✆ (02682) 61, opposite the hotel on Main Street, Clanwilliam, is a relaxed restaurant set in an old Cape Dutch house with polished yellowwood beams and a dark oak floor. There are outside tables in the garden in summer, and a Cape country menu interspersed with fresh seafood from Lambert's Bay. Try the succulent Karoo lamb, or springbok (in season).

cheap

If you need refreshment, try the **Clanwilliam Hotel** on Main Road, or the **Visser Street Coffee Shop** on Visser Street, (behind the town's Spa supermarket) which occupies the front room of a 1930s house and serves light meals and really good coffee. There are good books to read and no one minds if you read at table. The home-baked breads and the spinach and feta pie are particularly good. No need to book.

The Swartland

Once over the Piekenaar Pass south of Citrusdal, the mountains fall abruptly to the great wheat-growing plain of the Swartland (meaning 'black land'). Some sheep and wine farming goes on, but in general, the Swartland is known as the bread-basket of the Cape.

There are two theories as to how the region got its name; the first that it refers to the rich, dark soil, the second that it is named after the rhenoster bush which once covered the plain and which apparently turned black in summer. Whichever is correct, the first sight of the Swartland from the north is breathtaking, a vast flat plain seeming to stretch into infinity. Once on the plain, however, there is little drama for the eye. The farms are large and widely spaced between great, open wheat fields. The landscape soon becomes rather monotonous, though still impressive for its sheer scale. In winter the plain is green with winter-wheat, in summer a sea of shimmering gold.

Piketberg, nestled under the mountains, gets its name from the Dutch word 'piket', meaning guard, after the soldiers posted on the mountains above in the 18th century to defend the valley from bands of raiders made up of Khoi and deserters from the Cape garrisons. However, the settlers themselves were no saints, and often brought trouble down on their own heads by raiding the Khoi.

In 1739 a party of Swartland burghers went raiding into Namaqualand, driving cattle away from the Khoi living up there and snatching San (bushman) children for slaves. The burghers had taken their own Khoi servants along to do the fighting, promising them a share in the stolen livestock, but when they returned to Piketberg, the burghers kept the cattle, distributing only a few head to their neighbours. The Khoi servants got nothing. They complained to the Dutch East India Company at Cape Town, which officially disapproved of cattle rustling, and was always wary of rebellion among the Khoi. The Company ordered cattle to be given to the servants. The burghers refused, threatening their own rebellion, and the Company backed down. This outraged the Khoi. Farms all over the region were suddenly attacked. The Company, now seriously alarmed, reversed their tactics, and offered pardon to the burghers who had taken part in the Namaqualand raid, if they would form a commando against the rebellious Khoi servants.

The rebels were cornered in a mountain cave near Citrusdal, but repulsed the burghers with poisoned arrows. The revolt spread. Farms all over the Swartland and Oliphants River Valley were attacked, and their stock driven off to the mountains. Regular troops were then sent over the Piekenaar's Pass, and indiscriminately attacked Khoi kraals wherever they found them, killing whoever they found, men women and children. The rebel leaders were finally shot during a skirmish, but sporadic revolts came again in the 1750s and 1770s.

After this, gangs of Khoi and European bandits began using the mountains above Piketberg as a permanent refuge for seasonal raids on the Swartland, which were not finally put down until the early 1800s. Today, Piketberg's only relic of the frontier days is one rusty cannon mounted by the High School.

Mooreesburg is now the principal town of the northern Swartland. A prosperous place, mostly built in solid early 20th-century colonial style with ugly 1950s 'improvements', Mooreesburg nonetheless has a fine (if small) **Art Gallery** in the Dirkie Uys High School, with good Cape landscapes by well-known painters such as Pierneef, whose paintings capture the melancholy mood of the Cape mountains. On Main Street is the **Wheat Museum** (*open Mon–Fri 8–12 and 2–5*) a good example of South African eccentricity. The history of wheat is charted from its untamed beginnings as a wild grass to the present docile varieties.

Head reeling from the drama of wheat-growing, follow the R311 side-road to **Riebeek West**. Before reaching the village, there is a sign for **Jan Smuts' Birthplace** (*open daily 9–5*), a modest old white-washed Cape farmhouse. The statesman's chronology is well documented around the walls. Further along the same road is another ex-prime minister's birthplace, that of D. F. Malan—on **Allesveloren Farm**. Malan's premiership is not generally remembered with quite such nostalgia as that of Smuts. Visits are by appointment only. Call Mr S.F. Malan, ✆ (02246) 320.

Riebeek West itself is a quiet little farming town that seems to have changed little since the 1930s. There are two eccentric monuments here, the **Pieter Cruyhoff Monument**, which commemorates the first white man to set foot in the area in 1661, and the **Rooi Os Monument**, which was raised in memory of a red ox who acquitted himself particularly well during the Great Trek. Only in South Africa.

In **Riebeek Kasteel**, the next town on, is the **Swartland Wine-Grower's Co-operative** on Station Road (*open for tastings and sales Mon–Fri 8–12.30, 1.30–5.30*). From here, the R311 loops back to the N7 at **Malmesbury**, the largest town in the Swartland. It is also the dullest. Another victim of 1950s 'improvements', Malmesbury exists to supply the region's farmers and to process their grain. The **Communion Well** on Piet Retief Street is a hangover from the days when farmers used to drive their horses in from distant farms every Sunday for church. It was here that they watered their 'spans' (teams). The old **Dutch Reformed Church** on Church Street is, unusually for such churches, neo-gothic. The beamed ceiling is very fine.

Just outside town, on the Riebeeksrivier Road, is **Spesbona Farm**, which boasts the biggest oak tree in South Africa (that anyone has bothered to record, that is). It is a monster, and the farmer is happy to show it off.

From Malmesbury, either continue the last hour or so south to Cape Town or, if it is spring and time is not too pressing, take a detour west, past the **Mamre Road Wine Cellar** (*open for tastings Mon–Fri 9–5, Sat 9–12*). Further along is the small dairy-farming town of **Darling**. The town's setting lives up to its lovely name; its green pasture is irrigated all year and becomes a joyous frenzy of colour in the spring wildflower season. The name's origin is not so charming, being called after Charles Darling, Lieut. Governor of the Cape in 1851.

Being a dairy town, Darling naturally has a **Butter Museum** (*open Mon–Sat 9–12*) on Parsonage Street which, equally naturally, contains a variety of butter-making utensils. Fascinating stuff. The annual **Darling Flower Show** is more spectacular, albeit in a quiet way. It happens in the third week of September, when the surrounding wild flowers are at their peak. The **Tinie Versfeldt Wildflower Reserve**, 13km west of town on the road to Yzerfontein, is a wilder show of flowers in the season, particularly of the large, orange Namaqualand daisy.

On the Burgerspan road, 5km out of town, is the **Hildebrandt Monument**, commemorating the southernmost skirmish of the Anglo-Boer War. The Boers involved were Jan Smuts' famous Commandos that dodged around the Cape for a year, avoiding British columns, unfriendly farmers and facing the threat of hanging if caught. By the end of their campaign the local farmers were so terrified of the consequences of helping them that the Boers were, on several occasions, reduced to eating their boots. The Commandos finally surrendered in 1902 when called in by the other Boer generals at the end of the war.

South of Darling, heading back to Cape Town on the R307, is **Mamre** (*open 7 days, sunrise to sunset*), a Moravian Mission Station dating from the 1820s, and built in the lime-wash and thatch style of the time. The gabled church is austerely classical, while the thatched mission cottages cluster round it like hens. Shaded by tall oaks, the mission has been made a national monument. It still has a working water mill.

Where to Stay

expensive/moderate

Carollanns in Riebeek Wes, ✆ (02246) 245 offers very freindly accommodation in 5 rooms of a Victorian house on the corner of Voortrekker and Long Streets. All rooms have en suite bathrooms. In the same village but much more expensive is **The Lodge**, on Denerhoff Street, ✆ (02246) 211, which occupies a renovated 19th-century building originally designed as a municipal conservatoire.

In Malmesury, the **Swartland Tuishuis** is another 19th-century building now renovated and offering clean, comfortable rooms at the top end of the expensive scale. Better is to head for Piketberg, where the slightly run-down **Nederberg Hotel**, ✆ (0261) 314 645 offers a relaxed, old-fashioned atmosphere and a pub much frequented by locals, in the moderate price range. About 3km out of Piketberg, up the Versfeldt Pass road, is **Noupoort Guest Farm**, ✆ (0261) 5754, which offers about the best value in the immediate area, and has some superb mountain walks.

Also moderate is **Die Herberg** guest house in Porterville, ✆ (02623) 2416.

cheap

Malmesbury, ✆ (0224) 23266 and Piketberg, ✆ (0262) 31674/31126 both have municipal **camp sites** with ablutions blocks.

Eating Out

Carollanns in Riebeek Wes, ✆ (02246) 245, serves very good Cape country dishes—big servings and good value (upper moderate range). In Malmesbury, **Kontreispens** on Piet Retief Street, ✆ (0224) 21456, also serves Cape country, at slightly cheaper rates. If it's summer, ring

Die Lapa (in the countryside near Malmesbury), ✆ (0224) 77040, to see if they are running their open-air fish and poultry braais, at the lower end of the moderate range.

The Garden Route

The inhabitants of this country are tawny coloured. Their food is confined to the flesh of seals, whales and gazelles, and the roots of herbs. They are dressed in skins, and wear sheaths of olive wood over their virile members. They are armed with poles of olive wood to which a horn, browned in the fire, is attached. Their numerous dogs resemble those of Portugal, and bark like them.

The Portuguese explorer Vasco da Gama, on landing on the Garden Route coast, 1498.

Between Stilbaai and Port Elizabeth, a distance of about 500km, runs the coastal strip known as the Garden Route, a temperate zone of tangled hardwood forest, green pasture, beach town and lagoon separated from the interior by a continuous chain of high mountains. Down on the coast, the daytime temperature seldom drops below 15°C, and seldom gets higher than 30°C. Rain falls year-round all along the Garden Route, sup-

The Garden Route

1 Goudemond State Forest
2 Diepwalle State Forest
3 Ysternek State Forest
4 Gouna State Forest
5 Featherbed Nature Reserve
6 Knysna National Lake Area
7 Goukamma Nature Reserve

porting the largest indigenous forests in southern Africa on the seaward slopes of the mountains. The result is the lushest temperate landscape in the country—a patchwork of green pastures and greener woodlands that look almost European at first glance, and give the region its name.

Although the Garden Route towns have been on the tourist map for a long time, its mountain country and nature reserves are still very remote. Nature lovers flock here, whether for the incredibly diverse birdlife (a mixture of forest species, such as louries and wood hoepoes, and waterfowl), for the splendour of the forests, most of whose trees occur only in South Africa, or for the unspoilt, rugged coastline.

History

Unlike many other areas of the Cape, this region did not develop as a single unit, but sporadically, town by town. This was largely owing to the dense forest that, until the mid-19th century, covered most of the area except for a narrow strip along the coast. As a result, there was little inland infrastructure until quite recently and settlements were reliant on the sea for communication.

This said, the rich coast has been inhabited for many thousands of years. In the caves of the Robberg Peninsula archaeologists have found evidence of *strandloper* (beachcomber) culture, probably of KhoiSan origin, dating back to the 7th century BC. That there was habitation before this is likely, but the only material culture left behind by the *strandlopers* was shell middens (refuse heaps), which rot and leave no trace after a certain time. Some historians maintain that Khoi cattle and sheep herders were grazing their stock on the rich coastal strip as early as 1 AD. The forested mountain country behind was left largely uninhabited, except along certain trails beaten by large game migrating over the mountains from the north. Usually made by elephants, these natural roads were later developed into the modern road passes between the Garden Route and the Little Karoo.

The first Portuguese to round the Cape—under Bartholemieu Dias—stopped along the Garden Route to take in water and to barter for the cattle and sheep they saw from their ships. Dias' party landed at modern-day Mossel Bay, but could not communicate effectively with the Khoi, and the encounter ended in violence. Vasco da Gama also stopped at Mossel Bay but, after some initial success, also ended up firing a cannon at the Khoi. However, as the route around the Cape to the Indies opened up to general European trade, both Mossel Bay and Formosa Bay became regular stopping points for ships from all maritime nations, and the Khoi and the Europeans quickly established a trading relationship, once it became clear that the intruders were no threat. Iron, brass and copper seem to have been the most valued trade items. By the mid-16th century this trade had created a secure enough environment for ship's captains to leave messages for each other on 'post-office' stones and trees and by the 1650s, when the Dutch set up their Cape Town colony, the Khoi and the Europeans were on largely friendly terms.

This changed abruptly when the first permanent Dutch settlers began trickling into the region from the 1680s. As with the Khoi near Cape Town, Namaqualand and the Winelands (*see* **South African History**) those of the Garden Route were clear in not wanting strangers settling in their midst. But by 1730, Stilbaai, Mossel Bay and Formosa Bay (later Plettenberg Bay) all had permanent Dutch settlements, and the local Houteniqua, Gouriqua and Attaqua Khoi were reduced to a virtual slave caste, subdued by firearms and imported diseases such as smallpox. Today, the names of the region's rivers and mountain ranges are the only intact relics of Khoi culture. The people themselves, exploited sexually by the European masters, gradually lost their distinct ethnicity, and by the mid-19th century, had become the 'coloured' labouring class, an Afrikaans-speaking majority in most of the Western and Northern Cape.

Because of the forested terrain, European settlement of the coast continued slowly. In the late-18th and early-19th centuries, the town of George was developed by the British from small Afrikaner farming hamlets, and ports were established at Mossel Bay and Knysna. Timber from the interior began to be cut at a furious rate, and this, combined with a short-lived gold rush at Millwood, near Knysna, in 1880, denuded most of the wild interior of its cover and, by the 20th century the landscape had been dramatically transformed. At the same time, the forests' large elephant herds were wiped out and the land opened up to settlement.

However, even with the forests gone, the rugged nature of the hinterland confined most settlement to the coast, and by the 1950s, much of the forest had recovered—both with indigenous growth and imported eucalyptus and pine.

Under aparthied, and in the build-up to the 1994 changeover, the Garden Route, like many areas of the Western Cape, remained largely aloof from political strife. Although bad things certainly happened (in 1986, while visiting Knysna, the author was informed of a man being 'helicoptered'—hung upside down and beaten so that he spun—in the local police station), most of the political campaigning was confined to ritualized jousting between Afrikaner Nationalists and English-speaking liberals.

Today, the region retains its old tranquility. However, over the past 10 years, large numbers of Xhosa people from the poverty-stricken Transkei and Ciskei former 'homelands' seeking work have drifted into the area en route to Cape Town, and large squatter camps have appeared in the countryside near George and Knysna. With such a wealthy white population nearby, the unemployed, often desperate incomers, sometimes resort to crime. However, despite gloomy speculation by local residents, there has as yet been no evidence of this getting out of control, and the Garden Route remains one of the safest, as well as one of the most beautiful regions of South Africa.

Getting There

By road: The beaten track through the Garden Route is along the N2, whether from the west via Swellendam and Heidelberg, or from the east via Port Elizabeth. The N2 is fast and passes through all the major centres, but it is worth bearing in mind that, in terms of scenery, most of the best of the Garden Route lies away from the main road, on the coast and in the mountains. The exception is the town of Knysna, which should not be missed (though again, the best of Knysna's scenery lies in its coastline and montane forest).

By bus: Knysna and George and the other towns along the N2 can be reached by the Cape Town to Durban buses run every day by InterCape and TransLux. None of the towns have bus stations, only central bus stops. The local tourist information office will give directions, bus times and fares. Buses between George and Johannesburg are run by Garden Route Express three days a week, and TransCity (a cheaper branch of TransLux) run services between Kimberley and Plettenberg Bay, via Knysna and George.

By train: The only long-distance service is between Johannesburg and George, via Bloemfontein, Colesberg and Graaf-Reinet. At the time of writing, services are weekly only. Call George railway station, ☎ (0441) 773 8202, for deatils. Otherwise, the only train Garden Route train service is the Outenqua Choo-Tjoe, a steam train that runs daily across the lagoons between Knysna and George (*see* 'Activities').

Riversdale and the Langeberg Mountains

If entering the Garden Route from the Overberg in the west, follow the N2 to the small town of **Riversdale**. The small town itself is uninteresting except for the **Julius Gordon Africana Museum** (*open Mon–Fri 10–12 only*), which has some superb Cape landscape paintings by two of the better South African artists; Bowler and Volschenk. North of town, in the towering Langeberg mountains, are **Garcia Pass** and **Sleeping Beauty Peak**, reached via the R323 north. Garcia Pass is easy to drive and very beautiful, winding through forest to a series of small plateaux whose fynbos heathlands are cut with wooded kloofs and fast-flowing streams. This is a good place to observe the abrupt climatic switch from temperate to semi-arid that occurs between the the Garden Route and the Little Karoo. From the old tollhouse (now a hiking hut) on the east side of Garcia Pass, several good hiking trails snake away across the mountainsides.

Stilbaai and the Kafferkuils Estuary

South of Riversdale, the R323 twists for 30km along the Kafferkuils River to the small coastal resort of **Stilbaai**. Except at peak holiday times, Stilbaai is usually all but empty. Mostly composed of new-ish holiday homes, the village has one or two old buildings. One, the **Palinggat Residence and Fountain** (built in 1809) is an old Cape Dutch manor that now houses Stilbaai's **Publicity Association**, ☎ (02934) 42602. The house has a small museum (*open Mon–Fri 8.30–12.30, 2–4.30, Sat 9–12*), mostly devoted to the natural history of the local sea and shore. The fountain has some extraordinary residents—a population of tame eels (one over a metre long) which will come and take food from your hand. The former owners of the Palinggat Residence first started feeding the eels about 50 years ago, and the tradition has remained. The eels sometimes leave the fountain and glide over land down to the sea to mate. However, there are always some left, and occasionally the fountain fills up with the creatures. Visitors too sqeamish to dangle fishing bait in the water for the great black slitherers can watch them being fed at 11 every morning from Monday to Saturday.

There are two small nature reserves on the Kafferkuils estuary just north of the village; the **Pauline Bohmen Nature Reserve** and the **Krantzfontein Reserve**; both require a permit from Stilbaai Publicity Association. In the mouth of the estuary are the remains of some **prehistoric fish traps**, ingenious leftovers from early *strandloper* culture, constructed from boulders to create small dams between the high and low water marks. Again, contact Stilbaai Publicity to arrange a boat and guide.

An interesting contrast to prosperous Stilbaai is the 'coloured' fishing village of **Melkbosstrand**, reached by a dirt road not marked on the map, but signposted about 1.5km north of Stilbaai. Melkbosstrand is another of the early-19th century Moravian mission stations that dot the Cape, none of which have changed outwardly over the last 100 years. Most of the men who live here fish and sell their catch in Stilbaai.

After Melkbosstrand, the dirt road leads past **Gouritsmond**, a tiny farming, fishing, and holiday house hamlet at the mouth of the wide Gourits river. There is safe bathing in the bay, and an under-used beach. The reeds that grow along the estuary are in great demand for thatching Cape Dutch houses, and reed-gatherers can often be seen slashing away at the fringes of the marshy water margins.

Mossel Bay

Northeast of Gouritsmond is Mossel Bay, an unattractive town with a positively ugly industrial fringe. Unless you absolutely want to see its large museum, Mossel Bay should be avoided. However, the South African Tourist Board promotes the place, because of its size and historical significance as the site of the first two recorded Portuguese landings in South Africa in 1488 and 1510, after which it became a regular stopping point for European ships on their way to the East Indies (*see* 'Garden Route History'). The site was never developed as a port and remained a fishing and whaling backwater until its discovery as a holiday resort in the 1930s. Today, Mossel Bay retains a beautiful beach but the town itself has been sadly industrialized, mainly as the site of **Mossgas**, a large petrol refinery, visible from the N2, and set up by the South African government during the years of sanctions against apartheid, when no oil could be bought from abroad.

The **Bartolomieu Dias Museum Complex** on Market Street (*open Mon–Fri 9–5, Sat 10–1*) is the town's only point of interest. This comprises most of the surviving old buildings, including the remains of the original Post Office Tree, a large milkwood on which passing captains left messages for each other during the late 16th and early 17th centuries. You can still post a letter from here in a small postbox next to the tree. There is a maritime museum, which includes a replica of a Portuguese galleon, and an arts and crafts shop.

Mossel Bay has a pleasant beach (though there are better, wilder ones elsewhere on the Garden Route coast) looking out towards **Seal Island**, a large Cape fur seal colony, cruises to which leave from the harbour. Times and prices can be found at the museum.

Inland from Mossel Bay is some lovely mountain country, which can be seen from the R328 north towards Robinson's Pass, a good scenic drive. It is worth detouring east off the R328 on the dirt road about 2km after Ruitersbos. Drive slowly; there are precipitous drops away down to the Brak river, and a fair amount of loose rock. The road descends and ascends through 20km of forested gorges, crossing the river several times and passing isolated old farmsteads until finally joining the R102 at Groot Brakrivier. The R102 goes west, back to Mossel Bay, or east, parallel with the N2, to George.

The largest town on the Garden Route is another ugly, if bustling, town, much 'improved' during the 1950s and '60s, again with beautiful country all around. The **Outeniqua Mountains** (which get their name from the Khoi tribe living there in the 18th century) begin just north of here. Signposted from the R29, which winds up over the truly spectacular **Outeniqua Pass** connecting George with Outsdhoorn in the Little Karoo, is the Forestry Station from where begins the five day **Outeniqua Hiking Trail**, one of the classic South African trails (*see* 'Activities').

The town itself is only worth visiting for the **Dutch Reformed Church**, built in 1842, with elegant yellowwood pillars, ceiling and dome, and red stinkwood pulpit, and the **George Museum** in the Old Drostdy (built in 1813) (*open Mon–Fri 9–4.30, Sat 9–12.30*) This museum houses a remarkable collection of gifts given to ex-President P.W. Botha by various foreign heads of state. None of the gifts appear to have any economic value, prompting speculation as to the whereabouts of the gifts that did. A bust of the man, himself a resident of George, adorns the entrance hall.

Around George

About 15km east of George is the small resort of **Wilderness**, best known for its superb, if sometimes crowded, beach and the fabulously beautiful **Wilderness National Park** © (0441) 877 1197, an enchanting series of forest-fringed freshwater lagoons dotted with wooded islands and connected by great stretches of marsh, home to otters and waterfowl. The N2 runs along the southern boundary of the park, but the best route in is via the tarred turn-off from the north side of the N2, marked 'Hoekvil'. The next dirt road east winds through the lagoons, finally looping back to the N2 just west of Sedgefield, on the Knysna road. The lagoons are home to a vast array of birds; you are sure to see fish eagles and most of the South African waders. There are day-hikes, along which you can expect to encounter bontebok, bushbuck and duiker. In summer the area abounds with ticks, so wear long trousers. Maps of the trails, bird-watching hides and information on the wildlife are available at the park's **Ebb and Flow Camp** (telephone the park's main number, listed above), off the N2 3km east of town.

Along the N2, at the eastern edge of the Park, is **Sedgefield**, a small and unsightly holiday village. However, just east of here is the incomparable **Goukamma Nature Reserve**, © (04455) 31316. A huge freshwater lagoon, Groenvlei, the lower estuarine Goukamma River, and the sand dunes and rock-strewn coast, can be explored on foot or by boat. Fynbos and marsh alternate with large stands of milkwood trees. Again, expect to see fish eagles, green louries, bontebok, bushbuck, vervet monkey and, if you are lucky, bushpig. The coastline is not safe for swimming, and puff adders are common in summer, so be careful when hiking. There is no accommodation.

A peaceful contrast to George, Knysna lies at the head of a large saltwater lagoon at the foot of hills that sweep away to the great hardwood forests of the Outeniqua Mountains. For the last 150 years a furniture-making industry has flourished here, using the fine local hardwoods. **Knysna Lagoon** is almost entirely separated from the sea by a spit of cliffs, broken in the middle, through which narrow channel the lagoon is connected with the ocean beyond. These twin spits of land are known as the **Knysna Heads**. The Western Head is mostly covered by the privately-owned **Featherbed Nature Reserve** (*see* p.213), which can only be reached by boat from the old harbour.

Architecturally, Knysna is a mixture of Cape Dutch, 19th-century English and 20th-century jumble, all of which somehow combines to an attractive whole. The town is known for its tranquility and racial tolerance. A community of artists and craftspeople have settled here, giving the town a youthful, lively feel, and a major causes of the many good bars, restaurants and cheap accommodation. Knysna also has the country's only decent brewery. The lagoon and surrounding forest are administered by the National Parks Board to prevent over-development.

History

Knysna started life in the early 18th century as a settlement of Afrikaner farms, largely cut-off from the rest of the coast by deep forests and the difficult gradients of the few roads through them. In 1803 the largest of these farms was bought by a wealthy and eccentric Englishman called **George Rex**, whose name, opulent hospitality and flouting of social rules (he had two common-law wives, though not at the same time) generated a rumour, that quickly became legend, that he was the illegitimate son of King George III of England.

George Rex never made any such claims himself, but neither did he deny them outright, no doubt enjoying the cachet. In fact, although his English origins *were* obscure, he had come out to the Cape in the 1790s with the British occupation as a secretary to the Admiralty.

Rex managed to accrue an immense fortune while working as a civil servant, which the purchase of the farm at Knysna only served to increase. He was the first of many to exploit the seemingly endless hardwood forests of the area. The local tree species included the giant yellowwood and stinkwood, the former of which could grow to 40m and live 2000 years (a few such specimens survive today). He encouraged ships to call in at the sheltered lagoon and buy wood, building a harbour there and sometimes piloting the ships through the tricky channel himself. By the time of Rex's death in 1839, Knysna had grown up around the harbour and his homestead.

Meanwhile a community of Afrikaner woodsmen had grown up deep in the forest, itinerants who had mostly been attracted into the area to work for Rex, then set up on their own, with their own teams of workmen and oxen. Living deep in the forest, these men seldom came into Knysna itself, which grew ever more English. Younger sons of the English aristocracy, attracted by Rex's social status, the distance from the authority of the Cape, and the richness of the land, began building great homesteads nearby. But the forest

Afrikaners, cut off from the town's society, retreated into their own dark, superstitious world, haunted by Khoi nature spirits and the more real threat of death from the elephant herds that roamed the forest.

Originally, the foresters had done well, felling the timber and hauling it out over the difficult terrain. However, by the mid 19th century, agents had set up in town, buying the wood from the foresters and selling it either to the furniture factories further afield or as cargo for house-building and wagons. The agents kept the price of timber down and gradually forced the foresters to fell at a feverish rate. When they could no longer survive from the timber alone, the woodsmen turned to intensive ivory hunting, but this too soon became an artificially depressed market. By the 1870s, so much of the forest had disappeared that the Cape government appointed conservation officers to control the felling. But they misundertood the root of the problem and attacked the foresters rather than the agents, so that the rape continued unabated.

In the 1880s, gold was discovered deep in the Knysna forest and a short rush followed. Overnight, a mining town was established at Millwood about 40km into the forest from Knysna. Within a few years Millwood had six hotels, two newspapers, and several brothels. But most of the gold turned out to be alluvial. Only one or two real seams were found, and these quickly dried up. Although a few fortunes were made, most of the prospectors went bust or left for the richer Transvaal gold reefs. The activity had caused even more of the forest to be felled, and the once deep primeval Knysna Forest was reduced to patches of remnant woodland in the deeper kloofs. By the 1900s most of the woodsmen were gone, and most of the elephants with them.

However, since then, stringent conservation measures have been applied and the great Knysna Forest has reclaimed much of its range, and although only a few of the giant trees remain, the mountains north of town are once again cloaked with mature growth. The elephant have not recovered so well, and a mere three now survive in the forest.

Meanwhile, Knysna steadily lost its importance as a commercial centre. By the late 1920s, the port had ceased operations and today only the traditional industries of forestry, furniture-making, dairy and hop farming still flourish, though quietly. In recent years, Knysna has seen something of a tourist boom, coupled with an influx of young arts and crafts people, but despite the liveliness and youth of many of its inhabitants, the town's calm is still one of its chief attractions.

Tourist Information

The Knysna Publicity Association is on Main Road (look out for the big plate-glass window with the elephant skeleton in it), ✆ (0445) 21610.

The Town

Knysna has some good, small museums. The Old Goal, a Victorian building on Queen Street houses the **Angling Museum**, **Maritime Museum** and **Knysna Art Gallery** (*all open Mon–Sat 8.30–5*). Of these, the Angling Museum is the most interesting; apart from its history of non-commercial fishing, the museum has a display devoted to the coeleocanth, a surviving prehistoric fish species that lives off South Africa's Indian Ocean coast. Discovered back in the 1960s by one Professor J. L. B. Smith, the fish is famous among zoologists for providing a 'missing link' between land and sea creatures—the coeleocanth's fins are apparently mid-way along the evolutionary scale between fins and limbs. Smith called the fish 'Old Four Legs' and wrote a book about it using the nickname as a title. So popular was the book that Smith used its proceeds to buy Knysna's Western Head, which is now the Featherbed Nature Reserve, and is run by his son. A preserved coeleocanth is on display, but alas, not so the professor, who is only represented in photographs.

The Maritime Museum has a brief, concise history of Knysna's old port, while the Art Gallery houses displays by local artists and photographers that change each month. Some of the work, especially local landscape paintings, is very good, and it is always worth having a look at the latest exhibition.

Millwood House Museum, also on Queen Street (*open Mon–Fri 10–12 only*) was one of the only surviving buildings from the gold-rush town of Millwood. This cottage was brought down to Knysna in the 1960s after the Millwood fell into ruin and was reclaimed by the forest. It houses a collection of George Rex's belongings and a history of the pilots that used to guide the large boats through the Heads to the harbour. Should you wish to pay homage to the great man, George Rex's grave lies in a stone enclosure a kilometre down a footpath off the N2 east of town, just before the turn-off to the Heads. Two tall pines sway over the grave.

Opposite the church on Main Road is a permanent **flea market** of local crafts where it is fun to browse and chat with the stallholders. At around 5pm, most of these will start to drift down towards the old harbour, where, in one of the old warehouses is a bar and grill, called **Tapas**, which doubles as a local for the bohemian set (*see* 'Eating Out' and 'Nightlife'). Always lively, the place is often riotous by closing time, which is whenever the last person leaves.

Between Main Road and the Lagoon are several craft shops set up by creative incomers. Particularly good for browsing is **Mackintosh's Weaving and Country Store**, 6 Long Street, set in a large Edwardian trading warehouse. All the wool goods are hand-woven. In the same building, selling similar stuff, is **Bitou Crafts** weaving workshop. The **Carver's Gallery** at 18 Main Road, sells good carving in local wood. Across the lagoon, on the Western Head, is **Featherbed Nature Reserve** © (0445) 2693, home to the tiny, elusive blue duiker, as well as a host of birds.

The Knysna Forest

The Knysna Forest is a general term descibing all the woodland, indigenous and planted, that stretches from behind the town into the southern slopes of the Outeniqua Mountains. There are four nature reserves via which the public can gain access to the forest—**Gouna State Forest, Goudveld State Forest, Diepwalle State Forest** and **Ysternek Nature Reserve**—in the mountains about 25km north of Knysna.

The forest itself is magical. A permanent hush rules under the great trees, between whose trunks grow giant, (up to 10ft) prehistoric ferns. In some places the trees have been labelled and their names, like ironwood, assegai, hardpear and saffronwood, somehow add to the romance. There are a lot of mature stinkwoods and—in some places—some surviving yellowwoods giants. The largest of these, known as the King Edward's Tree, is 46m high and is reckoned to have been a sapling some time before the Norman conquest. The Knysna Forest's three surviving elephant (now possibly four; a calf has been spotted) live in and around Diepwalle, but you stand no chance of seeing them. Pastured next to the Forestry Station is a herd of grey Percheron draught horses, used for dragging the indigenous timber still harvested for sale out of the woods, causing less damage than machines. You can lose yourself in the forest for days, among the waterfalls and hidden streams, watching bright birds flash suddenly across the path and bushbuck leap from the trees as you turn a corner.

Gouna State Forest and **Diepwalle State Forest** are two extensive tracts of indigenous forest that are home to the forest's last surviving elephant, and are reached via the N2 as it passes through the western end of Knysna. From here a signposted dirt road winds tortuously into the mountainous forest. Neither reserve has accommodation, except for hiking huts of the **Outeniqua Hiking Trail**, which must be booked in advance (*see* 'Activities'). **Goudveld State Forest** is reached from the N2 about 5km west of town via the signposted turn-off north to Rheenendal, a village at the forest's edge. Hidden away here is the now overgrown site of Millwood mining town. One or two of the ex-streets have been signposted by the Forestry people; it's eerie to walk them. Eerier still is the cemetery, complete with the headstones of unfortunates from all over Europe, now the home territory of a troop of baboons. A few kilometres into the forest is a lonely rock pool deep enough to swim in. Again, part of the Outeniqua Trail passes through Goudveld and there is a hiking hut at Millwood that can be booked in advance.

Ysternek Nature Reserve is at the northern extent of the forest (reached via the R339, a rough road), where it meets the fynbos heath of the higher slopes. Here be leopards (as well as at Diepwalle), bushpig and bushbuck. For those who want to drive rather than walk, the R338 leads up through some of the densest forest before crawling up over the steep, ruggedly beautiful **Prince Alfred's Pass** into the Little Karoo. Make sure you have a full tank of petrol and a good spare tyre for this road. The **Passes Road**, the old main road between Knysna and George, was laid by Thomas Bains, the Victorian road engineer who opened up most of the Cape's major pass roads in the 1850s and '60s. This is a fascinating ride along the southern foothills of the Outeniquas, through alternate forest, fynbos, pasture, and over several steep passes, including Kaimans Pass, which was worn to a deep chute by ox's hooves before the present road was built. In those days it took two weeks to make the journey, presuming that your team could manage the gradients. Today takes about three hours if you do not rush. The road is not numbered, but is marked in red on the road map, leaving the N2 west of Knysna via Phantom's Pass (named after a species of moth, rather than a ghost) and the small village of Barrington.

The Coast Around Knysna

Buffalo Bay (or Buffelsbaii), 22km west of Knysna, has a long, often deserted swimming beach. The road is signposted south off the N2 about 15km west of town, and passes **Buffalo Bay Game Farm**, home to a variety of indigenous antelope as well as zebra and wildebeest. A look around the farm involves a 3km drive or a half-hour walking trail.

East of Knysna are **Brackenhill Falls** and **Noetzie**, also signposted south off the N2. The Falls, in fact a series of falls plunging steeply towards the sea, are surrounded by dense forest. A hiking trail runs alongside them. Noetzie is a small, rather exclusive resort of holiday homes fronting the beach at the end of the road that leads on south of the falls. It is remarkable only because of a fashion in the late 1920s, when these went up, to build houses that looked like castles. Otherwise, Noetzie is not very interesting, although the beach is good for swimming. Around the other side of the lagoon are **Belvidere** and **Brenton-on-Sea**, reached via the N2 west (about 5km), and signposted off south just after the road crosses an inlet of the lagoon. Belvidere's 19th-century church, built in neo-Norman style, whose rose window was fitted with shards from the great windows of Coventry Cathedral (in England) after it was bombed during the Second World War. Brenton-on-Sea is the closest swimming beach to Knysna (12km). The village is tiny and has a pleasantly isolated feel.

Plettenberg Bay

Known to most South Africans as 'Plett', this small, rather exclusive resort is crowded in summer, with wealthy holiday-makers, yet for all its fashionable status, Plett has nothing on Knysna. Its three beaches are very good for swimming, but the coastline has been marred by the building of a multi-storey hotel on one of the promontories between beaches. The town has one, very modern main street, with shops, restaurants and bars.

History

Evidence of early *strandloper* culture dating from around 700 BC to the 17th century has been found in caves by Plettenberg Bay's beaches. A KhoiSan settlement flourished here from about the first century AD, and these people were still herding their flocks here when a Portuguese ship, the *Sao Ganzalo*, ran aground here in 1630 (the site of the shipwreck is marked on the peninsula).

Once ashore, the Portuguese sailors did their best to survive, salvaging what they could from their ship, and seeking the help of *strandloper* seal hunters living on the long peninsula, west of the present town (later named the Robberg Peninsula by the Dutch—'rob' is Dutch for seal). Archeologists have excavated the Portuguese settlement and found fragments of Ming pottery, brought with them from the East to the wild shores of Africa. By the time they were rescued, they had christened the sheltered inlet Formosa Bay.

By the early 18th century, the modern Garden Route region was busy with trekboers on their way east, heading away from the Dutch East India Company's authority to the lush coastland of the Eastern Cape, and Formosa Bay became a small Dutch settlement. But officialdom followed, if slowly. The rough village became a magistracy in 1770, and was renamed Plettenberg Bay after the Cape Governor of the time. After the British annexation of the Cape in the early 1800s, Plett then grew into a small fishing, whaling and agricultural town until its second 'discovery' as a resort town in the 1930s.

Tourist Information

Plettenberg Bay Publicity Association: the Municipal Buildings, just off Main St, ✆ (0447) 34065

Around the Town

There isn't much in Plett itself besides the main street of shops. Around town, however, there is plenty. The **Robberg Nature Reserve**, on the Robberg Peninsula on the west side of the bay, used to be a colony of thousands of Cape fur seals (*see* above), but most were killed or driven away as the town became settled. Still, the bird-watching is still tremendous—especially on the cliffs of the north side of the 4km promontory. Great numbers of southern black-backed gulls, black oystercatchers and white-breasted cormorants breed here. The **Nelson Bay cave** (reached by a footpath) has stone-age *strandloper* shell middens still around its entrance.

Keurbooms Nature Reserve and **Keurbooms State Forest** are along the N2 east of Plett, (turn left on the R340 just before the N2 crosses the wide Keurbooms River mouth). Look out for bushbuck, dassies, baboons and vervet monkeys. Rare Caspian terns breed on a sand-bar near the river mouth.

The old **Plettenberg Whaling Station** (1831) is on Beacon Island, just offshore. Plettenberg's small whaling industry only closed down in 1916 and the slipway and blubber cauldron can still tbe seen. The island gets its name from a stinkwood sailing beacon put up there in 1771, later replaced with one of stone. Trips out can be arranged via the Publicity Association.

Waddrift Nature Reserve is a half-wild private farm in the small Bitou Valley, sign-posted on the northern side of the N2 east of town. The **Old Nick Trading Store**, on the N2 just east of town, dates from 1880 and now sells teas and crafts.

East of Plettenberg Bay, settlements become fewer and further apart, and the forest and mountains begin to crowd closer to the N2. A worthwhile detour 25km east of Plett is to **Forest Hall**, a stone manor house surrounded by a large estate of pasture and forest and overlooking its own stretch of coast. Forest Hall was built for Henry Newdigate, one of the younger sons of the English aristocracy, attracted to the area in the early 19th century by the legendary George Rex. Like the manor houses near Knysna, Forest Hall is superbly isolated. The present owner (descended from the Newdigates) breeds arab horses which can be hired for rides into the milkwood bush. You can walk in the nature reserve, which has bushbuck, duiker, bushpig, vervet monkey and louries. Less energetic fun is tea on the wide verandah.

Nature's Valley

East of Forest Hall there is only one more town before the Garden Route coast becomes wild. This is **Nature's Valley**, on the eastern edge of the **Tsitsikamma National Park** in the **De Vasselot Nature Reserve**.

Nature's Valley is incredibly beautiful. The road signposted to it from the N2 descends through mature yellowwood forest; the coastal forests from here eastwards were too remote to be exploited like those around Knysna and it was not until the 1860s that woodcutters began to appear. Having seen the rape of the Knysna forests, the Cape Governor appointed conservators for the Tsitsikamma region as early as 1880. The last of these, a Frenchman named the Comte Henri de Vasselot, lived at Nature's Valley, and gives the surrounding reserve his name. Fortunately, by the time of his appointment, the momentum of forest clearance had slowed and today the great trees survive from the Tsitsikamma Mountains to the sea.

Nature's Valley is now a very small resort town surrounded by milkwood bush and unde-veloped beaches. Visitors must check in to the office of the De Vasselot Nature Reserve to get maps of the coast and forest walks around the small town. One of these follows the beach, and then winds over rocks back into the bush and over a steep hill to a deserted, forested bay where the trees have been sculpted into wierd, dancing shapes by the wind.

De Vasselot Reserve is also the start of two long hiking trails into the Tsitsikamma National Park, the **Otter Trail** along the coast and the **Tsitsikamma Trail** into the mountains (*see* 'Activities').

If you haven't time to explore the Tsitsikamma coast and mountains by foot, the N2 runs between the two. Take the turn-off to **Storms River Mouth** for a half-hour stroll along a short section of the Otter Trail to the mouth itself, a spectacular, roaring flow of fresh water coming down between cliffs and into the open sea. A hanging bridge across the mouth allows you to photograph the head-on collision of waters. Storms River Mouth, as the one point in the wild coastline accessible by car, has been rather developed by the Parks Board, but that detracts little from the sheer natural force of the place.

At the Paul Sauer Bridge, a few kilometres along the N2 east of the Storms River Mouth turn-off, is the **Tsitsikamma State Forest Reserve**, a publically accessible point of the great forest. The Tsitiskamma Trail runs through here as does a short, circular hike. Look out for a forest giant, a yellowwood over 36m high, and the usual forest wildlife, though this tends to be shy, owing to the number of visitors. The narina trogon, a rare, brightly-coloured bird similar to a lourie, may be seen here, but only if you sit quietly for some time in a forest clearing. East of here, the N2 and the parallel, smaller R102 head straight through empty country between mountain and sea to **Cape St Francis**, which roughly marks the geographical end of the Garden Route, and the meeting of the official districts of the Western and Eastern Cape.

Cape St Francis is reached via Humansdorp. Now large resort, Cape St Francis is attractive enough with its mock Cape Dutch whitewash-and-thatch timeshare holiday homes, but unspectacular. The beaches of the bay are good for swimming and surfing. If you have time, take the dirt road turn-off to **Oyster Bay**, about 8km north of Cape St Francis. This leads for about 25km across the small cape to a small, seldom-used beach with a store and gas station. Big waves, but safe for swimming. **Jeffrey's Bay**, 20km east of Humansdorp on the R102, is another resort, a bit glitzier than Cape St Francis, and packed with surfers during summer. A good place to make friends or learn to surf, but otherwise, it has little to interest the traveller.

Between Jeffrey's Bay and the sprawling, ugly town of Port Elizabeth are several small nature reserves: the **Van Stadens Wild Flower Reserve** (signposted from the N2) covers about 500ha of coastal fynbos and forest. The fynbos flowers bloom between April and September, and there are walking trails, but no accommodation. **Maitland Nature Reserve**, on the Sea View road south of the N2, covers 127ha at the mouth of the Maitland River. A large stand of coastal forest and milkwood bush, with a hiking trail and camp site, it is known for bird watching. **Cape Recife Nature Reserve** covers 336ha of shoreline and dunes. Marine birds predominate, including great numbers of waders in summer. There are paths and bird-watching hides, but no accommodation.

The **Island Conservation Area**, is a stretch of coastal forest reached via the Seaview road from Humansdorp. Bushbuck, vervet monkey, bushpig and duiker are sometimes spotted from the reserve's 16km hiking trail. There is no accommodation.

Shopping

Knysna is the centre of the Garden Route's crafts tradition, and most craftspeople from the area sell their wares here. The Flea Market happens every day on the south side of Main Road opposite the church, selling good quality jewellery, hand-made shoes and clothes. For carvings, and utensils in the beautiful local hardwoods, try the Carver's Gallery at 18a Main St. For woven hangings, rugs, sweaters etc. try Bitou Crafts or Mackintosh's Weaving, both in Thesen House on Long Street. They also sell pottery, herbal products (locally produced) and work by local artists. New shops and galleries open and shut from year to year in Knysna, so it is worth exploring the small shopping centre behind the flea market for this year's galleries.

Hiking: Few areas of South Africa offer so much variety of scenery in such a comparatively small space. Almost all the Garden Route's nature reserves have walks and hikes ranging in length from half an hour to several hours, most of which can be broken into smaller sections. Trails of several days can usually be broken up into sections. Bear in mind that the Garden Route is very popular with hikers, and the overnight huts have limited space; it is always advisable to phone in advance. A mattress, bunk and water are always provided at the huts. Firewood and cooking pots are generally provided too, but this should be checked.

The Garden Route has several marked long-distance trails. The **Otter Trail**, ✆ (021) 222 810, runs for 48km (5 days) from the Storms River mouth to the Grootrivier mouth. Arguably the most popular trail in South Africa, it is usually booked up months in advance, but cancellations are common. Unfortunately, this trail cannot be broken into shorter sections. Huts are provided. Maps and permits from De Vasselot Reserve, Nature's Valley. If you are unable to get on the Otter Trail try the **Tsitsikamma Trail**, ✆ (0423) 51180, five days in the mountains and forests of the Tsitsikamma range with wide views out over the ocean. The trail eventually climbs out onto the fynbos high ground, skirting deep kloofs of cliffside forest where many hikers have seen leopard. The trail can be broken into shorter sections. Maps and permits are available from De Vasselot Reserve, Nature's Valley.

The **Outeniqua Trail**, ✆ (0445) 23037, is five days in the mountains and forests of the Outeniqua range. The trail climbs and drops for about 100km across high fynbos to the great forests behind Knysna, passing through Millwood ghost town and the range of the few remaining southern Cape elephant. Maps and permits from Southern Cape Forest Region Office, Main Road, Knysna.

Garcia Pass, north of Riversdale, is the starting point for two overnight trails (with huts) and two short hikes. These trails are under-used, and your only companions are likely to be wind and silence. Maps and permits from Garcia State Forest office on the R323 north of Riversdale, ✆ (02933) 32558. The **Sleeping Beauty Trails**, ✆ (02933) 32418, offer trails of 1–5 days through some of the loneliest, loveliest country in the Langeberg. All trails can be broken into shorter sections. Maps and permits are obtainable from Garcia State Forest office. **Keurbooms Nature Reserve** has lovely walks along the steep, forested banks of the Keurbooms River and good, cheap accommodation. For the energetic there is a 2-day hiking trail into the neighbouring Keurbooms State Forest. The **Keurbooms River Trail**, east of Plettenberg Bay ✆ (04457) 9309, winds through fynbos and forest. It too can be broken into shorter sections. Maps and permits from the reserve office.

On the Kafferkuils estuary, the **Pauline Bohmen Nature Reserve** has some nature walks, and the **Krantzfontein Reserve** has longer trails.

Gouna State Forest has a 1-day hike, the **Terblans Nature Trail**. Further along, **Diepwalle State Forest** has an overnight hut (part of the 5-day Outeniqua Hiking Trail), and three walks ranging from 1–5 hours.

The one hiking trail in **Ysternek Nature Reserve** is very short, but leads through some incredibly dense stands of timber and giant fern, with breathtaking views out over the bare fynbos to the highest peaks of the Outeniquas.

Two tour companies lead organized hikes and provide all equipment plus permits and transport: **Oxygen Tours** in Knysna, ✆ (0445) 826 234, guides hikes of one to five days in the Knysna Forest and Outeniqua Mountains, while **Judith Hopley's Forest Walks** (✆ (0445) 871133) offer day-walks guided by Judith Hopley herself—a well-known amateur botanist and author of a hiking book called *The Garden Route on Foot.*

Riding: Equi-Trailing, ✆ (04457) 9718, offers guided rides for beginners and the experienced through forest, fynbos and along the beach. Day, half-day and hourly rides, and moonlight rides leave from the stables in Wittedrift village, 10km north of Plettenberg Bay. **Forest Hall**, ✆ (04457) 8869, 15km east of Plettenberg Bay, offers hourly rides on arab horses. **Eight Bells Mountain Inn** on the R328 between Mossel Bay and Oudtshoorn (on the southern slopes of Robinson Pass) ✆ (0444) 951 544, offers hourly riding through local forest. The **Sleeping Beauty Guest House** in Riversdale, ✆ (02933) 31651, also has a riding stable. in Sedgefield, between George and Knysna, is **Cherie's Riding School**, ✆ (04455) 31575.

Canoeing: Knysna Adventures, ✆ (0445) 871133, offers guided trips of around 4 hours for beginners (longer for the more experienced) through the freshwater lagoons of Wilderness National Park. The **Krantzfontein Reserve** on the Kafferkuils estuary hires out canoes, as does the **Keurbooms Nature Reserve**, for taking down the Keurbooms River.

Freshwater Fishing: Superb angling for springer can be had in the **Wilderness National Park** (permits available at the park office, which also hires boats and tackle) and at **Hunter's Country House**, ✆ (04457) 7818, east of Plettenberg Bay, where you can fish for black bass.

Sea Fishing: At present, the largest operator is **Knysna Fishing Charters**, in Knysna ✆ (0445) 21548, who can offer line and big game trips. Otherwise apply to the tourist offices for information (*see* above). Recommended spots are: Knysna Lagoon; Nature's Valley beach (buy a permit at De Vasselot Nature Reserve), Storms River Mouth (by permission of Tsitsikamma National Park; permits from the Storms River office), Oyster Bay and Cape St Francis.

The Knysna Oyster Company, ✆ (0445) 22168, on Tuissen's Island in the Knysna Lagoon, offers tours and tastings in its oyster beds.

Scuba Diving: Diving and snorkelling in Knysna Lagoon is particularly rewarding as there are some unique fish species, such as the Knysna seahorse, which is larger than its ocean cousin. Trips are arranged via **Waterfront Scuba**, in Knysna, ✆ (0445) 22938.

Steam Trains: Afficianados of steam will delight in the Garden Route. The **Outeniqua Choo-Tjoe** runs daily between George and Knysna; an old steam train offering a 3-hour trip on raised tracks over the coastal lagoons. Tickets from George railway station.

Mitchell's Brewery Tours, ✆ (0445) 24685, at the Knysna brewery in the old harbour takes you around the place where the only decent beer in South Africa is produced. The brewery is quite liberal in its tastings, and you can expect a jolly time. Tours leave at 10.30 from reception Mon–Fri.

Bungi Jumping, off the bridge spanning the Gouritz River near Stilbaai, is organized from Cape Town, ✆ (021) 724 516. Yikes.

Where to Stay

With the exception of the budget range, the amount of accommodation to be found on the Garden Route is staggering. Listed below are the author's recommendations. Should these be full, any Garden Route tourist office will supply alternatives. Similarly, national parks and nature reserves usually have accommodation (always self-catering), from luxurious to basic, and most have camp sites. It is advisable to book. For telephone numbers of national parks and nature reserves, *see* individual listings above.

expensive

Forest Hall, ✆ (04457) 8869, a substantial stone manor house 15km east of Plettenberg Bay, was built in 1866 for the aristocratic English settler William Newdigate and is still run by his descendants. The manor has one of the most beautiful interiors of any house in South Africa, complete with original Cape Dutch furniture, a galleried hall, and ancestral portraits. It has its own stretch of coastline, a private forest reserve and an arab stud with horses available to ride. Above all, the hospitality is friendly, not at all stuffy. **Hunters Country House**, ✆ (04457) 7818, 10km east of Plettenberg Bay along the N2 between the Tsitsikamma Mountains and the sea, comprises a set of thatched white cottages furnished with antiques, including four-poster beds. There are forest trails, a river with bass fishing for guests and swimming holes, and a good library.

Also near Plett (signposted from the N2 16km east of town) is **Hog's Hollow Country House**, ✆ (04457) 8879, popular amongst birdwatchers for its location on the edge of dense forest, and with gourmets for its award-winning chef. Guests stay in individual cottages, each of which has its own wooden deck. Walking trails wind off into the trees.

Portland Manor, ✆ (0445) 4804, just north of Knysna on the road to Rheenendal, built by another aristocratic settler, Henry Barrington in 1864, is also still in the family. Its interior is more 'done-up' than Forest Hall and somehow less intimate. However, there is game wandering in the park (including hippo in the home lake). Bass fishing is available for guests. **Yellowwood Lodge**, ✆ (0445) 825 906, a country house built in 1897, overlooks Knysna Lagoon but is only a short walk from the town centre. There are curtained beds and much expensive, lacy chintzerie in the suites (there are no single rooms). Strictly no smoking.

Stilbaai River Lodge, ✆ (02934) 41317, is a very lovely white thatched house overlooking the estuary at Stilbaai. Set in its own estate, the place has tidal sea-fishing, small game spotting and good bird life. The rooms are comfortable, but not ornate. Deep leather chairs in the bar and dinner by candlelight. The **Eight Bells Country Inn** on the south side of Robinson's Pass (R328), ✆ (0444) 951 544, is modern, but not unpleasantly so. This is a collection of white rondavels and log cabins set in woodland. There is good access to both the Garden Route and Little Karoo, as well as horses to ride and trails to walk.

Hoogtekraal, ✆ (0441) 277/8 was built between the 1760s and 1820s. A particularly good Cape Dutch edifice. Its suites (again, no rooms) are period furnished. There is a working farm to wander in and the house borders the small resort of Glentana (midway between Mossel Bay and George) which has 20km of white sand beach. Glentana is signposted from the N2. **Sleeping Beauty Guest House**, ✆ (02933) 31651, another handsome late Victorian house in Riversdale, has 7 comfortable and unpretentious rooms, a 9-hole golf course and riding stables.

moderate

Ganzvlei Cottage, ✆ (0445) 830063, is the author's choice; a secluded, very comfortable old farmstead set on the farm Ganzvlei, 15km west of Knysna and overlooking the Goukamma River, with its back to milkwood forest. There are fish eagles, jackal buzzards, louries, bushbuck and perfect peace. Reached by rowing across the narrow Goukamma River, Ganzvlei cottage is self-catering only. Ganzvlei has a second cottgae, equally old, but closer to the main farm, which is worth staying in if the river cottage is booked.

Hunter's Moon Guest House, ✆ (0445) 830063, 3km from Knysna, offers B&B in comfortable en suite rooms overlooking the lagoon. There is a swimming pool and braai facilities.

Oak Tree Cottage, ✆ (0445) 21877, offers B&B for 6 in a timber cottage with a garden overlooking the lagoon. **Lud's Island**, ✆ (04457) 7818/7858, is a 30ha private island in the Keurbooms Estuary 3km east of Plettenberg Bay. Bird watching, antelope spotting, canoeing, fishing and swimming are offered, as well as B&B in modern cottages and optional evening fish braais in the summer.

At the bottom end of the moderate price scale is **Mike's Guest House**, ✆ (0445) 21728, which offers superb value rooms with en suite bathrooms and a big English breakfast on Knysna's Main St. Mike, the owner, is a mine of local information and can sometimes arrange transportation for guests needing to get into the mountains and forest. Also very good value is **The Caboose**, ✆ (0445) 825850, on Knysna's Grey St. A timber building constructed around a courtyard with a small pool. The tiny rooms are built to resemble old railway carriage interiors. B&B is offered.

cheap

The **Hiker's Home**, 17 Tide Street, Knysna, ✆ (0445) 24362 offers budget accommodation in shared dorms in the lower town near the lagoon. Popular with backpackers. Self-catering only. **Knysna Backpackers' Hostel**, 42 Queen Street, Knysna, ✆ (0445) 21877, offers much the same accommodation as the Hiker's Home in a converted Victorian house. Self-catering only. **George Backpackers' Hostel** on York Street, ✆ (0441) 747 807, makes a convenient stopover along the Garden Route, though George is not a very attractive town. Dorm accommodation only. **Mossel Bay Backpackers**, 1 Marsh Street, Mossel Bay ✆ (0444) 913182 is in the town centre, offering double rooms or dorms. Self-catering only. **Jeffrey's Bay Backpackers** ✆ (0423) 931739, at 12 Jeffrey Street, Jeffrey's Bay, is the place to stay if you want to hang out with surfers. Dormitory accommodation and double rooms are available. Self-catering only. More tranquil than any of the above is the **Hiker's Haven** on St Patrick's St, Nature's Valley, ✆ (04457) 6805, which has the advantage of excellent hikes more-or-less from the front door.

Eating Out

expensive

Portland Manor, on the N2 15km east of Plettenberg Bay, ✆ (04457) 8869, has a restaurant open to non-residents. As one of the Knysna area's original baronial manors, Portland carries the cachet of distant contact with the English aristocracy. The game, seafood and French cuisine are good, the vegetables and herbs grown on the estate.

Eight Bells Mountain Inn ✆ (0444) 951 544, on Robinson's Pass, north of Mossel Bay serves mostly Cape country cuisine. Game and seafood from the coast are specialities. The dining room is unpretentious and many locals eat here. The **Lake Pleasant Hotel** in Groenvlei, near Sedgefield, ✆ (04455) 31313, occupies a large country house. It is best to arrive early so as to enjoy the views over Groenvlei lake and its surrounding forest. The restaurant serves a good mixture of dishes, from traditional Cape, like *bobotie*, to French cuisine and the pick of the morning's catch.

Hog's Hollow Country House 16km east of Plettenberg Bay, ✆ (04457) 8879 has an award-winning chef whose Cape country recipes have been fetured in magazines and newspapers all over the country. **Hunter's Country House**, also east of Plettenberg Bay, ✆ (04457) 7818 has an elegant candle-lit dining room and serves a fantatsic roast guinea-fowl.

O'Pescador in the forest 6km west of Knysna, ✆ (0445) 871 386, is an excellent, informal Mozambiquan Portuguese seafood restaurant. Traditional shellfish and line-fish with hot food such as chicken peri-peri are specialities. Log fires in winter. On the moderate end of the expensive scale. In Knysna itself are two nouvelle cuisine restaurants in the same price range; **La Lourie** on Main St, ✆ (0445) 825401 and **Melville's** in the Knysna Lodge Hotel, also on Main St, ✆ (0445) 21616.

moderate

The Pink Umbrella, ✆ (0445) 22409 on the Knysna lagoon's Leisure Island has become famous among gourmets all over the country. At the upper end of the moderate scale, the restaurant serves lunches and teas only, and is strictly vegetarian. This does not sound promising, but the food is really superb and imaginatively presented. **Crab's Creek**, ✆ (0445) 871043, is a pub overlooking Knysna lagoon, about 8km west of town. The restaurant section does a lot of seafood, but there are also some pleasant surprises, such as Cumberland sausage with herbs. Knysna's excellent home-brewed beer, Bosuns Bitter, is served on tap. Long wooden tables and benches.

Jetty Tapas, ✆ (0445) 21927 is another pub/restaurant set at the far end of the old jetty in Knysna's small harbour. Make up your own dish from the spiced Portuguese seafood on display behind a counter. Tapas is Knysna's (and much of the Garden Route's) principle meeting spot, and always noisy and lively. A good place to meet locals. No need to book. The **Pelican Restaurant** on Woodmill Lane in central Knysna, ✆ (0445) 85711/3, is mainly an oyster bar that also serves seafood and some devastating cocktails. Very popular with locals, booking is advised.

The Islander, ✆ (04457) 7776, 8km west of Plettenberg Bay, serves fish, poultry and pork dishes, with herbs and vegetables grown in the restaurant's organic garden. Smoked fish and ham and home-made soups are specialities. Service is buffet-style. Simple, unpretentious and very tasty food.

cheap

The **Duck Inn** on Plettenberg Bay's Main St is the only cheap restaurant with any atmosphere in Plett. This friendly, diner-style place serves soups, toasted sandwiches, boerwors and beer and is much frequented by young holiday-makers. Garish wall murals. No need to book.

Nightlife

There are no nightclubs on the Garden Route. Pubs and hotel bars are used as meeting places by locals who tend to party later on either at each others' houses or, in summer, on the beaches. Most Knysna partiers kick off the evening at Tapas, on the jetty of Knysna's old harbour, as do a lot of people from George and Plett. Young South African travellers passing through tend to drink there, as the place has a reputation for fun.

The Little Karoo

Here the wild bees make their honey and the white, wild geese have their home.

The Little Karoo, Pauline Smith (1925)

North of the Garden Route's coastal mountains begins the Little Karoo. Divided into two valleys; the Little Karoo proper and the Langkloof (meaning 'long valley'), the region marks the transitional point between the Cape's temperate and arid climatic zones. Higher and drier than the lush Garden Route, but not as bone-bleachingly dry as the Great Karoo, the Little Karoo is a strange, contrasting world of green river meadows, dry, aloe-covered scrublands, high mountains and level, stony pastures grazed by flocks of ostrich.

In the east, the Little Karoo rises to a great wild massif that falls into the Eastern Cape province. To the west, it merges with the Breede River Valley. To the north and south tower dramatic, jagged ranges that seal off the Little Karoo from the rest of the country; with mountains on almost all sides, entering and leaving the region is always spectacular. Nestled under these protecting ramparts the countryside, away from the region's one large town—Oudtshoorn—has a peculiar, quiet charm, borne of long isolation from the rest of the country.

History

This quiet farming country, enclosed by its surrounding mountains, has never had a front seat in South African history. San hunters and Kammannassie and Inqua Khoi (winter pastoralists from the Garden Route coast), shared the region and its plentiful game before the first trekboers hauled their wagons over the western mountains in the early 1700s. Settling around the Gamka River, where a perennial water supply could keep their livestock alive through the arid summer, the trekboers laid out permanent farms, and, as was the custom, went vigourously about annihilating the local San and enslaving the Khoi.

Some of these back farming areas, often hidden away in remote mountain kloofs, have remained isolated even to this day, for example, Die Hel, a deep gorge cut by the Gamka River in the northern Swartberg Mountains (*see* p.232), was only reachable by foot or horse until the 1960s, and still receives few visitors.

However, down on the Little Karoo's central plain, larger towns had established themselves by the 1850s—the largest being Oudtshoorn, on the Kammannassie River. A quiet farming town until 1870, Oudtshoorn and its surrounding farmlands suddenly became one of the richest areas in South Africa after the local farmers began raising ostriches to supply first Cape Town, then the European fashion industry with feathers. Until the 1930s, when the fashion for ostrich feathers suddenly declined, the Little Karoo experienced something of a 'boom'.

In the past 10 years, the ostrich farms that still characterize the region have experienced a revival of their fortunes as ostrich meat has suddenly become very 'in demand' in the USA, as well as within South Africa. Costing next to nothing to raise (ostrich can thrive in the driest, most barren regions), the profits from their flesh are great. Wine farming has also taken off recently—especially in the richly alluvial area around Calitzdorp, west of Oudtshoorn, where award-winning fortified wines are produced.

Despite South Africa's dense and turbulent recent history, the Little Karoo has little to report from the apartheid years and the violent run-up to the government change-over. Too rural, too sparsely populated and too remote from the rest of the country, the Little Karoo continues with its quiet, prosperous farming life as uneventfully today as it has done since its first European settlement.

Getting There

By road: The N10 and R328 traverse the Little Karoo from north to south via Oudtshoorn, while the R62, R341 and N9 traverse it from east to west.

By bus: TransLux run a connecting service between Cape Town and Port Elizabeth via the Little Karoo every day. Regular services are also run by Transtate, between Cape Town and Oudtshoorn via the Breede River Valley. Call the **Oudtshoorn Visitor's Bureau** ✆ (0443) 222 221/8 for details.

By train: A service from Mossel Bay to Johannesburg via Oudtshoorn runs every week; again, call the **Oudtshoorn Visitor's Bureau**, ✆ (*see* above) for details.

Across the Little Karoo

It is west of Oudtshoorn , where the R62 enters the Little Karoo from the town of Montagu in the Breede River Valley, that most travellers enter, at the little town of **Barrydale**. Set in a narrow valley of orchards under aloe-covered red mountains, the town is not geared for tourism, but it is worth stopping at the signposted **Annie Roux Flower Garden**, where Little Karoo wild flowers are displayed and labelled.

About 20km east of Barrydale on the R62 is the **Warmwatersberg Hot Spring**. If you are in need of refreshment after a long drive, the mineral pool (40°C) will reduce you to a relaxed lump of sleepy bliss. Close your eyes and soak. The R62 then winds over 60km through an ever-drier landscape of flowering aloes, sheep farms and mountains, with the Witteberg to the north and the Langeberg to the south. Occasionally the eye is surprised by lush green pastures and lucerne fields flanking a willow-fringed river.

Ladismith, the next town along the R62, sits under the massive wall of the Little Karoo's second-highest range, the Klein Swartberg, which rise to over 6000ft (2000m). Like Barrydale, Ladismith is more a village than a town. Many of the houses have beautiful Victorian wrought-iron verandahs and balconies, and the surrounding countryside is a green jewel of pasture, orchard and perennial streams. The Little Karoo's ostrich farming country begins here, and it is strange to see, rather than four-footed livestock, these giant, awkward, wild-looking birds grazing as contentedly as sheep.

The R62 follows the southern wall of the Klein Swartberg through some of the most spectacular mountain scenery accessible by tar road. About 25km after the Moravian mission station of **Zoar**, (set 3km south of the main road) whose lime-wash and thatch cottages have changed little since the last century, the R62 leads into the breathtaking sheer, red cliffs of the **Huisrivier Pass**. Drive slowly, so as to take in the views while negotiating the bends, as the road leads through fold after fold of soaring flat-iron mountain wall.

If you are feeling adventurous, and are not in a hurry, head back up the pass to Zoar and take the dirt road north to the **Seweweekspoort Pass**, past the sleepy village of **Amlienstein**, an all but untouched relic of 19th-century Cape Dutch life. The Seweweekspoort Peak (2325m) rears up over the pass as the road follows the twisting course of the Seweweekspoort River, crossing it twice by low bridges. Both are safe swimming spots. The pass is known for its beauty and remoteness, but also for a particular kind of protea flower, the *protea aristata*, a brilliant red variety that grows only in this area.

The **Towerkop Conservation Area**, ✆ (02942) 325, is accessible from the Seweweekspoort road, and covers a dramatic chunk of the Klein Swartberg range, including several peaks of over 6000ft. You can hike from anywhere along the pass road or follow a marked trail near Ladismith (*see* 'Activities'). Two hiking huts allow for overnight stays. Look out for black, martial, and booted eagles on the mountain slopes, as well as sunbirds and sugarbirds among the fynbos flowers. Klipspringer, grey rhebok and baboon are common, and leopard hunt the kloofs. Take your own water.

Once over the Seweweekspoort Pass, you are in the Great Karoo. To re-enter the Little Karoo either head back over the pass, or head west 55km to where the dirt road joins the R327 and drive south through the furrow separating the Witteberg and Klein Swartberg ranges for about 70km until it rejoins the R62. At **Calitzdorp**, 24km east of the Huisrivier and Seweweekspoort Passes, the Little Karoo broadens out to a wide and well-irrigated plain. The town is surrounded by greenery; lucerne, ostrich pastures, wheat fields, orchards and vineyards watered by the Gamka River that flows down from the Groot Swartberg. Another victim of 1950s 'improvement', Calitzdorp is famous for producing port and has a small **wine route** leading off into the back roads of the surrounding plain, taking in several vineyards and more attractive to explore than the town itself. Maps are available from the Town Clerk, Voortrekker Street.

Calitzdorp Spa, about 20km east of town, was also developed in the 1950s into an ugly, over-priced resort. However, another 15km or so beyond is a small dirt road heading north between ostrich fields towards **Kruisrivier**. After about ten minutes drive you will see a set of massive red, rocky hills rising about a kilometre west of the road. These are worth climbing, especially at sunset. Head through one of the ostrich farm gates into the scrub (the ostrich fields give out at this point). The red hills are full of little holes that harbour birds of all kinds; you might find an owl staring at you at face-level. From the top is a sweeping view of the green valley below. At sunset, the hadeda ibises come winging across the plain, shrieking their distinctive call. The only other sound in the silence will be the wierd booming of male ostriches in the pastures below.

Gamka Nature Reserve, set up to protect the Cape mountain zebra, is a beautiful place to walk. About 46km east of Calitzdorp along the R62, double back west for 18km on the old Calitzdorp–Oudtshoorn road, then head 7km south on a signposted dirt track. There are six one-day trails of varying length, and a two-day guided hike (you must book in advance) leading through an isolated plateau and surrounding deep ravines in the northern slopes of the Outeniqua mountains. As well as zebra, there are grysbok, grey rhebok, klipspringer, duiker and steenbok. You might see leopard if you are very lucky. Black eagles are often spotted, as are their favourite prey, dassies.

Oudtshoorn

Oudtshoorn, about 60km east of Calitzdorp, is the economic centre of the Little Karoo, the heart of the ostrich farming industry and largest tourist draw. In the late 19th century, owing to the demand for ostrich feathers, many of the local farmers became fabulously wealthy, building grand mansions on their estates—knicknamed 'feather palaces'—and maintaining substantial townhouses for the weekends, when they came to Oudtshoorn to attend church and to meet their neighbours. However, when Anthony Trollope passed through here in the 1870s, he described it as 'an uninteresting village, about two miles long'. This still applies today but there is much to see around Oudtshoorn, and it has good, cheap accommodation, as well as some interesting old houses in its residential quarters.

Getting There

By road: Oudtshoorn can be reached via the spectular Outeniqua Pass from George in the south, by the R29 road. The R328 runs north/south, connecting the town with two more spectacular passes—the Swartberg Pass north into the Great Karoo, and the Robinson's Pass down to the Garden Route at Mossel Bay.

By bus: InterCape and Greyhound connect Outdshoorn with George in the south and Beaufort West in the north, via the R29.

By train: A railway runs south to George through the Outeniqua's, but services are poor. Better to go by bus.

The Visitor's Bureau, corner of Voortrekker and Van Reede Streets, Outdshoorn, ✆ (0443) 222221/8.

The Town

The **C.P. Nel Museum** on the corner of High Street and Baron Van Reede Street (*open Mon–Sat 8.30–1 and 2–5*) gives the history of the ostrich boom in an eccentric display that includes the preserved bodies of chicks born with four legs and biblical quotations referring to ostriches. The museum also has the preserved interior of a synagogue and a brief history of the town's Jewish community (now largely gone), as well as the usual Victoriana. In the main hall, old photographs of hunting parties in the area give an idea of how wild the Little Karoo was even up to the 1930s. You may encounter a particularly ardent female museum attendant who gets upset if you fail to follow the museum via the recommended route.

The **Tuinhuis Museum** at 146 High Street (*open Mon–Fri 8–1, 2–5*) is a well-preserved weekend townhouse belonging to one of the leading Edwardian ostrich-farming families, furnished in oppressively ornate style. The **Arbeidsgenot Museum** on Jan Van Riebeeck Road (*open Mon–Fri 9–12.30 & 2–5, Sat 9–12.30*) was the home of the Afrikaans poet and author C. J. Langenhoven, who was part of the early-20th century movement to gain official status for the Afrikaans language. However, his best-known work was much more light-hearted, a children's story called *Herrie op die Ou Tremspoor* (Harry on the Old Tramcar, published 1925), in which a man takes home an elephant and, his wife not wanting it in the house, teaches it to pull a tram. Langenhoven's house has a large carving of Harry as well as the more usual author's memorabilia.

Die Oude Pastorie is an arts and crafts shop on Baron Van Reede Street, selling a mixture of twee pottery, good leatherwork (particularly shoes) and Boer biscuits and preserves. In the town centre, look out for small brass plaques on the pavement that say 'No Spitting'.

Around Oudtshoorn

The countryside around Oudtshoorn is probably the lushest of the Little Karoo. Three local ostrich farms and their old feather palaces are open to the public, as are three wine estates.

Safari Ostrich Show Farm (*open daily 8–4*), ✆ (0443) 227311, offers 2-hour guided tours. Safari's home-stead, *Welgeluk*, is one of the largest of the feather palaces, complete with marble floors, dazzling wrought iron and general overblown Edwardian splendour. Visitors can ride an ostrich (worth it for the weird, rubbery bounciness of their surprisingly fast gait, though you are bound to fall) or watch the farmworkers (skilled jockeys) race them.

Highgate (*open daily 8–4*), ✆ (0443) 227115, is similar to Safari and offers tours, rides, races and a feather palace, as does **Cango Ostrich Farm** (*open daily 9.30–6*), ✆ (0443) 224623. Maps and directions to the ostrich farms are distributed free at the Visitor's Bureau in Voortrekker Street, Oudtshoorn.

The **Klein Karoo Wine Trust** offers tastings and tours of the local wineries, most of which grow grapes for ports and muscadels in the deep alluvial soils of the local river banks. **Domain Doornkraal**, ✆ (04439) 2556, where the Wine Trust has its office, is in the village of De Rust east of town at the meeting of the R341 and the R29 (*see* below).

Cango Crocodile Ranch and Cheetahland (*open Mon–Sat 8.30–5, tours leaving at half past each hour*), ✆ (0443) 22593, just north of town on the R328, is as kitsch as the name suggests but, for all that, it is an interesting place. There is something compelling about watching the big, reeking reptiles catch lumps of sheep tossed to them by the guide, and the Cheetahland part of the ranch is definitely worth seeing; visitors walk along a raised wooden walkway between cages of various big cats from around the world. At the cheetahs' enclosure they spring on you that—for an extra 20 Rand—you can get in and cuddle them. Amazingly tame, they will lie there while you scratch behind their ears, or rub their bellies, purring loud as a motor. Children are not allowed in. The ranch breeds cheetahs for re-release in the wild, so the extra charge is not a rip-off. Ask if you can see the cheetah cubs being fed: they make a chirruping noise like a loud chick. Few things can be so heart-stoppingly cute as a chirruping cheetah cub.

Rust-en-Vrede Waterfall is about 15km further north on the R328. Take the dirt road turn-off east marked Raubenheimer Dam. Worthy of its name (which means 'rest and peace'), the slender waterfall is set, unusually for the Little Karoo, in a wooded hillside. Trees fringe the wide pool, where you can swim. The falls are reached from the small dirt car park via a short path.

The Cango Caves

Tours leave on the hour 9am–4pm in the low season and 8am–5pm in the high season (Jan, Feb and April), seven days a week, except Christmas Day.

Under the massive Swartberg mountains, about another 25km north along the R328, lies a massive cave system. Not all of it is open to the public, but what is is definitely worth seeing, despite the development of the site as a first-class tourist trap. After exploring some way into the system in the 1870s, Trollope wrote 'the wonderful forms and vagaries of the stalactites are infinitely finer than anything I have seen elsewhere.' Trollope went on to say that certain of the formations reminded him of organ-pipes, a demonic orchestra conductor, and 'some wondrous animal of hideous form'. Unfortunately, the developers have taken such comparisons a stage further. For your amusement there is a sad little tableau, just inside the caves' entrance, of near-life-sized plastic bushmen, attempting to depict those who lived in the caves until they were driven out in the early 19th century. The guide then leads you, en masse, down into a massive, illuminated chamber, hundreds of feet long, about 100ft wide and almost the same high. The lights go off and a computerized voice-over starts telling you what each stalactite formation is supposed to resemble—mostly biblical analogies—as they are lit up one by one with garish coloured lights. The magic of the place immediately evaporates. However, stick with the tour because, at the end, those who want to can wriggle, crawl and climb through a series of narrow pipes and tunnels through almost total darkness, before being led back to the light.

The Swartberg Pass

This superb scenic drive is the continuation of the R328 as it turns to good dirt road north of the caves, and climbs up and over the Swartberg, to the Great Karoo on the other side. The Swartberg Pass is one of the most famous drives in South Africa. The seemingly endless series of sweeping curves leading up and up for several thousand feet is one of Thomas Bains' masterpieces of engineering, dating from 1888. On the way up, the views back over the agricultural patchwork of the Little Karoo are spectacular. As the road rises the temperature drops until, at the top, you can be seriously chilled in the high winds that buffet the Swartberg's summits. The trip down must be taken slowly; the gradients and bends will not forgive a wide skid. The descent leads into much drier country. Red rock faces, gorges and ravines soar or drop away on every side as the road twists down to the vast, unguessable distances of the dry Great Karoo.

The mountains are protected by the **Swartberg Conservation Area**, , which has marked out some one-day hikes from the top of the pass. The range can be explored in more detail via the 5-day **Swartberg Hiking Trail** (*see* 'Activities').

From the north side of the pass you can either continue on into the Karoo via Prince Albert, or turn east along the Swartberg wall (R407) to re-enter the Little Karoo through a lower pass via the R29 to De Rust, 35km east of Oudtshoorn. An alternative, parallel route to the R29 is a good dirt road which leads south through a hidden farming valley along the very foot of the Swartberg. (If you take the R407 east from the bottom of Swartberg Pass for about 3km, the dirt road turns south in front of a Cape Dutch farmstead.) The road leads for about 30km through several old pioneer farmyards, where ostriches and donkeys sometimes stray across the road, until it comes out on the R29. Drive slowly into any dips and riverbeds.

Meeringspoort Pass, a canyon formed by the Groot River, is where the R29 turns back into the Little Karoo. Much lower and quicker to drive than the Swartberg Pass, Meeringspoort is no less beautiful and should be travelled slowly to properly take in the towering, crimson cliff faces. At the southern end is the small village of **De Rust** ('the resting place'), an untouched Victorian gem. Stop for tea at the Blue Elephant café on the east side of Main Street. Ten kilometres from De Rust is **Meeringspoort Waterfall**, reached by a footpath from the small car park. The falls are 60m high, and surrounded by a deep hush.

Nature Reserves and Hell

Gamkapoort Nature Reserve, ✆ (0443) 291739/291829, is about 35km west of the north end of the Swartberg Pass along a signposted dirt road. An isolated reserve on the northern slopes of the Swartberg, Gamkapoort has no accommodation, but a walking trail leads to views out over the lonely Gamkapoort Dam, which sits at the confluence of the Gamka and Dwyka rivers. Below the dam, the trail drops into a deep, lonely gorge. A mixture of dry fynbos, aloes, succulents and thorn trees, the reserve is inhabited by kudu, rhebok, springbok, klipspringer, steenbok, duiker and dassies. Expect to see antelope if you walk quietly. Look out for black eagles. There are leopard and caracal in the kloofs.

Gamkaskloof, ✆ (0443) 733367, which used to be known as 'Die Hel' ('the hell'), is a remote farming valley cut deep into the northern Swartberg. This utterly remote country was a stronghold of Khoi and San until they were pushed out by trekboers in the early 19th century. The farmers remained cut off from the rest of the world until the 1920s when a school was built. But there was no drivable road until the 1960s. Even now, the farmers, who farm for prosperous subsistence rather than commerce, are an aloof lot. The kloof got its name from the intense heat that builds up in its deep cleft during summer. However, it is fertile, wooded and very, very, beautiful, and well worth the trip if you have time.

Nietgenaamd Nature Reserve, is 65km east of De Rust along the R341 towards Willowmore, then north for 16km along a gravel road. This is a gem: hot springs with no attendant resort, and walking trails through the aloe- and thorn-covered mountainsides, which turn to fynbos on the high ridges. A few cottages and a camp site make up the accommodation. Springbok, duiker, steenbok and klipspringer are often spotted on the trails.

In the Kammannassieberg, further east along the R62, is the **Langkloof Nature Reserve**, a 25,000ha expanse of wild mountain that is home to the Cape mountain zebra, grey rhebok, klipsinger and baboon. The hardwood forest and fynbos on the southern slopes change to a drier landscape to the north. Hiking is allowed, but visitors follow their own routes and take all their own provisions.

The Eastern Little Karoo's Wild Massif

The R62 through the Langkloof and the R341 from De Rust meet about 60km east of De Rust, north of the towns of Uniondale and Avontuur. East of here the land rises to a rumpled mass of mountains that run for about 150km, forming the boundary between the Little Karoo and the Eastern Cape. To the south run the mountains of the Garden Route. Few travellers explore these eastern Little Karoo ranges, but they are accessible by both road or foot. They comprise perhaps the wildest corner of the southern Cape and were one of the last strongholds of the Cape's free Khoi and San.

Uniondale, on their western fringe, is a small fruit-farming village. The **Old Water Mill** dates from the mid 1800s and has, oddly enough, the largest water-wheel in the country. There is also a **Boer War Fort**, built by the British to keep the Boers out of the Cape. A drive south through the **Uniondalepoort Pass** leads to **Avontuur**, an even smaller and rather uninteresting fruit-farming village in the Langkloof. Continue south and the road rises steeply over the almost conical **Prince Alfred's Pass**, through the gap between the Outeniqua and Tsitsikamma mountains, to Knysna and the Garden Route.

The Eastern Massif's Conservation Areas

There are two ways through the wild Baviaanskloof and Kougaberg massif. Directly east of Uniondale and Willowmore, turn from the R57 onto the R332 (a good dirt road) to the **Baviaanskloof Conservation Area**. Covering 70,000ha, the range contains a variety of different habitats, from montane forest and fynbos to bushveld and karoo scrub. Set hiking trails are being laid out, but visitors can hike anywhere and camp where they want. Large animals such as eland and the Cape mountain zebra thrive here, along with the more usual klipspringer, grey rhebok and baboon. Leopard and caracal are common. The conservation area's literature warns visitors to fill their petrol tanks before entering the Baviaanskloofberg, and to avoid the winter rainy season, when the dirt road in can be flooded.

Further east is the **Cockscomb Conservation Area**, which runs into part of the Groot Winterhoekberg, continuing on the dirt R332. The reserve begins beyond the hamlet of Andrieskraal. Cockscomb, even larger than the Baviaanskloof area, covers a similar transitional vegetation zone, and supports kudu, eland, Cape mountain zebra, bushbuck, grey rhebok, duiker and klipspringer. Again, leopard and caracal are common and the well-watered kloofs are hunted by fish eagles. Hikers can wander at will. Two equipped camp sites can be found along the R332 (with ablutions blocks), but otherwise visitors must camp in the wild.

To the south, where the Kougaberg fall into the Langkloof, is the **Formosa Conservation Area**. This vast (70,550ha) swathe of mountain is accessible from Joubertina in the Langkloof via a signposted dirt road. Again, hikers must choose their own routes, and the reserve's literature advises carrying water. Fires are forbidden. Mountain reedbuck and grey rhebok are the largest antelope in the ranges, otherwise the fauna is the same as for Cockscomb and Baviaanskloof. Formosa has a very basic camp site at its entrance which does not have an ablution block.

The remoteness of these mountains is summed up by one hiker's experience of hearing leopard cough next to his camp every night of his foray into the Baviaanskloofberg: while leopard are present throughout the Cape ranges (even in the well-populated Cape peninsula mountains), they have learned to steer well clear of humans. That a leopard should follow a hiker from curiosity shows how very few people ever penetrate these eastern ranges.

The Killing of Jan Prinsloo

Most hikers who have explored these mountains comment on their mysterious feel and it comes as no surprise that there is a gruesome ghost story attached to the area. The full version is well told in several story books the best being Alice Miller's beautifully illustrated *Myths and Legends of Southern Africa* (T.V. Bulpin Books, 1979), but here is the jist of the story.

Jan Prinsloo's Kloof lies in the northern foothills of the Kougaberg, over-looking the Baviaanskloof. In 1860, the one farm in the kloof was bought by a young Englishman. Despite its isolation, the farm had good grazing and commanded a great swathe of mountain, but the Englishman aquired the property for an unusually low price.

On the young settler's first night, under a waxing moon, screams were heard from the horse kraal. He rushed from his bed to investigate, and found the animals huddled together in a corner of the stone pen, plainly terrified. But whatever had disturbed them had vanished. Next morning, he questioned the farm's old Khoi foreman, but received only a shrug in reply. Determined to find out what had disturbed his livestock, the Englishman sat up with his musket for several nights until he heard the scream again, saw the rush of frightened horses, and glimpsed a large shadow slinking away from the kraal. Squinting in the moonlight, the Englishman fired, but the figure slipped away.

Again he questioned the old farmhand, but to no avail. However, late the next afternoon, the old man asked could he sleep in the house that night Guessing that he might learn something about the mysterious goings-on, the young man agreed, and asked no further questions. Around midnight, the young man woke to another piercing scream, jumped from his bed and saw the old Khoi farmhand standing at the front door, looking out.

In the moonlit kraal, the horses were again quivering with fright in a corner. Small wonder—a huge figure with a gun was running around, chased by five smaller men waving spears and knives. Grabbing his musket, the young man ran towards the intruders, but stopped dead when he saw empty eye sockets and livid flesh where their faces should have been. The big figure stumbled and the others fell on him, hacking out his entrails and dancing round the kraal. The moon passed behind a cloud, and when it reappeared, the figures had gone. The young foreman fainted.

Next day the old Khoi foreman finally told the story. He had been born on the farm, he said, which was then owned by the Jan Prinsloo after which the kloof was named. A cruel freebooter, Prinsloo, after the manner of the time, tortured, bullied and flogged his Khoi farmhands according to his whim. One day he whipped to death the husbands of two women who had left the farm to visit relatives without permission. Then he shot the women and retired to the house with a bottle of brandy. That night all his Khoi left the farm and Prinsloo woke to find himself alone. Feeling that the silence boded ill, he saddled up, but halfway down the kloof was ambushed by six of his ex-workers. He galloped back to the farm, took position in the horse kraal, and downed one man with his musket. But the others stormed the wall and the rest happened as the Englishman had seen. By a strange twist of fate, said the old man, the avengers were themselves killed during an insurrection that same year and since then the horrid drama had repeated itself every year on the night of the killing. The farm was sold again, and it is said that the new owner died on the way to claim it. and according to the story, it has stood empty ever since.

At the far east of these great massifs rises the **Groendal Wilderness Area**, in the Groot Winterhoekberg. Reached via the R329, R332, or N2 to Uitenhage, then via Caledon Street, Gibbon Street and the Groendal road to the Forest Station, the wilderness has a network of marked overnight trails of up to several days. Permits and maps are available at the Forest Station. There are no huts, but caves are used as overnight spots (many of which have bushman paintings) and most hikers carry tents. Like the Baviaanskloof area to the west, so few hikers make the trip that one stands a better chance of seeing the shy leopard or caracal here than in most Cape mountains. The vegetation is mostly fynbos with densely wooded kloofs. For the traveller who really wants to see the Cape wilds, there can be few better places.

Activities

Hiking: Apart from the trails in the Gamkapoort, Gamka, Nietgenaamd and Groendal Nature Reserves already listed, the Little Karoo's only marked hikes are the 3-day **Swartberg Hiking Trail**, ✆ (0443) 291 739/829, which can be broken up into 15 different shorter trails ranging from 4km to 21km, and the trails of the **Groendal Wilderness Area**, ✆ (041) 992 5418. Booking is essential for both. Wilder hiking can be undertaken in the **Baviaanskloof**, ✆ (04232) 30270 **Cockscomb** ✆ (04232) 30270, **Formosa Conservation Areas** ✆ (04427) 31530 and the **Langkloof Nature Reserve**, ✆ (04462) 110, with tents and maps. Again, booking is essential—you want the mountain rescue people to know that you are in there.

Wine Tasting: The Little Karoo has established a route that takes in nine wineries, beginning at Barrydale and ending east of Oudtshoorn. The region is best-known for fortified wines, especially port, although everything from *methode champenoise* sparkling wines to brandy are produced. The flagship estate is **BoPlaas**, out of Calitzdorp on Saayman Street, which makes a port that has won 25 medals in the last 15 years. For beauty, the **Domain Doornkraal** estate between Oudtshoorn and De Rust is king, sitting at the foot of the huge Rooi Krans (red cliff) and producing muscadels and fortified wines. The other wineries centre around Calitzdorp and Ladismith. Maps of the route can be found at the Klein Karoo Marketing Association on Voortrekker Street, Oudtshoorn, ✆ (0443) 226643, from the Oudtshoorn Visitor's Bureau on the corner of Voortrekker and Van Reede Streets, ✆ (0443) 222221, from the Calitzdorp Town Clerk on Voortrekker Street, Calitzdorp, ✆ (04437) 33312, or the Town Clerk, Church Street, Ladismith, ✆ (02942) 20.

Where to Stay and Eating Out

The Little Karoo lacks independent restaurants other than the burger and chips variety. Most hotels double as restaurants.

Rosenhof Country House, ✆ (0445) 222232/262, is a large 19th-century farmstead on the road north of Oudtshoorn, with yellowwood ceilings and antiques throughout. The place is small, with only four en-suite rooms built around a courtyard and large pool. The restaurant serves Cape country with some very good Cape wines. There is a rose and herb garden. Log fires in winter.

Oue Werf, ✆ (0443) 228712, is a beautiful Cape Dutch farm in the village of Schoemanshoek, 15km north of Oudtshoorn on the Cango Caves road (R328). This is one of the green valleys of the Little Karoo. B&B in two self-contained cottages. Swimming is allowed in the pool and farm dam. No restaurant though. Credit cards are not accepted.

Welgevonden Guest House near Calitzdorp, ✆ (04437) 33642, offers B&B and home cooking in the evenings, with excellent traditional Cape country; game, boerwors, home-made breads and home-grown fruits. There are four en suite rooms. In the centre of Oudtshoorn is the **Bed Stop B&B**, ✆ (0443) 224746, on Van der Riet Street, and the **Busy Bee B&B**, ✆ (0443) 224 784) on Church Street. Despite their rather alarming names, these places are quiet, comfortable and hard to beat for convenience.

The **Traveller's Oasis**, 3 Church St, Oudtshoorn, ✆ (0443) 291163, offers single and rooms. as well as dorm accommodation at very low prices. Clean and friendly, you can check in 24 hours a day. There is a pool, kitchen, braai and a free pick up from anywhere in Oudtshoorn for new arrivals. Most rooms have their own shower. Barrydale also has a cheap place, the **Tradouw Guest House**, ✆ (028) 572 1434, also offering dorms or double rooms, and has superb hiking within easy reach of the front door.

Camp sites with ablution blocks can be found at **Nietgenaamd Nature Reserve**, **Cockscomb Conservation Area** (*see* 'Activities' for telephone numbers) and wild camping without facilities is permitted in the other conservation areas.

The Northern Cape

'The full African moon poured down its light from the blue sky into the wide, lonely plain. The dry, sandy earth, with its coating of stunted 'karoo' bushes a few inches high, the low hills that skirted the plain, the milk–bushes with their long, finger–like leaves, all were touched by a wierd and almost oppressive beauty as they lay in the white light.'

Story of an African Farm, Olive Schreiner

The Great Karoo appears as a great emptiness on the map. Tourist offices offer little information on the area and consequently few people ever explore it. Its few towns are connected mostly by dirt roads that seem to pass through hundreds of miles of nothing and most visitors to South Africa never visit the region—at best they hurry across its southern fringe, along the N1, on the way to somewhere else. When the author first asked a representative of SaTour what the Karoo comprised, he was told 'Miles and miles of bugger-all!'

Nothing could be further from the truth. Blessedly free from dense human settlement the Karoo certainly is, but the vast thirstland (which is what its name means in the Khoi and San languages) is wide, silent and serenely beautiful. High mountains jut and fold along its western and southern spaces. The central pans stretch and shimmer to undiscernible horizons. A hot landscape of red, ochre, brown and black blisters in the flat light of midday. By night the skies are so clear, the stars so close and bright that it seems you could reach up and gather them in handfuls.

Some parts of the Karoo are well vegetated, others dry as a bleached skull. Occasionally you come upon a green, willow-fringed dam, whose tell-tale lone metal windmill marks the point of an undergound spring. For the Karoo is well watered. Under its dry, rocky surface lies enough water to support the thousands of sheep that browse the region's impossibly huge farms. And the Karoo's soil is very rich, having once been the floor of a vast lake system some millions of years ago. As a result, provided crops can be irrigated, almost anything can be grown, and the rare patches of Karoo alfalfa (clover) are among the richest in the world.

When it rains, the effect is almost mystical. The heavens open with thunder and sheets of water pour down. Tough Karoo farmers—who may have been waiting up to ten years for their dams to be replenished—fall to their knees in gratitude and cry and pray.

It is impossible not to react emotionally to the Great Karoo, its heat, its distances, its endless sun and thirst, its remote beauty. Even just driving across it, intent on the next horizon, the road running straight as a ribbon to the haze, you find yourself one moment oppressed by the desolation and silence, the next hugely liberated by the vast, unfettered space.

Climate

Somewhere around an invisible line between the towns of Beaufort West and Graaff-Reinet, the Great Karoo crosses the climactic zone between summer and winter rainfall. The western Karoo, from the Hex River mountains to Beaufort West, is the winter rainfall area. East of Beaufort West, rain falls in summer. In general the west is drier. The mountain ranges of both regions become very cold on winter nights and in the Sneeuberg, in the far-eastern Karoo, snowfalls are common on the highest peaks. Summers in both regions are very hot, with temperatures often exceeding 40°C, but it is a dry heat and easy to bear, provided you do not over exert yourself in the middle of the day.

Flora and Fauna

In places the Karoo is still surprisingly rich in wildlife, particularly in the protected reserves, though this is a shadow of the former numbers—until the mid-19th-century, migrating herds of springbok in excess of two million animals used to cross the Karoo. Today, kudu, gemsbok, Cape mountain zebra, mountain reedbuck, black wildebeest, klipspinger, duiker and springbok (still to be found in large herds in places) are the most common species. A few reserves harbour white rhino, the occasional cheetah (in the Bo-Karoo), eland, hartebeest and blesbok, while leopard and caracal are present through most of the mountain ranges, whether conserved or not.

Recently many Karoo farmers, concerned at the desertification of their land by sheep, have begun replacing their sheep farms with hunting ranches. While game ranching is by no means widespread, the trend may well result in a general increase in Karoo game populations in the next few years.

Birdlife includes large raptors, such as black eagle and secretary birds in the mountain areas, blue and crowned cranes by the dams and vleis (they often stop for water on their long, migratory flights). Ostrich are common, and there is a host of smaller species, including rarities like sand grouse and white-faced owl.

Look out for some of the more spectacular invertabrate life, like baboon spiders (a kind of tarantula), scorpions and solugifids, or 'sun spiders', fearsome-looking arachnids that hunt lizards and have the most powerful jaws in the invertabrate world.

Plant life is specially adapted to the Karoo's low rainfall; aloes, euphorbias and other water retaining species (collectively known as 'succulents') have to survive the extreme heat of summer (up to 45°C) and sub-zero winter nights of hard frost. The Karoo's present super-arid appearance is largely due to overgrazing by sheep. A visit to one of the nature reserve or hunting ranches reveals a very different landscape of dry grasses—the Karoo can support a large number of indigenous grazers without becoming overgrazed.

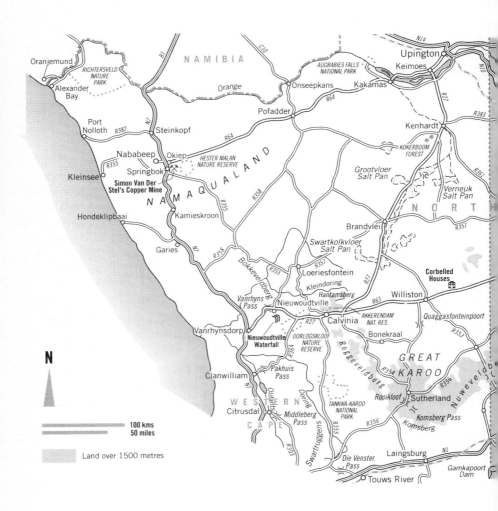

N

100 kms
50 miles

Land over 1500 metres

Cultivated land is very uncommon, owing to the low rainfall, but where there is sufficient underground water, you will be surprised to see small fields of alfalfa in the middle of the semi-desert.

The Western Karoo (Hantams Region)

The Western Karoo begins north of the Cape mountain ranges that form the northern extent of the Winelands and Little Karoo. To the west, it ends at the great Cedarberg Mountains that run parallel to the West Coast, eventually merging into Namaqualand in the northwest, near the border with Namibia. The region gets its name from the Hantams mountains around the small farming town of Calvinia, roughly the Western Karoo's central point. One of the most sparsely populated areas of South Africa, the Hantams region is full of solitude and space.

History

Unlike the rest of South Africa, the western Karoo's past is relatively easy to trace. San (bushmen) and wandering Khoi tribes followed the seasonal game migrations that crossed the area for thousands of years before the arrival of the first white hunters.

The first white settlers were generally trekking further east, towards the Fish River country, and took a route via the Karoo because the coastal routes east from the Cape were too thickly forested for easy travelling. Some stopped here and built homesteads around sites of permanent water, which brought them into immediate conflict with the Khoi and San, generally dispossessing the former and driving the latter into the mountains.

Game tended to congregate around these watering points and the trekboers slaughtered the herds both for meat and to protect their sheep herds. Deprived of the game on which they depended, the San began raiding farm stock and through the 18th and early 19th centuries, fought a running war with the settlers, coming down from the mountains at night to raid, and vanishing back into the kloofs by day. In some places, like the eastern Sneeuberg mountains (*see* '**Eastern Karoo** History'), they were sufficiently effective to force many burghers to abandon their farms.

The settlers retaliated with counter-raids. At first these were simply expeditions to recover lost stock, but by the 1750s the Boers and their Khoi servants were snatching San men, women and children to work on their farms. But the San would only work until their new masters became used to them, then simply escape into the great emptiness. Meanwhile the stock raiding continued and the Boers began to turn their raids into murdering sprees. Hunting the bushmen seems to have become something of a sport; accounts from the 1790s to the 1850s even tell of the 'bag' accounted for at the end of a trip. The 18th-century traveller Anders Sparman wrote, 'Does a colonist at any time get sight of a Boshieman, he takes fire immediately and spirits up his horses and dogs, in order to hunt him with more ardour and fury than he would a wild beast.' The Boers spared the young children, who they trained as farmworkers. By the 1860s the San had been annihilated or pushed north towards the unsettled Kalahari Desert. From this point on, the western Karoo lapsed into a kind of rural, apolitical vacuum. Even during the Anglo-Boer War little happened, barring a brief occupation of Calvinia by Boer commandos, who skirmished a few times with the British columns before surrendering in 1902. Since then neither the western Karoo farmers, nor their workers seems to have taken much interest in politics, though this was probably more a matter of lack of opportunity than desire.

Even through the intensely violent years building up to the 1994 elections, the Western Karoo remained somehow remote, both by culture and by geographical distance. Today, as ever, the region pursues its timeless course and makes a peaceful change from the hustle and energy of the country's more populated regions.

Getting There

The main route is via the N1. From the south this includes a spectacular climb up through the Winelands to Worcester and on over the Hex River mountains to **Touws River**. Most of the main Karoo roads, many of which are dirt or gravel, lead due north from the N1 into the Hantams. The other way in is over the Swartberg Pass from the Little Karoo to Beaufort West, the region's only large town, through which the N1 also runs.

The Southern Fringe

Before heading into the Hantams proper, it is worth detouring east along the N1 to **Matjiesfontein** (pronounced 'Mikeysfontein'). Visible south of the N1, Matjiesfontein is, like many Karoo towns, a Victorian set piece. Founded in the 1880s as a health spa (the dry air being good for chest complaints), Matjiesfontein attracted a fashionable international crowd for a few years. Centrepiece of the town's high Victorian architecture is the **Lord Milner Hotel**, a museum piece that was used as a military hospital during the Anglo-Boer War and still takes guests. The story of the hotel and of the few Victorian celebreties that came here for their health is told in the nearby jumbled and eccentric **Matjiesfontein Museum**.

The R354 heads due north from Matjiesfontein, over the tall buttresses of the **Komsberg Mountains** to the small town of **Sutherland**, famous for some of the coldest winter temperatures in South Africa, and for the clarity of its night skies (there is a small observatory in the town).

An alternative route north is via **Hottentotskloof** (west from the N1 on the R46 southwest of Touws River, then north on the R355). This long, lonely road leads to Calvinia, running along the western edge of the **Roggeveldberg Mountains** and passing one of the Karoo's more interesting guest farms, **Elandsvlei**, site of one of the Cape's few Anglo-Boer War skirmishes. The antelope that gave the farm its name have long since gone, but smaller game can be spotted on the farm's walking and riding trails (*see* 'Activities').

Some 70km further north, the emptiness flows up to the **Hantamsberg**, under which huddles **Calvinia**, which, though quiet, is a large town by Karoo standards. Calvinia is one of the few towns in the western Karoo to have played any direct part in South African history. During the Anglo-Boer War, the town's 'coloured' population, having long suffered at the hands of their Afrikaner 'employers', became open supporters of the British. One Abraham Esau, a leading light of

Calvinia's 'coloured' community, tried to organize a small defence force to be on hand in the event of any Boer attack, but was refused by the local British magistrate, who feared it might excite rebellion among the district's Afrikaner farmers. In early 1901 a Boer commando did enter the town, unopposed except for a force raised by Esau, which attacked with whatever was to hand. They were quickly beaten off, and the Boers, perhaps alarmed by this unexpected 'native' resistance, began a reign of terror, flogging and incarcerating 'coloureds' on flimsy charges. Many local farmers relished the chance to take the 'coloureds' down a peg, especially Esau Abraham, who was regarded as a 'cheeky hottentot'. They kidnapped him and handed him over to Nieuwoudt, the Boer commandant. Over a period of about a week, Abrahams was publically flogged and beaten, then finally dragged by his heels from a horse and shot. Ironically, the Boer occupation only lasted another week, when the commando left town in front of an approaching British column.

Today, Calvinia is one of the Karoo's main sheep-breeding centres, although it has none of the bustle one would normally associate with a prosperous market town. There are some handsome buildings on the wide, dusty streets, including the **Hantam Huis** on Main Street (*open Mon–Fri 9.30–1, 2–4.30*), a museum of Victorian life (with ex-fashion boutique mannequins dressed in bonnets and shawls to add an inauthentic note), and a small restaurant and craft shop selling the usual pottery, wooden spoons, veldskoens and Boer preserves.

The **Calvinia Museum** (*open Mon–Fri 9–1, 2–5*) ranks as one of the most eccentric in the country. Housed in the roomy Old Synagogue (the town's Jewish population drifted to the cities long ago), the museum includes such gems as a biscuit tin struck by lightning inside a local farm kitchen, which hurled the farmer's wife across the floor, and a stuffed sheep with wool so long that it trails the ground. This was a farm escapee that lived wild on the Hantamsberg for some 15 years, dodging leopard, lynx and all attempts to catch it. It finally died peacefully on the mountain.

Akkerendam Nature Reserve, 4km north of town, takes in part of the Hantamsberg, the southern slopes of which form an amphitheatre of red rock. From here two walking trails overlook the brown and red Calvinia flats, in which the Akkerendam itself makes an inviting circle of blue. Gravel roads bisect the reserve. Expect to see springbok and perhaps mountain reedbuck and duiker. Migrating waterfowl stop at the dam and, though fenced off, it also makes a welcome swimming hole after a hot walk on the mountain. The reserve has no accommodation.

There is no road north from Calvinia. The R355 (gravel) and R27 (tar) go west 100 lonely kilometres to the towns of Nieuwoudtville and Loeriesfontein in Namaqualand. East of town, the tarred R27 bears north into country that becomes flat and desolate, opening into vast white salt pans north of the little town of **Brandvlei** (meaning 'burnt lake'). The town—a few baking hot streets of ugly buildings—does not warrant a visit, except perhaps as an example of somewhere you would not want to live, and as a pit-stop for drinks and petrol. The R27 then runs straight as an arrow 150km across the **salt pans** to Kenhardt, in Bushmanland. The largest pan, named Grootvloer, was the scene of Sir

Malcolm Campbell's tragic 1929 attempt to break the land speed record in his car, the *Bluebird*, which tipped over, killing him. This incredibly barren area was also the unlikely scene of one of the Anglo-Boer War's lesser-known campaigns when, in 1902, General 'Mannie' Maritz led his commando into the region in an attempt to forge a supply-line into South West Africa (Namibia). In order to stay one step ahead of the British, Maritz stayed in the Karoo, somehow finding enough water and food in the waterless, scorched landscape, until the Boer surrender at Vereegening allowed him and his exhausted troops to come in from the veld. Maritz was unhappy with the surrender and later joined the Boers' last, ill-fated revolt against British rule in 1910 (*see* **South African History**).

Just over 100km due east of Calvinia the tiny, quiet town of **Williston** is built around a huge sandstone church that used to attract up to 400 farmers every Sunday, who would drive a horse and cart as far as 90km to attend the service and chat with their 'neighbours'. Today, most 'coloured' farm-workers still use horse and donkey carts to travel these distances; the carts you pass on the roads may be making journeys of several days. The church still attracts a good 100 or so locals, demonstrating the continuing power of the Bible in this biblical landscape. Williston is very old-fashioned; one or two of the older Boer women still wear Victorian sun-bonnets. Horses and carts are more common on the streets than cars, largely because the 'coloured' population greatly exceeds the white. There is a small open-air **swimming pool** where you can float in cool water under the red hills. Swifts and swallows swoop to drink as you revel in the water after a dry, dusty drive.

The farms around Williston are known for their many surviving **corbelled houses**. These, the first permanent structures put up by the trekboers that settled the area in the early to mid 1800s, resemble celtic brochs in construction; flat stones piled one atop the other in a conical beehive shape. The one-roomed dwellings, which would have housed the entire family and servants, have hard floors of beaten dung. **Arbeidsfontein**, a farm 30km east of town, has the most easily accessible corbelled house, now a national monument. The owners, the Esterhuizens, have farmed Arbeidsfontein for over a hundred years and their ancestors used to inhabit the sparsely furnished corbelled house. By permission, they occasionally allow visitors to stay the night (*see* 'Where to Stay').

From Williston you can either head east 140km to Carnarvon, a small town set among high mesas rising from a flat plain, or southeast on the R353 to **Fraserburg**, a well-known fossil site. The **Fraserburg Museum** on Main Street (which also doubles as the local tourist information office; *open Mon–Fri 8–12 and 2–5, closed Wed pm*), has displays of fossilized skulls and eggs of very early (pre-Triassic) dinosaurs found on local farms. The museum issues a map of where to see **dinosaur footprints** on a farm 1km north of town on the Williston road, and the woman at the Tourist Office can also arrange visits to farms in the **Nuweveldberg Mountains** south of town, on which there are hidden waterfalls and herds of game, despite the apparent dryness.

The R353 south of Fraserburg leads through the Nuweveldberg back to the N1. If you have time, take the dirt road west to **Merweville**, another tiny town about 70km south of Fraserburg. About 40km through the low hill country east of Merweville, is **Nova Vita**, a farm offering five **walking trails** through the wild hills around.

Once back on the N1 highway, one can either head west back to Cape Town or east to the Western Karoo's largest town, **Beaufort West**. Beaufort West itself is a traditional pit-stop for drivers travelling from the Cape to Johannesburg, and as such the main street is quite busy. There are some handsome 19th-century buildings, including the **Museum Complex** on Donkin Street (*open Mon–Fri 9–5*) which has pioneer displays. The complex also doubles as the Tourist Information Office.

 The **Karoo National Park** covers much of the Nuweldberg mountain country north and west of town. It is interesting to note the difference in vegetation between the park and the farms on the other side of the game fence. The park is covered in grass, while the surrounding farms only support low Karoo-scrub—a direct result of over-grazing and an illustration of how the Karoo might have looked when only game wandered its expanses.

The park supports a lot of game. Cape mountain zebra, red haartebeest, mountain reed-buck, gemsbok, springbok (including the larger sub-species of Kalahari springbok), grey rhebok, steenbok, duiker, klipspringer, kudu and ostrich are common. Leopard and lynx stalk the kloofs and dry river beds. Bat-eared fox and jackal come out at dusk. The rare blue crane (South Africa's national bird) often uses the park as a foraging spot.

Leaving Beaufort West for the north, the **Molteno Pass**, on the R381 north towards the town of Loxton, is surprisingly well vegetated. Great boulders jut from grass-covered hill-sides and here and there are even small planted woodlands. The northern entrance to the Karoo National Park is on the left, about 5km after the head of the pass. To the right stretches a vast private game farm, so expect to see antelope on either side of the road, especially at evening.

Prince Albert, about 140km south of Beaufort West, is the last town in the Great Karoo before the mighty Swartberg mountains. Another well-preserved 19th-century town, its **Fransie Pienaar Musuem** (*open Mon–Fri 9.30–1, 2–5*) is a gem; an intimate history of the town, it includes children's exercise books from the turn of the century until the 1930s, badly stuffed local reptiles, weapons and other memorabilia. There is an old **water-mill** just north of town on a tributary of the Gamka River, which flows down from the

Swartberg, whose dark wall rises behind the town. The mill and stream contrast oddly with the dry country stretching north of town.

Activities

Hiking: Elandsvlei, ✆ (0273) 411712, a guest farm on the R355 south of Calvinia has walking trails, while **Akkerendam Nature Reserve** has two hiking trails—one gentle (4km), one quite demanding (10km)—through the low Karoo scrub. **The Karoo National Park**, ✆ (0201) 52828, has several walking and hiking trails; the **Fossil Trail** and **Bossie Trail** are very short, paved strolls with labelled fossils and Karoo plants on view. There is also an 11km hike up into the first dry kloofs and river beds near the camp, a 7km hike on the highlands (reached by another entrance to the park on the R381 north of town), and the 3-day **Springbok Trail**, complete with overnight huts, though this is not open during the blistering summer months.

Riding: Riding is offered at Elandsvlei Farm, *see* above.

Where to Stay

expensive

The **Lord Milner Hotel**, Matjiesfontein, ✆ (0220) 3, is a set piece of late Victoriana in a town that is a living museum of the period. Built in the early 1900s as a spa hotel—for clean, dry air, rather than for mineral baths—its original interior has been carefully preserved, even down to the bath taps. Further south, the **Prince Albert Protea**, ✆ (04436) 332, is an old Victorian hotel south of Prince Albert with only 20 rooms. A little bland inside, as are all the hotels of this chain, the rooms are clean and comfortable rather than luxurious. There is good access to the Swartberg mountains and Little Karoo, and a swimming pool.

moderate

Karoo National Park, ✆ (0201) 52828/9, has self-catering thatched chalets built in Cape Dutch style around a swimming pool, under the Nuweveldberg mountains. The park entrance is about 10km west of Beaufort West on the N1. **Elandsvlei Guest Farm**, ✆ (0273) 411712, is about 60km south of Calvinia on the dirt R355. The farm has game and a house built into a cave for visitors. Self-catering or farm cooking are offered. The **Dorphuis** on Main St in Calvinia, ✆ (0273) 411606/059, is a small Victorian townhouse still furnished in period style; big brass beds, lithographs and polished wooden floors. Self-catering or farm cooking are offered.

De Rust Gasthuis, ✆ (02052) 2104, is a small, 4-bedroomed farmhouse 11km along the Sutherland road from Williston. Its small restaurant is possibly one of the most authentic for Cape country cooking in South Africa.

BrakRivier Guest House, ✆ (02052) 2104, 70km from Calvinia on the R364 towards Clanwilliam, is another lonely guest farm surrounded by the wide, hot emptiness. There are good walks on the farm, and, of all things, a tennis court. **Meltonwold Guest Farm**, ✆ (02042) 1430 just outside Victoria West has very good value accommodation in the middle bracket of the moderate scale. You can walk on the farm, ride the horses, swim or play tennis.

cheap

Vine Lodge, 23 Meintjies St, Beaufort West, ✆ (0201) 51055, is useful for breaking a trans-Karoo journey. There are no frills, but the dormitory and double rooms are clean and comfortable.

Arbeidsfontein, a farm 30km east of Williston, has a corbelled house whose owners occasionally allow visitors to sleep there if asked politely, and may even provide water and firewood. There is an old brass bed covered with a kaross (skin blanket), a beaten earth floor and a candle for light. The owners normally refuse payment, but a donation is polite. There is no telephone.

All the above towns have **camp sites**, as does the Karoo National Park. More interesting is to camp on farms in the veld, but always ask first. Often you will end up being given a beautiful spot for free, and maybe even supper with the family.

Eating Out

The Western Karoo has few restaurants, except for those attached to hotels, and take-away places. All the accommodation listed above provide food, except for Arbeidsfontein. Make sure you try the Karoo mutton, which is sweet with the flavours of the wild herbs and Karoo-scrub upon which the local sheep graze. Justly famed throughout South Africa, Karoo mutton is as organic as farmed meat can be, has very little fat, but is tender as a good steak. The **De Rust Gasthuis**, *see* 'Where to Stay', serves some of the best Karoo mutton specialities, such as sheep's tails in mustard sauce, sheep's head and *spitbraaid* sheep as well as the Boer breads and cakes such as *vetkoek* and *roosterbread*. The **Matjiesfontein Museum Coffee Shop,** next door to the museum, is little changed inside since the 1900s, and a good place for a drink and a light meal before ploughing on into the interior.

The Eastern Karoo

And like other deserts and semi-deserts, ours is a country of life. The squat, fat, angled plants; the hunting spiders that flicker between them; the ground squirrels upright beside their burrows; the vultures; the pale gladioli; the cobras, the scorpions; the mantis coloured like a flower; the black beetles rolling balls of dung. Here moves a steenbok, a duiker, a springbok, a lark clapping its wings above us; here are the tracks of an antbear (aardvark) in the soil; red dust and a mottled egg upon it; arrowheads; the smell of rain; Karoo bush, wild asparagus, mountains and hills floating in a mirage of water; a white hot sky; the sound of cicadas and wings and wind.

Plains of the Camdeboo, Eve Palmer

With a higher rainfall than the Western Karoo, this landscape is better vegetated and richer in game. The towns are larger and the farms more prosperous. The Nuweveldberg, Bankberg and Sneeuberg mountains are higher than those in the west, one range crumpling into another towards the distant Drakensberg, whose foothills, the Bamboesberg, fall into the northeastern corner of the Great Karoo, beyond the town of Cradock. However, the Karoo's wide emptiness still prevails.

Between the Sneeuberg mountains and the Orange River is an area known as the **Bo-Karoo**, meaning Upper Karoo, forms a triangle between the towns of Prieska, Colesberg and Victoria West. Until recently, the Bo-Karoo ranked as one of South Africa's least known regions, a vast back-country of semi-desert farms.

History

As in the Western Karoo, the Khoi and San were masters of the region until late-18th-century trekboers on their way to the Eastern Cape frontier stopped and laid out farms by the springs and permanent water sites. Many trekboers settled the mountain slopes of the Nuweweldberg, Sneeuberg and Bankberg, fighting, enslaving and gradually absorbing the Khoi into their farms and annihilating the San, who raided their cattle .

The Dutch East India Company, ever desirous of bringing the trekboers back under colonial control, founded a magistracy at Graaff-Reinet in 1786 and appointed a *landdrost*. By then trekboers had already settled far beyond, in the Xhosa country of the Eastern Cape, and were busy trading, raiding and hunting there. The little village of Graaff-Reinet had to administer the whole Eastern Karoo and much of the Eastern Cape coast, a vast, anarchic region of Khoi, San, Xhosa and trekboer, all jostling to keep their semi-nomadic lifestyles intact.

The frontier trekboers were a rough bunch. Their cruelty to their Khoi servants (who less than a generation before had been freeholders of the land) became legendary. By the mid 1790s, increasing frustration with their inability to crush the San caused them to drift eastward at the same time as the Xhosa, drifting west, were entering the Eastern Karoo.

The frontier Boers forced the first Graaff-Reinet *landdrost* to form official commandos to attack the Xhosa. However, *landdrost* Maynier (the second Graaff-Reinet *landdrost*) was a liberal product of the enlightenment. Known to have sympathy for the Khoi, he enforced the Company's edicts that farmers guilty of ill-treating their Khoi servants should be punished. The resentful Boers, under Adriaan Van Jaarsveld, Marthinius Prinsloo and Conraad De Buys, rebelled against the Company and expelled Maynier in 1795.

The Company retaliated by cutting off all supplies of powder and shot to Graaff-Reinet. When Britain annexed the Cape Colony in 1796, the Boers allied with them against the Company. The British demanded unconditional surrender from the Boers which they got in 1797. Van Jaasveld and Prinsloo were imprisoned but Conraad De Buys escaped and went to live among the Xhosa, where he became a principal courtier to the frontier chief Ngqika, before finally heading north into the Transvaal, where he settled in the Soutpansberg mountains.

In 1799 and again in 1813 the Graaff-Reinet Boers rebelled against the British, even attempting to get support from the western Xhosa. But they failed; after a short campaign the new British-appointed *landdrost* captured the ringleaders. Their trial three took years, but they were hanged in 1816 on a ridge called Slagters Nek, an event that engendered early hatred between Boers and the British government (*see* **Eastern Cape** 'History').

Meanwhile, during the 1799 rebellion, many Khoi saw their opportunity in the chaos and ran away from their brutal 'employers'. They formed their own rebel army and joined the Xhosa in the Zuurveld, near present-day Port Elizabeth. The British, already using Khoi in their own colonial forces at Graaff-Reinet (a cavalry regiment called the Cape Corps), were suddenly caught in a confused position as referee to the Boer, Khoi and Xhosa power struggle.

After a hard but inconclusive campaign many rebel Khoi were persuaded by the British to return to the Eastern Karoo. But they feared retribution and mostly converged on Graaff-Reinet, so as to be under the protection of *landdrost* Maynier, who the British had re-appointed. The Boers foresaw renewed attacks. Armed burghers from all over the region rode to Graaff-Reinet and demanded that the British Khoi soldiers (the Cape Corps) and the great mass of ex-rebels be dispersed. Maynier managed to placate them but the continued plunder of the Eastern Karoo farms by isolated bands of rebel Khoi caused the Boers to besiege Graaff-Reinet in 1801.

The British again put this down, but Khoi bandits remained on the loose. Events became even more confused when the British handed the Cape back to the Dutch. In 1803 the Boer commandos failed to quell a resurgence of Khoi rebellion, which renewed panic among the settlers and caused mass abandonment of many farms. The new Dutch Governor subdued the rebels by granting their leaders land on the colony's frontier. However, much of the abandoned farmland had now been occupied by roving Xhosa bands. When the British returned to the Cape and to Graaff-Reinet in 1806, and expelled the Xhosa by force, they became locked into a series of Frontier Wars with the Xhosa that were to last into the 1870s. However, the scene of the fighting soon shifted east to the country around the Fish River and after the 1820s Graaff-Reinet and the Eastern Karoo ceased to be so strategically important.

Graaff-Reinet settled into its modern existence as a prosperous agricultural centre. The Eastern Karoo Boers continued their warring with the San in the Sneeuberg mountains, finally annihilating them by attrition in the 1860s and '70s. Many of the Khoi drifted north, away from the Boers, to the free country around the Orange River, and their place on the farms was gradually taken by Xhosa, who continued to drift west despite, or sometimes because of, the continuing Frontier Wars. By the turn of the century the Eastern Karoo was as much Xhosa as Afrikaner, though small pockets of Khoi (by now much mixed with white blood and generally referred to as 'coloured') remained—and still do remain—in the smaller farming settlements.

Today, the Eastern Karoo is something of a peaceful backwater, but its largest towns—Graaff-Reinet and Cradock—have a great support for the ANC among the farmworkers. Whether this will eventually result in a white/black sharing of land in the Karoo, or whether the tradition of white farmer and black labourer will continue, is open to speculation. Certainly it is hard to imagine the wide, empty spaces as the scene of political strife.

Getting There

By road: Three main roads cut across the Eastern Karoo; the N1 between Beaufort West and Colesberg, the R57 between Colesberg and Aberdeen (along which route lies Graaff-Reinet, the region's centre) and the N10 between Middleburg and Cradock. The Bo-Karoo is bisected by the N12 between the Orange River (at Hopetown) and Victoria West.

By bus: Graaff-Reinet and Cradock can be reached direct by bus from Johannesburg or Port Elizabeth, and Colesberg can be reached from Johannesburg and Cape Town. Local transport by black taxi can be risky, and travellers should either hire a car in Graaff-Reinet or Colesberg or try to arrange local lifts through the tourist information offices.

By rail: Beaufort West can be reached by train from Johannesburg or Cape Town, with a bus connection through to Graaff-Reinet.

Graaff-Reinet

The late-18th century frontier town and original administrative capital for the Eastern Cape is now a quiet farming town and tourist draw. Huddled around the Sundays River, one of the few perennial rivers to flow through the Karoo (though it is often little more than a trickle), Graaff-Reinet has little in its present atmosphere to suggest the town's turbulent early history.

Early Graaff-Reinet was described by one British officer as a 'miserable collection of dusty cottages'. It did not prosper until the 1800s, two decades after its founding, when the colony's eastern frontier had moved deep into the present Eastern Cape, and the town's oldest buildings date from this time. Many of the old buildings survive, making Graaff-Reinet one of the most architecturally attractive towns in South Africa. White-washed cottages and houses, some humble, some grand, make up the central streets, while the surrounding residential neighbourhoods are late-19th and early-20th century. The only modern buildings are on the edges of town.

The high hills that rise on three sides of the town are conserved as wild country by the large Karoo Nature Reserve, which includes the Valley of Desolation west of town. To the south stretch the hot, dusty plains of Camdeboo.

Parsonage Street, in the very centre of town, has been declared a national monument. A perfectly preserved early-19th century Cape Dutch street, the buildings are all still in use.

Reinet House on Parsonage Street, (*open daily 9–5*), was built in 1812. A splendidly-proportioned mansion with (unusually for Cape Dutch manors) a grand ornamental staircase leading to the front door, the interior, with its yellowwood ceilings, stinkwood floors and period furniture, is now a museum. More interesting is the cobbled yard at the back, which has (reputedly) the world's largest grapevine (and it is huge) and a pioneer farming museum in the outbuildings.

The **Residency** (*open Mon–Fri 9–5*), another manor house from the same period, contains a museum of early-19th century life, including a collection of hunting rifles. Worth looking at are the heavy, unwieldly large-bore muskets that the early ivory hunters used in their semi-legal forays into Xhosa country. Given the intelligence and agility of the great animals, and the inefficiency of the guns, it is easy to see why early big-game hunters had such short life expectancy.

The **Drostdy** on Church Street was the first residence of the *landdrost* (though the present building, built on the original site, dates from only 1806) and is now a hotel. The building is simple, gracious and well-proportioned—typical of its designer, Thibault (*see* '**Cape Town** History'). **Stretch's Court**, behind the main building, is a small street of elegant early-19th century cottages that are now self-contained suites of the hotel. The **Reinet Museum** (*open Mon–Fri 9–12, 2–5*) is on the corner of Church Street and Somerset Street. Its most interesting exhibits are the fossil and early dinosaur bones collected from the area, ranging from small molluscs to large skulls and semi-intact skeletons, and an explanation of the formation of the Karoo-shale strata from which the fossils come. Around the walls of the main room are enlarged reproductions of the some of the finest San art currently known.

The **Hester Rupert Art Museum**, a few doors down from the Reinet Museum, (*open Mon–Fri 9–1, 2–5*), houses a mediocre collection of South African paintings, mostly by white artists imitating European styles. However, there are some emotive Karoo landscapes, an unusual subject in traditional South African landscape paintings, where Cape and Drakensberg scenes are more the norm. The **Jan Rupert Centre** on Middle Street is a craft workshop producing woven goods from the local Merino sheep wool, using dyes produced from Karoo plants. The project was started about 10 years ago as unemployment relief for the local Xhosa and it seems to have been commercially successful. There is also some pottery and woodwork.

The Karoo Nature Reserve and Valley of Desolation

The Karoo Nature Reserve comprises all the land immediately north, west and east of the town, over 30,000 acres. High, aloe-covered hills predominate, though there is a grass-covered plain north of town, past the Graaff-Reinet dam and camp site. Inside the reserve kudu, bontebok, black wildebeest, springbok, reedbuck, duiker and steenbok are the most common game species. Less numerous are eland and red hartebeest. Look out for bat-eared fox and secretary birds.

The reserve is divided into three parts: the western section includes the high Spandau Kop and Valley of Desolation; the middle section comprises the central plain and game-viewing roads; the eastern section includes Hangklip mountain and an overnight hiking trail with a sleeping hut. The **Valley of Desolation**, a deep, narrow gorge in the mountains above Graaff-Reinet, is what most people come to see. Walk or drive up a steep mountain road about 2km northwest of town to reach the look-out point, from which great, sweeping views stretch away to the south over the Camdeboo. Immediately below the look-out point runs the deep gash of the Valley of Desolation. A hiking trail leads down through it, while the shorter **Cape Crag trail**, named after a lizard species found only in the Valley of Desolation, winds along the ridge from the look-out point. Hikers are likely to see game if they are quiet. Look out for vervet monkeys and dassies.

Nieu Bethesda and the Sneeuberg Mountains

About 60km north of Graaff-Reinet, at the foot of the great Sneeuberg range, is a fertile, isolated valley watered by a tributary of the Sundays River. The village is divided into two; the old white section has a population of just 23, whereas 400 live in the 'coloured' location on the hillside above. There is a great feeling of peace in Nieu Bethesda, perhaps because of the green valley, a relief to the eye after the endless browns, ochres and reds of the Karoo, or perhaps because of the high, encircling mountains and the resulting quiet.

Nieu Bethesda has no tarred road (though its dirt road south connects with the R57 after 23 mountainous kilometres), but the tiny place is famous in South Africa for having been the home of **Helen Martins**, a reclusive sculptor whose house in the village, known as the **Owl House**, has become a strange monument to her half-biblical, half-occult view of the world. When Martins came to live at Nieu Bethesda in the 1950s she began to transform her garden into an outdoor studio, working in concrete to produce naive figures. Some have an obvious biblical origin, such as her Three Wise Men and their camels. Others are moon-worshippers, and are constructed around poems written in letters cut from metal and hung on griddle frames. Everywhere there are owl sculptures, inside the house and out.

Martins and her eccentric life have been the object of much scrutiny. One play about her suggests that she supported herself through quiet prostitution to local burghers. Other sources refute this, suggesting that she and her 'coloured' servant (in fact her friend and helper) were having an affair. Others again say this was nonsense. However, her work attracted enough attention during her life to ensure its loving conservation and, after initial rejection by those seeking to conserve the house, Martins' 'coloured' friend, who in her arthritic old age became her hands for the last sculptures, now helps to maintain the Owl House.

Nieu Bethesda gets a steady trickle of pilgrims to the Owl House every year, and some similarly artistic recluses have settled in the village or on the farms outside. At the full moon every January there is a festival of music and dance, loosely organized and informally run, to which young hippies, musicians, New Agers and generally interested people come. But there has been no development around the Martins myth and on an average day in Nieu Bethesda there will be very few people. The village remains remote, jewel-like in its greenery, and isolated behind its hills and bad roads.

The **Sneeuberg Mountains** rising to the north of the village were for over 100 years a bastion against northern colonial expansion. The San used it as an impregnable natural fortress in their incessant raiding wars with the Boer settlers, who gave up trying to penetrate the country beyond the range between the 1700s and the 1870s. The name means 'snow mountains', and indeed, despite the dry Karoo climate, these mountains see snow most winters. Their highest peak, the **Compassberg**, rises close to Nieu Bethesda, while the main massif rolls away wild for almost 100km beyond. The Sneeuberg have some perennial springs, and hence good game populations. Hiking and riding trails into the Sneeuberg have been organised by the local farmers (*see* 'Activities' and 'Where to Stay').

The Bo-Karoo

The Bo-Karoo is hardly geared for even the most basic of tourism. However, the very small town of **Orania**, on the banks of the Orange River near Hopetown, is of interest to those fascinated by the more eccentric political vagaries of the country. Orania was the subject of a well-known Channel 4 television documentary (produced in England in 1990) about life among radical right-wing Afrikaners. It is also the proposed capital of the Boer Homeland that many right-wing groups are demanding. A word of warning: Orania is a working town that has been beset by visitors since the less-than-flattering documentary. Avoid gawping at people. More important still, avoid making political statements, which will at best be met with indifference. Afrikaner tempers can be short.

 Colesberg, founded in 1829, is just off the N1 at the southeast end of the Bo-Karoo. If you are making a Cape Town–Transvaal trip, break it at Colesberg. Perhaps more than Graaff-Reinet, this town evokes the isolated feel of the early Karoo towns, and many of the buildings are national monuments. It was founded by the British in an attempt to pacify the once anarchic and violent frontier region of TransOrangia (the country around and north of the Orange River), which at the time was populated partly by wandering bands of 'Bastaards', groups of free half-white, half-Khoi people who could find no place in colonial society. They were later renamed 'Griqua' by missionaries who found 'Bastaard' distasteful. The rest of the sparse population was made up of free Khoi fleeing their cruel Boer masters, Boers fleeing the British, and errant bands of Xhosa and Tswana warriors. Raid and counter-raid of the different groups' herds, pastured on the fertile islands in the middle of the river gave the area an almost mythical reputation for lawlessness (*see* 'Bushmanland' and 'West Griqualand History').

Unlike Graaff-Reinet, Colesberg never expanded beyond its original size, even once the area had settled down in the mid-19th century. Its bright, white-washed buildings reflecting the harsh sunlight are reminiscent of the Mediterranean.

Doornkloof and **Rolfontein Nature Reserves** are two large, seldom-visited reserves set close to each other on the west bank of the P. K. le Roux Dam on the Orange River (reached by the R369 north of Colesberg). Doornkloof—which covers more than 10,000ha—is remarkable for having woodland in some of its sharp riverside kloofs; woodland is almost unheard of in the Karoo. The reserve supports kudu, reedbuck and small antelope such as duiker. Baboons and vervet monkeys are also common. Waterfowl live in the reedbanks and trees along the dam's shore, and look out for fish eagles. There is no accommodation. Rolfontein, about 20km north of Doornkloof, is half the size of its neighbour, but supports more game, including big animals such as white rhino, zebra, eland, kudu and blesbok. There are also a few shy cheetah still living here. Like Doornkloof, Rolfontein has some kloof and riverine woodland.

Oviston Nature Reserve lies on the south shore of another Orange River dam, the Hendrik Vervwoerd Dam, reached by the R58 from Colesberg. Oviston follows the dam's entire southern coastline, but only a limited area is open to visitors. There are herds of black wildebeest, springbok, blesbok and hartebeest. Ground squirrels are common, and their frenetic bursts of play (playing a very fast tag with tails held stiffly erect) are fun to watch. The reserve has a small, ugly town, **Oviston**, in the middle, with shops and a swimming pool that is blessed relief on a hot day. At the eastern end of the Hendrik Verwoerd Dam is another, larger reserve, **Tuissen Die Rivieren** (meaning 'meeting of rivers') where the Orange and Caledon rivers converge. This reserve is densely populated by game and has very good walking but is officially in the Orange Free State (*see* **Orange Free State**). **Victoria West**, at the southern end of the Bo-Karoo, straddles the N12. Although the town is unattractive, the **Victoria West Nature Reserve** just to the south makes a good place to stretch the legs if you are passing through. The reserve is home to Burchell's zebra, springbok, eland, black wildebeest, gemsbok and blesbok. There is no accommodation.

Cradock and the Mountain Zebra National Park

Cradock is another 19th-century set-piece, though with more modern building on its outskirts than Colesberg or Graaff-Reinet. Large by Karoo standards but small by any other, Cradock (named after Sir John Cradock, one of the first British Governors of the Cape) lies at the easternmost extent of the Eastern Karoo, just north of the unpopulated massifs of the Bankberg and Winterberg mountains on the N10 highway. Cradock is a very handsome town, but less quiet than others in the Karoo.

A very large black—mainly Xhosa—'location', lies just south of town along the N10. Unemployment here is high, and the poverty is obvious. By the roadside, children make and sell exquisitely-constructed wire windmills based on the kind that pump water above ground in the Karoo. These are unusual in South African township art, where wire bicycles and vehicles are the norm, and this will probably be your only chance to buy one.

The **Mountain Zebra National Park**, in the Bankberg mountains about 30km west of town, is one of the loneliest and most beautiful of South Africa's national parks. The Bankberg sweep away for over 100km of upland emptiness to Graaff-Reinet. Although the usual reds and ochres prevail, the park is far better vegetated than is normal for the region. Trees, grass-covered hillsides and Karoo-scrub make for a distinctive landscape. The wild country is inhabited by kudu, mountain reedbuck, eland, red hartebeest, black wildebeest, springbok, blesbok, klipspringer and, of course, the Cape mountain zebra that the park was formed to protect. Birds of prey are much in evidence, particularly black eagle (who feed on the many dassies), booted and martial eagles and eagle owls. Leopard and caracal are common, and there is a small research station into the hunting behaviour of these cats.

The village of **Aberdeen** is 55km southwest of Graaff-Reinet, where the R57 crosses the vast, flat, hot plains of Camdeboo en route for the Little Karoo. Popular among enthusiasts of late Victorian colonial architecture, the village's verandahed houses present an eclectic mix of styles with little turrets and half-timbered houses among the more orthodox Cape gables and tin roofs. Just west of town is **Aberdeen Nature Reserve**, under whose sweet thorn trees and Karoo-scrub are springbok, kudu, gemsbok, red hartebeest and black wildebeest.

Activities

Hiking: The Karoo Nature Reserve, ✆ (0491) 23453, has a 3-day trail to the east of town. Overnight huts, water and firewood are provided, but must be booked in advance. **Sneeuberg Farm Trails**, ✆ (04923) 749, run a network of guided and non-guided hiking and climbing routes. The 12 co-operating farmers are familiar with the mountains and their wildlife, San history and geology. The individual farms provide information about local **bushmen paintings**. **Trails of the Camdeboo**, ✆ (0491) 23046, is a similar set-up in hill country east of Graaff-Reinet offering hiking and good opportunities for wildlife photography. **Aberdeen Nature Reserve**, just west of Aberdeen, has a short trail. **Doornkloof Nature Reserve**, ✆ (051752) 1304, has good trails, including a **5-day trail** to Rolfontein reserve. **Rolfontein Nature Reserve**, ✆ (05782) 160, about 20km north of Doornkloof, has a guided 2-day trail and some shorter self-guided day walks. **Oviston Nature Reserve**, (0553) 50000), on the south shore of the Hendrik Verwoerd Dam has a 2-day trail, and various day walks. Short walking trails through the Karoo-scrub of the **Victoria West Nature Reserve** take you close to Burchell's zebra, springbok, eland, black wildebeest, gemsbok and blesbok. The **Mountain Zebra National Park**, ✆ (012) 343 1991, has a 3-day hiking trail. For those who don't want to hike (and the going is tough), there is a network of game-viewing roads and 1-day trails.

Riding: Sneeuberg Farm Trails, ✆ (04923) 749, and **Trails of the Camdeboo** near Graaff-Reinet, ✆ (0491) 23046, both offer riding trails of between half a day and several days (guided). The **Mountain Zebra National Park**, ✆ (012) 44 1194, also has horses for hire.

expensive

Thibault's **Drostdy**, on Church St, Graaff-Reinet, ✆ (0491) 22161, was built to house the *landdrost.* A street of early-19th century cottages behind the Drostdy (Stretch's Court) have been incorporated as self-contained suites. Guests can sit in a formal garden around a fountain, and there are two period-furnished restaurants serving Cape country and Karoo dishes, and specializing in Karoo lamb.

moderate

Cradock Tuinhuise, ✆ (0481) 5098, a terrace of old artisans' cottages in the centre of Cradock, give the feeling of staying inside an old pioneer museum. B&B is the main service, but evening meals can be arranged; the owners cook a good leg of mutton, Karoo-style with herbs and garlic.

Sneeuberg Farm Trails, north of Nieu Bethesda, offers accommodation on several farms, either self-catering or with home cooking. The most established are Gordonville and the Groenvlei Gasthuis. **Gordonville**, ✆ (04923) 727/720, the closest to Graaff-Reinet has game on the farm and offers riding. In the outbuildings is a wool-spinning workshop and the farmhouse has a library of 2000 books, many of which pertain to Africa. It has been in the same family since 1903. Further into the Sneeuberg, **Groenvlei Gasthuis**, ✆ (04925) 627, has no horses, but you can play tennis.

Trails of the Camdeboo offer similar facilities on farms in the hills east of Graaff-Reinet. **Camdeboo Safaris**, ✆ (0491) 23038, 50km east of Graaff-Reinet at Sondagsrivierhoek, is the largest guest farm on the list, offering good B&B or full board in chalets. **Pardjiesberg Farm**, ✆ (0491) 23050, is an old farmhouse that sleeps 7 and offers hiking, climbing, horses and hunting.

The only accommodation in the **Rolfontein Nature Reserve** is in the overnight hiking hut, which has water and firewood.

Fountains, ✆ (0424) 61492, is on Cranemere Farm, near Pearston, 75km east of Graaff-Reinet. A 4-bedroomed farmhouse, Fountains offers self catering accommodation (cook available), with walking trails, good birdwatching and game spotting.

Mountain Zebra National Park, just west of Cradock, ✆ (012) 343 1991 (between 9 and 4.45) has self-catering cottages for 4 or 6 in its rest camp. With the exchange rate, these work out to a moderate price for two. Very comfortable bedrooms set under the wild Bankberg mountains. The rest camp also has a pool and restaurant, as well as guest chalets.

West of Colesberg (7km along the Tzamenkomst road, then turn right at the red tractor and continue for 28k to the farm signpost) is **De Poort Guest Farm**, ✆ (051) 753 1323, an old farmstead offering excellent value B&B, farm walks, donkey-cart rides and other such delights, as well as the requisite space and silence you would expect from a Karoo farm.

The **Oviston Nature Reserve**, south of the Hendrik Verwoerd Dam, has untempting chalet accommodation or an overnight hut. However, Parks Board cottages can be found about 33km east, over the Free State's border at the eastern end of the dam, at **Tuissen Die Rivieren Nature Reserve** (*see* **Orange Free State**, 'Southwest'). If shared between a group, these self-contained cottages fall into the cheap category.

cheap

There is no budget accommodation as such, although all the towns and most of the nature reserves listed have **camp sites** with facilities, and there is always free camping on farms (with permission) if you have your own equipment.

Eating Out

 As with the Western Karoo, there are no listed restaurants other than fast food and take-away joints except in hotels, which usually have an à la carte restaurant serving tolerably good food.

The **Drostdy Restaurants** in Graaff-Reinet, ✆ (0491) 22161, warrant mention. These two restaurants in the old *landdrost*'s manor have long, spacious rooms with polished wooden floors and ceilings and are furnished in period. Karoo mutton is the house speciality. The atmosphere is friendly but formal. Expensive/moderate.

A good, very cheap eatery in Graaff-Reinet is the **Trail Inn** on Caledon St, which though unlicensed serves as a meeting point fot most of the town's youth and for many backpackers passing through. Pizzas are good value here, and the atmosphere is more that of a fun bar than a restaurant.

Nieu Bethesda has a **Coffee House and Restaurant** run by a single man in one of the village houses serving very cheap and very good home-made breads and holistic meals.

Namaqualand and the Richtersveld

> *'Father ... says, 'Ja-nee' with the sense of the equivocal born out of watching rainclouds gather over the earth and then disperse. 'Ja-nee', he repeats, 'that's a place now, hey!' and with a whistling extraction of marrow from the neck of the goat, he laughs the satisfied laugh of one who has come to see the hidden blessings of drought'*

> *You Can't Get Lost in Cape Town*, Zoe Wicomb

South Africa's far northwest is a semi-desert area with low winter rainfall, barely vegetated shale hills, giant aloe trees and bare rock. Namaqualand (named after the Nama, the Khoi tribe that originally inhabited this region and now lives in the south of Namibia) is vast, with merino and dorper sheep farms that stretch over scores of kilometres to a desert coast on the cold Atlantic ocean.

For most of the year, people breeze through Namaqualand as fast as possible on the straight-as-straight-can-be N7 that connects Cape Town with Windhoek in Namibia. But for a few weeks in spring, tourists flock to Namaqualand to watch the desert flower.

This it literally does. Once the July and August rains have fallen, specks of bright colour begin to dot the brown surface of the veld. In the first week of September, the flowers come out en masse, a scarcely credible carpet of yellows, oranges, pinks and blues covering almost every inch of ground. Some flowers, like the orange and white Namaqualand daisy, are easy to identify. Others, like the delicate, purple lapeirousia silenoides, and the cheridopsis pillansi, a pink-and-white flowering succulent whose leaves look like living stones, require a local guide to identify them (see 'Activities'). The flowers stay until October, then die back and the land returns to its parched state for another year.

History

Namaqualand was not colonized until the 18th century, until when its dry land was sparsely inhabited by nomadic KhoiSan who followed the grazing down to the hot plains during the winter rains and retreated to the cooler Bokkeveld and Cedarberg mountains during the long summer droughts. The region was first explored by Europeans in the 1680s when the Cape Governor Simon Van Der Stel, who had heard from Khoi tribesmen that copper could be found in the region, took a prospecting party north and successfully sunk shafts into a mountain a few kilometres east of the present-day town of Springbok. The largest shaft—now a national monument on the dirt road to Carolusberg—bears the faint impression of Van Der Stel's carved initials. But no harbour could be found on the Namaqualand coast suitable for getting the ore out of the region, and the venture was abandoned, not to be resumed until 1852, when several mines around Springbok, such as Nababeep and Okiep, were opened up, and small harbours constructed at Port Nolloth and Alexander Bay.

Trekboers from the Cape colony began to establish themselves in Namaqualand from the end of the 18th century, and by the 1850s small farming villages were emerging wherever there was accessible underground water. The farmers hunted out the San, pushing them north into the Kalahari, and forced the local Nama Khoi to work on their farms. The young Khoi women were generally pressed into the farmers' beds and, as happened all through the Cape colony, the Khoi gradually developed into the 'coloured' population of today's Cape Province—a largely landless, Afrikaans-speaking people traditionally exploited as cheap labour.

In the 1860s, diamonds were discovered on the Namaqualand coast and the towns of Port Nolloth and Alexander Bay experienced a brief boom. Small-scale diamond mining still goes on, but Namaqualand is not a wealthy region. The huge farms suffer acute seasonal drought and the main economy remains agricultural, at a level not much above subsistence.

Inland Namaqualand

Springbok is the principal town of the region. The nearby **Goegap Nature Reserve** (formerly the Hester Malan Nature Reserve), ✆ (00251) 21880, is one of the best places to see spring flowers. The large reserve (15,000ha) is made up flat plains between domed granite outcrops, hiking trails and gravel roads. Wierd desert succulents, such as the halfmens (a humanoid water-holding 'tree' the name of which means 'half man') and kokerboom (giant aloe) grow on the dry hillsides. The reserve is excellent for photographing flowers, particularly at Hartmann's mountain where zebra, eland, gemsbok, springbok and klipspringer graze amongst them. The reserve has no accommodation.

Kamieskroon, about 70km south of Springbok, is where connoiseurs of the flower season head. Guided hikes of up to three days into the flowered veld are led by local experts who can identify all the flora and know which farms to head for at which particular time. People in the know come from all over the world to Kamieskroon, a tiny, one-street dorp, and stay at the Kamieskroon Hotel before going out into the veld (*see* 'Where to Stay'). The hotel organizes hikes with local guides which must be booked in advance (*see* 'Activities'). While waiting for a tour it is worth taking the dirt road 8km north of Kamieskroon to **Bowesdorp**, the original site of the village, now a ghost town.

South of Kamieskroon the land flattens to a dry plain, with the only greenery lying on the sandy river beds running along the western wall of the **Bokkeveld** escarpment. At **Vanrhynsdorp** (about 200km south of Kamieskroon along the N7, past the village of Garies), the R27 crosses the straight N7. Vanrhynsdorp itself is not much to look at—the first thing you see is a 24-hour truck-stop and petrol station—but east of town the R27 heads straight for the Bokkeveld escarpment, which it climbs via the **Vanrhyns Pass**. The look-out point at the top gives views back over the dry, blasted landscape stretching to the coast, while to the east, on the plateau, the scene changes suddenly and dramatically. A landscape of irrigated pastures and pine trees, reminiscent of the countryside around Cape Town, makes a sharp contrast with the unremitting dryness of the region below. It is hard not to feel a lift of the heart at the sudden greenery, after the hours of parched driving.

The village of **Nieuwoudtville** is roughly 10km east of the pass. At its eastern end is the **Nieuwoudtville Flower Reserve**, a 120ha stretch of grassland that explodes into colour in the spring. **Oorlogskloof Nature Reserve**, ✆ (02726) 81010, a few kilometres south of Nieuwoudtville, is larger and wilder. To get there follow the dirt road southwest from Nieuwoudtville towards Clanwilliam. The road is signposted but if you have trouble finding it, ask at the garage at the west end of the Main Street. Follow the dirt road for about 7km, then turn right onto a smaller dirt road, signposted to Oorlogskloof. The reserve lies in a spectacularly deep-cut kloof formed by the Oorlogs River (one of the few perennial rivers in the region) as it falls through the Bokkeveld plateau and over the escarpment into the dry flats below via a beautiful waterfall, active most of the year except in high summer. Leopard and caracal hunt in the kloof's vegetation. Klipspringer, grey rhebok, duiker, grysbok, baboon and dassie are common and the rare aardwolf is a nocturnal resident, as are smaller cats and foxes. The bird life includes Cape eagle owls, black eagles, booted eagles, and lanner and peregrine falcons which nest on the cliffs. The reserve has hiking trails and swimming holes in pools of the Oorlogs River. Accommodation is in permanent tents.

As you travel east of Nieuwoudtville, you soon realize how narrow is the vegetated belt surrounding the village. Before long the road enters the arid Karoo, meeting the R357 north to **Loeriesfontein** at its western edge before heading back into the parched landscape and vast horizons of Namaqualand. After Nieuwoudtville, about 20km along on the right, is a signpost for the **Kokerboom Forest**. This, the southernmost large collection of these giant aloes in South Africa (forest is rather a wishful word for such a blasted landscape), lies on a range of low but steep shale hills, about 5km down the signposted farm track. There are several gates and some steep humps in the road to take the driver by surprise. Be careful. Loeriesfontein itself has few houses, but its Spar supermarket supplies all the surrounding farmers. The owners stock everything from food to televisions, guns and coffins; everything that an isolated Namaqualand farm could need. From Loerisfontein, the R357 and R355 east lead back into the Karoo, while the R355 west heads straight along the Bokkeveld escarpment, a lonely drive with views over some the Bokkeveld's higher peaks, before dropping back to the lowlands at the junction with the R358 (which leads northeast to Pofadder or west to the N7).

The Namaqualand Coast

Like the West Coast, of which the Namaqualand coast is the northern extension, this is a barren, sandy coastline of cold Atlantic beaches and treacherous currents. Wilder than the West Coast, most of the coastline is privately owned, although there are some points of access which make interesting side-trips.

Port Nolloth, about 150km northwest of Springbok, was founded in 1854 as a port for shipping copper from the Namaqualand mines. The discovery of loose diamonds in the surrounding sandveld let to a brief diamond rush in the 1860s, which survives today in the form of a rough crew of seasonal prospectors who use underground hoses to suck the sea-floor sand into boats for sifting, and dive offshore for the elusive stones. The town itself is windy, dusty and temporary-looking, its corrugated iron houses painted bright colours to alleviate the monotony of the surrounding browns. The town's few bars are lively at night. The road to Port Nolloth from the N7 (R382) passes through some of Namaqualand's loveliest scenery. It crosses the Buffels River at the village of Steinkopf, then winds over the folded hills that comprise the **Ananous Pass**. On the west side of the hills wheat fields (the last thing you would expect to see in Namaqualand) stretch to the further hills. From here though, the land becomes steadily drier until you hit the coastal sandveld.

An alternative route back to the N7 from Port Nolloth is via the dirt road south from the N382 (about 20km east of Port Nolloth) to **Kleinsee**, a tiny coastal settlement at the mouth of the Buffels River. The R355 then takes you east back to Springbok along the river, which is usually flowing—a welcome glimpse of water in the dry landscape. The road climbs up another pass with attendant spectacular views (the appropriately named **Spektakel Pass**) before turning back to tar for the home run to Springbok.

Hondeklip Bay, roughly 170km southwest of Springbok (via the Messelpad and Wildeperdehoek Passes), is a coastal village where little seems to have changed since the 19th century. Whereas Port Nolloth is small but lively, Hondeklip Bay is tiny and almost inert. 'Coloured' fishermens' cottages cluster round the little windswept bay and small harbour. Crayfishing, trawling from small boats and seasonal trade keeps the town alive. Hondeklip Bay is a good place to spend a few days and forget about the rest of the world, though most people spend no more than an afternoon here before driving back to the N7 and Kamieskroon via the Grootvlei Pass.

Far Inland Namaqualand

The R64 from Springbok to **Pofadder**, the region's only inland centre, passes through a landscape so apparently devoid of life that it is hard to understand how it was ever settled. However, in spring the veld is carpeted with flowers, even at Pofadder (150km inland) and beyond to the Orange River at Kakamas (*see* 'Bushmanland'). The perennial springs around Pofadder provided hide-outs for various Griqua chiefs and cattle rustlers who operated in the area during the mid-19th century. Today, Pofadder is a true 'dorp'—a desolate, forgotten interior town where there is little to do but pass through on the way to the Orange River and the national parks further north. However, 'dorps' such as Pofadder are central to the South African (and particularly the Cape's) culture. It does no harm to visit one, to take in the stoic, patient atmosphere of such places which somehow survive, despite the pull of the cities and the difficulty of ekeing a living from the unforgiving land.

The Richtersveld

This huge tract of empty, mountainous desert in the far north of Namaqualand has recently been proclaimed the **Richtersveld National Park**. It occupies the stretch of territory between Alexander Bay (a closed diamond mining town north of Port Nolloth) and the Orange River border with Namibia. The land is savagely desolate, its beauty intimidating. Even by African standards this is an untamed territory. However, it should be said too that the Nama and 'coloured' graziers of the wild area resisted the formation of the park, and it is worth asking what moves have been made to accommodate these people, now that the park is 'official'.

Access is via the N7 from Springbok to Steinkopf. From there take the R382 to Port Nolloth, then the restricted road north to Alexander Bay at the Orange River Mouth. From Alexander Bay follow the signs to **Sendelingsdrift**. The total distance from Springbok is 326km. The last section of road has sharp bends and bad gravel patches which can make a car spin, so drive slowly. The Parks Board office for the Richtersveld is at Sendelingsdrift. The Richtersveld has not yet been developed for tourism in the same way as the more established national parks and there are no fuel stations or grocery shops after Alexander Bay, so stock up there. The Parks Board do not allow traffic on the Richtersveld's few gravel roads by night, when broken-down vehicles cannot be located, so make sure you arrive at the office with plenty of daylight to spare.

The office provides a map of the existing roads with specific overnight camping spots marked. Remember to take your own food and water. The reason for the controlled camping is to protect the areas wide variety of fragile plant life, which thrives despite the Richtersveld's barren appearance. The rocks in fact support small lichens and succulents, as well as the larger, more distinctive kokerboom and halfmens trees. However, walking is freely permitted, as is swimming in the Orange River, although bathers are warned not to swim out too far, as there are treacherous currents in the centre. You can buy fishing permits for the camp site along the Orange River at the office.

Summer temperatures can shoot up above 50°C, so it is worth getting up at dawn, enjoying the morning, and having a lengthy siesta through the heat of the day before getting up again for the evening cool, when you should spot the gemsbok and springbok herds that somehow manage to thrive here. As always in deserts, nights are much colder, so take a good sleeping bag.

Activities

Wildflower viewing: Apart from the reserves listed above, Colla Swart at the **Kamieskroon Hotel** offers hiking trails of 3–5 days into the deep valleys and hills of private farms around Kamieskroon.

Hiking: Trails can be found in the **Hester Malan Nature Reserve**, the **Nieuwoudtville Flower Reserve**, the **Oorlogskloof Reserve** (near Nieuwoudtville) and in the **Richtersveld National Park** (free walking in the veld around the camping spots).

Canoeing: Trips of 3–5 days down the Orange River in the Richtersveld are offered by two Cape Town-based companies, **Felix Unite**, ℂ (021) 762 6935, and **River Runners**, ℂ (021) 762 2350.

Riding: It is possible to hire horses for guided forays into the Richtersveld. Details can be had from the National Park office at Sendelingsdrift, 94km northeast of Alexander Bay.

Fishing: Permits for fishing in the Richtersveld can be obtained in person also from the National Park office at Seledingsdrift.

Where to Stay
expensive

The **Narries Guest Farm**, ✆ (0251) 22748/462, near Springbok offers full board with superb home cooking (the lamb and venison raised on the local veld is succulent) in 4 comfortable rooms. Further south, the family-run **Kamieskroon Hotel**, ✆ (0257) 614, offers clean, comfortable accommodation at the moderate end of the expensive scale. As the centre from which most flower spotters organize their hikes, the hotel's atmosphere is less provincial than is usual for a small Northern Cape town, and some interesting folk pass through.

moderate

At Port Nolloth, on the coast, is the excellent **Bedrock Lodge Guest House**, ✆ (0255) 8865, a small family house owned by one of the local diamond divers. In Springbok, the **Springbok Café**, ✆ (0251) 21321, has rooms. The owner is a mine of local information, and the place is popular with the younger crowd visiting for the flower season.

Around Vanrhynsorp, there is a good selection of guest farms and town houses: **Gifberg Holiday Farm**, ✆ (02727) 91555, offers accommodation on a farm below the Bokkeveld escarpment: in town, the **Van Rhyn Guest House**, ✆ (02727) 91429, an old house on Voortrekker St, offers traditional B&B; if the guest house is closed, try the **Van Rhijn Inn**, ✆ (02727) 91003, which has more rooms but is slightly less personal.

cheap

Oorlogskloof Nature Reserve, ✆ (02726) 81010, south of Niewoudtville has a permanent tented camp, but this is often booked up and you should ring beforehand. Otherwise there is a lack of cheap accommodation in Namaqualand. However, all the larger towns have camp sites with ablution facilities, and camping can usually be had on farms by permission.

Bushmanland and West Griqualand

> *'I was born near the great river, in the heart of what for thousands of years had been great Bushman country. The Bushman himself...had already gone, but I was surrounded by so many fragments of his race and culture, that he seemed extraordinarily near.'*
>
> *Lost World of the Kalahari*, Laurens Van Der Post

Bushmanland and West Griqualand form the top section of the Northern Cape, between the Karoo in the south, the Orange Free State and Transvaal to the east, the Botswana border in the north and the Namibia/Namaqualand border in the west. The Orange River forms both an eastern boundary for the two regions, and a central focus, cutting through them on its way to the Atlantic.

Bushmanland, the more northern and western section, is a mixture of arid semi-desert in the south (except for the fertile floodplain around the Orange River) and Kalahari camel-thorn savannah mixed with red sand dune country in the north. Most of the population lives alongside the great river, where the wine farms and large towns, such as Keimos and Upington, give the impression of a prosperous, peopled land, belying the great tracts of dry emptiness behind. In the northwest, forming a jutting tongue between Namibia and Botswana, is the huge Kalahari Gemsbok National Park, home to great herds of game and their predators.

West Griqualand also has a narrow strip of fertile country along its stretch of the Orange River, with dry, under-populated country beyond, a great chunk of which—the former Bophuthatswana—belongs to the Tswana people. Kimberley, the town that grew up around the diamond diggings that made South Africa's fortune, sits at the extreme east of the region, hard by the border with the Orange Free State.

History

Bushmanland and West Griqualand take their names from the people that occupied them until the late 19th century. The San (bushmen) retreated north into the Namibian and Botswana Kalahari during the late 1800s, but the Griqua of West Griqualand remain, and in a few places have even kept their patrimony, despite colonial expansion and the apartheid years.

'Griqua' was the name given by English missionaries to the people of mixed Khoi and European (mainly Afrikaans) blood that trekked up to this barren region in the early 19th century, in an attempt to distance themselves from the encroaching white man. The missionaries were offended by the peoples' own name for themselves—Bastaards. Griqua was the name of one of the first Bastaard leaders that the missionaries came into contact with, and first the preachers, then the Bastaards themselves, began to use the name.

At that time the general area around the Orange River was known as TransOrangia, a vague, undefined territory into which people who wished to escape the confines of colonial society had been drifting since the 1770s. The Griqua were among the first to do so, having no place in either white or Khoi society. Nomadic herders of sheep and cattle, they

Land over 1500 metres

150 kms
100 miles

became the first trekboers to open up the northern routes and establish their own nation in a country where no colour lines existed. Using horses, wagons, and guns, they soon established mastery over the indigenous KhoiSan groups, and raided the Tswana villages and cattle herds to the north. Some even trekked into northern Namibia to escape the society that had both created them and cast them aside.

By the 1790s TransOrangia was peopled by various bands of Griqua, free Khoi, escaped Khoi bondsmen, European army deserters, renegade Boers, Tswana and some Xhosa, while the great emptiness on either side was hunted by the San. There was plentiful game in the desert and sufficient water and pasture along the river and on its islands to support cattle.

Most groups along the river lived by plunder, using the river islands as fortresses or stationary pirate ships, preying indiscriminately on other people's herds. Most of these groups were made up of any number of different race and colours. Only the Bastaards (Griqua) and the Tswana remained ethnically distinct, being sufficiently numerous to both protect and preserve their own cultures.

Although various Government officials and explorers passed through TransOrangia in the late 1700s and early 1800s, there was no permanent colonial activity until the Griqua began to invite missionaries to come and live among them. The first, John Campbell, (who arrived from London in 1814),was followed in 1820 by Robert Moffat and his wife, Mary. By encouraging the nomadic Griqua and Tswana to settle around permanent waterholes, it was these missionaries who were to establish the region's first towns.

The arrival of missionaries attracted the attention of Government House in Cape Town, where there was worry that the general instability of the TransOrangia region would attract Afrikaners wishing to flee British rule, and involve the government in costly native wars, such as were already being fought in the Eastern Cape. Governor Cradock also wanted to harness the TransOrangia raiding peoples as a pool for raising army conscripts and asked the missionary Campbell and his assistant, William Anderson, to enforce this. Both missionaries warned that such demands would only bring trouble. The few Boers who had already settled in the region warned the Griqua that this was just the beginning of a process which would eventually end in annexation of their territory by the English. Sure enough, in the 1820s, British soldiers and government agents arrived in Trans-Orangia, and a fierce anti-colonial reaction followed. But the missionaries, who helped the Griqua to dodge the draft and took no sides in the light skirmishing that followed, remained popular, and the British gave up the project as too expensive.

Meanwhile, at Lattakoo, north of modern Kuruman in northwest Bushmanland, Robert Moffat had established another mission among the Tswana, and colonial expansion into TransOrangia began, with neither troops nor government officers to enforce it. Although Christian converts were pitifully few (Moffat achieved no more than eight in the many years he spent at Lattakoo), the missionaries built on the trust they had achieved with all the TransOrangia peoples, managing to stay on friendly terms with the Griqua, Tswana Koranna (mixed Griqua/Tswana) and even the Ndebele, despite these groups' continual raiding of one another.

During the 1830s large groups of Sotho and Tswana, displaced by the general warring on the highveld (*see* **South African History**), followed by the Boers of the Great Trek, and began to settle around the Orange River. Still the Griqua held their territory, cleverly allying with different groups and relying on their military expertise and horsemanship, and knowledge of the country. They were again helped by the missionaries, who did everything they could to keep the Boers from taking the permanent water sites around Kuruman, Griquatown and Lattakoo, and began calling on the British Government to make the area a protectorate. However, some of the Griqua were pushed out by Boers— one group, under Adam Kok, trekked as far east as Natal (*see* 'Natal History'). Meanwhile, the San, alarmed at the rapid disappearance of the game, retreated north to the Kalahari. The combined missionary/Tswana/Griqua attempt to keep the Boers out was largely successful, and most trekked east to found the Orange Free State, under President Brand in the 1850s. Griqualand was then recognized as a separate territory by the Boers and the British, both of whom signed treaties with Nicolaas Waterboer, the Griquas most influential leader. However, wrangling over the exact borders became a problem as each group vied for the narrow strips of fertile land amid the great dryness. A measure of how established the Griqua had become is the fact that Nicolaas Waterboer had a Scottish South African land agent operating on his behalf, David Arnot.

In the 1860s diamonds were found in the Kimberley area, on territory disputed between the three groups. The Orange Free State asked the Cape authorities to mediate in their dispute with the Griqua, with a view to making a later deal with the British, once the troublesome Griqua were dealt with. But Arnot managed to persuade the British Cape Governor that this was Griqua land (the extent of the diamond deposits were not yet known), which was placed under protection as nominal British territory.

The Orange Free State did not give up, forcing several new surveys of the boundary in question, but the British kept asserting their right. Finally the Free State's President Brand travelled to London to present his claim to Parliament, but to no avail. The British Government paid the Free State £90,000 and bought off Brand with private land grants and pensions.

For the Griqua, this was the end of independence. With the diamond-boom of the 1870s, diamond diggings erupted around the hastily constructed town of Kimberley. The mission centre of Kuruman lost its importance, Moffat returned to England, and British occupation became complete. The Griqua, like the Tswana and Sotho who had moved to the area, were gradually stripped of their seasonal grazing lands, and absorbed into employment by the overwhelming number of diamond diggers moving in. Through the 20th century they lost their recognized status, were classified as 'coloured' under the laws of apartheid and stripped of most of their civil rights. During the 1970s large areas of the far north were designated part of the former tribal 'homeland' of Bophuthatswana (now re-absorbed into the union of South Africa), and most of the region's Tswana were forcibly removed there after 1973, mostly to live in dire poverty with insufficient water and grazing.

However, quietly and unobtrusively, many descendants of the Griqua have managed to hang on to property and even to prosper, particularly around the town of Keimos on the

Orange River in central Bushmanland, near Upington, where many 'coloured' wine farms survived both apartheid and the political upheavals of the years since its abolition.

West Griqualand: Kimberley

This large, unattractive town on the border of West Griqualand and the Orange Free State was where South Africa's commercial boom began. The diamond rush (and the later gold rush in the Transvaal) transformed South Africa from a collection of economically stagnant states to a land where extreme wealth could be found, and laid the foundation for the country's great prosperity through much of the 20th century.

History

There are many stories of how the diamond-digging began. The most popular is that the first main diamond find in the area was made by a 16-year-old Afrikaner boy near Hopetown, on the banks of the Orange River, in 1866. He gave it to a farmer, who in turn passed it on to a doctor in Grahamstown. The stone—named the 'Eureka' diamond—weighed 21.25 carats. The same farmer, one Schalk Van Niekerk, was given another stone of 83½ carats in 1869 by a Griqua in exchange for 10 oxen, a portent of what the diamonds were to mean for the Griqua. This diamond, the famous 'Star of Africa', precipitated a rush of prospectors to the Vaal and Orange Rivers around present-day Barkly West.

Then, in 1870, several veins of kimberlite (diamond-bearing rock) were found in the low hills on the farm of two Afrikaner brothers named De Beer. One of these hills, Colesberg Kopjie, was tapped in 1871. The haul it produced was staggering. The farm was sold and, by 1872, a tent-town of over 50,000 inhabitants was centred around the kopjie, which had been divided into over 3500 claims, all one next to the other. The kopjie soon began to look more like a hole. A confusing network of ropes and pulleys allowed each claim to be worked, but in reality there was chaos.

At first, the free-for-all was surprisingly democratic; anyone, including blacks, was allowed to make a claim, and many hundreds of local Tswana took advantage of the opportunity. However, the white diggers soon banded together to disallow black claims, and the resident Tswana were forced to seek work for white prospectors. Still, for some years, Kimberley's mining was controlled by no central company, only a host of small operations jostling for space, and thousands of black migrant labourers from all over South Africa drifted to the diggings, seeking work, swelling the town's population.

In the 1880s Cecil Rhodes, a young English immigrant who had arrived in Kimberley in 1872 from a failed farming attempt in the Eastern Cape, began buying up the smaller syndicates using borrowed money and cash made from his own prospecting. He concentrated on those held by a company called after the original farming brothers, De Beers. Rhodes' business momentum was phenomenal. After buying out De Beers in 1887, he raised funds from the European De Rothschild family to buy the largest operation, the Kimberley Mine, owned by Barney Barnato, a Jew from the East End of London known for his opulent style, love of sport—especially boxing—and success at the diggings. After a year's wrangle, Rhodes incorporated the mine into De Beers at a cost of over £5 million, an incredible sum for those times. De Beers gradually secured control of the mining, and the town began to settle into more established life. Three lasting South African phenomena had been established: the status of the De Beers Company (which later secured much of the Transvaal gold fields—*see* p.491), the importance of mining to South Africa's economy, and the drift of black people away from their rural homelands to, and subsequent reliance on, the cities that grew up around the mines.

Although its boom days are long past, Kimberley has steadily continued to make money since the original diggings opened, apart from a period of siege during the Anglo-Boer war in which many of the town's black workers were press-ganged into military service and killed, while at the same time being starved as most food was requisitioned for whites. Four diamond mines still operate in the area, though not at Colesberg Kopjie, which is now a huge water-filled depression known as the 'Big Hole'—and it is big.

The Town

Modern Kimberley is ugly, having been much 'improved' in the 1950s and '60s, but around the Big Hole is the **Kimberley Mine Museum** at the west end of town, on Tucker Street (*open daily 9–5*), a large open-air museum incorporating 50 of the original buildings, still laid out in street form. The best way to get there from town is on the **Kimberley Tram** which runs from the City Hall to the Big Hole (*roughly every hour from 9–4, more at weekends, 7 days a week*). The cottages, churches, shops, offices, surgeries, pubs used by the mining community have been well preserved, including the cottage originally inhabited by the De Beers brothers when it was just a farm. It takes at least an hour to get around what really is a fascinatingly and intimate (if rather romanticized) look at late Victorian and Edwardian colonial life. A tea room and restaurant break up the concentration of exhibits.

The **Star of Kimberley Pub**, another preserved relic of the frontier town, is located in the main town, just outside the Mine Museum. Follow Tucker Street and turn right on North Circular Road, the pub occupies half a block on the left. Still serving drinks, the pub has an untouched Edwardian interior.

There are several smaller museums in town. The **McGregor Museum** on Atlas Street (*open Mon–Fri 9–5, Sat 9–1, Sun 2–5*) is housed in a hotel and health spa built by Rhodes in the 1870s and where he lived during the Boer's siege of Kimberley (1900). The displays are mostly of local natural history. An eccentricity is the Hall of Religions, an educational summary of several of the world's better-known belief systems, which for some reason has been placed here. The **Alexander McGregor Memorial Museum**, round the corner on Chapel Street, (*open Mon–Fri 9–5, Sat 9–1, Sun 2–5*) is another Edwardian building housing a colonial history of the Northern Cape and a collection of rocks and minerals.

The **William Humphreys Art Gallery** in the Civic Centre, off Jan Smuts Boulevard (*open Mon–Sat 10–1, 2–5, Sun 2–5*), houses a collection of South African painting and sculpture by the better-known artists like Pierneef and Irma Stern, with some reasonable Dutch and Flemish landscapes and portraits. There is a furniture collection, mainly Cape Dutch. The more interesting **Duggan Cronin Gallery** on Egerton Road (*open Mon–Fri 9–5, Sat 9–1, 2–5, Sun 2–5*) is an ethnographic museum of black South African life at the turn of the century, albeit from a colonial and very general point of view. The most valuable exhibits are the photographs taken by Cronin of Griqua, Tswana and Sotho (as well as settlers), whose cultures in the area were eroded and squashed by the success of the mines.

Kimberley has several Victorian houses open to the public among the more assertive modern buildings. The interiors are still furnished in period, but there are no specific displays. These include: **Dunluce**, 10 Lodge Road (built 1897); the **Kimberley Club** on Du Toitspan Road, where the mining magnates used to meet; **Rudd House** at 5–7 Loch Road, a large colonial bungalow; and **7 Lodge Road**, the house where Harry Oppenheimer was born and lived before the family moved to Johannesburg in 1915. This last house can only be viewed from the outside. The others are viewed inside by appointment only, but generally you can turn up and ask to be shown around during office hours.

Around Kimberley

Magersfontein battlefield is 32km south of town, with a small museum displaying weaponry and a brief history of the long battle fought here in 1899 during the early period of the Anglo-Boer War, when Britain was getting the worst of the fighting. At Magersfontein, Boer general Koos de la Rey's commandos dug into position and surprised a large British column under the command of Lord Methuen. Precision sniping from the Boers' Mauser rifles brought the column to a complete halt. Magersfontein was one of the first recorded effective uses of trench warfare to hold a geographical line.

Barkly West, about 40km northwest of Kimberley, is where the area's diamond diggings were initially centred. The miners, in an attempt to secure the diggings for themselves, declared their own republic in 1870, but it fell apart within the year. People still prospect in the gravel along the Vaal in summer and finds are common enough for several diamond dealers to operate in the town. The town, which fronts the Vaal river, has a stone bridge dating from 1884; the first bridge over the Vaal, it is still in use. More interesting is **Canteen Kopjie**, a nature reserve and open-air archaeological and geological museum. Miners in the area have turned up a lot of early Stone Age tools and bones, as well as fossils which are displayed here and at the small **Mining Commissioner's Museum** in town.

 The newly created **Vaalbos National Park**, ✆ (0531) 806264/5, a huge area of wild veld west of Barkly West, is watered by the Vaal River and marks the meeting point of Karoo vegetation and that of the Kalahari. Rhino and buffalo are being re-introduced, and the area already supports plains game such as kudu, springbok, giraffe and eland. At the time of writing there was no accommodation but tourist facilities may be in place by publication.

Stellaland is a huge tract of Kalahari grassland stretching north of Barkly West, in which are two large chunks of what was Bophuthatswana, centred around the town of **Vryburg**. This area proclaimed itself a republic in 1882, but it lasted less than a year and today is almost entirely given over to cattle ranching. However, about 5km north of Vryburg on the R378 is the **Leon Taljaardt Nature Reserve**. Although not large, the reserve has white rhino, buffalo, both kinds of wildebeest, gemsbok, hartebeest and several large antelope species. A much larger stretch of wild country, the 24,000ha **Molopo Nature Reserve**, ✆ (0020) and ask for 1322, sits in Stellaland's far northwest, south of the tiny dorp of **Voorstershoop**. Molopo's thornveld is watered from under ground—the Molopo river, which forms its western boundary (and the border with Botswana) flows only once every 50 years on average. However, game concentrations are fairly dense, with gemsbok, red hartebeest, kudu and springbok predominating. Leopard and cheetah are the main predators, though brown hyena are common. Large raptors, including bateleur eagles and white-backed vultures, are often seen. Visitors can hike in the large reserve, but *must* carry a plentiful water supply, and arrange their route with the reserve's office before setting off. There are no chalets or camp sites at Molopo—you are really on your own.

Bushmanland

For the purposes of this guide Bushmanland, west of Griqualand, can be divided in two sections: the green, fertile strip along the Orange River, and the semi-desert Kalahari to the north.

Orange River

This bright corridor of startling green is reached by three main routes: the N10 from the south, the R54 from Kimberley via Griquatown, and the R27 from Vryburg and the Transvaal via Kuruman. The N10 runs along a 120km section of the Orange River, whose alluvial banks from Groblershoop to Upington are given over to small, intensive wine and fruit farms with dry rocky hills stretching away on either side. West of Upington, the R359 continues along the river through similar country to the **Augrabies Falls National Park**, where the river plunges suddenly into a deep, narrow gorge, creating an angry churning wall of water whose roar is deafening against the surrounding silence. West of Augrabies, you can continue down river by raft or canoe (*see* 'Activities') or by road (R64), into the empty spaces of Namaqualand.

To the south, near the town of Groblershoop and 120km south of Upington on the R32 is **Witsand**, a weird white 'island' of sand dunes known as the **Roaring Sands**. During the summer months the 100m high dunes make a sound like a human moan if disturbed. The wind usually does this, but even kicking at the white sand can produce the sound, the origin of which lies in the loose composition of the sand, through which air moves continuously. There is a hutted camp at the foot of the dunes for those wanting to break their journey here.

Upington, Bushmanland's main centre, is another town that was ruined by 'improvement' in the 1950s and '60s. An important wine-growing centre, it has a **Wine Route** that follows the N10 east towards Groblershoop. Originally a mission station (like most of the towns in the area), there is little to see in the Upington itself, despite its river frontage and the beauty of the surrounding fruit farms and vineyards. The **Kalahari Oranje Museum**, (054) 26911, is housed in the church of the old mission station (built in 1875). The usual pioneer life exhibits are displayed. More fun is the Donkey Monument, a bronze statue paying just tribute to the Southern Africa desert regions' principal worker. The **Hortentia Windmill** (1879), by the bridge on the Groblershoop Road, can only be viewed from the outside.

Spitskop Nature Reserve, 13km north of town on the R360, lies amid the rocky, barren landscape north of the Orange River. As a testament to just how much game the landscape can support, the reserve boasts zebra, gemsbok, hartebeest, eland, steenbok and many, many springbok. There is no accommodation, but there is a short walking trail.

Keimos, 40km southwest of Upington along the river, was founded by a Griqua band known as the 'Koranna River People', pirates and brigands that had two punitive raids sent against them during the 1860s. The village was named Keimos, which means 'mouse's nest', after the colonies of tree mice discovered in the vegetation fronting the river. Keimos is remarkable in that it is one of the few places where the Griqua managed to hang on to prosperous land through the fiercely racial policies of the late 19th and 20th centuries. Many of the farms around are still owned by 'coloureds' descended from the Griquas who originally moved here to escape white domination of the Cape. The town has a waterwheel (still in use) on the Main Road, and the original mission church (also on Main Road). Outside town is the **Orange River Wine Cellars Co-operative**, offering wine tastings and tours of the cellars. Four kilometres west of town is **Tierberg Nature Reserve**, a very small reserve teeming with springbok and noted for its tall aloes, some of which flower a spectacular red in winter. There is a walking trail to the summit of the hill that gives the reserve its name, a perfect place from which to observe the green river valley set against the harsh reds and browns of the hills around. **Kakamas**, another fruit and wine village a further 40km west, has several operational wooden waterwheels (through which run several irrigation canals) and a series of water tunnels bored from farm to farm in the alluvial lands around the village. Kakamas was also one of the few sites of skirmishing between German Southwest African troops and South African soldiers during the First World War. Just west of town is a monument to the several Germans killed.

Augrabies Falls National Park centres around the spectacular 300ft-deep gorge into which the broad, peaceful Orange River plunges, kicking up spray into the bone-dry air. A bridge spans the ravine, allowing for fantastic photographs. The accessible part of the park covers about 10,000ha, but a vast 70,000ha, hinterland also falls under park protection. Black rhinoceros are currently breeding in this back-veld, but the public cannot go in.

Away from the river banks, dry thorn bush predominates, supporting springbok, steenbok and klipspringer. Baboons and vervet monkeys, ground squirrels, jackal and bat-eared fox are also likely to be seen. The resident leopard and caracal remain hidden. Black and martial eagles are often sighted. The best thing about the park is its 3-day **Klipspringer hiking trail** (*see* 'Activities').

To the west of Augrabies begins Namaqualand, a great arid borderland between South Africa and Namibia that lies along the Orange River (*see* 'Namaqualand'). The wild emptiness between Bushmanland and Namaqualand has few roads, but can be penetrated either by **canoe or camel safari** for guided trips of about a week (*see* 'Activities').

On the R27 south of Keimos lie the great white salt pans of the upper Western Karoo. At the edge of these, 85km south of Keimos into the bleached dry country, is the small, remote town of **Kenhardt**. Its perennial springs and desert location made the place a haven for Griqua, Boer and Tswana cattle rustlers during the early 19th century, but in the 1860s the British decided to curb the activities of the raiders, sending in a magistrate and some police who set up camp under a camel-thorn tree. The town developed around the tree, which still stands, despite being over 500 years old. Eight kilometres south of town is the **Kokerboom Forest**, one of the southernmost points where these strange giant aloes are found. There is a marked 4km trail through the 'forest', which consists of about 5000 giant aloes, each of which grows taller than a man.

The Kalahari

Bushmanland's northern reaches form a transitional zone between the Karoo scrub typical of most of the northern Cape, and the game-rich Kalahari. Red and grey dunes of fine sand alternate with camel-thorn trees so tall and wide that they resemble a man-made parkland. In between stretch dry grasslands the colour of spun gold.

The best way in is via the N14 to **Kuruman**, hard by the westernmost section of the former Bophuthatswana. Kuruman, one Bushmanland's only well-watered spots, was taken from the San (bushmen) by the Koranna (a Griqua band who lived by raid and conquest) in the late 18th century, and in the early 1800s became the site of the first mission to penetrate the region, under John Cambell of the London Missionary Society. It was taken over, around 1816, by the energetic and influential missionary Robert Moffat (*see* p.268), whose daughter later married the legendary David Livingstone (who also spent some time preaching here before heading north).

In a park on the Main Road in Kuruman, water gushes up from the ground through a crack in a tall rock known as the **Kuruman Eye** into a deep, clear pool in which live large shoals of freshwater fish. Over 20 million litres of water pour out every day.

The **Kuruman Moffat Mission** was begun just after the Napoleonic Wars and completed around 1840. For a long time there was no larger building in the Northern Cape. Moffat, the missionary in charge, designed it to seat 800, even though he only had 8 converts from the local Tswana and Khoi. However, after his daughter married David Livingstone (in the Mission church), the Mission's status was assured. Moffat retired in 1870, just before the Kimberley diamond boom caused Kuruman to lose its importance in the area and slip into its present-day regional obscurity. Today, the mission is a national monument, and occasional services are still held there.

In the hills 84km south of Kuruman are a set of caves known as the **Wonderwerk Grotte**. Some of South Africa's best preserved bushman art is etched onto the rock wall of the main cave (though some has been desecrated with graffiti). Beautifully detailed animals and hunting scenes are scattered across the stone. The cave can be viewed by permission of the farmer at Wonderwerk Farm, signposted from the R31.

Just outside **Danielskuil**, a tiny dorp 60km further south, is a dolomite sinkhole into which the local Griqua raiders reputedly cast their prisoners. Snake-ridden and waterless, the thought sends a shiver through anyone standing at the lip. So far, no one has excavated the hole for human remains, and the legend remains unconfirmed. Danielskuil also has a ruined British fort on a hill overlooking the town, built during the Anglo-Boer War.

However, it is north of Kuruman that most people head, to the vast Kalahari Gemsbok National Park. The road there, the R31, leads for 61 lonely kilometres through dry country, the distant, jagged outline of the uninhabited Korannaberg mountains (named after the Koranna people—*see* above) forming the western horizon. At the tiny, excellently-named mining town of Hotazel (meaning exactly what it sounds like), the R31 becomes a sandy dirt road, which leads to the tiny town of **Van Zylsrus**. Drive carefully, as cars can spin very easily on this section. At Van Zylsrus, the character of the landscape changes from thorn scrub to a gracious natural parkland of giant camel-thorn trees, which continues all the way to the Kalahari Gemsbok National Park. Van Zylsrus is a good place to stop the night before travelling the next 200-odd kilometres on bad dirt roads to the turn-off for the park. It has an old hotel, a camp site under the trees, a post office and precious little else. Despite the amount of travellers who pass through on their way to the park, Van Zylsrus has never grown beyond its few buildings. After a long, dusty drive, a cool drink on the hotel verandah is recommended, watching the sun set over the tall camel-thorn trees.

The R31 from here to the turn-off at Andriesvale should be done in daylight only. Varying in condition from deep sand to bald corrugations, this is a dangerous road. Make sure you have a full tank—the deep sections make the car use more fuel than usual, and the first petrol station is not until the tiny settlement of Askham, just 20km from the turn-off.

From here there are another 61km of dirt road, with occasional dangerous bends, before the camp entrance. The parkland gives way to the dry river bed of the Nossob, which runs parallel with the road. The first red sand dunes appear, some of them with little tin-shack farms owned by Nama people (the only Khoi group that managed to retain some land in South Africa, though most now live in Namibia) standing hot and bright against the sand. These farms are a far cry from the rich alluvial domains along the Orange River. The Kalahari's Nama farmers scratch a living from the sand and dry grasses, keeping cattle, sheep and goats. Few have motor transport.

The **Kalahari Gemsbok National Park** is entered at Twee Rivieren, where there is a rest camp (beautifully built from local stone and thatch), restaurant, shop (which does not sell camera film) and camp site. The two other camps, at Nossob on the Botswana border, and Mata Mata on the Namibian border, are both about 120km north of Twee Rivieren. Bear in mind that it takes around 3–4 hours driving to reach them.

The Kalahari Gemsbok park is enormous, and adjoins an even larger protected area in Botswana. Game is plentiful, despite the lack of ground water. Huge herds of springbok, blue wildebeest, and gemsbok predominate. Eland and red hartebeest also occur. Lion, cheetah and spotted hyena are common, and the visitor can expect to see them from the park's three roads even in broad daylight. By night, leopard, brown hyena, jackal and bat-eared fox wander the veld.

One drawback of the park is that there are no walking trails and you are confined to your vehicle. But the rich, golden landscape, interspersed with red dunes and camel-thorn park-land, and the density of game and bird life (kori bustards, secretary birds and bataleur eagles are common) make it all worthwhile. The park has very little rainfall, and herbi-vores derive most of their moisture from succulent plants and desert fruits, such as the Kalahari melon, which grow on the veld floor, while predators get their water from the bodies of their prey. However, the park authorities have recently installed water troughs and pumps as well, and these make good point for photographing large concentrations of game. Look out for the huge, unmistakable nests of the sociable weaver birds, colonies of up to 200 of which build communal nests the size of small houses in the camel-thorn tree tops. Avoid the park in summer, when the temperatures usually exceed 40°C. In winter, take a good sleeping bag, as the night time temperature often falls below freezing. The only way out of the park is the way you came in, via the R31. At the junction with the R360 at Andriesvale (61km south of the park) you can either head south to Upington, east to Van Zylsrus and Kuruman or west into Namibia via the border post at Rietfontein (70km).

The route to Namibia is a spectacular and lonely journey. Again, make sure you have a full tank (fill up at Askam, Twee Rivieren or Rietvlei) before penetrating into Namibia, as there is no petrol station until Aroab, 40km on the other side. The R31 leads abruptly out of the camel-thorn country into a wide salt pan that stretches off to cliff-edges on the horizon that glow with an almost electric red, like the rings on a stove seen through haze. Rietfontein, when you finally reach it, is one of the most desolate of all South African towns, a string of shacks with a trading store and petrol station in a wide, blasted emptiness of dry veld. To the west are distant mountains and eroded hills with exposed rocky spines like the fossilised vertebrae of dinosaurs. Into that western Namibian land-scape the road stretches like a ribbon to the horizon for 200km, until the town of Keetmanshoop.

Activities

Hiking: In West Griqualand, day trails can be found at Canteen Kopjie Reserve, Barkly West, at Klaarwater Reserve near Griquatown and on the private guest farms listed below. Wild hiking at Molopo Game Reserve in northern Stellaland is allowed, but there are no marked trails, and hikers must cary a good water supply. In the Orange River section of Bushmanland day trails can be found at Spitskop Nature Reserve, Keimos, at Tierberg Reserve, Kakamas, and at Augrabies Falls National Park, ✆ (012) 343 1991. Hikers should look out for the brightly coloured Cape flat lizard, which often basks on the trail, waiting until the last moment before moving. Overnight huts with firewood, cooking pots and water are provided. There are also some shorter walks into the veld and along the gorge. The national park has chalets and a camp site. In the Kalahari section of Bushmanland, Kuruman Nature Reserve has short walking trails in flat, rocky terrain among Karoo-thorn bush with chances of viewing antelope.

Camel and horse safaris: Camel Runners, ✆ (011) 403 2512, organize camel trips of 5 days, as well as horse and canoe trips, into the Orange River wilderness west of Augrabies.

Canoeing: *see* p.263

Bushman art: Very detailed rock etchings can be seen in the Wonderwerk Cave on Wonderwerk Farm, on the R31 south of Kuruman in the Kalahari Section of Bushmanland.

Where to Stay

West Griqualand

expensive

The **Halfway House Hotel** in Kimberley, ✆ (0531) 25151, is a survivor of the Edwardian age. Its 12 en suite rooms are still decorated in Edwardian style with much use of heavy reds and maroons for wallpaper and curtains. The bar has a strange quirk; a drive-in section where people can drink without getting out of their cars, a left-over from mining days when people could drink without getting out of the saddle.

moderate

De Beer's Gasthuis, 28 Pickering Ave, Kimberley, ✆ (0531) 612192, is a colonial bungalow in the quiet suburb of Lindene, west of downtown. Meals are available by request, and the house is clean and friendly. **Pembury Lodge**, 11 Currey St, Kimberley, ✆ (0531) 24317, is another Edwardian survivor. There are 5 en suite bedrooms. B&B is offered, with dinner by arrangement. The house is within walking distance of downtown.

Kimberley Youth Hostel, on Bloemfontein Rd, ✆ (0531) 28577, has both dorms and private rooms, as well as a cheap restaurant serving good, simple food.

Bushmanland: Orange River

expensive

The **Upington Protea Hotel**, ✆ (054) 25414, fronts the river. It offers good service, good food and is a convenient place to break a journey west, but lacks atmosphere. The **Waterwiel Protea**, ✆ (011) 484 1717, about 80km further on in the town of Kakamas, occupies a more tranquil setting. Also by the river, the hotel is near the village's old wooden water-wheel. Slightly more luxurious (and pricier) than the Upington Protea, the Waterwiel offers the usual efficient service and good food with mediocre decor verging on the quietly tasteless.

moderate

Augrabies Falls Game Reserve, ✆ (0020) and ask for Gemsbok 901, has a number of self-contained cottages and huts, sleeping 4, all at moderate prices. There is a shop and restaurant at the rest camp. Augrabies, with its spectacular falls, big game viewing and wild landscape is the best place to stay at in Bushmanland's Orange River region.

cheap

Apart from sharing a Parks Board cottage or chalet at Augrabies, the only cheap accommodation on offer is **camping**. All towns have a municipal site, as does Augrabies Falls National Park.

Bushmanland: Kalahari

moderate

Van Zylsrus is the best place to break the journey between Kuruman and the Kalahari Gemsbok National Park.

The **Van Zylsrus Hotel** is old and a bit run down. Few rooms have bathrooms. But it has a shabby charm, not having been altered much for the last 30 years, and a verandah to sit out on while the sun sets over the camel-thorn trees out front. Alternatively there are various guest farms in the vicinity, but as roads are bad, it is advisable to call first to check availability and road conditions. **Korannaberg Estate**, ✆ (01475) 215, lies at the foot of the Koranna Mountains. It is a game farm on a 19th century farmstead, it has opportunities for walking and game-viewing (plains game only). **Avontuur Guest Farm**, ✆ (01475) 416, is on the road to the national park, as is **Caledonia Guest Farm**, ✆ (01475) 442.

Kalahari Gemsbok National Park, ✆ (054472) and ask for Waterfall 4, has cottages and chalets at its 3 rest camps. All are self-catering, but there is a restaurant at Twee Rivieren camp at the park entrance, plus a shop and petrol pump.

As with the Orange River section, there is no budget accommodation except for **camping** at the municipal town sites, in the national parks or on farms (by permission).

Eating Out: West Griqualand and Bushmanland

expensive

The **Halfway House Hotel** in Kimberley, ✆ (0531) 31791, has an *à la carte* restaurant in the Edwardian dining room, which is informal for an expensive restaurant. The speciality is spiced, aromatic Karoo mutton, with some French cuisine and game.

Tiffany's at the Savoy Hotel, Kimberley, ✆ (0531) 26211, is more pretentious, though not as tempting; French cuisine dishes alternate with meat-and-two veg on the menu. The restaurant also pipes irritating muzak at you.

moderate

Kimberley has the usual South African chain restaurants (Spur, Mike's Kitchen etc.) as does Upington. Most of the regular town hotels do food (toasted sandwiches, burgers etc.) at reasonable prices.

The **Kalahari Gemsbok** and **Augrabies Falls** National Parks both have moderately-priced restaurants at their rest camps that specialize in game culled from the parks themselves. Particularly good is gemsbok in a creamy pepper sauce. Game is culled all year, so there is no set season.

cheap

The region's towns have take-away joints serving the usual sandwiches, burgers and salads.

The Eastern Cape

The Eastern Cape, Ciskei and Transkei comprise a borderland in every sense, a gradual transition between South Africa's temperate and sub-tropical climatic zones, between the arid Karoo plateau and the Drakensberg, between the predominantly 'coloured' west and the predominantly Black east.

In few other parts of southern Africa can you find so many natural contrasts crammed into one region. Rich grasslands fall to the coast; dense thorn bush fills the game-rich river valleys; the Amatola mountains, covered in majestic hardwood forest, rise just inland, giving way to the higher Winterberg, Bamboesberg, Stormberg, Witteberg and Drakensberg ranges in the north; dry vegetation reminiscent of the Karoo contrasts with areas so lush that they resemble Europe or the tropics rather than southern Africa; along the coast of Transkei, empty white sand beaches stretch for hundreds of kilometres; there is big game in the reserves.

The diverse terrain and sheer size of this mountainous territory make the Eastern Cape one of South Africa's most rewarding areas for walking, hiking and riding. The bush and mountain trails often take you to within a few yards of the plains game and sometimes even to larger animals such as rhino. Try to allow time to explore the Amatola forests, the Cape Drakensberg to the north, and the Transkei Wild Coast.

Climate

As elsewhere in South Africa, the Eastern Cape's climate changes with altitude; the higher, the more temperate, the lower, the more humid. Summers are blindingly hot, but winter snowfalls on the higher ranges are common. Summer is the rainy season, winter the dry. Despite the region's lush vegetation and perennial rivers, localized drought strikes about once every five years, turning the surrounding country into a dust-bowl, and radically altering each landscape's appearance from year to year.

Fauna and Flora

Here, the fynbos heath of the Cape Floral Kingdom gives way to the thorn vegetation more typical of the rest of Africa. Thick, green acacia and euphorbia bush blankets the river valleys near the coast (if they have not been cleared for cattle). Prehistoric plants such as giant cycads and giant aloes grow on the hills. In the eastern reaches, wild banana mixed with hardwood forest gives the landscape a semi-tropical look.

South Africa's southernmost viable elephant population (as opposed to the few Knysna Forest elephants of the Garden Route, who are considered 'non-viable', or of insufficient number to ensure future survival) inhabits the dense thorn bush of Addo Elephant National Park, north of Port Elizabeth. Rhino, both black and white, are found in many reserves through the region, as are the larger plains game such as buffalo, kudu, eland, zebra, wildebeest, hartebeest, blesbok and impala. Leopard and occasional hyena make up the region's large predators, except at Shamwari Game Reserve, near Port Elizabeth, where lion have recently been re-introduced.

A regional oddity is the tree dassie of the coastal forests, similar in looks to the more common rock dassie, but known for its spine-chilling night-time scream.

Bird species include most of those found in the temperate south-western Cape, plus some from the hotter east. The woods are alive with the chattering of wood hoopoes, or the growling boom of louries. Hornbills are a common sight, while large raptors thrive in the mountain ranges.

History

The Eastern Cape's 200-year colonial history has been one of continual war and struggle. Many of South Africa's black freedom fighters, including Steve Biko, Nelson Mandela and Walter Sisulu, were born in this troubled area, and the region's bitter past offers many clues to South Africa's turbulent recent history. The best telling of the tragic, complicated saga is in Noel Mostert's superb book *Frontiers* (Pimlico 1991). However, for those without the time to read the 1300-odd page book, the following will have to do.

Until the 18th century, the Eastern Cape was populated by Khoi in the west (around Port Elizabeth and the eastern Karoo), San (bushmen) in the mountains to the north, and several large clans of Xhosa people from east of Port Elizabeth to the eastern Transkei. Apart from a few shipwrecked sailors who had been succoured by the Transkei Xhosa in the 17th century, no white man had yet settled in the Eastern Cape. The region's Khoi were still freeholders of their own land west of the Fish River, and shared the grazing of the Zuurveld, the grassland area immediately west of the Fish, with seasonal Xhosa herders from across the river.

The Xhosa nation is known to have been riven by endless warring between the clans. All Xhosa owed nominal allegiance to the paramount **Gcaleka** clan in the Transkei, with the next most powerful being the **Rharabe**, east of the Fish River, and the **Gqunkwebe**, who seasonally pastured cattle west of the Fish. However, individual chiefs of sub-clans acted independently when it came to local politics, carefully shifting allegiance as each situation demanded. The many petty wars resulting from this were of a contained nature, involving neither mass butchery, nor the the killing of women and children, an ethic that continued through most of the later Frontier Wars, despite no such restraint on the colonists' part.

During the 1750s and '60s, large numbers of trekboers, intent on escaping the authority of the Dutch East India Company, began settling west of the Fish River, near modern Ciskei. For the next 20 years, they busily enslaved and dispossessed the Khoi, but treated the Xhosa (who greatly outnumbered them) with a healthy respect. Some Boers, like the

1. Hogsback Forest
2. Amatola Forest
3. Katsberg & Readsdale Forest
4. Pirie Forest
5. Kologha State Forest
6. Amatola Mountains

Land over 1000 metres

60 kms
30 miles

legendary Conraad de Buys (*see* p.249), even lived at the courts of Xhosa chiefs as client subjects and councillors.

By 1780, so many Boers had settled in the Eastern Cape, that the Dutch East India Company feared it might lose control of its colony, and extended its frontier to the Fish River. But not until 1786 did it found a *landdrost* (magistracy) and garrison town from which to control the vast swathe of country. Even then the new administrative town, Graaff-Reinet, was unable to really govern the trekboers, being built in the eastern Karoo, about 300km from the Fish River, too far from the frontier to contain its settlement. A land conflict between the growing numbers of trekboers and the Xhosa was inevitable.

The Frontier Wars (1780–1878)

Confused, unjust, and sharpened by race-hatred, the Eastern Cape's nine Frontier Wars between Boer, Briton, Xhosa and Khoi lasted almost 100 years, destroyed the Cape's last free Khoi tribes and brought tragedy and humiliation to the Xhosa.

The earliest wars were fought over the good grazing country of the Zuurveld, west of the Fish River near modern Port Elizabeth. In 1781 the Dutch East India Company ordered several Xhosa clans in the Zuurveld to move east of the Fish River. More numerous than the settlers, the clans ignored the order. With cynical expedience, the Zuurveld Boers formed their own commando, invited the Xhosa chiefs to parley and opened fire on them unexpectedly. From there it was a simple matter to fall on the unsuspecting villagers and drive them west of the Fish. Such was the **First Frontier War**.

But the Xhosa nation was expanding, and the number of settlers growing, and it was only a matter of time before conflict came again. In 1789, the large Gqunkwebe clan migrated into the Zuurveld. Outnumbered, the Zuurveld Boers pragmatically allied with the Rharabe Xhosa, (who, under their chief, Ndlambe, were old rivals of the Gqunkwebe), and opened the **Second Frontier War** late in 1789. But after some initial victories, civil war broke out in the Rharabe's home country east of the Fish and the warriors left to go and fight at home. The Boers lost their allies and the Gqunkwebe, now hostile, stayed put.

Disgruntled, the frontier Boers turned on the Dutch East India Company, whom they saw as unable or unwilling to keep the Xhosa at bay. In 1795 they abandoned the Zuurveld and rebelled—first against the Dutch, and then against the British (1799) after their annexation of the Cape. Both rebellions failed, and the second was put down by the British with Khoi cavalry raised near Cape Town, making the frontier Boers fearful that their own Khoi servants, having seen a Boer defeat, would be inspired to revolt.

This fear was confirmed late in 1799 when the British sent an army to clear the Gqunkwebe from the Zuurveld. As soon as the redcoats arrived, Khoi farmhands from all over the eastern Cape abandoned their cruel masters to join the British army, which happily absorbed them as guides and sharpshooters. The joint force began the **Third Frontier War** in 1799, and soon forced the Gqunkwebe east of the Fish. But the British then returned to the Cape, unwittingly abandoning their Khoi allies to certain Boer retaliation for having left the farms. The Khoi had little choice but to throw in their lot with the Gqunkwebe, and in 1800 the two forces re-invaded the Zuurveld.

In the middle of this confusion, Britain handed the Cape colony back to Holland. The new Dutch Governor, seeking a quick end to the tiresome wars, granted the Khoi rebels land near present-day Port Elizabeth, founded Uitenhage, a new military town, at the western edge of the Zuurveld, and with this assurance of military protection, persuaded the Boers to resettle the Zuurveld and share it with the Gqunkwebe, who were also sick of war.

However, the Rharabe's civil war east of the Fish had caused the clan to split into two—the Ndlambe (under the chief of that name), and the Ngqika, under Ndlambe's nephew. In 1809 following a drought, the 20,000 strong Ndlambe clan crossed the Fish in search of new pasture, and spread across the entire settled region. With such a large Xhosa presence, the raiding of settler herds was inevitable. Boers began abandoning their farms again, calling on Britain (who had re-annexed the Cape in 1806) to eject the Xhosa by force.

The British took three years to respond, but finally did so with alarming ferocity. In 1812, Colonel John Graham's large army, supplemented with Khoi and Boer auxilliaries, began the **Fourth Frontier War**. The idea was to push the Ndlambe east as quickly as possible, and the army killed indiscriminately, massacring uncounted Xhosa women and children and enlarging the military post, Grahamstown (built three years before), in the Fish River valley. The Ndlambe, deeply shocked, were driven east inside a year, and the brutal war established a kind of peace, despite a short-lived Boer rebellion over being forced to pay their Khoi workers a minumum wage (*see* Slagter's Nek, p.307). Over the next few years, Xhosa and Boer still crossed the Fish to raid cattle, but there were no open hostilities.

It was the British, so confident of their ability to govern, who were to destroy the hard-won peace. In 1814, they sent a dangerously autocratic new Governor, Lord Charles Somerset, to the Cape colony. Determined to make his mark by bringing proper law and order to the frontier, Somerset launched an ill-advised scheme to stop Xhosa cattle-raiding, creating a system of cavalry patrols who were to track stolen cattle east of the Fish and demand restitution from the first Xhosa village they came to, regardless of its innocence or guilt. He then sought out the most powerful of the Frontier chiefs—Ngqika—and, overestimating the extent of the chief's authority, ordered him to take responsibility for all Xhosa cattle raids. Ngqika had no control over the other clans, but was intimidated into accepting.

Somerset's raiding patrols could not fail to provoke trouble, and in 1818, the **Fifth Frontier War** erupted when the Ndlambe clan, who had lost thousands of cattle to the patrols in just four years, lost patience and (unsuccessfully) attacked Grahamstown with 6000 warriors. This gave Somerset an excuse to meddle even further. As part of a grand experiment to 'whiten' the frontier, he confiscated a large tract of prime grazing land *east* of the Fish from Chief Ngqika as 'punishment' for not having prevented the invasion, even though Ngqika had had no control over it. Somerset christened the area Albany and brought out 5000 English colonists to populate it. But the 1820 Settlers, as these new colonists became known, proved unfit for frontier life. Youths from Ngqika's clan raided the settlers' herds. This, combined with the harsh climate and wild animals, forced most to abandon their farms and drift to Grahamstown and Port Elizabeth. By 1825 most of Albany lay empty, but the Ngqika were still denied grazing rights to the territory.

Somerset seems to have wanted war; in 1829, he provoked the Ngqika again, this time by expelling Maqoma, Ngqika's warlike brother, from land near the Kat River, also east of the Fish, to make way for a self-governing Khoi settlement. The Khoi were proven bush fighters and, by settling them on the frontier, Somerset thought to redress the failure of his Albany colony, and secure the frontier against invasion. But it could never work on land stolen from the Xhosa. In 1834 Maqoma declared the **Sixth Frontier War**, stating that he would fight only until the confiscated lands had been returned. Taking refuge in the high forest of the Amatola mountains, Maqoma successfully kept the new British general, the firebrand Sir Harry Smith, at bay. Frustrated, Smith took his soldiers far to the east across the Kei River into Gcaleka territory, where no whites had yet settled. Without any orders from Cape Town, he captured Hintsa, paramount chief of all the Xhosa, thinking to hold him hostage until the Ngqika surrendered. But the plan went wrong and Hintsa was shot while trying to escape. Smith then illegally claimed part of the Gcaleka territory as British, setting up military bases at King William's Town and East London.

For the Xhosa, the murder of Hintsa was an act of outrage greater even than John Graham's killing of women and children. In even the smallest clan, a chief and his property were inviolate. By murdering the Xhosa's paramount chief, Smith (and by extension the British), had irreparably insulted the whole Xhosa nation. Britain had unwittingly committed herself to a war to the death. Meanwhile, the Amatola campaign degenerated into exhausted stalemate and Maqoma, prepared to bide his time, offered peace, but without surrender. The war was emptying the treasury so the British government forced Smith to accept and appointed a man called Stockenstroom (an ex-*landdrost* of Graaff-Reinet) to draw up the treaty. Somerset and Smith were both recalled to England, and Stockenstroom, a rare Boer humanitarian, put a long overdue end to Somerset's provocative cattle patrols. In the teeth of oppostion from the Grahamstown settlers, who wanted a full and final crushing of the Xhosa, he then restored to the Gcaleka the land around King William's Town and East London. But to Stockenstroom's immense frustration, Britain retained part of the land that Smith had stolen and stirred further resentment by offering it to the Mfengu people, refugees from Zulu raids (*see* **Natal** 'History'), who had been succoured by the Gcaleka in Transkei, but treated as subordinates. The Mfengu jumped at the chance of having their own country under British protection, and swore to fight in any subsequent wars against the Xhosa.

Through the 1830s, Stockenstroom's live-and-let-live policy enraged the frontier whites; many Boers abandoned the Eastern Cape to join the Great Trek in 1836 and the British settlers called continuously for his resignation. But he kept the peace until 1842, when yet another bad drought re-started the cycle of Xhosa cattle raids. Tension mounted. In 1844, the **Seventh Frontier War** (known as the War of the Axe) broke out between Maqoma, Sandile (Ngqika's son) and the British, after one of Sandile's subjects was imprisoned for stealing a cheap hatchet from a shop in the new garrison town of Fort Beaufort. Some friends broke him out of jail and when the British demanded his return, Sandile refused. A British column sent into the Amatolas to find Sandile was attacked, and his clan, backed by thousands of Gcaleka warriors, invaded the Cape colony, raiding and burning as far as Port Elizabeth. The insult to Hintsa had not been forgotten.

The advance was only checked when a cavalry regiment chanced on 500 Ngqika warriors near Peddie and cut them down. The Gcaleka retaliated by burning the grass around the British columns, starving their oxen and horses. Pressing their advantage, Maqoma and Sandile offered peace if their confiscated lands (Kat River and Albany) were returned. But Cape Town and Britain could not allow such a reversal. Harry Smith, who had been distinguishing himself in India against the Sikhs, was recalled to the Cape, this time as Governor, and told to bring the Xhosa to heel.

Smith promptly re-occupied the land around King William's Town, called in the local chiefs, forced them to kneel to him and humiliated them in front of their people. He supported the Grahamstown settlers' view that the Khoi's Kat River settlement was too good for non-whites, and in 1850, sent troops to evict hundreds of people accused of being squatters. But then Smith went too far and deposed Sandile from the Ngqika chieftaincy. Late in 1850, a military column crossing the Amatolas was cut to pieces by Sandile's warriors, who suddenly poured into the colony once more. Smith, besieged in King William's Town, ordered the Kat River Khoi to mobilize, despite his recent persecution of them. Disgusted, the Khoi levies promptly took the field with the Xhosa, who now rose en masse, with all but two of the clans joining the war.

This, the **Eighth Frontier War**, lasted three years, claimed far more lives (British, Xhosa and Khoi) than any before, and the expense cost Smith his military career. But by 1852 the Xhosa had lost all their territory except the Transkei, and the Kat River Khoi were evicted and forced to seek work with the contemptuous whites who now occupied the settlement. Maqoma was captured and sent to Robben Island, where he died. The insults to the Xhosa chiefs were unavenged and the best of the land had been lost. Contemporary accounts talk of a despair coming over the nation.

Many historians link this catastrophic defeat with the Xhosa's great, irrational, national near-suicide four years later, when a millenarian prophetess of the Gcaleka people in Transkei declared that if all Xhosa clans destroyed their cattle and crops, their ancestors would rise and sweep the British into the sea. Tragically, Sarili, son of the murdered Hintsa and paramount chief of the Xhosa, became a convert and ordered this done. A few clans held onto their stock, but tens of thousands starved (*see* **Transkei** 'History').

In a single year, the Xhosa had lost their independence. Transkei was opened up to settlement and most of the chiefs (except for Sandile and Sarili, who fled), imprisoned. Yet this was not quite the end. Over the next 20 years, the Xhosa population gradually recovered. Sandile and a few other chiefs were 'forgiven' and appointed magistrates, and put on the British pay roll. But there was to be one last campaign. In 1877, Sandile and some Gcaleka chiefs attended an Mfengu wedding. The Mfengu had fought for the British in the last three wars and were now hated by the Xhosa. There was a brawl, and some Mfengu were killed. The Government, bound by treaty to protect the Mfengu, sent troops to arrest Sandile, who took his followers back to Amatolas (in the Pirie Forest, near King William's Town), where he fought until he was killed in 1878, ending the **Ninth and last Frontier War**.

Recent History

Throughout the Frontier War period, English, German and American missionaries had been active among the Xhosa clans. Although late 19th-century prejudices had made most of these mission stations priggish affairs, the schools attached to them gave the Xhosa a non-military means of resisting white oppression. The last decades of the 19th century saw many alumni of these mission schools go on to universities abroad, and several Xhosa (such as the gifted future politician Alan Soga) later graduated from Edinburgh, entering the professional world on their return to South Africa. One, John Jabavu became a journalist and in 1884 published a newspaper called *Imvo Zabantsudu* ('Native Opinion') from King William's Town. The journal became a forum for Black political thought and, after Jabavu's death, it continued under his son Davidson, until the 1930s. In 1908, Jabavu and his circle fought successfully for a black franchise in the Cape, and in 1916 formed a black college near Alice in the former Ciskei, later to become the University of Fort Hare, whose subsequent graduates include Robert Sobukwe, founder of the PAC, and Nelson Mandela. Despite his political influence, Jabavu was not in favour of blacks forming their own political parties, and was opposed by Alan Soga who published another newspaper, *Izwi Labantu* ('the People's Voice'), to espouse the cause of active black power. Soga and his supporters had formed the South African Native National Congress in 1898, and this gradually gathered support, eventually becoming the African National Congress in 1923.

Military action against blacks in the Eastern Cape had not abated by the early 20th century. For example, in 1920, police fired on blacks gathering to organize better wages in Port Elizabeth, killing about 25 people. In 1921, members of a black Christian cult called the Israelites gathered at Bulhoek, near Queenstown, apparently to await the end of the world. About 800 police were sent to move them, and in an ensuing skirmish, killed almost 200 of the unfortunate Israelites.

However, the ANC and other black political groups from the Eastern Cape moved into the national political arena during the 1930s and '40s—especially in the Transvaal, where increasing numbers of Xhosa (and other nations) now worked on the mines. Following the arrival of apartheid in 1948, black political groups began to organize direct action, but in the 1960s and '70s, following the famous Rivonia trial (*see* **Gauteng** 'History'), most were forced underground. During this time large chunks of the region were designated tribal 'homelands' (Ciskei and Transkei), and it was these parts of Eastern Cape that produced most of the freedom fighters: many political commentators claim that, while the ANC and PAC have never been specifically Xhosa organizations, the core of their leadership and support has always been found in the Eastern Cape. The early 1990s saw sporadic strife, with faction fighting between the ANC and PAC and attacks on whites threatening always to upset the balance so painstakingly sought by South Africa's main political leaders, and it remains to be seen whether the new government can settle the conflicts which have shaped the province's bitter history. However, since April 1994 the region, like much of South Africa, has been remarkably quiet, and a long-awaited peace seems to have settled on the beautiful, troubled, Eastern Cape.

Port Elizabeth marks the coastal transition point between the Garden Route and the Eastern Cape. The third-largest port in South Africa, Port Elizabeth is, it must be said, one of the country's least attractive towns. Except for a small collection of period buildings in the very centre of town, car assembly plants, freeways and ugly concrete buildings predominate. You should spend as little time here as possible.

However, the country around Port Elizabeth is beautiful indeed, with a sub-tropical, forested coastline and a hinterland of game reserves harbouring big game. Port Elizabeth is therefore convenient as a jumping-off point for the area around it, and you may find yourself having to spend a day or two in the city *en route.*

History

Port Elizabeth was founded in 1820, on the site of the British Fort Frederick (1799), just south of the Dutch military town of Uitenhage, to receive the 5000 English settlers sent out to populate the country between Algoa Bay and the Fish River (then known as the Zuurveld), from which several Xhosa clans had been forcibly evicted (*see* 'Frontier Wars') This was Britain's first serious attempt to regularize the Eastern Frontier, after inheriting an endless cycle of Boer, Xhosa, Khoi and English settler raiding that the Dutch had found insoluble. Port Elizabeth was named by Sir Rufane Donkin, (the acting Cape Governor sent to welcome the 1820 settlers), after his wife, who had died in India.

The town remained a small village and military post for some years, until the failure of many British settlers to make a living from the fickle Eastern Cape veld forced them to abandon their plots and come into the settlement for work. Like Grahamstown further east, Port Elizabeth soon began to thrive on the commercial opportunities opened up by the escalating warfare between the British and the Xhosa. Increasing numbers of troops passing to and from the Cape and the frontier gradually augmented trade, and the town became rich. By the 1850s, grand public buildings were being erected. Few Boers lived in this British imperial atmosphere, but one, the famous Piet Retief, leader of the 1836 Great Trek from Eastern Cape to Natal lived here during the 1820s.

Port Elizabeth did not begin its transition to a major port city until the late-19th century, when farming in the frontier region became sufficiently established to create a regular supply of meat, maize and wool for export to Cape Town and beyond. In particular, Angora wool (still a mainstay of the eastern Karoo farmers, both black and white) helped establish the town's fortune. In 1920, Port Elizabeth entered big-time commerce when Ford Motors opened a plant there. The city grew quickly thereafter, attracting more factories and a massive population drift of Xhosa labourers from the Ciskei and Transkei. Today's population is around 800,000.

Port Elizabeth saw much political unrest through the 1980s, causing many commercial companies to leave the city. This, coupled with South Africa's recent recession, has caused a downturn of the city's fortunes, and unemployment is rife. But for all that, the city centre is generally safe to wander by day and is well policed by night.

by bus

Port Elizabeth is on the N2 highway linking the Garden Route with the Eastern Cape, Transkei and Natal. Buses follow this route from Cape Town, Durban, Grahamstown, Umtata and East London, stopping at all large towns in between. The **bus station**, ✆ (041) 558 751, is below Main Street between Donkin Road and Whites Road, just east of the Market Square. The big bus companies operate to and from other major cities: TransLux, InterCape, Greyhound and Transtate. More local companies are: Whippet Express (PE/Graaff-Reinet), Copper Rose (PE/East London) and Leopard Express (PE/Grahamstown). Two tour companies make excursions out to the game reserves of the Port Elizabeth hinterland—**Springbok Atlas**, ✆ (041) 351 038, and **Algoa Tours**, ✆ (041) 558 751.

Port Elizabeth's compact city centre and old town can be crossed in about 15 minutes. Buses for the beaches and suburbs leave roughly every half hour until about 10pm from platform 5 of the bus station. Port Elizabeth also has an airport.

by car

Apart from the main east/west route along the N2, Port Elizabeth is connected to the north via the R75 along the Sundays River to Graaff-Reinet, or the R32 via Cradock and Middelburg to the Orange Free State and Transvaal (the N2/R32 junction is 70km east of town). More interesting ways to enter the Eastern Cape are via the R75 and R329 along the dry north wall of Baviaanskloof mountains, via the R332 through the wild, lonely Baviaanskloof itself, or via the R62 through the fruit-growing Langkloof behind the Garden Route.

Car hire: Apart from the large chain car rental agencies, Port Elizabeth lacks really cheap car hire. However, **Dolphin Car Rentals**, ✆ (041) 541 221, offers slightly cheaper rates than the mainstream companies.

by rail

Port Elizabeth is connected with all major centres via the Spoornet railway, as are the larger towns in the region. Steam enthusiasts will delight in two narrow-gauge steam lines that leave from the main station. One chuffs along the Langkloof; the other goes east for a short distance along the coast (*see* 'Activities').

Tourist Information

Donkin Park, between Belmost Street and Western Street, ✆ (041) 521 315.

Old Port Elizabeth

Fort Frederick (*open Mon–Fri 8–5*), the original fort on the Baakens River mouth where the 1820 settlers had their tented camp, is on modern Port Elizabeth's Belmont Terrace. A large, square, stone fortification, it was one of the few British forts in the Eastern Cape never to be attacked. The **Campanile** (*open Mon–Fri 9.30–5, Sat 9.30–12.30*), is next to the fort at the entrance to the docks on Strand Street A tall monument built in the 1920s to the 1820 Settlers, it has a very long spiral stair leading to a platform with good views of the city and bay.

The **City Hall** and **Market Square** form the most handsome part of town, a collection of solid mid-Victorian buildings all recently done up and cleaned. An **Open Air Market** operates on the square every day. **Fleming Square**, a smaller square off the Market Square has the **Prester John Monument**, a tribute to the mythical Christian African King and his land of gold that lured so many medieval adventurers south (*see* **History**). Various national monuments are still in use around the two squares, including the **Feather Market Hall** (1885), a large stone building originally used for auctioning luxury goods, such as ostrich feathers and game skins, and now a concert hall. The **Opera House** on Whites Road (just uphill from Market Square) is still an opera house today.

Uphill, behind Market Square, is **Donkin Park**, an open area designated as 'a perpetual open space' by Acting Cape Governor Donkin in 1820, and the location of the Port Elizabeth Publicity Association. **Donkin Street**, which leads from the town centre to the park, has a well-preserved terrace of handsome colonial houses built between 1860 and 1870. Behind Donkin Park are a few blocks of period houses before the modern, ugly city takes over again.

The Sea Front

Port Elizabeth is known for high winds. Consequently, its beaches and coast, while popular with windsurfers, yachtsmen and the like, can be uncomfortably blowy. There are four main beaches (*see* 'Activities'), but in general the sea front is better visited for its **Museum Complex** by Humewood Beach.

The **Port Elizabeth Museum** (*open Mon–Sat 9–1, 2–3*) presents a history of the town and the 1820 Settlers, and has a maritime hall dedicated to shipwrecks and their treasure. Fossil bones and Early Man tools found in the Eastern Cape, are also on display along with the usual natural history and Victoriana.

The **Oceanarium** (*open Mon–at 8–4.30; dolphin shows between 9 and1*), next to the museum building, is part of the same complex, but requires a separate ticket. Trained dolphins, seals and penguins are the main attraction, but there are also sharks, turtles and most local sea fish in the aquarium. The **Snake Park and Tropical House** (*open Mon–Sat 8–4.30*) also require a separate ticket. The Snake Park has the usual spine-shivering poisonous snake-handling shows. Also on view are crocodiles, giant tortoises and other reptiles. The Tropical House connects the main museum with the Snake Park; brightly-coloured tropical birds flit amongst the luxurious plants.

Happy Valley, along the beach front road between the town centre and the museum complex (by Humewood beach), is a strange piece of high kitsch, and worth visiting, especially in the evening. This pleasure garden (signposted from the road) was designed in the 1950s as a kind of suburban family theme park. The lawns are divided by footpaths, ponds, a river and a giant, open-air chessboard. At night it's illuminated with fairy lights. Oddly enough, Happy Valley does achieve a kind of plastic romance after dark which, despite oneself, it is hard not to enjoy.

Settler's Park, in the north end of town, is an area of fynbos heath, hardwood coastal forest, and grassland that follows the Baakens River along a series of small cliffs. Bushbuck still thrive here, even though the park is bordered on all sides by the city; the quiet walker may well be rewarded with a sighting.

St George's Park is more formal, housing South Africa's first cricket club among its orchids, indigenous flower gardens and wide-spaced, mature trees. The **George VI Gallery** (*open Mon–Sat 8–4, Sun 11–2.30*) is housed in a building called the Cenotaph, inside the park. Its permanent collection of indifferent 19th- and early 20th-century English painting include some good South African landscapes and a collection of oriental miniatures. More interesting is the monthly art market, **Art In The Park**, held on the first Sunday of every month, ✆ 561 356/7. Apart from the usual arts and crafts, some very good township artists sometimes sell their work here.

The **Historical Museum**, 7 Castle Hill, parallel with and one block west of Whites Road (*open Mon–Fri 8–4*), is a Victorian house furnished in period. Nearby, the **South African Horse Monument**, at the junction of Russell and Cape streets is a rather touching statue of a trooper watering his horse. Erected in honour of the horses that died in the Anglo–Boer War, it's worth reflecting on the anonymous 19th-century poem:

> *Look back at our struggle for freedom*
> *Trace our present-day strength to its source*
> *And you find that man's pathway to glory*
> *Is strewn with the bones of a horse.*

Activities

Beaches: Port Elizabeth has 4 main beaches, just west of town along Marine Drive via the Museum Complex. The most developed and the safest for swimming, **King's Beach**, is also the closest to town, and offers mini-golf, fast-food outlets, water-slides and a miniature train. **Humewood Beach**, next along, is the most popular with swimmers. Its waves are good for body-surfing, and it's a little more sheltered than PE's other windy beaches. **Hobie Beach** is rougher and mainly used by surfers, windsurfers and Hobie-cat sailors. **Pollock Beach**, the furthest along, can be really rough and isn't much fun for swimming.

Watersports: Windsurfers, bodyboards and Hobie-cats can be hired (though the last should only be handled by an expert) through the Publicity Association.

Walking: Settler's Park on Valley Road has some lovely trails through natural woodland where bushbuck can often be spotted.

Steam railways: The **Apple Express** runs from Port Elizabeth along the Langkloof to the town of Loerie. It includes a spectacular chuff along the Van Stadens gorge, views of the Winterberg mountains and the gentle Loerie Valley. At the time of writing, the line had been temporarily closed, but plans are afoot to re-open it by 1995. The **Dias Express** is a much shorter ride, from the station to the Campanile and a small rail museum where you can watch the locomotives being maintained. The Dias Express must be reserved, ✆ 520 2260.

General crafts and jewellery, as well as some good township art are sold at the **Art in the Park,** held on the first Sunday of every month in St George's park.

Port Elizabeth ✆ (041–)

expensive

PE has the usual expensive chain hotels, but the clear choice within this price range is the independent **Edward Hotel,** on Belmont Terrace, ✆ 562 056, within walking distance of the city centre, a charming survivor from the late 1920s, a combination of Art Deco, mock Tudor and mock Cape Dutch. It is large, with 126 rooms, mostly en suite, overlooking the ocean. There is also an inner courtyard, and the restaurant serves fresh seafood. The **Walmer Gardens Hotel,** ✆ 414 322, in the suburb of Walmer Gardens, 12km from the city centre, is also independent. Built in a 1930s hacienda style (South Africa has the climate for such buildings not to look out of place), there are 27 rooms, all en suite, with a courtyard and pool, and an outdoor grill in the garden. The restaurant also does good seafood, with some French dishes. The **Humewood Hotel,** 33 Beach Road, ✆ 558 961, fronts the popular Humewood beach. Also a 1930s building, 64 rooms, all en suite. The Museum, Oceanarium and Snake Park are behind; the beach with its mini-golf and water-slides in front.

moderate

Langerry, 31 Beach Rd, ✆ 552 654 is next to the Humewood and has all the surrounding facilities at less expense. It is clean and comfortable and offers self-catering only. In the town centre, **Trocadero Lodge** at 2 Parliament Street, ✆ 522 651, is a large guest house offering B&B or self-catering. It's not fancy, but it is comfortable. **Pine Lodge** on Marine Drive, ✆ 534 004, has a choice of chalets, caravans or self-contained apartments. There are outside braai facilities and the beaches are within reach by bus. **Rema Apartments** are also in the city centre, at 45 Western Road, ✆ 521 772. These self-contained flatlets have their own bathrooms and fridges. B&B is optional.

cheap

Port Elizabeth Backpackers on 7 Prospect Hill, ✆ 560 697, is a friendly, well-run place with dormitory accommodation near the centre of town.

Port Elizabeth ✆ (041–)

expensive

The **Sir Rufane Donkin Rooms** on George Street, ✆ 555 534, are not as formal as the suggests. Seafood and Cape dishes are served in a Victorian style dining room. **Nelson's Arm** on Trinder Square, ✆ 559 049, does not, sadly, serve preserved limbs of the late admiral. It does serve seafood though, in a room done up in period naval style, complete with telescopes, naval pictures and polished wood. **Bella Napoli**, ✆ 553819, at the moderate end of the expensive scale, is on Hartman Street and serves good pasta and very fresh seafood antipasti. Also at the low end of the expensive scale is the **Havelock Street Restaurant**, on Havelock Street, which serves traditional steaks, seafood and French dishes in a relaxed atmosphere.

moderate

Up The Khyber on Western Road, ✆ 522 200, isn't run by the *Carry On* team, but serves good traditional Indian food. **Blackbeard's Seafood Tavern and Pier** on Western Road, ✆ 555 567/341 424, serves fresh seafood amid the standard fishing-net and lobster-pot decor. The adjoining bar gives the place an informal feel. **Rumours** on Burgess and Zareba streets, ✆ 338 216, is at the expensive end of the moderate scale. The menu varies, so it is worth asking for the day's specials. The room is small and intimate; deep colours and candlelight. **Sabatino's** on Westbourne Road, ✆ 331 707, serves good Italian food in unpretentious surroundings. Good service, relaxed clientele. Excellent calamari, and a fillet in garlic sauce are specialities of the **Coachman** ✆ 522 511, on Lawrence Street in the town centre. More solid meals can be had at the **Rand Steak House** on Russell Road, ✆ 559 684. Just out of town, at Pine Lodge, Cape Recife, is **A Stone's Throw**, ✆ 533514, a tapas and seafood bar and grill that serves as a hang-out for local surfers and fishermen as well as diners.

cheap

It's Country on Evatt Street, ✆ 523 835, attracts a young crowd and stays open 24 hours, serving wholesome pasta, seafood, steaks and burgers. Good Chinese food can be had at the **Little Swallow** ✆ 307 382 in the Cape View Centre on Cape Road, just out of the town centre. **Rio Hamburger Hut and Game Centre** on Russell Street, ✆ 522 440, is handy for the backpackers hostel and serves American and spicy Indian fast food, burgers and bunny-chows (curry served inside a hollowed loaf of bread) and stays open till 2am.

Nightlife

The **Red Lion Hotel**, on the eastern end of Main Street, is a little rough, but often has local live acts, ranging from dull cover bands to some really good rock and township sounds. Live bands also play at the **Clarendon Hotel** on Leutman Street. Check in *Splash Magazine* for listings. The **Limelight Supper Club and Disco** in The Corner House, Evatt Street, has less atmosphere and plays Top 40 dance music.

The charm of the countryside and coastline near Port Elizabeth make up for the ugliness of the city. Here you can explore orchard country, coastal forest, thick thorn-bush and montane forest and grassland, dotted with nature reserves and national parks preserving some of the larger fauna. The **Addo Elephant National Park**, ✆ (0426) 400556, in the thorn-bush country about 50km north of town on the R335, is home to Africa's southernmost viable wild elephant herd, along with buffalo and black rhino. In 1931, when the park was proclaimed, the local elephant were down to just 11, having been mercilessly shot out by the local fruit and potato farmers, whose activities the elephant naturally interfered with from time to time. Now protected, today's elephant population has recovered to over 100.

The Addo bush is dense and high, so game-viewing can be difficult. Elephant are usually at the water holes, and sometimes buffalo, but the rhino are shy and tend to stay out of sight. Other game includes kudu, eland, red hartebeest, and bushbuck, and the usual wide variety of bird life. In summer, look out for groups of white storks. There are hides near the office, rest camp and restaurant overlooking a small vlei where red bishop birds nest. Walking is not permitted, except inside a fenced, 1000 acre section from which large game is excluded. Look out for the road signs asking you to drive around, rather than over, any large black beetles that may be rolling balls of elephant dung along the road. Their mixing of dung with earth is vital in breaking up the soil and letting rain soak in properly. So don't run them over. The park has chalets, rondavels, a camp site, restaurant and shop.

Zuurberg National Park, attached to the Addo Elephant National Park, is reached via the R335 dirt road, and spreads over the entire range of low, grass-covered mountains to the north of Addo. The park covers a vast area of steep, deeply wooded kloofs and high, rolling downs which provide cool relief from the baking hot plain below. Among a number of day-hikes are several leading to remote waterfalls. Horses can be rented by the hour and ridden wherever you like. The rare cycad, a prehistoric tree-fern, grows on the Zuurberg's higher reaches. Cape mountain zebra, kudu, baboon, grey rhebok, duiker, bushbuck, grysbok, caracal and leopard are to be found. The deep milk-wood forest in the kloof is home to ticks, so if visiting in summer, remember to check yourself every few hours. At present, Addo's big game cannot roam freely into the Zuurberg, but the Parks Board is constructing a game fence around the hills, so that in the near future the downs and forests will again be home to elephant, buffalo and rhino. The park has no accommodation.

Addo Village, the small settlement where most people stock up before going into the national parks, has an interesting shop called **Elsa's Little People**. Despite the twee name, it sells good African crafts, as well as exquisite small ceramic figures of Xhosa, Sotho, Venda, Tswana, Tsonga and other South African people in traditional dress, all hand made by Elsa, the shop's owner.

Where to Stay and Eating Out
moderate/cheap

The old **Zuurberg Inn**, ✆ (0426) 400 583, a moderately-priced, charming old hotel by the entrance to the Zuurberg National Park, offers the only accommodation in the area. It has been a resting place on the road north for over 100 years. The rooms and self-contained rondavels are clean and comfortable, and there is a lively bar, with resident parrots and assorted dogs. Cheap camping can be negotiated, and riding and hiking in the Zuurberg can be arranged from here. Apart from the Zuurberg, the only place to eat out in the area is in the restaurant in the Addo Elephant National Park.

Algoa Bay and Inland between Port Elizabeth and Grahamstown

Algoa Bay, named after the needle-shaped rocks off Port Elizabeth (*algoa* means 'needles' in old Portuguese), runs east of the city for 100km. **Sardinia Bay**, an inlet from the main bay 18km east of Port Elizabeth, has a nature reserve of coastal forest and dune, with safe swimming and a walking trail (the Sacramento Trail) known for wildflowers in spring. **Woody Cape Nature Reserve and Alexandria State Forest**, ✆ (04652) 1103, are at the further end of Algoa Bay, beginning at the Sundays River mouth, about 50km east of Port Elizabeth, and running a further 50km east along a wild coastline of white dunes, coastal bush, and forest. Bushbuck and duiker are often spotted, as are a variety of birds. The two-day **Alexandra Hiking Trail**, with an overnight hut, runs through the reserve, but needs booking through the Eastern Cape Forest Region, Forestry Branch, Dept of Environmental Affairs.

Shamwari Private Game Reserve, ✆ (04285) 11196, midway between Addo and Grahamstown, covers a huge area along the Bushman's River and is the only reserve in the eastern Cape where all of the **Big Five** may be found. Follow the signs from the N2 to Paterson then Alicedale, and from there to the reserve. Here you can see elephant, white rhino, buffalo and most of the large antelope, as well as lion, leopard, hyena, warthog and bushpig. Fish eagles hunt the river, which is also the haunt of hippo and croc. The reserve offers guided day-hikes with accommodation in comfortably-appointed 1820 Settler cottages.

Recently, a luxury steam line has opened connecting the reserve with Johannesburg via Port Elizabeth, ✆ (041) 311 1127. Reserve accommodation is in the expensive category.

Settler Country: Grahamstown and the Fish River Valley

... their chief object is to oppose and render odious all authority and to sow the seeds of discontent whever their baneful influence can extend

Cape Governor Lord Charles Somerset to Colonial Secretary, Lord Bathurst in 1825

The Settler Country takes its name from the 5000 settlers brought out by the British government in 1820 to populate the land from the Fish to the Keiskamma Rivers (christened 'Albany' by the Cape government), from which the resident Xhosa clans had been forcibly ejected in 1812. One of the most fought-over stretches of country during the Frontier Wars, today's Settler Country is a quiet rural patchwork of farm, forest and wild bushveld, at whose centre lies the Settler capital of Grahamstown and its satellite villages of Bathurst, Salem and Fort Beaufort.

History

During the mid 18th century the resident Khoi tribes and seasonal Xhosa graziers had been joined by an increasing number of Dutch trekboers. At this time, the region was known as the Zuurveld, after its coastal grassland which could turn sour and ungrazable in certain seasons. Much of the inland area was, and still is, covered by thick acacia bush, especially around the Fish River itself. During the various raiding wars between Boer, Xhosa, Khoi and Briton that flared across the Zuurveld from the end of the 18th century, the Xhosa used the bush as a fortress from which to raid and into which to drive cattle.

In 1809, three years after the British annexed the Cape for the second time, a garrison village was built at Grahamstown, in the eastern Zuurveld, 60km west of the Fish River. In 1812, during one of the frontier's interminable wars, the Ndlambe and Gqunkwebe clans of the Zuurveld were driven east of the Fish River in a scorched-earth campaign of indiscriminate slaughter. In order to stop the Xhosa clans from cattle raiding once they had been forced east of the Fish, a system of patrols and *commandos* was set up from Grahamstown by Henry Somerset, the local military governor, and arrogant son of the Cape Governor, Lord Charles Somerset. Whenever a farmer reported a loss, the cavalry would ride into the Fish River bush, following the tracks of the stolen beasts, and demand payment from the first Xhosa homestead they came to. This unfair system provoked the Ndlambe, under the leadership of a millenarian prophet, Nxele, to re-enter the Zuurveld in 1819, attack Grahamstown and lay waste the entire countryside (*see* p.287).

In 1820, Lord Charles Somerset attempted to turn the region into a working British colony overnight, renaming it Albany and persuading Britain to use £50,000 of the public treasury to send 5000 English settlers to the region. But the harsh climate and fickle rainfall (alternate floods and drought), wild animals and continued Xhosa raids (the land had been summarily appropriated from the Ngqika clan) were too much for most of the settlers, who, with a few exceptions, gradually abandoned their farms and drifted to

Grahamstown. As the British continued to invade east of the Fish River and penetrate further into the heart of Xhosa country, the town prospered. Troops had to be supplied and fortunes were made.

From the 1830s, Grahamstown grew to become the Cape colony's second town, and a centre of anti-Xhosa feeling during the later Frontier Wars. Indeed, the surrounding country was invaded three times by various Xhosa clans between 1842 and and 1853, each time with increasing ferocity. However, many of the wealthier Grahamstown settlers, such as Robert Godlonton, who published anti-Xhosa propaganda in his influential *Grahamstown Journal* had a vested interest in continued warfare—land occupied by the British after each war could be bought up cheaply by Grahamstown speculators and sold later at great profit. The newspaper actively supported Henry Somerset's legalized cattle raiding, and stirred up hostility to the residents of the Kat River settlement—an area of prime land east of the Fish River given to the local Khoi in the late 1820s. The Kat River Khoi were continually accused of treachery and thieving, were racially snubbed by the settlers, and were only protected by liberal administrators such as Andries Stockenstroom, who himself became the object of derision in Grahamstown's colonial society.

Naturally, the reactionary Grahamstown residents eventually got their way, seeing the full annexation of all the Xhosa land west of the Kei River and the confiscation of the Kat River settlement after the Eighth Frontier War (1852). By the end of the Ninth (and last) Frontier War in 1878, Grahamstown was a solidly English outpost in a British-dominated part of South Africa; the local Xhosa and Khoi were reduced to farm labourers. Centred around its large, neo-Gothic cathedral, Grahamstown became the country's second city until the discovery of the Transvaal gold reefs caused Pretoria and Johannesburg to mushroom in the 1890s.

Today Grahamstown is much quieter. Rhodes University (one of South Africa's most prestigious) was founded in the 1900s, and Grahamstown is now principally a university town of some 20,000 people. Most of the old buildings, fine examples of late Georgian architecture, still stand, giving the town a period air. In term time, the huge number of students make Grahamstown lively, but it lapses into torpor during the holidays. Every July, the Grahamstown Arts Festival causes the city to overflow with visitors for a fortnight. One of the least troubled towns of the often violent Eastern Cape, Grahamstown and the surrounding bush country are a pleasure to visit and a relief from the tense atmosphere of the larger Eastern Cape towns.

Grahamstown

Getting There

By car: Grahamstown lies on the N2 highway midway between Port Elizabeth and the Fish River.

By bus: Greyhound, InterCape, TransLux, Transtate, Copper Rose and Leopard Express connect Grahamstown with Cape Town, Durban, Umtata and East London along the N2, stopping at all large towns in between.

By train: Grahamstown is linked to Cape Town, Port Elizabeth, East London and Durban by the coastal railway line.

Tourist Information

Grahamstown Publicity Association, Church Square, ✆ (0461) 23241.

Festivals

For two weeks every July, Grahamstown goes mad. The Grahamstown Festival is South Africa's most prestigious arts festival and attracts theatre, music, cabaret and other performance artists from all over Africa. Like the Edinburgh Festival in Britain, this festival distributes itself around various locations through the town. Finding accommodation can be very hard. For more information, contact the Grahamstown Publicity Association.

Grahamstown has so many old and attractive buildings that simply wandering the streets around the huge central cathedral is satisfying. The **High Street** is the central thoroughfare, running east-west, with Rhodes University campus at the west end and the cathedral at the east. Still largely Georgian, the street is a working one, with grocers, bookshops and general stores. At the west end is the **Yellow House**, Grahamstown's oldest building and originally a prison, now a public hall. The **Village Market**, now a bazaar and coffee shop, is also on High Street, and has one of the loveliest 19th-century yellowwood ceilings in the country. The nearby **Grand Hotel**, a fine piece of high Victoriana, is still in use.

Somerset Street, which runs north-south at the far end of High Street, along the eastern end of the campus, has most of the town's museums. The **Albany Museum** (*open Mon–Fri 9.30–1, 2–5, Sat and Sun 2–5*), founded in 1885, has a fairly detailed history of the 1820 Settlers, although the information cards fail to say that many of the settlers were drifters and ne'er-do-wells pushed into emigrating to South Africa by their families and communities, that most lied about their agricultural experience (the colony was to be one of farmers, re-creating an English rural society) and that those who prospered either adapted to the Boer way of life or exploited the many Frontier Wars against the Khoi and Xhosa. The wars themselves are also depicted from the standard colonial viewpoint.

Next door, the **National History Museum** (*open Mon-Fri 9.30–1, 2–5, Sat 2–5*) is mostly devoted to displays of early Man in South Africa, and the early San, Khoi and black African cultures. The nearby **Institute of Ichthyology** (*open Mon–Fri 8.30–1, 2–5*), also on Somerset Street, is an eccentric museum dedicated to South African fish, in particular the coelacanth, a prehistoric survivor discovered off South African coasts in the 1960s. The **Provost's House** (*open Mon–Fri 10–1, 2–5, Sat 2–5*), another early prison, built around a small tower, is on Lucas Avenue, west of Somerset Street, houses a permanent craft shop. The **Botanical Gardens** on Lucas Avenue, next to the Provost's House, have a wide variety of South African plants and trees and spacious lawns. A flea market is held here at weekends; Grahamstown attracts craftspeople, and some of the jewellery and clothing are of very good quality.

The **Observatory Museum** on Bathurst Street (*open Mon–Fri 9.30–1, 2–5, Sat 9–1*) is a stunning piece of Victorian colonial architecture, with a three-storey verandah of wrought iron running up the back of the building. It was here that the Eureka Stone, the first big diamond to be found in the Kimberley area, was identified in 1867. Apart from the early astronomical equipment on display, the museum has a lovely, fragrant herb garden. **Fort Selwyn** (1836), on the evocatively named Gunfire Hill above the university, was one of a series of forts built by the British from the 1830s throughout the Amatolas and the country between the Fish and Keiskamma Rivers—an attempt to partition and control Xhosa territories there. It was abandoned in 1870, but visitors can still see the heavy cannons with which the British pounded the Fish River bush in their clumsy attempts to drive the Xhosa from cover during the later Frontier Wars (*see* **Eastern Cape** 'History'). The **Settlers' Wildflower Reserve**, also on Gunfire Hill, covers 61ha. Cycads, ponds, proteas, aloes and other wild flowers make it a pleasant place to wander. The **Settlers' Monument** sits atop Gunfire Hill; a huge, ugly brick building, complete with gift shop, pub, restaurant and fountain, its main function is as a theatre.

Grahamstown ✆ *(0461–)*

Where to Stay

expensive

The **Cock House** (built in 1820) at 10 Market Street, ✆ 311 287, has 4 en suite rooms in one of the town's most handsome period houses. **Oatlands**, ✆ 23058, is a large manor, once surrounded by the estate belonging to Henry Somerset, who lived here until 1852. The entrance is in Caroline Close, off Florence Street. B&B is provided in rooms furnished in high Cape Dutch style. The **Cathcart Arms** on Market Square, ✆ 27111, has been a hotel since 1825. Again, its 14 rooms decorated in period. There is an à la carte restaurant, a bar and a garden with a swimming pool. The new **St Aidan's Court Hotel** on Milner Court, ✆ 311 188, occupies what used to be the old Jesuit's College. The town's most expensive hotel, St Aidan's has 24 luxurious rooms, all en suite.

moderate

The **Guest House**, 16 Jacobus Van Uys Way, ✆ 23393, offers B&B in a late 19th-century cottage with a quiet garden overlooking the town. **Longleat**, 9 Mount Street, ✆ 26163, is a larger 19th-century house offering B&B in old rooms with new, but not jarring furniture. No smoking is allowed. **Suffield House**, 21 Oatlands Road, ✆ 26033, also offers B&B and will bring you tea or coffee in bed. Another pleasant 19th-century building with garden.

cheap

Grahamstown lacks cheap accommodation, although there is a town **camp site**, ✆ 29112. You could also try your luck on the university campus by chatting to students and seeing who has a spare room or floor.

expensive

Grahamstown's best restaurants are both attached to hotels. The restaurant at the **Cock House** is late Georgian, and serves good Cape cuisine, game (in season) and cordon bleu. Relaxed, and very good food. At St Aidan's Court Hotel is **Il Tinello**, ✆ 311 188. Despite the name, this restaurant serves not only Italian food, but also some French, seafood and Cape dishes.

moderate

The **Copper Kettle** at 7 Bathurst Street, ✆ 24358, serves light suppers in a small Georgian cottage. **Peacocks** is a health food/wholefood restaurant on the corner of High and Hill Streets (by the Church Square). A young crowd in a scrubbed pine atmosphere. Very good, filling food. No need to book. The **Monkey-Puzzle Bistro**, ✆ 25318, in the Botanical Gardens is a new restaurant specializing in game. The ostrich and kudu dishes are recommended.

cheap

The **Rat & Parrot**, ✆ 25002, on New Street serves pub food to a largely student crowd. **Gino's Pizza and Steak House**, ✆ 27208, on Hill Street serves exactly what it says. Apart from these, there are few cheap restaurants in Grahamstown. But there is no shortage of fast food and take-away places on Market and High Streets.

cafés

Grahamstown has some good cafés. The **Copper Kettle** serves coffee, waffles pastries and light meals on an outside terrace. The **Village Market**, on the High Street, also has a coffee shop, though the decor is a bit twee. The **Cock House** serves excellent coffee on the verandah.

Around Grahamstown

South and east of Grahamstown, the rolling farmland around the old Settler villages of Bathurst and Salem gives way to dense milkwood and euphorbia forest near the coast and wild thorn bush in the Fish River Valley. Large nature reserves and state forests have conserved sizeable stretches of wild land and, despite its proximity to 'civilization', this area offers some of the Eastern Cape's best opportunities for 'going bush'.

Tourist Information

Port Alfred Publicity Association, Pascoe Crescent, Port Alfred, ✆ (0464) 41235.

Salem, Bathurst and the Farmlands

Salem and Bathurst lie south of Grahamstown, near the sea. They and their surrounding farms are considered the heart of Settler Country. **Salem**, 15 km south of Grahamstown, is a well-preserved early Georgian village. It came under siege twice during the Frontier Wars, when its larger houses and church doubled as forts.

North of town is the **Thomas Baines Nature Reserve**, a stretch of bush country on either side of the Palmiet River that harbours white rhino, buffalo, eland, bontebok, black wildebeest, reedbuck and impala. The reserve is named after the settler artist Thomas Baines, whose ink and gouache landscapes, scenes from settler and Khoi/Xhosa life and wildlife portraits comprise one of the best records of the mid-19th century frontier. Many of them have been used to illustrate South African history books, and a collection of his work is housed in the Rust-En-Vreugd museum in Cape Town. The nature reserve has game viewing roads, but guided walks can be organized by prior arrangement (*see* 'Activities'). There is only hostel accommodation.

Bathurst is larger than Salem, a town of late Georgian houses shaded by large fig trees. The **Pig and Whistle Hotel and Pub** is the reason why most people come to Bathurst. It has been open since 1831 and served as a fort during the Frontier Wars. Bathurst has various historical buildings, including a powder magazine (on Bird Street), a double-pulpitted church (which also served as a fort on occasion) on Donkin Street, and an **Agricultural Museum** on Trappes Street (*open Mon–Fri 9–4.30*). A short walk from town (2.4km from the Pig and Whistle) is **Bradshaw's Mill** (1822), which claims to be the first place in South Africa where cloth was woven from wool. The wooden water-wheel still works. The countryside immediately around Bathurst is known for its pineapples.

The Bathurst Conservation Area protects a huge sweep of euporbia and milk-wood bush between Bathurst and the coast, mostly following the west bank of the Kowie River. The conservation area includes the small **Horseshoe Bend Nature Reserve**, 7km west of Bathurst, which follows a stretch of the beautiful Kowie River, along whose wooded banks graze small herds of antelope. There are walks, but no accommodation. Also part of the conservation area is the much larger **Waters Meeting Nature Reserve** which follows the Kowie River north of the Horseshoe Bend Reserve. There are walking trails through the dense vegetation, from which an occasional bushbuck or duiker may spring, and an overnight canoe trail (canoes hired from the reserve office) up to Horseshoe Bend and back. At night, tree dassies scream, and if you are very quiet and patient, you might spot otters in the early morning. There is a camp site for tents only, and an overnight hut for canoers.

Kowie Nature Reserve, a stretch of dense aloe, euphorbia and milkwood bush, is only 199ha in extent, but follows a particularly lovely stretch of the Bloukrans River, a tributary of the Kowie. Bushbuck, vervet and samango monkey and otter are common. Walking trails have been laid out but there is no accommodation. The reserve is along the R67 to Port Alfred, about 15km south of Grahamstown.

The Settler Coast

Port Alfred, at the mouth of the Kowie River, is a small resort town with safe swimming beaches. The town itself is not of particular interest, but the Kowie can be canoed (a two-day paddle) and in **Kowie Nature Reserve**, just outside town, an 8km hiking trail leads through tranquil wetlands haunted by fish eagles. The town's harbour was never actually finished and Port Alfred was never a port. **Kenton-on-Sea**, west of Port Alfred, is an even smaller resort (also with safe swimming beaches) where the Portuguese explorer Bartholomew Dias (*see* **South African History**) erected one of his stone crosses in 1481. A replica still stands, reached by a 2km trudge across the dunes.

The Fish River Valley

The Fish River was designated the official eastern boundary of the Cape Colony in the 1760s in a futile attempt to halt the eastward advance of the trekboers and ivory hunters. For the next 100 years it remained the official boundary. Apart from the towns that grew up around the British forts, there is little in today's Fish River bush country to recall the 100 years of continual warfare that the region suffered. The landscape, with its tall acacias and yellow grasses, looks more East than South African, and much of it was never settled—today large areas have been set aside as nature reserves.

Ecca Nature Reserve is the first reserve of the bush country, just 16km northeast of Grahamstown on the R67. This small reserve (120ha) has a marked trail through the bush, with information boards on rock and vegetation types. It is famous for fossils; very early dinosaur bones have been found here. Kudu, bushbuck, duiker and steenbok are common. There is no accommodation. The **Andries Vosloo Kudu Reserve and Sam Knott Reserve** form a huge sweep of over 45,000ha. On the opposite bank of the Fish River is the large Double Drift Game Reserve in the former Ciskei, making this a vast area over which game can move, hunt and browse at will, including black rhino, buffalo, eland, impala, kudu, bushbuck, duiker, springbok and steenbok as well as bushpig, warthog, baboon and vervet monkey. Leopard and caracal hunt the reserve. There are game-viewing roads, walking trails (booked in advance) and bird watching hides (*see* 'Activities'). Accommodation is in chalets or a permanent tented camp.

The **Great Fish River Wetland Reserve** at the mouth of the Great Fish River, just off the N2 on the former Ciskei border, is a haven for waterfowl, waders and seabirds. There is a gorgeous, unspoilt beach, safe if you stay in the shallows, and a camp site hidden among the dunes (with an ablution block).

Activities

The Settler Country and Fish River Valley are best known for their reserves and walking/hiking trails from which to spot game.

Day Hikes: Kowie Nature Reserve, Waters Meeting Nature Reserve and Thomas Baines Nature Reserve offer trails south of Grahamstown near Salem, Bathurst and Port Alfred, as do the Andries Vosloo and Sam Knott Nature Reserves in the Fish River Valley.

Overnight Hikes: The Andries Vosloo and Sam Knott Nature Reserves, ✆ (0461) 27909, have a connecting overnight trail (with hut) that must be booked. Woody

Cape Nature Reserve, ✆ (04652) 1103, has a beautiful 2-day hike through coastal forest. Access is from Alexandria Village, south of Salem.

Riding: Horses are available from Glenthorpe Farm, 10km west of Grahamstown, ✆ (0461) 28868.

Where to Stay

expensive

Kariega Park, ✆ (0461) 311 049, on the R343 between Kenton-on-Sea and Salem, is a private reserve with self-contained log cabins tucked away in the bush. There are walking trails through the riverine forest. Giraffe, zebra and bushbuck are common, as are most antelope species. Look out for martial eagles.

moderate

The well-known Georgian **Pig & Whistle Hotel**, ✆ (0431) 53273, Bathurst, has been an inn since 1831. The dining room and pub are period-furnished, but the rooms are more modern. **Glenthorpe Farm**, ✆ (0461) 28868, sits in an oak-shaded valley, signposted from the N2, 10km west of Grahamstown. It offers B&B and meals by request. There is a swimming pool, some woods, and horses to ride.

The nature reserves of the Fish River Valley also have moderately-priced accommodation. (*See* above for listings.)

cheap

Top House Guest House on Bucklands Farm, ✆ (0461) 26055, on the road from Grahamstown to Fort Beaufort, is handy for the Fish River Valley reserves. Clean and simple, the guest house is self-catering only. There is a **camp site** at **Waters Meeting Nature Reserve** for tents only and at the **Great Fish River Wetland Reserve**.

North of Settler Country: The Karoo Fringe

Getting There

There are two main routes into the northern reaches of the Eastern Cape. The most interesting is via the R335 over the Zuurberg mountains on a good dirt road that winds for a spectacular hour through the forest and open grassland of these high hills to Somerset East, roughly 80km north. The second, quicker, way is via the R32 to Cradock, and then on up the R390 to Burgersdorp, Aliwal North, Lady Grey and the Drakensberg Region.

Somerset East is more or less the point at which the Karoo meets the grass veld. Depending on the season, the surrounding country can be parched or green. Behind the town rise the **Bosberg**, a range of low mountains cloaked in yellowwood and milkwood forest, cut by streams and waterfalls that make a dramatic contrast to the dry country below (there is an overnight hiking trail through here). As you enter Somerset East, a sign invites you to 'Stop Awhile, You'll Like It Here'. However, though the town has some attractive Georgian and Edwardian buildings, there is little of interest save the **Somerset East Museum**, dedicated to church history, with the usual collection of pioneer tools, clothes and other artefacts and the **Walter Batiss Art Gallery**, displaying work of a landscape artist who was well known in South Africa earlier this century, and who was born in the town.

Adelaide and **Bedford**, are east of Somerset East. Adelaide is a large, pretty village set below the Winterberg Mountains. It's worth driving a short way north into the foothills to see the aracadian **Mankazana Valley**, whose green, well-watered farms front a winding, tree-fringed river. Thomas Pringle, a Scot who came over in 1822 and made a mark as an espouser of the early missionary cause to 'enlighten', rather than directly enslave, the local Khoi and Xhosa, farmed this valley for a while. An enemy of the reactionary Grahamstown settlers, Pringle moved to Cape Town and published a liberal newspaper called *The South African Journal* during the 1820s and '30s, which called for better treatment of the Khoi, and indirect rule of the Xhosa through their existing chiefs. He also attacked the British Governor Lord Charles Somerset's tyrannical policies, and eventually had the pleasure of seeing Somerset recalled after the costly, inconclusive sixth Frontier War (1834). However, Pringle didn't much like Africa and went home after a few years to work for the Anti-Slavery Society and lobby parliament to reform colonial mismanagement of the Cape.

Bedford is famous for nearby **Slagter's Nek**, the ridge where the first British execution of Boer rebels took place in 1815 after one Fanie Bezuidenhout led an ill-fated rebellion against British restriction of movement across the Fish River and the ill-treatment of the Boers' Khoi servants. Interestingly, the Boers tried to enlist Xhosa support for the venture, but failed. Bezuidenhout and four others were executed in 1816 at Slagter's Nek, and the event subsequently went down as a landmark date of Anglo–Boer hatred. Certainly, the execution itself was a cruel farce: the condemned were too heavy for their ropes, which broke on the first attempt. Although they pleaded for their lives, they were marched back to the scaffold for a second, successful hanging. Andries Stockenstroom, *landdrost* of Graaff-Reinet in the early-19th century, and a man who shaped many of the events in the history of the Eastern Frontier, farmed nearby when he retired from public life (*see* **Eastern Cape** 'History').

Fort Beaufort, on the Kat River, is the next town east. A small Georgian town surrounded by citrus farms, it began life as a garrison fort in 1823. The original officer's mess on Durban Street is now the **Fort Beaufort Museum** (*open Mon–Sat 9–5*), with a small collection of Victoriana and local natural history and some paintings by Thomas Baines, an early settler who recorded what he saw in watercolour. Fort Beaufort was attacked in 1851, during the long Eighth Frontier War, but today is a quiet country town, except on Friday and Saturday nights, when the local citrus workers come in to spend their wages. Nearby is the **Lovedale Mission Station**, still open to visitors, founded in 1841. Several alumni from here, like the famous Alan Soga, went on to become the first black South African university graduates, being sent by the London Missionary Society to Edinburgh University in the late 19th century.

In the high uplands north of Fort Beaufort is the **Fort Fordyce Conservation Area**, an expanse of montane hardwood forest and wild pasture inhabited by bushbuck, baboon, klipspringer and duiker. A hiker's paradise, the protected mountains are criss-crossed with marked trails. However, these forests were not always such a joy to foreign walkers—much of the fighting of the Eighth Frontier War (1850–3) between Sandile and Maqoma and Sir Harry Smith took place here (*see* p.289), with the British columns lumbering through the impenetrable forest after the fleet and silent Xhosa. The horror of hand-to-hand fights in the half-dark under the great trees, and the constant struggle of the over-equipped British troops with the terrain earned the uplands the title of '**Mount Misery.**' Lieut.-Col. Fordyce, after whom the hills are now named, was one of the many British soldiers to lose his life in the fierce campaign.

North to the Drakensberg

North of the Winterberg, Afrikaans signs re-appear on the farm gates. To the west and north, stretches the dry Karoo. To the east and northeast rise the first tiers of the Bamboesberg and Stormberg, the foothills of the high Cape Drakensberg itself.

Leaving the R32 at Cradock (*see* 'Eastern Karoo') and taking the R390 north, head for the mountains via the small town of **Hofmeyr**, which has hardly changed in outward aspect since the mid-19th century. The general store sells delicious home-made ginger beer, lemonade, Boer breads and biscuits. Alternatively, you can head north over the Witteberg to **Tarkastad** (R344), a small town surrounded by vast game farms. Some of these offer accommodation, with marked hiking and riding trails leading through the game-rich hills.

You come out on the R56, in country that is part Karoo, part grassland, and lies at the foot of the Bamboesberg and Stormberg. From the Hofmeyr route, either go north along the R391 and R58 to Burgersdorp and Aliwal North, or east via Molteno (R56) to hook up with the N6 highway, which also goes north to Aliwal North. If coming over the Witteberg route either head east to Dordrecht, on the R56, which skirts the southern wall of the Cape Drakensberg and the northern edge of Transkei, or go up the N6 to Aliwal North, and enter the Drakensberg from here.

Aliwal North is a strange town; staunchly Afrikaans, despite its name, which celebrates Sir Harry Smith's victory over the Sikhs at Aliwal in India, before he came out to the Cape as Governor in the 1840s. The town sits on the Orange River, on the border between the Cape and the Orange Free State. There is a **Hot Springs Resort** on the eastern edge of town, unfortunately housed in a grey concrete building, and the town has an ugly Main Street, but a pleasant, old residential district behind. A gem is the **Old Library Museum**, now a museum of local history. When the author visited, the old library books, many of them first editions from the 1930s and '40s, as well as a large collection of Victorian editions, were being sold in the museum for R1 each. There are some treasures to be picked up here, and as few people visit the town, it will take a long time before the collection is seriously diminished.

The last farm on the right as you leave town, on the road to the Drakensberg, belongs to Martin Vogel, a farmer and horse trainer known to the town as 'Oom Martin' (Uncle Martin). Mr Vogel trains horses in the traditional *boerperd* fashion that harks back to the classical riding traditions of 17th-century Holland. If asked politely, Mr. Vogel may show you the horses being put through their paces.

Lady Grey, a charming village set in the high foothills of the Cape Drakensberg, is again, despite the name, a primarily Afrikaans settlement of wrought iron and sandstone Victorian houses clustered round a large church. On the Main Street is a small **museum** (*open Mon–Fri 9–2*) which displays a Victorian hearse designed to be drawn by people rather than horses. So steep are the hills surrounding Lady Grey that a **narrow-gauge railway**, constructed in 1911 from Aliwal North to Barkly East via Lady Grey, was constructed as a series of reverses, the only one of its kind in the world. The high, lonely train ride is worth taking for the scenery alone, ✆ (0551) 41362. For hikers, the **Lammergeier Trail** winds for two days through the mountains above the town, with accommodation in a refuge hut (*see* 'Activities').

Cape Drakensberg

All kinds of monsters, cannibals, even the legendary unicorn, were rumoured to roam those heights

Stormberg, Johannes Meintjies

East of Lady Grey begin the Drakensberg proper. The range, South Africa's highest, stretches from here all the way through northern Transkei, Natal and the Eastern Transvaal. Most tourists only visit the latter two regions: the Cape Drakensberg, towering and silent, remain largely unexplored by tourists. Hiking and riding trails abound, passing though vast uplands scattered with sandstone outcrops, boulders, overhangs and caves, often painted with bushman (San) art—the Cape Drakensberg were one of the last strongholds of the San in the 19th century, until combined white, Xhosa and Sotho migration into the area in the 1840s and '50s caused their demise.

Unlike the Natal and Transvaal Drakensberg, the Cape section has no big hotel complexes, golf-courses or camp sites, and only a few tarred roads. Visitors tend to be hikers, climbers, trout fishermen, riding enthusiasts and skiers (there is a ski-lift at the village of Rhodes). Still, there is no shortage of moderately priced guest farms and small hotels in the villages, and camping can always be had by permission on the huge mountain sheep farms.

Despite the largely Afrikaans farming population of the region, the names of the mountains are mostly borrowed from Scotland (for example the 3000m Ben Macdhui, rising above Rhodes) which the Cape Drakensberg resembles in its higher reaches, especially in summer, when the hillsides are green from the summer rains, and during the winter snowfalls. The highest driveable mountain pass in South Africa, the **Naudesnek Pass**, connects Rhodes and Maclear in the east of the region. Worth driving just for the scenery and solitude, the pass gives views over Transkei and Lesotho. A word of warning though: the small, triangular section of the former Transkei 'homeland' between Lady Grey and Lesotho is known for being dangerous for white drivers.

Barkly East is a small town on the R58, with little for the traveller except a hotel that arranges trout fishing on streams owned by surrounding farms, but the little town is also the start of a two-day wild hike, the **Ben Macdhui Trail**, which climbs over the mountains to the remote village of Rhodes (*see* 'Activities'). About 20km further along the R58 is a farm called **Denorben**. Just behind the farmhouse is a sandstone overhang that shelters the longest set of bushman paintings in South Africa. The paintings are mostly of animals and hunters, but there is one half-man, half-animal, representing a shaman in trance communicating with animal spirits. The cave in which the present farmer keeps his sheep was used by the San to hide cattle rustled from the lowland farmers. The stronghold was discovered by settlers in the 1850s, and the San raiders were massacred in the cave, but the soot from their fires still blackens the cavern's ceiling. About 10km beyond Denorben is the magnificent **Barkly Pass**, which connects the mountains with the lowland town of Elliot. Falling thousands of metres, the road passes vast outcrops of sandstone that resemble misshapen giants. Long-tailed wydah birds hover low on the mountain pastures. Driving the pass is spectacular, but it is better to get out and walk. The **Ekowa Hiking Trail** winds through the mountains of the pass (*see* 'Activities').

Rhodes is the gem of the region. A perfectly conserved, tiny Victorian village, it has a white population of 23, and a Sotho/Xhosa village just outside, of about 200. Sotho horsemen frequently cross the mountain wall north of the town, where Ben Macdhui rises. Rhodes has a small, beautiful hotel, a Victorian wood and corrugated iron set piece, furnished in period, whose pub (still serving beer) used to be a rest spot for 19th-century brandy, cattle and gun smugglers between the Cape colony and Lesotho. Horses can be hired from the hotel, there are some marked hiking and riding trails and shooting (for francolin and mountain reedbuck) is available in autumn. There is even a small ski lift on Ben Macdhui that is open through June and July. Despite the range of activities, there is no modern development to the town and hotel and Rhodes is one of the most tranquil spots in the entire country.

The **Naudesnek Pass** connecting Rhodes with Maclear is South Africa's highest road pass (2027m). The views are breathtaking, but the condition of the road deteriorates in summer when the rains turn parts of it into a mud-slide, and in winter when the pass sometimes snows up. However, if the weather is reasonable, it is worth driving the 80km pass for the scenery and solitude: you are unlikely to pass another vehicle on the way over. Don't hurry, it can take two days to get over the pass in an ordinary car, so be prepared for a long haul and to camp if need be. Look out for red-hot poker flowers in summer and beware of rock-falls. The hotel at Rhodes can usually give up-to-date information on the state of the pass road: if they tell you it's safe, then it's safe.

Maclear lies at the eastern end of the Naudesnek Pass. Although small, it seems a hive of activity after the loneliness of the preceding drive. In fact, the town is pretty lively, being the only trading post for miles around for the local Sotho, Xhosa and white farmers. Maclear's surrounding mountains have several good hiking trails, including the **Tsitsa Falls** (a half-day hike) and the **Woodcliffe Trails** (hikes of several days with accommodation in huts set in caves, with donkeys available to carry packs and pots). Early dinosaur tracks can be seen on the Pot River near town (*see* 'Activities'). **Ugie**, the next village on from Maclear (back on the tarred road), nestles in the Prentjiesberg, a foothill chain jutting out from the main Drakensberg, and known for its forests of rare protea trees. **The Prentjiesberg Hiking Trail** leads two days through the mountains country (*see* 'Activities').

Elliot, next town along the R56, lies at the foot of the magnificent Barkly Pass: Apart from this, there is not much to recommend the town, which serves as a small banking and shopping centre for local farmers and houses some of the offices of the Mondi Forestry company, whose vast plantations cover the mountains northwest of town.

Further west, **Dordrecht** is handsome and Victorian, with the reputation for being South Africa's coldest town in winter (although many Karoo towns make the same claim). The **Anderson Museum** on Grey Street houses the usual pioneer stuff, plus a more interesting photographic collection of some of the best examples of the Cape Drakensberg's bushman rock paintings. Just north of town, the lovely **Dordrecht's Kloof** has gentle walking trails. A harder hike is the **Kranskop Trail**, on the farm Gelegenfontein, where hikers overnight in a huge cave, climb to some remote waterfalls, then stagger back to Gelegenfontein via a series of narrow, beautiful kloofs (*see* 'Activities'). East of Dordrecht the R56 crosses the N6 highway, from where you can head north to Aliwal North and the Orange Free State, or south through the Stormberg mountains to Queenstown and the Settler Country that runs between the former Transkei and Ciskei 'homelands'.

Activities

Hiking: The following trails all offer overnight accommodation in huts with firewood, water, cooking pots and sheepskins to sleep on. The **Woodcliffe Cave Trail**, ✆ (045322) 1222, a 5-day trail through the Drakensberg near Maclear, can be divided into sections of one or more days. The **Kranskop Trail**, ✆ (045312) 6330, runs for 3 days through the mountains near Dordrecht. The **Ekowa Hiking Trail**, ✆ (045312) 11, winds 3 days through the mountains and protea forests above the Barkly Pass. The **Lammergeier Trail**, ✆ (0423) 19, named after the rare, bearded lammergeier vulture found nearby, is a 2-day walk above Lady Grey. The **Ben Macdhui Trail**, ✆ (04542) 7021, is a tough one, but beautifully remote; 2 days in the mountains above Rhodes, on the Lesotho border. The 2-day **Prentjiesberg Hiking Trail**, ✆ (045332) 42/44, in the mountains above Ugie, has some good bushman paintings and game-spotting.

Riding: The Rhodes Hotel hires horses by the hour or day. Simply show up at the hotel to book.

Skiing: Rhodes is one of the few places in South Africa that has sufficiently reliable snow to warrant a ski lift. All arrangements, including hire of gear, are made through the Rhodes Hotel.

Steam Railway: This area is famous among train-spotters for having a unique series of railway reverses, necessary to get the narrow-gauge steam trains up the steep gradients. Enthusiasts come from all over the world to ride this slow train through the spectacular Cape Drakensberg, past stations that service only hill farms and miles and miles of uninhabited upland scenery. To book, phone the Mountain View Hotel at Lady Grey, ✆ (05551) 112.

Where to Stay and Eating Out

expensive

The **Rhodes Hotel**, ✆ (04542) 21, is at the moderate end of the expensive range, and well worth the price. This undeveloped 19th-century hotel in the undeveloped 19th-century village of Rhodes is beautiful, furnished with period pieces throughout. The bar used to be popular with brandy smugglers and cattle rustlers in the last century and was the scene of more than one shoot-out. The Cape food served in the small restaurant is exquisite, as is the choice of wine. If the hotel were not so isolated, it would command far higher prices.

moderate

The **Mountain View Hotel**, Lady Grey, ✆ (05552) 112, is a 1930s establishment with simple, comfortable rooms and a dam for swimming. The nearby steam railway is bookable from here. The **Drakensberg Hotel**, Barkly East, ✆ (04542) 277, is gloomy and overpriced, but a convenient place to break the journey if you arrive too late to go up into the mountains proper. It also arranges trout fishing on local farms, with accommodation in cottages.

cheap

There is little cheap accommodation in the Cape 'Berg. However, Rhodes has a quiet, equipped camp site, or you can camp on just about any farm, with permission. Alternatively, as tourism has dropped off in the area lately, it is always worth bargaining with the hotels, which often have empty rooms.

The Former Ciskei

My heart is far-off between the peaks
Away off where the south wind speaks

Vusumzi's Song, L.T. Manyase

The former 'republic' of Ciskei (re-incorporated back into South Africa in April 1994) forms a rough triangle, with the base between the mouths of the Great Fish and the Chalumna Rivers at the coast (about 75km) and the apex in the Stormberg and Winterberg Mountains near Queenstown, about 200km to the north. The tiny regional capital, Bisho (built in 1981 and not worth visiting), lies to the extreme east of the region, within sight of the much larger King William's Town. In the centre rise the beautiful, forested Katberg and Amatola Mountains, heartland of the Ngqika Xhosas in the 19th century, and the scene of much bitter fighting between Xhosa, British, Boer and Khoi from 1800 to

1870. The central Katberg and Amatola mountains are still densely forested, while the Winterberg area to the north and much of the Fish River Valley are also fairly wild, and have some excellent private game reserves. The rest of the region is overpopulated, over-grazed and eroded, due to the forced overcrowding resulting from its recent history as a 'homeland'. By contrast, the coastline is beautiful and undeveloped, especially around the Keiskamma and Chalumna River mouths, where long, white sand beaches and coastal bush fall to a sea known to harbour huge, unexploited shoals of fish.

History

Much of the Eastern Cape's violent history was played out in this area. The territory between the Great Fish and Keiskamma Rivers was known through most of the 19th century as the Ceded Territory, referring to a series of treaties made between the British and the Ngqika Xhosa after the first Frontier Wars in the 1790s and early 1800s. In the 1820s the Ngqika were expelled from everywhere in the region, with the exception of the Amatolas, but were given back the territory when the British government realized that the volatile frontier could not absorb a homeless, wandering Xhosa clan. From this time, the area was known to the colonists as 'British Kaffraria'.

The Ngqika became the most militant of the Xhosa, suffering the brunt of colonial misman-agement of the frontier, as first the Dutch and then the British tried to force the chiefs Ngqika, Maqoma and Sandile to answer for the raiding and/or wars of the entire Xhosa nation. The colonists were jealous of the magnificent Amatola country and, having put the Ngqika in an impossible position, applauded as the Government launched campaign after campaign against the Ngqika, gradually stripping them of the territory.

However, this was a slow process. The British found campaigning in the Amatolas to be ineffective and costly; the regular troops were unused to the terrain and were never able to come to grips with their foe, relying on the Khoi troops to do the bush fighting. By the 1840s, the entire region of what became southern and central Ciskei was dotted with a series of forts, centred around the Amatolas, which the British used as centres from which to partition ever-increasing amounts of Ngqika land. Most of the region's larger towns are on the sites of these old forts.

During the 1840s Ciskei was the scene of the final tragedy of the Cape colony's free-holding Khoi. In 1828 the Cape Governor Lord Charles Somerset gave a large group of Khoi their own self-governing colony on well-watered pastureland at the foot of the Katberg, to be administered by the humane but unpopular missionary James Read who had married a Khoi woman, and was ostracized by most frontier whites. Read had campaigned passionately for the Khoi since his arrival on the frontier in the early 1800s.

But, unfortunately, the land had been confiscated from Ngqika chief Maqoma after yet another war. Over the following two decades the resentful Ngqika raided the settlement at will, while white settlers, outraged that such good land should be given to mere Khoi, clamoured to have the settlement annulled. On top of these difficulties, the Kat River Settlement, as it was known, was required to provide soldiers for the Frontier Wars of the 1830s and '40s; 90 per cent of its males between 16 and 60 were pressed into service as part of the **Cape Corps**, the 'coloured' regiment started by the Dutch in the late 18th-century and which went on to fight for the British in the two World Wars. But despite a loyal war record, many influential white settlers suspected that the Kat River Khoi were liable to ally with the Xhosa and turn on the colony, even though this flew in the face of evidence to the contrary: on two occasions, it was the Kat River Khoi who tipped off the British about forthcoming Xhosa hostilities. But the frontier whites insisted that the Kat River land be annexed and sold to the highest bidder.

In the late 1840s, colonial mistrust of the Kat River Khoi became outright persecution. White colonists claimed that many of the settlement's inhabitants were illegal squatters and not proper Khoi, but mixed race 'coloureds', an indication of how the continual mixing of races in the colony was beginning to undermine the Khoi, marking the start of their final slide from an officially equal race to a disenfranchised group of colonial dependants.

Sir Harry Smith, the egocentric new Cape Governor, who hated the frontier missionaries (especially the liberal James Read), saw Kat River as a chance to undermine them. He sanctioned the removal of the 'squatters' from the settlement, which was carried out in the worst of a severe winter (1849). Huts were burned and families driven into the veld. The Kat River Khoi, by now as educated and 'westernised' as any white frontier community, bore this latest humiliation as stoically as ever. But in 1850 when Sir Harry Smith was worsted by a combined force of Ngqika, Gcaleka and Ndlambe warriors in the violent, drawn-out Eighth Frontier War, and called on the Khoi to fight for the British once again, the Khoi's patience finally snapped and in desperation the young men allied with the Xhosa. For the following three years the joint Khoi/Xhosa force kept the British bogged down in an expensive and inconclusive campaign, but eventually the colonists brought in massive reinforcements and the combined Khoi and Xhosa forces were brutally subdued in 1853. The Kat River Settlement was taken away and its inhabitants, whether they had rebelled or not, reduced to wandering the countryside seeking employment as farm labourers, while their land was bought up by frontier whites.

In the 1860s, the Ngqika Xhosa were also expelled once and for all from the Amatolas. Sandile, the last Ngqika chief, led his people back to the mountains for a brief campaign in 1878, but he was killed there, and his people again expelled. Much of the country was then given over to European settlers (predominantly German) and Mfengu from Transkei. Not until the late 20th century, when Ciskei was declared an 'independent' republic (1973), were Xhosa people allowed to move back. As a puppet state, Ciskei's government toed the apartheid government's line and suppressed black political organisations like the ANC, a fact that came to the world's attention when Ciskei troops opened fire on an ANC march from King William's Town (just over the the Ciskei/Cape border) to Bisho, the republic's small capital. The pictures, published in journals around the world, brought home the fact that South Africa's 'homelands' were nothing more than military dictatorships propped up by apartheid.

On the other hand, some Ciskei residents claim that the ANC itself was less than ethical in using violence to force people to join the organisation. However, in general, Ciskei suffered less political violence than some of South Africa's other 'homelands', and even through the troubled build-up to the 1994 elections, remained a tranquil place to travel. Today, although Ciskei (and the other former 'homelands') are back 'inside' South Africa, having been separate for a generation, the place offers an alternative view of South African life to the white-owned areas of the Eastern Cape, and, for both its village life and its superb landscapes, should not be missed.

Xhosa Culture

In his book of South African oral history, Credo Mutwa, a Zulu witch doctor and historian writing in the 1960s said this of the Xhosa:

> The Xhosa are not a tribe, they are a true nation, a group of tribes inhabiting one land and united by a common language... The Xhosa are an ancient people. In Southern Africa they are older than the Zulus.

Certainly, the Xhosa are a large, diverse people of several distinct groups, the most prominent today being the Tembu, Ngqika, Gcaleka, Qayi and Mfengu (Fingo). Traditionally, the Gcaleka were the paramount clan, and all deferred to the Gcaleka chief. Having said that, the Gcaleka chief would not interfere directly in the political affairs of other chiefs. In general, authority still rests with chiefs and headmen of inherited lineage, both in the villages and in the bureaucratic and business hierarchy of the towns.

The Xhosa are primarily a cattle-owning people. Cattle equals wealth; brides must be paid for in cattle, and a rich man can therefore have several wives. In the countryside, sheep and goats provide the staple meat, but cattle are generally never slaughtered except on special occasions.

Rural Xhosa culture, as everywhere in Africa, still revolves around reverence for the ancestors. Although evangelical Christianity has mostly replaced traditional worship, diviners have not lost their function as mediums between the human and the spirit world, from which comes everything that affects human life. Diviners and traditional healers are important members of society and will generally be consulted before a medical doctor.

The most well-known Xhosa spirit is the *tokoloshe*, characterized by a short, sturdy form and an immense phallus that can be thrown over his shoulder when running. The *tokoloshe* is neither good nor bad, but can be enslaved by a witch/wizard and made to act malevolently. Rural people fear the him and often stand their beds on bricks, so that the *tokoloshe* can pass underneath.

Water has always held ritual importance for the Xhosa. It was formerly believed that the dead lived at the bottom of rivers and lakes, and there are gentle water-dwelling spirits who look after the drowned. Less benevolent is the Lightning Bird (*Impundulu*). Tall as man, it can assume any shape, and is traditionally used by witches (rather than diviners; historically, people accused of witchcraft were the only people traditionally executed under the Xhosa's otherwise tolerant law, and always by torture) to perform the most evil deeds. If one among you will not drink beer at a gathering, beware, it is the *Impundulu* in human guise.

Rural beliefs have been eroded among many urban Xhosa, whose involvement in the modern world is replacing tradition. Many of the older generation regret this, fearing a concurrent breakdown of moral and social codes. However, even in townships near large cities, you will always spot Xhosa boys painted with white clay. This is evidence of the circumcision rite, perhaps the strongest Xhosa tradition, which has survived everywhere. When boys turn 13 (or when they can spare the time) they are taken in groups by elders to secret camps in the bush and put through rigorous survival tests, culminating in painful, ritual circumcision. The initiates are then daubed in white, the colour of light and goodness, and turn from boys to men. So strong is this tradition that a taunt from Xhosa to Zulu men during their often lethal faction fighting in the townships is 'Uncircumcised Ones', which translates roughly to 'not men'.

Perhaps the strongest facet of Xhosa culture is their lack of xenophobia and nationalism, and their great pragamatism, forged strong under the endless wars with the British and subsequent semi-enslavement following their near mass-suicide during the Great Cattle Killing of 1856 (*see* p.316). Although closely rivalled, the Xhosa are arguably the most politically successful black group in South Africa, despite the many petty rivalries between clans.

The Ciskei Coast

The R72 crosses the Great Fish River within sight of its mouth, passes the Fish River Sun Hotel and Casino, (with its own swimming beach) and continues across several more estuary mouths to the small settlement of **Wesley** (which has a large arts and crafts store), where the road curves inland. After about 20km, a dirt road (R345) turns sharp south along the Keiskamma estuary to the coastal village of **Hamburg**. A white resort before the inauguration of Ciskei as a 'republic', Hamburg's old hotel (and many of the beach houses) now lie derelict while cattle graze around them, and traditional huts dot the surrounding hillsides. A tranquil spot, Hamburg is known to fishermen and a few holidaymakers, but is completely undeveloped. A trading store, a kiosk that doubles as a bar after dark, a camp site and some two-roomed guest cottages comprise the facilities. If you do not have fishing tackle, you can usually borrow or hire a prawning net from the locals (as well as buying their fresh catches). It takes about an hour to learn how to cast the net so that it lands on the water in as near-perfect a circle as you can manage. Cast along the estuary for an hour or two after dark, when the large river prawns are running, and you will catch enough for supper and breakfast.

The **Shipwreck Hiking Trail** runs along the whole Ciskei coast from Great Fish Point to Chalumna Mouth, crossing 14 estuaries, including the wild, forested Mtati and Mgwalana river mouths. The 3-day trail passes several beached wrecks. Day-long sections of it are accessible from where roads meet the coast at the Fish River Sun, Hamburg, Kilwane and Chalumna mouth.

The Fish River Bush

Double Drift Game Reserve, ✆ (0401) 952 115, covers 22,000ha of Fish River mimosa, thorn and euphorbia bush about 10km north of the small town of **Peddie**. Originally Fort Peddie, this was the site of the Frontier Wars' only massed cavalry charge, during the War of the Axe (The Seventh Frontier War 1844–46), and the area to which the British moved the Mfengo clan (today's Fingo) in the 1830s, as a reward for fighting with the British against the main body of Xhosa chiefs during Sir Harry Smith's murderous Transkei campaign (*see* **Eastern Cape** 'History').

Double Drift, entered at Breakfast Vlei on the R345, forms part of a massive wild area backing onto the Andries Vosloo and Sam Knott Game Reserves on the west (Cape Province) side of the Fish River. Big game includes black rhino, buffalo, hippo, eland, kudu, bushbuck, blesbok, impala and blue wildebeest.

Facilities include two luxurious game lodges (*see* 'Where to Stay') with a network of game-viewing roads. A hiking trail of 1–3 days (with overnight huts) that visits a series of cliff caves along the Fish River. These have good bushman paintings, and evidence of much earlier inhabitants (as early as 20,000 years ago), whose stone tools can be found lying on the cave floors. Two ruined British forts, Fort Wiltshire and Fort Montgomery, both scenes of fighting in the 1830s and '40s, lie in the bush, and can be reached on foot.

The Katberg Mountains

The Katberg are best reached by the R67 from Fort Beaufort, just over the Cape border to the south-west, or from Whittlesea and Queenstown in the north. The massive, almost sheer, forested upland is accessible via two nature reserves: Mpofu, to the south, bordering the Cape, and the Katberg and Readsdale Forests, a few kilometres further north.

Mpofu, ✆ (0401) 952 115, 12,000ha of rolling grassland and forest in the foothills of the Katberg, supports a lot of game—blue and black wildebeest, red hartebeest, eland, bushbuck and duiker abound. Bushpig, grysbok and blue duiker (as well as leopard and caracal) tend to be more shy and keep to the forest. There is a horseback trail and hiking (the reserve is linked to the Katberg Hiking Trail, *see* below), and the lowland section of the reserve has game-viewing roads and a lodge (Mpofu Lodge). The upland section also has a lodge (Ntloni Lodge), and a hiking hut. The horseback trail camp is in the west of the reserve, on the banks of the Blinkwater river.

The **Katberg and Readsdale Forests** are in the high Katberg, a massive amphitheatre giving fabulous views out over the Eastern Cape and southern Ciskei. Clear mountain streams, waterfalls, ferns, huge yellowwood trees and clean, cool air make this a heaven after the heat of the lowlands. The two forests (accessible from Katberg and Buxton Forest Stations on the R67, a bad dirt road) have hiking trails of one 1–4 hours, as well as the 2-day **Katberg Trail** that links the forests with Mpofu Reserve. Green louries, samango and vervet monkeys, baboon and bushbuck are the most usually spotted game, and the lack of regular visitors to the Katberg makes it one of the best places to see the shy bushpig by day. Leopard and caracal hunt by night.

Just below the Katberg Forest is the **Katberg Protea Hotel** (also on the R67), a fairly luxurious establishment that offers horseback trails up into the mountains (*see* 'Activities' and 'Where to Stay'). The lowlands at the foot of the Katberg were the site of the ill-fated Kat River Settlement, home of the Cape's last freeholding Khoi in the 1840s. At **Seymour**, on the R67 south of the Katberg, one of the British forts survives intact; the ghostly **Eland's Post**, built in 1846, and beseiged by the Kat River Khoi in 1850, is open to visitors.

The Amatolas

The most bitterly contested territory of the long Frontier Wars, is now one of the Eastern Cape's most tranquil areas. More extensive than the Katberg, the Amatolas consist of dense forest, mountain pasture, clear streams, waterfalls and some of the country's cleanest air. The 6-day **Amatola Hiking Trail** (*see* below), reputedly South Africa's hardest, winds through the wilder portions of the range.

Amatola Forest Reserve, ✆ (0401) 91131/2/3, covers a vast area of mountain north of the town of Keiskammashoek, with three access points along the R352 gravel road; the Cata, Dontsa and Zingcuka Forest Stations. The game is shy, but bushbuck, baboon, samango and vervet monkey, bushpig and rock dassie are common. There is good birdlife, including green lourie, the rare, brightly-coloured narina trogon, crowned eagle, sunbirds and sugarbirds. At night you might be woken by the scream of a tree dassie. The Amatola Hiking Trail, all six days of it, passes through the Amatola Forest Reserve into the lower reserve of **Pirie Forest** (no office or phone), reached by travelling 13km north of King William's Town along the R30, then turning north onto the gravel road to Maden Dam and Trout Hatchery. Do not turn into the hatchery but keep going on the rough road, and you will reach the forest entrance. As well as access to the Amatola Trail, Pirie Forest has several walking trails. The most interesting leads 7km up through the forest to cliffs where Chief Sandile, the last Ngqika Xhosa chief to fight the British, made his stand in the Ninth, and last, Frontier War (1877–8), after which the Xhosa of the Ciskei territory were stripped of their independence.

The Pirie Forest does not receive a lot of visitors, and so the forest tends to crowd densely over the trails. Watch out for large, three-dimensional spider's webs at face-level: these are the webs of golden orb spiders, a large arachnid that won't bite if you blunder head-first into its home, but may freak you out by scuttling across your face. Green louries, samamgo and vervet monkeys, bushbuck, bushpig and duiker are all common.

Alice is a large town in the Tyumie Valley below the Amatolas (on the R63), now housing Fort Hare University (*see* **History**). Its handsome Victorian streets, well-kept houses, neat park and bookshops contrast sharply with the usual straggle of hut, house and garden that make up most Ciskei towns. The campus itself has a superb collection of black artists (*see* **People and Culture** 'Art and Architecture'). The surrounding Tyumie Valley was the scene of fierce conflict between settler and Xhosa in the 1840s and '50s, when the British settled ex-soldiers on one side of the valley, and allowed the Xhosa to herd on the other. The settlers had the provocative habit of impounding any Xhosa cattle that 'trespassed' on to the wrong side of the valley, despite the fact that neither group used fences. The Ngqika Xhosas' mounting resentment against this and other provocations within their own territory helped to spark the disastrous last frontier wars of the 1850s and 1870s. Today's Alice and Tyumie Valley are more peaceful, though the student bars in town can get rowdy in the evening, and it is best to visit them by invitation.

Hogsback, a village in the Amatolas north of Alice along the R345 is, strictly speaking, in Cape Province, but only just, and is most easily reached via Ciskei. Hogsback is one of South Africa's loveliest spots. Around the village stretch high pastures and forest through which a series of walking trails lead to waterfalls, some of them quite large. Most spectacular is the Madonna and Child Falls, reached by a trail leaving the road on the south end of the village. Hogsback gets its name from the high, rocky ridge that runs above the village (also accessible by walking trail), and resembles the spine bristles of a bushpig.

The village itself is very quiet, strung out along about 3km of gravel road, the forest hiding most of the buildings. However, there are, two old country hotels and several more moderate places to stay, as well as a forest camp site. Along the road, young Xhosa men sell animals fashioned from unfired red clay, usually horses, bushbuck or busgpigs. Some of these are very beautiful, and it is worth stopping when they hail you to see what they have.

Reckoned as one of the least developed of South Africa's mountain tourist spots, Hogsback is worth taking time over. Walk or ride the forest trails, drink in the fresh scents, and take tea on the sunny lawns of the old hotels.

Those interested in Xhosa history will be tempted to drive south of Hogsback to **Sandile's Grave**, via a signposted detour down a long, straight dirt road (used by forestry trucks) north of the R346 from King William's Town to Stutterheim. Sandile lies in a field under an ornate tomb surmounted by a bust, having fallen here after being driven from the caves of the Pirie Forest in the Ninth Frontier War. Two British troopers he killed at this last stand are buried next to him.

The Winterberg

The high, wide-horizoned plateau between the Stormberg and Winterberg ranges comprises northern Ciskei. In the western section, is **Tsolwana Game Reserve** ✆ (04582) 5402, a high, wild grassland stretching toward the Karoo. Rock-strewn, and overshadowed by the Winterberg mountains, Tsolwana is home to large herds of antelope, zebra and wildebeest, it also harbours white rhino (more than 30 breeding wild in the reserve) and giraffe. Visitors from Europe might be surprised to see fallow deer wandering the reserve. They are there as trophies for hunters; Tsolwana is one of the few game reserves open to sport hunting, ploughing the money back into the reserve and the local communities, from whom the land is rented, as a way to prevent poaching. Its policy seems to be working: Ciskei is extremely poor and one rhino horn represents a huge sum to any prospective poacher, yet the rhino flourish unharmed and the reserve is popular locally, even though its 17,000ha would normally be used for grazing. A 3-day hiking trail winds through the reserve, bringing the walker very close to game—in the case of the rhino sometimes uncomfortably close (although white rhino are not irascible and are unlikely to charge). There are also horses for hire, two comfortable safari lodges, game-viewing roads, two bush camps and a small shop selling game curios, camera film, food, etc.

Hiking close to rhino in the Tsolwana Game Reserve

Whittlesea, a small market town on the R67 to Queenstown, is the nearest point to Tsolwana (about 20km) for buying supplies and petrol. At weekends there is an open street market, and in the lively, friendly atmosphere a new face will be hailed and joked about loudly. Hang onto your wallet if the market is crowded. **Shiloh Mission** near Whittlesea is a Moravian Mission built in 1828 and still active, with a fine, stuccoed church and a working water-mill. The Moravian missionaries were less active in frontier politics, and less censorious of Xhosa nudity and 'feckless' pastoralism than some of the more meddling, pompous English missionaries.

Activities

Hiking: amongst game or in mountain forests is undoubtably Ciskei's most attractive feature. This can be done at Double Drift Game Reserve, Tsolwana Game Reserve and Mpofu Game Reserve, each reserve offering trails of between 1 hour and 2–3 days. Hiking in mountain forests can be done at Hogsback (several hikes of 1–4 hours). In the Amatola Mountain Forest (hikes from 1 hour–6 days), Pirie Forest (hikes from 1 hour–6 days), Mpofu (hikes of 1 hour–2 days) and in the Katberg and Readsdale Forests (hikes of 1 hour–2 days). For details of the above reserves, see individual listings.

Riding: The Xhosa are a horse-owning people, and tourists to Ciskei will see many people going about their everyday business in the saddle. For tourists, Mpofu and Tsolwana Game Reserve both offer riding amongst herds of game. The Katberg Protea Hotel, at Balfour, also offers horses for trails into the Katberg Forest.

Swimming: Ciskei's coast does not have many safe beaches. Exceptions are found at the Fish River Sun, which has its own beach, at the Mpekweni Sun Marine Resort, just a few kilometres to the east, and Kiwane, the next coastal village east of Hamburg, has a lagoon. Elsewhere, fooling around in the shallows is fine, but avoid river mouths when the tide is going out (ask locals if you are unsure of the tide), and never swim far out, as there are cross-currents and sharks.

Game Viewing: Double Drift Game, north of Peddie, has some large game; black rhino, buffalo, hippo and most of the large antelope species. Tsolwana Game Reserve, west of Whittlesea, has white rhino, giraffe and most large antelope species. Mpofu Game Reserve has mainly large antelope. All the reserves have hiking trails and in the case of Mpofu and Tsolwana, riding trails (for details *see* individual listings above).

Where to Stay and Eating Out
expensive

King's Lodge, ✆ (04542) 24, is a wooden hotel just off the Main Street in Hogsback, with quiet gardens, a trout pool by the entrance, and Cape country cuisine (the excellent lamb is taken from local sweet-grass Amatola farms). The rooms are done up in imitation Victoriana style, and are somewhere between very comfortable and luxurious. The **Katberg Protea Hotel**, ✆ (0404) 31151/2, at the foot of the Katberg, between Balfour and the Katberg State Forest, is a large, neo-colonial affair set in parkland bordered by forest. The interior is a little bland, as with all the Protea hotels, but the surroundings are idyllic; green lawns, crowding evergreen woods, and the peaks of the Katberg, a vast amphitheatre, towering above. There is a pool and hiking/riding facilities. **Imvubu and Mbabala Lodges** at Double Drift Game Reserve, ✆ (0401) 952 115, are a collection of four cottages on the Fish River, overlooking a hippo pool, and an old Victorian farmstead in the heart of the bush. Both lodges are self-catering, but staffed. **Ntloni Lodge** in Mpofu Game Reserve, ✆ (0401 952 115, is modern, panelled in yellowwood, and is within walking distance of some bushman paintings below the Katberg mountains. Also self-catering and fully staffed. **Lilyfontein Lodge**, in Tsolwana Game Reserve, ✆ (0401) 952 115, is a late 19th-century Afrikaner homestead. Quite grand, the house is surrounded by a verandah overlooking Ntabethemba mountain, a massif cut off from the main Winterberg range. Tsolwana has two smaller lodges: **Indwe Lodge** and **Otterford Lodge**. Indwe is also a late 19th-century gabled farmstead, next to the offices and reception, while Otterford is on the banks of the Swart Kei River. All three can be self-catering or full catering by request.

moderate

Hyde Park Cottages, in Hogsback (Dinwiddie Lane, off Main Road, ✆ (04542) 069) are self-catering cottages, two new and one old, in the mountain village. There's a pool and an orchard, with the forest crowding behind. **Hogsback Mountain Lodge**, also on Main Road, ✆ (04542) 5, comprises several thatched self-catering rondavels looking out from the forest to the Tyumie Valley below the

Amatolas. **Double Drift Hiking Lodge**, in Double Drift Game Reserve, ✆ (0401) 952 115, is a bush-camp on the Fish River, surrounded by dense euphorbia bush, and providing basic, self-catering accomodation. **Mpofu Hiking Trail Camp**, ✆ (0401) 952 115, a 10-bed dormitory-style refuge hut with water, wood and cooking utensils, sits below the Katberg mountains in Mpofu Game Reserve. **Fundani Trail Camp** and **Pumlani Trail Camp**, both in Tsolwana Game Reserve, ✆ (0401) 952 115, are also dormitory-style refuge huts with basic facilities (including a bucket-shower heated by a wood stove). Self-catering only, the camps are surrounded by large herds of grazing game.

cheap

Hamburg Municipal Cottages, at Hamburg, are incredibly good value, the cheapest for such facilities that the author found. These clean, 2-room (one single, one double bed) cottages have a kitchen and bathroom, and overlook the Keiskamma Estuary. You cannot book, but there's seldom any need. Ask at the wooden kiosk (small store/bar) on the left before the filling station. Hamburg must be one of the most relaxed places on the planet; few people know about it. Get chatting with some of the fishermen that come up from Port Elizabeth, and you may be offered a boat-trip and a chance to catch the big cob and king-clip that teem in the river-mouth. There is also a **campsite** in Hamburg.

The Border Region

The Border region is a narrow corridor running between the former Ciskei and Transkei. A green land of sheep farms, forestry and cattle pastures, its central section is mountainous—the Amatolas—while the south gives way to a coastline of green, rounded hills and wide estuary mouths known as the Cape Wild Coast, a wistful appellation for this more developed extension of the more spectacular Transkei Wild Coast, further east. The N6 runs through the region, from Queenstown in the north to East London in the south.

History

Until the 1850s the Border Region was the home of the Gqunkhwebe clan of the Xhosa people, whose chief, Pato, led them there after being ejected from the Ciskei coast by the British in the early 1820s. Pato then steered an awkward course with the colonists— sometimes fighting them—sometimes remaining neutral, in the series of Frontier wars between 1824 and 1856.

When Sir Harry Smith invaded the area in the 1830s, he set up a military village, King William's Town, and a supply port, East London, in Pato's country, which he claimed (without orders from Britain) as British territory and named Queen Adelaide's Land. Smith was sent to India for his rash antics, and the territory was abandoned by the British for a while. However, in 1847 Smith returned to South Africa as Governor, to 'save' the frontier after the massive Xhosa re-invasion of the Eastern Cape during the War of the Axe (*see*

Eastern Cape 'History'), and King William's Town was re-occupied. The name of the region was then changed to Victoria East, after the young English queen. Once the war was over, Smith used the settlement as his private court. Seated on a throne, he repeatedly called in the various Xhosa chiefs to swear him fealty, to the point of kissing his boots under threat of bayonetting. He even forced the powerful warrior-chief Maqoma (*see* 'Frontier Wars') to kneel in front of an audience of thousands, placed his boot on the fighter's neck and publically called him a dog.

But these theatrics did not impress the Xhosa, who again fought Smith in 1850, after he had sent a patrol into the Amatolas to depose Sandile, chief of the Ngqika Xhosa. Maqoma and Sandile persuaded most of the frontier chiefs to join in this war (which lasted until 1853), and although Pato kept his Xhosa neutral, chief Siyolo, of the neighbouring Ndlambe clan, laid siege to King William's Town and blockaded the roads in and out so that Smith could not reach his troops, nor supply them from East London.

This war, bloodier in terms of British and colonial losses, and costlier to the British treasury than any frontier war before it, dragged on for three years. Smith's consistent failure to decisively beat the Xhosa ended his military career. He and the arrogant, ineffectual Henry Somerset (the son of Lord Charles Somerset and the frontier's military commander for almost 30 years), were recalled, to be replaced by Henry Cathcart, who methodically drove off the Xhosa cattle, burned their crops and imprisoned the women (who tilled the land and supplied the warriors in the bush), until the chiefs, already exhausted by the long war, capitulated. At this point the Ngqika clan were forcibly removed from the Amatolas to a small reserve in present-day Border Country, which created serious overcrowding. Lung sickness hit the Xhosa cattle in 1854, and this coincided with the suicidal Great Cattle Killing of 1856, when, in despair most of the Xhosa clans, including the Ngqika, destroyed their herds and grain in the belief that this would summon their ancestors and drive the hated British into the sea.

After the nation had reduced itself to starvation, Sir George Grey, Cape Governor at the time, treated the Xhosa chiefs as criminals. Among those he brought to 'trial' (on the shaky charge of inciting their people to a desperation that would force them to invade the Cape Colony and attack farms) were Pato and Siyolo of the Border Country, and Maqoma of the Ngqika. All three were sent to Robben Island, the bleak penal colony off Cape Town.

With the chiefs out of the way, Governor Grey planned to turn the Border Country and neighbouring regions into a 'chequer-board' of black and white farmers living in harmony. For this he wanted British immigrants, similar to those brought out to Albany Region near Grahamstown in 1820. Instead, he got Germans, mostly a rough crew of bachelor soldiers from a volunteer regiment that had fought as part of the British army in the Crimea. After a feckless few years this rowdy lot eventually settled down, capitalizing on the cheap labour of Xhosa rendered dependent on the settlers for employment after the loss of their herds, land and crops. Today, many Border Country farmers still bear German names.

The area's tradition of Xhosa resistance continued through the apartheid years, King William's Town producing perhaps the best-known martyr of them all, Steve Biko. After death while in police detention in September 1977, Biko's body was brought back to King

William's Town for burial. In the years leading up to the 1994 interim government, the region's proximity to the 'homelands' of Ciskei and Transkei made it subject to occasional political strife; evident in the APLA (Azanian People's Liberation Army—the terrorist wing of the PAC) attacks on white restaurants in Queenstown and King William's Town in 1992, and some isolated killing of white farmers. But for the most part, the area's rural hinterland remains quiet, a region of tranquil farms that carry no outward sign of the bitter struggles that once raged across their green acres.

Queenstown

This northern region of the Border Country has little to offer the tourist, except the N6 highway leading to the Cape Drakensberg and Orange Free State, and the wild Stormberg mountains. Queenstown, which lies at the foot of the Stormberg, is a large regional centre, useful for stocking up and resting, but with little to see. Dubbed the 'Rose Capital' of South Africa, for summertime blooms in its parks (though Bloemfontein in the Orange Free State also makes this claim), Queenstown was proclaimed in 1847 by Sir Harry Smith, flush with his victory over the Xhosa chiefs during the War of the Axe. Originally a military village, Queenstown was one of the few on the eastern frontier never to be attacked. The town settled into prosperity early, and since the 1860s has held an agricultural show that is still one of the country's largest.

It is worth strolling along the two marked hiking trails at the the **Berry Reservoir** on Milner Street, which wind through a large garden of flowering aloes, all identified. The **Collector's Museum**, at 4 Reservoir Street (*open Mon–Fri 9–5*) is an excellent monument to one man's quiet eccentricity. The private home of a Mr Rex Abbott, this museum exhibits his vast collections of telephones, dolls, car badges, teaspoons and old kitchen implements, all labelled with any appropriate anecdotes. The garden is a collection too— of exotic cacti and indigenous Karoo succulents. The car badge collection claims to be the biggest in the world. The **Frontier Musuem** on Shepstone Street (*open Mon–Fri 8.30– 12.45, 2–4.45*) is more conservative—the usual monument to pioneer life and how hard it was. The museum has constructed a rough-and-ready frontier cottage to prove it. The Frontier Wars are given several rooms of paintings and regimental regalia. The accompanying labels tell the colonists' version of events, rather than that of the Xhosa and Khoi. The **Old Market Business Plaza**, to the west side of the **Hexagon Park** on Cathcart Street (the town's main drag) is a redeveloped, but handsome, market building (built in the 1850s), whose inside has been partitioned into shops and craft workshops.

Around Queenstown

In the **Lawrence De Lange Game Reserve**, numerous plains game species (including kudu, black wildebeest, zebra, ostrich, blesbok and springbok) wander the hillside among the flowering aloes for which the reserve is known. The best time to visit is in winter, when the *aloe ferox*, which flowers a vivid red, covers the hillside in bright colour. There is no accommodation, but hikers are allowed to pitch tents.

The **Koos Ras Game Reserve** is about 40km north of town along the N6, then 10km west on the R56 towards Sterkstroom. A small reserve, it has hiking trails through transitional grassland/karoo scrub terrain. Kudu, blesbok, eland, impala, black wildebeest zebra and springbok are common. **Carnarvon Estate** is a family-owned farm 50km north of Queenstown along the N6, and 8km east towards the village of Haseleton. The farm incorporates a large private wetland reserve, with two hiking trails and two lodges. The reserve has springbok, waterbuck, reedbuck, lechwe (introduced from Botswana), steenbok, black eagle and ostrich, as well as waterfowl, particularly fish eagle, snipe, various duck species, heron and egrets. Blue cranes sometimes stop here on their migratory flights.

Where to Stay

expensive

Carnarvon Estate on the road from Queenstown to Sterkstroom, ✆ (04592) 3311/3320, offers full board in an old homestead at the foot of the Stormberg. There is hiking, riding and game-viewing for guests. Expect to be pampered, especially with the food; game and Karoo mutton being the speciality. **Eagle's Ridge Mountain Inn**, ✆ (0433) 31200, by the Kologha State Forest west of Stutterheim, is an old-fashioned country hotel complete with a library of old novels in the lounge, horses to ride, forest walks and a tennis court. The hotel itself is not particularly attractive, but the surroundings are very lovely, being at the forested foot of the Amatolas. The rooms are pretty standard; clean, neat and en suite without any special luxury.

moderate

Aloe Grove Guest Farm, ✆ (0451) 5910, 17km from Queenstown along the Dordrecht road, is a Victorian farmstead set in mountain country. There are rondavels or a double room in the farmhouse, with breakfast (lunch and dinner by request). Facilities include a pool, good bird life and mountain walks. **Bradford Guest Lodge**, ✆ (0451) 3313, is 18km from Queenstown towards Tarkastad, in another farmhouse offering full board in airy, comfortable rooms with a farm to wander. Good home cooking. Fishing and watersports can be arranged, as well as daycare for children.

cheap

Koos Ras Nature Reserve, ✆ (04592) 8, on the R345 near Sterkstroom, north of Queenstown offers chalets and camping.

Eating Out

The **Grand Hotel**, Queenstown, ✆ (0451) 3017/8, has a restaurant serving big juicy steaks and seafood amid a strange mixture of plastic chairs and wood-panelled walls. **Hotel Bagatelle**, just north of Stutterheim, ✆ (0436) 31220, is a country restaurant offering game, some Cape dishes and the usual steaks in an olde worlde atmosphere, with much dark wood and a blazing log fire in winter. King Williamstown lacks good independent restaurants, and the only eating out to be had is either in the town hotels, which offer the standard à la carte fare, or at the chain Spur and Mike's Kitchen restaurants.

The Border Country Amatolas

Cathcart, a village off the N6 some 55km south of Queenstown, is one of the jumping-off points for the Amatolas. The village itself is just a small farming centre. However, in the mountains nearby is **Benghoil**, a guest farm offering horse trails and hikes (*see* 'Activities', p.332).

Stutterheim, a 19th-century German town, is another 48km south along the N6. Useful as an entry point to the Amatolas, the nearest slopes are about 15km west of town at the **Kologha Forest Reserve**, which has a short walking trail following a series of waterfalls through the woods. There is a camp site just outside the gates to the reserve. Following the R346 southwest of Stutterheim, the road re-enters Ciskei and the **Pirie Forest** (part of the Amatola Hiking Trail), passing Sandile's grave (*see* p.318).

King William's Town is 50km southwest of Stutterheim on the R346. 'King' is a strange town. Founded in war by Sir Harry Smith in the 1830s, abandoned, then re-occupied after the War of the Axe in 1847, it has always been something of a hot-bed of Xhosa/settler tension, hiding under the guise of a quiet regional town. Steve Biko was born and buried here. In **Bisho**, the hurriedly built capital of Ciskei (1981) that sits on the opposite hill, former Ciskei's then president Oupa Xhosa ordered his troops to fire on ANC supporters during a march in 1991, killing several and injuring many. The following year, APLA blew up the Spur restaurant in King William's Town, killing two whites. But a sense of exterior calm is maintained by the handsome façades of its older buildings, and its quiet, tree-lined residential streets.

The **Kaffrarian Museum** on Main Street (*open Mon–Fri 9–12.45, 2–5*) is one of the few museums in South Africa to depict history from a non-colonial viewpoint. The museum is housed in two adjacent buildings: the newer section has a Xhosa history put together by Xhosa historians, dealing plainly with Britain's role in shattering the Xhosa culture during the endless Frontier Wars. But the account is not completely partisan; the section on modern Ciskei and Transkei is frank about the factional in-fighting that has plagued black politics throughout this century, and tells how traditional culture, particularly folk medicine, has survived the breakdown of most of the old traditions. Xhosa mythology and art are well represented.

The main building houses a very good collection of stuffed South African mammals. If you are still unsure of the differences between the numerous small antelope species, or want to see just how many rodents inhabit the veld, this is the museum for it. Also displayed is Huberta the Hippo, who wandered down the coast from St Lucia in Zululand to the Border Region between 1928 and 1931 (a distance of more than 1000km) until a local farmer shot her, and the museum stuffed her. With Huberta are the press cuttings that charted her progress; she was a national personality until her demise, being the only hippo to venture into the Eastern Cape for about 50 years. Today, hippo have been reintroduced in some game reserves. The museum also has a history of the Cape Mounted Rifles, better known as the Cape Corps, a Khoi cavalry regiment founded in the early 1800s. Frontier commanders relied the Cape Corps to do the bulk of the fighting during the Frontier Wars, yet treated them as second-class citizens and exhibited obvious distrust of them. Some units did finally rebel in exasperation, and fought with the Xhosa in the Eighth Frontier War (1850–53), but the regiment was kept on and was later sent to Europe to fight in both World Wars. They aquitted themselves heroically, but little was said of it at the time, the South African establishment being ever-uneasy of praising 'coloureds'.

The **Missionary Museum** on Barkly Street (*open Mon–Fri 9–5*) is a must for any serious student of South African history. More than the colonial governments and even the trek-boers, the early 19th-century missionaries from Moravia, London and Glasgow opened up the interior to colonial expansion. Frequently at odds with the military governments, the missionaries began as a humanistic bunch, unwilling to break down indigenous traditions such as nudity and polygamy, concentrating instead on the 'soul'. Stephanus Van der Kemp and his assistant, James Read who, in the early 1800s became the Eastern Cape's first missionaries (first to the Khoi and then to the Xhosa), were particularly high-profile advocates of this approach and did their best to stop the white settlers from abusing the inidgenous people. This made them very unpopular with the colonists. Van der Kemp died in 1812, but James Read continued his liberalist methods and, by the 1830s, the frontier settlers were demanding a more Europeanist type of missionary, who equated the material trappings of 'civilisation' (i.e. clothes, working for money, becoming British subjects) with salvation. The frontier was duly evangelized by a number of incredibly narrow-minded, reactionary men who did much to provoke the frayed patience of the Xhosa. However, these missionaries unwittingly trained the first generations of black activists (who began to campaign as early as the 1870s), by pioneering black education, and opening a path for the slow journey from conquered subjects to citizens. The museum gives a more colonial view of the missionaries' work, but there are plans to change this, and the present exhibition at least provides an accurate chronology.

East London

Tourist Information

East London Publicity Association, ✆ (0431) 26015.

This port, on the N2 at the mouth of the Buffalo River, was founded by Harry Smith in the 1830s to supply his military headquarters at King William's Town. Now a small city with a still-active dock, East London is used by most travellers as a jumping-off point for the Cape Wild Coast and Transkei. The small town centre is quite handsome (a lot of imposing Victorian buildings survive), but rather unexciting, despite its bustle. The main thoroughfare is Oxford Street, which runs north/south to the docks. East London has a beach and a seafront: but the latter was, alas, re-developed in the 1960s, and is now a series of concrete block buildings with no real charm, despite having lively bars. In short, East London is a town to pass through quickly. However, there are some points of interest. The **East London Museum** on Oxford Street (*open Mon–Fri 9.30–5, Sat 9.30–12, Sun 11–4*) has the stuffed body of the first coelacanth to be found. A prehistoric fish species has survived in South African waters since the Mezoic Period, 250 million million years ago; this modern specimen was netted by an East London trawler in the 1960s. The museum also has a dodo's egg from Mauritius, apparently the only known surviving egg in the world.

The **Gately Museum** on Queen Street (*open weekends only, 3–5*) was the house of East London's first mayor, John Gately. The period furnishings are intact. The **Anne Bryant Gallery**, off Oxford Street between St Mark's Road and St Luke's Road, (*open Mon–Fri 9–5, Sat 9.30–12*) has some good Pierneff landscapes and some mediocre sporting sculpture. About 13km east of town on the Maclean Town Road, is the **Calgary Museum** (*open Weds–Sun, 9–4*), which conatins a collection of old horse-drawn vehicles. The **Dog Box**, on Oxford Street, is a strange place. Ostensibly a pet shop, many black East Londoners buy live poultry here: The shop is alive with the birds and their chicks. Run by an energetic, elderly woman from Sussex, whose prize-winning alsatian dog is memorialized in a large colour photo above the counter, the Dog Box is not something you would expect from such a staid town. Look for the Victorian building with painted cartoon dogs on the front.

The **Old Lock Street Gaol**, on Fleet Street (in fact one of the old garrison forts, and later South Africa's first women's prison), has been turned into a small complex of shops and cafés. All the old buildings remain, while some of the gaol's original features have been preserved, including the hanging chamber.

Orient Beach and Eastern Beach, next to the town, are safe for swimming, have good rock-pool life and are excellent places from which to see dolphins, whole schools of which sometimes appear in the surf.

East London ✆ (0431–)   **Where to Stay and Eating Out**

expensive

East London has the standard chain hotels, the most popular being the **King David Hotel** on Inverleith Terrace, ✆ 23174. **Le Petit**, ✆ 353 685/6, at 54 Beach Road, Nahoon (a suburb of East London) is rather self-consciously upmarket with expensive chintz decor, but nonetheless serves very good classical French dishes. The service is very formal and correct. **Bellami's**, 18 Marine Terrace, ✆ 432 145, offers nouvelle cuisine without being overly pretentious (and the helpings are a bit larger than the average nouvelle restaurant). The dining room is rather stark but the service is friendly and the atmosphere relaxed. The fish dishes are the best. Superb seafod can be had at the **Sunset Restaurant**, ✆ 474 821, in the Blue Lagoon Timeshare flats on Beacon Bay, a few kilometres from town.

moderate

The **Tug and Ferry**, ✆ 431 188, on Latimer's Landing, in the old harbour, serves a mixture of seafood, steaks and pasta to a predominantly young clientele. Also down on Latimer's Landing is **Hunter's Jetty** (✆ 438 410), a grill which offers you a choice of skewered, seasoned meat which is then cooked at your table. **Casbah**, ✆ 23174, in the King David Hotel, is at the expensive end of the moderate scale and serves an à la carte menu of French dishes, seafood and steaks. **Tropics** at the Osner Hotel on the Esplanade, ✆ 433 433, is more fun, and specializes in stir-fry dishes. The **Prawn Inn** on Clifford St, ✆ 24253, is a good seafood joint with the standard nautical bits and bobs on the walls offering fresh linefish and shellfish caught that morning. **Finnegan's**, 40 Terminus St, ✆ 25585, is a decent restaurant serving steaks, seafood, good burgers and the odd French dish. A bit bland inside, but good value for money.

cheap

The **Spud Rock Café**, 21 Devereux St, ✆ 57298, does baked potatoes and kebabs. Some of the seafood fillings are really delicious. Bring your own booze. **Platform One**, ✆ 420 185, is a bar in one of the ugly modern buildings on the Esplanade, offering bar meals. Surfers and business people gather here in the evening. The bar is nothing special, but the window tables look out over the ocean. **Santa Monica** is a cheap seafood, steak and fried chicken place on the Esplanade (another ugly building). As the name suggests, the Santa Monica caters for surfers, with big music video screens and young beach folk drinking beer. There is a camp site just outside the gates to the **Kologha Forest Reserve**.

cafés

East London has a couple of continental coffee houses. **Café Wien**, in the Patcyn Centre, Frere Road, does home-baked pastries and really good coffee, while **Stephanie's Coffee Shop** on St Luke's Road offers the more standard toasted sandwiches and hot drinks.

Nightlife

East London has a few clubs, all of which play a standard mix of oldie rock and Top 40. If you want to dance, try **Jaggers Nightclub** in the King David Hotel, Inverleith Terrace, (mostly students and yuppies) or **Numbers Disco** in the Quigley Centre on the Esplanade. The **Beach Hotel**, 12 Kirkpatrick Street, hosts a 'Weekend Rave' in its Seaview Bar. Surfers hang out here. Lively bars are: **Santa Monica** (on the Esplanade; a young crowd), **Platform One** (also on the Esplanade; an older, yuppie crowd) and the **Rose and Crown** (in the Patcyn Centre, Frere Road) a straightforward pub.

Around East London

Mpongo Park, a game reserve some set in rolling grassland along the Pongo River, some 29km from East London, has some big game; elephant, white rhino and giraffe as well as the usual complement of large antelope species. At the park office is a small animal orphanage for creatures that have been injured or abandoned. Visitors are sometimes allowed into the pens with a staff member, and even to handle the animals. Mpongo has a **camp site**.

Bridle Drift Nature Reserve is set around a dam about 10km west of town along the R346. There are only walking trails, and you cannot drive inside the reserve. You are unlikely to spot any game, but the bird life is prolific; Fish eagles in particular are often seen. **Gonubie Nature Reserve** is a tiny (8ha) piece of wetland next to the holiday resort and beach of Gonubie, a short drive east of East London along the N2. Crowned cranes nest here (as well as a host of other birds) and there are observation platforms built into the vlei. Of further interest is a small indigenous herb garden, called the Witchdoctor's Garden, from which local Xhosa herbalists and diviners gather their stock. Some of the plants are labelled, and their medicinal properties listed.

The Cape Wild Coast

Between East London and Transkei, is the stretch of coastline known as the Cape Wild Coast. Neither as wild nor as beautiful as the Transkei Wild Coast, the Cape section is mainly composed of small resorts clustered around old-fashioned hotels, reached from the N2 by dirt roads through the bush. However, if you know where to go, this coastline has some lovely, unspoilt bits, listed below.

Bosbokstrand Nature Reserve is about 40km east of East London along the N2, then a few kilometres south on the gravel road to Haga-Haga, a small beach resort with a very ugly hotel. Set along the coast west of the resort, Bosbokstrand comprises forest, beach and estuary. Bushbuck, eland, blesbok and impala wander the reserve, and even browse along the beach. There is safe swimming, a camp site, rondavels and a shop for general supplies. **Cape Henderson Nature Reserve** sits immediately next to Bosbokstrand, by Haga-Haga resort. Also composed of coastal forest and beach, the reserve is good for spotting green lourie and sunbirds. There are a few shy bushbuck and duiker; vervet monkeys live in the trees.

Morgan's Bay, on the coast about 90km east of East London (follow the N2 for 66km, then turn south on the gravel R349 to Kei Mouth) is a small resort village comprising a hotel, a few houses and little else. Set beneath great cliffs, Morgan's Bay is undoubtedly the most attractive resort near East London. From the hotel, several good walks (east to Kei Mouth or west to a wild lagoon) lead along beaches known for their rich shell deposits..

Kei Mouth, a slightly larger resort village 10km east of Morgan's Bay, looks across the Kei estuary to Transkei. The best way to visit is to stroll about an hour along the beach from Morgan's Bay. The estuary mouth itself is very wide, and a fabulous view of it can be had from atop a small wooded hill in the centre of the village, which has a marked footpath leading to the summit. East of here, the real Wild Coast begins. Kei Mouth has some shops, a bank (*open Tues, Thurs only*) and a petrol station. Its hotel is more modern than, but not as attractive as, the one at Morgan's Bay.

Ocean View Guest Farm and Nature Reserve, ✆ (04372) 2603 in the bush along the R349 to Morgan's Bay and Kei Mouth, is a working farm, but with a large stretch of forest that is great for bird-watching. Crowned and long-crested eagles (two rare species) breed here, as do massive ground hornbills—the rottweilers of the bird kingdom—and elegant crowned and blue cranes. There are also bushbuck, duiker and samamgo monkey. The forest is cut through with walking trails and there are bird-watching hides. (*See* below.)

Where to Stay
expensive

The **Morgan's Bay Hotel**, ✆ (0155) 62, is an Edwardian hotel built round a small inner courtyard, filled with plants and caged parrots, and overlooking the sea. It has a good pub, fresh seafood in the restaurant, fishing tackle for hire, and a free pick-up from East London. The rooms are not fancy, but are comfortable, have en suite bathrooms and most have a sea view.

moderate

Buccanneer's Retreat, ✆ (0431) 383 012, at Cintsa, 35km east of East London, is a group of 8 small self-contained cottages overlooking a freshwater lagoon and the sea with their own stretch of private beach, safe for swimming. Birds flit among the coastal bush separating the cottages. Buccaneer's Retreat is very tranquil; guests can cook for themselves or eat in a central dining house, and the limited number of cottages makes for a limited number of people. Fishing and watersports can be arranged. **Crawford's Cintsa Beach**, ✆ (0431) 385000, on the north bank of the Cintsa River mouth, across from Buccaneer's Retreat, is slightly more expensive. Crawford's has some 30 white-washed, thatched cottages surrounding a large central house set in coastal bush, with a restaurant (mostly seafood) and good views over the ocean. In summer, you eat on a terrace. There is a bar, sauna, jacuzzi and a private beach.

cheap

Ocean View Guest Farm and Game Reserve is on the R349 to Haga-Haga and Morgan's Bay, about 75km from East London. The farm and forest reserve has self-contained chalets, as well as a small camp site with an ablution block. The air is full of the incessant chatter of wood hoepoes and the booming of louries. Excellent value, and a beautiful place to stay. **Bosbokstrand Nature Reserve**, ✆ (04372) 4512, next to Haga-Haga, about 75km east of East London, has chalets that, if split between two or more, fall within the cheap price rangeas well as a **camp site**.

Walking and Hiking: The Border Region has several good trails. The Lawrence De Lange Nature Reserve near Queenstown has overnight trails (hikers must bring a tent and a camping stove). Carnarvon Estate, near Sterkstroom, north of Queenstown, also has an overnight trail with two camping huts. Both these trails are good for game spotting. Dayhikes can be found in the Lawrence De Lange Reserve, the Kologha State Forest, near Stutterheim (forest and waterfalls) and Bridle Drift, Bosbokstrand, Cape Henderson and Ocean View reserves near East London.

Riding: Benghoil Horse Safaris, ✆ (04562) 2203, in the mountains above Cathcart, offers trails from a couple of hours to several days through wild country rich in birdlife, exotic plants—such as cycads—and antelope, to caverns rich in bushman paintings. Welcome Stables, ✆ (0461) 462511, at Igoda Beach, near East London, offers beach rides. Mpongo Game Reserve, ✆ (04326) 669, 29km north of East London, also arranges game-spotting horse trails by prior arrangement.

Swimming: Safe beaches can be found at East London (Orient Beach, Nahoon Beach and Kidd's Beach) and at many places up the coast between East London and Transkei. The most attractive of these are Gonubie (10km east along the N2), Buccaneer's Retreat (35km east along the N2), Bosbokstrand near Haga-Haga (72km east along the N2) and Morgan's Bay (90km east along the N2).

Transkei

There is a world of roving grass
White-faced huts looking down on paths and cattle
... Beyond and beyond, afloat
Topple the blue peaks of the Drakensberg

The White-Faced Huts, H. F. Sampson

East of East London and the Cape Wild Coast begins the great sweep of upland pasture, mountain and wild sub-tropical coastline of Transkei, heartland of the Xhosa people. The N2 highway winds across the hills and valleys of central Transkei, linking the Cape Province with Natal. In between is Africa. Transkei has few modern towns, despite running its own civil service from the small capital, Umtata. Here, traditional Xhosa life goes on in a way that has largely disappeared inside the borders of Cape Province. Xhosa herdboys and horsemen use the grass verge as their own turf road, and cattle and goats graze alongside the highway, making fast driving extremely dangerous. Round huts, often brightly painted, dot the green, rounded hills.

Away from the highway, life is slow and superstition and folklore strong. Spirits and ancestors are very much present in the minds of rural Transkeians. Life is still lived around the cattle kraal, and wealth is still calculated in head of cattle. Traditional dress has largely disappeared (except among the long-braided, enigmatic diviners that exist in every community), but the tenor of rural life has changed little.

The traveller's main reason for visiting Transkei is the **Wild Coast**, over 300km of verdant, sometimes forested downs fronting white sand beaches so unspoilt that shoals of fish can be seen swimming in the surf. Great estuary mouths and freshwater lagoons cut across the beaches every 20km or so, along whose mangroved banks live small communities of fishermen. The Wild Coast has a few quiet resorts and a hiking trail running along its entire length that is ranked as one of the best in Southern Africa.

History

In the early 19th century, the Xhosa clans living in Transkei (i.e. east of the Kei River) were the Gcaleka, paramount clan of the Xhosas, and their satellite clans, the Mfengu and Mpondo. Protected from the struggles of the Eastern Cape frontier by geographical distance, they were left pretty well undisturbed by colonists (with the exception of missionaries and the odd emissary from the Cape Governor) until 1835, when Sir Harry Smith rashly decided to invade the Transkei.

The immediate results of this invasion were tragic, and the long-term effects disastrous for the whole Xhosa nation. Sir Harry Smith had been bogged down, campaigning inconclusively against the Ngqika Xhosas near the Fish River (*see* **Eastern Cape** 'History'), and only in exasperation turned his attention to the Gcaleka, paramount clan of the Xhosa, mistakenly believing that he could demand compensation from Hintsa for cattle stolen from colonists by the Ngqika, despite the fact that Hintsa was not involved in any border raiding, living over 200km east of any white farmer, and that the Ngqika acted independently of any direction from Hintsa. Moreover, Smith demanded that Hintsa order the frontier Xhosa to cease warring with the British, even though, again, he was not involved in the war and had no direct influence over the frontier chiefs. Weak though his reasoning was, Smith marched into Transkei, demanded a vast amount of cattle, and when this was only tokenly met, took Hintsa prisoner, making him promise to stop the Ngqika from continuing the war. Hintsa, seeing the impossibility of his position, tried to escape but was pulled from his horse by Sir Harry Smith, then shot in cold blood.and his ears cut off as trophies.

The outrage and insult was indescribable. To the Xhosa, a chief and his property were inviolate and, until Hintsa's murder, most colonists had respected this. It was now clear that no chief could trust the British, whose arrogance was seen to be lethal. Hintsa's murder did not stop the war. The Ngqika only ceased hostilities later in the year, after both they and the British had been ground down into stalemate. But the Xhosa's cease-fire was voluntary, and there was no surrender.

Transkei then remained untouched by the colonists (again, except for missionary activity) for more than a decade. However, the British invited the 16,000 strong Mfengu (Fingo) clan, then living in Transkei, to settle in the new province of British Kaffraria (modern Ciskei) on land confiscated from the frontier Xhosa clans. The Mfengu were not proper Xhosas, but a refugee tribe that had fled west from Natal during Shaka Zulu's wars of the 1820s. The Gcaleka had allowed them to settle in Transkei, but treated them as second-class citizens. The Mfengu were therefore very open to British influence and, when the chance came to move out of Transkei onto land of their own, they readily accepted, giving the colonists both Xhosa allies in time of war, and a buffer zone between colony and the Transkei in times of peace.

Transkei remained peaceful through the Frontier Wars of the 1840s, but in 1850, Sir Harry Smith (now Cape Governor) again invaded. But this time the Gcaleka, under Sarili, Hintsa's son, were ready. They joined the general war west of the Kei, then retreated back to the Transkei and led the British columns a merry dance in the region's northern mountains. Driving their cattle into safe mountain hideaways, the Gcaleka threw boulders down on the British, and harryied them with ambushes always remaining one step ahead of the pursuit.The British gave up and withdrew in 1851, to concentrate on fighting the Ngqika and Ndlambe clans further west.

However, by 1853 the tables had turned. The British had forced the Ngqika and Ndlambe to surrender by burning their crops and imprisoning the women, who kept their men in the field supplied with food (a ruthless tactic that was later to win the Anglo–Boer War for the British, *see* **South African History**). By the end of the war (1853) the Xhosa clans west of the Kei had lost their land, and the Gcaleka found themselves isolated, the last pocket of Xhosa resistance on the eastern frontier.

The Great Cattle Killing

Sarili seems to have known that the days of his Gcaleka independence were numbered, and in his desperate search for a solution, he was perhaps susceptible to irrational influence. Certainly, through the mid 1850s, which were marked by drought, famine and low morale caused by the loss of the Eighth Frontier War, he and his people were slipping towards despair. But in 1856 came the event which caused the collapse of the entire Xhosa nation. A young woman called Nongqawuse, niece of a diviner living near the Qolora River mouth (just east of the Kei), claimed that strange voices had spoken to her from one of the river pools, telling her that if the Xhosas would destroy all their grain, kill all their cattle, the ancestors would rise, bringing new herds and filling the granaries, and sweep the white man into the sea. A few months later, another adolescent seer made similar claims, and soon news of the prophecies spread across the entire Xhosa nation.

The Xhosa chiefs had heard about Britain's war in the Crimea, and of her heavy losses there, and fostered a naïve, desperate hope that the British South Africans might be defeated by Russians invading in ships, with whom the Xhosa could ally. This combined with the millenarian claim of the young woman and her diviner uncle seem to have convinced Sarili, who, after some initial scepticism began to slaughter his own herds and sent word to all other chiefs to do the same by 11 August 1856.

The order met with various reactions from the Xhosa chiefs in Transkei and on the Frontier, and caused much strife between believers and unbelievers. Still, vast amounts of cattle were killed, and granaries destroyed. When the ancestors failed to rise on the appointed day, the failure was attributed to the disobedience of unbelieving chiefs. A second date was set for February 1857.

The reactions of white frontier colonists ranged from horror to glee. The Governor, Sir George Grey, admitted that this was a chance for the British to settle the Xhosa once and for all without spending a single penny, while their inevitable self-imposed destitution would reduce them to dependence on white farmers for employment. He made no move to stop the killing.

By the end of February, many frontier and Transkei Xhosa were already starving. By July, thousands had died, including Nongqawuse's uncle, and Sarili renounced his belief. In just under a year and a half, the Xhosa had lost everything. Many streamed into towns on the frontier looking for food. It was common to see Xhosa dead in the streets. Cannibalism broke out in the more remote districts and those Xhosa who had not destroyed their grain and cattle found themselves under attack from those who had.

Some British missionaries set up famine relief centres, but Grey shut them down. Nongqawuse away for questioning (and for her own safety). Instead, Sir George Grey set up a series of courts to try the Xhosa chiefs who had taken part in the cattle killing on loose charges of inciting their people to war through putting them in such desperate staits, and sent them to Robben Island. Sarili remained free but, despite his pleas for food for his people, was warned that the British government now regarded him as hostile and that he would be arrested at the slightest provocation.

There is still confusion as to why the Great Cattle Killing happened. Governor Grey asserted that Sarili saw this as a chance to force the Xhosa to band together and fight a decisive war against the British to take back their confiscated lands. Others maintain that his belief was sincere, and that the movement was an attempt to unify the nation to a cohesive unit that could properly resist white incursions. In his chapter on the Cattle Killing in the *New Illustrated History of South Africa* (Human & Rousseau, Cape Town 1986), the historian John Benyon suggests that the killing was a pre-meditated political strategy on the part of Sarili: 'Instead of victory in war, as in 1847, the old Xhosa order in 1856–7 aimed at victory through reconciliation, and this resulted in the so called "Great Cattle Killing". Still other historians believe that the situation was manipulated by wealthy settlers and the British government. The only thing that is certain is the extent of tragedy.

The Transkei was declared a British magistracy and opened to colonization, and the destitute Transkei Xhosa provided a ready market for white traders and livestock speculators, and towns grew up around the mission stations at Butterworth, Umtata, and Port St Johns, as well as around the larger trading posts of Flagstaff and Willowvale. As the price of wool rose steadily through the 1880s Transkeians showed a remarkable resilience; by concentrating on sheep farming, they were soon prospering again, albeit as British dependents.

The government became alarmed, seeing the unexpected Xhosa prosperity as endangering the cheap labour pool on which the Cape Colony depended, especially for the newly booming mines up at Kimberley. In an attempt to force the Transkei Xhosa to seek employment with whites, legislation was passed in 1887 to curb their voting franchise, and to make 'squatting' (i.e. occupation of non-privately owned land, such as village common land) an offence.

But by now, many mission-educated Xhosa were beginning to enter the professional classes in the Eastern Cape, and resistance to government interference was strong. Individual Xhosa farmers resisted by refusing to have their land valued to see if their possessions qualified them for the vote, or as freeholders of their acreages. But through the early 1900s, increasing pressure from white farmers and industrialists caused more and more repressive legislation to be passed, including the infamous Native Land Act of 1913 which set aside just 13 per cent of the new South African Republic for black Africans, dispossessing hundreds of thousands of people. The Transkei Xhosa, like blacks everywhere, found themselves pushed onto smaller and smaller parcels of land, with chiefs being gradually stripped of their power. Severe droughts through the 1920s, coupled with cattle sickness and locust plagues, reduced them to desperation again.

By the 1920s, political campaigning by Xhosa leaders began to have violent repercussions. White Transkei magistrates jailed one Wellington Buthelezi, a Natal-born black campaigner active in Transkei (no relative of today's famous Zulu leader of the same name), whose urges to the rural population to resist colonial government were so successful that taxes had become almost impossible to collect. However, good land was now too scarce to support significant populations, and more and more Transkei Xhosa drifted to the mines. The government's attempts to make the place into a cheap labour pool were succeeding.

By the time the Nationalists took power in 1948 and introduced apartheid, Transkei had firmly established its present status as the power-base of black action among the military wings of the ANC and PAC. After the Sharpeville riots of 1960 eastern Transkei erupted into violence and a state of emergency was declared. Although many of the young ANC activists at the time were Transkei born (including Nelson Mandela), the ANC was not very active in Transkei. However, the PAC's military wing, *Poqo*, largely based in the Transkei (*see* **South African History**), favoured direct attacks on whites. Police stations in the Cape were targeted, but also white civilians and in 1963, the first of many murders of whites in Transkei occurred at Mbashe Bridge, where a group of people, including women and children, were attacked and killed. Arrests followed, but a precedent had been set that still makes Transkei a potentially dangerous area for whites.

In 1976 Transkei was declared an independent state, along with several other South African black 'homelands', in a move both to ensure the region's export of cheap labour to the cities and mines (by making Transkeians foreigners, the government would have no obligations to provide services, while setting favourable labour prices in their own territories) and to curb Xhosa militarism by setting up puppet rulers from the existing hierarchy of chiefs. The plan backfired. While the cheap labour pool was ensured, Transkeian activists had, with the removal of South African police and army, a freer base from which to act. In the 1980s, Bantu Holomisa, the Transkei's military commander, began to take an increasingly confrontational stand against South Africa. By the early 1990s attacks on whites within Transkei by APLA (or Azanian People's Liberation Army, as the terrorist wing of the PAC was then called) had become commonplace, and fewer and fewer whites dared venture there. Meanwhile, South Africa's recession caused thousands of Transkei Xhosa men to lose their jobs in the mines and to drift home penniless and landless, a ready pool of disaffected youth for the political organisations to draw on.

While the Transkei government denied any encouragement of terrorist groups, most South Africans believe that Transkei remained the base of APLA, whose 1993 'one settler, one bullet' slogan made travelling there very hazardous. Many Transkei Xhosa, unable to make a living in the Eastern Cape, have drifted to the South African cities, particularly Cape Town, to look for work, living in large squatter camps. Transkei was re-absorbed into South Africa in 1994, but the region, though outwardly calm in the countryside, is still one of South Africa's most volatile.

Safety

The political climate in Transkei has calmed down considerably since 1993. However, many travellers are shy of the region, and even the largely peaceful Wild Coast—for a long time of Southern Africa's most established travellers' playgrounds—now receives few visitors, leaving the small resorts that used to flourish there in financial trouble. However, for the adventurous, the tourist infrastructure still exists and confidence is returning among travellers. It is worth seeing the Transkei, and particularly the heavenly Wild Coast, if at all possible. The bottom line is; avoid the cities, where mugging is frequent (theft is general throughout the region), and get as much local information as possible from the hotels and hostels within Transkei before going in. One of the best ways to get around safely is to arrange a Xhosa guide through one of the Transkei local government offices in South Africa (they have one in most cities), usually at little or no cost.

When travelling in Transkei, always carry your passport, particularly if driving. Police checkpoints are common and cars with South African licence plates will almost always be stopped. Usually the police will take a cursory look at your passport and wave you on, but it is important to have it to hand.

The N2 highway runs through central Transkei, a rolling country of rounded, grass covered hills, plateaux and sudden uplands, vivid green in summer, pink and golden-yellow in winter. Along the north-west horizon marches the distant blue line of the Transkei Drakensberg, a region inaccessible to the traveller who does not speak Xhosa or have a guide and a horse to get about on.

The majority of Transkei's population lives in this central zone, and the region's only large towns lie along the route.

Butterworth has grown from the original mission station (1827) to a reasonably sized market town. It was near here that the faithful Xhosa gathered to await their ancestors after the great Cattle Killing in 1856. Today, Butterworth is a compact, lively place of shabby old buildings and raw, new industrial structures. The University of Transkei has a campus here, but the town has little for the traveller, except petrol stations and shops to stock up at before heading down to the southern Wild Coast. Bear in mind that wandering the side streets can be dangerous here, especially after dark.

However, a short drive from town are the spectacular **Bawa Falls** and the **Butterworth River Cascades**. Tradition has it that one section of the falls was used up to the mid-19th century as a place of execution for people who had been 'smelt out' (found to be witches)—the only capital crime among the Xhosa, who almost never executed people—even murder and rape were punished by fines.

Umtata, the capital of Transkei, is roughly in the geographical centre of the region. Founded by the British in the 1860s, it marks the boundary between the Mpondo and Tembu Xhosa clans, today's dominant clans. A bustling, rather unfriendly town (especially after dark), Umtata must be visited to collect permits for the Wild Coast Hiking Trail from the Transkei Department of Agriculture and Forestry. Umtata also has such essentials as mechanics and tyre shops for those whose vehicles have suffered on the rough roads to and from the coast.

There is no question that Umtata is a rough town, and that anti-white feeling is strong. Avoid the taxi-ranks, particularly at rush hour when there is a large crowd. These are classic mugging spots and you can expect no help from bystanders, and seldom even from policemen. The same goes for bars after dark. By night, always park your car in hotel car-parks and stow your belongings in your room. Obviously, do not walk around with cameras and jewellery.

Libode off the N2, on the R61 to Port St Johns is very small and unremarkable except for its position near a high mountain called Executioner's Rock, a lone massif that juts unmistakeably from the surrounding landscape. Like the Executioner's Falls near Butterworth, this was a place where witches were hurled into oblivion in olden times.

Despite its wonderful name, **Lusikisiki** is not much more than the usual collection of falling-down colonial buildings and assorted shacks, with a petrol station and a general trading store. The old hotel has a functioning bar that used to be a well-known stopping point for fishermen on their way through to the coast. But since the recent troubles the atmosphere has changed somewhat, and few travellers stop there now. Some interesting graffiti adorns the walls of the police station: rather than the usual 'One Settler, One Bullet' slogan seen elsewhere, Lusikisiki's youth appeal to the police to 'Stop Killing Us', giving an insight into the Transkei's own internal problems.

Lusikisiki is the town from which to approach the northern Wild Coast spots such as Emboyti and Mkambati. From Lusikisiki the road becomes really terrible; drive very cautiously unless you are in a truck, and always have a couple of spare tyres.

Umtata ✆ (0471–) **Where to Stay**

expensive

The **Umtata Protea**, 36 Sutherland St, ✆ 25654, is expensive and new, but has the town's safest car park. All the rooms are done up in tasteless comfort (bright blue curtains and bed spreads) with TV, en suite bathrooms, fridge bars, etc. The hotel bar is used as a general meeting place for businessmen and, like the restaurant, it is open to non-residents. The **Umtata Holiday Inn**, ✆ 22181, on N2 the west of town, is much the same as the above, only bigger, with a tennis court and swimming pool.

moderate

The **Sutherland Arms Hotel**, ✆ 312 281, just round the corner from the Umtata Protea, is run down but safe for white travellers, though things can get pretty rowdy in the bar (itself barred off from the main hotel) which the owners recommend you do not use. There is safe parking. Very basic rooms, sometimes clean, sometimes not. Breakfast is optional; a grim serving of porridge and toast in a grey-carpeted
room without windows; better to eat out at one of the many take-aways in the town centre. Round the corner, and slightly more expensive, though also a bit run down is the **Royal Hotel**, ✆ 22231, some of whose rooms are en suite, the **Grosvenor Hotel** (on Sutherland and Madeira Streets) ✆ 312 118, which has an old-fashioned feel, with rather formal service, and the **Transkei Hotel**, ✆ 24445, on Elliot Street. All the above offer B&B, with dinner as an option.

There is no safe cheap accommodation in Umtata. The best bet is to share a room in one of the moderately-priced hotels between several people. Most of the hotels are amenable to this, owing to Transkei's recent fall-off in tourism.

Umtata ✆ (0471–) **Eating Out**

Umtata is not known for its restaurants. Most of the hotels have à la carte eateries, varying in price according to the standard of the hotel. The **Grosvenor Hotel** serves reasonable food in a dining room that has changed little since colonial times, and is something of an island of calm in the chaotic town centre. Cheap eating is available at the take-away places which can be found on any street.

Superlatives spring to mind when trying to describe the Wild Coast. The green hills of central Transkei fall steeply to the Indian Ocean, their seaward slopes often covered with the dense sub-tropical forest that used to cover much of Transkei. The human population then thins out, reduced to small villages among the trees, on the cliff-tops or at the wide estuary mouths. Antelope, monkeys and exotic birds live among the trees, while fish jump in the mangrove-fringed rivers and swim in clearly visible silver shoals just off the endless, empty beaches.

Living off fish and shellfish is a relatively new experience for the Xhosa of the Wild Coast. Even 50 years ago, the sea was considered unclean. Tradition has it that once a year a chosen woman from coastal villages would ceremoniously cleanse herself in the surf, thus cleansing the menstrual juices of all the women of the village. As a result, fish and shellfish were taboo. The taboo has faded now, and with good reason. The pure, unpolluted waters of the Wild Coast support vast beds of shellfish that can be cut from the rocks of any cove. The density of estuarine and marine fish is so great that anglers from all over South Africa flock there. For the traveller, a few rand exchanged with any Xhosa fisherman or woman can buy large amounts of fresh mussels, oysters, crayfish, prawns, and a huge range of fish. It is worth remembering to take lemon, butter and garlic with you.

Flora and Fauna

The Wild Coast has several game reserves, through which the Wild Coast Trail passes (*see* below). Most harbour antelope, such as eland, kudu, blesbok, bushbuck, eland and duiker, and Dwesa Game Reserve has larger animals such as buffalo, crocodile and wildebeest. Bird life is abundant, with louries, trogons, sunbirds and a wide variety of raptors providing the most spectacular sights.

Much of the coast is covered with evergreen, sub-tropical hardwood forest of great beauty, mostly composed of yellowwood, milkwood, stinkwood, hardpear, assegai and the other South African hardwoods. Some species are found only in Transkei, such as the Pondoland coconut palm, found on the coastline around Port St Johns. More intriguing are the night-flowering creepers. It's worth walking in the forest after dark to sea these large, enigmatic flowers hanging from the trees. Shaped like trumpets of white petals, the ghostly blooms are pollinated by moths and close their buds at dawn.

Getting There

There is no road running along the coast, but various dirt roads connect points of the coast with the N2 highway, approximately 70km inland. These are often in appalling condition and it advisable to carry two spare tyres. All of the Transkei's nature reserves are on the Wild Coast, as are its resort hotels, which occupy isolated spots at various river mouths. The coast has one large-ish town, Port St Johns, in the northern stretch. Reckoned by most travellers who have been there to be the mellowest town in South Africa, many people arrive at Port St Johns for a few days and stay weeks, months, or sometimes even settle there; various artists and craftspeople from South Africa have found the cheap living, gentle climate and sheer beauty of Port St Johns addictive enough to stay.

The Wild Coast Hiking Trail

Without doubt, the best way to see the Wild Coast is to walk the Wild Coast Hiking Trail, or at least a section of it. The trail runs the full length of the coast and takes 25 days to complete. But shorter sections, even of just one day, can be walked. Accommodation is in rondavels set at roughly 20km intervals along the coast. The most popular sections are the five days between Port St Johns and Coffee Bay (which can involve swimming two estuary mouths at low tide, with packs floated across in inflated plastic bags) and the two-day cliffside walk through Mkambati Game Reserve, where waterfalls plummet over the cliffs into the sea. Unfortunately, permits issued from Umtata have to be purchased before starting the trail, and shown to the custodians of each rondavel where you stop for the night. These can be bought from the Department of Forestry and Agriculture in Transkei, either direct from the office or by post, if you have a month to spare.

Safety on the Trail

Once again, a word of warning on personal safety. The Coast should not be hiked alone or even in couples. Groups are best. Expect attempts at theft from the rondavels (which do not lock), no matter how isolated they seem. Some places are known for trouble; particularly Mpande rondavel (between Port St Johns and Coffee Bay) where several groups of hikers have been attacked at night. The best way to ensure personal safety is to request a guide from the Transkei Department of Forestry and Agriculture when applying for a permit (you will have to pick up the guide from Umtata when you go there for your permit), or to hire a reliable guide at Port St Johns (*see* below).

Swimming

Away from the hotels, the Wild Coast beaches are remote, so do not swim far out. There are sharks and treacherous currents out there. Within the surf, one is generally safe. Avoid river mouths when the tides are changing or ebbing.

Villages and Reserves along the Coast

Qolora Mouth is the southernmost point of the Wild Coast accessible by road. Two large, old fashioned hotels, Trennery's and Seagull's are comfortable and safe (*see* 'Where to Stay'). A beached ship, the *Jacaranda*, a Portuguese vessel that foundered here in 1971, is a beautiful hour's walk north along the beach. Near Qolora Mouth is the river pool where, in 1856, the young prophetesss Nongqawuse claimed to have spoken with the ancestors prior to the Great Cattle Killing (*see* **Transkei** 'History').

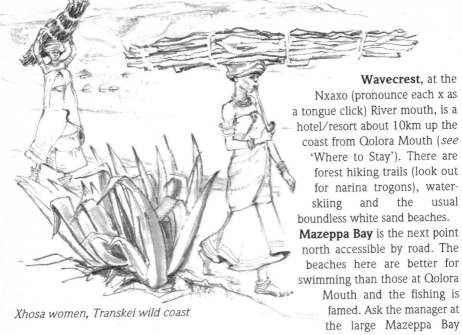

Wavecrest, at the Nxaxo (pronounce each x as a tongue click) River mouth, is a hotel/resort about 10km up the coast from Qolora Mouth (*see* 'Where to Stay'). There are forest hiking trails (look out for narina trogons), water-skiing and the usual boundless white sand beaches.

Mazeppa Bay is the next point north accessible by road. The beaches here are better for swimming than those at Qolora Mouth and the fishing is famed. Ask the manager at the large Mazeppa Bay

Xhosa women, Transkei wild coast

Hotel about hiring tackle for the barracuda, kob and hammerhead shark for which the bay is famous. Bushbuck and duiker lurk in the coastal forest, and wood hoopoes chatter incessantly.

Qolora Mouth, on the coast south of Willowvale, has a less fancy hotel called the Kob Inn, with safe bathing and good fishing (*see* 'Where to Stay'). The superbly-named pignose grunter (a large, heavy fish that actually grunts when landed) runs in shoals near the Qolora Mouth in winter (July and August). Inland from Qolora Mouth, the land is hilly and cut with deep kloofs through whose dense forest wind a series of hiking trails.

Dwesa Nature Reserve, accessible from Nqabara, north of Qolora Mouth, is a large stretch of coastal forest still populated by large game. Buffalo, eland, red hartebeest, blesbok, warthog, wildbeest and kudu live among the trees, while crocodile bask on the mangroved mudbanks of the Mbashe River, which runs at the northern end of the reserve. This is not a river to swim in. Birdlife includes green lourie, narina trogon, fish eagle and mangrove kingfisher. The Wild Coast Trail passes through. Be careful of buffalo when walking about. Bear in mind that no fuel is available at the reserve.

Cwebe Nature Reserve, on the north side of the Mbashe River from Dwesa, is accessible via the Haven, which is linked to Elliotdale (also called Xora) by a gravel road. Unlike Dwesa, Cwebe has no big game, though there are crocodiles. Smaller game, such as bushbuck and duiker, are common. Listen for tree dassies (which scream at night) and samango monkey (which call with a loud 'Ak' sound). Waterfalls run through the kloofs towards a large freshwater lagoon where you may spot otters if you are quiet. The birdlife is the same as in Dwesa. Inside Cwebe is The Haven, a hotel with the feel of a small frontier settlement, surrounded by virgin bush (*see* 'Where to Stay').

Hole in the Wall, a huge rock arch standing in the sea north of Cwebe (accessible from Coffee Bay), appears on the cover of most brochures promoting the region. The arch is much larger than the photographs suggest, the top being a plateau about the size of a football pitch. The noise the sea makes as it crashes through the gap has given Hole in the Wall a place in Transkei mythology as a place of angry spirits.

About 10km north of Hole in the Wall is the tiny settlement of **Coffee Bay**. The surrounding geography is dramatic; mountain forest and high cliffs fall to a narrow bay and river mouth, with the usual vast sweep of golden beach, coastal bush and aquamarine surf. Coffee Bay is one of the most favoured tourist spots on the Wild Coast.

Hluleka Nature Reserve, north of Coffee Bay and accessible by dirt road from Libode inland via the village of Notinsila, is a small reserve of high coastal hills concentrated around the Hluleka River mouth. Forest and grassland cover the hills, which are grazed by zebra, eland, blesbok and duiker. Louries, narina trogon, wood hoopoe and sunbirds are common sights. The reserve has chalet accommodation which must be booked in advance (*see* 'Where to Stay') but no fuel. There are walking trails (again, the Wild Coast Trail passes through), and fishing is permitted, but bring your own tackle.

Umngazi River is a small resort of thatched bungalows set around a main restaurant and overlooking a wide river mouth. There is good walking down to a mangrove forest and along the river to deserted cliffs, and small, hidden coves. Fishing tackle can be hired.

Port St Johns is the Wild Coast's only town of any size. Connected with the Transkei capital, Umtata, by the tarred R61, the town got its from a ship wrecked just off the bay. Port St Johns sits at the mouth of the Umzimvubu River, beneath towering, forested mountains, where lie two nature reserves, the **Mount Thesiger Nature Reserve**, west of town, and the **Silaka Nature Reserve**, south of town, where begins the Port St Johns–Coffee Bay stretch of the Wild Coast Hiking Trail. On the road into town, children sell large bags of avocado, banana, guava and mango for next to nothing.

There is a fixed community of white South Africans living in Port St Johns, many of them artists and craftspeople who sell their work in Cape Town and Johannesburg. It is not hard to see why they have settled here; the atmosphere is relaxed to near inertia, and the town itself is gentle, decaying and lively. Many of its 19th-century colonial buildings have fallen down, or been burnt out and left, the vegetation gradually reclaiming them. Travellers often find it hard to leave Port St Johns, and locals call this sudden langour 'Pondo fever'.

If you want to hike along the coast from Port St Johns, reliable guides can be arranged through a man called Kirk, an Australian who runs the Backpackers Hostel in Port St Johns, and who is now something of a public figure there (*see* 'Where to Stay').

Embotyi (pronounced Emboyki) is a quiet spot on a river mouth on the coast north of Port St Johns. Access is via the inland town of Lusikisiki (a truly awful road in its last stretch) or via the R61 from Umtata (turn right over the bridge as you approach Port St Johns). From its very small resort of wooden bungalows, forest walks lead to various mountain views and waterfalls. The resort also has horses, and offers guided rides to a grassy plain where wildebeest graze.

Port Grosvenor, a tiny place north of Embotyi (also accessible from Lusikisiki via a bad dirt road) gets its name from a ship that went down off the coast near here in 1782. The event is remembered because its survivors were succoured and absorbed by the coastal Mpondo people. Travellers visiting the area in the early 1800s encountered white women living as Mpondo, who had been little girls when their ship was wrecked. Oddly enough, Port Grosvenor was the scene of an earlier, similar shipwreck in the 1550s, when a Portuguese ship went down: her crew were also helped in their distress by the Mpondo. However, the Portugese decided to try and walk over 1000km north to Delogoa Bay (modern Maputo) in Mozambique, then a Portuguese trading station. Out of an original party of almost 500, only 25 made it through the foetid, tropical journey.

Mkambati Nature Reserve marks the final wild access point to the Wild Coast before Transkei ends and Natal begins. In the early part of this century Mkambati used to be, of all things, a leper colony, but there is no trace of such tragedy today. The forest is more noticeably tangled and jungle-like than further south, as Mkambati is close to the more tropical Natal coast. The grasslands of the reserve support large herds of eland, wildebeest, hartebeest, blesbok, gemsbok and reedbuck. There are horses for rent, trails to walk and wild beaches to swim from. Most spectacular, however, are the **Horseshoe Falls** which plunge down a series of cascades and finally over a cliff directly into the sea. Access from the N2 is via a dirt road through the town of Holy Cross.

The **Wild Coast Sun**, the final northern point of the Wild Coast, comes as a brutal shock to anyone who has travelled up the coast through Transkei. The quiet African pace and beauty is abruptly changed by this brash, crass overpriced casino of the most noisy, taste-less, glitzy variety. Unless you have an irresistable urge to gamble, it is best avoided.

Where to Stay

The hotels are listed in order, south to north. Travellers should bear in mind that due to the fall-off in tourism in Transkei, most hotels are open to bargaining.

expensive

Trennery's, ✆ (0474) 3293, is an old-fashioned colonial hotel at Qolora Mouth whose thatched cottages have picture windows overlooking the Indian Ocean. A short walk takes you down to the beach. There is a shipwreck to visit, tennis courts, windsurfing, fishing tackle for hire, a good bar and a better seafood restaurant. **Seagull's**, ✆ (0474) 3287, is on the other side of the bay at Qolora Mouth. Not quite as attractive as Trennery's, but closer to the beach. The facilities are much the same, with the addition of canoeing, horseriding, a waterfall walk and snorkelling/scuba diving. Accommodation is in large double rooms, rather than separate cottages.

Wavecrest at Nxaxo River Mouth, ✆ (0474) 3273, offers luxurious rondavels with some good forest hiking, birdwatching, water-skiing, bar and seafood restaurant. It also has its own airstrip. **Mazeppa Bay** resort/hotel, ✆ (0474) 3287, is surrounded by thick coastal bush. Sub-tropical flowers such as hibiscus and bougainvillea are in abundance. Thatched cottages surround a central lodge. Activities include scuba-diving, snorkelling, safe swimming, tennis and snooker. Perhaps the biggest attraction is the hotels' own island, linked to the mainland by a chain-bridge. Here, there are forest trails and a shore-line where dolphins play. Traditional Xhosa dancing is often arranged at night, and though one can feel a little uncomfortable being performed for, it is a compelling, beautiful sight.

The **Kob Inn**, ✆ (0474) 4421, is smaller and more remote than the other hotels on this list, which, although seldom full, are nonetheless small settlements in themselves. Once again there are thatched bungalows to sleep in, fishing tackle and scuba equipment for hire, and waterskiing, canoeing and windsurfing are offered. Below the Inn are magical rock pools full of brightly-coloured life. It has a bar and seafood restaurant, though your can cut your own mussels from the rocks and dive for crayfish, if you know how.

The **Haven**, ✆ (0474) 25344, a large resort set in the bush of Cwebe Nature Reserve, has some of the best day-hikes for bird-and game-spotting in Transkei. The Haven has less to offer from the swimming and water-sports point of view, but has beaches within walking distance through the bush. Of particular interest are boat trips among the crocodile infested mangroves of the Mbashe River.

Hole in the Wall Holiday Village, ✆ (031) 258263, a 2km walk from the famous rock arch, has thatched cottages in landscaped gardens around a central lodge. Horses, forest and beach hiking, water-skiing and fishing are available to guests.

The **Ocean View Hotel**, ✆ (0471) 25344, near the tiny settlement of Coffee Bay, occupies a promontary between two rivers. Excellent shell-fish gathering, fishing for kob and grunter and beach hiking are the main attractions. **Umngazi River Bungalows** (at the time of writing there was no available telephone number (just show up) for Umngazi Mouth, are set in forest fronting the Umngazi estuary. The thatched bugalows and central lodge sit under palms and trailing hibscus. Windsurfing, waterskiing, tennis and snooker are on offer, as well as the usual bush and beach hiking.

Embotyi River Bungalows, ✆ (0471) 25654, break the thatched cottage tradition and house their guests in log cabins with verandahs. There are good walks to waterfalls and horses to ride. Bear in mind that the last section of road from Lusikisiki to Embotyi is very bad.

Mkambati Lodge (no telephone), in Mkambati Game Reserve, is a handsome 1920s sandstone building (the house in which the governors of the old leper colony lived) overlooking a deserted cove and river-mouth inside the game-rich reserve. The rooms of the lodge have been comfortably done up in semi-period fashion, and there is a large staff to pamper you. Mkambati has horses, game viewing, and one of Africa's most unusual waterfalls (off a cliff into the sea). Mkambati has a variety of accomodation, from basic self-contained rondavels to the lodge, where servants and full board are offered. Mkambati is not a reserve where accommodation must be booked in advance.

moderate and cheap

Hluleka, Dwesa and Silaka Nature Reserves all have moderately-priced chalet accommodation, but it must be booked through the Department of Agriculture and Forestry in Umtata, ✆ 0471 249 111. There are ablution blocks and cooking facilities, but take your own food. **Mkambati Nature Reserve** has moderate and cheap chalets and rondavels (*see* above). There are ablution blocks, cooking facilities and a restaurant. **Second Beach Cottages, Port St Johns**, ✆ (04752) 61, are in bush behind the beach, 4km south of town. There are forest walks (bushbuck and duiker are common), and canoes can be hired. Each cottage has a bathroom, kitchen and cooking utensils.

Wild Coast Hiking Trail rondavels are found every 20km or so along the Wild Coast. Again, they must be booked from Umtata. Reaching them entails a day or half-day's walk, but the hikes are beautiful, and if taken at a leisurely pace (particularly in summer), not over-tiring. Firewood and cooking pots are provided. Local fishermen and shellfish gatherers usually come by to sell you your supper very cheaply. Avoid the rondavels at Mpande between Port St Johns and Coffee Bay, where several travellers have been attacked.

Port St Johns Backpacker's comprises a set of permanent tents in the town, on the road to Second Beach, offering cheap, safe accommodation, with a kitchen and a central sitting area covered with thatch. Reliable guides for the Wild Coast Hiking Trail can be arranged through here, and children selling crayfish often visit. At the time of writing, the hostel was re-opening after a period of closure due to the political situation. There is no telephone. Also ask the locals if the very cheap guest farm (also with permanent tents) called **Mbekeni** is still running. With boat trips down through mangove swamps and accommodation set beneath a grove of guava trees, this is paradise.

Kwa-Zulu/Natal

*Everything grows immediately, and just as immediately stands still.
Time and the climate both combine to growth and growth's
suspension.*

Riotous Assembly, Tom Sharpe, talking about Natal

For most South Africans, who live in landscapes that are dry and brown
for at least half the year, Natal provides verdant relief from the seasonal
droughts of their own region. Much of Natal is blessed with South
Africa's highest rainfall, and a warm, often humid climate that plants
like; green rounded hills and flat-topped mountains fall through forested
kloofs to a sub-tropical coast of flowering trees; Natal's perennial mantle
of green is dear to the parched South African heart.

However, like most romantic ideals, this one of all-year green does not
stand close scrutiny. True, the foetid, often stifling Natal coast gets year-
round rain and never loses its luxuriant, sensual verdure, but inland the
scenery changes colour with the season. During the dry winter the
grasses turn pink, brown and gold and the trees lose their leaves. But the
forests never shrivel and the many rivers, though they may slow to mere
trickles, seldom fail. And with the summer rains, the whole province
turns a vivid, startling green that out-emeralds Ireland.

Natal can be divided into roughly five regions: the well-settled south, up
to and including Durban and the southern coast; Pietermaritzburg and
the Natal Midlands, whose temperate upland pastures rise steadily to the
western mountains; the Drakensberg mountains; Zululand, which
includes most of the province's big-game harbouring nature reserves, and
the wild, tropical northern coast; and northwest Natal, a high, lonely
region of mountain foothills, space and isolated game reserves.

Most Natalians mean the southern part of the province (i.e. not including
Zululand) when they talk of Natal. This can be confusing for travellers—
especially those visiting the coast. Roadsigns near Durban, the province's
biggest city, will point you to the Natal North Coast and the Natal South
Coast. These refer only to the coastline on either side of Durban: the
South Coast stretching to the Transkei border, and the North Coast to
the Tugela River mouth. North of this 'North Coast' lies the majority of
the Natal province's coastline, but this is referred to as the Zululand or
Tsongaland coast. Confused? Don't be—avoid the official North and
South Coasts entirely—their resorts are brash and have long been a
haven for crowds of Transvaal holiday-makers. Head straight for the
Zululand/Tsongaland coast instead, where the wild beaches and forest
are largely intact.

Natal is South Africa's smallest province yet vast areas of it, particularly in the Drakensberg and northern Zululand, are still sparsely settled, even though, agriculturally, Natal is a land of plenty. Sugar cane fields cover the hills just inland from the coast, while the good pastureland of the Midlands supports rich cattle ranches and racehorse studs. Sorghum, millet and maize are intensively cultivated in Kwa-Zulu and forestry has come to most of the higher uplands of the central region. But for all this, each region has large swathes of wild country, often protected by giant nature reserves and supporting healthy game populations.

Natal's human landscape is not so diverse. With the exception of the Tsonga in the far north, the Hlubi in the Drakensberg and some Xhosa near the border with Transkei, almost the entire black population is Zulu-speaking. But this was not always the case. Up until the 1830s, the population was divided into scores of separate clans, all of whom were gradually absorbed into the Zulu nation during the conquests of Shaka, the first Zulu king, and his son Dingane. The result is the country's largest single black language group, and the one that has inherited the most militaristic identity, still theoretically subject to a single monarch.

As for whites, Natal was mostly settled by the British in the mid-to-late 19th century, so Natalian whites are predominantly English speaking. However, many Voortrekkers settled here during the Great Trek of 1836 and the northwest part of the province is staunchly Afrikaans.

Natal also has a uniquely large Asian population, mostly the descendants of Indians brought over in vast numbers in the 1860s and '70s to cut the new sugar cane fields (plus a smaller population of 'free' Indians who came over a traders). This community of agricultural labourers slowly worked its way out of pauperdom (with no help from Briton or Boer) and Durban now claims to have the highest concentration of Indian residents outside of India. Mosques and Hindu temples abound in the city, and the spice markets and bazaars can make you feel that you have misplaced continents.

Climate

Natal is wet in summer and dry in winter, except on the near-tropical coast, where it rains year-round. Coastal summers are humid and breathless (Durban in summer is unbearable for those not used to it) and winters are warm with mercifully cool nights. Just inland the terrain rises from the cane fields to bushveld, also hell's hot (a South African phrase) and humid in summer, but warm and dry in winter, with bitter nights. The Natal Midlands are temperate, with warm to hot summers and cold winters with regular frost and occasional snow. The Drakensberg gets very cold in winter, with a sustained (if thin) coating of snow up high. Zululand verges from the sub-tropical to the tropical (up near the border with Mozambique). Depending on altitude, the climate can be steamy or temperate. Some of

Natal and Kwa-Zulu

80 kms
50 miles

Land above 1500 metres

N

EASTERN TRANSVAAL
Piet Retief

Volksrust
Charlestown
Balelesberg
Paulpietersburg

R543

R33

R34

Utrecht

Newcastle
Vryheid

ORANGE FREE STATE

CHELMSFORD NATURE RESERVE

Bethlehem

R720

N3

Harrismith

Chelmsford Dam

Talana
Dundee
Bloedrivier

Blood River

N5

Fort Mistake
Glencoe

Rooiberg

STERKFONTEIN DAM NATURE RESERVE

Sterkfontein Dam

Elandslaagte

Rorke's Drift
Rorke's Drift

R68

Fouriesberg

ROYAL NATAL NATIONAL PARK

N3

Spioenkop Dam

Elandslaagte

Isandhlwana

R26

R74

Ladysmith
Wagon Hill

Sundays

Pomeroy

Butha-Buthe

Woodstock Dam

Bergville

Colenso
Spion Kop

Colenso

Tugela

Weenen

KWA ZULU

Keate's Drift

A1

Winterton

WEENEN NATURE RESERVE

Tugela Ferry

Maluti Mts

Loskop

MLABONJA AND MDELELO
KWA ZULU

Weenen

Drakensberg

Estcourt

R74

Mokhotlong

GIANT'S CASTLE NAT. RES.

Mooi

Greytown

R622

R74

LESOTHO

A14

KAMBERG NAT. RES.

Rosetta

Mooi River
Nottingham Road

Albert Falls

A3

A3

LOTENI NAT. RES.

Balgowan
Lidgetton

Dargle

Howick
Howick Falls

Valley of 1000 Hills

R614

MZIMKULWANA AND MZIMKULU WILDERNESS AREAS

Midmar Dam
PIETERMARITZBURG

Tongaat

A4

Himeville

Edendale

Inanda

Underberg

Bulwer
KWA ZULU

Phoenix

N3

Mpumalanga
Kwa Mashu

Umhla

COLEFORD NATURE RESERVE

Richmond

R624

KWAZULU

R603

DURB

Qacha's Nek

R617

Ixopo
KWA ZULU

NATAL

Umkomaas

Amanzimtoti

TRANSKEI

Umzimkulu

R56

Cedarville

R612

Umzimkulu

Umkomaas

MOUNT CURRIE NAT. RES.

WEZA FOREST

VERNON CROOKES NATURE RESERVE

Scottburgh

EASTERN CAPE

Kokstad

Weza
Harding

ORIBI GORGE NATURE RESERVE

Hibberdene

N2

N2

Umtamvuna

Port Shepstone

R61

KWA ZULU

Margate
Ramsgate

TRANSKEI

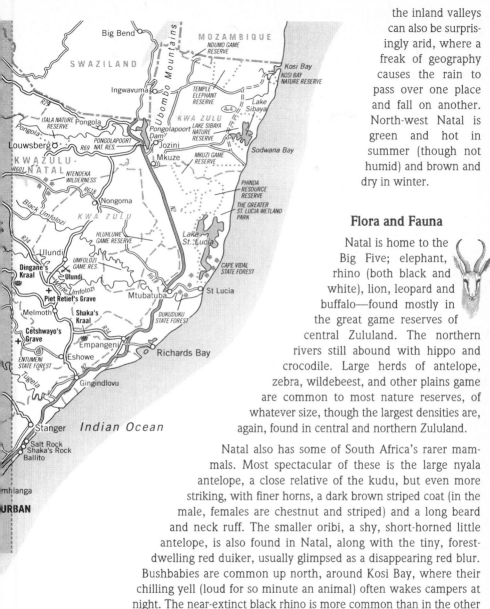

the inland valleys can also be surprisingly arid, where a freak of geography causes the rain to pass over one place and fall on another. North-west Natal is green and hot in summer (though not humid) and brown and dry in winter.

Flora and Fauna

Natal is home to the Big Five; elephant, rhino (both black and white), lion, leopard and buffalo—found mostly in the great game reserves of central Zululand. The northern rivers still abound with hippo and crocodile. Large herds of antelope, zebra, wildebeest, and other plains game are common to most nature reserves, of whatever size, though the largest densities are, again, found in central and northern Zululand.

Natal also has some of South Africa's rarer mammals. Most spectacular of these is the large nyala antelope, a close relative of the kudu, but even more striking, with finer horns, a dark brown striped coat (in the male, females are chestnut and striped) and a long beard and neck ruff. The smaller oribi, a shy, short-horned little antelope, is also found in Natal, along with the tiny, forest-dwelling red duiker, usually glimpsed as a disappearing red blur. Bushbabies are common up north, around Kosi Bay, where their chilling yell (loud for so minute an animal) often wakes campers at night. The near-extinct black rhino is more common than in the other South African provinces.

Natal's birds are colourful and diverse. Bright, jewel-like sunbirds, parrots, rollers, twinspots, nicators, louries and trogons, bee-eaters and a host of other species flit among the trees, with the general rule that the further north you go, the more colourful the birds become. Hadeda ibis are everywhere, as are the large raptors, especially in the wind-blown, silent heights of the Drakensberg (good for black and booted eagle, jackal buzzard, lammergeier vulture and bald ibis, as well as sugar-birds and other smaller beauties). In the dense coastal forests live the more exotic-looking crowned, snake and long-crested eagles. Natal has some avian oddities, among them the Pel's fishing owl, which snatches fish from estuary marshes, and the palm nut vulture of Kosi Bay, which eats the fruit of the raffia palm.

Reptiles abound, particularly snakes. Although you have to be very unlucky to be bitten, be aware of mambas, boomslangs and other nasties when climbing tress or striking off into dense bush. In the Drakensberg, keep an eye out for berg and puff adders. Having said this, most of Natal's reptiles are harmless—there are hundreds of lizards, from the tiniest bright-coloured skinks, to the leguaans (or rock monitors) that can grow to a metre long. On the sands of the Tsongaland beaches, sea-turtles crawl ashore to lay their eggs.

If one had to be re-incarnated as a plant, Natal would be the place to come back to. There is an exuberance to the plant-life that is astonishing for those used to a temperate climate. Entire trees that flower pink and white, creepers that grow wooden spikes ten centimetres long, wild fig trees the size of buildings (especially dense in Mkuzi Game Reserve) and a host of exotic species run riot here. The Drakensberg has subtler wonders, particularly its small wild orchids, the lilies that grow by the mountain streams, and the protea wood-lands of its lower slopes.

Natal has some superb forests, from the coastal jungles to the wider-spaced hard-wood forests of central Zululand, where yellowwood, stinkwood and assegai thrive. Around Sibaya in the far north is a dense, cathedral-like, and largely uncharted thorn and wild fig forest.

However, large areas of Natal are simply bushveld and aloe scrub, and oddly enough it is these, rather than the more spectacularly vegetated zones, that support the most wildlife species.

History

Natal's well-watered, fertile land was the undisputed hunting ground of San (bushman) clans until cattle-herding, Bantu-speaking clans began moving in from the north. The San were gradually pushed towards the Drakensberg (where they remained until the 19th century). The Nguni-speakers were undisputed masters of the region by the time the first Portuguese mariners sailed by the Natal coast in the 15th and 16th centuries.

It was the Portuguese who gave the land its present name. In 1497 the explorer Vasco da Gama rounded the Cape and, after landing around present day Mossel Bay in the Garden Route, kept sailing east. On Christmas Day, 1497, he sighted a lush, green coast which he christened Natalia—the day of Christ's birth. Da Gama did not land however, but sailed on to Mozambique and the East African coast.

There was then no European landfall on the Natal coast for almost two hundred years; the coastline lacks the natural harbours of the southern and eastern Cape coasts. A few ship-wrecked Portuguese crews made land, and on being rescued, reported maltreatment at the hands of the Natal Nguni. However, such tales may have been propaganda; the crew of two English ships *The Good Hope* and the *Bonaventino* wrecked on the south coast of Natal in 1685, set up camp on the Bluff overlooking the bay of present-day Durban, and found conditions so good that many elected to stay on after help arrived. Other ship-wrecked sailors later joined them, and established a small village. The Englishmen joined forces with the crew of a Dutch ship—the *Stavenisse*—that had also been wrecked nearby. The combined crews managed to build a makeshift boat capable of handling the coastal waters and sailed back to Cape Town (an impressive feat) having been amply provi-sioned by the local Natalans.

Their favourable reports made to the Dutch East India Company officials at Cape Town, of Natal's fertile country, friendly inhabitants, and abundance of game (particularly elephants for ivory), persuaded the Dutch East India Company to aquire the little post as a pro-visioning point. They sent a ship called the *Noord* to the Bay of Natal with an official aboard who duly negotiated a land grant from the local chief. Following the tradition of South African coastal shipping, the *Noord* was wrecked on its return, and only a few survivors returned to Cape Town. The document was received, then forgotten and fortunately for the indigenous inhabitants of the Bay of Natal, no colonial office or settle-ment was established there.

But by about 1750 this bay was well-known to ships from all over Europe, and various temporary settlements of shipwrecked sailors (particularly English, for some reason) seem to have thrived on the Bluff, so that the site acquired the nicknames among Dutch sailors of *Engesche logie* (English village). But it also became famous for a great underwater sand bar that made the bay unsafe for large ships and its commercial potential continued to be ignored by the Dutch and after them (in the early 1800s) by the British.

In fact, by the 1800s, the reports of sailors' villages die off—perhaps because at this time began a wave of political and social upheavals that were to thoroughly disrupt Natal's peaceful existence. Several dominant clans had emerged from the mass of small chiefdoms in Natal, gaining sufficient power to maintain standing armies of warriors (known as *amabutho*) used to mount large-scale raids on their neighbours. Many historians now believe that these clans rose to prominence by establishing control over the inland trade routes—for ivory to the Dutch and British in the Eastern Cape, and slaves to Delagoa Bay (modern Maputo) in Portuguese Mozambique—that had grown up through the 18th century. By the early 1800s, two clans, the Mthethwa and the Ndwandwe, had become dominant north of the Tugela River. Around 1810, contemporary reports tell of heavy warfare between the two.

It seems that the stronger clan were the Mthethwa, led by one Dingiswayo. Colonial histo-ries relate that he was a violent man who seized power from his father after aquiring a horse and gun from a luckless white traveller, whom he had murdered. However, this is now being refuted as myth—certainly Dingiswayo was a charismatic figure who organised his army, by whatever means, into a number of highly-disciplined regiments, each of which could act independently. One of his generals was a young man called **Shaka**, the illegitimate son of a chief of the then unimportant Zulu clan, an offshoot of the Mthethwa (*see* **Zululand** 'History'). Again, tradition has it that in about 1816, Dingiswayo awarded Shaka with the Zulu chieftaincy in reward for his continual success in battle.

With the Zulu section of Dingiswayo's army now at his disposal, Shaka seems to have hatched plans for creating his own state. In 1818, the Ndwandwe attacked Dingiswayo, who called on Shaka to bring up the Zulu regiments for war. However, Shaka held them back, sitting by as the Ndwandwe routed the depleted Mthethwa army. Unable to escape the storm, Dingiswayo was killed. This was Shaka's opportunity—he brought up his Zulu regiments, assumed command of the defeated, leaderless Mthethwe army, and managed to hold out until 1819, when he turned the tide against the Ndwandwe in one great, pitched battle. Pressing his advantage, Shaka then took his forces north and successfully attacked the Zwide clan, who blocked the trade route from modern Zululand to Mozambique. By 1820, there was no group in Natal powerful enough to challenge Shaka. He began exacting tribute from every chiefdom and homestead, and sent raiding parties as far as Pondoland to the south and Swaziland to the north.

The southward raids caused havoc among the clans around the Bay of Natal. The site had not been forgotten by South Africa's trading community; in 1824 two English Naval officers, Francis Farewell and Henry Fynn, decided to try their luck at trading with the new Zulu empire. Trade and control of its revenues had been at the root of the original power struggle in Natal, and Shaka received the Englishmen well, granting them the Bay of Natal as a neutral trading post, to be called Port Natal. The two men hoisted the Union Jack over the settlement (rather cheekily, as the land had been granted to them, not King George IV) and opened for business. They were soon joined by other traders, and a small, independent-minded community formed, supplemented by waves of refugees from the various Zulu wars. The traders prospered, but their accounts of Natal under Shaka dwell on mass executions and general blood-letting. Many historians now suggest that this was mere propaganda designed to convince the Cape authorities to extend military protection to Port Natal.

However, given the volatile nature of the Zulu state, this was understandable. The traders weathered several alarms after Shaka was murdered by his half-brother Dingane in 1828. Dingane sent troops into southern Natal to put down local tribes, and once to attack the traders themselves, suspecting them of plotting his deposition. Forced to flee overland towards British Pondoland in the south, some of the traders were overtaken and killed. Realizing how much he depended on the Port Natal trade, Dingane hurriedly recalled his troops, apologised to the traders, and persuaded them to return to Port Natal, but he had convinced them that they needed protection. The British were initially unwilling to interfere with Natal, being already bogged down in a series of expensive, inconclusive wars against the Xhosa in the Eastern Cape. However, history was on the traders' side—for in 1836 a large Voortrekker wagon train arrived in Natal, seeking to found a free republic away from British rule. Wherever the Voortrekkers went, British authority was soon to follow, intent on thwarting any rival colonies to the Cape.

Dingane, too, became concerned about this sudden white presence in his country. In 1837, the two Boer leaders, Piet Retief and Gert Maritz (and their party) were massacred while visiting Dingane'skraal to negotiate for a land grant, and Dingane'stroops wiped out the two northernmost Voortrekker parties. Rightly suspecting that the traders and the Boers might be in cahoots over plotting to take over Natal, Dingane then sent a Zulu regiment to attack Port Natal but the traders took refuge in a ship. Inland, the Voortrekkers rallied and in 1838, beat the Zulu army decisively at Blood River in northwest Natal. Dingane retired north of the Tugela to lick his wounds and think.

Meanwhile, a British force had landed at Port Natal, with orders unclear as to whether to proceed against the Zulus, the Voortrekkers, or simply to establish Port Natal as British territory. They stayed a year, annoying the Voortrekkers by negotiating with Dingane for areas of Natal that the Boers now considered theirs by right of conquest. In retaliation, the Voortrekkers approached Mpande, a brother of Dingane, and offered to help him seize the throne. Greatly pleased, Mpande promised the Boers most of southern Natal in anticipation of victory, while Dingane, unaware of any treachery, granted the same land to the British. The plot was revealed after a few weeks, and Dingane ceased all negotiations, calling out his army against his brother and the Boers. The British, deciding that this was all too complicated and potentially expensive, retired to Port Natal, and then left for Britain, having achieved nothing.

The Voortrekker Boers, under Andries Pretorius, rejoiced, and declared the Republic of Natal. The traders at Port Natal had to pretend to be pleased, as Mpande and the Boers drove Dingane far north to the Lebombo mountains on the Mozambique border where he was killed, probably by the Swazis, whom he had continually raided during his reign. He was buried near present-day Mkuzi Game Reserve.

However, life soon became complicated for the new Boer republic. Nguni clans like the Hlubi, who had fled southern Natal during Shaka and Dingane'sferocious raiding campaigns, began flooding back—and the Boers were at a loss where to put them. Then, in 1841, they made a blunder that would eventually cost them their hard-won land. They raided Pondoland, to 'punish' a chief who had accused a Boer party of cattle theft. Pondoland was British territory. In 1842 a British force was despatched against the Boers but, lost with heavy casualties, and had to hole up at Port Natal. The Boers laid siege, but a British trader named Dick King managed to ride through the Boer lines and galloped all the way through Transkei to Grahamstown in the Eastern Cape in just 10 days (a distance of over 1200km) where he alerted the British Governor, Sir Benjamin D'Urban. A ship of reinforcements was sent, and the siege raised by bombardment. Natal became British territory (1843) and Port Natal was renamed Durban, after the Cape governor that had sent the troops.

The Boers then founded their own town, Pietermaritzburg, at the beginning of the Drakensberg foothills, about 100km northwest of Durban, naming it after Retief and Maritz, who had been killed by Dingane in 1838. But the old Boer desire to get away from the hated *Engelssman* re-asserted itself, and gradually the Boers trekked away north, to the Transvaal, abandoning the land they had shed so much blood to win, and nursing their resentment of the British.

For the next three decades, the Zulu king Mpande remained friendly and open to trade in the north, giving the Zulus their first (and last) period of tranquil prosperity. Southern Natal continued to fill up with returning Nguni clans as well as with several thousand Griqua from north of the Orange River, who settled around modern-day Kokstad (*see* 'Kokstad History'). In addition, about 5000 English settlers were brought out between 1849 and 1852 to open the Natal Midlands for farming. Sugar cane plantations (worked by poor Indian labourers imported on 10 year contracts) began to creep up the coast though the 1860s. By the early 1870s, southern Natal was 'full', and both the settlers and the Natal Government began looking covetously towards Zululand to the north.

Sir Theophilus Shepstone, the Natal High Commissioner, hoped to force a war with the Zulus, and placed several clans of returned Nguni clans along the Tugela River. Ostensibly, these were to provide a 'buffer' zone between Zululand and Natal, but Shepstone knew that cross-border raiding would be inevitable. In 1873 Mpande died, and Shepstone formally 'crowned' his warlike son Cetshwayo king of the Zulus. This seemed the opportunity that the Natal settlers were waiting for—sure enough, Cetshwayo could not resist raiding the buffer-zone tribes placed on his frontier. The 'buffer-zone' settlements were under British protection, and Britain was forced to send troops into Zululand in 1879. (For the full Zulu War history, *see* 'Zululand History'.)

The Zulu War did not go well for the British straight away, and a series of initial reverses culminated in the massacre of almost 1000 British and Native auxilliaries at a place called Isandhlwana, where they had been left by the commander, Lord Chelmsford, without adequate entrenchments or look-outs. However, despite an offer from Cetshwayo for peace (who must have realised that his victory would bring down the full wrath of the British), the war dragged on and Chelmsford finally caught the Zulu army in the open at Ulundi and destroyed it with cavalry and cannon.

But to the chagrin of the white Natal settlers, the British refused to annex Zululand—the war had been costly enough. Instead they removed Cetshwayo to Cape Town, and established 13 sub-chiefs as paid British magistrates, with the idea of fragmenting and destabilising the Zulu state. Unfortunately, the plan worked all too well, and Zululand plunged into a savage civil war that many claim lies at the root of the continuing violence between clans that still afflicts the region today. Worried that the unrest would spill into southern Natal, the authorities put Cetshwayo back on the throne in 1883, but this only caused the fighting to intensify, and the king only lived another year. Finally, the Natal settlers' long-awaited annexation of Zululand came in 1887, and speculators were allowed to buy up land at knock-down prices.

A last, short-lived Zulu rising was brutally put down in the 1900s, and permanent troops were left in the region. But strangely enough, the bulk of Zululand was never densely settled by Europeans, except for parts of the coast and northwest, perhaps because of the malaria and tropical disieases that affected livestock. All that had been achieved was the destruction of the Zulus' prosperity.

Natal saw war again in 1899 when the Boers made the Tugela River their line against the invading British forces in the first months of the Anglo–Boer War (1899–1902), during which the British lost thousands of men before dislodging the Boers and pushing them back into the Transvaal.

Since then, Natal has remained one of South Africa's most prosperous regions—sufficiently so for its local leaders to threaten seccession from the union on more than one occasion. The Zulu nation, despite its incessant and violent internal wranglings (*see* above), has survived as the largest and most nationalistic black group in South Africa. In the 1970s under apartheid, large tracts of Zululand and Natal (60 per cent of the entire province), were designated part of the 'self-governing tribal homeland of Kwa-Zulu', which has done much to promote Zulu nationalism (for better or worse). Since the 1994 elections, Buthelezi, leader of the Inkatha Freedom Party (IFP), has been absorbed into the national government as the Minister of Home Affairs, and the IFP still has the majority of electoral support. The province's new Premier, Frank Mdlalose, is IFP, as are most members of the local government. Unless the ANC's local support grows at a faster rate than the present, Natal looks set to become the seat of official opposition to the ANC in the next decades.

Getting to and around Natal

By car: Most of the province's roads are accessible by ordinary car.

By bus: Buses from Durban and Pietermaritzburg connect with most of the regional centres, from which local tour companies (contacted through local tourist offices) can take you into game reserves or into rural Kwa-Zulu if you have no private transport. The Drakensberg are easier to reach by bus than the game reserves. The larger towns of the foothills (Kokstad, Underberg, Winterton and Bergville) are all reachable by bus from Durban and Pietermaritzburg, and local lifts to camp sites and trail-heads in the mountains can be arranged through the tourist offices or hotels and garages. The trick is to ask first, rather than to hitch. One or two Drakensberg hideaways even arrange their own pick-up and return transport to Durban.

By train: Trains are limited in Natal. The one main line goes due north from Durban, through the province's least interesting bushveld country, to the Transvaal and Jo'burg. A steam train, the **Banana Express**, runs from Port Shepstone in the south, through to Paddock, at the entrance to the spectacular Oribi Gorge Nature Reserve (*see* 'South Coast'). Other than this, trains run from Durban up to Richard's Bay and the north coast, and through central Zululand, but the few remaining services are erratic, chaotic and very slow, owing to massive cut-backs in the national rail system. You may wait a week for a train.

By black taxi: Of course, there are always black taxis, which connect every town in Natal with the outside world. But these do have a propensity for crashing, and depending on the political situation, the sections of Kwa-Zulu they travel through are not always safe.

Southern Natal is the most populated part of the province, with most of the population centred around Durban or strung along the coastal towns, which merge into each other along the N2 highway. Inland, however, the country gets hilly, empties, and reveals some surprises for the traveller with enough time to explore. Two large chunks of Kwa-Zulu (known for ANC/Inkatha trouble) and another of Transkei limit travelling possibilities. But the areas around them, especially near Harding and Kokstad, are very beautiful indeed.

Durban

Durban is the third largest city in South Africa, and the country's sea, surf and kitsch capital. The hideous concrete hotels fronting its four beaches (known as the Golden Mile), the beaches themselves and the bars and nightclubs between hotels and beach are crammed with beautiful-bodied surfheads, beach bums, sunburnt holiday makers from the Transvaal (known as 'Vaalies' by the Durbanites), bikini-clad beauties, beer drinkers and pot smokers. Of course, however kitsch and shallow this may be, it is also great fun, and one cannot help feeling that other South Africans, who may sneer at the brash city, secretly envy Durban its relaxed, unashamed hedonism.

Of course, that is only one side of Durban. The city is also the Asian capital of South Africa: mosques and bazaars take up whole blocks of the compact city centre. These, combined with the tropical heat of the place (insupportable in summer) and the luxuriant vegetation, create a genuine feeling of exoticism. But do not be fooled into thinking that Durban is not an African town. Despite the predominantly white beach culture and the Asian flavour of the city centre, Durban belongs to the Zulu. The townships surrounding central Durban stretch for almost twenty miles, and the highways pass some of the worst poverty in southern Africa. Behind the orderly Indian Bazaar on Victoria Street sprawls a huge African market where you can buy anything from groceries to (illegal) guns, spare parts for cars, animal parts for witchcraft, medicinal herbs, electronics, clothes, beads, baskets, you name it. Traditionally, blacks have been kept out of Durban's city centre, but that is changing, and the place is beginning to have a much more African feel.

History

(*see* History of Natal pp.352–356)

Durban acquired its name in 1843 when Port Natal was renamed after Sir Benjamin D'Urban, the Cape Governor who had ordered the British annexation of Natal.

Through the 19th century, Durban prospered, even though the port was slow to develop, owing to a large sandbar cutting across the entrance of the Bay of Natal. Not everyone had faith in the town's future, for example, the indefatigable British writer and traveller Anthony Trollope, who visited the city in the early 1870s. He speculated that the Durban businessmen would eventually lose their shirts because of the sand bar. At a dinner given in his honour, when one of the guests light-heartedly toasted the bar, Trollope reported that he had his eyes vehemently damned by his fellow diners. However, the battle against the bar was eventually won in the 1900s, and since then, Durban has thrived as South Africa's largest port after Cape Town. But it would be hard to decide whether the city's 20th-century economy has grown more from cargo or from the thousands of Transvaal holiday makers who, since the 1930s, have turned the city's beach-front into a gigantic playground.

Despite the city's light-hearted reputation, 20th-century Durban has seen some major events—such as the founding of the Phoenix Peace Commune (now swamped by the Kwa-Mashu squatter camp) by Gandhi in 1903. However, against the usual South African tradition, violent political events have never been a great feature of Durban's life. Even during the widespread rioting in 1993, in the long build-up to the 1994 election, Durban got off more lightly than the other South African cities, including Cape Town.

Today, this slightly apolitical feeling continues—and most western travellers fall headlong into the beach-culture for which the city is justly famed. The only real observable difference to the place has been the long-overdue integration of its beaches. And perhaps this is the way it ought to be—too often in this over-politicized country, you find yourself judging the worth of towns and cities by their history of political struggle, regardless of the suffering it has caused on all sides, instead of concentrating on lighter aspects. Give in to Durban's seductive pleasures and relax.

Getting Around

by bus

Buses connect the city centre with the the beachfront and the residential neighbourhoods to the west and north. The Mynah Minibus links the beachfront with the city centre, and is the best for visitors. The Mynah bus stop is on the corner of Gardiner and West Streets, ✆ 309 4126. Fares are still generally under R1 for anywhere inside the city centre.

Durban

1000 metres
1000 yards

by black taxi

They are also useful in the city centre, but are not too safe outside this area, as the townships can be rough for travellers, even if just passing through. Black taxis are usually more expensive than buses, about R1 for a ride anywhere in the city centre, but the service is much faster.

by taxi

For late night travel, take a taxi. These have to be picked up from the taxi ranks in West Street (central Durban's main drag), or (safer) you can phone for one by looking in the *Yellow Pages*.

car hire

Durban has all the big name companies, but the best deals are local. Try Forest Drive Rent-a-Car, ✆ 582 8433 (or 423 547 after hours), Master Rent, ✆ 561 1296, or Maharani Car Hire ✆ 370 211.

long distance train and bus

Durban Railway Station is on Umgeni Road (the R102) at the west end of the city centre. Regular services north to the Orange Free State and Transvaal leave from here, as well as local services up and down the coast. Durban bus station is also here: services include; Greyhound ✆ 376 478 for Joburg, Bloemfontein and Port Elizabeth; TransLux and Transtate, ✆ 361 7461 or 8283 after office hours for all major cities and points in between; Golden Wheels ✆ 292 894/285 032 for Jo'burg only; Interport ✆ (0322) 58055 for Richard's Bay and Zululand.

Publicity Association: Durban Unlimited, ✆ 304 4934, has its main office at 22 Gardiner Street and also has an office on the Beachfront, opposite the Beachfront Hotel (*open Mon–Fri 8–4.30, Sat 8.30–12.30*).

Hospital: The Addington Hospital, ✆ 322 111, on South Beach Avenue (facing the beachfront) is a public hospital. The private Entabeni Hospital, ✆ 811 344, on 148 South Ridge Road, Berea, also takes outpatients but is quite expensive.

Emergency Ambulances: can be called on ✆ 582 252 or 10177.

Post Office: The Main Post Office is on the corner of Gardiner Street and West Street in the old town centre.

Durban's Golden Mile

Durban's brazen, rather than golden, monument to kitsch gets its name from the sands of its four beaches. The whole beachfront has been pedestrianized, with a few large car parks at various points along the 'mile' (in fact it runs for almost 6km). The best access from town is by the Mynah minibus. Durban's young social life is most active here; the beachfront bars are lively and busy by day as well as night. Apart from the beaches (which have clean, safe swimming with large breakers for body-surfing), the Golden Mile's day-time attractions are magnificently kitsch:

Seaworld (*open daily 9–9*), with its performing dolphins and seals, is the largest attraction along the Golden Mile (where it meets West Street). It also has an aquarium complete with sharks, turtles and other Indian Ocean exotica. You can watch the sharks being fed on Mondays , Wednesdays and Fridays.

Snake Park (*open 9–4*), on the Snell Parade, North Beach has all the poisonous slitherers plus crocs, giant tortoises, leguaans and other toothy reptiles.

Minitown (*open Tues–Sat 9.30–8.30; Sun 9.30–5.30*), also on the Snell Parade, is exactly what it says, a miniature town complete with cars, planes and other machines. For fun, try the mini drive-in in the evenings. **Funworld** Oh boy, an all-day amusement park on the beachfront in front of the Marine Parade Highway Inn. The dodgems are good, and there is an overhead cable-way, like a seated ski-lift that takes one aimlessly from one end of the beach to the other. **The Little Top** is a miniature red and white striped theatre tent on South Beach. Puppet shows for kids are the usual fare, with the occasional concert.

On Gillespie Street, just behind the beachfront, is **The Wheel** a much publicized shopping mall that has been done up to look like a ship inside, with a working ferris wheel over the entrance. This is expensive schmaltz of the highest order. Tens of millions have been invested to encourage the public part with their money. **Water Wonderland**, between Snell Parade and the North Coast Highway (*open daily 9–5*) is for those tired of the ocean. The place has all kinds of water shutes and artificial rapids to scream your way down.

The fabulously dressed **Ricksha** drivers you see plying for trade up and down the beach-front have been a feature of Durban since the 1890s. The rickshas have the stigma of political incorrectness attached to them, despite the fact that their drivers rely on them for a living, so they may disappear from the beach-front soon. This is a classic Third World Catch 22 situation; the clash between what is acceptable to the western eye and what is economic. The sight of the sweating, puffing ricksha drivers ferrying indolent whites about might offend you, but then if you take a ride yourelf, you will at least contribute something other than moral support to the people that labour to keep Durban's tourist industry going.

Durban City Centre

Like all of South Africa's city centres, the compact downtown area of Durban is laid out along a grid. The business centre, which begins immediately behind the beachfront, is not terribly interesting by day, but has many lively bars and clubs to enjoy at night. The most interesting part of Durban is around Grey, Victoria, Russell and Queen Streets, which comprise **Oriental Durban**.

Durban's massive Indian population originates mostly from southern India, but several cultures and languages are represented, as are both Hinduism and Islam. The most easily recognizable landmark of Oriental Durban is the handsome **Grey Street (Jumah) Mosque**, © 306 0026, the largest in the southern hemisphere, but the hub of Oriental Durban's town life is the **Victoria Street Market**. This is a modern, functional building (the old Victorian one burned down about 10 years ago) mostly filled with spice and herb sellers, butchers and fishmongers. Latterly, the market has taken on an African flavour too; of particular interest are the *muti* (medicine) sellers, who sell various herbs, charms, bones, skins and other, wierder animal bits and pieces to diviners and traditional healers.

Durban's downtown Asian culture is mostly Moslem. Hindu Durban lies in the old Indian townships north of town. Most interesting of these is the **Phoenix Park Settlement**, which is where, in 1903, Mahatma Gandhi set up his retreat centre. It was from here that the moral support was drawn for the Indians' anti-Pass Law demonstrations of 1913 (*see* 'History'). Unfortunately, Phoenix has had to be abandoned due to the growth of Kwa Mashu squatter camp next door. The residents of Kwa Mashu have already destroyed much of the old settlement, and it has become a shanty town. Tours of the settlement and surrounding townships can be arranged by calling © 304 8893.

Colonial Durban

This is the downtown area immediately surrounding the main square (Church Square) where stands the ornate, Victorian City Hall.

The **Natural History Museum** (*open Mon–Sat 9–5, Sun 9–4*) occupies the first floor of City Hall. The usual stuffed denizens of the African bush stand frozen behind glass cases. But of particular interest is the skeleton of a dodo (the last one died in 1790). **Durban Art Museum**, on the second floor of City Hall has some surprising European treasures, including several Constables and some of the minor Impressionists. Look out for the Rodin sculptures. There is also a changing exhibition of local art, and it is worth taking pot luck on what's on offer. Some Black artists from the local townships have begun successful careers from exhibitions in Durban's Art Museum.

The **Local History Museum** (*open Mon–Sat 8.30–5, Sun 11–5*) on Aliwal Street (where it joins Church Square) gives a colonial's-eye perspective of the history of Natal, concentrating on the days of Shaka (portraying him only as a bloody tyrant), the Voortrekkers' brief attempt at a republic, and the Zulu Wars. There are some interesting old photographs of early Natal, as well as the usual rooms done up as Victorian houses and pioneers' cottages. The **Killie Campbell Museum** (on the corner of Essenwood and Marriott Roads) is an old Victorian house with a large library of Africana, open to the public by prior arrangement only ✆ 207 3432. The **Old House Museum**, (on Andrews Street) is another colonial set-piece (*open Mon–Sat 8.30–5, Sun 11.50*).

Whysall's Camera Museum (*open Mon–Fri 8–4*) on Brickhill Street is an eccentric's private collection of thousands of old cameras from the 1840s until modern times. The **Old Fort** (*open Tues–Fri 11–3, Sat 10–12, Sun 11–3*) on Old Fort Road, comprises the old barracks and chapel of Durban's original British fort (built in 1842) where the boers of the short-lived Natal Republic besieged the British for almost a year before capitulating. **Warrior's Gate**, also on Old Fort Road (*opening times as for Old Fort*) houses a collection of military artefacts from Natal's many battlefields. At the time of writing, a new museum, the **Kwa-Muhke Museum**—dedicated to 20th century African urban life— was still undergoing final work before opening. By the time of publication the museum may have opened. The site is on Ordnance Road.

Durban's Parks and Nature Reserves

Central Durban has some very quiet spots of glorious vegetation, both wild and tended, most of which still support small game and good bird-life.

The Bluff Nature Reserve on Tara Road, Jacobs (*open 7–4.30*) covers 45ha of The Bluff, the promontary that rises above the Golden Mile. The reserve is thickly wooded, and is still home to some little buck. There are footpaths and bird-watching hides.

The **Botanic Gardens** (*open daily sunrise to sunset*), Sydenham Road, Berea (the residential neighbourhood due west of the city centre), were founded in 1849, and are a formally laid-out haven of ordered quiet and soft colour amid the humid bustle of central Durban. The **Kenneth Stainbank Nature Reserve** (*open daily 6–6*), on Coedmore Road, Yellowwood Park (the neigbourhood behind Berea, reachable by bus) is a large block of coastal forest, surrounded by metropolitan Durban. The reserve is big enough to support some quite large game, notably nyala, zebra, impala, the rare red duiker, reedbuck, impala and bushbuck. Walking trails wind through this lovely green lung of the sweaty city.

Pigeon Valley Nature Reserve, © 213 126 (*open daily 7–4.30*), is on King George V Avenue, in the suburb of Bulwer (north Durban), is a clump of unbuilt-on forest that makes a pleasant place to wander. **Beachwood Mangroves Nature Reserve** is just north of Durban proper, off the M4 highway, before the turn-off for Umhlanga. Despite the over-developed nature of the coast near Durban, this sizeable strip of mangrove forest has somehow survived. All the mangrove exotic denizens are there: mudskipper fish that can survive out of water, fiddler crabs with their one outsize claw, and dense bird life. The best way to see the reserve is by guided tour in a boat.

Silverglen Nature Reserve (*open daily sunrise to sunset*), at the Clearwater Dam, Silverglen (a suburb in southwest Durban) unwittingly supplies many of Durban's local herbalists, who poach plants from the reserve. Moves are afoot to stop this plant theft, but you would never know there was anything wrong, the vegetation is so lush. This large chunk of forest has beautiful walking trails and good birdwatching.

Shopping

Durban lacks outdoor activities apart from walking in the nature reserves listed above, and swimming on the Golden Mile beaches. But shopping is a big activity in this town. The **Asian Markets** are a good place to browse. Victoria Street Market, the largest, is probably the most culturally vibrant part of Durban. Other Indian markets can be found on Warwick Avenue and in the old Indian 'townships' of Clairwood and Chatsworth.

The **African Arts Centre** on Gardiner Street (in the Guildhall Arcade) was set up as a race-relations project to bring arts and crafts from the black townships and squatter camps into town. Superb Zulu beadwork, weaving (grass and wool), fabric prints, pottery and sculpture are sold.

The Workshop, just north of Church Square, is a big mall housed in a large Victorian building that was once the maintenance centre for Natal's railways. The shops are mostly upmarket boutiques, but the place has some pleasant, shaded outdoor cafés in which to escape the heat.

The **flea markets** are more interesting, both for merchandise and atmosphere. Durban has several: **The Amphimarket** (*open Sun*), in the Amphitheatre on the Golden Mile's North Beach, sells jewellery, crafts and clothes. **South Plaza Market** (*open Sat and Sun*) is in Durban Exhibition Centre, on Aliwal Street, in the city centre, sells less ethnic, more slick goods. Some very good African artefacts and printed cloths can be found, though. **Farepark Market** (*open daily 9–5*), on the lawns between Pine and West Streets, is a permanent market housed in log cabins, with crafts people making shoes, fabric prints, jewellery and suchlike. The **Station Fleamarket** (*open daily, no fixed times*), on top of Durban Station, sells more electronics and modern goods than arts and crafts.

Township Tours: ✆ 304 8893 or 259 645, make an alternative to beaches, nature reserves and shopping, are the guided tours around Durban's black townships and squatter camps. Although there is something distasteful in the idea of a human safari, this is the only really safe way for a tourist to go into the townships. The guiding is done by locals. Despite the violence that Durban's townships are celebrated for, they are vibrant, friendly places if visited by day, and not during times of political strife. Tours include visits to the remains of Mahatma Gandhi's Phoenix settlement (now a squatter camp), Kwa-Mashu and Inanda (Durban's largest townships, with visits to the single men's hostels), Richmond Farm and Lindelani.

Deep Sea Diving and Fishing: A number of operators give diving courses and take people out to catch the big game fish, like marlin, dorado, kingclip and sharks, that teem in the Indian Ocean, call Durban Unlimited ✆ 304 4934.

Durban ✆ (031–)   ***Where to Stay***

luxury

Durban's Golden Mile has several brash, ugly five star tower-block hotels. The **Maharani**, ✆ 327 361, on 81 Snell Parade, is the most famous. The **Tropicana**, ✆ 373 341, on Marine Parade is a close rival. One star down, though it's hard to understand why, are the **Edward Hotel**, ✆ 373 681, also on Marine Parade, and the **Elangeni**, ✆ 620 133, on Snell Parade.

expensive

The **Royal Hotel**, on Smith Street, in the city centre, ✆ 304 0331, carries the most cachet of any hotel in town. Like the Mount Nelson in Cape Town, this is a tangible survival of Victorian colonial days, from the architecture, to the potted palms, to the white liveried waiters and pictures of the soldiers of the Queen campaigning in Zululand. The rooms are simple, but rather beautiful, with dark mahogany furniture and high ceilings. **Lillieshell Manor**, ✆ 561 1511, is a restored country house in the Berea District (just west of the city centre). Bed and breakfast only in rooms furnished in Victorian style. There's a large, beautifully leafy garden.

moderate

Braeside B&B, 206 Chelmsford Road, ✆ 253 115, is a large, white double-storey suburban house, about five minutes' drive from the beachfront, looking out over the ocean, with a pool and a small garden. Rooms are clean and bright, but simply furnished. Smoking is not allowed. **Newton Hurst Guest House**, 267 Chelmsford Road, ✆ 256 151, also in Berea, is a large, Victorian double-storey house with en suite rooms, a pool and bar and convenient public transport for the beach and city centre. In the suburb of Morningside, near Berea, is **Phezulu B&B** ✆ 233 167. Situated at 71 Silver Avenue, Phezulu offers a large double room in a family house. Overlooking the bright blue Indian Ocean, about 10 minutes' drive south of the city centre at Brighton Beach is **Beach Getaway B&B**, ✆ 472 486. Two large rooms are offered.

cheap

Tekweni Youth Hostel, ✆ 231 695, 169 9th Avenue, Morningside, near the Berea neighbourhood, has dormitory and double room accommodation, with shared bathrooms, and a games room (including pool table). You can check in any time of the day or night. To reach it by public transport, take a bus to Mitchell Park Circle or Musgrave Road Circle, and ask from there (it's a short walk). After 9pm take a taxi.

In the same price bracket is the **Beach Youth Hostel**, ✆ 324 945 at 19 Smith Street, 2 minutes from the Beachfront. Double rooms and dormitory accommodation are offered.

Durban ✆ (031–)   ***Eating Out***

expensive

The **Palm Court Restaurant**, 16 Stamford Hill Road, ✆ 309 4017, is housed in the old British Middle Eastern Sporting and Dining Club, a small but rather grand Victorian building built in mock-classical style. The Palm Court has always been famous for Indian food, and still is, while the formal, colonial atmosphere has changed little. Dress smartly. **Saagries**, on the Beachfront, ✆ 327 922/373 511, is another fine Indian restaurant. More modern in decor and informality than the Palm Court, Saagries specializes in southern Indian dishes.

Api Taki, 320 West Street, ✆ 305 4451, serves Indonesian, Chinese and Polynesian food, all highly spiced (the spices are specially imported from the Far East), served with fresh vegetables picked that day. The food is hot, but not heavy, and perfect for Durban's humid climate. The **Colony**, in the Oceanic Hotel on Sol Harris Cresent, ✆ 322 913 celebrates the British, rather than the Oriental side of the Empire. Victorian furnishings, excellent game dishes (in season) and seafood.

The **Royal Hotel** on Smith Street, ✆ 304 0331, has two restaurants in Victorian colonial settings: the **Royal Grill**, which serves French cuisine, and the **Ulundi**, which serves a mixture of Indian food, game (in season) and seafood. Both are very formal.

Cloud 9 is on the Beachfront, ✆ 372 231, in the Malibu Hotel (part of the Holiday Inn chain). The setting is very modern and glitzy, in true Durban beachfront style, but the seafood is fabulous, as is the game (in season). The **Maharani Hotel** (also part of the Holiday Inn chain), Marine Parade, ✆ 327 361, has two restaurants: **Les Saisons**, a rather pretentious (but very good) French restaurant complete with piped Vivaldi and dimmed lights, and **Papadum**, much less formal, serving good southern Indian curries. **Villa D'Este**, Gillespie Street, ✆ 370264, is a small place set in a courtyard, serving very tasty pasta and seafood dishes.

moderate

O Pescador, a Portuguese seafood restaurant on Albany Grove (opposite the Durban Playhouse), ✆ 304 4138, is informal and popular with the younger crowd. Take your own wine. Also unlicensed is **Wolfgang's** on Florida Road, ✆ 232 861, which serves nouvelle cuisine. Portions are not huge, but it can be just the thing on a hot, humid Durban night. A bit self-consciously sophisticated, but friendly and informal. The **Greek Taverna**, 213 Musgrave Road, Berea, ✆ 215 433, serves superb Greek salads with fresh feta cheese, stuffed vine leaves and light fish dishes. Again, bring your own wine. **Trawler's Restaurant**, at the Ocean Terminal, Durban Harbour, ✆ 373 737, serves simple line fish and shellfish platters amidst standard seafood restaurant decor; ropes, nets and stuffed fish. But the food is as delicious as you would expect from fish caught that day.

Stax on the first floor of the Marine Sands Hotel on Marine Parade, ✆ 325 291, is an American-style steak and seafood joint with piped rock music. Popular with the beach crowd. **Lord Prawn**, on the second floor at 47 West Street (the beach end), ✆ 372 928, is very good value—huge helpings of shellfish and steak (the big swimming prawns being the speciality). Also very popular with the beach crowd. The **Orient**, 191 Marine Parade, ✆ 372 083, serves very good Chinese food (the Peking duck is worth trying, but must be ordered in advance) and sharp Malay satays. The chefs are from Hong Kong, and know their business. (*Closed on Tuesdays.*)

cheap

O'Reilly's, at Shop 1A, in the Westguard Arcade, Gardiner Street, offers fried food, grills and steaks. It serves breakfast and lunches only through the week, and suppers at the weekend (*open until 12.30am*). No need to book. **Spaghetti Junction**, at 243 Marine Parade, ✆ 324 913 is a pizza, pasta and seafood place, with a chain-restaurant feel and piped mainstream pop, but the servings are large and the prices lowish. The **Porterhouse**, 66 Gillespie Street (opposite The Wheel), ✆ 368 1821/2, also serves steaks, seafood, pizza and pasta, this time in an attempt at an English pub setting (mock tudor beams inside and hunting prints). Good-sized helpings and low prices make up for the interior and the irritating music.

Entertainment

Durban has a symphony orchestra, a theatre company and a ballet/modern dance company. All perform a range of work, from Shakespeare, classical ballet and classical music, to more up-to-the-minute political plays, musicals, experimental dance and modern compositions. Their home is at the **Natal Playhouse**, ✆ 304 3631, on Smith Street, which has two large auditoriums. Visiting orchestras, theatre and dance companies also play here. The Natal Playhouse was built in the 1920s, in two adjoining buildings, one built in Disneyesque Tudor Style, the other resembling a Moorish mansion. Both get away with it, and are excellent examples of successful Art Deco fantasy. Watch the press—particularly the *Natal Witness* and the *Natal Mercury*—for upcoming concerts and shows.

Nightlife

Durban is a pleasure-seeking city, and bars and clubs abound. They mostly come and go with the season, so it is worth asking around for what is good at the moment when you arrive. However, some places have become institutions.

Bars: Joe Kool's, on the beachfront's North Beach, is where most people start off the evening if they've been on the beach (though it's just as popular as a day-time bar). Light rock is generally played, and the bar's outside and inside tables are crammed with young beach-heads and students, all trying to out-cool each other, However, the place is quite friendly, and useful for finding out what is new on the nightclub circuit. **Bonkers Pub** ✆ 303 1146 on Florida Road stays open day and night, and gets quite lively. Also on Florida Road, though more conservative, with a slightly older crowd, is **Trawlers Pub** and, catering to the same crowd is **Calico Jack's** ✆ 280 239, in the beach suburb of Overport City. Both have a small dance floor with Top 40 music. **Sandpebbles,** ✆ 368 2447 on South Beach Walk is more of a dive, and attracts a very young crowd. Rock, Top 40 and assorted oldies blast out over the drunken hubbub. Fun but crowded.

Live Music: Durban has a vibrant music scene. Excellent township jive and African jazz bands play at **Jam & Sons** in the Belmont Arcade, 1 West Street (✆ 370 497), downtown Durban. Reggae bands also feature here. The **Rainbow Restaurant** at 23 Stanfield Lane, ✆ 729 161, and the **Moon Hotel,** ✆ 465 1711 on South Coast Road, in the suburb of Clairwood, also host township jive bands. More Western-influenced jazz bands play at the **Octagon** ✆ 304 4018, on the corner of Queen and Field Streets, at **Club Zoom** ✆ 374 752, on Dick King Street and at the **Bassline,** ✆ 322 603, on the corner of Gillespie and Rutherford Streets.

Rock, metal and indie bands have also become popular in the last few years, and some of Durban's bands are quite original. Try **Jam & Sons** in the Belmont Arcade, 1 West Street (✆ 370 497) and the **Vic Bar** (✆ 374 645) on 241 Point Road. The **Aliwal Lighthouse** on Aliwal Street is a small bar that stays open right through the night, and showcases local original rock and reggae. The **Rift Club** on St George's Road, by the Belgica Hotel also hosts indie and reggae groups, with some hardcore thrash. For more mainstream rock (and sometimes weekend jazz), the **Queen's Tavern** (✆ 309 4017) is a safe bet.

Dance Clubs and Discos: Durban's clubs are very changeable. However, standard favourites include the **Bassline** on the corner of Gillespie and Rutherford

Streets, which plays funk and house on nights when bands are not showcased. The same goes for the **Club Zoom** on Dick King Street. After dark, **Bonkers Pub** on Florida Road plays oldies to a drunken crowd. The **Hard Rock Café** on Berea Road, Berea, plays loud pop, as does the **Westville Hotel**, in the old Indian suburb of Westville, just north of the town centre (bands also play here on occasion). For indie, rock and metal, the **Rift Nightclub** on St George's Street is one of the best clubs in South Africa for checking out sexy people in black clothes and mascara.

Cabaret: The **Drostdy-Hof Cellar**, ✆ 304 6713, at the Natal Playhouse, has cabaret acts in a café-type atmosphere (little tables, candles in bottles). The **Millionaire's Club**, ✆ 379 145, at the Palm Beach Hotel, Gillespie Street, has naughty cabaret—strippers and topless waitresses. Comedy bands play at **Father's Moustache** on North Beach.

Around Durban

The Valley of a Thousand Hills

North of Durban, to the north of the road to Pietermaritzburg, lies a chunk of Kwa-Zulu whose landscape ranks among the greatest natural wonders in Africa. The Valley of a Thousand Hills is a vast natural depression formed by the course of the Umgeni River. From the floor of the valley rise a confusing array flat-topped green hills round with traditional Zulu villages clustered at their feet.

Despite the splendour of the scenery, the Valley of a Thousand Hills is little troubled by tourism; there are few good roads through it, and the valley has seen political trouble, particularly around the highest of its hills, the massive Natal Table Mountain (over 1000m high). This is a shame, because the forests and waterfalls that crown Table Mountain's vast summit used to be accessible to hikers. Indeed, the rest of the valley harbours equally spectacular vegetation and rural African life far removed from the modern urban scene of nearby Durban.

The ordinary traveller can drive a road that skirts the southern end of the valley, running parallel with the N3 highway. You reach it from the N3 by taking the signpost for the Valley of a Thousand Hills at Hillcrest, just north of Durban. There are several spectacular lookout points over the valley. From the same road, look out for the sign to **Phezulu**, ✆ 777 1405, a Zulu show-village and rural crafts centre. While the village itself is a contrived tourist attraction, the crafts for sale are some of the best to be found in Zululand, especially the beadwork and baskets, and guided trips further into the valley can be arranged from here. This is especially worth visiting for travellers who have no time to go exploring in Zululand proper.

The Natal South Coast

The developed South Coast stretches from Durban down to Port Edward on the Transkei border, a long string of beach towns and resorts all running into each other. Most of the towns consist of holiday homes and have reduced the coastline to an extended suburb.

The first of these beach towns is **Amanzimtoti** (known locally as 'Toti'), about 30km south of Durban. With its good, safe swimming, lively bars and formal Japanese garden on Fynn Road, Amanzimtoti gets very crowded at weekends. Nearby are a couple of small nature reserves: **Ilanda Wilds** (signposted from the town centre) is a small area of riverine forest containing some short hiking trails; **Umdoni Bird Sanctuary** is another coastal forest reserve, good for viewing river birds, especially herons and kingfishers. Umdoni has a hide and a short walking trail.

Kinsburgh, just south of 'Toti', has a very long beachfront (10km), which has shark nets for safe swimming. **Scottburgh** is more of a town in its own right. Again, there is safe beach bathing, and the usual bars and seafood restaurants overlooking the beachfront, as well as a tidal pool with a big water slide. About 4km north of town is **Croc World**, a typical bit of South Coast kitsch, comprising a mock-up Zulu village (with the obligatory dancers), poisonous snakes and crocodiles.

The **Vernon Crookes Nature Reserve**, inland from Scottburgh, is a natural haven away from the ugly buildings and noisy roads of the coast. The reserve is one of rounded, grassy hills, cut by deep forested kloofs that are full of ticks in summer. Zebra, impala, bushbuck, duiker and blesbok graze the reserve. Visitors can walk at will, or drive the game-viewing roads. There are chalets and a camp site.

Hibberdene is the next town south of Scottburgh, although the 40km of coast in-between is built up. The beaches here are quieter than those further north, largely because Hibberdene is a popular retirement centre. Again, there is safe sea swimming and a tidal pool. **Umzube**, south of Hibberdene, is a much smaller resort clustered around one rather ugly hotel. This bit of coast is better for fishing than for swimming, though safe beaches can be found at **Banana Beach**, a few kilometres to the south. Banana Beach is fairly undeveloped by South Coast standards, with a narrow belt of forest fronting the sea and screening the holiday homes behind.

Port Shepstone, a large, sweaty town at the mouth of the Umzumkulu River, is the gateway to the beautiful inland areas near Harding, Kokstad and Oribi Gorge (*see* p.375). The town itself was developed as a small port in the 19th century. It was named after Sir Theophilus Shepstone, the first Governor of Natal, and the man responsible for pushing the London Colonial Office into war against the Zulus in the 1870s. Today, Port Shepstone is a mixture of holiday resort and industrial centre, with few of the old buildings still standing. There are some good beaches south of town, however, including **Shelly Beach** (inclined to get crowded with ski-boat enthusiasts at weekends), **St Michael's-on-Sea**, a lagoon resort good for windsurfing, **Uvongo**, a larger resort with a small nature reserve that protects a forested waterfall, and **Margate**, a large, brash beach town and the busiest beach resort south of Scottburgh. Margate is very similar to Durban's Golden Mile in feel. Beach bums and beautiful people flock here, as well as 'Vaalies' on holiday. The beachside bars are busy and there is a fun nightlife.

Margate has its own modern legend: in 1921, crowds gathered on the beach to watch two whales fighting with some other giant sea creature, generally described as a huge polar bear, as it seemed to be covered with white fur. After three hours, the whales left, and the creature floated still on the surface. That night it was washed up on the beach between Margate and Ramsgate. Hugh Ballance, a resident of Margate described the creature as '47 feet long, ten feet in breadth and five feet high. At one end it had a trunk about 14 inches long. At the end was a tail two feet thick and ten feet long. This horror was clothed in snow-white hair and seemed to be devoid of blood'. The creature lay on the beach for ten days while people tried to move it with oxen. Each day the smell rose higher. Scientists were called in to identify it, but a spring tide took the corpse away. Today, most people believe that it was the half-decomposed body of a whale, the white hairs in fact strings of blubber, and the trunk and tail also lumps of blubber detaching themselves from the carcase.

Ramsgate, just south of Margate, is for the rich, with large, private holiday homes, particularly grand around **Southbroom**, a beach just to the south of town. The small **Frederika Nature Reserve**, a stretch of surviving coastal forest, makes a pleasant place to wander and Margate's Main Street has a lively feel, full of the adolescent children of the rich drifting among the curio shops and bars.

Port Edward, the farthest spot south on the South Coast, marks the border with Transkei. Just across the Umtamvuna River to the south (the official territorial boundary), is the horrible, loud, expensive and rather boring Wild Coast Sun Hotel and Casino.

However, Port Edward is one of the more pleasant South Coast towns. It has the usual suburban look, with bars and restaurants behind a safe swimming beach, but the atmosphere is a little more relaxed, less frenetic than at the other towns elsewhere on the coast, where status-symbol cars and clothes and brash displays of wealth are the norm. Perhaps because of its proximity to the Transkei, Port Edward is quieter and less pretentious.

The little town also has a historical incident attached to it. In 1831, all but a few members of the family of Henry Francis Fynn (the trader who lived with Shaka, and whose son was one of the pioneers of Durban) were killed by Dingane's troops at a large, scrub-covered dune south of town, thereafter called **Tragedy Hill**. The killing was for nothing; Dingane thought that the traders were plotting a British invasion of Zululand, and the traders had seemed to confirm this by running away when the Zulu troops appeared at Durban. Dingane later apologized to the family survivors for the error.

Umtamvuna Nature Reserve, a few kilometres inland from Port Edward, is another escape from the extended suburb of the South Coast. The reserve is large (over 3000ha) and follows the deep gorge of the Umtamvuna River. The cliffs, kloof forest and grass-covered heights are home to reedbuck, duiker, bushbuck, baboon and leopard, and the bird life includes crowned eagle and peregrine falcon. Flowering orchids are a feature of the reserve. There are walking trails, but no accommodation. Don't bathe in the river, which is known to carry bilharzia.

The Natal North Coast

This name is misleading, for it refers only to the coast north from Durban to the mouth of the Tugela River, which marks the regional boundary between the old colony of Natal and Zululand. North of here, the much wilder coastline that stretches to the border with Mozambique is known as the Zululand or Tongaland Coast. This is confusing for travellers, who are not aware that Natal and Zululand are still regarded as separate by most Natalians, even though both regions fall within the Province of Natal—a typically bewildering legacy of the chopping and changing of boundaries and region names that has been South Africa's lot since the earliest colonial days.

The Natal North Coast immediately north of Durban (along the N2) is as built up as the South Coast, and again, from a traveller's point of view, there is little to see until the Zululand coast north of the Tugela Mouth. However, if only for the purposes of orientation, it is worth knowing the main North Coast resorts.

Umhlanga (pronounced 'Umshlanga') is a large suburb and beach town about 20km north of Durban along the N2. Umhlanga has a safe beach much favoured by surfers and pleasure-seekers from Durban, but otherwise the town is nothing much; a collection of ugly modern buildings with restaurants, bars and shops, surrounded by equally ugly modern apartment blocks. However, it is worth stopping at the **Natal Sharks Board**, © (031) 561 1001, on Umhlanga Rocks Drive, whose aquarium is stocked with some of the Indian Ocean's fiercest inhabitants: tiger sharks, great whites, hammerheads, blue sharks and others. Sharks can be seen feeding on Tuesdays at 9, Wednesdays at 9, 1 and 2.30 and on the first Sunday of each month at 2.30.

Umdloti has a good swimming beach and tidal pool about 5km further north, as does **Ballito**, about 15km north, next to the sugar-processing town of Tongaat. Ballito also has a camp site and small shopping centre among the large, ugly holiday homes crowding the hillsides behind the beach.

Shaka's Rock and **Salt Rock** were secluded until recently, but suburbia has caught up with them. The beaches are safe but have very slippery rocks under the surf, so tread carefully when wading out. The waves are big quite close to shore though, so body-surfing is good. Both have hotels and camp sites behind the beaches.

Stanger, another sugar town just inland from the coast about 16km north of Salt Rock, marks the end of the North Coast, and the beginning of the interesting coastline. Stanger has a prime place in Natal's history; it stands where Shaka had his last, and biggest, royal kraal, *Dakuza* (the word means 'labyrinth' and gives some idea of the scale on which Shaka lived). Shaka was killed here, prudently stabbed in the back by his half-brother Dingane in 1828. A small garden marks the spot. Apart from this, there is little in Stanger except for shops and fuel stops for the journey north into Zululand and its wilder shores.

Where to Stay

South Coast

Both coasts are crammed with places to stay. Most are very bland, but here is a pick of the bunch.

expensive

Selborne Country Lodge at Pennington (15km south of Scottburgh), ✆ (0323) 51133, is a 1930s mock Elizabethan mansion with 7 bedrooms furnished with Victorian antiques. Famous for its beautifully groomed golf course, Selborne also offers tennis courts, pools, walking and fishing, a private beach, a restaurant and beach braais. The **Crayfish Inn** at Ramsgate, ✆ (03931) 4410/1, has been a family hotel for years, but it's small and doesn't feel too institutionalized, even if it is a little bland. The Crayfish Inn has 14 clean, comfortable rooms, and a very good seafood restaurant. The **Beach Lodge** at Margate, ✆ (03931) 20372, is a modern Spanish-style place set around a pool. The beach is few minutes' walk away, and all rooms are en suite. At the cheaper end of the expensive range.

moderate

The **Dumela Resort** in Margate, ✆ (03931) 73301, has self-contained chalets with central facilites including a pool, sauna and gym. The rooms are clean, neat and comfortable, and the resort is close to the beach. The **Blue Marlin** at Scottburgh, ✆ (03231) 21214, is large (92 rooms) and at the expensive end of the moderate range. Rather glitzy and dull, but a good place to meet people, mostly friendly Transvaal families on holiday. All rooms are en suite. The **Bedford Inn** at Port Shepstone, ✆ (0391) 21085, is a much smaller, private house with 10 en suite rooms. The hotel is in town, but the beaches are within walking distance.

cheap

Umtamvuna Nature Reserve, ✆ (03930) 383, and **Uvongo Nature Reserve**, ✆ (03931) 51222, have self-contained chalets which, if shared by a couple, fall within the cheap range; surrounded by nature rather than suburb, they are far nicer places to stay than almost any other on the South Coast. Both reserves also have **camp sites**, as do Banana Beach, Hibberdene, Margate, Scottburgh, and Port Edward. There are two budget hostels on the South Coast offering cheap dormitory bunks and double rooms: the **Banana Beach Club Tropicana**, ✆ (0391) 83547, and the **Margate Youth Hostel**, 2 Bank Street, Margate (no phone).

expensive

Shortens Country House near Ballito, ✆ (0322) 71140/1/2/3, is an Edwardian bungalow with an all-round verandah set in a large, luxurious tropical garden. There's a bar and small restaurant specializing in fresh seafood. Guests sleep in their own garden cottages. **Westbrook Beach Hotel**, at Tongaat Beach, ✆ (0322) 42021, has 24 rooms and a good seafood restaurant. Otherwise a very ordinary hotel with clean, bright rooms, and a pool.

moderate

Ballito Apartments are self-contained flats overlooking the sea, among the general suburbia on the hillside behind the beach. Unfortunately, you cannot just turn up, but have to book a few days in advance by calling the central agency in Jo'burg, on ✆ (011) 678 2480. It is easier to arrange rooms in the **Umdloti Beach Hotel**, about 10km north of Umhlanga, ✆ (031) 568 1611, which is right on the beach and rather bland, but offers good rates and lets you eat as much as you like at breakfast.

cheap

The Natal North Coast has no cheap accommodation apart from **camp sites**, which can be found at Umhlanga Rocks, Ballito and Blythdale beach in the north and on the coast east of Stanger.

Southern Natal: Inland

Much of inland southern Natal is occupied by large chunks of Kwa-Zulu, which are inaccessible to the traveller. However, the area around Harding and Kokstad (both of which are along the inland section of the N2) is beautiful and worth exploring if you are passing through.

Oribi Gorge Nature Reserve is signposted from the N2 between the coast and Transkei, and is the first stop if travelling inland from the Port Shepstone. Oribi Gorge follows the deep, deep ravine cut by the Mzimkulwana River through the surrounding uplands. Waterfalls, cliffs, giant boulders, forest and grassland are home to reedbuck, baboon, bushbuck, duiker, dassies and vervet and samango monkeys. Crested and crowned eagles are often sighted perching on the trees of the forested kloofs. Black eagle and jackal buzzard are also sighted frequently. Oddly enough, there are no oribi in Oribi Gorge; presumably someone mistook a duiker, which looks not dissimilar, for the oribi antelope, which occurs further north in Zululand and the Eastern Transvaal. Leopard hunt the kloofs. The gorge has walking trails, chalets and camping. Do not bathe in the river, which has bilharzia. If staying, try to arrive before 4.30, as the gates sometimes shut at this time.

Harding is a timber town about 42km inland from Oribi Gorge along the N2, and is indistinguishable from many such small country towns scattered throughout the country. However, west of town (along the N2 towards Kokstad) is the beautiful **Weza Forest**, a dense hardwood forest with walking trails through fantastic vegetation. One extraordinary tree found here is the knobwood, whose trunk is covered with blunt spikes. Look out for bushbuck and crested and crowned eagles. The trailheads begin at the Weza Motel, which sits by the N2, about 10km northwest of Harding.

Kokstad lies just below the foothills of the mighty Drakensberg, whose southern section rises along the skyline west of town. Despite being one of Natal's backwaters, Kokstad has an sad, epic story.

History

Kokstad was founded in 1861, by Adam Kok, a Griqua (mixed Khoi and Boer, what today would be called 'coloured') leader, who trekked away from the Orange River, on the western side of the mountains after large parties of Boer trekkers from the Cape started settling the land traditionally occupied by the Griqua. The Boers renamed the territory the Orange Free State (1854) and established their own republic there. Kok, wisely deciding that his people would have no future living under Boers, appealed to the British Cape Governor for some land under British protection (itself a pretty unsure guarantee). The Governor (Sir George Grey) offered Kok a piece of country called Nomansland, where modern Kokstad now stands.

To get there, Kok had to lead 2000 of his people and 20,000 cattle right across the jagged, steep mountains of Lesotho and over the precipitous cliffs of the Drakensberg, a journey which took two years. But the fertile land of southern Natal was worth the terrible journey, and only thinly populated by Pondo and Sotho clans. The Griquas erected a turf fort on the slopes of nearby Mount Currie, outspanned their wagons, built a church and set themselves to live in this green, well-watered country. In 1872, Kok moved to the site of present-day Kokstad, setting up an unofficial Griqua republic, far from the grabbing hands of white settlers.

But such good country was coveted by the Briton and Boer alike. The Cape Colony annexed it in 1874, calling it East Griqualand (West Griqualand was in TransOrangia, near present-day Kimberley). Kok was bought off with a magistracy and given a salary, and he tried to safeguard his people as tax-paying British subjects. But Kok was killed in an accident with a cart in 1875. He had decreed that no land should be sold to white settlers, and had also exerted strict control over liquor. But with his death, the commmunity began to fragment. The British began try paying for Griqua livestock in alcohol, and the local police started raid Griqua houses, on spurious 'treasonable' suspicions (the Griqua made no secret of their dislike of the British).

Thus provoked, rebellion eventually broke out and a Griqua/Pondo force skirmished with British Frontier Police on Mount Currie. They lost. Survivors of the battle were imprisoned and sent to Robben Island. Almost all the Griqua had their land confiscated and within three years, Boer and British settlers owned most of the farmland, bought cheap from the Government.

The later 19th century saw the local Griqua decline into alcoholism and despair, as they were forced to beg for work on the farms they had previously owned. But the final chapter in the brief, sad history of East Griqualand came this century. In 1917, a group of Griqua bought wagons and trekked again, this time to the Karoo, but their attempt to form a village failed, due to lack of all-year water, and most returned. Then again in 1928, a group walked and rode in donkey carts to Plettenberg Bay, on the temperate southern Cape Coast, where a few still survive among the farmworker families. As always in South Africa's history, those of Khoi descent had been dispossessed.

Today's Kokstad hardly matches its epic history. It is a quiet, rather handsome Edwardian town surrounded by rich farmlands. Worth visiting nearby is **Mount Currie Nature Reserve**, a large chunk of isolated mountain east of town, where the first Griqua pioneers made their ill-fated skirmish against the British Frontier Police in the 1870s. Today there is a dam with a camp site, with footpaths over the grassy spurs. Look out for grey rhebok, and mountain reedbuck. Springbok, blesbok, reedbuck, duiker and bushbuck also graze the hills.

Inland Southern Natal   **Where to Stay**

Kokstad has three rather grim and over-priced town hotels. Better is to stay at the moderately-priced **Rivermead Manor Guest Farm**, ✆ (0372) 3801, just outside town, a beautiful, relaxed place with home cooking in an old farmstead.

Cheap accommodation can be found **Oribi Gorge Nature Reserve**, ✆ (0331) 471 961, which has self-contained chalets and camp sites and **Mount Currie Nature Reserve**, which has a camp site only. No need to book. The gates for both reserves close at 6.

Pietermaritzburg and the Natal Midlands

Free of mosquitoes, the air invigorating, the streams clear of bilharzia... the bushmen, when they found this highland, must have thought of themselves as having passed through the gates of heaven.

Natal and the Zulu Country, T.V. Bulpin

Natal's provincial capital is a small city of handsome brick and wrought iron Victorian buildings lying at the foot of a high escarpment, about 100km north of Durban. Pietermaritzburg (or 'Maritzburg for short) is often referred to as 'sleepy hollow' by Durbanites. But sleepy 'Maritzburg is not. The large University of Natal on the city's southern fringe, coupled with a vibrant mix of Zulu, Indians and mostly English-speaking white, give 'Maritzburg a streetlife and nightlife unusual for a regional South African city. The compact Victorian city centre has an air of civic grace of which its people are rightly proud, and its surrounding old neighbourhoods have largely escaped the terrible 'town improvement' that erased so much of South Africa's best colonial architecture in the 1960s and '70s.

This grace does not extend to the surrounding townships of Edendale and Sweetwaters, which have suffered much inter-clan and political fighting among the inhabitants. However, their geographical distance from the town centre means that the traveller to 'Maritzburg will neither see nor experience this side of the Natal Midlands.

History

Pietermaritzburg's Victorian exterior and English-speaking business life belie its origins. The well-watered site below the first escarpment of the Drakensberg foothills was settled by the Voortrekkers on land then controlled by the Zulu king Dingane, following the hard-fought war of 1838 between Dingane and the Voortrekkers that culminated in the Boer victory of Blood River (*see* 'Northwest Natal History'), after which the Boers declared the whole region of southern Natal their own Republic of Natal. They erected a small stone church (the Church of the Vow) in the bowl under the escarpment of the Drakensberg foothills as a thanksgiving for the victory and around the church grew the new capital— Pietermaritzburg—named for the Voortrekker leaders Piet Retief and Gert Maritz (Retief had been killed by Dingane early 1838 and was already a Boer martyr—*see* 'Natal History'). But 'Maritzburg was a Boer capital for only three years. In 1842, the Republic was annexed by the British following a three-year camapign and in early 1843, after much shuffling of papers between Cape Town and London, the Union Jack was hoisted over the little Voortrekker town, which became the administrative centre for the new British colony of Natal.

'Maritzburg and the Midlands suffered a depopulation immediately after the annexation. Between 1843 and 1849, most of the Boers trekked away north, being unwilling to live under British rule. However, they were soon replaced by thousands of people who had fled Natal during the Zulu raids of Shaka and Dingane (*see* 'Natal History') and who, now that the Zulus had been pushed out of southern Natal, were returning. These clans sought, if not to have their original homelands back, at least a livelihood with the settlers. Martin West and Theophilus Shepstone, appointed to govern the new territory, were alarmed at the departure of the Boers, and now had to find a way of accommodating the returning clans without allowing them to occupy the prime land, which was to be reserved for future colonists. West and Shepstone placed the returnees in 'locations' along the Tugela River border with Zululand and the Drakensberg mountains, there to act as buffer zones between Natal, the Zulus and the new Boer republics of the Orange Free State and Transvaal, which lay beyond the Drakensberg.

However, the problem of the Natal's now empty Midlands still had to be addressed. Benjamin Pine (who succeeded West in 1849) and Shepstone hit on the idea of filling Natal with settlers imported from Britain, as had been attempted in the Eastern Cape in 1820. That venture had failed, owing to continual wars with the Xhosa people (whose land the settlers had been given) and seasonal droughts. But Natal, being peaceful, well-watered and now full-of refugees ready to be put to work on white farms, was surely a different matter. Between 1849 and 1858, thousands of British settlers, mostly from northern England, arrived in Durban, made the 100km journey up to 'Maritzburg and its surrounding farmlands by ox-wagon, and took over plots of prime land granted to them by the British Colonial Office.

But, like most colonial strategems, this one proved to be full of holes. The plentiful labour that Pine and Shepstone had counted on was not forthcoming. The returned Hlubi and other clans had established a prosperous subsistence agriculture in the 'locations' during the few, brief years they had been there, and saw no reason to come onto the white farms. Through the 1860s Pine and Shepstone struggled to force them into employment, introducing hut taxes, marriage taxes, and even forbidding the men to appear on the streets of 'Maritzburg without trousers on, all of which required money, which in turn could only be earned through working on settler farms. These ploys were only partially successful. Through the 1850s, the settler farms struggled, while the Hlubi and others earned money to pay the taxes by producing cash crops and livestock which they sold to the very settlers that the government wished them to work for! The resentful settlers pressurized the government into taking action against the Hlubi (see 'Drakensberg History') who were gradually forced into servitude on the farms by a steady increase of punitive laws and taxes. Their labour brought a long-awaited prosperity to the Midlands. From the 1860s 'Maritzburg flourished as a trading station en route to the southeast African interior, where ivory hunters, cattle dealers and general goods merchants would gather to trade in the town's market square.

As befitted the administrative capital of a British colony, some fine new buildings were built in 'Maritzburg, among them the Cathedral St Peter (now merely St Peter's Church). Once the British had installed John Colenso as bishop it seemed that 'Maritzburg had everything a colonial capital needed. But here again things did not go quite as the Natal government intended them. Bishop Colenso was, unusually for the period, an arch-humanitarian and defender of black rights. He recognized the government's measures as pure tyranny, and began saying so from the pulpit.

Despite censure from most 'Maritzburgers and even being locked out of the cathedral by his own dean, Colenso found enough liberal goverment supporters in Natal and London to retain his position into the 1870s. His countless acts of individual humanity to black labourers who came to him needing legal and medical help earned him the Zulu nickname of Sobantu ('father'). In the 1870s the English writer Anthony Trollope heard him preach and wrote that the visit 'allowed me to come into contact with that clear intellect, the gift of which has always been allowed to him. He is still bishop of Natal and will probably remain so until he dies'. 'Maritzburg's civic authorities have done little to preserve Colenso's memory, but his name lives on in the town of Colenso, northeast of 'Maritzburg on the Tugela River. The Zulu War of 1879 only served to further enrich 'Maritzburg's tradesmen, who supplied the British army and, some historians claim, also sold guns to the Zulu. Similarly, the Second Anglo–Boer did not touch 'Maritzburg; although the Boers invaded Natal in 1899, they drew their battle line at the Tugela River northest of the city, and again, its inhabitants and local farmers made money from supplying the huge British army that trundled up from Durban.

Pietermaritzburg's 20th-century life has been remarkable mainly for its upholding of British colonial institutions, such as the Victoria Club, and nearby Michaelhouse, a prestigious private school modelled on Eton. Hereford and dairy cattle farms and thoroughbred horse studs thrive in the Midlands. Trout fishing, bird shooting, and even a pack of foxhounds provide the recreation of many wealthy English-speaking 'Maritzburgers, and the city's annual Royal Agricultural Show provides a spectacle reminiscent of an English county gathering.

However, this picture of tranquil colonial privilege is all veneer. Much of 'Maritzburg's commercial life is dominated by Indians, who arrived as paupered indentured labourers in the 1860s, and have slowly clawed their way to prosperity, despite active white legislantion aimed at hampering their prosperity from the early 1900s until the demise of apartheid in 1994 (see **History**). The northeast part of town is almost entirely dominated by Indian businesses and Indian suburbs, a quarter disparagingly referred to as 'Coolietown' by many whites. 'Maritzburg's black townships (the largest being Edendale to the west) suffered appalling black to black violence during the 1980s and early 1990s, with the Inkatha Freedom Party (IFP) and ANC supporters waging a war that has claimed more lives than in any other part of the country. The violence has put many of the townships' businessmen out of operation, and whole tracts of the townships have been reduced to wastelands.

What is extraordinary is that these conflicts have stayed almost entirely within the Zulu community, hardly touching 'Martizburg's centre. Only on two occasions, both in 1993, did mass political action spill out of the townships. The first was when the ANC youth sacked the city centre after the South African Communist Party (SACP) chief, Chris Hani, was assassinated by a white supremacist (see **History**), the second when the IFP marched with their 'cultural weapons' of assegais and knobkerries, although no fighting occurred until the demonstrators returned to the townships, 10 minutes' drive away from the city centre. Central Pietermaritzburg is thus something of an ivory tower. Although the town's crime has become worse over the last few years, as unemployment has risen dramatically in the townships, the city centre remains one of the safest of any South African city, and walking at night around the bars and music clubs clustered around Church and Commercial Streets (almost all patronized by English-speaking whites) is safe enough.

Getting to and from 'Maritzburg and the Midlands

By road: 'Maritzburg is connected with and Johannesburg by the N3 and by the parallel R74, which used to be the main road north. The R56 runs southwest towards southern Natal and the Transkei, while the R33 heads northeast into Zululand.

By bus: TransLux, InterCape and Greyhound all run luxury long distance services between Durban and Johannesburg via Pietermaritzburg, as well as services to and from Bloemfontein Transtate, Golden Wheels and Eagle Liners offer the same route but for less. Travellers from the Cape should take a Greyhound, TransLux or InterCape bus up the N2 to Durban, and transfer to a 'Maritzburg bus from there.

Transtate run several local daily services between Durban and 'Maritzburg, and also connect both cities with Umtata in the Transkei, Maseru in Lesotho (via the Eastern Free State Highlands) and Welkom in the Free State, as well as up into Zululand. A local minibus service runs to Underberg and Himeville at the foot of the southern Drakensberg (see below). Transtate buses pick up and set down opposite the railway station on Church Street in 'Maritzburg. Eagle Liner buses stop at the municipal bus depot on Havelock Street, just off western Longmarket

Street near the railway station (be careful here at night). All others stop on eastern Longmarket Street near the junction with Commercial Road. For information and bookings for Greyhound, TransLux, Golden Wheels, InterCape and the minibus to Underberg © (0331) 423 026. For information on Transtate, © Durban (031) 361 8333, and for Eagle Liners, © (031) 507 6363.

By rail: 'Maritzburg's railway station, © (0331) 958 2272, was where Ghandi was thrown off the train for occupying a whites-only first class carriage. Today, the sleepy Victorian edifice runs limited services—once a week to Cape Town via Durban or Bloemfontein, and daily to Johannesburg via the northern Natal and Free State towns. There is also an infrequent run to Kokstad at the foot of the southern Drakensberg.

By black taxi: The black taxi rank is at the Havelock Street bus depot. The taxis pass through and stop in the Natal Midlands townships around 'Maritzburg, which are known to be violent. Better to take a bus or train out to the countryside and then switch to black taxi.

Tourist Information

Pietermaritzburg Tourist Association, corner of Commercial Road and Longmarket Street, © (0331) 451 348.

The City Centre

Running east–west through the centre of town is the pedestrianized section of **Church Street**, a parade of Victorian and modern shop fronts between **Commercial Road** (where stands the huge, clock-towered, red brick Victorian town hall) and **Chapel Street**, where stands the Church of St Peter. Church Street's pedestrian section is the main area for shopping, off which lead a series of narrow lanes with some of the best Victorian colonial architecture in Africa: the courtyards, bridges between buildings, and stucco mouldings (usually of elephants, a motif that occurs on many of 'Maritzburg's older buildings) are designed in an understated mock-Italianate style. Some interesting bars, cafés and night-clubs can be found here, and just off the largest, **Theatre Lane**, is a fine arcade housing a huge second-hand bookshop, where collectable books can be found at prices way below those in Britain or North America.

On **Longmarket Street**, which runs parallel with and south of Church Street is the huge **Central Post Office**, a massive grey stone edifice, and the **Victoria Club**, open to men only, which can be visited if you ask the doorman. The club's fusty old rooms, smelling of leather armchairs and pipe tobacco, hung with trophy heads and lined with Victorian first editions, exudes an atmosphere of outdated privilege. The **Tatham Art Gallery**, on the corner of Commercial Road and Longmarket (*open Mon–Sat 9–4.30*), was once the Supreme Court. Today it houses a surprising collection of work by 19th- and 20th-century European impressionists and modernists, including Renoir, Degas, Sisley, Chagall, Picasso and Henry Moore. The **Natal Museum** on Loop Street (*open Mon–Sat 9–4.30*) (parallel with Longmarket and one block south) has the usual stuffed wildlife collection typical of South Africa's provincial museums, as well as local geology and fossil history, an introduction to Zulu life, culture and beliefs, and a history of the Zulu Wars presented from a colonial perspective. This latter exhibit is being changed and, by publication, the ethnology displays should be less biased. Such British colonial emphasis in architecture and museums makes one forget that 'Maritzburg was founded by Boers trying to escape British rule. But on **Lower Church Street** (east of the pedestrianized section and opposite the modern, red-brick local government buildings), stands the **Church of the Vow**, a modest whitewash-and-thatch affair, built in 1839, the year after the battle of Blood River, was the Boers' first permanent monument to their fight for their short-lived Republic of Natal (*see* 'Natal History'). The day of Blood River—the Day of the Vow—(16 December) was instituted as a public holiday by the Afrikaner government in 1948, but has now been abolished—or rather replaced—by a new public holiday known as the Day of Reconciliation, which occupies the same date, but is aimed at erasing the Afrikaner nationalist stigma attached to the Day of the Vow.

Today, the church houses a small **museum** (*open Mon–Sat 9–5*). Exhibits include Piet Retief's diary, found on his unburied body two years after his murder (though its authenticity is disputed by historians). A welcome note of humour has crept into this rather solemn museum: on display is a mannequin of a Boer in typical wide-awake hat and bandeliers, but no lean hero this. The museum has chosen to depict him as a different kind of Boer stereotype—enormously fat and ungainly—despite the Church's central place in Boer tradition.

The stone **Voortrekker House** on Boom Street, north and east of Church Street (*open Mon–Fri 9.30–4.30, Sat 10–12.45*), is another survivor of Boer 'Maritzburg. Built in the early 1840s, the rooms are sparsely decorated in pioneer style, with saddles, skins, uncomfortable-looking beds and lithographs of stern, bearded Church elders. By contrast, the **Macrorie House Museum** on the corner of Loop and Pine Streets (*open Tues–Thur 9–4.30, Sun 10–12.15*), celebrates British Victoriana with period clothes and furniture.

Two other 'Maritzburg buildings open to the public are the small ornate **Hindu Temple** on the east end of Longmarket Street (part of the Indian quarter of town unvisited by most Western travellers), and the **Natal Archive** on Pietermaritz Street (*open Mon–Fri 9–5*), whose huge collection of Africana books and old documents are open to researchers and those just wanting to browse.

Pietermaritzburg's Parks and Nature Reserves

'Maritzburg has some superb parks, some of which connect with the indigenous forests on the escarpment northwest of town, which provide showcases for the spectacular vegetation that thrives in Natal.

For peace and quiet, the **Botanical Gardens**, out of the town centre on Church Street (open sunrise to sunset all week), are hard to beat. Take a reflective wander across the wide lawns beneath stands of huge exotic trees. A bridge crosses the small ornamental lake, and leads to a footpath up into the forest of the escarpment.

Alexandra Park, just south of the town centre (reached via Park Drive from Loop Street) has a wide open section of lawns along the small Ununduuzi River (locally known as the 'Duzi'), at the east end of which is a flea market every Sunday, around the Victorian pavillion and bandstand. It also has a superb formal rock garden and trellis walk lined with indigenous flowering aloes.

The city's loveliest park is **Queen Elizabeth Park** (*open Mon–Sat 9–6*), about 6km outside 'Maritzburg (drive north up the Howick Road towards Hilton, and look out for the signpost). Sitting halfway up the escarpment, the park overlooks the 'Maritzburg bowl and on a clear day you can see as far as the Valley of a Thousand Hills. The Natal Parks Board has its headquarters here (including a small natural history museum and curio shop), and has stocked the park with antelope and zebra, which wander freely among the large trees. A specially constructed *boma* houses two white rhino, which can be observed from a wooden viewing platform. You can also get very close to antelope—particularly the delicate, soft-eyed impala and white-blazed, snorting blesbok, and walking one of the woodland trails can bring you face to face with a bushbuck for a split second before it crashes off into the undergrowth.

Ferncliffe Forest (*open daily sunrise to sunset*) also rewards anyone willing to drive half way up the escarpment west of Queen Elizabeth Park (follow Town Bush Road up past Grey's Hospital for about 4km, then turn right onto a bad dirt road at the Waterworks). Ferncliffe's woodland is all indigenous (unlike the massed pine and eucalyptus plantations that occupy much of the escarpment slopes) and full of natural wonders: creepers with wooden spikes 10cm long, luxuriant wild flowers and small waterfalls. Rock dassies, bushbuck and duiker may be encountered on the short walking trail that leads up to a rock with sweeping views out over the city.

Where to Stay

expensive

The more interesting accommodation is out in the countryside of the Natal Midlands (*see* p.389) and Zululand (*see* p.417). However, there are a few good, expensive hotels in Pietermaritzburg itself. The **Imperial Hotel** on Loop Street, ✆ 426 551, is an early Art Deco building with 50 en suite rooms, unfortunately not decorated in Art Deco style. The **Karos Capital Towers,** ✆ 942 761, is an ugly modern tower block (one of the few in 'Maritzburg) on Commercial Street. The hotel has over 100 en suite rooms and is decorated in typical expensive chain hotel style with simple, suburban furnishings. The **Royal Hotel,** towards the station on upper Loop Street, ✆ 428 555, is a Victorian building, unfortunately much modernized inside. Next door, in the old stable, is the **Stables Night Club**—very popular with students and teenagers.

moderate

On the south side of town, just south of the University campus, is **21 Isabel Beardmore Drive B&B,** ✆ 68743, a suburban family house offering comfortable double rooms and a large garden. On Taylor Road in the suburb of Scottsville is another such house, **Scottsville B&B**, ✆ 460 133, which offers a 2-roomed cottage in a garden with use of a swimming pool. Just northwest of the town centre, in the Wembley neighbourhood, is **1 Pape Drive B&B**, off Armstrong Drive, ✆ 420979, offering 2 double rooms in a large, pleasant house.

cheap

Summer Place Youth Hostel, ✆ 945 785, offers clean dormitory bunks and double rooms in the city centre, at 86 Pietermaritz Street, north of Church Street.

Eating Out
expensive

White Mischief on Loop Street, ✆ 424 579, has two dining rooms on two floors of an elegant Victorian town house, complete with wrought-iron verandah and high ceilings. The candlelit atmosphere is relaxed and subdued. Although the name and the prints of the Zulu War on the walls seem rather provocative, the restaurant is patronized by both black and white. The menu consists of traditional meat and game dishes, very well prepared. Try the fresh trout from the Drakensberg foothills.

Despite its Mediterranean leanings, **Els Amics**, on Longmarket Street, ✆ 56524, is in a Victorian house and has a faintly colonial feel. The menu is generally Mediterranean, and specializes in poultry and fish. Also offering dishes from the Midi is **La Provence** on Loop Street, ✆ 424 579, whose best dish is, predictably, chicken provençale. Much more formal is the **Oak Room** in the Imperial Hotel, also on Loop Street, ✆ 426 551. In season, the game dishes are superb, especially francolin and venison (usually reedbuck from the Natal Midlands), and the fresh trout with almonds is available all year.

moderate

The **Plaka Taverna**, ✆ 947 727, a Greek restaurant on upper Church Street towards the station, is informal and favoured by the younger crowd. The falafels and kebabs are very good value. Upstairs is a small concert hall where local folk bands play regularly. Take your own wine. Another good-value Greek restaurant is the strangely-named **McDaniel's Greek Taverna**, in the small arcade of shops called the Joshua Doore Centre, off Commercial Road south of Longmarket Street, ✆ 423 929. The menu offers an even stranger mix, with spicy oriental dishes competing with Greek, and not a word to explain why the restaurant has a Scottish name. However, the food and the prices are good, and McDaniel's is popular with the city's students. **Da Vinci's**, on Commercial Road north of Church Street, ✆ 56632, is also a regular student hang-out, and its bar gets very crowded at weekends. The food is nothing special; good, filling traditional pasta and pizza, but the atmosphere can be festive.

Bimbos on Chapel Street stays open very until about 2am, sometimes longer, and is very much a late-night stop for the city's young pleasure-seekers. It serves mostly burgers and chips, but also does good bunny chow (curry in a loaf of bread). Piped rock and cartoon murals. No need to book. For light lunches, try the **Botanical Gardens Tea Rooms** on Mayor's Walk (*open 10–4*), opposite the ornamental lake in the Botanical Gardens, which serves toasted sandwiches and other simple fare, but the setting is very lovely.

'Maritzburg is full of good take-away places, but the best is the **Upper Crust** on Longmarket Street, opposite the black taxi ranks. Italian run, the place bakes its own pasties and pies, which can be bought hot from the oven. It has a special meaning for the author, who took shelter here during the riots following Chris Hani's asassination, when the ANC youth sacked Longmarket and Chapel Streets.

Bars and Clubs

For a town of its size, 'Maritzburg is surprisingly well stocked with bars and clubs, and there is a lively local music scene.

Drifters, on Theatre Lane (off the pedestrianized bit of Church Street) is a small live music bar (usually two guitars and an appreciative, drunken crowd) that rocks after midnight. The regulars are friendly, and it is a good place to meet people. There is a small courtyard with outside tables if you need to come up for air. **Take Five** is a larger bar/club down an alley between the pedestrianized bit of Church Street and Timber Street. Local rock bands play at weekends, when the place gets packed to the gills with students. There's a large balcony to drink on and enjoy the summer nights. There is a small cover charge.

Stables, next door to the Royal Hotel on Loop Street plays house and techno. This place gets packed at weekends, but is rather dead during the week. The crowd, though young, tends to be a little conservative.

Sax, on Commercial Road, is the hang-out for 'Maritzburg's Afrikaans youth (a minority in this English-speaking town) and has a reputation for vulgar, raucous fun. On a busy night, Sax's dance floor is packed, with much hard drinking (there is often a special on sambuka or tequila) and occasional fights taking place on the periphery. If you keep a low profile in this shameless pick-up joint, it can provide a classic view of the Great South African 'Jol' (pronounced 'jawl'), which means a huge, drunken blow-out. The most spectacular example is on Miss Wet T-Shirt nights (usually Wednesdays) notorious in 'Maritzburg, when most of the city's young Afrikaans policemen, with their regulation clipped moustaches and bulging jacket pocket concealing guns, gather to get furiously drunk. They can barely be contained by the MC, who encourages the girls to behave as outrageously as possible while the plastered mob howls and bays for more. Amazingly, these nights attract as many female as male spectators, and contestants seem very easy to find.

Upstairs at the Plaka, above the Plaka Taverna on upper Church Street, is more relaxed, a folk music club (usually on Thursdays, but check the posters around town, or ask at other bars) that often has very good musicians playing.

The Natal Midlands

Travel up the escarpment north or east of Pietermaritzburg and you enter the Natal Midlands. Wide sweeps of high, green downland grazed by sleek cattle and thoroughbred horses create a landscape more European than African. Many Midlands farms have planted European trees, and in some places even hedgerows. Clear trout streams wind through the cattle pastures and in April the country lanes are lined with clouds of pink and white cosmos flowers.

Riding, walking and trout fishing are the best way to see the country, although the local villages have also co-operated to form the Midlands Meander, a driving route which takes in tourist attractions over the whole region. The route offers a structure for those wanting to explore by car and some of the stopping points are definitely worth visiting (*see* below).

The most extensive area of the Midlands lies west of the N3 to the Drakensberg. This most beautiful part of the Midlands is a country of steep hills, sometimes rugged and strewn with boulders, sometimes covered with gentle grassland that seems to have been smoothed by hand. This area has few villages and some lovely, isolated nature reserves, and always the dim blue line of the Drakensberg marching along the western horizon. Northeast of the N3, around Greytown, the Midlands landscape alternates between upland pasture and forest, and lowland bushveld along the Tugela River, which marks the border with Zululand.

The Central Midlands

The area from Pietermaritzburg to Mooi River is the most developed part of the Natal Midlands. The area's small towns and villages set up the **Midlands Meander**, which allows travellers (with their own vehicle) to visit various craft studios, riding stables, restaurants, small hiking trails, farms, studs and galleries of local artists. A Midlands Meander map is available from the Pietermaritzburg Publicity Association and at the principal Midlands villages of Nottingham Road, Mooi River, Greytown and Howick.

Howick is the first Midlands town north of 'Maritzburg, a small agricultural centre that grew up in the 19th century around a ford in the Umgeni River. This ford is dangerously close to the 100m Howick Falls, which have claimed the lives of scores of people, both in accidents and suicide. The falls can still be visited, but there is little else to explore in the town except a small museum of Victorian farm life (*open Mon–Sat 9.30–4.30*). The Howick Hotel, built in 1873 only a few hundred metres from the falls, makes a good place have a drink before moving on. Many of the falls' victims were swept away by the Umgeni's fast current as they staggered back across the ford after a heavy night at the Howick Hotel. About 7km west of Howick (signposted from the N3) is **Midmar Dam**, a resort popular with Natal fishermen and watersports enthusiasts. There is a rather lame theme village supposedly recreating Zulu, British and Indian pioneer life. Both should be avoided, especially at weekends, unless you are keen to waterski—you can sometimes beg a go from one of the many boats. But surrounding the dam is a nature reserve that is worth visiting midweek; it is stocked with white rhino and various antelope species. Horses are hired out, and the dam is safe to swim in. Midmar also has chalets and a camp site, and makes a good place to break a journey north/south along the N3.

Less heavily touristed is the **Umgeni Valley Nature Reserve**, a few kilometres east of Howick along the Karkloof road, which follows the Umgeni River and has cool walking trails through riverine forest. The reserve is great on a hot day, as its stretch of river is safe for swimming and game (giraffe, nyala, kudu, eland, reedbuck and bushbuck), is plentiful. The reserve's Information Centre has some good educational displays concerning Natal's wildlife and habitat conservation.

Game Valley Private Nature Reserve lies just below the impressive **Karkloof Falls**, also reached by the Karkloof Road from Howick, following the Game Valley signs. A private game reserve with mixed woodland and grass-covered downs, Game Valley has a large buffalo herd and some of the rarer antelope, such as roan and sable. White rhino wander the valley, as well as the more common game species such as zebra, kudu, nyala, reedbuck, bushbuck, duiker and warthog. Guided bush walks and game drives are offered, as well as a forest trail up to the high Karkloof Falls, where you can bathe in its large pool. Game Valley is also a hotel, with isolated bush camps by water-holes (*see* 'Where to Stay').The Karkloof Falls are best viewed from Game Valley, but if you want to get close to them follow the Karkloof Road out of Howick, and look for signs to the right down a minor road that winds through forestry plantations. There is a picnic site, but limited exploring.

The next town north is **Nottingham Road**. The N3 goes there but the parallel R74, the old main road north, is much prettier. Thoroughbred studs abound, as do country hotels—two of which, **Granny Mouse's**, and **Fern Hill**, rank among South Africa's best (*see* 'Where to Stay'). Nottingham Road itself has little except for its old coaching inn, which does good Sunday lunches. From Nottingham Road, you can make a loop back to 'Maritzburg through rolling countryside (covered in pink and white cosmos flowers in summer) via the tiny hamlet of **Fort Nottingham**, which has one of the best points of the Midlands Meander—a restaurant set among trees called **Café Le Fort** (*see* 'Eating Out'). A dirt road heads southwest from Fort Nottingham back to 'Maritzburg southwest via the village of **Dargle**. This route passes through deep Midlands country, similar to the more remote western Midlands. For those without time to explore, the road to Dargle gives a good idea of its high, empty downland, forest kloofs, fresh air and silence. At Dargle, you hit the main R617 road which leads back to the N3 at Howick.

West to the Drakensberg Foothills

West from Nottingham Road winds one of the loveliest roads in South Africa, the road to the **Little Berg**, the first heights below the main Drakensberg. The road leads through progessively higher uplands, cut through by bright streams. Occasionally a track leads off to a distant farm, but otherwise the landscape is unpopulated and always there is the great blue wall of the Drakensberg up ahead. **Kamberg Nature Reserve** lies at the end of the road, under the Little Berg. The infant Mooi River passes through, and you can fish for trout in its narrow course or wander the trail along its banks. Look out for kingfishers and reedbuck. Another trail leads up to a sandstone outcrop called Gladstone's Nose, where some good bushman paintings of eland hunting can be found. Eland still graze the reserve's higher slopes, and bushbuck, hunted by lynx and leopard, inhabit the wooded kloofs.

Also in the Drakensberg foothills is **Loteni Nature Reserve**, to the south of Kamberg. Access is by dirt road via the hamlet of Lower Loteni. Trout fishing is allowed here, and there is a 12km hiking trail, as well as horses for hire. Even more isolated than Kamberg, Loteni is sometimes cut off during the summer rains, when the dirt roads can become liquid mud. The game includes leopard, reedbuck, grey rhebok eland, bushbuck , duiker and oribi. Look out for black eagles.

South of Loteni are two villages, **Himeville** and **Underberg**, both reached from 'Maritzburg via the main R617 road through Bulwer. The two settlements are just 6km apart and lie under Sani Pass, the one point of road access (only in a 4x4) over the Drakensberg between Natal to Lesotho. Himeville has a hotel with a good pub, and a small nature reserve around a dam with boats for hire and trout fishing available. Waterfowl such as Egyptian geese and black duck congregate here. Underberg is a little bigger, with a bank and supermarket. South of Underberg along the R617 is the **Coleford Nature Reserve**, also known for trout fishing, walking and riding. There are cottages set among the grassland and hills where black wildebeest, blesbok and reedbuck graze. East of Underberg (on R617) is the the **Swamp Nature Reserve**, set around a wetland known for rare birds such as the wattled crane. Reedbuck live in the marshes, and the swamp has a walking trail, but no accommodation.

Underberg is also known for its annual folk/rock bash, the **Splashy Fen Music Festival**, which attracts South Africa's best musicians, black and white, for a Woodstock-style weekend of music, peace, love and *dagga* (marijuana), although LSD has become popular over the last few years. The festival is one of the few occasions where you stand a chance of socializing across the (now unspoken) South African race barrier, and some of the music is very fine indeed. Splashy Fen is usually held in May, but the Pietermaritzburg Tourist Association will know the exact dates.

Between Pietermaritzburg and Zululand

The northeastern stretch of the Midlands, which borders Zululand, centres around **Greytown**, a prosperous country town surrounded by forested hills and reached by the R33 from 'Maritzburg. On the way is the **Albert Falls Nature Reserve**. Like Howick, the Albert Falls are on the Umgeni River. A variety of plains game grazes the reserve, including blesbok, zebra, red hartebeest, bushbuck, duiker, reedbuck and oribi. Walking trails cut through the bush. However, Albert Falls is over-popular with 'Maritzburgers at weekends; those seeking solitude would do better to go on to Greytown, then take the mountainous R74 via Muden to **Weenen**.

Weenen ('the place of weeping') marks the turning point between the high downland of the Midlands and the harsher thornveld of Zululand, although the village itself sits in a green, fertile bowl of intensive farmland on the Little Tugela River. It was here that, in 1838, Dingane'simpis massacred 500 Boer women and children, shortly after Piet Retief had been killed in Dingane'skraal while negotiating for a grant for the Boers to settle in Natal. The massacre has become an integral part of Afrikaner mythology, and was often cited as a warning against power sharing with blacks during the apartheid years.

Weenen Nature Reserve, to the north of the quiet village, is very lovely. A mixture of grassland, thornveld and high hills, it harbours a healthy white rhino population, as well as eland, kudu, reedbuck, duiker, giraffe and a few shy, rarely-seen black rhino. There are also buffalo (but very few), ostrich and the little steenbok. The reserve has three good walking trails, one of which has spectacular views out over the Little Tugela Valley from a high escarpment. There are also bird-watching hides; blue cranes often come down to the reserve's water holes, whose reeds are home to bright yellow and red bishop birds.

Plans are afoot to declare the vast farming district around Weenen a biosphere, which will mean taking the land out of farming and put it back under game. This would result in one of the largest game reserves in the country, big enough for elephant and lion to range. The rough date for opening the first of the ex-farms (which back onto the nature reserve) is 1996. So it is worth visiting Weenen to see how the plan has advanced, and what new game species have been introduced since the time of writing.

Activities

Walking: Almost all the nature reserves of the Natal Midlands run good one day-trails (*see* above).

Riding: Good hill riding, with occasional sightings of antelope, can be arranged at the Vlei Stables at Nottingham Road, ✆ (0333) 36287. The Midlands Trout and Saddle Resort, near Mooi River, ✆ (0333) 3275, has an equestrian centre for serious riders who want to brush up their technique. Also, Loteni and Midmar Dam nature reserves hire horses.

Trout Fishing: The Natal Midlands were first stocked with trout in the 1870s. Since then they have established themselves as one of the southern hemisphere's best fly-fishing regions. Fishing is allowed in Kamberg, Himeville and Loteni nature reserves, as well as at some of the larger country hotels listed below, and tackle can be hired from The Fisherman's Hut, Nottingham Road, ✆ (0333) 36151.

Where to Stay

expensive

Granny Mouse's Country House, ✆ (03324) 4071/4532, at Balgowan, on the R74 just south of Nottingham Road is an old thatched building set on a rise above the Lion's River. Despite the name, the hotel is superb. Most rooms have their own balcony and fireplace, and there is trout fishing, a pool and lovely walking along the river. **Fern Hill Hotel**, ✆ (0332) 305071, just north of Midmar on the R74, is an old colonial trading post with 19 en suite rooms and a formal garden. Riding, swimming and tennis are available. **Game Valley Lodge**, ✆ (03393) 787/800, in the valley below Karkloof Falls, is a private game reserve with individual bush camps set by waterholes where you can watch buffalo come down to drink without seeing or hearing another human. The game drives and walking/swimming around Karkloof Falls are recommended.

Old Halliwell Country Inn, ✆ (0332) 302 602/573, near the hamlet of Curry's Post (east of Mooi River along the R114) is another Victorian house converted to a small hotel with 12 rooms in imitation Victorian style. A verandah runs around the building giving views out over the Karkloof Valley. Log fires in winter make this a cosy place. The cooking is good—all vegetables, milk, eggs and most of the meat comes from the farm next door. The **Trout Bungalow**, ✆ (0333) 36417, is a small (only 5 guest rooms) wooden Victorian house in what was an old officer's mess on the banks of the Mooi River, about 22km west of Nottingham Road along the Himeville road. The bungalow owns a 10km trout-fishing beat, and a small, beautifully-tended garden set amid the surrounding farmland.

moderate

The **Nottingham Road Hotel**, ✆ (0333) 36151, a substantial Victorian building, was established in 1854 as a coaching inn. It is popular as a Sunday lunch spot with weekenders from Durban and 'Maritzburg. Hunting prints and chintz make up the decor, and the pub is lively. **Hawklee Country House**, ✆ (0333) 36008, offers B&B in the tiny hamlet of Fort Nottingham, near Nottingham Road. The thatched house has riding, fishing, cycling and walking for its guests, as well as a scaled down model railway. The **Happy Hill Guest House**, ✆ (03324) 4380, at Balgowan, south along the R74 from Nottingham Road, is a clean and bright whitewashed house offering B&B, with pleasant gardens to wander in.

cheap

Loteni Nature Reserve, **Midmar Dam** and **Albert Falls Public Resort** all have self-catering chalets and cottages that fall into the cheap category if shared, and into the bottom end of the moderate range if taken alone. There are also camp sites with ablution blocks at the above reserves and at Weenen Nature Reserve. **Kamberg Nature Reserve** is divided into two sections; the main area has a group of thatched chalets and a camp site, but ask for the stone cottage, which overlooks its own valley in the southern, more isolated part of the reserve.

Eating Out

expensive

 Granny Mouse's, ✆ (03324) 4071, on the R74 at Balgowan, south of Nottingham Road, serves country dishes to residents and non-residents. Try the fresh trout from the river cooked in herbs. All dishes come with home-baked bread, and meals are served in a Laura Ashley fantasy of a dining room. **Fern Hill,** ✆ (0332) 305071, also on the R74 south of Nottingham Road, offers similar fare—fresh trout is again a speciality, but game also features on the menu. Meals are served in a roomy Victorian dining room with a polished wooden floor.

moderate

The Natal Midlands' best restaurant must be **Café Le Fort,** ✆ (0333) 36354, a small cottage restaurant in Fort Nottingham hamlet, serving genuine *provençale* food with imported French wines. Moroccan and Corsican dishes are also on the menu, and the restaurant holds theme evenings when the entire menu is changed to suit a Pagnol story (entire menus are invented around books such as *La Gloire de mon Père* and *Le Château de ma Mère*), or to celebrate Napoleon Bonaparte's birthday. Delicious local cheeses and home-baked bread add to the fun. For such a good restaurant, prices are very reasonable (at the expensive end of the moderate range), but booking is essential. The **Nottingham Road Hotel,** ✆ (0333) 36151, serves substantial, well-cooked meat-and-two veg dishes in a Victorian atmosphere of sporting prints and old wooden chairs. Again, the trout is good—always fresh and served with lemon and garlic.

The Natal Drakensberg

uKhalamba—the Barrier of Spears

The old Nguni name for the Natal Drakensberg

The highest range of South Africa's Great Escarpment curves eastwards from Lesotho into Natal in a giant buttress whose cliffs fall sheer to the bare, green foothills of the Natal Midlands. From a distance, only the highest ridge (which tops 10,000ft) is visible, a thin blue line suspended above the western horizon and hung with shifting cloud.

The 'Berg, as most South Africans refer to the range, is the country's most popular wild hiking area, and with good reason. Their scale is dwarfing. At some points, river gorges fall over a thousand feet away from the trail, while above soar cliffs of equal height. There is a crystal quality to the air (locals call it 'champagne air') that leaves you light-headed and exhilarated. Waterfalls and cold streams cascade down hidden forest kloofs to wild, open plateaux of montane grassland grazed by small herds of shy antelope. Balancing rocks and jagged, tooth-like columns hundreds of metres high jut from the great massifs of the square-topped basalt peaks. The landscape is fabulous in the true sense of the word, its quality reflected in the names of the best-known landmarks: Giant's Castle, Giant's Cup, Cathedral Peak, the Sentinel and the huge Amphitheatre. The mountains have a central place in both black and San (bushman) myth, and the author J. R. Tolkien, who was born in South Africa, is said to have found the inspiration for his imaginary world of Middle Earth in the Drakensberg ('Dragon-stone') landscapes.

Climate

Because of the abrupt rise in altitude, the lower Drakensberg slopes have a much more temperate climate than the hot Natal plain below. Midday temperatures in the green, rainy summer can be blisteringly hot, but evenings are always cool and even summer nights get cold. Winter nights are bitter and usually frosty. Above the 2000m line, extremes of temperature occur year-round. Violent rainstorms can blow in at any time, and in winter snowfalls are common.

Flora and Fauna

Eland, blesbok, mountain reedbuck, grey rhebok, klipspringer, and sometimes black wildebeest, are often seen skittering across steep slopes away from the hiker. Secretive bushbuck inhabit the forest kloofs. Leopard, caracal, and serval cat live in the more remote caves and rock overhangs. Dassies leave great heaps of droppings anywhere there is a cluster of boulders large enough to support a colony. The sharp bark of baboons, echoing along the cliffs of a deep gorge, is a familiar sound to anyone who has walked in the 'Berg. Black, martial, crowned eagles, buzzards, ibis and the smaller falcons cruise the heights, while sugarbirds and sunbirds flit among the wild-flowers of the lower slopes. Hikers should watch out for plump berg adders sunning themselves on the trails. Lizards by the thousand bask on the rocks and paths.

Most of the Drakensberg is dressed in a smooth coat of montane fynbos (heath) and grassland, brilliant green in summer and pinkish gold in winter. Protea woodland—groups of strange, gnarled, flowering trees that grow to stunted, crazy shapes, as if frozen in mid-dance—is common at low altitude. In the forest kloofs, hardwood trees such as yellowwood and assegai cover the steep slopes. Delicate wildflowers, purple orchids and ericas, dot the fynbos grasslands in spring and summer.

History

The sandstone caves and overhangs of the 'Berg often have galleries of bushman rock paintings, many of which can be reached via the Berg's hundreds of walking trails. Traditional San hunting and ritual pictures sometimes alternate with scenes from the white settler invasion, such as ox-wagons and horsemen with guns; the San had inhabited the Drakensberg since being driven there by black African pastoralists around the 14th century. Eventually it was this range that provided the South African San with their last mountain stronghold, before being wiped out by both white settlers and black tribesmen in the mid-19th-century, neither of whom would tolerate the San's practise of hunting cattle when there was insufficient game. Today, the San survive only in the Kalahari, almost 2000km to the north.

During the rise of the Zulu empire through the 1820s and '30s, various Nguni tribes from Natal fled into the Drakensberg to escape the *impis* of Shaka and his brother (and successor) Dingane. Some, like the Hlubi and Ngwane, crossed the mountains and dispersed onto the highveld beyond, either raiding other tribes or being assimilated by them. Some smaller refugee clans, like the Bele, stayed in the Drakensberg and turned to cannibalism as game became too scarce, the climate too harsh and the time too chaotic to allow for settled farming. Some cannibal caves can be explored along a few of the 'Berg's many hiking trails. The Bele and other cannibal clans represented such a danger to travellers and clans living at the foot of the mountains that first Zulu and Sotho war parties and then white settlers began hunting them out. By 1850 the cannibal bands had disappeared from the Natal Drakensberg, though a few held out in the wild uplands of Lesotho for another decade.

The last of the San hunters were finally exterminated by farmers and by Hlubi tribesmen returned from exile in the 1860s, after Natal became a British colony and the Zulu were confined to the country north of the Tugela River. The Hlubi were settled in 'native locations' in the Drakensberg foothills and in pockets further into Natal. Taking advantage of the plentiful water and temperate climate, they soon became prosperous farmers, and by 1870 were supplying the new colonial towns at the foot of the 'Berg (such as Estcourt, Winterton and Bergville) with meat and vegetables. The Hlubi's prosperity began to excite the envy of Natal's white settlers, who were often struggling, being little experienced in African farming.

After the 1871 Kimberley diamond boom, mineworking recruitment agents travelled all over South Africa looking for labourers, and many young Hlubi men left their 'locations', went to Kimberley to work for a year, returning with the statutory pay-off of a small lump sum and a gun, while the Hlubi women continued to produce crops for the local farmers' markets. By now, both the local settlers and the Natal government, were uneasy at the thought of a prospering nation of armed natives sitting in the mountain foothills. The assumption was that the Hlubi might one day decide to join forces with their old enemies the Zulus and attack the white settlers, though there was absolutely no evidence to support this.

In 1873, John Macfarlane, the magistrate of Estcourt, demanded that all firearms in the Hlubi 'location' be brought into town to be registered. The Hlubi, under their chief Langalibalele, guessed that this was simply a ploy to confiscate their guns. So the old chief ignored the order. Macfarlane then persuaded Theophilus Shepstone, then the Secretary for Native Affairs and later the Governor, to summon Langalibalele to Pietermaritzburg to explain his non-compliance with the order.

The young Hlubi men forced their old chief to stay at home, in case the British arrested him in Pietermaritzburg. Macfarlane sent officials with a second and a third summons. The young Hlubi men, by now confused and suspicious, searched the envoys, kept them under guard, and ejected them from the 'location' next day. Macfarlane saw this as his opportunity for action, and demanded to know if the Natal government meant to tolerate such high-handedness from its black subjects. His strategy worked; a force of over 10,000 regulars and native levies were sent to arrest Langalibalele, to confiscate his land and cattle, and to disperse the Hlubi among other 'locations'.

The Hlubi warriors got wind of the force and fled into the mountains. An advance troop of soldiers under Major Anthony Durnford (later to be killed by the Zulus at Isandhlwana in 1879) was sent to block off the Bushman's River Pass, in the vast present-day Giant's Castle Nature Reserve. They were too late to stop Langalibalele but were in time to confront a mass of armed Hlubi warriors. Most of Durnford's troops fled, but the major and a few volunteers vainly attempted to block the pass. All but Durnford were killed.

In retaliation, British troops annexed the Hlubi's main location, drove off some 15,000 head of cattle, kidnapped the women and children and gave them as virtual slaves to surrounding farmers. So too the land. Unable to suvive in the harsh uplands, Lanaglibalele and his men surrendered. The old chief was sent to Robben Island for a year and the clan dispersed.

However, the Natal government did not get away scot-free. Native sympathisers, among them the influential bishop of Natal, John Colenso, caused an outcry in the British press about barbarous colonial tyranny, and Benjamin Pine, the Natal governor who had sanctioned the use of force in the Langalibalele affair, was recalled. The British Colonial Office sent orders to restore the Hlubi land and cattle, but these were quietly ignored. The Hlubi returned to the Drakensberg foothills, where some remain today, but their prosperity had been broken.

Despite its history, the Drakensberg have been among the least politically eventful areas of South Africa through the 20th century. Apart from the villages and resorts that line its feet, and the transitory Sotho, Zulu and Hlubi people crossing the mountains, like most of South Africa's ranges, the 'Berg are all-but uninhabited. Only the town of Estcourt, 30km east of the range and now the site of a large Nestlé factory, and the Kwa-Zulu 'location' near Loskop, have seen any real unrest during the struggle against apartheid. Today, the Drakensberg continues to be South Africa's most peaceful region, a place where the conflicts and problems of the country can be forgotten, and where the traveller can look down from the heights and simply feel exhilarated by being on the roof of Southern Africa.

Hiking in the Drakensberg

The 'Berg has so many different hiking and climbing routes that they warrant a book of their own. The most authoritative guide available is Jaynee Levy's superbly thorough *Guide to Walks and Hikes in Southern Africa*, which deals with the scores of individual trails in the 'Berg, as well as in other areas of South Africa. Here, there is only room to outline the main trails. Some of these are well hiked and can become quite crowded, especially in Giant's Castle Nature Reserve and Royal Natal National Park. But there is a wealth of remoter trails, particularly in the Mzimkulwana Wilderness Area of the southern 'Berg, and the Mkhomazi and Mzumkulu Wilderness Areas of the central 'Berg. On these you may not meet another soul.

Safety on the Trail

The Drakensberg Mountains should be treated with particular respect on account of their sudden changes of weather. Mist and low cloud are particular hazards. It is imperative that you stick to the marked trail; the Drakensberg's uplands are vast and many hikers who wander off-track get lost, sometimes with fatal consequences.

If camping or sleeping in caves (rather than in overnight hiking huts) do be aware that Sotho and Zulu tribesmen do sometimes pass through the area, so do not leave tempting hiking and camping equipment lying around, and always remember to greet whoever you meet confidently and with friendship, as the mountain people can be touchy and have had experience with frightened travellers being apparently rude by ignoring their greetings. Learning the Sotho and Zulu forms of greeting is a good idea.

The Three Drakensberg Regions

The Drakensberg is usually divided into three sections, southern, central and northern, for easier orientation. The signposts from the N3 highway use this system, and this guide will follow the same pattern.

The Southern Drakensberg

The southern section of the Natal Drakensberg runs from the southern Natal border north to Sani Pass, near Underberg. Most of this area is protected by the vast **Mzimkulwana and Mzimkulu Wilderness Areas**, and include the high mountains visible from the towns of Underberg, Cedarville and Kokstad. Hiking trails through the valleys and lower passes can be easily reached from two resort hotels, the **Bushman's Nek Hotel** and the **Drakenberg Garden**. Both hotels also hire horses for guided rides of up to four hours.

One of the best things about this massive block of wilderness is that no vehicles are allowed except near the hotels. Hikers who penetrate deep into the wilds can stay in designated caves (marked on the trail maps available from the hotels). From Bushman's Nek, there is a superb two-day walk up to the Selabethebe National Park in Lesotho, with overnight huts along the way.

Up on the highlands, the cold streams tumble and mixed grassland, montane fynbos and kloof forest supports a healthy population of eland, mountain reedbuck, klipspringer and bushbuck. Baboon are plentiful on the steeper slopes, as are dassies. Predators include leopard, lynx, black and crested eagle and jackal buzzard. Lammergeir (bearded vulture) and bald ibis (which has iridescent green feathers) are rarer sights.

Sani Pass, just north of Mzimkulwana Wilderness Area, is the one road directly linking Natal and Lesotho (a second road, via Qacha's Nek in the south, passes through Transkei). It's a rough road, only accessible for 4x4s, but a steady stream of traders from Lesotho come regularly down the pass to buy supplies for their mountain stores. Hitching a ride up Sani Pass is easy; the best point to pick up lifts being about 15km along the dirt road to the pass from the village of Himeville at **Sani Lodge**, the last point accessible by ordinary vehicle (*see* 'Where to Stay'). A number of very beautiful trails begin and end at Sani Lodge, some of which lead to superb bushman paintings, or to natural swimming pools of crystal springwater. It is best to spend a couple of days at Sani Lodge so as to try at least two of the trails, each of which take about half a day to walk. Eland and reedbuck are common, and hikers often have the trails to themselves. Those without transport can pick up a minibus service to/from Sani Lodge from either Durban or Pietermaritzburg, ✆ (0331) 423 026. If you intend to travel up Sani Pass, you will need your passport to cross the Lesotho border, which is halfway up. At the top of Sani Pass is a small lodge, a hiking hut (a three-day trail leaves from Sani Top) and horses for hire.

The Central Drakensberg

Giant's Castle Game Reserve is a huge protected area (about 35,000ha) of mountain north of Sani Pass, accessible from Estcourt on the N3 or Winterton on the R74. The reserve is named after the central massif that dominates the mountain horizon—at 3314m it is one of the higher peaks in the 'Berg—which is said to look like a sleeping giant. The Little Tugela River rises in these mountains and cascades down to the plain below, eventually joining the mighty Tugela River, whose waters mark the border between Natal and Zululand. Giant's Castle has three camps, with self-catering cottages or camp sites available. The largest is **Main Camp**, whose entrance, called **Witteberg Gate**, is accessible from the town of Winterton on the R74. Petrol is available here. **Injasuthi Camp**, the second-largest, is also accessible from Winterton along the Cathkin Peak road, and **Hillside Camp**, the smallest, is reached via Loskop. Be aware that Loskop is a volatile area, and that the road can be dangerous at times of political unrest.

Due north of Giant's Castle Nature Reserve and Sani Pass is the combined **Mlabonja and Mdelelo Wilderness Area**, a great sweep of wild mountain reached via the R600 from Winterton (on the R74) or from Estcourt, on the N3, via the Loskop road. The famous **Cathedral Peak** is here, a 3004m massif resembling a gothic cathedral with twin towers. **Cathkin Peak** (3181m), famous among climbers, is also found here, as is **Champagne Castle** (3377), which was christened by two British officers who climbed it just after the Second Anglo–Boer War (1902), having towed a champagne picnic along with them. God knows how—it's a gruelling 2-day walk to the top. The foot of this wilderness area has more resorts and hotels than the Southern

'Berg—mainly along the road from Winterton—but the mountains themselves are as wild as anywhere else in the range. The principal points of access are from **Champagne Castle Hotel** or the adjacent **Monk's Cowl Camp Site** (*see* 'Where to Stay'). The walking is spectacular. In the northern section of Mlambonja Wilderness Area is **Ndedema Gorge** (also called Rainbow Gorge). A particularly beautiful hiking trail leads along the river bed of the Ndadema (a tributary of the Tugela), between great rock walls that eventually become so narrow that they have caught a great boulder in mid-fall. Standing beneath this rock offers one of the classic photo-opportunities in the 'Berg.

The Northern Drakensberg

The Northern 'Berg is the most spectacularly scenic part of the range. The highest accessible point, **Mont aux Sources** (3282m), juts from the rampart of a 3000m cliff wall called the **Amphitheatre,** where the Tugela River rises.

Royal Natal National Park and the smaller, adjoining **Rugged Glen Nature Reserve** (accessible from Bergville via the R74) are the best points from which to explore the mountains around, whether on foot or horseback (*see* 'Activities'). With its protea woodland, fast-running streams, waterfalls and flat-topped heights, Royal Natal is picture-postcard Drakensberg scenery. Hiking trails snake through the mountains, and, while walking, you may meet Zulu women cutting reed grass for basket-making, as they have done since before the park existed.

Fauna in the park includes mountain reedbuck, bushbuck in the forested kloofs (often seen by the camp site at first light), grey rhebok, klipspringer, duiker and baboon. Leopard hunt the more remote areas.

Qwa Qwa, just east of Royal Natal, is South Africa's smallest 'homeland'. It covers only about 60,000ha, half of which has been set aside as a conservation area between Mont Aux Sources and the Maluti Mountains in Lesotho. Apart from providing quicker access to Mont Aux Sources than the hike from Royal Natal, the reserve has a 3-day hiking trail, a small hotel (**Witsieshoek Mountain Resort**) and a camp site. Much of the reserve is over 3000m, so be aware of the altitude and expect sudden changes of weather. Access is via the R74 from Bergville to the R712 to Phuthaditjaba (pronounced 'put-a-ditch-arba'), the tiny, scrubby Qwa-Qwa capital, from where the Witsieshoek Mountain Resort is signposted, 30km down a good dirt road.

Activities

Walking and Hiking: NB: Before setting off on any Drakensberg hike, make sure that you have a waterproof, map and some warm clothing, no matter how sunny it is. Weather can change quickly, dragging the temperature down. If hiking above 2000m, carry a full pack with survival gear such as a bivvy bag, food, compass etc.

The **Main Camp** at Giant's Castle is the access point for several walks and hikes. The most popular is up to Giant's Castle itself, a 2-day journey to and from a refuge hut at the foot of the cliffs that make up the final massif. Once up there, hikers can continue north/south along a contour path for several days, sleeping in overnight huts (maps from the camp office). Anyone attempting the high paths *must* inform the camp office, which involves giving details of your leaving time and expected return time. Make sure you have warm clothing for the higher hikes. A gentler walk leads from the camp to a cave of bushman paintings that has been declared a museum of rock art, so dense and varied are the pictures. Guided tours leave about three times daily, but you can go up independently. The Main Camp also offers guided walking overnight trails (from September to May only), and birdwatching from hides (particularly good for lammergeier vulture). Injasuthi Camp has more walking trails (short day walks or access to the longer, high hikes). Black wilde-beest, blesbok, oribi, duiker, red hartebeest and grey rhebok may be seen nearby, and are often encountered on trail.

Mlabonja and Mdelelo Wilderness Area has 12 marked trails leading up through waterfall and forest to the high plateaux. As well as eland, mountain reedbuck and baboon, look out for the elegant, straight-horned grey rhebok in the kloofs. It is worth taking a tent for the overnight trails, although some of them do have designated caves for sleeping.

The best walk in the **Royal Natal park** is the 2-day hike up Mont Aux Sources (one day in, one day out, with an overnight hut at the top). Start early to ensure you have plenty of time to scale the chain ladders that make up the final 200m or so to the summit. Another much shorter walk is up to the Mudslide, also reached by a chain-ladder, at the top of which is a hidden waterfall that plunges 200ft over a cliff. Maps for all the park's hikes can be had from the main office. Qwa Qwa has a 3-day trail with overnight huts. Much of the reserve is over 3000m, so be aware of the altitude and expect sudden changes of weather. Access is via the R74 from Bergville to the R712 to Phuthaditjaba.

Riding: Horses are available at any of the resort hotels listed below, all of which rent by the hour, as do the stables at Rugged Glen Nature Reserve, which adjoins the Royal Natal National Park. Hillside Camp, in Giant's Castle Nature Reserve, runs 3-day horse trails into the 'Berg between September and March. These have to be booked in advance via the Natal Parks Board in Pietermaritzburg, ✆ (0331) 471 961.

Fishing: Injasuthi Camp has trout fishing in the Little Tugela River (tackle not provided).

Where to Stay
expensive

The **Drakensberg Garden**, near Underberg in the southern 'Berg, ✆ (0020) 1, is one of the old-fashioned family hotels that one finds throughout the 'Berg. There are 80 rooms, horses, tennis courts, a pool, a restaurant and bar. Hikes and short walks lead off into the mountains from the hotel (open to non-residents too). Further north, near Winterton, the **Champagne Castle Hotel**, ✆ (0364) 468 1063, is an old-fashioned gem with 49 en suite rooms set in a park of fragrant pines and looking out on the Champagne Castle massif. Again, there are horses, tennis, walking and hiking trails, and a feeling of being back in the 1930s. The **Cathedral Peak Hotel**, ✆ (0364) 381 381, also reached from Winterton, is from the same era, with similar facilities of riding, hiking, tennis and clean air.

For solitude, try **Giant's Lodge** in Giant's Castle Nature Reserve, ✆ (0331) 471 981, a self-catering lodge let to individual parties. It has 7 en suite rooms, and, although you bring your own food, a cook and domestic servants are provided. The Lodge is set into the hillside like a luxurious bunker, hidden by turf, yet with spectacular views out over this central section of the high 'Berg. **Tendele Lodge** in the Royal Natal National Park, ✆ (0331) 471 981, is also turfed over, though not built completely into the hillside. The three en suite bedrooms look out to the Ampitheatre and Mont Aux Sources. Again, bring your own food, but there is a resident cook.

The **Royal Natal National Park Hotel**, ✆ (036) 438 6200, is another old-fashioned family hotel. Set under the requisite tall trees, with the requisite riding stables (for guests only), tennis courts, pool and bowling green, the hotel has 49 en suite rooms. Bushbuck can often be seen stealing across its lawns in the early morning. The hotel makes a convenient place to have a drink or a meal if you are staying in the adjacent Parks Board chalets or camp site. North of Royal Natal, along the R74 is **Little Switzerland**, ✆ (036) 381 175, a small private resort of thatched cottages around a central lodge. The place sleeps 50, and has some superb hiking trails into the 'Berg, a trout stream (tackle available), and guaranteed peace.

moderate

Bonny Glen B&B ✆ (036) 488 1222 a beautiful stone-built dairy farm in the Drakensberg foothills near Winterton (on the D187, north of the R600), which makes a good base for walking in the Champagne Castle area 20 minutes' drive away. Further north is **Sandford Park Lodge**, ✆ (036) 448 1001, a late-19th century thatched bungalow set in woodland near Bergville with a pool, restaurant and bar. **Uitzicht Farm**, ✆ (036) 488 1492, on the west side of the R74 south of Winterton, has a self-catering cottage that sleeps 8, with walking, swimming, fishing (tackle available) and canoeing on the Little Tugela River. Near Bergville (6km along the Ladysmith road, R616) is **Hunter's Rest**, ✆ (036) 448 1412, which offers a comfortable self-catering cottage that sleep six. You can either drive to the 'Berg for hiking or walk on the farm.

Natal Parks Board Cottages and Chalets are found in all the reserves and adjacent state forests listed above. There is seldom any need to book unless you are intend to be there during school holidays (particularly over Christmas), when it is advisable to book accommodation at the Natal Parks Board in Pietermaritzburg, ✆ (0331) 478 961. All cottages and chalets are self-catering only.

Sani Lodge, in the southern 'Berg, ✆ (033722) 1330, is the last point accessible by ordinary car on the Sani Pass road from Himeville. One of the cheapest and best value places to stay in South Africa, Sani Lodge used to be an old trading store, and has a choice of dormitory bunks or double-bed rondavels painted with traditional designs. Russell, the owner, is a mine of local information and can advise on where to walk, where to see bushman paintings, where to organize riding or mountain biking, and also makes superb fudge and chocolate cake. Guests gather round a roaring log fire in the evenings. The Lodge arranges pick-ups and drop-offs from Durban or Pietermaritzburg for travellers with no transport; call them for the timetable. Guests range from backpackers to local Sotho and Zulu traders journeying up and down Sani Pass. You can often hitch a ride up the pass with these people. Take your own food, and be prepared for a long-drop toilet.

Natal Parks Board camp sites offer a cheap way to explore the Drakensberg nature reserves. All of the reserves listed above have camp sites with ablution blocks. A separate Parks Board camp site can be found at Monk's Cowl, further along the road from Champagne Castle Hotel. All Parks Board camp sites are at the trailheads for day and overnight (or longer) marked hiking trails.

Zululand

Command the warring king
to lay aside his deathful lance awhile
and seek his consort of the shining smile
and with her fight and win a sweeter war
where shield is kiss and assegai desire

Indaba My Children, Credo Mutwa

VISITORS SHOULD BE AWARE THAT ZULULAND IS MALARIAL

Until 1994, most of the land from the Tugela River north to the border with Mozambique, was administered by Kwa-Zulu, one of the 'tribal homelands' invented by the Nationalist Party in the 1970s. Kwa-Zulu was divided into scores of fragmented chunks, some large, some tiny Although now no longer 'separate', when driving through Zululand you cannot fail to notice the ever alternating difference between land owned by white farmers and land belonging to the Zulu villages of what was Kwa-Zulu 'homeland', creating sharp contrasts in an already spectacular landscape.

Zululand is divided into three main chunks; the inland section, the coast and Tsongaland. The inland section houses the massive **Umfolozi** and **Hluhluwe Game Reserves** (home to the Big Five), and among its high hills and valleys traditional Zulu life continues more or less as it always has. To the east, the foetid and sub-tropical coast is dominated by the massive lake complex of **Lake St Lucia,** one of the largest wetlands in Southern Africa. Tsongaland sits north of the main coast, in a rough square formed by the Mkuze River, the Lebombo Mountains, the Mozambique border, and coastline even wilder that around St Lucia. Remote from the rest of the country, most of Tsongaland is dense sand forest shared by cattle and game. It too has large game reserves and a tropical coast whose few accessible points, such as **Kosi Bay** and **Lake Sibaya,** are unspoilt. The Tsonga still consider themselves a separate people, though most speak Zulu and are administered by Kwa-Zulu.

Visitors to Zululand should try allow a week at the very least in order to have a look at all three regions; as the distances between those places open to travellers can be great, and the country itself is very beguiling, both for its beauty and for the friendliness of its people. Despite the Zulu reputation for inter-clan violence, fighting is usually contained within groups that have a specific quarrel with each other, and travellers are generally treated with much warmth and respect, particularly in Tsongaland, which is only nominally part of Zululand and largely apolitical.

Flora and Fauna

Zululand's inland section is mostly savannah and bushveld, with a wet, humid summer, and warm, dry winter that becomes parched just before the first rains. The Big Five—elephant, lion, leopard, buffalo and both rhino species—abound in the large Umfolozi and Hlulhuwe Game Reserves, which used to be the Zulu kings' hunting ground in the 19th century. Rarites such as wild dog, spotted hyena and brown hyena also occur, as do most of the antelope and grazing species, which roam in large herds through all the inland reserves. Some of the upland areas have large stretches of temperate hardwood forest, supporting small numbers of shyer game.

The coast is mostly forested with dense, sub-tropical growth. Some big game, such as buffalo, rhino and leopard, still thrives there, as well as plentiful antelope. Hippo and crocodile are found in most of the lakes and rivers. Wild fig trees and wild fruits such as the monkey orange and marula tree feed a host of colourful songbirds, while forest raptors such as fish and crowned eagle are common.

The dense forest of Tsongaland is still home to elephant, most of which now inhabit the new Tembe Game Reserve. At nearby Ndumo Game Reserve, rhino, hippo and crocodile make up the bigger game, and at Kosi Bay and Lake Sibaya, sea turtles crawl onto the beaches to lay their eggs on summer nights. The coast has some rare birds, such as Pel's fishing owl and the vegetarian palm nut vulture, while inland Tsongaland has spectacular birdlife, especially at Ndumo, where rollers, nicators, bee eaters and sunbirds attract serious bird-watchers from all over the world.

The Zulu People

Much has been written of the Zulu people. Their military tradition and apparent national solidarity have held a fascination for academics, historians, and the generally curious public throughout the world, and their fiercely independent character has changed little over the years, becoming if anything more consolidated under South Africa's oppressive white regime. Today, despite, a recent rise in ANC support within Zululand, the reigning monarch (King Goodwill X) and the local chiefs still inspire great respect and obedience through much of Zululand—evident even among those living away from Zululand in the big cities, where support of the Inkatha Freedom Party (IFP), the Zulu political party under the leadership of Dr Mangosotho Buthelezi is almost as strong as within Zululand itself.

Most rural families still live in the traditional round, woven-grass hut or, in drier areas, clay rondavels. Cattle represent wealth and are given as payment (*lobola*) for a bride. Although clinics now operate throughout Zululand, *sangomas*, or witch doctors, still tend to the medical and spiritual needs of most rural Zulus and it is not uncommon to see their distinctive braids and inflated animal bladders (a sign of office), even in the larger towns.

Having said this, the Zulu are anything but 'backward' (although there are people in some of the remoter parts of Zululand who have never seen a white person), despite their tragic tendency to inter-clan feuding which today manifests itself most violently in the bloody clashes between ANC and IFP in the townships around Durban and Pietermaritzburg. Under Mangosotho Buthelezi, Kwa-Zulu has been welded into what is probably the most powerful single ethnic minority in South Africa.

History

Until about 1820 the Zulu were an insignificant clan in a large confederation of cattle-herding Nguni-speaking peoples who, through the 18th century, had traded ivory and slaves with the Dutch and English at Port Natal (modern Durban) and the Portuguese and English at Delogoa Bay (modern Maputo). Amongst these clans the Ndwandwe and the Mthethwe (*see* 'Natal History') competed for dominance, organizing their young men into permanent regiments (known as *amabutho*) and raiding, first within present-day Zululand, then further afield. By plundering smaller clans the Mthethwe and Ndwandwe could provide supplies for their soldiers while at the same time augmenting their number with captives. By 1800 the two clans were intermittently at war, with most young men of the small Zulu clan levied to fight for the Mthethwe, under chief Dingiswayo.

Chief of the Zulu at this time was Sezangakhona who, in his youth, had made pregnant a girl from the neighbouring Langeni clan—an unhappy accident; Nguni youths and maidens were encouraged in non-penetrative sex-play before marriage, involving friction between the girl's legs. But to impregnate a girl before her marriage was to strip her of status, cutting the bride-price, and bringing scandal to her clan.

The girl's name was Nandi, meaning 'sweet'. According to the oral tradition, Nandi began to swell a few months after her encounter with Sezangakhona. An accusation of paternity was duly sent but the Zulus denied it, claiming that the swelling was caused by a parasite, called *ishaka*. But a child was born and, with ironic jest, Nandi called him Shaka. Mother and baby were dumped at the small Zulu capital, where Nandi was given a menial domestic position, though she was still kept as a concubine by Sezangakhona.

The various accounts of Shaka's childhood all agree that he was persecuted by the Zulus. In his book *Chaka* (an alternative spelling of the name), Thomas Mofolo, himself a Zulu, relates how the young Shaka was victimized, even in his sleep:

> *Twice or three times, Chaka had his hands tied right there in the young people's hut, and was made to sleep outside near the door tied up like that, so that the hyena should see him as soon as it came. This would be done when a hyena was seen near the village, and it was expected that it would catch some people after dark. But on those occasions, the hyena would feast on goats and leave the people alone. Chaka's growing-up was truly painful.*

Shaka and Nandi were finally banished from the Zulu village after Shaka was accused of allowing a sheep to die while in his care. They went back to the Langeni clan. But again, Shaka was persecuted. After some years, when Shaka was in his late teens, a severe drought forced mother and son to forage abroad again, and they eventually wandered to the main village of the Mthethwe clan.

Shaka was conscripted into the army and proved an heroic and ferocious soldier on Chief Dingiswayo's raiding campaigns. Tradition has it that at around this time he invented a short stabbing spear for personal use in combat against champions of opposing clans, which was later adopted by the whole Mthethwe army. (The spear made battles bloodier, more hand-to-hand and more decisive; larger numbers of the enemy could be killed than by the traditional light throwing spear.) Dingiswayo rapidly promoted the young fighter, and Shaka took advantage of his growing influence to perfect a new fighting strategy, known as the 'horns of the bull', in which the enemy was attacked in a pincer movement, surrounded and destroyed.

In 1818, news came to Shaka (now a general) of his father's death and Dingiswayo gave him permission to claim the Zulu chieftaincy. Shaka duly killed his rivals and assumed both the chieftaincy and command of the Zulu and Langeni regiments of the Mthethwe army. Shaka reorganized the men into four regiments divided by age. His idea was that the youngest should remain bachelors until they had proved themselves on campaign, the incentive of acquiring a wife making them fight harder. After marriage they would join a veteran's regiment of experienced warriors who, as they aged, would move to the two older regiments, there to provide back up and carry out specialized tasks. In this way no able-bodied man, young or old, would ever be out of the army.

Shaka now made his own bid for power. In the 1819 Ndwandwe invasion of Mthethwe territory, Shaka ignored Dingiswayo's call to arms, stood by as his patron was defeated and killed, and then stepped in to assume command of the broken Mthethwe army. The following year, Shaka ejected the Ndwandwe, defeated them while on retreat and became the undisputed master of modern Zululand.

From this point on Shaka never let up campaigning, as far afield as modern Natal, Transkei, Swaziland and even the Eastern and Northern Transvaal, hundreds of miles to the north. His own clan, the Zulu, replaced the Mthethwe as dominant, and absorbed it, swelling the Zulu clan. Shaka's incessant wars caused many small clans to flee Natal into Transkei or over the Drakensberg to the highveld, both areas that were themselves undergoing their own political upheavals at the time (*see* 'Ndebele' and **Lesotho** 'History'). Some of these refugee clans, like the Bele, were so reduced by this cycle of warfare and famine that they turned to cannibalism; others, like the Ngwane and Mfengu, merely wandered until absorbed into other, larger clans (*see* 'Transkei' and **Swaziland** 'History'), while still others, like the Hlubi, managed to dodge the disturbances and to return eventually to Natal long after Shaka's death (*see* 'Drakensberg History'). The whole process , combined with its parallel upheavals on the highveld, became known to historians as the *Mfecane* (the Zulu word for 'crushing') and caused widespread dislocation of the peoples of southern Natal—the reason why the Voortrekkers of the 1830s claimed to have found large tracts of it apparently empty.

Shaka built himself two great capitals: the first, *Bulawayo* ('place of killing'), was just east of the modern town of Empangeni. After a few years, he moved to the Natal North Coast, building a large capital called *Dakuza* ('labyrinth') near the modern town of Stanger. Traditional histories depict Shaka as a bloody tyrant; mass execcutions, the impaling of defeated warriors and 'smellings-out' (execcution on suspicion of witchcraft) have been cited as regular atrocities. But recent historical opinion tends to dismiss these stories as fiction. What is clear is that Shaka was an able ruler who united the shattered fragments of Natal's Nguni clans, organized his army into mining for iron ore and, more importantly, reopened the trading station at Port Natal (abandoned during the Mthethwe/Ndwandwe wars) through the maverick British traders Henry Francis Fynn and James King (*see* 'Natal History').

Shaka was eventually assassinated by two of his half-brothers, one of whom, Dingane, took the Zulu throne. Dingane carried on the raiding campaigns but pursued a placatory foreign policy with the British in Pondoland, and even communicated with Cape Town via the traders at Port Natal. The resulting white interest in his domain was to prove Dingane'sdownfall. The first trouble came in 1838 when a large Voortrekker party, under Piet Retief and Gert Maritz, crossed the Drakensberg. Dingane, rightly fearing that this might lead to a general occupation, decided to get rid of the Boers. He invited Retief and Maritz to his capital to discuss land grants but had them and their party killed before sending his warriors to wipe out the two wagon-trains waiting on the south side of the Tugela, at a place now called Weenen ('the place of weeping'). But a few months later the Boers rallied under a new leader, Andries Pretorius and lured the Zulu into frontally attacking a defensive *laager* (corral) of wagons. The charging *impis* (regiments) were felled by the Boers' guns before their spears could get to work. The nearby river run red with the blood of thousands of Zulus, and the encounter was thereafter known as Blood River (*see* 'Northwest Natal'). Not a single Boer died in the engagement, which the Voortrekkers regarded as proof of divine intervention. Until 1994 they observed the day of Blood River in a thanksgiving cermony and public holiday the Day of the Vow—celebrated each year in the monolithic Voortrekker monument in Pretoria. Since the 1994 elections, the Day of the Vow has been abolished, but the holiday kept, with the new name of the 'Day of Reconciliation'.

Dingane was forced to acknowledge southern Natal as the new Boer Republic and drew his boundary at the Tugela River. The Boers then approached Dingane'sbrother Mpande, and offered to help him usurp the throne in return for a guarantee of peace. So Dingane was attacked from within his own kingdom, driven north, and killed on the border with Swaziland. The Boers did not keep their new republic long; the British annexed Natal in 1842 after a two-year campaign (*see* 'Natal History'). The Zulus had lost half their kingdom but under their new king, the peace-loving Mpande, there was no further trouble with the white settlers for over 30 years.

However, in the 1870s, the Natal authorities determined to force an annexation of Zululand. Mpande had died, and his son, Cetshwayo, his successor, made no attempt to disguise his dislike of the British (though he regarded them as a lesser evil than the Boers). He tolerated, but longed to cleanse his country of, the missionaries that Mpande had allowed to settle, rightly thinking that the new religion eroded Zulu culture and belittled the people by criticizing their customs and forcing them to wear cheap European clothes. Cetshwayo was restrained by his advisors (one of whom was an English adventurer called John Dunn) and he continually asserted to the Natal authorities that he had no desire for war or quarrel with the British

But nobody could prevent Cetshwayo from raiding the non-Zulu clans placed by the British along his southern border and by the early 1870s he had accumulated an unfair record of 'hostile' action against these British subjects. Nevertheless, despite the Natal authorities' avid desire for war, the British government only agreed to send troops in 1878, after being perusaded by colonial administrators such as Sir Bartle Frere and Theophilus Shepstone that an annexation of Zululand would both secure Natal from a 'native' threat and move British troops closer to the coveted Boer South African Republic (SAR) of the Transvaal. Troops were moved to the Zululand frontier in October 1878 and Cetshwayo was presented with a trumped-up 'Ultimatum' demanding that (among other impossible things) the entire Zulu army be disbanded within 20 days. This Cetshwayo could not do, with hostile neighbours to the north and west, and even had he been willing, the time given was insufficient. British troops crossed the Tugela and the Anglo-Zulu War had begun.

The Zulu War

The invasion of Zululand cost the British dear. The British general, Lord Chelmsford, vastly underestimated Cetshwayo's military might and, for the first few months, the Zulu won every engagement. The British failures culminated in the historic defeat of 22 January

1879, when Chelmsford and his adjutant, Colonel Glyn, rode out with a column of several thousand to scout enemy positions, leaving about 1500 British and 'native' auxilliaries encamped in the open under a lone hill called **Isandhlwana**. Unbeknownst to Chelmsford, on the previous day over 20,000 Zulu had quietly moved into position just to the north, and were watching every British move. Once Chelmsford and his troops had ridden out of sight, a small Zulu force ranged itself on the ridge above the British camp.

A company despatched to drive off these Zulu discovered the huge army behind the ridge. For the Zulus, attack was now imperative and, as the British scouts galloped back, the officer-in-charge, Colonel Pulleine, saw the *impis* massing on the ridge. He and his second-in-command, Colonel Durnford, organized the troops and repelled this first attack but, with no pallisades or entrenchments, the camp was hopelessly vulnerable.

In mid-afternoon the entire Zulu army poured over the ridge and engulfed the camp in the classic 'horns of the bull' pincer movement. Despite organized fire the British were over-whelmed and only a few managed to escape the slaughter, galloping full tilt for the British military hospital at Rorke's Drift, just over the Natal border 10km to the south. Cetshwayo had instructed his army not to go cross into Natal but 4000 Zulu troops disobeyed, pursuing the fleeing British and attacking Rorke's Drift. The 150 or so defenders, many of them badly wounded, managed to repulse the now tired warriors with sustained rifle fire and the *impis* retired, having lost about 500 men.

Isandhlwana claimed the lives of over 1200 British and auxilliary troops, including commanding officers, with roughly the same number of Zulu fallen. The largest single military defeat of the British colonial forces (excluding the battle of the Indian Mutiny), Isandhlwana and Rorke's Drift have inspired two feature films—*Zulu Dawn* and *Zulu*, both of which give romanticized but reasonably accurate accounts of the slaughters.

It took the British some months to turn the tide, leaving the main army holed up in the Norwegian mission station near the modern town of Eshowe, while the Zulus laid siege from the surrounding forest. Massive re-inforcements were brought up from the Cape, but unfortunately for Chelmsford, the embarrassment of the Isandhlwana defeat was com-pounded by the later loss of the young Louis Napoleon—the French Prince Imperial, heir to the throne, and great-nephew of the great Bonaparte himself—who blundered into a Zulu ambush with his escort while on his way to join the army at Eshowe. Young Louis was officially under the protection of the British Crown and his death ensured both Chelmsford's full military disgrace and a full deployment of modern military technology against Cetshwayo.

The main Zulu army was finally caught in the open at Cetshwayo's capital of Ulundi (the regional capital of modern Zululand) and Lord Chelmsford, now under the shadow of a shameful recall, unleashed a merciless artillery barrage. Cetshwayo was deposed and Zululand's most powerful chiefs put on the British Government payroll, relying on the divide-and-rule principle to keep the Zulus down. The policy worked too well—Zululand promptly sank into a series of civil wars (which continued even after Cetshwayo was re-instated in 1883) from which the region has never fully recovered: many say that the endless clan warfare still afflicting the Zulu nation has its roots in this time.

The Zulus staged a last, ill-fated rising in the early 1900s, which was put down with brutal reprisals. The various white governments consistently failed to lure Zulu men to Natal to work; they understandably scorned to labour on farms (regarded as women's work), and took off in force to work in the Transvaal gold mines through the early 20th century, establishing a Zulu majority among mineworkers on the Reef that persists today.

Even under apartheid, Zululand cut a largely independent path. The largest noticeable change in the region has been the passing of direct political power from the monarchy (under King Goodwill X) to the chiefs under Mangosotho Buthelezi, leader of the Inkatha Freedom Party (IFP). Meanwhile, the ANC has claimed many Zulu converts in southern Natal, exacerbating the traditional feuding with frequent clashes between IFP and ANC supporters. This may creep up into the Zulu heartland before long. But then, feuding and abrupt power shifts have always been a feature of Zulu political life and have yet to diminish the nation's overall cohesion.

Inland Zululand: The Umfolozi and Hluluwe Game Reserves

The Umfolozi and Hluluwe reserves back onto each other to form a vast swathe of wild country north of Mtubatuba in central Zululand. This is often the first spot travellers head to, and with good reason. The combined area exceeds 80,000ha and the terrain varies from savannah plains to riverine forest and broken hills, supporting lion, cheetah, leopard, buffalo, wild dog, white and black rhino, elephant, giraffe, hyena, wildebeest, hartebeest, zebra, and almost all the South African antelope species. Birds amount to almost 500 species, including colourful trogons, louries, sunbirds, hornbills and some of the more spectacular raptors, such as bataleur eagle and chanting goshawk, as well as vultures. Both reserves were proclaimed in 1897 to protect what had once been the hunting preserves of the Zulu kings, and into which white ivory hunters poured after the Zulu War.

Umfolozi has a **five day guided bush hiking trail** into deep wild country, one of the best bush experiences available in South Africa. Otherwise there are game viewing roads. Umfolozi and Hluhluwe are popular, so it is important to book if you want to stay overnight (*see* 'Where to Stay'). Also, be aware that both reserves' rivers carry bilharzia.

Ubizane Game Ranch is a private reserve about 7km northeast of Hluhluwe (accesible from the N2). Apart from white rhino, this bushveld reserve mostly harbours antelope (though leopard and hyena pass through). However, there are walking trails and horses to ride.

Mkuzi Game Reserve lies in the far north of Zululand, where it borders Tongaland. The Lebombo Mountain escarpment rises above the small town of Mkuze, dominating the 35,000ha reserve. A particularly prominent lofty white cliff—*Tshaneni*, or Ghost Mountain was the burial place of the Ndwandwe chiefs before they were absorbed into the Zulu tribe in the mid-19th century. The mountain is said to be haunted, and strange lights are sometimes seen on it. The reserve is about 10km down a roughish dirt road from Mkuze. Famous for its large rhino population (both black and white), Mkuzi also harbours hippo and crocodile, giraffe, zebra, blue wildebeest and almost all the South African antelope. Nyala are particularly common. Much of the reserve is thick bush, with many light-coloured fever trees, but there is also a large forest of wild fig trees—spectacular things the size of small buildings. There are also bird-watching hides—the reserve surrounds the Mkuze River and a large lake, and waterfowl are much in evidence, including Egyptian geese, pelican, gallinules (like colourful moorhens) and jacanas (also like colourful moorhens), a variety of herons, fish eagles, bright red bishop birds and storks. Among a number of wilderness trails is a five-day guided hike that takes you very close to rhino.

Ntendeka Wilderness Area is west of Mkuze, on the R618 to Vryheid. This forest (about 5000ha) of dense, subtropical hardwoods, giant ferns and trees in excess of 30m makes a surreal backdrop. There are walking trails and it is worth doing at least two of the day-hikes through this fabulous forest. It was here that Cetshwayo hid from the British after his defeat at Ulundi, and it is easy to see why. Not only is the forest dense, but there are steep ravines and cliffs pockmarked with caves and hidden by hanging forest. Bushbuck, duiker, bushpig, leopard and baboon live in here, as do some of the more spectacular forest birds, like trogons, the rare purple-crested lourie and iridescent sunbirds, which look like winged jewels. Monkeys and baboons live among the cliffs.

The Zulu Heartland: Battlefields and Villages

The most scenic way into Zululand is the R33 from Pietermaritzburg, via Greytown. This is an area known for clan fighting (read the Msinga chapter of *My Traitor's Heart* by Rian Malan—*see* 'Further Reading'), but the traveller need not worry. High mountain, arid, aloe-covered slopes, spectacular patterns of soil erosion from overgrazing, and thick thornveld characterize this southern region of inland Zululand, which begins at **Keate's Drift** on the Mooi River, about 30km north of Greytown. Keate's Drift is little more than a single-lane bridge across the river, plus a few shacks and a permanent market where Zulu women sell fruit, vegetables and cloths, and some of the best beadwork and pottery you can buy in South Africa. You will be expected to bargain. Here and at Tugela Ferry, another single-lane bridge and market 15km north on the Tugela River, visitors should see Zulu women wearing the traditional headdress or isicolo, a large, fan-like affair with a beaded browband. Some young women still go bare-breasted (indicating that they are unmarried), though this is becoming less common. Remember to ask before photographing anyone, and will normally be expected to pay R2 to R5 for the pleasure.

Pomeroy, a small town 25km to the north, is little more than a dusty street of falling-down houses and an old fort left from the Zulu War. However, on Thursdays there is another regional market here that is known for pottery. After Pomeroy, the road leads through the small farming hamlet of Helpmekaar where you can turn east on dirt road to **Rorke's Drift**, the second of the Zulu War battlefields.

Tourist information: Guides can be hired locally for detailed tours of Isandhlwana, Rorke's Drift and the other Natal/Zululand battlefields (*see* 'Activities').

From a makeshift military hospital inside the small fort at Rorke's Drift, protected only by a breast-high stone wall, 100 British soldiers, many of them badly wounded, held two Zulu regiments at bay after the towering Zulu victory earlier on in the day—22 January 1879—at Isandhlwana. More Victoria Crosses were handed out to the soldiers of Rorke's Drift than to those any other battle since. The fort is now a museum (*open daily 9–5*) with the story told from both perspectives.

Northeast of Rorke's Drift, via the same dirt road back to the tarred R68 then along another dirt road, is the battlefield of **Isandhlwana** scene of the disastrous confrontation between the British and the Zulus earlier on the day of Rorke's Drift. Both sides lost over 1000 men in the engagement, the biggest single loss of British Empire troops in one go, bar the Indian Mutiny. The defeat was a disgrace for Britain; as one surviving officer said, 'There will be a frightful row about this back home'. In an attempt to offset the disaster of Isandhlwana, the Victorians celebrated (and romanticized) the deaths of Lieutenants N. Coghill and T. Melville, two officers killed trying to carry the colours of the 24th Regiment to safety across the Buffalo River, at a place now called Fugitive's Drift. Scattered all over the landscape are hundreds of white-painted cairns marking the exact spots where men fell and where they lay unburied for several months.

From near Isandhlwana a dirt road leads 110km south through hilly country of Zulu villages and past a high mountain overlooking the small town of **Kranskop**. Zulu tradition has it that a siren lived on the mountain who lured travellers into a cave with her song, never to let them out again. The mountain dominates the Tugela Gorge, which in summer is a thundering torrent where some of the world's best white-water rafting happens.

Southeast of the Zulu War battlefields, is the old heart of Zululand, where the kings Shaka, Dingane and Cetshwayo had their main royal kraals, and where the graves of Piet Retief and some of his party may be found.

To reach them from Isandhlwana head southeast along the R68 through mixed hill, grassland and thornveld, to the site of **Dingane'sKraal**, the site where he ordered the killings of the Voortrekker leaders Gert Maritz and Piet Reitief (and their party) in 1838—the act that led to the Boers' defeat of Dingane'sarmy at Blood River later that year, and to Dingane'sdeposition at the hands of the Boer's and his own half-brother, Mpande, who took the Zulu throne and allowed the boers to settle natal (*see* 'Natal History').

From Dingane'sKraal, the R68 leads southeast to the little trading village of **Melmoth**, from which you can either go north on the R34 and R66 (continue past the R66 turnoff to pass Piet Retief's grave, which is marked on the road maps) to **Ulundi**, or head southeast towards Empangeni and the coast (*see* below). Ulundi is where the British destroyed Cetshwayo's Zulu army with artillery, and has lately been developed into a small town housing the administrative offices for Kwa-Zulu. At **Ondini**, just east of Ulundi, is a reconstruction of King Cetshwayo's kraal and a Zulu cultural museum with Zulu-designed displays (*open Mon–Fri 9.30–5*).

Southeast through forest from Melmoth, the road forks again. The south fork leads past Shaka's first great capital—**Bulawayo**, (meaning 'the place of killing') now a short distance from a small Zulu theme village and hotel called **Shakaland**. Despite the terrible name, it is a good place to stop for a drink and look around. The site of the film set for the visually spectacular but historically dubious TV series *Shaka Zulu*, the place looks out over the wide Tugela Valley and there are 'witch doctors' and people in traditional dress. Although the recreation is shamelessly artificial, and not as culturally accurate as the Zulu museum of Ondini, the place is nonetheless very attractive, and provides employment for many people in the area.

Continue along the R68, and you come to **Eshowe**, where Cetshwayo established his first capital (1860) and where the British army was beseiged by the Zulus after the defeat at Isandhlwana in 1879 (they took refuge in the Norwegian mission station that Cetshwayo had allowed to be built before the war). Sitting on a high ridge, Eshowe is pleasantly temperate after the heat of much of Zululand, and it has a remarkable feature—a forest in the middle of town. **Dhlinza State Forest** is an indigenous hardwood stand of about 220ha, harbouring bushbuck, bushpig, duiker, monkeys and a variety of birds. There are two shady walking trails under the great, silent trees. **Entumeni Nature Reserve**, a forest surrounded by sugar-cane fields, lies about 15km from town on a dirt road. It too has great hardwood trees harbouring game. At 400ha it is twice the size of Dhlinza.

These reserves are all that survive of a much larger forest that once covered the whole surrounding area, but was felled in the late 19th century to make way for sugar-cane fields. It was in these forests that the Zulus hid while besieging the fortified Norwegian mission station at Eshowe. **Eshowe Fort** is now a museum (*open Mon–Sat, 9–4.30*). More interesting than its history of the Zulu War is the story of John Dunn, an English privateer who established himself as an advisor to Cetshwayo before the war (*see* 'Zululand History'). He quickly changed sides once British troops invaded and was later re-instated by the British as one of the 13 chiefs left to govern (or rather feud over) Zululand after Cetshwayo's deposition.

East of Eshowe, before reaching the Zululand coast via the large agricultural town of Empangeni, the R68 leads past **Ocean View Game Park**, a private park of only 50ha where reedbuck, kudu, impala, wildebeest and other antelope graze. There are guided walks around, offering good opportunities for photographing animals that are very used to people. The park has no accommodation.

The Zululand Coast

North from the village of Tugela Mouth to Sodwana Bay (where the Tongaland Coast begins) is a protected strip of wild, tropical beach, coastal jungle and freshwater lake systems, accessible by several large nature reserves.

The **Harold Johnson Nature Reserve** on the south bank of the Tugela estuary is a good place to break the journey if heading north on the N2. This riverine forest reserve is small but has lovely walking trails. One, the 2km **Rituals and Remedy Trail**, passes some 30 numbered trees and bushes; an accompanying handbook details the medicinal and ritual uses of each plant. The reserve also has the Ultimatum Tree, a huge fig under which (in 1879) the Natal authorities informed Cetshwayo of their intention to launch the Zulu War, unless he allowed them to annex his kingdom as a British territory. Impala, bushbuck, bushpig, duiker and vervet monkey live in the reserve.

Umlalazi Nature Reserve, on the other side of the Tugela mouth from Stanger and the Harold Johnson Reserve, marks the first point accessible to visitors on the southern Zululand coast. There are walking trails through mangrove swamp and coastal forest, and rowing boats for hire. However, be wary of crocodiles near the banks and do not swim, even near the mouth, where there are sometimes sharks. Umlalazi is peaceful in the week, but tends to be invaded by Durban fishermen and water-skiers at weekends. There are log cabins hidden in the bush and a small camp site.

Empangeni and **Richards Bay** are two large towns between Tugela Mouth and St Lucia. Richards Bay, an industrial port, is strangely out of place on this wild coastline and rather depressing to visit. Empangeni is further inland and, as the N2 cuts through its suburbs, is a good place to stock up with petrol and supplies before heading north. The town itself is a regional shopping and administrative centre for eastern Zululand, composed mainly of modern, ugly buildings. However, south of town, at **Gigindlhovu**, is a quiet beach and superb hotel converted from a 19th century sugar baron's mansion (*see* 'Where to Stay'). It was at Gingindlovu that the Zulus staged their only serious attempt to stop the second invasion force that was sent into Zululand to relieve Lord Chelmsford's beleaugured army after Isandhlwana. The battle was the usual story of unequal odds—warriors armed with *assegais* (stabbing spears), shield and wooden mace charging against massed blocks of riflemen. Needless to say the battle was a heavy defeat for the Zulus.

North of Empangeni there is also a pleasant private reserve, **Nyala Game Ranch**, a permanent bushveld camp with walking trails through bush populated mostly by antelope. The ranch is also open to day visitors.

Dukuduku State Forest sits astride of the road between Mtubatuba and St Lucia. The protected area is about 6000ha of jungle-like forest, most of which is impenetrable, but there is a short walking trail from the picnic site (signposted from the road). Dukuduku is home to bushbuck, bushpig, leopard, red and common duiker. The gaboon viper, a highly venomous snake usually found in Central Africa, also occurs here. The gaboon viper scents warm-blooded creatures and camouflages itself into the leaf-mould of the forest floor, so tread carefully.

St Lucia Nature Reserve, a lake system east of Dukuduku, is one of the largest wetlands in southern Africa. Lake St Lucia alone covers almost 13,000ha, including the protected strip of forest and beach around it. Also part of the reserve are the coastal forests running for about 30km up the coast from there the lake meet the sea. Crocodile and hippo cruise

through the entire lake system and there is plentiful game in the forests around. St Lucia is a sub-tropical wilderness of great beauty, and no trip to Zululand is complete without a visit.

However, of the several ways into St Lucia, avoid the main entrance, in the south (east of Dukuduku and Mtubatuba). The Natal Parks Board have allowed a small, glitzy holiday resort to grow up around this entrance, complete with a massive camp site stuffed with Transvaal holiday makers whose greatest love is to drive their 4x4s aimlessly up and down the beach all day. Speed-boats are also popular; in the evenings, when the mullet are running in the lake mouth, people drive up and down at speed, making the fish jump from the water in their hundreds, while someone on deck swings a bat at them. Even the huge crocodiles at the lake mouth retreat to the banks while this goes on.

If you have to go in at the south end, head straight past the camp site up the coast for about 20km to **Cape Vidal**. This much quieter stretch of wild beach and jungle has a small freshwater lake—Lake Bangazi—and an offshore marine reserve of coral reef teeming with tropical sea fish, which provides outstanding snorkelling. Cape Vidal's 12,000ha forest has frequent clearings where antelope, black rhino, kudu and buffalo roam. Reedbuck occur in great density, and there are a few hippo in the marshes. Cape Vidal has log cabins, chalets and a camp site. Trails in the forest include the five-day guided Mkizi Trail from Cape Vidal to St Lucia and back.

St Lucia has two other camps further north, reached from the N2. **Charters Creek** and **Fanies Island** both have a few cottages and a small camp site. Be careful of hippo wandering among the tents at night and crocs on the lakeshore. However, there are safe walking trails, and you can generally hitch a ride on a someone's fishing boat and explore the lake from the water. A three hour boat trip leaves from the main camp every day at noon. It is common sense not to swim anywhere at St Lucia, except on marked beaches. The lake has plentiful hippo and croc, and sometimes sharks near the mouth. Also, the St Lucia wetlands are an ideal breeding ground for mosquitoes, so do not go near unless you have been taking malaria tablets for at least three days prior to arrival.

False Bay Nature Reserve is a separate reserve around the northwest corner of Lake St Lucia and accessible from the N2. Among the great walking here is an overnight trail, a 7km walk and a 10km walk through forest and lakeshore meadow. The reserve has the rare suni antelope—smaller even than the red duiker or grysbok—as well as zebra, nyala, waterbuck, reedbuck, bushbuck and duiker. Fish eagles are common on the lake.

Phinda Private Nature Reserve is a large private game reserve north of St Lucia, just inland from the coast (signposted from the N2), covering a vast area of coastal forest, grass-land and swamp. Home to big game, including lions, Phinda does not take day visitors and is very expensive to stay in, being modelled on the luxury private reserves bordering the Kruger National Park in the Eastern Transvaal. However, the wilderness area is extremely beautiful, and its sub-tropical forests and grasslands are grazed by large herds of game. Apart from lions, big predators—such as leopard and cheetah—inhabit the Phinda bush, and the reserve made itself famous in 1992 by losing one of its guests to a lion that wandered into the luxury camp. However, since then, fences have been erected and the camp is now 100% safe. Game drives and guided walking trails with an armed game scout are features of the reserve, and the accommodation is truly luxurious (*see* 'Where to Stay'). If you have the money, Phinda is one of the most rewarding pieces of wild Zululand that you can visit.

Sodwana Bay is the next accessible point up the Zululand coast, and marks the border between Zululand and Tsongaland. Despite its relative remoteness (from the N2, you have to drive for two hours down a long dirt road through dense sand forest), Sodwana Bay has, sadly, become much like the southern end of St Lucia—a beach playground for 4x4 drivers causing much noise and rutting the sand. The vast camp site has 600 stands. In holiday seasons, this is packed, and the beach is too noisy and crowded to bear. In general it is better to head further north to Kosi Bay Nature Reserve—which is more remote and lacks the crowds (*see* below). However, out of season during the week, Sodwana can be very quiet, and reverts to being a sub-tropical paradise. There is a coral reef offshore, and a diving school can take you out there to swim among the bright-coloured fish and coral (*see* 'Activities'). Sodwana has a state forest attached, with some short walking trails. Bushbuck, red duiker, suni antelope, reedbuck, bushpig and steenbok live under the trees.

The rare Tsongaland red squirrel is another inhabitant, but is unlikely to be seen. Sodwana Bay has petrol, a permanent Zulu craft market, a shop, log cabins and a private lodge for those who want to be pampered, as well as an enormous camp site.

Tsongaland (Northern Zululand)

The man who does not travel will marry his own sister

Tsonga Proverb

This area of dense forest between the Lebombo mountains in the west and the Indian Ocean in the east and the Mozambique border in the north is the far northeast of Zululand and of the Natal province. The few accessible points are all nature reserves. Although conquered by the Zulus in the 19th century, and for long administered by the Kwa-Zulu government, the Tsonga people of Zululand have only been semi-absorbed into Zulu culture and retain both their own language, and a more relaxed attidude to life—the clan fighting and militarism of the Zulu heartland is almost unknown in Tsongaland. The one tarred road through the territory (from Jozini in the Lebombos to Kosi Bay) passes hundreds of villages, and cattle on the road are a problem—almost all settlement is along the forest fringe next to the road. Unless you have a 4x4 you have to use this road, but it does provide access to three of Tsongaland's four superb nature reserves.

Ndumo, the first, lies between the road and the Mozambique border, 80km from Jozini. The last 14km stretch is sand road and can be heavy going, so go in low gear, but not too slow. Ndumo's 10,000ha is mostly acacia forest with fever trees and wild fig. Black and white rhino, hippo, crocodile, nyala, bushbuck, suni and impala are the most common animals, but Ndumo is known for its birds. Broad-billed rollers, Pel's fishing owl, parrots and some of the colourful tropical species such as nicators and twinspots are just a few. There are guided game walks, game-viewing roads and bird-watching hides at the many pans where the birds tend to gather.

Tembe Elephant Reserve, 30km further down the tar road to Kosi Bay, was set up in the late 1980s to protect one of the last herds of wild Tsongaland elephant, which used to roam freely through the surrounding sand forest of Tsongaland and Mozambique, but which were poached almost to extinction in the 1980s. Because of this Tembe's elephants were more aggressive than usual, and the park was initially tentative about allowing the public in, which they only did as recently as 1993. The elephant now seem to behave themselves with the tourists, although their shyness, combined with the thick forest, can make them difficult to spot.

Apart from the elephants, Tembe has much the same game species as Ndumo, as well as leopard, but lacks the variety of birdlife. At the time of writing there was no accomodation on offer, but plans were afoot to build a camp, and this might be in place. Either ask at the gate or telephone the Kwa-Zulu Parks Board in Ulundi ✆ (0020) and ask for Sihangwana 3, or call the Natal Parks Board in Pietermaritzburg, ✆ (0331) 428 101.

Kosi Bay Nature Reserve is the last stop before the Indian Ocean. The tar gives way to sand about 13km from Kosi Bay. The road forks about 9km along. The signposts are regularly stolen, so bear in mind that the left hand track is good only for 4x4s.

Kosi Bay is not a bay at all, but a series of freshwater lakes surrounded by coastal jungle and open to the sea only at a small mouth where there is a coral reef. The jungle is very beautiful—wild fig trees, monkey orange and clearings of close-cropped greensward grazed at night by hippos. There is a 22km guided day hike on very flat terrain from the camp site at Third Lake down to the Fourth Lake, where a forest of raffia palms makes a natural pillared hall reminiscent of the Moorish Alhambra mosque at Granada in Spain. This forest is home to the palm nut vulture, a rare creature that feed on raffia palm nuts. Pel's fishing owl is another resident, as are crocodiles and hippos in the lakes and bushbuck, duiker, bushpig and samango monkey in the jungle. There is also a short trail near the camp site and a three-day guided trail around the whole lake system (bookable in advance). Kosi Bay teems with fish and fishermen and it is worth hitching a ride with a fishing boat out to First Lake to see the wicker fish-traps still worked by the local Tsonga people, and to have a go on their rods. A boat is the easiest way to reach the mouth (otherwise a hot 15km walk from the camp site) where there is superb snorkelling on the reef.

Lake Sibaya is an even larger freshwater lake system on the coast between Sodwana Bay and Kosi Bay (the largest freshwater lake in South Africa). Accessible only by 4x4, Sibaya is very wild and seldom crowded. Boats are hired out, and there are walking trails, birdwatching hides and fishing with a permit. Hippo and crocodile abound in the lakes, but otherwise there is little large game. Reedbuck are plentiful, but the real attractions are the dense and varied bird population and the peace and quiet.

Shopping

Zululand is famous for its beadwork jewellery, its pottery, basketwork and its coloured cloths. The best places to buy from locals are at the markets at Keate's Drift and Tugela Ferry, Ulundi, Sodwana Bay and sometimes at Mtubatuba. There is also a large Zulu-run curio shop just before Shakaland just off the road between Eshowe and Empangeni (signposted) that sells Zulu crafts.

Activities

Game Viewing: This is the primary tourist activity in Zululand (*see* above for nature reserves, their game and facilities, also 'Where to Stay'). Only Umfolozi, Hluluwe and Phinda have big predators, however. Rhino are found in most reserves, but are densest at Mkuzi. Elephant are also found at Tembe in the north.

Walking: All the above listed reserves have one-day walking trails. Overnight wilderness trails (March to November only) are found at Umfolozi (3 days among big game including lion, cheetah, leopard, buffalo and elephant), St Lucia (2 days—you'll see a lot of hippo), Mkuzi (3 days, good for rhino, nyala and birds), Ndumo (2 days, superb for birds and plains game), and Kosi Bay (3 days through jungle, good for birds and hippo). To book for Umfolozi, St Lucia and Mkuzi, ✆ (0331) 471 961. For Tembe and Kosi Bay, ✆ (0331) 946 696/7/8/9. The five-day guided Mkuzi Trail, ✆ (03592) 1104, leads from Cape Vidal to St Lucia and back.

Riding: The foetid coast is not kind to horses, but in the bushveld at Ubizane Game Ranch, ✆ (03562) 3602, between the N3 and Hlulhuwe Game Reserve, horses can be hired for rides out to view wildlife. Nyala Game Ranch, north of Empangeni, ✆ (0351) 924 095/24543, also has game-viewing rides. Longer riding trips of up to five days are available in the hills of Qwibi, near Melmoth through Jacana Trails, ✆ Pretoria (012) 346 3550/1/2.

Scuba diving: For those without their own equipment, there is a diving school at Sodwana Bay which offers trips on the reef for experienced divers courses for beginners. Courses last about 4 days and start at around R900, including accommodation, instruction and all equipment.

Fishing: Zululand's coast and lakes are full of exotic and big game fish. The problem is, unless you can hitch a ride on a boat and use someone else's tackle, fishing is difficult to arrange. An exception is Zululand Coastal Adventures in Richards Bay, ✆ (0351) 41541/2, which can put travellers in touch with fishing operators.

Canoeing and white water rafting: In summer, the Tugela Gorge in central Zululand becomes a roaring torrent. Rafting and canoeing trips are arranged through Kwa-Zukela River Adventures in Johannesburg, ✆ (011) 463 3167/8 or 706 1079/80, Sunwa Ventures in Durban, ✆ (031) 561 4429, or Felix Unite in Durban, ✆ (031) 304 6806.

Tour groups: Most Zululand reserves are inaccessible without your own transport. Zululand Coastal Adventures in Richard's Bay, ✆ (0351) 41541/2, and Wild Adventure Expeditions in Durban, ✆ (031) 821 409, offer reasonably priced tours into the Zululand reserves. You could also try Overland Safaris, who book their trips from Johannesburg, ✆ (011) 442 8007 or the more expensive is Ingwe Safaris who also book their trips from Johannesburg, ✆ (011) 464 1758.

Battlefields and Historical Sites: Maps of the various sites in Zululand and neighbouring Northwest Natal are given out for free at most Kwa-Zulu/Natal tourist offices. Guides can also be aranged via the tourist offices.

Most visitors to Zululand stay in Parks Board accommodation in the reserves they visit. The majority offer moderately-priced accommodation in chalets or cabins (mostly self-catering, although a few of the larger reserves have restaurants) and a cheaper camp site. The exceptions are the **Umfolozi** and **Hluhluwe** reserves, which have luxury lodges and no camping facilities. **Ubizane Game Ranch** has a choice of moderate self-catering or expensive accommodation, but no camp site. The **Harold Johnson Nature Reserve** and the **Ntendeka Wilderness Area** both have camp sites only. **Tembe Elephant Reserve** and **Ndumo** have cottages but no camping. Some reserves—like Umfolozi, Hluhluwe and Mkuzi—get booked up well in advance, but there are usually cancellations, so it is always worth just turning up. **Kosi Bay Nature Reserve** has a camp site and several beautiful wooden chalets half-hidden in the forest near Third Lake. These must be booked in advance through the Kwa-Zulu or Natal Parks Boards (*see* below), as the reserve is popular and the number of people allowed in at any time deliberately limited.

NB Plans are afoot to bring all the Kwa-Zulu parks under the administration of the Natal Parks Board in Pietermaritzburg, ✆ (0331) 946 696/7/8/9), but this may take some time to effect and until that happens Tembe Elephant Reserve, Kosi Bay Nature Reserve, Ndumo and Lake Sibaya should all be booked through the Kwa-Zulu Parks Board in Ulundi, ✆ (0020) and ask for Sihangwana 3.

However, if you want to break the journey elsewhere, or stay on a private game ranch, here are some pointers:

expensive

Mine Own Country House, at Gigindhlovu, on the coast between Tugela Mouth and Richards Bay, ✆ (0353) 301 262 is a beautiful a sugar estate mansion built in 1927 and similar to a Southern United States plantation manor; white stucco, tall pillars and a convincing neo-Georgian front. The sugar estate still functions. The owner will play the piano in the living room if you ask. The house has extensive tropical gardens, a pool and a tennis court. **Fugitive's Drift Lodge**, at Rorke's Drift, ✆ (0425) 843, stands on the Buffalo river, overlooking the ford where the fleeing survivors of Isandhlwana crossed. The small late-Victorian house has 6 simple, clean, airy rooms lit by gas lamps rather than electricity. The owner is a registered guide to the Zulu War battlefields and has a fund of anecdotes.

Babanango Valley Lodge, ✆ (0358) 350062, is a 1930s farmstead in the Nsubeni River Valley in northern Zululand, off the R68 northwest of Melmoth. Pleasant rooms, delicious home cooking and a pool. The surrounding valley bushveld and hill woodland is open to walking with good birdlife. At the cheaper end of the expensive range, and a convenient place to break a journey across north Zululand (the owner is also a registered guide). **Shakaland**, ✆ (03546) 912, the reconstructed Zulu kraal (the remains of a film-set) lying west of the

Eshowe–Empangeni road, is owned by the Protea hotel chain. Accommodation is in large, traditionally-built Zulu grass huts with very comfortable beds and bathrooms, beautifully constructed and fun to stay in. **Phinda Private Game Reserve**, ✆ (011) 803 8421, lies inland from St Lucia, south of Mkuze. Famous for its luxurious cottages, rich food (much venison on the menu) and big predators, Phinda is at the highest end of the expensive range. If you can afford it, the game viewing is excellent. **Sodwana Bay Lodge** at Sodwana Bay, ✆ (031) 304 5977, organizes diving and game fishing in luxurious log cabins overlooking Lake Shabize, just inland from the bay. Seafood beach braais at night are a speciality.

Ndumo Safari Lodge in Ndumo Game Reserve, Tongaland, ✆ Jo'burg (011) 884 1458, is a luxury tented camp on the Banzi Pan, a good site for bird-watching and regularly visited by game that comes down to drink in the evenings. By night, hippos graze nearby. **Rocktail Bay Lodge**, ✆ Jo'burg (011) 884 1458, is off the dirt road (for 4x4's only, or arrange to be picked up) between Sodwana Bay and Lake Sibaya. Accommodation is in 'Robinson Crusoe' style chalets in the trees. Facilities include a wild beach, reef snorkelling, forest walking and trips to Lake Sibaya.

moderate

Sungwane Game Lodge at Bayala, near Mkuze, ✆ (03562) 1220/2831, has private rondavels around a pool. Venison braais are a speciality, and there is walking in the surrounding private game farm, as well as trips to Mkuzi and Hluhluwe.

Nyala Game Ranch, north of Empangeni, ✆ (0351) 924095/24543, also has rondavels, walking and riding trails into the bush and braais of culled game.

Eating Out

 There are few restaurants in Zululand, apart from in town hotels or in the expensive accommodation listed above, most of which are too remote to visit for just a meal and so cater for guests only. The exception is the small town that has grown around the southern end of Lake St Lucia, which has some small, moderately-priced restaurants;

The **Tropicana** on Main Street, St Lucia, serves Italian and Portuguese seafood fresh from the ocean, as well as standard pasta and pizza dishes. Rather tasteless and plasticky inside, but very good food.

Street Pizza on McKenzie Street, St Lucia, makes good pizzas in a wood-burning oven. The dining room is unpretentious with checked table-cloths and candles.

The **Captain's Cabin**, also on Main Street, St Lucia, serves standard seafood at moderate prices. Very fresh fish and shellfish make up for the nautical decor of nets and stuffed fish.

"Why", said I, "Mrs Joubert, do you accompany the General on all his campaigns?"
"Oh yes", said she. "Piet [Joubert] couldn't get along without me... I have been with him in every battle since Majuba Hill. I shall continue following him around until one or the other of us is killed. "Yes", said the General. "I try to keep mother [Mrs Joubert] at home, but it is useless to try."'

An American journalist interviewing General Joubert (commander-in-chief of the Boer forces in 1899/1900) after the battle of Elandslaagte (extract taken from *Thank God We kept the Flag Flying*— a history of the siege of Ladysmith by Kenneth Griffith).

Between the Drakensberg, Zululand and the Transvaal border is an obscure (though much fought over in the past) strip of Natal that few travellers visit. True, Northwest Natal's principal towns—Ladysmith, Dundee, Glencoe, Newcastle, Utrecht and Vryheid—are all rather ugly, small semi-industrial towns with little architecture to speak of, but the countryside, a beautiful upland of Drakensberg foothills, high grassland, forestry plantations and game reserves, has a lonely, exhilarating sense of space and freedom. Big game still thrives in the superb Itala Game Reserve (one of the largest in the province) and the region's many mountains (in fact, eastern foothills of the Drakensberg) offer some of South Africa's least explored hiking trails.

Unusually for the province, Northwest Natal's white population is historically staunchly Afrikaans, and even declared itself a republic in 1884 following the decisive defeat of a small British army during the First Anglo–Boer War by the Transvaal (SAR) Boers at Majuba Hill, which lies in the west of this region.

Battlefields are two-a-penny in Northwest Natal—one of the most fought over regions of South Africa. Since the first recorded encounter, when Dingane'sZulu *impis* hurled themselves to disaster against the *laagered* wagons and disciplined musketry of Andries Pretorius' Voortrekkers at Blood River in 1838, this part of Natal has witnessed several heavy engagements of the Zulu War of 1879 and many of the pitched battles from the opening months of the Second Anglo–Boer War of 1899, including the bloody British defeat of Spioenkop.

Getting There

By road: Most people enter the area via the north/south N3 highway from Harrismith, Estcourt or Colenso. A more interesting way in is via northern Zululand along the R68 between Empangeni and Vryheid, through high downland, forest and battlefields. Travellers from the Transvaal should head southeast over the Balelesberg via the N11 or R33.

By bus: TransLux, Greyhound and Transtate run buses from Durban and Pieter-maritzburg to Newcastle, Dundee, Vryheid, Glencoe and Utrecht. The number varies from town to town, and can be found in the *Yellow Pages*.

By rail: Daily services between Johannesburg and Durban stop at Harrismith and Estcourt. From Harrismith, infrequent local services connect with the area's main towns. In general it is more convenient to take a bus.

Tour groups: A number of small tour companies offer trips to the smaller towns, nature reserves and battlefields. These can be contacted through the Publicity Offices of the main towns.

Itala Game Reserve

The Itala, reached via the R69 between Vryheid and the N2, is all that survives of the once huge Pongola Game Reserve, declared by Jan Smuts in the 1900s, but subsequently opened up for farmland. This huge bowl beneath an upland amphitheatre remained wild and was finally declared a park in 1973. Crocodiles still swim in the Itala stretch of the Pongola River, and elephant browse the riverine forest. The reserve is known for its large white rhino population, while the denser bush harbours a few shy black rhino, cheetah and leopard as well as spotted and brown hyena. Most of the bushveld antelope species occur, as well as klipspringer on the cliffs of the amphitheatre and the rare red duiker near the river. Wildebeest, tsessebe, zebra and giraffe are common, as are baboons and vervet monkeys. Caracal lynx and honey badger may be seen at evening. The reserve runs excellent guided walks from an hour to five days in length (*see* 'Activities').

Vryheid

Tourist Information

Vryheid Tourist Information, Corner of Mark and High Streets, ✆ (0381) 812 133

Vryheid itself is not an attractive town, but makes a useful stopping point for petrol and supplies if heading to or from Itala or up into the Transvaal and Swaziland. Since its five year stint as capital of the Boer Republic of Vryheid (1884–9), the town has settled into an ugly, though prosperous, minor industrial town. However, of interest to shoppers is the **Knabbelhuisie Craft Centre** on President Street, where Zulu crafts and Boer biscuits, pastries and preserves are sold. There is a small nature reserve on the hills north of town where zebra and various antelope species graze. You can walk where you please, but there is no accommodation.

Blood River, the famous Boer/Zulu battlefield, lies just south of the R33 between Vryheid and Dundee. A life-size bronze wagon laager (64 of them) marks the site (*see* 'Natal History').

Dundee itself is even less attractive than Vryheid, but its position on the R33 makes it unavoidable if heading down towards Ladysmith and the northern Drakensberg. Southwest of Dundee is the **Elandslaagter battlefield**, where in 1899 the British invaders were routed by sniper fire and mown down in flight by the bush-wise Boers.

Talana battlefield also lies near Dundee, on the R68 to Melmoth. It was here, also in 1899, that the British finally broke through the Boer trenchs and artillery of the Tugela Front and penetrated the Transvaal, changing the character of the Second Anglo–Boer War from a conventional one to a drawn-out guerilla fight.

Natal Spa, a small hot springs resort set in the hills just north of Vryheid, has two outdoor pools of about 40°C, horses, tennis and squash courts, a bar and restaurant and moderate to expensively-priced accommodation. It is a bit staid, being mostly used by local Afrikaans farmers and their families, but is a good place for a relaxing plunge before driving on to a game reserve or guest farm.

Ladysmith

Tourist Information

Ladysmith Publicity Office, Murchison Street, ✆ (0361) 22992

Ladysmith is a large agricultural town of interest mainly for its role in the Anglo–Boer War, when it suffered a four-month siege that resulted in several bloody battles as the lumbering British columns tried and repeatedly failed to relieve the town. There is a small museum dedicated to the siege next door to the Publicity Office on Murchison Street (*open Mon–Fri, 8–4, Sat 8–1*).

The Siege of Ladysmith lasted 115 days, from October 1899 to February 1900 and was a classic example of the Boers' lack of experience with conventional warfare. Like the war's other two sieges of British garrisons, Kimberley and Mefeking, Ladysmith was of little strategic value. The Boers were right to try and take the town, lying as it did behind their defensive line at the Tugela River, but the artillery and manpower invested could have been better expended against the main British invasion force south of the Tugela.

As it was, that front held for almost a year and breaking through it cost thousands of British lives. However, once the line had broken, the Boers abandoned most of their heavy artillery and took to the bush where, although they held out for a further two years, they could never win any decisive action, and the British victory, if slow in coming, was assured.

The siege was romanticized by Victorian Britain as an example of British fortitude in the face of overwhelming odds, and its raising was of immense propaganda value. But, as so often with colonial history, the real victims were the many Zulu and Hlubi who acted as messengers and skirmishers for the British (many of whom died) and who bore the brunt of the food and water shortages.

Southwest of Ladysmith on the R74 to Colenso is **Spioenkop**, a classic South African kopje where on 24 January 1900 three hundred British troops on their way to break the seige of Ladysmith died in their trenches at the hands Boer sharpshooters on higher ground. Instead of charging, the poor soldiers were ordered to wait it out, and finally, when so many had been killed as to make an assault impracticable, to retire. A waste of life in true colonial style.

Many of the British defending Spioenkop that day were members of the Kings Liverpool Regiment and the main stand at Liverpool United Football Club's newly-built Anfield stadium was endowed with the name in honour of the dead. Known ever since as 'The Kop', the old terrace has witnessed some of the greatest moments in British football. But it is unlikely that many of the fans who crowd into the Kop every Saturday remember the 300 men who died, crouched and thirsty in the South African heat.

Today, the site of the battlefield has been absorbed into a game park and water-sports resort—**Spioenkop Dam and Nature Reserve**, ✆ (0368) 78. The dam (on the Tugela River) gets crowded at weekends, but the reserve is worth visiting for its white rhino and larger antelope, walking trail and horses. Guided tours of the battlefield are available. Accommodation in self-contained chalets and camping (with ablution block) is available

Northeast of Ladysmith lie **Newcastle**, a bleak coal mining centre, and **Utrecht** a small country town close to the high Balalesberg Mountains. An old frontiersman and hunter called Loxton (great great great uncle of the author) retired to Utrecht in the early 1900s with his wife and two playful lion cubs, Saul and Deborah. When the cubs were half-grown, old man Loxton was visited by an English adventurer, Major Tudor Trevor. Trevor was sitting on Loxton's verandah, when he saw the town's Dutch Reform Church minister walking by. Deborah saw him too, slipped through the garden hedge and followed him. The minister, hearing breathing, turned, saw the young lion and set off up the street, yelling. Deborah loped after him and, with an easy swing of her paw lopped off first one coat tail, then the other. The minister redoubled his pace, just as Saul jumped out of the hedge in front of him and roared. The minister fainted, and Saul sat on top of him, licking his face. Trevor ran to the rescue, kicking Saul, who snarled and tore off a chunk of trouser-leg with a cuff of his paw. It was old Mrs Loxton who saved the situation by driving the young lions off with a sjambok while Trevor and the minister fled to the house. Next day the outraged minister brought a law-suit. Loxton was ordered to destroy the lions, but he and Trevor smuggled them out of town by night, back to the Zululand bushveld, where they set them free.

Utrecht was the headquarters of the British army for a while during the 1879 Zulu War, when Lord Chelmsford was commander-in-chief. The **Chelmsford Nature Reserve**, southwest of town on the N11 carries his name. Another reserve set round a large dam, Chelmsford is known for wildfowl, particularly spurwing and Egyptian geese, which congregate here in large numbers. Nomadic blue cranes often visit the dam on their journeys to and fro across southern Africa. Avoid the reserve at weekends, when large numbers of water-skiers from Newcastle and Utrecht come out to play; on weekdays you are likely to have the veld to yourself. The walking trails may lead you past white rhino, hartebeest, zebra, blesbok and the smaller antelope (duiker and steenbok) which graze the fringes of the dam.

Ncandu Waterfall, on the dirt road to Muller's Pass (on the border with the Transvaal), is a beautiful place to walk in the lower slopes of the Balalesberg mountains, an offshoot spur of high Drakensberg foothills. Horses can also be hired from here.

Along the N11 north of the range are the sites of two fairly minor skirmishes of the Second Anglo–Boer War; **Laingsnek** and **Ingogo** (near Volksrust). **Majuba Hill**, the site of the only battle of the First Anglo–Boer War of 1881 (a major humiliation for the British), is also alongside the N11 just north of the Laings Nek Pass. Majuba Hill is open to the public (i.e. there is a small admission charge) and visitors are given a small booklet to take around a self-guided trail, the gist of which is how foolish the British General Colley was to allow his 400 troops to be driven from the hill and out of the Transvaal by just 150 Boers.

No visitor to Northwest Natal should leave without taking at least a day-hike into the wild **Balelesberg**, which rise in a blue wall northwest of Utrecht and Newcastle. This range is one of the least visited in Natal and its trails are uncrowded. Day and overnight hikes wind through several parts of the range among trails offer waterfalls, protea woods, cycads, secret gorges, baboons, eagles, small antelope, but above all, silence and clean air.

Activities

Walking and hiking: Itala Game Reserve, ✆ Pietermaritzburg (0331) 471 961, runs four one-day trails from March to September, all following circles leading back to the same bush camp, so there is no carrying of heavy packs except for the hike between the camp and the park office. Sightings of large game are guaranteed. Spioenkop and Chelmsford reserves both have self-guided trails with good chances of seeing game. The Balelesberg Mountains, ✆ (0433) 3041, have a series of 2-day trails (accommodation in huts with mattresses, firewood, water and toilet) in the cool heights of this seldom-visited range.

Battlefield tours: Majuba Hill (off the N11 north of Newcastle) has a self-guided walk, as do most of the battlefield sites listed above. Fugitive's Drift Lodge and Babanango Lodge offer qualified guides for the local Zulu War sites and the Boer war ones further afield, with transport laid on (*see* p.417). If you want to follow the battlefields independently, pick up the detailed map of all the sites issued by the Publicity Offices in Northwest Natal's main towns.

Where to Stay

expensive

Ntshondwe Lodge, ✆ Pietermaritzburg (0331) 471 961, is a thatched brick house inside Itala Game Reserve with 6 en suite rooms looking out over forested and boulder-strewn slopes grazed by a variety of game. You have to take your own food, but there is a cook. The lodge also has a sun-deck and pool. Less remote is **Magdelena Game Ranch**, ✆ (0386) 71865, in the uplands near Vryheid, which has a small lodge overlooking a waterfall, as well as a self-contained cottage, a pool, walking, horse-riding, and various species of antelope (including nyala, bushbuck and blesbok) roaming its open hills.

moderate

Itala Game Reserve, ✆ (0331) 471 961, has a variety of self-catering chalets and cottages. It is worth spending at least two nights here to make sure of seeing game in the reserve's thick bush. These are seldom full, and most visitors simply turn up. There is also Natal Parks Board accommodation at **Spioenkop Dam** and at **Chelmsford Nature Reserve**, between Newcastle and Dundee.

The **Penny Farthing,** ✆ (03425) 925, is a country guesthouse in the heart of the Natal battlefields country near Dundee on the R33 to Helpmakaar. The chintzy late 19th-century farmhouse has been in the same family for 150 years. There are antelope on the farm, and walking, fishing, and guided battlefield tours are offered. The farm also has a set of caves that were inhabited by Bele cannibals during the Mfecane upheavals of the 1830s.

cheap

Mambasa Hutted Camp, ✆ (036) 488 1524 or (03682) 1122, is on the banks of the Tugela River down a 2km farm track off the R600 between Spioenkop and Winterton. The traditional Zulu grass dome huts have permanent beds, cooking and ablution facilities and bushveld all around. The camp is managed by an old Zulu man, and there is none of the irritating 'theme park' Zulu culture that so often accompanies this sort of place and local Zulu families go about their daily business regardless of tourists. The camp has two walking trails up into the surrounding wooded hills. Take your own food.

Chichester Bushveld Holidays, ✆ (03841) 41146, 45km east of Itala on the R69, has a basic bush camp (though there is a hot shower) with hiking trails through bushveld inhabited by a healthy antelope population (nyala, kudu, bushbuck etc). Take your own food.

Chelmsford Nature Reserve and **Spioenkop Nature Reserve** both have camp sites. The **Balelesberg Hiking Trail Huts** are all one day's walk into the Balelesberg range behind Utrecht, cost little and have water, toilets and firewood, but you must hike in with your own food.

Lesotho

On the navel of the Boer's domain
...stands an antheap, an eye-catching target,
a goad to the white one slackened in plenty
where he sits like a king down on the plains...

Lesotho, B. Makalo Khaketla's epic poem

The mountain kingdom of Lesotho (pronounced Le-soo-too) sits high above the surrounding plains of South Africa, remote from its great neighbour in altitude, if not in actual distance. From a small, well-populated, arable Lowland plateau—where lies the capital, Maseru—rears the vaster Highland region, whose treeless moors, deep-cut with narrow gorges, culminate in peaks exceeding 3000m. From these spring a host of infant rivers, including the great Orange, which flows away west a thousand miles to the distant Atlantic.

Travellers wise enough to journey into the Highlands find themselves in a world of horsemen, whose sure-footed ponies dance along the rugged trails like goats, their riders wrapped tight in coloured blankets, sitting with the careless ease that comes of a lifetime in the saddle. Lonely villages of stone and thatch sit perched on hillside spurs. The herdboys carry long sticks, hollowed through the middle, which serve as flute or staff or club as need demands. Fierce heat at midday drops to freezing cold by dusk, and the morning frost burns from the thatch in spiral plumes of steam. Lesotho carves its memories deep—of waterfalls and torrents, distant cow-bells and narrow valleys planted with meagre crops, of eagles hunting silent along the cliffs, of high, clean air and the drifting scent of woodsmoke, and the sky framed ahead between the twin crescents of your pony's ears.

Climate

The Lowlands have a hot, rainy summer, and a warm, dry winter, but Lesotho's Highlands are subject to extremes of temperature at all times of year. Rain falls most heavily in summer, usually in the afternoons. Daytime temperatures can be very high, but fall fast when the sun goes down. Winter days are warm with occasional rain and snow, but the temperature drops well below freezing at nights. Waterproofs and good sleeping bags will be required for hiking or horse trekking. Summer rain and winter snow can make some roads impassable, so try to get local information on the state of the roads before you go, particularly to the Highlands.

Flora and Fauna

Despite the wild landscape, Lesotho's game has been largely hunted out, with the exception of the grey rhebok, which for some reason is considered inedible. However, at **Sehlabethebe National Park** in the southeast Highlands, eland, mountain reedbuck, duiker, caracal and leopard still thrive. Bird life is abundant, especially large raptors, which prey on young sheep and goats. Tawny eagles and

Lesotho

50 kms
30 miles

Land over 2000 metres

N

ORANGE
FREE STATE

Oxbow H

Butha Buthe
Moteng
Pass

Hlotse (Leribe)

KWAZULU-
NATAL

Caledon

R26

R26

A1

A1

Drakensberg

MASERU

Maluti Mountains

Highlands
Water
Scheme

Mokhotlong

Rafolatsane

Thaba Bosiu

God Help Me Pass
(Molimo Nthuse)
Government pony
trekking centre

Bokong

4x4

Molumong

Thabana
Ntlenyana

Roma

Molimo
Nthuse

A3

Central Ranges

4x4

A13

4x4

3482

Sani
Pass

Cheche Pass

Thaba
Tseka

Sani Top

Sani Lodge

H

4x4

Sehonghong

Drakensberg

A2

Mafeteng

Malealea

H

Semonkong

H

4x4

Sehlabathebe

4x4

SEHLABATHEBE
NAT. PARK

Thaba Putsoa

Maletsunyane
Waterfall

4x4

A5

Qabane

Cannibal
Caves

Nohana

A4

A13

4x4

Mohale's
Hoek

A5

Quacha's
Nek

Quacha's
Nek

A2

Orange

A4

Quithing
(Moyeni)

EASTERN CAPE

lammergeier vultures are not uncommon sights in the mountains. The rare bald ibis is also widespread in the narrow river valleys.

As for flora, Lesotho has few trees except along rivers and the Lowland roads. Most of the Highlands are covered in high grassland that is vivid green in summer and golden in winter. This barren beauty is not unlike Scotland or the Welsh uplands, but on a far larger scale.

Practical A–Z

currency

Lesotho's own currency, the **maloti**, exchanges 1 to 1 with the rand. Rands are accepted everywhere in Lesotho, but you will often be given change in maloti. Maloti will not be accepted in South Africa, so spend whatever you have before re-crossing the border to South Africa.

language

Sesotho, part of the Sotho/Tswana language group, is the national language, and it is useful to learn the formal greetings and their responses (*see* **Glossary**). However, Lesotho was long a British protectorate and English is widely spoken, even in the remote Highlands. Lesotho's education system has been closely modelled on the British.

safety

Owing to its independent status, Lesotho never suffered apartheid, and has been spared the political violence of South Africa, though there have been a few failed coups in the last two years, and visitors should always consider whether there is any current unrest. The Highlands and rural Lowlands are generally safe for travellers, despite the occasional case of theft. Travellers might be asked for money by strangers, but this is seldom aggressive and a smiling 'no' usually ends the matter. Maseru has some violent crime and mugging, though not as much as most South African cities. It is best not to go alone after dark, although the city is safe by day.

History

Lesotho's history is a remarkable tale of independence sustained in the face of appalling odds, largely because of the tireless energy and statesmanship of the kingdom's founder, Moshoeshoe, Mosheshwe or Moshesh (depending on which of the many sources you read). In the early 1820s Moshoeshoe, a minor chief of a Sotho-speaking clan, fled the chaos of the wars raging across the highveld at that time (*see* **South African History**), and moved his villagers from the plains to the broken country of the Lesotho Lowlands. With a good eye for a defensive spot, he first chose an isolated, flat-topped mountain near modern Butha Buthe, but after narrowly repulsing a fierce attack from the neighbouring Tlokwa (a Tswana clan), Moshoeshoe moved to another, larger mountain overlooking the long, fertile Caledon River valley near modern Maseru. He named the natural fortress Thaba Bosiu ('the mountain of the night'). From there he defended his flocks and people against successive waves of other migrating peoples displaced by the aggressive raiding armies of the Zulu, Ndebele, Rolong Tswana and Pedi, who were ravaging the whole eastern half of modern South Africa. Among the refugee tribes that unsuccessfully attempted Thaba Bosiu in the early days were the Ngwane, Hlubi, and various Tswana clans, all reduced to raiding since the loss of their land. The Sotho chief fought off all advances, gradually attracting a following of warriors who became part of his own BaSotho army. At a time when no part of the highveld or mountains was safe from marauders some sort, and some tribes, like the Bele from Natal, were reduced to becoming cannibals, Thaba Bosiu was a sanctuary.

By 1830 his people numbered around 5000; enough for him to raise an army and begin annexing large areas of the fertile Lesotho Lowlands from the Ngwane, who had settled there after trying to take Thaba Bosiu. Moshoeshoe's warriors won a series of decisive victories that pushed them north towards modern-day Swaziland, where they still live. Following these successes, refugees poured into Moshoeshoe's enlarged kingdom. By 1840, Moshoeshoe was king of about 40,000 people, all calling themselves BaSotho.

As his power base grew, Moshoeshoe found himself having to fight off hostile groups intent on rustling his ever-growing herds and settling the good arable land around the Caledon River that he had taken from the Ngwane. Large armed and mounted war parties of Griqua and Koranna attacked from the west during the 1830s. Moshoshoe also had to repel raids from various Tswana clans, such as the Rolong in the northwest and the Ndebele in the east.

Moshoeshoe managed to trade for guns with the Voortrekkers, who arrived in the region around 1836, and again managed to beat off his attackers, allying with the powerful Taung Tswana who had occupied the country directly north of Thaba Bosiu. Finally able to keep marauders at bay, the BaSotho began producing grain on their fertile river valley. With grain in short supply on the highveld, the Taung/BaSotho state aquired a powerful trading influence and the surrounding states became increasingly dependent on Basutoland for food.

The early 1840s saw several attempts by Boer settlers to invade Moshoeshoe's kingdom, and some applied for client status as a pretext for settling the fertile lowlands. At first Moshoeshoe accepted them, but as more and more clustered into the kindgdom, he became alarmed, fearing they would eventually usurp him.

Fortunately for Moshoeshoe, the British Cape authorities were also unwilling to have a Voortrekker republic in the volatile western highveld; it was too close to the Orange River, the Cape Colony's northern boundary, for comfort. In 1843 Moshoeshoe appealed to Sir George Napier, the Cape's High Commissioner, for help. Napier helped set up two treaties, one ensuring Basutoland's boundary with its Tswana neighbours (1843) and one giving the Boer settlers a deadline by which they had to leave (1845).

The Boers and the Tswana ignored the order, and Moshoeshoe appealed to the Cape again—this time to Sir Harry Smith, the new Governor and High Commissioner. Smith, a military man rather than a statesman (his troops knew him as 'Hurry-along-wackalong-smite'), had, as a general during the Sixth Frontier War, murdered the Gcalaka Xhosa chief Hintsa and illegally annexed large areas of Xhosa land (*see* **Eastern Cape** 'History').

With his usual arrogance, Smith imagined he could settle the highveld conflicts and in 1848 asked Moshoshoe to allow his country to become a British protectorate, with British arms to stave off the Boers and anyone else who might intrude. Moshoeshoe accepted this nominal loss of independence and Smith, against his promise, annexed Basutoland and all the country around it as imperial domain. Smith then bullied the British government into accepting the new territory, which he called the Orange River Sovereignty (ORS).

The Boers deeply resented the British annexation of the surrounding territory and blamed Moshoeshoe for inviting the British in. They duly invaded late in 1847. Moshoeshoe called on Smith, who sent a force which drove them away. Smith himself now started showing interest in settling Basutoland. British land speculators began to appear along the Orange and Caledon River Valley, and approached Moshoeshoe about selling parts of his kingdom, which, they reminded him, was now British territory anyway. Realising that Smith had tricked him, Moshoeshoe drove the speculators away. Smith promptly sent two armies north. But here, Moshoeshoe showed his teeth, defeating both British forces in 1851.

Moshoeshoe knew to expect further trouble from the British, and that it might yet cost him the kingdom. Another force invaded his land in 1852, under the new Governor Sir George Cathcart, and again, Moshoeshoe's large, well-disciplined BaSotho and Taung army drove them away. But the BaSotho king then displayed his masterful statesmanship with a placatory letter to Cathcart, asking to be considered an ally, rather than an enemy of the British. Cathcart was already looking for an excuse to wash his hands of the troublesome kingdom, and this allowed him to do so without losing face. Cathcart 'pacified' the region, re-arranged the boundaries (allowing the Boers to take some of Moshoeshoe's best arable land) and left. The old king kept quiet and let the land go in return for his assured independence.

Moshoeshoe was now almost 70 years old, but still there was no rest for him. With the British withdrawal came a renewed Boer threat. The infant Orange Free State now lay just over his western border. Fortunately, the BaSotho had bought thousands of guns from the Pedi tribe, who had passed through Moshoeshoe's kingdom in the late 1840s. The Free State Boers attacked in 1858 and were driven off. Moshoeshoe again appealed to the British who did little but growl at the Free State Boers, and in 1865 the Boers attacked again in greater numbers, calling thousands of freebooting Afrikaners and British up from the Cape Colony with a promise of rich pickings. The British at the Cape sat by. In desperation, Moshoeshoe appealed to the new colony of Natal for protection, even offering his kingdom for annexation. Meanwhile the Transvaal Boers under Paul Kruger joined the invaders, and the combined army plundered through the lowlands at will. But Moshoeshoe's own army, which matched the Boers in numbers, horses and guns, and trained through the incessant warfare of the previous 30 years, won several battles and kept the Boers from Thaba Bosiu. The Cape Governor finally intervened in 1868 and declared Basutoland to be British territory.

The British allowed the Orange Free State to keep almost all of Moshoeshoe's good arable land, and the BaSotho began to settle in the harsh Highlands, cultivating the river valleys as best they could, but never managing to acheive the prosperity that their lowland grainlands had given them.

Moshoeshoe died in 1870 at Thaba Bosiu, unconquered at the age of 84. Basutoland was never invaded by British settlers, and the Boers threat was now permanently removed. Peace reigned until 1879 when the British, following their massive defeat by the Zulus in the same year, decided that all their black subjects should be prevented from carrying guns. The BaSotho were indignant, as they relied on their guns to defend their country. Rebellion broke out, and a few whites were killed. A British force engaged the rebels at Mafeteng in western Basutoland with little result, and a hurried truce was declared. The BaSotho were now only to register their guns, but most refused. The Cape government had by now spent £3 million for nothing, and appealed to London to take Basutoland directly under Crown rule, which duly happened in 1884.

Basutoland quietened. The BaSotho remained neutral during the Anglo-Boer War, and voted to retain its Crown status when the Union of South Africa was declared in 1910. The territory escaped apartheid, gaining its independence from Britain in 1966 at a time when blacks over the border in South Africa were being oppressed as never before. Lesotho declared itself a constitutional monarchy, with the present King Moshoeshoe II as head of state. Democracy lasted until 1986, when Major General Lekhanya staged a military coup. He was thrown out in 1991, and today Lesotho is run democratically again by Prime Minister Ntsu Mokhele. The king has kept his throne throughout. Politically, Lesotho is one of the most peaceful areas of Southern Africa. Brief fighting did break out between rival factions of the army in January 1994, but soon died down. Modern Lesotho is blessedly free of the civil strife that affects so many areas of its neighbour.

BaSotho Culture

The BaSotho people have a mode of dress that is markedly different from South Africa's other nations. The three most obvious characteristics that set them apart are their brightly-coloured, patterned blankets, worn like togas, their conical straw hats (though these are seen less and less) and their horses. The BaSotho are a passionate horse people, relying on their mounts to take them across the difficult terrain of the Highlands. They have even evolved their own breed, the BaSotho Pony, from mixing Javanese ponies, brought out by the British in the 1900s, with English thoroughbreds and the Boer horses of Dutch descent. These sturdy, elegant beasts are trained to a high standard, and most BaSotho men own several. English thoroughbreds are also kept, even in remote mountain villages, for running at monthly horse races that are a central part of Lesotho's social life.

After horses, the BaSotho value livestock above all. Cattle (and horses) represent wealth. Goats are kept for slaughter, and Angora goats and Merino sheep provide most of the rural cash income from their mohair and wool. These flocks are tended by young shepherd boys in their early teens, who are sent into the hills for a few years before returning to their villages as men to be given land of their own. Shepherd boys live an isolated and independent existence on the highest ridges in summer. Left alone for long periods, their great sport is to rustle each-other's flocks, which often ends in fighting and, occasionally, death. If you hike or ride in the Highlands, you will often come across these boys, usually accompanied by a large dog or pack of dogs, playing music on long sticks hollowed out to make a rudimentary flute (held sideways from the mouth while playing) that also double as a weapon and walking stick.

Despite great military prowess in the 19th century, the BaSotho have not fostered an overtly aggressive warrior cult. Being a mountain people, and never having lost their independence, they are proud and hospitable, and visitors are treated with great courtesy. Villages consist of a number of stone family homesteads clustered around cattle kraals. Village headmen control the land around, and allot grazing and arable acreages as they see fit. However, headmen must refer to the village council before making any decisions, and the process is very formally democratic.

Most young BaSotho men go away to find work in the Rand gold fields for a few years after serving their time as shepherds, and it is generally women who work in the fields. However, recent lay-offs at the South African mines have forced many young men to return home and unemployment is becoming a problem. Overpopulation has also hit the Lowlands, where soil erosion from over-grazing is common. Even the Highlands are more populated than before. It remains to be seen whether this can be curtailed.

BaSotho education tends to be of a high standard, with most children being taught English at primary school, most of which are attached to numerous mission stations scattered throughout the country. Cambridge 'O' and 'A' levels are taught at secondary school, but mostly it is girls who take these, as the boys have usually been sent into the hills by then. Lesotho has a university of international standing at Roma in the Lowlands.

Look out for a white flag flying from a pole outside huts; this means that *joala*, or sorghum beer, is being sold. Green and red flags mean meat and vegetables.

Getting There and Around

You must have a passport to enter Lesotho. All visitors technically require a visa (with the exception of South African, British, Danish and Israeli passport holders), but this is generally not enforced; presenting your passport at a border post should get you a stamp allowing a stay of two weeks or a month.

By car: Most of Lesotho's entry points are in the Lowland region bordering the Orange Free State. All Lowland entry points give access to the A1 and A2 highways, which connect with Maseru and the main Lowlands towns, which in turn give access to the Highlands. There are only two road entry points in the Highlands; Sani Pass, from Natal, and Qacha's Nek, via the Transkei. Both require a 4x4. Of the two, Sani Pass is the safest and most travelled, and has a lodge at the top. Qacha's Nek involves travelling a short distance through the Transkei, which can be dangerous for white travellers.

Most of Lesotho's roads are accessible by car, although in the Highlands progress will be slow. Those roads accessible by 4x4 only are Sani Pass, the Makunyapane–Sehonghong road and the Sehonghong–Sehlabathebe road.

By bus: Transtate run buses to Maseru from Jo'burg and Durban. Buses from both Jo'burg, ✆ (011) 488 1359, and from Durban, ✆ (031) 361 7504, leave 3 times per week. Drakensberg Express, ✆ (033) 710 1017, run small buses from Durban and Pietermaritzburg to Sani Lodge © (03372) 1330 on Sani Pass, from where you can hitch a ride or arrange a lift into Lesotho to Sani Top and Mokhotlong. The journey takes about 4 hours from Durban.

Lesotho has a good internal bus system between the major towns, including the Lowland towns along the A1 and A2 and the Highland towns of Semonkong, Thaba Tseka, Molimo Nthuse and Mokhotlong. The **Maseru Bus Station** is on Main Road South.

By air: Lesotho Airways, © (09266) 312 813, flies from Jo'burg to Maseru.

By rail: There is no rail link from South Africa to Lesotho.

Hitch-hiking: Once on the Highland roads hitch-hiking is easy and fairly safe. You may be asked to pay a small fee towards petrol.

By horse: Horse is the most widespread form of transport in the Highlands. The BaSotho have evolved their own breed of mountain pony and an entire culture around it. Trekking can be arranged from just about any lodge, and through the government's own pony breeding centre on God-Help-Me Pass (*see* 'Activities').

A very good guide book, the **Backpacker's Guide to Lesotho**, written and published by Russell Suchet of Sani Lodge © (03372) 1330 on the Natal side of Sani Pass has the most up-to-date details on public transport (internal and external), where to stay and hiking routes—the author has spent years travelling the country. Published in booklet form, the guide is handy to carry but is not yet widely available, though some South African backpacker's hostels now carry it. Give the author a ring at the above number to find out where you can pick it up.

Maseru

Tourist Information

Lower Kingsway opposite the BaSotho Hat Craft Centre, © (09266) 323760 or 322 896. Do not park your car out front when visiting the tourist information centre. You will return to find it badly washed (i.e. wet), with a young man demanding an exorbitant sum. You will probably have to pay him something to go away, and he may become intimidating.

The capital is a large, bustling, lively town strung out along a central road called the Kingsway. Owing to its easy accessibilty by road from South Africa and its tourist information centre, Maseru is the point from which most travellers begin their exploration of Lesotho. The town started life in 1869 as a British administration post built to keep watch on Thaba Bosiu, Moshoeshoe's mountain fortress and capital which lay just to the east.

Opposite the tourist information is the **Basotho Hat**, a large craft shop that sells the best of the regional crafts, in particular woven rugs and clothes, pottery and jewellery, as well as books on BaSotho culture by Sotho authors. The shop, built in a round and crowned with a thatched roof that resembles the hat that gives it its name, is unmistakable and makes a good rendezvous point.

Next to the BaSotho Hat is a small shopping centre with fast food joints, banks and most of the South African chain stores—a good place to get supplies. West along Kingsway on the same side of the road is the **Post Office** (although you may want to wait to post letters from South Africa, which is quicker) and an open fruit and vegetable market with very good produce at cheap prices. Hold onto your wallet. Opposite the market on Kingsway is a café and restaurant run by Germans called **L'Auberge**. This is another convenient spot for meeting that incidentally serves really good coffee and food in a very continental atmosphere. Go in at lunch time and you will meet young Westerners working in Lesotho, and thereby tap into the local information network.

The Department of Land, Surveys and Physical Planning on Lerothili Road (take the third left off Kingsway after the Post Office, then left again and immediately right) sells very good hiking and road maps with the relief clearly marked. The bus station and taxi rank are on the west end of Kingsway, near the large, Art Deco, Roman Catholic cathedral. The bus station is generally safe, but it is better to be in a group.

Maseru/Lesotho ✆ (09266–) **Where to Stay and Eating Out**

expensive

The **Lancer's Inn Hotel**, ✆ 312114, on Kingsway, near the Post Office, has long been the place for non-tourists to stay. The bar is usually full of businessmen, both BaSotho and South African, and you can meet interesting characters here. The rooms are fairly standard, and all en suite.

More expensive are the **Maseru Sun** and **Lesotho Sun**. Like all the Sun hotels, they are modern, ugly, bland and overpriced, but offer great comfort. The Maseru Sun, ✆ 312 434, is on the road that runs north from the BaSotho Hat Craft Shop. The Lesotho Sun, ✆ 313 111, is set in 100 acres of park on a hilltop at the west end of town.

moderate

Maseru has two comfortable, moderately priced hotels, the **Victoria**, ✆ 312 922, on Kingsway, and the **Lakeside**, off the Main North Road, ✆ 313 646. The Victoria has a pool, bar, restaurant and a disco that is quite lively at weekends. The Lakeside is smaller, also with a pool and restaurant. Both hotels have safe parking.

cheap

The **Anglican Training Centre** off Assisi Road (take the third left off Kingsway after the Post Office, then first right, first left, and left again onto Assisi Road, and look for the sign) has beds in shared rooms. Meals can be arranged and the place is spick and span, but you must turn up before about 7pm to get a room. The **Lesotho Work Camps Association** is behind the cathedral. Go west on Kingsway to the cathedral, then turn onto Main North road until you reach a dirt road that is also a taxi-rank. The Association is down this track. Dormitory accommodation and a small kitchen are offered. Be aware that this area can be rough.

Apart from the hotels, which generally serve reasonable à la carte fare, Maseru's restaurants are fast food places found in the shopping centres along Kingsway. However, **L'Auberge,** on Kingsway, opposite the street market and west of the Post Office, is a good, moderately priced German-run restaurant serving really good French and German dishes and game (in season). There is a formal dining room and a café for light meals. No need to book.

Nightlife

Maseru has several discos along Kingsway that can be fun at weekends, although you will mostly hear western Top 40 and very little African jive. The Victoria Hotel and the Lancer's Inn are safe for foreigners but are known pick-up joints.

South of Maseru

The A2 west of Maseru provides several jumping-off points for the western Highlands, including the A3 to the Government Pony Trekking Centre at God-Help-Me Pass and the A5 to the lodges of the Thaba Putsoa Mountains.

The first major town along the A2 is **Mafeteng,** some 80km south of Maseru. Although Mafeteng is a large town by Lesotho standards, it consists of little bar a few shops for stocking up on supplies and petrol. From Mafeteng, the A2 curves south, around the Thaba Putsoa range to **Mohale's Hoek,** another jumping off point for the Thaba Putsoa lodges, and a rest stop for those on the way round to Qacha's Nek and Sehlabethebe National Park. Signposted from the A2 between Mafeteng and Mohale's Hoek are a set of **Cannibal Caves.** There is little to see, but it sends a shiver down the spine to think that just over a hundred years ago you may have been caught and eaten when travelling along this road.

North of Maseru

The A1 is the main road north, leading eventually to the Maluti Mountains, their lodges, and the remote town of Mokhotlong, deep in the Highlands. On the way, there is one other access point to the mountains; a tarred road leading up to the Lesotho Highlands Water Scheme, but this is a there-and-back road providing no access to the Highlands.

There are several large towns on the A1 north of Maseru. The first is **Hlotse,** also known as Leribe, which is famous for weaving and knitwear, and has two craft centres where you can buy straight from the workshops. The **Leribe Craft Centre,** which sells rugs, table-cloths and shawls beautifully made by disabled women, and **Lesotho Knits,** which sells wool and angora sweaters, are both signposted from the A1.

About 30km north of Hlotse is Butha Buthe, the only town in Lesotho with a reputation for unfriendliness. Whether this is true or not, there is little reason to stop at this small industrial centre, except perhaps for **Lesotho Handknits,** signposted from the A1, which has very good sweaters and scarves in angora and wool.

North of Butha Buthe, the A1 curves west into the Malutis and soon becomes a tortuous climb up the Moteng Pass to Oxbow and the northern Highlands. This pass is demanding on petrol, so fill up at Butha Buthe beforehand.

Riverside Lodge, ✆ (5191) 2681/3173, just outside Maseru, provides a good alternative to staying in the city. The lodge has comfortable thatched rondavels set under large trees, with blesbok grazing nearby, a pool, a good restaurant and a large garden. The **Hotel Mount Maluti,** at Mohale's Hoek, ✆ (09266) 785 224, is at the opposite end of the Lowlands from the Maluti Mountains. But never mind. This fine country hotel, set in gardens, offers hikes and pony treks into the nearby Thaba Putsoa range, albeit on the expensive side of moderate. The quiet **Trading Post Guest House** at Roma, southeast of Maseru on the A5 to Semonkong, ✆ (09266) 340202/340267, has bedrooms in the old house or self-contained rondavels. The management can also arrange riding. The old sandstone **Leribe Hotel,** ✆ (09266) 400362, in the hills just west of Hlotse (Leribe) on the A1 north of Maseru, makes a good rest stop on the way to the northern Highlands. Wisteria climbs around the verandah, there is a tea-garden, and the hotel sits under large trees. Also at the expensive end of the moderate scale.

cheap

The **Farmer's Training Centre** at Mohale's Hoek offers dormitory accommodation for travellers heading south towards Qacha's Nek. **Ha Thabo Ramakatane**, a hostel run by one Mr Ramakatane in a village called **Ha Sechele** about 4km from Butha Buthe, is one of the best places to stay in the Lowlands. With its gas lighting, water from an outside pump, and friendly villagers, it makes a good introduction to Lesotho village life. Ask for directions in Butha Buthe. The last section of road to the hostel is very rough, so drive slowly, or walk.

The Lesotho Highlands

The Lesotho Highlands, the roof of Southern Africa, are the real reason for coming here. The rugged mountain country is divided into three main areas: the Thaba Putsoa Mountains to the south, the Central Ranges, and the Maluti Mountains in the north, all of which converge at the Drakensberg escarpment on the border with Natal. Most of this paradise of high moorland, deep-cut river valleys, soaring peaks and remote villages is inaccessible to vehicles and the BaSotho horse culture is at its strongest. Blanketed horsemen riding through the wild country between stone villages give the landscape a medieval feel.

The few towns have a frontier feel, owing to their remoteness. Most visitors ride in over the mountains, rather than by car or truck, and horses tied up outside shops and bars are the norm. Do remember that even vehicles are likely to be very slow on the rocky Highlands roads, and so short geographical distances can take many hours.

The Lesotho Highlands are one of the few trekking areas in Southern Africa where drinking water is not a problem. As long as there is no human settlement immediately upstream, then water from the mountain streams is not only drinkable, but is probably among the cleanest water in the world. However, it is still advisable to take purification tablets in case you have no choice but to take water from a stream near a village.

The Southern Highlands: Thaba Putsoa Mountains

The southern end of the Highlands is reached via the A2 and A5, and are best explored from the two lodges at the villages of **Malealea** and **Semonkong** (*see* 'Where to Stay'). Semonkong is the more remote, taking four hours up and over a series of spectacular passes along the A5 (mostly dirt road) from Maseru via Roma. The lodge sits in a narrow valley, at the end of a small farming village. Nearby is a deep gorge into which plunges a mighty waterfall of over 200m. This, apparently, is the highest set of falls in Southern Africa, although there is some confusion over whether this means the highest in altitude or in the length of the fall. Either would seem to be plausible.

Horse races are held on the mountain plateau above the lodge on the first weekend of every month. These are great fiestas, with throroughbred horses being ridden for days over the mountains to be raced, dressed in expensive travelling blankets and leg bandages. The young male jockeys risk life and limb to bring their horses in first. A lot of money changes hands at these events, and they offer a glimpse of the robust social life of the Highlands.

The Central Highlands

The Central Highlands are reached via the A3 from Maseru, which becomes dirt after Molimo Nthuse (God-Help-Me Pass), and can only be driven by ordinary car as far as Cheche Pass, 20km further on. However, most visitors will only be going as far as the **BaSotho Pony Project**, or Government Pony Trekking Centre, at God-Help-Me Pass.

The BaSotho Pony Project

This is Lesotho's most widely used pony trekking centre. It was designed, and is still run, by Irish consultants brought in by the government to monitor the breeding of high-class BaSotho ponies. It is worth asking to see some of their impressive stallions, which are used to compete in endurance competitions as well as for breeding.

Treks of one to five days are offered very cheaply—far cheaper than at any of the lodges. Having said that, the standard of pony is much lower here than at the lodges, which hire the best of the local horses. But for inexperienced riders who would nevertheless like to see Lesotho from the saddle, these quiet, rather underfed government horses are ideal. If you can ride, these beasts will prove better trained than they appear and it is worth asking your guide to show you the special BaSotho tricks that put the horses through their gaits. The routes taken by these treks are beautiful indeed, following rivers along precipitate hill-sides, over incredibly steep passes, stopping at waterfalls, and sometimes finding level tracks where you can canter. You will often be passed by BaSotho horsemen, or even whole families on the move, and shy shepherd boys playing their home-made pipes are a common sight. Eagles and vultures cruise the heights. Be prepared to spend about six hours a day in the saddle.

The centre provides a guide and pack mule, but you must supply food and sleeping bags. You will be expected to tip the guide afterwards, usually about R10 per rider. On the overnight trails you will be required to pay an extra R7 per night for accommodation in huts in the remote villages. Treks are supposed to be booked a month in advance, but in fact, just turning up is almost always enough to book a trek of several days, usually beginning the day after your arrival. This is just as well, as the telephone to the centre does not work. To pass the time between booking your trek and setting off, you can either camp at the centre or stay at the hotel just down the pass towards Maseru. This hotel is expensive, but it lacks custom and the price can sometimes be negotiated.

The Northern Highlands: the Maluti Mountains

From the Lowlands, there are two ways up into the Malutis. The first is a there-and-back road from the A1 at Hlotse (Leribe) to the massive dam being constructed by the Lesotho Highlands Water Scheme. This good tarred road makes an easy and spectacular drive, but once up there there is little to do except look at the ambitious Water Scheme which aims to pump water from four huge dams up to Johannesburg via the Vaal River. What effect this will have on the environment is anyone's guess, and the project is, understandably, subject to much controversy among environmentalists and the BaSotho who live in the valleys that are to be flooded.

A more interesting route into the Malutis is along the A1 to Butha Buthe and then up the incredibly steep Moteng Pass to **Oxbow Lodge**, where the tarred road ends. This is more upmarket than the other Highlands lodges, though the rates are still moderate. Oxbow is one of the few places in Southern Africa's mountains that receives enough snow for skiing, and the lodge has a ski-lift in the mountains behind which is usually open between June and July. Oxbow also offers the usual Highlands activities of guided hiking, pony trekking and trout fishing. From Oxbow there is almost no settlement for about 100km (or five hours of driving or bus ride) until the remote town of **Mokhotlong**. Do not attempt this drive after dark, as the road can be treacherous in places, and allow plenty of daylight before starting the journey from Oxbow. Until the 1950s no vehicles could reach Mokhotlong, and even now the road on from there to Sani Top, on the Drakensberg Escarpment, can only be driven in a very tough 4x4. Up here, the horse is king.

The Drakensberg Escarpment

 This, the western edge of Lesotho and the country's highest point, can only be reached by ordinary car at **Sehlabethebe National Park**, near Qacha's Nek on the A4. All other roads require a 4x4. Sehlabethebe is one of the only areas of Lesotho that still harbours a healthy game population. Eland, grey rhebok and mountain reedbuck graze the mountainsides among flowering aloes and forested kloofs. Eagles and vultures are common, as are bald ibis and sugarbirds. Sehlabethebe has several hiking trails, including a 2-day trail out of the park, over the escarpment to Bushman's Nek in Natal. North along the escarpment from Sehlabethebe is **Sani Top**, sitting at the head of Sani Pass, the only direct road access from Lesotho to Natal, which also requiries a 4x4, good legs or a quadruped.

South along the escarpment from Sehlebethebe is **Qacha's Nek**, accessible by ordinary vehicle (in fact, you have to pass through Qacha's Nek to reach Sehlebethebe), and with road access to Natal via a short stretch of Transkei. This has been said to be dangerous for private vehicles (although the author could find no evidence of any attacks on the Transkei side), but is recommended by South African backpackers as being safe for taking black taxis from Lesotho into South Africa. On the tarred section of the A4 between Qacha's Nek and Mohale's Hoek is the town of **Quthing** (also known as Moyeni), a good place to break a journey.

Where to Stay and Eating Out

Readers will note that there are no telephone numbers in this section. Where a number is listed, it will not connect with the lodge, but with a booking office, usually in Maseru or South Africa. This is because most of the Highlands are without telephones. Do not worry; the lodges are rarely full and expect visitors just to turn up.

expensive

The **Oxbow Lodge** at the end of the tarred road over Moteng Pass can arrange riding, hiking, trout fishing, and (in season) skiing. **Semonkong Lodge** is one of Lesotho's best. Friendly, informal, tranquil and well run, it lies next to Semongkong, a remote village in the Thaba Putsoa mountains, near the highest waterfall in Southern Africa. The lodge can arrange hiking and trout fishing, and every month there are horse races on the plateau above the lodge. Attached to the lodge is a pub where visitors can drink and chat to local BaSotho, who tether their horses outside. The bar gets very lively and most of the drinkers must trust to their mounts to take them safely home.

Malealea Lodge is an old trading post in a small oak forest at the foot of the Thaba Putsoa, which dreams away on the close horizon in a sheer wall of orange and gold. So beautiful is this view that the last ridge on the road into Malealea is known as the Gates of Paradise. Malealea can arrange just about anything from pony trekking on good BaSotho ponies to hiking (with pack donkeys) and 4x4 expeditions, all guided, for between an hour and 6 days.

moderate

The three lodges above all have more moderate accommodation. **Oxbow Lodge** does B&B, while **Semonkong** and **Malealea** both have self-catering rondavels. **Selhabathebe Lodge** in Selhabethebe National Park offers very comfortable self-catering accommodation, but must be booked at the office at the park's entrance. The **Mokhotlong Hotel** in Mokhotlong and the **Mountainside Hotel** in Quthing make good rest stops when driving to Sani Pass and Selhabethebe respectively. Both have modest, comfortable rooms with shared bathrooms. The gloomy **Central Hotel** in Qacha's Nek has a few en suite rooms. All three have à la carte restaurants and bars.

cheap

Semongkong Lodge and **Malealea Lodge** both have cheap dormitory and rondavel accommodation for backpackers with bedding available. **Molumong Lodge** (not as you might expect in nearby Molumong village, but in Rafalotsane village, 15km down the Thaba Tseka road), has similar accommodation but you must provide a sleeping bag and food. The **Farmer Training Centre** in Mokhotlong itself offers shared rooms with bedding. Take your own food. **Quthing Merino Stud Farm** has clean, self-catering double rooms on a farm 3km from the town (signposted from the road between Qacha's Nek and Mohale's Hoek). Sehlabethe Lodge has a cheap bunkhouse, and visitors can camp in the mountains. If you arrive late and need to stay overnight before entering the park, the **Range Management Centre** in nearby Sehlabethe village has dormitory accommodation in a clean hostel. Bring your own sleeping bag. It can be worth spending a couple of days here, as there are good walks to local bushman paintings.

Sani Top's **Mountaineer's Chalet** overlooks the magnificent pass and has self-catering accommodation in dormitories and cheap double rooms, with bedding provided. At the foot of Sani pass, on the Natal side, is **Sani Lodge**, a very cheap, very good value, self-catering lodge with either dormitory accommodation or double beds in rondavels in an old trading post that also has access to hiking trails and horses.

The Orange Free State

'We learned to ride, shoot and swim almost as soon as we could walk'

Deneys Reitz describing his Free State childhood
in his Boer War memoir, *Commando*

The Orange Free State, forming a rough oval on its side, plumb in the middle of South Africa, is the province least visited by tourists. Even many South Africans avoid it unless to drive between the Transvaal and the Cape, and certainly its central flat farmlands, northern industrial towns and old-fashioned rural Boer culture are not to everyone's taste. However, the Free State has landscapes that are among the most beautiful in South Africa, as well as several game reserves of great size, some of which support big game, and in which you can walk at will. The mountainous grasslands of the Eastern Highlands, where the Free State borders Lesotho, are heavenly beautiful, blessedly free from tourists, cut through with hiking and riding trails, and small, secluded country inns.

History

The Orange Free State was proclaimed in 1854 by Boers who had gone north with the Great Trek of 1836 to look for settlement away from British rule. The empty highveld grassland, temperate climate, fertile soil and plentiful game made the area highly attractive. Moreover, large tracts of the country (though by no means all) had been temporarily abandoned by fleeing tribes during upheavals that followed the rise of the Zulu empire of the 1820s and the Ndebele and Tswana ravaging of the highveld in the 1830s (a process generally known as the *Mfecane—see* **South African History**). Despite this, the Boers still found plenty of resistance to their settlement from groups living in the area; the BaSotho, under King Moshoeshoe in the east, the Rolong, and Taung Tswana in the drier west, and the Griqua, or free bands of Dutch-speaking 'coloureds', who had migrated into the southern area, near the Orange River, in the late 18th century, to escape the racism of the Cape Colony.

With their firearms, horse and wagons (which could be laagered into a makeshift fort), the Voortrekkers set out to break the Ndebele power in the highveld, inflicting a crippling defeat on them at Vegkop, in the northeast of the region, in 1836, after having been sheltered and provisioned by the Rolong Tswana's chief Moroka.

PRETORIA

JOHANNESBURG

N12

N17

Potchefstroom

NORTHWEST PROVINCE

Orkney

Vaal

Sasolburg

EASTERN TRANSVAAL

R59

Vredefort

BLOEMHOF NAT. RES.

Heilbron

Vrede

Christiana

Hoopstad

SANDVELD NATURE RESERVE

WELKOM

Kroonstad

Lindley

Reitz

Newcastle

Hertzogville

WILLEM PRETORIUS GAME RES.

Bethlehem

Harrismith

MOUNT EVEREST PRIVATE GAME RES.

R708

Senekal

Rooiberg

Clarens

GOLDEN GATE NATIONAL PARK

Van Reenen Pass

SOETDORING NATURE RESERVE

Witteberg

Winburg

Fouriesburg

QWA-QWA

Ladysmith

Modder

Marquard

Rustler's Valley

KWAZULU-NATAL

Petrusburg

BOPHUTHATSWANA

Clocolan

Ficksburg

BLOEMFONTEIN

Thaba Nchu

Ladybrand

MASERU

Maluti Mountains

Drakensberg

MARIA MOROKA NAT. PARK

LESOTHO

CALEDON NAT. RES.

Wepener

N

TUSSEN DIE RIVIERE NATURE RESERVE

Zastron

Bethulie

Rouxville

Land over 1500m

TRANSKEI

80 kms
40 miles

Aliwal North

OVISTON NATURE RESERVE
HENDRIK VERWOERD DAM RESERVE

EASTERN CAPE

443

After Vegkop, there was little to challenge Boer supremacy, and in 1854, the region's Voortrekkers proclaimed the Orange Free State on the central plains around their small capital of Bloemfontein, a settlement that had existed since at least the 1830s.

Ever hungry for land, they soon began to look with envy at the fertile lands around King Moshoeshoe's mountain fortress at Thaba Bosiu near the Caledon river, at the eastern end of the Free State, in modern Lesotho. Moshoeshoe resisted several Boer attempts to dislodge him, even when the Free Staters advertised for adventurers in the Cape Province and attacked with a combined force of burghers and English colonists. Unable to get rid of Moshoeshoe, the Free State burghers then simply began settling in his valleys west of the Caledon. Moshoeshoe appealed to the British for protection (even though the British army had also made three attempts at taking Thaba Bosiu). The Cape Government agreed the present border of the eastern Free State after declaring Moshoeshoe's kingdom (modern Lesotho) a British protectorate. The fertile country west of the Caledon was awarded to the Free State burghers, much to Moshoeshoe's chagrin, and the Free State's eastern high-lands were secured.

But trouble came to the western border in the 1870s after diamonds were found on several farms near the Orange and Vaal Rivers, followed by a large deposit on a farm called Vooruitzicht near present-day Kimberley. The Free State president, Brand, a Boer expansionist, who had led a commando during the Great Trek and organised the attacks against Moshoeshoe in the eastern Free State, claimed the diamond-bearing land for his republic. The British, naturally, did the same. But the land itself was officially outside both the Free State and the Cape Colony, being part of a British protectorate called West Griqualand, whose Griqua ('coloured') people were governed by Nicolaas Waterboer, a fighter who had successfully protected his peoples' land from white settlement for over 20 years. Waterboer employed a land agent called David Arnot, to represent his claim to the diamond land at Cape Town. President Brand, on studying the maps, insisted that the deposits lay clearly within the Orange Free State. But the British surveyor, G. Gilfillan, fiddled with the name of the ranges of hills near the deposits, swapping one name for another, so that the Cape Colony was stretched east by the few kilometres necessary to enclose the diamond-rich farms. This knocked Waterboer out of the game, as he had neither the financial nor the military back-up to challenge the decision. But Brand did not give up, and went to London to protest. Britain dug in its heels and offered the Orange Free State £900,000 in compensation if it let the claims go. President Brand reluctantly complied, and was given 37 well-watered farms, a lump sum of £4000 and a pension of £500 a year. The Orange Free State was not to benefit from the diamond diggings at Kimberley.

Instead, the little republic remained a loose-knit agricultural community of giant sheep farms as the burghers gradually shot out the game in most areas of the plains and intimidated the local Sotho and Tswana-speaking clans into working on the farms. Blacks were not permitted to own land, and many drifted west to look for work at the Kimberley diggings. Nonetheless, enough remained for the Orange Free State to prosper slowly. Britain's attention was focussed on the larger Boer state to north, the South African Republic (today's Transvaal), which it occupied in 1877, leaving the Free State be.

However, when Paul Kruger ousted the British during the First Anglo–Boer war (1880–1), and proclaimed the South African Republic independent again, the two states drew much closer together, despite the fact that the Free State lost even more of its African labour to its northern neighbour when the Rand gold fields began to flourish in the 1890s.

When the Second Anglo–Boer war broke out in 1899 the Orange Free State allied with the South African Republic and sent more than 20,000 men to war against the British. Commandos from the Free State laid siege to Kimberley, Mafeking and Colesberg and the Stromberg mountains in the Cape, while the combined main army under General Joubert occupied Natal east of the Free State border. Things went well for the Boers during the first year of war, but the British broke through Joubert's line in 1890, after the British General Roberts was sent out to replace General Buller. More than 60,000 British troops invaded the Free State, forcing the besiegers to withdraw.

The Orange Free State commandos, under General De Wet, could not stop the British from taking Bloemfontein, which opened up the road and rail route for the British to invade the South African Republic. Pretoria and Johannesburg were occupied, and the two Boer republics became effectively British territory. However, the commandos then split up into a mass of highly effective guerilla bands and dispersed over the Free State and South African Republic, while large, unwieldly British columns lumbered after them, unable to bring the Boers to direct battle. General De Wet's Free State commandoes managed cut the British supply lines to the Cape, and the Boers decided to fight on until a foreign power could be persuaded to intervene against the British. This was not altogether unrealistic, as Britain was receiving much censure in Europe for making war on colonial whites. Free State commandos began to raid far into the Cape Colony and occupied several towns in the Karoo, such as Calvinia and Kuruman during 1900–1901, living off the veld, raiding African homesteads and farms, and getting help from Cape Afrikaner sypathisers.

The British, under Field Marshal Kitchener, responded by systematically burning the farms of the Free State and South African Republic, and removing the women and children who had remained behind when their men had gone to fight in the commandos; this destroyed the Boers' supply base. The woman and children were put into 'concentration' camps, the first of their kind, where tens of thousands died from disease and malnutrition, creating a Boer hatred of the British that is still felt to this day. African farming communities were also uprooted and put in camps, to prevent the Boers from surviving by raiding African villages and homesteads. Many thousands of Africans thus imprisoned also died. Bloemfontein had two of the largest such camps. The British then criss-crossed the Free State and South African Republic with long barbed wire fences to impede the comman-does' mobility, and set up a system of blockhouse forts across the Cape Colony to monitor any movement in the more fertile districts, especially where there were large Afrikaner populations who might assist the fighters. Anyone found doing so was hanged.

Still, De Wet, commanding the Free State commandos, fought on with some success, capturing enough British rations and ammunition to keep his men in the field. However, an increasing number of the smaller commandos were captured, some of whom were then recruited by the British to fight the commandos at their own game. They became known as *hensoppers*, or 'hands-uppers'. This discouraged the fighting Boers. Meanwhile, huge British columns began to sweep tracts of country between one barbed wire fence and another, forcing the commandos into a continual retreat. The British then began to recruit regiments from African clans who had scores to settle with the Boers. Zulu and Tswana forces became active on the fringes of the Free State, while others helped the British in the South African Republic.

The Boer generals capitulated in 1902, though the Free State commandos, still under General De Wet, wanted to continue. After the war, the Free State crawled slowly to its feet as the surviving Boers returned to their burned farms and tried to get back their African labour force. The Transvaal immediately began to prosper once the gold mines re-opened, and Johannesburg and Pretoria quickly became as cosmspolitan as they had been before the war. Meanwhile, after the Union of South Africa in 1910, the Orange Free State became the centre of the growing Boer nationalist movement. The Nationalist Party was formed in Bloemfontein in 1914.

Gold and platinum were discovered in the northern Orange Free State around the modern town of Welkom in the 1920s and '30s, and the Free State began to share in the country's mineral wealth. During the Second World War, this new prosperity, combined with undi-minished Boer nationalism, made Bloemfontein one of the hot-beds of the *Broederbond* ('brotherhood'), a secret society of Boer industrialists and wealthy landowners sworn to oust the British through the National Party, and to remove voting rights from the Free State's more numerous black population. The *Broederbond* soon spread across the nation. Eventually, the society managed to permeate all levels of the country's administrative, judicial and industrial institutions, in a successful attempt to make the South African estab-lishment more Boer than British.

Once the National Party came to power in 1948, these objectives became possible. The Orange Free State and Transvaal became South Africa's political power centres, particu-larly after the opening of the northern Free State's gold fields in the 1950s, augmenting the more established gold fields of the Transvaal.

During the apartheid years from 1948 to 1990, the Free State resisted sanctions through its synthetic petrol-producing plant at Sasolburg on the Transvaal border. However, today most of the Free State is still farmland and mountain, and many white South Africans regard the Free Staters as yokels. The Orange Free State's image may change dramatically under the Government of National Unity, as the province's black majority (of mostly South Sotho and Tswana) will now control local government despite the region's entrenched Boer nationalism. So far, the sleepy, agricultural Orange Free State has adapted peacefully.

The Eastern Highlands

This region of the Free State, where it borders Lesotho, should not be missed. High grass-lands roll beneath table-like mesas; sandstone outcroppings jut from the soil almost anywhere you look, and the air here has a quality of raw health that makes you almost light-headed. The area's national parks and nature reserves (and many of the farms) still support large game populations, and offer hiking and riding through the wild hills and tended valleys, whose orchards and poplar-fringed fields make stark contrast with the hills behind. Bushman paintings can be found in almost any range of hills; whose sandstone overhangs and caves provided sanctuary for these hunter/gatherers until the early 19th century.

In spring, the valleys are white with cherry blossom; in summer, when most of the rain falls, the country shines a vivid green. In the drier, cold winter (snow is not uncommon on the hills), the region turns a deep gold, tinged with red as the grasses die. Along the eastern horizon (in Lesotho) marches the long, blue line of the Malutis, southern Africa's highest mountains. Relatively few tourists reach the Free State's Eastern highlands, and so you will often see no-one else if exploring on foot or horseback, and the region is a convenient jumping-off point for Lesotho. Even the towns are pretty, generally composed of handsome single-storey 19th-century sandstone buildings clustered around a central square.

Getting There

By car: the R26 runs through all the towns along the border with Lesotho and can be picked up from the N5 at Bethlehem in the north or from Rouxville on the N6 in the south. The R708 via Marquard connects the Eastern Highlands with the N1 highway at Winburg, just north of Bloemfontein.

By bus: twice weekly Transtate services run along the R26 towns (Fouriesburg, Ficksburg, Clocolan and Ladybrand) to/from Johannesburg. Unfortunately, bus services to/from Bloemfontein are non-existent, unless you take a Greyhound out to Senekal or Bethlehem and pick up a Transtate service from there (alternatively, hitch or take a black taxi). Call Rennies Travel in Bloemfontein for details, ℂ (051) 302 361.

Golden Gate National Park

This mountain reserve is at the northern-most point of the Eastern Highlands, where the Drakensberg and Maluti foothills meet, just below the tiny mountain 'homeland' of Qwa-Qwa (now re-absorbed into South Africa, but still marked on the road signs).

Golden Gate is named after two massive sandstone outcroppings which command the northern entrance to a spectacular valley that links the Free State with Qwa-Qwa.

A tarred road runs along this main valley, and a graded dirt road leads up the slopes on the border with Qwa-Qwa, but otherwise the 12,000ha upland park is an unbroken swathe of unspoilt montane grassland, grazed by eland, black wildebeest, red hartebeest, blesbok and springbok. Alongside these live smaller groups of zebra and smaller antlelope such as mountain reedbuck, grey rhebok, klipspringer and oribi. Eagles and vultures are not as common here as in some of the other mountain reserves, but jackal buzzard are well in evidence, and the many sandstone cliffs and overhangs are home to thousands of doves. Dassies thrive here and feed a sizeable but nocturnal population of caracal and a few shy leopard. You can explore the park via numerous day walks, an overnight trail (with a refuge hut supplied with firewood and water), and guided horse trails from one to three hours, and a limited network of game roads near the main valley.

To reach the park follow either the R712 from Clarens in the Free State, or the R74 from Bergville in Natal. Watch out for the signs to the park from either road. Trails can be booked on arrival or in advance via the National Parks Board in Pretoria ✆ (012) 343 1991.

The Heart of the Eastern Highlands: The Rooiberg and Witteberg

Clarens, nearest town to the Golden Gate National Park, lies on the R711 at the foot of the Rooiberg, (or 'red mountains', named for the golden russet colour of their winter grasslands). This tiny, picturesque sandstone town has been occupied by many of the foreign workers contracted to manage the building of the Lesotho Highland Water Scheme, a massive set of dams currently in construction just over the border in Lesotho. As a result, this little town has a good restaurant in the main square, called the **Guinea Feather**, and some good craft shops of local Sotho and Tswana artefacts. About 10km east of town, on the road to Golden Gate, is **Bokpoort Farm**, which offers guided horse trails and hikes into the Rooiberg.

South and then west along the R26, which follows the Lesotho border, is **Fouriesburg**, slightly larger than Clarens. The 19th-century **Fouriesburg Hotel** (*see* 'Where to Stay'), is a good place to break a journey or to visit in the evening. Otherwise it is worth wandering Fouriesburg's few streets; the trading stores are old-fashioned, with dark wooden counters and the stock piled up on old panelled shelves. At the time the author visited, two small craft shop/cafés selling Sotho handiwork, Boer breads and pastries and serving tea and coffee were opening.

South of Fouriesburg, the R26 winds to Ficksburg through a wide valley between the low Witteberg (meaning 'white mountains', because of their winter snows) and the Caledon River that borders Lesotho. About 20km out of Fouriesburg is a sign for **Rustler's Valley**, one of the most beautiful and unusual places to stay in South Africa.

Rustler's Valley (*see* 'Where to Stay') is a large, well-watered private farm and guesthouse commanding a whole valley of the Witteberg foothills. Perhaps because of the hills, which rise on three sides of the valley, hiding it from the rest of the world, the farm has developed with an individualism seldom encountered in South Africa. From the original farmhouse, Frik, the owner, has built a series of beautiful, highly individual buildings that blend with, rather than jar against, the landscape. The farm has accommodation for all budgets, and a very good restaurant and bar where local farmers mix surprisingly well with the rather hippyish atmosphere. The farm still produces vegetables, such as asparagus, and horses graze the wide pastures. Blesbok wander at will, and in the bush-covered slopes of the Witteberg there are caracal and a few nomadic leopard.

As a polo player, Frik keeps good horses: there are a few quiet schoolmasters for beginners. For the experienced rider, it is pure heaven to take off into the surrounding country on one of his throroughbreds. Hiking at Rustler's Valley is also excellent; there are short walks to rock formations and caves (including what purports to be a cannibal cave) and a two-day hike around the entire valley that involves sleeping in a sandstone overhang.

Once a year, at Easter, the tranquility of Rustler's Valley is broken by a three-day music festival—one of only a handful in the whole country—which attracts some of South Africa's best musicians. South Africa's hippy/bohemian culture comes out to play, and it would be hard to find a better setting for a party.

Ficksburg, south of Rustler's Valley, is a very handsome little town surrounded by cherry orchards, which in spring (Sept–Oct) fill the air with a rich scent of blossom. The town itself has little for the tourist besides rural atmosphere, sandstone buildings and shops and petrol for supplies. But every spring there is a Cherry Festival, and the whole town parties. It is a moveable feast, but Rustler's Valley should know the date.

The R26 then cuts west to the town of **Clocolan**, another 19th-century sandstone farming town set under the Witteberg. There is a very good weaving centre in town, **Lethoteng Weavers** on First Street, which employs local Sotho and Tswana women on a profit-share basis, producing rugs, hangings, sweaters and cardigans from local wool and mohair. Outside Clocolan is a private game farm, **Ikebana** (*see* 'Where to Stay'), with hiking and riding trails into the Witteberg.

North of Clocolan, the R708 winds for about 35km through empty hill country to **Marquard**, a village at the western end of the Witteberg. Several good hiking and riding trails lead into the mountains from local farms, which offer B&B, refuge huts, or cave overhangs to stay in. South of Clocolan, the R26 continues to **Ladybrand**, the closest South African town to Maseru, capital of Lesotho. Ladybrand is larger than the other Eastern Highlands towns, but has little beyond the basic amenities; most tourists just pass through on their way to Maseru.

Eland

West of Ladybrand is a section of what was Bophuthatswana, whose small central town, **Thaba Nchu**, forms an unexpected island of ugly glitz in this otherwise beautiful region. Thaba Nchu has a casino: Bophuthatswana was exempt from South Africa's prudish anti-gambling laws, and capitalized on this lucrative income. A holiday park sits next to the casino which, unless you have an irresistible urge to gamble, is best avoided. However, its present-day ugliness belies Thaba Nchu's history—during the 1830s, the flat-topped mountain above the resort (after which the place is named), was a stronghold of the Rolong clan of the Tswana, who sheltered the Vootrekkers, under Andries Potgieter, in 1836. Thaba Nchu gave the Voortrekkers a secure base from which to challenge the powerful Ndebele people, breaking their monopoly of power on the highveld at the battle of Vegkop later that year (*see* 'Ndebele History' pp.526–7).

The vulgarity of Thaba Nchu is made up for by the nearby **Maria Moroka Wilderness Area** ✆ (05265) 2161, which covers a great swathe of classic Eastern Highlands hill country. The beautiful park supports a lot of game; mostly eland, zebra, red hartebeest, black wildebeest, blesbok and springbok, as well as some of the smaller antelope. Twitchers flock here to see the rare blue korhaan—a miniature bustard—and raptors such as black and martial eagle. There are game-viewing roads, and walking trails that can take you very close to game. Unfortunately there is no accommodation except for the casino hotel at Thaba Nchu (see above phone number); it is best to visit early in the morning and drive back to Ladybrand (about 50km) in the evening, rather than stay in Thaba Nchu.

Golden Gate National Park offers accommodation to suit all budgets. The expensive rooms are in the large Brandwag Lodge, and include full board in very comfortable rooms overlooking the Golden Gate rocks. The self-contained rondavels are moderately priced, and there is cheap camping with ablutions. To book, telephone the National Parks Board in Pretoria, ✆ (012) 343 1991. Except for at the height of the summer holidays, it is usually safe to just turn up, as the accommodation is seldom full. **Rustler's Valley**, ✆ (05192) 3939, is one of the country's most unusual imaginative places to stay and caters for all budgets. Hiking and riding are offered, and the food is almost all home-produced and very well cooked. The half-Boer, half-bohemian atmosphere of the place, coupled with its quiet beauty, make it hard to leave.

expensive

Oaklands Country Manor, ✆ (05867) 883, sits in oak woodland atop the Van Reenen Pass where the Eastern Highlands flatten into a plateau overlooking the province of Natal. The old colonial house has simple, comfortable rooms and offers riding, shooting, bass fishing, walking and a superb view down over Natal. The country cooking is hearty and excellent. **Mount Everest Private Game Reserve**, ✆ (05861) 23493, near Harrismith, is spread over three entire mountains. The game, which includes white rhino, walks freely among the guest rondavels. There are several hiking trails and horses for hire, and guests can fish for bass or trout. **Ikebana**, ✆ (05194) 30516, a private game reserve south of Clocolan on the R26, is at the moderate end of the expensive scale. Its thatched chalets and rondavels surround a central lodge. Full board or B&B is offered. Hiking and riding among the game can be arranged.

moderate

The **Fouriesburg Hotel**, ✆ (058222) 30, occupies the oldest house in town. Owned by a Swiss family, the interior is quietly decorated in period. The food is good and guests are invited to make their own selection from the excellent wine cellar. **Nebo Holiday Farm**, ✆ (05192) 3947, deep into the Witteberg, consists of an old sandstone farmhouse and self-contained rondavels surrounded by cherry orchards and woodland. You can help to milk the cows.

Franshoek Mountain Lodge, ✆ (05192) 2828/3938, at the foot of the Witteberg, offers B&B in a sandstone farmhouse more secluded than Nebo. The farm has a 22km hiking trail during which you overnight in a large cave at the head of a beautiful gorge. Bass fishing, riding and swimming in the dam are offered. **Cranberry Cottage**, ✆ (05191) 2290, in the centre of Ladybrand, has 4 double rooms in an old sandstone townhouse, renovated in Victorian style. Home cooking is available.

Bokpoort Farm, ✆ (058) 256 1181, about 17km east of Clarens on the road to Golden Gate, offers comfortable B&B or self-contained backpackers accommodation in an old farmhouse. There are riding and hiking trips of 1 to 4 days into the Rooiberg. **Hoekfontein Guest Farm**, ✆ (05192) 3915, offers cheap accommodation in a camp at the foot of the Malutis, signposted from the R26 between Ficksburg and Fouriesburg. There are 3 rondavels and 6 thatched chalets. Venison braais are available, and there is riding and hiking. The game is mostly antelope, but there are hippo in the dam.

Liliehoek Resort, ✆ (05191) 40656, in the wheat and sunflower fields east of Ladybrand, is very good value, with 14 comfortable, thatched rondavels and even cheaper camp sites with ablutions in a landscaped setting among trees and giant sandstone boulders. Hikes of an hour to 3 days can be made from here, with overnight huts in the surrounding hills. All accommodation is self-contained, and there is a large swimming pool. The **Fanny Press House**, in Louis Trichardt Square, Marquard, ✆ (05272) 126/384, offers straightforward, self-contained backpackers accommodation, despite the rather spectacular name. Dormitory beds or double rooms are available.

The Southeastern Highlands

South of Ladybrand and Thaba Nchu, the R26 follows the western bulge of Lesotho's border to the small town of Wepener, about 20km east of which as the **Caledon Nature Reserve**, which surrounds a large dam on the Caledon River. Here the high grasslands of the Eastern Highlands merge with Eastern Karoo veld, offering a mixed landscape of thornbush, high grassland and riverine hardwood forest. Game thrives here, notably black wildebeest, reedbuck, springbuck and blesbok. Bird watchers come here for the waterfowl, particularly the handsome black stork. There are no marked trails, but there is nothing to stop you walking at will. Unfortunately, there is no accommodation (though if you camped quietly, no one would notice), so it is better to visit in the morning and continue south to **Zastron**, a little town at the foot of the **Aasvogelberg** (meaning 'vulture mountains'). Zastron has a little hotel, and there are marked trails into the mountains from here, where vultures still breed.

Zastron is famous for a set of legends concerning one of its first white inhabitants, Renier Du Wenaar, who lived to be over 100 years old, as his gravestone in the old churchyard testifies; Renier Du Wenaar, 1781–1883. The stories of Du Wenaar and his faithful Khoi servant, Boesman, are numerous, and most seem to have originated from the old man himself, but the most famous (told and beautifully illustrated in Alice Miller's Myths and Legends of Southern Africa, T.V. Bulpin Press 1979) warrants retelling here.

In the middle of the rocky outcrop that forms its summit off the Aasvogelberg is a round hole resembling an eye, apparently the result of one of Du Wenaar's exploits. One day he and Boesman were walking near the mountain when they noticed the devil—cloven hoofs, horns and all—sitting amongst a large troupe of baboons. The devil wished Du Wenaar good morning and, pointing to his large, old-fashioned musket, asked what the funny-looking object was. Du Wenaar resented the devil poking fun at his ancient gun and answered that it was his pipe, which, owning to its size, had to be smoked out of doors, as the smell irritated his wife.

The devil laughed, saying, 'So let's smoke. Light it up.' Du Wenaar loaded the musket and told the devil to put it to his mouth and draw, while he struck a light from the flint. The devil sucked at the barrel as De Wenaar lit the fuse; the gun went off with an almighty bang, blowing the devil's head clean off and straight through the Aasvogelberg. 'Hell!', came a faint voice from the other side of the mountain, 'That's strong tobacco!' The body sprang up and ran off stumbling over the mountain. Du Wenaar and Boesman laughed until they cried.

Zastron has hardly grown since Du Wenaar blew the devil's head off, but there is a marked hiking trail up into the Aasvogelberg where you can inspect the hole from the foot of the outcropping. However, as a qualification to Du Wenaar's claim, different versions of the story crop up in other locations in South Africa, the closest one being told in the eastern Karoo, near the town of Graaf Reinet—except that there it is a Khoi hunter and his old flintlock who are the heroes. Perhaps old Du Wenaar heard the story from his Khoi servant Boesman. Either way, the devil seems to have lost a lot of heads in South Africa.

℗ (05542–)

Where to Stay

There are few places to stay in the southeast Highlands. Visitors to the Aasvogelberg and the Caledon Nature Reserve could try **Quaggafontein**, ℗ 3212, near Zastron. This self-catering farm has a beautiful wrought-iron verandah, a log fire and candle-light only. Canoeing can be arranged in the nearby Orange River, and there are some short hikes.

Also recommended by travellers is the **Tienfontein Guestfarm**, ℗ 2931 and the nearby, **Champagne Guestfarm** ℗ 2713, offers great home cooking, riding, walking and hikes into the mountains. If the above are full, try the **Maluti Hotel** in Zastron, ℗ 107, which, despite being rather ugly, offers comfortable, moder-ately-priced accommodation with breakfast and good traditional Boer dishes like Karoo mutton, in the small restaurant. The bar is touchingly twee—done up to resemble the front of an old Frontier hotel. You could also try the **Vogel & Sons B&B** in Zastron, ℗ (05542) 3431.

Hiking: All the guest farms listed offer hiking trails of between 1 hour to 2 days. The longer Brandwater Trail, ✆ (014332) 115, covers 5 days (with a shorter, 2-day option) in the Witteberg, with accommodation in sandstone caves and overhangs. The trail starts from the Meiringskloof Nature Reserve, just outside Fouriesburg. The Bokpoort Farm Trails near Clarens, ✆ (05826) 1181, offers trails of up to 5 days into the Rooiberg, sleeping in caves and huts.

Riding: Again, all the guest farms listed below offer riding. Rustler's Valley, ✆ (05192) 939, has the best quality horses for experienced riders, while Bokpoort Farm, ✆ (05826) 1181, offers guided riding trails of up to 4 days on good *boerperd* horses.

Canoeing: Quaggafontein near Zastron, ✆ (05542) 3212, offers canoeing in the nearby Orange River.

The Southwestern Free State: The Karoo Fringe

Southwest of the Eastern Highlands, around the grasslands bordering the wide Orange River, the Free State widens into great plains which are dry for most of the year, but receive sufficient rainfall to keep the land grass-covered and to support a variety of game. Around the huge **Hendrik Verwoerdt Dam** on the Orange River are three large nature reserves. Oviston Nature Reserve sits on the Cape Province side of the river, where the Great Karoo begins (*see* 'Bo Karoo'). The two reserves on the Free State side are slightly lusher: the **Hendrik Verwoerdt Dam Nature Reserve**, which fronts the dam's shoreline, is mainly flat with sparse game populations, but bordering this is **Tussen Die Rivieren Nature Reserve**, ✆ (051762) 2803, also known as Tussen Die Rivieren Game Farm. This vast sweep of country, surrounding the convergence of the Orange and the Caledon Rivers (the name means 'between the rivers'), is one of South Africa's best-kept secrets. The grassland, scrub, riverine woodland and broken hills support a huge game population, and there are several hiking trails that take you past or through great herds of animals. White rhino, eland, gemsbok, kudu, zebra, black and blue wildebeest, blesbok, springbok, impala, reedbuck, steenbok and red hartebeest are all common and, because of the mixed terrain, the bird life is varied and prolific. Small predators such as caracal, bat-eared fox and jackal, occur throughout the reserve, and there are a few shy hyena. The rare, nocturnal aardwolf, a large hyena-like dog that eats termites, is common. The 3 one-day hikes are worth walking, as they take you very close to the game, in an ever-changing terrain. The reserve is only 50km from Aliwal North and the N6, so makes a convenient side-trip for anyone travelling to the Cape Drakensberg or into the Eastern Cape.

Where to Stay

Tussen Die Riveieren, ✆ (051762) 2803 has moderately-priced, comfortable self-contained cottages, and very cheap hiking shelters (with very hard floors!) whose only mod cons are ablution facilities and firepits.

Bloemfontein

The Free State's capital and largest town is situated on a plain beneath a line of broken hills, Bloemfontein's modern tower blocks are incongruous against the surrounding landscape—the result of the Free State's mineral wealth coming into its own in the 1960s and '70s. Bloemfontein is an ugly town, and not one to stay in.

Getting There

by air

SAA, ✆ (051) 47 3811, and Airlink, ✆ (051) 333769, fly to Bloemfontein Airport from Johannesburg and Port Elizabeth. SAA also fly from Cape Town, Durban, East London, Kimberley and Upington.

by car

Bloemfontein sits astride the N1 highway, roughly two-thirds of the way from Cape Town to Johannesburg. The N5 highway links Bloemfontein with Natal via Bethlehem and Harrismith. The N6 highway heads south to Port Elizabeth, while the R64 connects the city with Kimberley and the Northern Cape.

by coach

Greyhound (book through Rennies Travel, ✆ 302 361), TransLux and Transtate, ✆ 408 3242, all run services from Bloemfontein to the country's major centres, while the city's limited Transtate services connect with several smaller regional centres in the Orange Free State (useful for getting to/from the Eastern Highlands towns) and Lesotho.

Greyhound Buses pick up and set down from Shell Ultra-City pit stop on the Bultfontein Road, about 4 inconvenient kilometres north of the city centre, necessitating a taxi for journeys to and from Bloemfontein itself. TransLux pick up and set down from Cricket Street in the city centre. Transtate uses the Railway Station on Maitland Street, close to the city centre.

by rail

Bloemfontein Station on Maitland Street, ✆ 408 2941 runs daily services to Cape Town, Kimberley and Johannesburg, and weekly services to Durban, Port Elizabeth, Queenstown and East London. Less frequent services run south to Mossel Bay via Outdtshoorn and George in the Garden Route.

History

The well-watered site was probably named by Jan Bloem, a Griqua leader who lived here before the Voortrekkers settled it in the early 1840s and built a tiny capital for their nascent Orange Free State. Life continued peaceably for the Bloemfontein Boers until the Second Anglo–Boer War (1899–1902). When the British invaded Bloemfontein in 1900 they used the town as a centre of British operations, chasing down the elusive Boer guerilla commandos dispersed across the veld. However, the Free State's military commander, General Christian de Wet, was so effective in disrupting the British army's communications between the Cape and the Transvaal that the invaders were forced to retaliate strongly. Farms were attacked; Boer women and children and thousands of Africans were interned in two 'concentration camps' in Bloemfontein (*see* p.445). By 1902, most of the internees of the two huge Bloemfontein camps, both black and white, had died.

However, after the Boer War, the town seems to have recovered quickly. Money from the Rand gold fields found its way into Bloemfontein as thousands of people travelled through on the way to and from the mines and the Cape. When the Nationalist Party was formed in Bloemfontein in 1914, the town's wealthy businessmen began organizing themselves into a secret Nationalist brotherhood (*broederbond*) with a view to ousting the British and taking the voting franchise away from the Free State's black majority.

During the later years of apartheid, although the northern Free State industrial towns of Welkom and Sasolburg saw a lot of trouble, Bloemfontein remained largely untouched by the political violence. Despite the town's hitherto rabidly right-wing stance, day-to-day life was more relaxed than in the mining towns; Bloemfontein, lacking mines, has always been an administrative, rather than directly political centre. Since the fall of apartheid, and the accession of the ANC, Bloemfontein has continued to grow and prosper quietly. Whether the country's new administration will shake the Free State capital's solid calm remains to be seen.

Tourist Information

Hoffman Square © (051) 405 8911. Another knowledgeable source is Bloem Tours, © (051) 302 184 on the corner of Zastron and De Villiers Streets.

Old Bloemfontein

The compact old town centre, which radiates outward from **Hoffman Square**, still contains several handsome buildings amongst the post-war concrete ugliness. These are all to be found within a couple of minutes walk from the junction of Aliwal and Henry Streets. The **Old Raadsal** (*open Mon–Fri 10.15–3, Sat and Sun 2–5*) on St George's Street, an adobe and thatch cottage with a beaten dung floor, dates from the 1840s, and is all that remains of Bloemfontein's frontier past. The building served various public functions simultaneously; the headquarters of the army and civil service, town hall, school, church and dance-hall. However, Bloemfontein prospered sufficiently fast for this building soon to prove too small for the centre of the republic's government. Three more raadsals were constructed, each larger than the one before. The first two still survive as national monuments, while the third now houses a literary museum (*see* below) and the **Fourth Raadsal** (built 1893), an imposing structure, still operates as a government building which visitors can look over by arrangement, *©* 478 898. This marble and stained glass edifice, also on St George's Street, is as solid and substantial as any British colonial public building of the same period. As if conscious of this, Bloemfontein's few British settlers built a large **Anglican Cathedral** on the same street between 1850 and 1890, and embellished it after the British invasion of 1900. On nearby Brand Street (named after President Brand, who tried to claim the Kimberley diamond area for the Free State in the 1870s) is the **Old Presidency** (*open Tues–Fri 10–12, 1–4, Sat and Sun 2–5*), home to the three Free State presidents from 1885 until the British invasion. A simple, handsome building, it is now a concert hall housing a small collection of early presidential paraphernalia such as documents pertaining to the province's original land grants and some old clothes.

Also on Brand Street is the **National Afrikaans Literary Museum** (*open Mon–Fri 8–12, 1–4, Sat and Sun 9–12*). The wealth of poetry and fiction written in Afrikaans is unknown to many foreign readers (*see* **People and Culture**), though they may well have unwittingly read some in translation. Original manuscripts by such novelists and poets as Chris Barnardt and Eugene Marais are housed here. It is worth reading some of Marais' work in translation; writing around the turn-of-the-century he became famous for his semi-mystical books of natural history—on the lives of termites (*The Soul of the White Ant*) and baboons, whom he referred to as 'Twilight People'. Original manuscripts by Afrikaans writers still active today can also be looked at, and there is a a brief chronology of 19th- and 20th-century Afrikaans literature (some liberal, some pro-apartheid) and its central place in South African society.

On Aliwal Street is a museum of local natural history, the **National Museum** (*open Mon–Sat 8–4, Sun 1–6*), which is small and rather dull, with rows of old stuffed animals and shelves of minerals and fossils. The **Freshford House Museum** on Kellner Street (*open Mon–Fri 10–1 Sat, 2–5*) is a preserved Victorian townhouse. On McDonald Street, at the south end of the city centre is **Hertzog House** (*open Tues–Sat 9–12, 1–4*), the home of the Boer General and later prime Minister Barry Hertzog, famous as the founder of the Afrikaans-supporting, right-wing National Party in 1914, Barry Hertzog was one of the most vociferous voices in the country's early 20th century politics for taking away the black and 'coloured' franchise. He became Prime Minister in 1929, and again (with Jan Smuts) in 1934, but resigned over Smuts' decision to aid the British war effort. In 1940, the reactionary old Hertzog was pushed out of his own party and he retired from public life. But his championing of the poor white cause by urging continued legislation against non-whites made him something of a hero in Afrikaner history.

However, as is so often the case with these old presidents' house museums (there are several such in South Africa), there is little in the collection of memorabilia and furniture that gives clues of the personality of the man himself, nor to the turbulent events of his time. But students of white/black history may be able to extract anecdotes about the man from the museum's curator.

A reminder of the hard fighting that marked the Free State's early history is the **Queen's Fort** on Church Street (*open Mon–Fri 8–4*) built in 1848 to protect the Voortrekker town from BaSotho raids—most of which, it must be said, were provoked by the burghers (*see* **Lesotho** 'History'). On Monument Street the **Military Museum** (*open Mon–Fri 9– 4.30, Sat 9–5, Sun 2–5*) deals with the military history of the Orange Free State and Transvaal from an exclusively Boer viewpoint. On view are photographs of stern, starving Boer fighters from the second Anglo–Boer War, the prison camps of the period, the slightly better-fed fighters of the earlier 'native' wars and first skirmishes against the British, as well as weapons and brief personal histories of the military commanders involved in these wars.

Next door to the museum is the **National Women's Memorial**, commemorating the 26,000 Boer women and children who died in British 'concentration' camps between 1899 and 1902. The ashes of Emily Hobhouse, an Englishwoman who campaigned for better treatment for the internees, are buried under the monument. The many thousands of Africans who also died in such camps are not remembered here.

Bloemfontein's Parks

Bloemfontein's rose gardens and parks, both public and private, are undoubtedly the ugly city's most attractive feature. The biggest rose garden is in **King's Park**, just west of the town centre (reached by Henry or St Andrew's Street). The park has a small zoo and a boating lake, incongruously named Loch Logan. The largest park, **Naval Hill**, sits above the old town centre. At the top is a small theatre around which spreads the park, which covers several hundred hectares. About 200ha of this form the **Franklin Game Reserve**, where antelope such as eland, red hartebeest, blesbok and springbok graze. You can wander the reserve from sunrise to sunset every day. At the bottom of the hill is **Hamilton Park**, a formal garden famous for its Orchid House, a giant conservatory through which flows and artificial stream. **Signal Hill** is a smaller park on the opposite (westward) hill from Naval Hill. Less formally laid-out than Naval Hill, this is fine to wander by day, but is best avoided at night.

About 11km northwest of the town centre, adjoining the N1, is the **National Botanical Garden**. Laid out below a large dolerite outcrop, the garden is small, covering only 45ha. However, the displays of indigenous vegetation vary greatly and give the impression of a much larger area. There is a small hardwood forest of widely-spaced trees, a section of formalized Karoo veld with flowering thorn trees and aloes, and open grassland. The place has been carefully prepared, with an eye for beauty, and the effect is marred only by the roar of traffic from the N1.

expensive

Bloemfontein has the usual expensive chain hotels, but nothing else of any interest within the price range. The **Bloemfontein Sun** ✆ 301 991 is on East Burger Street, the **Holiday Inn** ✆ 301 111 is on Union Avenue and the Protea-owned **Halevy House** ✆ 480 271 is on the corner of Charles and Magraaf Streets. Better, and with facilities almost as good, are Bloemfontein's B&Bs (*see* below).

moderate

The **Waverley Gasthuis B&B**, on Peter Crescent in Waverley, ✆ 312 622/463 118, is a pleasant 1930s colonial house set in a large garden. A choice of B&B or full board is offered in 3 very comfortable en suite rooms. **Dagbreek B&B**, ✆ 332 490/463 118, a large, modern suburban house built in neo-Classical style at the north end of Bloemfontein, about 7km from the N1, has a small restaurant and pool, as well as a garden. **Unitas Herberg** on Logemanstraat, ✆ 226 874/5/6/7, is in the west end of the city, near the university. The rooms are simple, clean and comfortable, and there is a small restaurant. The **Elsa Calitz Gasthuis B&B** in Bayswater, ✆ 332058/463 118, has truly kitsch rooms upholstered in draylon plush. However, the food is very good.

If you are simply breaking a cross-country journey and don't need to be in the town centre, then about 40km south of Bloemfontein is a very pleasant farmhouse, **Die Oude Kraal**, ✆ (05215) 636/733, which offers a few en suite rooms on a working farm. The house is set in gardens, and has a small pub attached, that the locals drink at. The home cooking, especially the mutton and home-made breads, is superb, and guests can wander the farm.

cheap

Bloemfontein has some good-value places at the cheap end of the accommodation scale. Try **Die Herberg**, ✆ 307 5000, on Barnes Street, just north of the city centre. Not to be confused with the Unitas Herberg (*see* above), this one has 48 en suite rooms, which, if shared, fall into the cheap price range. The **Roberto Hotel**, ✆ 483 601/484 601, has 52 en suite rooms, but is about 3km south of the city centre (catch a number 11 bus from Hoffman Square). Again, if you share a room (some rooms have four beds), you can bring the price down quite considerably. Both the above hotels can provide breakfast for an extra charge, and the Roberto has a cheapish à la carte restaurant.

The city's cheapest deal is Bloemfontein **YWCA**, 167 St Andrew's Street in the city centre, ✆ 304 574, has safe accommodation with a shared kitchen and bathrooms. You have to be female to stay here. There are single rooms only.

expensive

C'est La Vie, ✆ 474 022, on St Andrew's Street in the city centre is a French restaurant of great charm. A little formal, but with an excellent menu and wine list, this is one of the few Bloemfontein eateries of any quality. In the C. R. Stewart Building on Elizabeth Street is **Carousel**, ✆ 80251, a more consciously upmarket place serving good Continental dishes, with some Cape country cooking. **La Dolce Vita**, ✆ 81625, on the corner of Charles Street and Wes-Burger Street offers Italian food using fresh herbs in the pasta sauces and excellent seafood in the antipasti.

moderate/cheap

Il Pescatore, ✆ 304 832, on Burger Street East serves the standard, but delicious, Portuguese Mozambiquan fare of fresh, fried seafood dishes and spiced, Continental cuisine, such as chicken peri-peri.

A cheaper, Italian restaurant is **Schillaci's Trattoria**, ✆ 473 829, on Zastron Road. Schillaci's is great in summer as it has outdoor tables. But the best value food in town is probably **St Mary's Kitchen** on the corner of Fichardt Street and Charles Street is a very cheap place used by black workers. Traditional African food like mealie-pap with beans (very filling and keeps you regular) or deep-fried junk food predominates. You can eat there or take away.

Nightlife and Entertainment

Despite its stolidly provincial feel, Bloemfontein has a good theatre, and regular classical concerts and ballet/modern dance at the **Sand Du Plessis Theatre** on Markgraff Street, ✆ (051) 477 771.

Bloemfontein cannot compare to other South African cities for nightlife. Clubs come and go each year, but two stalwarts are **Arthur's Club** and **Simply Red**, both on St Andrew's Street, and both of which cater for live blues and local reggae, with the occasional visit by a township band. The crowd is not heavy at these clubs, but the drinking can be.

The Northern and Central Free State

Many South Africans denigrate the wide, level plateau of flat farmlands that make up the central and northern Free State. Certainly, the countryside is unspectacular, but the skies are big and the muted ochres and browns of the highveld grassland have a quiet beauty.

Soetdoring Nature Reserve is on the R64, about 70km north of Bleomfontein, and surrounds the Krugerdrif dam on the Modder River. The R64 connects Bloemfontein with Kimberley, and the reserve makes a good place to break the journey and stretch your legs. The riverine woodland, thorn scrub and grassland supports zebra, blue and black wildebeest, blesbok, springbok and duiker, and there are plans to re-introduce more species. The dam is home to large flocks of waterfowl, particularly spurwing and Egyptian geese. Look out for secretary birds in the grasslands. Unfortunately, there is no accommodation.

Further into the highveld, about 40km north along the N1 from the town of **Winburg,** is the **Willem Pretorius Game Reserve,** ✆ (05777) 4229, a large reserve surrounding a large dam. Large game, such as buffalo, white rhino, giraffe, eland and kudu, and most of the medium and small antelope species thrive here. The reserve is a good place to stop if driving north to the Transvaal, and there are chalets and a camp site, as well as boating on the dam. A small restaurant, shop and petrol station complete the facilities. Waterfowl thrive here, and fish eagles are a common sight over the water. Large raptors, such as martial eagles, chanting goshawk, and secretary birds, are common in the thornbush of the main reserve.

Further north, towards the Vaal River begin the ugly Free State mining fields. This area, which surrounds the hideous industrial towns of Welkom, Orkney, Kroonstad and Sasolburg, should certainly be avoided. However, in the dry west of the region, where it borders the Western Transvaal, are two large nature reserves surrounding a massive dam; the **Bloemhof Dam Nature Reserve** and the **Sandveld Nature Reserve** (for both reserves ✆ (018022) 1103) both west of Welkom along the R34, or the N12 between Johannesburg and Kimberley. Both reserves are largely thornveld, with many tall, yellow-flowering camel-thorn trees and grassland, and support large numbers of giraffe, eland, red hartebeest, blue wildebeest, gemsbok and smaller buck such as duiker and steenbok. The dam supports great flocks of ducks and geese, and blue cranes and white storks are regular visitors. Vultures, small hawks, sociable weaver birds (which build vast nests housing whole flocks) and hornbills are common sights. There are hiking trails and both reserves have basic accommodation; camping with an ablution block.

Further north, where the farmlands meet the fringe of the industrialized Vaal Triangle is a place that historians will find interesting—**Vegkop Battlefield**. Set just outside the small village of Vegkop, reached by dirt road from the town of **Heilbron** on the R34 between Kroonstad and the N3

South Sotho Painted House

highway, Vegkop is the site where the Voortrekkers under Andries Potgieter repulsed a massive Ndebele attack with devastating musket fire in 1836. The ferocity of the of the Ndebele's attack convinced the Voortrekkers that they must break the power of Mzilikazi, the Ndebele chief, and the most powerful warlord on the highveld. The Voortrekkers spent the next 20 years pushing the Ndebele northward, and eventually forced Mzilikazi into modern Zimbabwe where most of the people still live today (*see* Ndebele History). Today, like so many of South Africa's great battlefields, there is little on the lonely site of Vegkop to suggest the great event that took place there, but the high, lonely landscape has great presence and the battlefield makes a good detour if travelling through the northern Free State to the Transvaal.

Where to Stay
moderate

Should you find yourself having to overnight in the northern Free State, try the self-catering thatched chalets at **Free State Safaris**, near Kroonstad on the N1, ✆ (05612) 25657/23900 (be warned, it can be difficult to get through to this number), a game farm in unspoilt bush, supporting several species of antelope. The small town of **Heilbron**, near the border with the Transvaal (on the R34) has a thatched cottage called **Mooidraai**, ✆ (01614) 30443, next to a river on a farm offering swimming, riding and hiking. **Vredefort**, a small town west of the N1 near the Transvaal border has **Rietpoort Farm**, ✆ (05692) 1512, which also offers self-contained accommodation, riding, farm walks and swimming in the dam. Good parks board accommodation at all three budgets can be found at the **Willem Pretorius Game Reserve** near Winburg, ✆ (05777) 4229, though to stay cheaply you will have to camp.

In the great, flat farmlands of the central Free State, travellers can find a variety of moderately-priced accommodation. The town of **Bethlehem**, on the N5 connecting Bloemfontein with the Rooiberg in the Eastern Highlands, has the **Fisant Gasthuis**, ✆ (058) 014 1512, a sandstone suburban house, very twee, but comfortable inside and offering B&B. **Lindley**, northwest of Bethlehem on the R76, has the **Vaalhoek Guest Farm**, ✆ (05612) 1512, an old farmhouse providing B&B, riding and farm walks. **Senekal**, on the N5 between Bloemfontein and Bethlehem, has **Arcadia**, ✆ (05848) 2867, a neo-Cape Dutch farm offering B&B, riding, walks, and a swimming pool.

Swaziland

*The Ox rushes out wild. The young men must catch it and with bare
hands pummel and drag it back into the sanctuary*

A History of Swaziland, Dr J. S. M. Matseluba

TRAVELLERS SHOULD NOTE THAT SWAZILAND IS MALARIAL

Tucked between the Transvaal, Natal and neighbouring Mozambique,
the Kingdom of Swaziland has never been a part of South Africa. The
country is small enough to drive across in a day, but there is within this
area a great variety of landscape; from high, cool mountains to sub-
tropical lowveld, temperate grasslands and montane forests. The area
around the capital, Mbabane, is westernized, but in the rural areas
traditional life goes on as ever, and there are large stretches of very wild
country designated as nature reserves supporting big game.

Swaziland has a modest but healthy economy—based primarily on sugar
and forestry—and the country moves to its own, relaxed rhythm,
regardless of any troubles in neighbouring South Africa. This difference
is noticeable from the moment you cross the border. People smile more
and the slight tension that you have become used to in South Africa
miraculously lifts. Most visitors to Swaziland remark on this fact, and
many lament that they did not allow enough time to explore the little
country properly.

Climate

The uplands of western and central Swaziland have a generally temperate climate of hot,
rainy summers and warm, dry winters. The mountains can be cold at any time of year,
especially at night. Eastern Swaziland is lowveld, and has a sub-tropical climate of humid,
blisteringly hot summers and a dry 'winter' where mid-afternoon temperatures can still be
very high indeed.

Flora and Fauna

Despite Swaziland's small size and comparatively high population, the country has a very
successful nature conservation policy and big game flourishes in the several large reserves
which comprise most of the country's diverse habitats and landscapes. This success is
largely due to the efforts of a man called Ted Reilly, who pioneered the country's first
game reserves in the 1960s. The king of Swaziland has also been instrumental in financing
and promoting nature conservation, to the point that Swaziland's natural resources are
among the best managed in Southern Africa. Elephant and rhino have been re-introduced
to Mkhaya, in the lowveld, as have some of the rarer antelope, such as sable and roan.
Leopard still inhabit the mountain reserves and remoter reaches, and there are plans to re-
introduce lion. Plains game species are common in all the reserves, and in the Mkhaya and
Mlilwane reserves hippo and croc can still be found.

Swaziland's flora varies greatly, due to the different altitudes and their corresponding climates. Hardwood forest and grassy downland dominate the western uplands, while bushveld with sub-tropical riverine woodland cover the low-lying east. The Lebombo mountains bordering Mozambique are also forested, and giant wild fig trees are a common sight throughout the country, especially along river banks.

Practical A–Z

currency

Swaziland has its own currency, the elilangeni, which exchanges 1 to 1 with the Rand. Rands are accepted everywhere in Swaziland, but you will often be given change in Swazi currency. This is not accepted in South Africa, so spend all your elilangeni before leaving Swaziland.

language

Siswati is the Swazi language, but the visitor will seldom need to use even the simple greetings, as English is spoken almost everywhere; the Swazi education system emphasizes learning English and even in the countryside most people learn it very young. However, a few greetings and phrases are always useful, if only for politeness (*see* **Language** p.636).

safety

Swaziland is one of the safest places in Southern Africa. Despite sporadic recent strikes and student political action, racial and political strife have not affected the country on anything like the same scale as South Africa. Most crimes against travellers involve simple thieving and the occasional mugging after dark in the large towns, though this is still rare. However, it is best to avoid the side-streets of Mbabane and Manzini at night, unless there are two or more of you.

History

Swaziland is known to have been inhabited for over 100,000 years. In the 1960s some of the earliest *homo sapiens* remains ever found were excavated from the eastern Lebombo range, and from a site known as Castle Cavern in the western mountains near Malolotja Nature Reserve, where evidence was found of mining activity dating back 30,000 years. By the late Stone Age, it seems that the majority of the country was inhabited by San (bushman) groups, whose paintings can still be seen in some of the mountain caves. The San were eventually pushed out of the region by the southward migrations of large numbers of Nguni-speaking peoples between the 12th and 14th centuries.

The Swazi as a composite nation only appeared in the early 19th century, when the Ngwane tribe, displaced by the emerging Zulu empire in Natal, was led north by its paramount chief Sobhuza into modern Swaziland and the Eastern Transvaal. In the 1820s the southern end of Swaziland was overrun by repeated Zulu raids as Shaka sent his *impis* to ravage neighbouring lands. The Swazi, under King Mswati, Sobhuza' successor, retreated to the mountains in the north of the country. Some of their number migrated up to modern-day Malawi to become, in time, the Maseko tribe, whilst those that stayed held their own until the death of the Zulu king Dingane in the 1850s, when they re-settled the southern reaches. By 1860, Mswati had re-established his people over their former range.

Now it was the turn of the Voortrekkers to make incursions into this fertile land. After Mswati's death in 1868 the Swazi were unable to prevent the Boers from annexing their land as part of the short-lived South African Republic (SAR). And when, in 1877, the SAR was taken under British control, the new King Mbandzeni was similarly powerless. Britain returned Swaziland to independence in 1881, but did nothing to stop whites from settling where they wished. As most of the country was, and still is, owned by the king, this undermined the monarchy's prestige, and Swazi culture seemed threatened with fragmentation.

In 1889 Mbandzeni died, leaving his queen and infant son to deal with the increasing white settlement. The SAR resumed government of Swaziland in 1895 but Mbandzeni's surviving queen, Libotsibeni, set out to get the land back, actively encouraging young Swazi men to go to the booming Transvaal gold reefs and to make money with which to buy land back from the white settlers. Libotsibeni was helped in her quest by the Anglo–Boer War, which forced the Boers to withdraw from Swaziland, to be replaced in 1903 by a loose British administration. Her strategy of buying land went unopposed by the British Special Commissioners appointed to govern the country and, by 1921, when her son Sobhuza II acceded to the throne, Swaziland was largely owned by the Swazi, with title deeds that would stand up before a British court.

Sobhuza continued to work quietly towards independence, absorbing British institutions into the traditional Swazi government of absolute monarchy. In 1960 he proposed the forming of a Legislative Council based on European law, and a National Council based on Swazi culture to work side by side—a sort of double house similar to Westminster, with the monarch as head of state. The king also held the right of veto, but political parties were allowed. When elections were eventually held in 1964 and 1967, the National Movement (called Mbokovdo), a party that preached independence, won both.

When independence followed in 1968 Swaziland slipped into it with few of the problems that have beset other Southern African countries shrugging off colonial rule. This is partly because the clan in power represents almost all the country's inhabitants—unlike most other African countries, where independence has often been followed by wars to establish which of several clans should take power.

Some claim that this lack of social strife has been no more than subservience to monarchical rule, but it is hard to contest the apparent good reasoning behind many of the monarch's decisions, and the people's apparent satisfaction with them. For example, King Sobhuza and the two councils adopted a strictly non-racist policy for their legislature in the 1960s, re-wrote the British-proposed national constitution in 1973, making it conform to Swazi culture, and formed a parliament. Nature conservation, progressive agriculture, water conservation and forestry were all promoted, and today Swaziland's natural resources are among the best-administered in Africa.

This rational approach has continued under King Mswati III (acceded 1986), who has tolerated political parties opposed to the monarchy, even though they are officially illegal.

He continues to maintain rule with a comparatively light hand, despite his immense power in terms of Swaziland's natural wealth, almost all of which is owned by the crown. As a result the monarchy continues to be popular with the majority of Swazis, though there is a growing anti-monarchist movement that may yet emerge into a fully-fledged opposition.

Swazi Culture

Swaziland is one of the few African countries that seems to have successfully married Western culture with its own. Despite its westernized towns, rural life in Swaziland is, like most Southern African cultures, based around cattle, a patriarchal system of headmen and elders and ancestor worship (mixed now with evangelical Christianity). However, the most striking aspect of Swazi culture is the absolute power that still rests with the monarchy. Not only does the Swazi king still directly control the government and economy, but the nation still swears him fealty every year at a great festival known as the *Ncwala*, a moveable feast which usually occurs at the end of December or beginning of January, when the rainy season is in full swing. The *Ncwala*, or 'First Fruit' ceremony is a combination of harvest festival and symbolic remewal of the monarchy and Swazi nation presided over by the king. The *Ncwala* lasts for four days, but its preparation time is in fact, much longer, as holy water must first be gathered from the sea at Maputo in Mozambique, and from the Crocodile River in the Eastern Transvaal. A large number of chosen youths then spend three days building a royal kraal from acacia branches—which must not wilt or die after being cut from the tree, as this is taken to mean that the youth in question is impure—having seduced a married woman or impregnated a virgin—both crimes in Swazi culture. On the third day a young bull is released among the youths who must attack, fell and kill it using only their fists. On the fourth day, the king eats the first fruits of the new harvest in front of his youths, the hut of acacia branches and the king's bedding and household items are burned, and the king dances before his people. Great fires are built on the surrounding hills—offerings to the rain gods, and amid feasts and general dancing, the new year can then begin. The *Ncwala* always takes place at the royal Kraal at Lobamba in the Ezulwini Valley. Spectators are allowed at some parts of the ceremony, but photographs are forbidden.

Another annual ceremony is the *Umhlanga*, or Reed Dance (held in August or September), a festival to initiate unmarried maidens into womanhood and eligibility for marriage. Again, a large number of the nation's young unmarried women gather at the Royal Kraal, and ceremony is presided over by the Queen Mother. The *Umhlanga* used to double as a sort of human livestock show of potential wives for the king. Young women related to the royal family are particularly in evidence, and are identified by the purple lourie feathers they wear in their hair. The ceremony lasts for about a week. Spectators of the *Umhlanga* are free to take photographs.

Swaziland also has its own traditional popular culture in the form of a dance known as *sibhaca*, which has evolved into something of a national sport. Teams of young men, often from schools and colleges, compete at traditional ceremonies and agricultural shows all over Swaziland, with an annual championship at the Manzini Trade Fair, every August/ September. The Swazi Sun Hotel in the Ezulwini Valley near the capital, Mbabane, maintains two teams of *sibhaca* dancers and displays are put on twice a week (*see* below). *Sibhaca* dancing is a thrilling sight: the troupe provides a rhythmic backdrop for each member in turn to come forward and perform a fast, high-kicking solo, before returning to the troupe as another takes his place without a break in the rhythm. One white Swazilander I spoke to dismissed the dancing as 'all for the tourists', but that hardly seemed to dim the enjoyment of either the dancers or the audience.

Like many other Nguni-speaking cultures in and around the east and north Transvaal, Swaziland has a strong tradition of rural occultism. The government even has a national school to train *Inyangas* (diviners—usually male) and *Sangomas* (herbalists and healers—usually female) at Siteki in the far east of the country, under the Lebombo Mountains, and travellers can visit the school by prior arrangement through Swazi Tourism in Mbabane, the capital (*see* below). However, not all of Swaziland's traditional *Inyanga* and *Sangoma* culture is so high profile, and some aspects are downright morbid. The most extreme evidence of this darker side are '*muti*' murders—ritual murders to aquire human body parts for magical purposes. As recently as the 1980s, several cases of '*muti*' murder came to light, usually of children. Most people who have lived in Swaziland for any length of time will have a story of brushing with the occult, in however intangible a form, but they tend to over-emphasize this side of Swaziland's strong spiritualist culture, and it has never reached the epidemic proportions said to have occurred in Venda and Lebowa further north.

Getting There and Around

All visitors must have a valid passport to enter Swaziland and visas are issued gratis at the border posts. Drivers will be expected to pay a small charge for road tax.

by air

Royal Swazi Airlines run daily flights to Mbabane from Johannesburg and Durban, as well as from Harare in Zimbabwe, Gaberone in Botswana, Lusaka in Zambia and Maputo in Mozambique.

by car

Of the four main entry points into Swaziland, Oshoek, Mahamba and Lavumisa are open 7am–10pm. Josefsdal and the several minor entry posts are generally open 8am–4pm. The most direct way in from Johannesburg is via the N4 to Carolina, then the R38, R451 and R39 to Mbabane, through Oshoek, the largest and busiest of the border posts. In the north, Jeppe's Reef (called Matsamo in Swaziland) is reached by the R570 which connects with the N4 just south of the Kruger National Park. Mahamba entry point is along the R29 from Piet Retief. There are two entry points from Natal; Lavumisa at the very end of the N2, and another from northern Zululand via the Cecil Macks Pass over the Lubombo mountains. This is rough, and not always passable for ordinary vehicles. The most picturesque route is the dirt R40 over the Saddleback Pass, winding up through forest and grassland and with breathtaking views out over the Transvaal and the large Songimvelo Game Reserve. The border post (Josefsdal) on this road shuts at 4pm.

Swaziland has good roads; even the gravel roads are generally in good condition and do not require a 4x4. Mbabane and Manzini are connected by the Enzulweni Valley Road, along which most of the country's traffic goes. There is one border post with Mozambique, at Namaacha in the east of the country, an easy 85km drive to Maputo. Visas must be bought from the Mozambique embassy in Mbabane before leaving Swaziland. These take about a week to process and cost around R40 with two photographs.

by bus

Transtate, ✆ (011) 283 562, a sub-company of TransLux, runs buses to and from Johannesburg and Manzini, Swaziland's second city, via Piet Retief and Mbabane. Transtate buses also run between Durban and Pongola. If you get off at the little town of Golela, it is an easy taxi-ride or hitch across the border at Lavumisa. Both bus services run several times per week.

Swaziland has a good, if irregular internal bus network between the main towns. Buses are cheap, but slow.

by rail

There is no passenger rail link between South Africa and Swaziland and no passenger service within the country.

black taxis

Black taxis are quicker and more frequent than buses and cost a little more, but have a high accident rate.

hitch-hiking

Swaziland is one of the best areas of Southern Africa for hitching. Drivers are generally not afraid to pick up hitchers, even after dark. However, some mountain roads see little traffic and hitchers may experience long waits. As anywhere, women should think twice about hitching alone.

tour group

Swaziland has two good local tour companies, both whom know the country intimately, and both of whom also offer forays into neighbouring Zululand and the Eastern Transvaal. **Umhlanga Tours**, ✆ 61431, are based in the capital Mbabane, is the easiest to reach for those without transport. However, **Eco-Africa Safaris**, ✆ 71319, based at Phophanyane Nature Reserve near Pigg's Peak also has its own private reserve at Muti-Muti in the Swaziland lowveld, and can arrange trips into Mozambique.

Mbabane

Tourist Information

Tourist Office, Swazi Plaza, ✆ 42531 or 44556, at the south end of Mbabane on the road parallel to and west of Western Distributor Road.

The **Post Office** is on Warmer Street, which connects with the south end of Allister Miller. You can make international calls from here.

Mbabane, capital city of Swaziland, lies at the north end of the Ezulwini Valley, the traditional seat of the Swazi Royal Family since the mid 18th century. Although a pleasant town, Mbabane has little in its tiny centre to interest the traveller, beyond shopping for supplies before heading off to the nature reserves, or visiting the restaurants and/or nightclubs. There are no museums or indeed any specific tourist facilities in Mbabane, except for the **Tourist Office** in the brand new Swazi Plaza which sits opposite The Mall, just out of the town centre. The Tourist Office has detailed information on nature reserves, hikes, traditional Swazi activities etc. It is also worth going to one of the hotel bars at night, as people are very approachable, and you can tap into the local information network with ease.

Swaziland did not change its street and town names after independence and the main street is still called **Allister Miller** after the first European to be born here. Most of the banks, shops and take-away places are found here. For those shopping for authentic Swazi crafts, the **Mbabane Market** is worth a morning visit. Prices are cheaper than in South Africa. Head for the Jabula Inn on Allister Miller, and cross over to Msunduza Street.

The **Mozambiquan Embassy**, ℂ 43700 (*open Mon–Fri 9–1*), is useful for buying visas for Mozambique at far cheaper rates than in South Africa. The embassy is on a dirt road reached from the town centre by following the Manzini road to the sign for the Mountain Inn, turning left, left and left again. Visas take about a week. Spend no more than a night in Mbabane, as Swaziland's real pleasures lie further afield.

ℂ *(09268–) from South Africa*

Where to Stay

expensive

Mbabane lacks expensive accommodation. However, just south of town, overlooking the Ezulwini Valley, are the **Swazi Inn**, ℂ 42235, and the **Mountain Inn**, ℂ 42781. The Swazi Inn is posh and rather formal, mostly filled with wealthy South African tourists, while the Mountain Inn seems to attract more business travellers, and can be good for bar-room conversation. Both offer clean, comfortable rooms with private bathrooms, decent restaurants, a pool and gardens. Prices for both are at the lower end of the expensive range.

moderate

In the town centre, on Johnstone Street (parallel to and east of Allister Miller Street) is **Maxim's**, ℂ 45011, a good spot for meeting locals and finding out about nightlife. Accommodation is in comfortable, unpretentious suites with enough beds to sleep several people, which can bring the price down considerably. There is a generally lively disco attached and local bands sometimes play at weekends. The restaurant has tables inside and out.

cheap

The **Jabula Inn**, ℂ 42406, on Allister Miller Street, is the most popular with travellers. Prices range from cheap to moderate and some rooms have en suite bathrooms. Be warned, the bar and nightclub behind the hotel can thump out noise into the early hours.

Further out of town are **Kamtshwane Lodge**, ✆ 45256, and **Hill Street Lodge**, ✆ 43730. Kamtshwane is south of town on the corner of Ilunga Street and Jo-Jo Street. The rooms are a bit run down, but clean, and the bar is a good place to meet Swazis living and working in Mbabane. Although things can get riotous, the atmosphere is friendly and safe. If you are without a car, take a taxi from Allister Miller Street rather than walk, as the streets on this end of town can be rough at night. Hill Street Lodge, on Hill Street, is in a residential district west of the town centre. There are pleasant, comfortable rooms with shared bathrooms.

Dirt cheap accommodation can he found at two hostels, the **Thokose Centre**, ✆ 46681, on Mhlanhla Road, which runs parallel with Allister Miller and is reached from there via Walker Street, and the **Youth Centre**, ✆ 42176, on Isomi Street at the far south eastern end of town. Both require a short taxi ride, and offer clean, safe accommodation. Ring first to make sure there is space. If these are full, try the even cheaper **Sebenda Institute** on Sitwanshini Street (no telephone number was available at the time of writing).

✆ *(09268–) from South Africa*

Eating Out

expensive

Most of the area's good expensive restaurants are out in the Ezulwini Valley. The **Swazi Inn** ✆ 42235 and **Mountain Inn** ✆ 42781 have good à la carte restaurants offering a standard range of dishes. More popular with the locals is the **Hwa Li** Chinese restaurant on the corner of Walker Street and Tin Street, which serves really good Chinese food.

moderate and cheap

Oddly enough, Mbabane has an interesting range of cheaper restaurants. At the lower end of the moderate scale is **Maxim's** which serves steaks, pizzas and pasta (at indoor and outdoor tables) in a friendly atmosphere. Locals often eat here before going to the nightclub attached to the hotel.

The **Indinglizi Gallery and Restaurant** on Johnstone Street, ✆ 42613, serves wholefood breakfast and lunch only in a friendly, bohemian atmosphere. Inside and outside tables. Local Swazi artists and craftspeople exhibit here regularly. **Marco's Trattoria** on Allister Miller, ✆ 45029, serves good, cheap Italian food with a choice of tables inside or on a balcony. The oddly named **Mediterranean Restaurant**, ✆ 43212, also on Allister Miller, is an Indian restaurant serving reasonable southern Indian food at very low prices. Good Portuguese food is offered at **Lorenço Marques**, ✆ 43097, again on Allister Miller, with the standard spicy chicken peri-peri and fried seafood dishes predominating. In the Mall, opposite the Swazi Plaza, is the **Casserole**, ✆ 46425, which serves decent German and French dishes. Cheapest of all is the **Copacabana**, on the corner of Warmer Street and Allister Miller Street. Run by Mozambiquan Portuguese, the restaurant serves basic but very tasty food.

Mbabane has a few lively clubs, some of which have live music. **Maxim's** is one of the most popular, with a disco through the week and live acts at weekends. The **Jabula Hotel** has a weekend disco. Smaller nightclubs come and go and it is worth asking locals in the bars. About 15km out of town, on the Ezulwini Valley Road, is the **Why Not Disco**, in the Happy Valley Motel, an unashamed pick-up joint that is light-hearted and fun. Bands from Johannesburg are sometimes booked to play here, and these can range from township jive, to hard rock, to easy listening.

The Ezulwini Valley

Between Mbabane and Manzini runs Swaziland's vibrant Royal Valley, site of the Royal Palace. Traffic streams continually between the hotels, restaurants, camp sites, curio shops, health spas and craft workshops that crowd along the road. Yet despite such densely-packed human activity the valley is still green and beautiful and you do not have to venture far into the hills on either side of the road before finding yourself again surrounded by traditional rural land or wild country.

It only takes about half an hour to drive the valley, so it is worth cruising along once just to take it all. By picking up one of the many locals who hitch regularly along between the two towns, you will have access to any local information you need.

In the centre of the valley is **Lobamba**, the large, modern royal palace for the king and his household, and the **National Museum**. Both are signposted from the main road, opposite the entrance sign for the Mlilwane Nature Reserve. Lobamba is not open to visitors, and photographs are prohibited. However, it is here that the *Ncwala* and *Umhlalanga* dances are held, and on the latter occasion tourists can enter the Royal Kraal in front of the palace and take as many photos of the dancers as they wish. The National Museum has a good, concise display explaining Swazi customs, both royal and commoner, Swazi ritual and belief, and some history.

Further up the road from here are the **Mantenga Falls**, an impressive set of large cascades. Sadly, this is one of Swaziland's few tourist spots to have a reputation for danger; people have been attacked here. So be vigilant and visit in a group if possible. The road up to the Falls is badly maintained and can be difficult to negotiate in an ordinary car.

Off the main road, opposite the turn-off to Lobamba, is **Mlilwane Nature Reserve**, ✆ 461 037. This large stretch of grassland, forest and mountainside was the first of Swaziland's wildlife refuges to be pioneered by Ted Reilly, the man behind most of the country's nature conservation programmes. Mlilwane used to be his family's massive estate, and Reilly donated it to the country for the preservation of wildlife back in the 1960s. Despite being so close to the busy Ezulwini Valley the reserve is quiet and wild and is home to white rhino, buffalo, giraffe, impala, zebra, blue wildebeest, eland, waterbuck, duiker and mountain reedbuck. There are a few shy leopard and spotted hyena. Warthog are so common that one family has become semi-tame and has taken up residence at outside the reserve's office, shop and picnic area, which overlooks a hippo pool. There are crocodiles in the lakes further into the reserve.

Mlilwane has excellent **hiking and horse trails** among the game. There is self-catering accommodation in cottages and a camp site. Prices range from cheap to moderate. Tame blue cranes wander between the cottages.

The Ezulwini Valley is a good place to buy Swazi jewellery, wool and mohair clothing, printed cloths, baskets and carvings. There are several shops along the main road all selling work by locals, and run by locals. **Siswati Crafts**, on the east side of the main road just north of the turn-offs to Lobamba and Mlilwane, is a good place to start; its range is wide and its prices are very low compared to the more upmarket craft shops in Mbabane, while its goods are as authentic as those in the Mbabane and Manzini markets.

The **Swazi Spa Health and Beauty Studio** is a real gem. On the west side of the main road north of the valley's two Sun hotels, the spa offers a very reasonably priced sauna, qualified masseurs and other treats, but its real attraction is the large outdoor mineral bath; a pool fed by a mineral spring that bubbles out at about 40°C. It has an awful name—the Cuddle Puddle—but anyone can swim there for about R2 (buy your ticket at the entrance). It is a good place to meet locals, especially in the evenings when people go there for a relaxing dip after work. There are changing rooms and a safe place to leave clothes and valuables.

Activities

Walking and Hiking: **Mlilwane Nature Reserve**, ✆ 461 037, has self-guided walking trails through montane forest and upland grassveld. Trails are from 1 to 3 hours, and the game/bird spotting is good.

Riding: Mlilwane offers guided riding trails through its lowland grassland, taking the rider quite close to game. Trails last about an hour. **High Hopes Riding Stables**, ✆ 84364, at the far southern end of the valley, just before the town of Manzini (look out for the signpost on the western side of the road), has very good horses for trail rides into the surrounding mountains, and lessons in dressage and jumping by well-qualified, friendly staff. All riding levels can be catered for.

Where to Stay and Eating Out

expensive

Swaziland's most expensive hotels are on the valley's main road; the **Royal Swazi Sun**, ✆ 61001, the **Ezulwini Sun**, ✆ 61201, and the **Lugongo Sun**, ✆ also 61201 all offer the usual bland 5 star luxury of the Sun chain, but have bars and restaurants that are convenient to visit after a dip in the mineral pool at the Swazi Spa. All hotels have casinos.

moderate

The **Mantenga Falls Hotel**, ✆ 61049, is a small, family-run hotel in a colonial villa just east of the National Museum on the road to the Mantenga Waterfall. The rooms are cosy, and the food very good. Back on the main road, the **Happy Valley**

Motel, ✆ 61061, is a notorious pick-up joint and prostitute's hang-out. The **Why Not? Disco** attached to the hotel is, for this reason, the area's most popular. You will hear so much about this place when in Swaziland and it should be visited. You are likely to be smoothly approached in the bar by any number of prostitutes, some heart-breakingly beautiful. The rooms are clean and some have separate bathrooms.

The **Mgenule Hotel**, ✆ 61041, is cheaper, and very close to Mbabane with clean, unpretentious rooms, a pool and (of all things) an Indian restaurant, while **Smoky Mountain Village**, ✆ 61291, has a group of attractive, self-contained A-frame log cabins set well back from the road.

cheap

Mlilwane Nature Reserve (to book accommodation ✆ 44541), has clean, neat self-catering accommodation in huts, and a cheaper camp site with ablution blocks. All overlook a hippo pool, and tame warthogs root around between the buildings. If you do not have a car, hitch or take a bus/taxi to the Mlilwane signpost on the valley's main road, then walk the ten minutes to the park entrance from where the ranger will arrange transport into the reserve.

Jimmy's Bar and Paradise Caravan Park, ✆ 84935, is 7km north of Manzini on the main road and offers very cheap camping, or a bed in a caravan. **Timbali Caravan Park**, ✆ 61156, has a variety of accommodation, from camp sites with ablution blocks to self-contained chalets that are cheap if shared.

All the hotels in the valley have reasonable restaurants priced according to their level of accomodation. However, it is worth visiting the moderately-priced **First Horse Restaurant**, ✆ 61137, and **Yen Saan**, ✆ 61051/2, both in the same enclave of shops signposted west of the main valley road near Mbabane. The First Horse is an Indian restaurant with a very colonial feel that serves excellent curries. The Yen Saan offers good Chinese food in an informal atmosphere, and is popular with Mbabane's younger crowd. Also moderate is the **Calabash**, ✆ 61187, at Timbali Caravan Park, and which despite its African name serves German and Austrian food.

Manzini

At the southern end of the Ezulwini Valley, Manzini is Swaziland's commercial hub and is slightly larger than the capital, Mbabane. Newly-built industrial complexes surround the old centre that in 1890 was the Boer capital of the region. When the British took over, they moved the capital to Mbabane for its cooler climate (Mbabane sits higher than Manzini). Today Manzini is known as the only seriously rough town in the country, though only at night.

However, Manzini does have a **Craft Market** on Thursdays and Fridays on Mnlakuvne Street, one block south of Ngwane, the main road. Country people travel for miles to sell their wares, some of which are very beautiful indeed. Apart from this, there are banks, shops and some restaurants, but Manzini is not recommended as a place to stay; rather visit the craft market on your way through.

Whether visiting or just passing through Manzini, it is worth timing your arrival outside of peak hours, when the main road through town is solid with traffic.

Where to Stay and Eating Out

The Enzulwini Valley's accommodation is conveniently close to Manzini, but if you do have to stay in town the **New George Hotel** on Ngwane Street, ✆ 52061, offers fairly expensive accommodation in a bland, uninteresting modern complex. More moderately priced are the **Prince Velebantfu Hotel**, ✆ 46465, at the Mbabane end of the Ngwane Road on the south side of town, and the **Mozambique Motel** on the corner of Meintjies Street and Mahleko Street, ✆ 52489 or 52586, one block north of Ngwane. The bars of both hotels are patronised by locals, and both have safe parking.

Alain's Restaurant and Nightclub on Nkoseluhlaza Street, one block south of Ngwane, ✆ 53598, offers a moderately-priced Swiss à la carte menu and is frequented by locals. **Gil Vicente's Restaurant** on Mahleko Street, ✆ 53871, one block north of Ngwane, offers Portuguese Mozambiquan dishes such as chicken peri-peri and spiced seafood at good prices. No need to book.

The Malkerns Valley

Just southwest of the Ezulwini Valley, runs the Malkerns Valley, a more rural area of stock farms, orchards and forest, all quite beautifully landscaped under the western mountains. The valley is not long, but it has one small town, **Mhlambanyatsi**, an old-fashioned farming settlement with three very good small hotels and restaurants (*see* below). All can arrange **hiking and riding** through the valley and into the mountains and sometimes **trout fishing**. One of the most tranquil areas of rural southern Africa, the Malkerns Valley hotels are favourites among Swazilanders from the city, and driving out to Mhlambayatsi for Sunday lunch has become something of a tradition.

Where to Stay and Eating Out

Mhlambanyatsi has three charming country hotels offering walks and rides up into the farmlands. **Meikles Mount**, ✆ 74110, has a moderately-priced, self-contained cottage at the foot of a forested mountainside, with walking, riding and trout fishing.

The **Forester's Arms Hotel**, ✆ 74177, is more expensive, and justly famous for its food, particularly the hearty Sunday lunches of roast beef and Yorkshire pud. **Malandela's**, ✆ 83115, offers full board at the top end of the moderate scale in a farmhouse in the centre of the valley, with lovely walking on the farm.

North of Mbabane the landscape changes dramatically, rising to high mountains and huge sweeps of empty country. On the road to the small town of Pigg's Peak is the fabulously beautiful **Malolotja Nature Reserve**, © 61171, a huge chunk of open upland cut by deep, forested valleys where cold, clear streams run, and game abounds. Malolotja is a paradise for the hiker: a series of trails wind through the 18,000 acre reserve. On these you are unlikely to meet any other humans, but zebra, warthog, vervet monkey, baboon, grey rhebok, reedbuck, oribi, klipspringer, blesbok, hartebeest, blue and black wildebeest and duiker can be encountered at any time. There are marked camping spots under trees, and you can walk for up to four days without exhausting the trails. Leopard, lynx and jackal thrive in the reserve, as do a host of birds, from the large raptors such as black and crowned eagle, to small sugarbirds. Blue cranes breed here, and the large Stanley's bustard is a regular sight. Protea forests, similar to those found in the Drakensberg, crowd close to the streams. Rare cycads—prehistoric giant tree-ferns—dot the grasslands.

For those who do not want to hike overnight, there are chalets and camp sites with an ablution block near the park. But the really beautiful country begins about two hours walk from here, and it is worth making the effort to see it. If you are planning to make a hiking trip at some time during your holiday, this should be high on your list. Trails must be booked in advance and you must have your own tent and stove, as fires are not allowed. The water from the mountain streams is safe to drink. The mountains in Malolotja are high; two of the peaks exceed 1800m, and the area is known to archaeologists for its relics of early man found in the Lion's Cave, where people were mining over 43,000 years ago. Bear in mind that this reserve can be very cold at night, and remember to take a water-proof in case of sudden weather changes.

Further along the road from Malolotja, after Pigg's Peak, the country becomes forested. Most is commercial, but a hidden stretch of magical indigenous forest lies along the 3km-long Phopanyane Waterfall, inside the **Phopanyane Nature Reserve**, © 71319. Look out for the signposted turning after the sign for the Pigg's Peak Hotel. This leads about 10km down a forestry road to another sign for the reserve entrance, a further 2km down a steep hill. Phopanyane is friendly, relaxed and one of the loveliest places to stay in Southern Africa. Although you can enter as a day visitor, the place is so beautiful that a stay of at least one night is recommended (*see* 'Where to Stay'). The reserve is run privately by Rod de Vletter, who was born and brought up in Swaziland and has been closely involved in education and nature conservation for the past 20 years. Phopanyane has been lovingly created by him; there are trails through the hardwood forest and bushveld on both sides of the falls, wildflowers grow in abundance, and there are landscaped gardens. Bushbuck and duiker are abundant, and the reserve is a good place to spot the colourful narina trogon, as well as green and (if you are very lucky) the rare purple lourie. De Vletter also organizes tailor-made safaris into Mozambique, and is closely involved with that country's slow rehabilitation of its game reserves and national parks, which still support large game populations. Phopanyane should not be missed.

Phophanyane Nature Reserve, ✆ 71319, has superb moderate to expensive accommodation in three luxurious cottages or comfortable safari tents (fully equipped with electricity and water) hidden in the forest close to the Phopanyane Falls. There is a choice of self-catering, half or full board, but the small restaurant and bar is very good, serving light to full meals with an emphasis on tasty wholefood, served with home-grown vegetables and home-cooked breads. Teas with home-baked cakes are also a speciality.

Malolotja Nature Reserve, ✆ 61171, offers moderate to cheap self-catering accommodation in comfortable log cabins, as well as camping.

The **Pigg's Peak Protea**, ✆ 71104, about 5km further up the road from Phopanyane towards the northern border, is a glitzy casino hotel full of noisy fruit machines and with a few gaming tables and expensive, rather bland rooms. While the hotel is comfortable enough, it should only be used if the above two places are fully booked.

Eastern Swaziland: the Lowveld

The hot, subtropical eastern Lowlands are a world apart from the temperate hills of western Swaziland. Along the main road from Manzini to the sugar-cane processing town of **Big Bend**, the altitude falls dramatically and the temperature rises by the minute. Bushveld replaces the grassy plains, interspersed with vast sugar-cane growing estates, the produce of which are processed at Big Bend. Despite its name, Big Bend is no more than a mill surrounded by houses for the plant workers, with a couple of small hotels. It is for the lowveld's superb stretches of wild country that travellers visit the area, particularly its three game reserves, Mkhaya, Hlane and Mlawula.

Mkhaya Game Reserve, ✆ 40957, 55km along the road from Manzini to Big Bend, is a centre for breeding rare African species. The reserve gets its name from the Swazi word *mkhaya*, which is the name of the wierd, spike-trunked knobthorn tree, which thrives here. Bookings must be made in advance, whether for overnight stays or for a day visit, as only very small parties are allowed in. Accommodation is in a luxurious tented camp in a wild fig forest. Mkhaya is known for rhino—both black and white—and harbours such rare antelope species as roan, sable and tsessebe. There is a small elephant herd, and buffalo are common. Crocodile and hippo swim in the pools. Zebra, giraffe and other plains game are prolific. There are leopard, hyena, and transient packs of wild dog. The game drives at Mkhaya are particularly good for getting you close to game, sometimes uncomfortably so, and there are guided walks in the evening. The catering is of the highest standard, despite the kitchen being in the deep bush. No vehicles other than those belonging to the reserve are allowed in Mkhaya, and visitors must leave their cars at the entrance lodge, from which one of the reserve's open-top Land-Rovers will take them to the bush camp, and out into the veld for a game drive. those staying overnight can also take a guided game-walk in the evening.

Mkhaya also offers **white-water rafting** trips in the Bulungu Gorge nearby, an experience rated by white-water enthusiasts as one of the best south of the Zambezi. These are also bookable in advance.

All in all, Mkhaya, although not cheap and despite the fact that it has no big cats as yet, offers a similar quality of safari as the very expensive private game reserves of the Eastern Transvaal, at far cheaper rates.

Hlane Game Reserve, ✆ 61597, about 100km north of Big Bend, is cheaper than Mkhaya. This large reserve of classic bushveld country supports elephant, white rhino giraffe, zebra, kudu and most plains game. Cheetah have been re-introduced and there are plans to bring in lion. Spotted hyena and leopard are present, but shy. The lakes have a few hippo. Hlane was donated by King Sobhuza II in 1967, having been one of the royal hunting preserves. There is a network of game-viewing roads, and guided early morning walks. Accommodation is in self-catering chalets and there is a camp site with ablution blocks. Elephant and rhino often visit the water-hole by the camp, and semi-tame ostriches wander about, sometimes unnervingly close. Be aware that Hlane has no shops or fuel. Gates are open sunrise to sunset.

Mlawula Game Reserve, ✆ 61151 or 61178/9, lies just east of Hlane, in the foothills of the Lebombo mounatins bordering Mozambique. The two reserves are linked via a good dirt road straddled by the small town of Simunye, where all supplies can be bought, and which has a bank and post office. The reserve is seldom visited, and worth going to for seclusion. Accommodation is in two camp sites with very basic ablution blocks, and which are often left unattended. Walking trails run thoughout the reserve, which supports mostly antelope and zebra though there are (shy) spotted hyena and leopard, and hippo and crocodile in the Mbuluzi river, which runs along the northern boundary. At the camp site by the railway which traverses the reserve you can arrange game drives, guided walks to a 'vulture restaurant'—a baited rock where you can watch the huge scavengers jostle over carrion—and canoeing on the river (guided, to make sure you don't run too close to hippo). Be aware that the water carries bilharzia, so do not wade in the shallows.

Like Malolotja Nature Reserve, the mountains at Mlawula have yielded some important archeological finds; human remains dating back to about 110,000 years ago have been found here. These are among the earliest human remains found anywhere in the world. Although not quite so primitive now, Mlawula still lacks fuel and supplies, so stock up before you go.

Siteke is a tiny town at the far eastern end of the country, set under the Lebombos, and is connected with Manzini by a good, tarred road. Although town is so small, it is known for its *Inyanga* **and** *Sangoma* **School**, which is run by the government to train traditional doctors and diviners (over 80 per cent of Swazilanders regularly consult the holders of both offices). The school is a fascinating mix of spiritualism, botany and natural science, all held in a strangely ordered, institutional framework. A visit here is imperative if you are in the area. Visits to the school must be arranged in advance either through the Siteki Hotel ✆ 34126 or Swazi Tourism in Mbabane ✆ 44556.

Outside Siteki is the appropiately named **Muti-Muti Nature Reserve**, run by Eco-Africa Safaris at Phophanyane, ✆ 71319. The word *muti* is generally used for both folk-medicine and magic in South Africa, and the reserve's proximity to Siteki's *Inyanga* and *Sangoma* School only partly explains the name. Within the reserve grow a variety of herbs and roots used by *Sangomas* for part of their work, and the Eco-Africa guides who take you into the reserve can point out many of them, and know their remedial and ritual uses. Muti-Muti covers an extensive wild area of differing landscapes, including hardwood forest, savannah, rocky hills and cliffs. Over two hundred bird species have been recorded.

Activities

Hiking: Day and overnight trails (without overnight huts) can be found at Mlawula Game Reserve, ✆ 61151/61178/9. The trails wind through dense buch, well populated with game, and climb up into the Lebombos. Otherwise, if you get detailed maps from Swazi Tourism in Mbabane, ✆ 44556, you can hike from village to village in the lowveld, and either camp by permission, or rent a hut for the night at each village you arrive in. Guided game walks are offered in Hlane Game Reserve, ✆ 61597, with a good chance of seeing elephant or rhino, and short evening walks are part of the package at Mkhaya Game Reserve, ✆ 40957.

Canoeing and White Water Rafting: Mkhaya Game Reserve organizes trips down the Bulungu Gorge.

expensive

Mkhaya Game Reserve, ✆ 40957, offers a luxurious tented camp with first-class chefs and a bar, set under the giant trees of a wild fig forest. You have to book at least a day in advance, however, and leave your car at the reserve's gate (there is safe parking here), before being taken in by an open Land-Rover.

moderate

Hlane Game Reserve, ✆ 61597, offers self-contained stone cottages in its main camp, which overlooks a waterhole where elephant and rhino gather in the evenings, while the **Siteki Hotel**, ✆ 34126, offers more standard accommodation in an old-fashioned family-run hotel with an à la carte restaurant and bar. The **Bend Inn**, and the **Riverside Motel**, ✆ 36012, both offer good, clean rooms, some en suite, with a bar and restaurant. Of the two, the Riverside Motel is the more popular with locals, who use the bar as a pub, and discos are occasionally held here.

cheap

Mlawula and **Hlane** Game Reserves both have camp sites with ablution facilities, and Hlane's cottages, if divided between two or more people, fall into the cheap category. Accommodation in both reserves is self-catering only.

The Grand Valley and Usutu Forest

From Manzini south to the little town of Hlatsikulu runs the Mkhondvo River, whose valley (known as the **Grand Valley**) is forested, with an overhanging mountain and giant fig trees growing on the riverbanks. This route is accessible via a good tarred road connecting Manzini with the southwestern border post of Mahamba and the Transvaal town of Piet Retief.

The Grand Valley serves as more of a scenic drive than a place to be explored in depth, unless you speak Siswati, or have a Swazi guide who can take you into the villages. You can make it a round trip by heading south past **Hlastikulu** for about 6km, then turning off onto the good dirt road heading north to **Mankayane**, which also passes through some very spectacular country. From here continue north to **Loyengo**, where you meet the tarred road. Head west, through the little town of **Bhunya** and look out for the signs for the massive **Usutu Forest**, whose 65,000ha of plantation and indigenous trees hide a wealth of interesting things, such as bushman paintings, forest trails and waterfalls. The signposted road takes you to the forest station, from where maps can be obtained, but it is easier to take a guide, as getting lost in the forest is easy. Either Eco-Africa Safaris (based a Phopanyane), ✆ 71319 or Umhlanga Tours (based in Mbabane), ✆ 45222 can arrange this, and provide transport if you have none of your own.

From Usutu, head back to Bhunya, where the tarred road forks, and take the north road to Mhlambanyatsi and the Malkerns Valley. You can either stay here (*see* above) or make the short trip back northeast to Mbabane.

Hiking: the Usutu forest has a good network of day trails, some of which follow the course of the fast-flowing Lusutfu River, while others head off to caves with bushman paintings. Follow the signs to the forest station, or take a guide (*see* above).

Gauteng (PWV)

Gauteng (PWV)

20 kms
10 miles

Gauteng—the Sotho for 'Place of Gold'—is the new name for the area comprising Pretoria, Johannesburg and the Witwatersrand (previously called PWV). After much prevarication and and a choice of over a dozen possible names, the province has finally been given a name that reflects the region's black majority—the first time this has happened in South Africa's history.

Founded after the 1994 elections, the new province takes in what is generally known as the 'Vaal Triangle', that is Johannesburg, and its surrounding industrial belt (which stretches south to the Vaal River—hence the name), the 'Rand' or Witwatersrand ('White-water's Ridge'), the range of low hills running west and east of Johannesburg where most of the goldmines are found, and the South African capital of Pretoria, which lies 60km north of Witwatersrand.

The vibrant city of Johannesburg, quiet, handsome Pretoria, and some of the surrounding country—in particular the Magaliesberg mountains—are definitely worth seeing, and if you have time to take in one of the subterranean mine tours, a half-day's immersion in the fiercely hot, cramped tunnels, amid the clanging of drills, a full kilometre under the earth, will explain better than any book the savage energy, frustration and quest for money that has dominated South Africa's turbulent 20th-century history.

Johannesburg

> One of the men points for him
> —Johannesburg umfundisi
> ...His heart beats like that of a child. There is nothing to do or think to stop it. Tixo, watch over me, he says to himself. Tixo, watch over me.

Cry the Beloved Country, Alan Paton

Johannesburg, Jo'burg, Joeys or Egoli (meaning City of Gold in the African lingua of the mine —all names for the same city) is Africa's most aggressively Westernized city, and one of its most vibrant. There is nothing in the mix of late 19th and early 20th century buildings dwarfed by post-war concrete and glass skyscrapers, to remind you that you are in Africa. But despite the physical ugliness of much of its downtown area (though some of its suburbs are very pretty, with wide-tree-lined streets, cafés and bars), and the fact that most South Africans run it down, *and* the fact that it can be dangerous, Johannesburg should not be missed, if only for a weekend. Almost all aspects of South African culture can be found here in the people drawn to the city for work, creating an atmosphere of intense human activity that can be very exciting. Anything happening in South Africa in terms of art, culture, music, drama, literature, happens in Johannesburg first, or at least finds its outlet to the public through the great city. This, coupled with the fact that geographically the city has nothing to distract its inhabitants (no beach, no mountain, few parks, not even a river), Johannesburg's nightlife and entertainment are what people live for. Music, especially, thrives here like nowhere else in South Africa, and, except for the city centre, which becomes something of a combat zone after dark, it is only at night that Johannesburg really comes alive.

Like Cape Town three hundred years before, Johannesburg suffered an artificially accelerated evolution from a confused mixture of race and culture. But while Cape Town's origins lie in its strategic importance for Europe's empire builders, Johannesburg is the result of private enterprise, and its history is only loosely connected with Europe. The city evolved from the pursuit of fortune, pure and simple, and was never intended to be a defensive or administrative centre. Perhaps because of this lack of pretence to anything but the quest for money, Johannesburg is somehow freer than other South African cities, a place of greater possibility, where all the elements of South African culture; urban black, traditional black, urban Afrikaner, rural Afrikaner, 'coloured', English, Indian, Chinese, bohemian, reactionary, all come together, however uneasily, to form a society based entirely around the individual endeavour, in whatever sphere.

Contrasting with Johannesburg's white suburbs, is the huge 'township' (almost a city in its own right) of Soweto, which lies just south-west of Johannesburg, and houses most of the city's black workers. Soweto, created in the 1950s, is not an African name, but merely an abbreviation for 'south-western townships', and although grindingly poor in some districts, it shares Johannesburg's quest for money; most people live in Soweto not by choice, but because they were banned (until 1990) from living in Johannesburg itself, which was reserved for whites only. Since the breakdown of apartheid, many Sowetans who have the money have moved into Johannesburg, especially the Jeppestown, Hillbrow, and Bezuidenhout Valley areas. But for most blacks on the Witwatersrand, Soweto is the cultural centre, the place from which the most effective anti-apartheid resistance was organised, and, despite frequent police raids, a place where life could be lived away from the eyes of white authority. Unfortunately however, Soweto and Johannesburg's other large 'townships' of Alexandria (east of the city) and Katlehong have suffered from intense violence since the mid-1980s, factions within the PAC (see p.494), ANC and IFP (the latter mostly composed of Zulu migrant workers living in hostels) fought out their political differences, leaving an uncounted death-toll behind them. Organized crime has also flourished during the recent chaos in the Witwatersrand townships, and wars between rival black taxi companies and general lawlessness and violence have also claimed hundreds of lives. The result is that Soweto and the other townships are largely out of bounds for the visitor, unless travelling with a group of locals or on one of the organized township tours during a period of political stability.

This is a shame, as much of the Johannesburg area's best music and culture is therefore inaccessible. Whether Soweto will become reasonably safe for travellers under the new ANC government, remains to be seen.

Johannesburg

N

Main nightlife areas

1000 metres
1000 yards

ATHOL-OAKLANDS

ATHOL

PRETORIA

LOUIS BOTHA

HAIGORN

IVY

IVY

LOUIS

NINTH

GRANT

NORWOOD

ORANGE GROVE

TENTH

EIGHTH

GOODMAN

SYLVIA

CLUB

FIRST

FREDERICK

COOPER

Fisherman's
Village

FRIEDLAND

BRUMA

OBSERVATORY

OBSERVATORY

MARCIA

Bruma
Lake

ALLUM EXT

BELLEVUE

HUNTER

ROCKEY

OBSERVATORY

HOMESTEAD

QUEEN

BROADWAY

ALLUM

RALEIGH

YEOVILLE

BECKER

GILL

NORTH
BEZUIDENHOUT

MARATHON

BROADWAY

BEREA
GORDON

BEZUIDENHOUT VALLEY

KITCHENER

KITCHENER

MILNER

LANGERMAN

HARLTON

BERTRAMS

DOORNFONTEIN

BEZUIDENHOUT

APOLONIA

ROBERTS

QUEEN

MONMOUTH

BEZUIDENHOUT
OP DIE
BERGEN

COMMISSIONER

JEPPESTOWN

JULES

JULES

JOHN PAGE

MAIN REEF

MARITZBURG

MAIN REEF

CHILVERS

RUEN

N 4

VICKERS

In short, Johannesburg has the best and the worst of human South Africa openly on view; all its conflict and creativity, poverty and obscene wealth, open-mindedness and reaction, race hatred and racial mixing, violence and indolent tranquility, all thrown together in one confused mass driven by money with all the human energy that goes into its pursuit. Whether exploring Johannesburg's grey, treeless centre, its few bohemian suburbs (Yeoville, Berea and Bellevue) with their relaxed street life, or, if you have an invitation, its vast 'townships', the traveller cannot but be aware of all these elements continually shifting around each other, and will come away with some insight into the intense, complicated human web that makes up South African society.

History

Before White Settlement

The highveld, South Africa's treeless, high grassland plateau, was populated around the 12th century by groups of semi-nomadic Bantu-speaking cattle herders (the ancestors of today's Tswana and Sotho people), some of whom lived a pastoral life, wandering with the seasonal grazing, some of whom built permanent stone villages, tilled the soil and worked with iron. Wildlife wandered at will, clustering around the region's perennial streams, which incised the flat landscape with narrow ravines.

This timeless cycle was suddenly devastated in the 1800s, when an abrupt series of political upheavals plunged the highveld into warfare and chaos. Modern historians claim that the wars were caused by clans fighting to control ivory and slave trading routes that had become established across the eastern side of South Africa in the late 18th-century with the arrival of European traders at Port Natal, the Cape and Delagoa Bay. Powerful clans in the highveld included the Taung, Rolong, Tlokwa and Thlaping (all Tswana-speaking), and these began to fight amongst themsleves, creating standing armies and raiding each other incessantly for livestock and captives.

In 1820, a renegade clan called the Ndebele (meaning 'fleeing ones') arrived in the highveld from the south under their king, Mzilikazi, who had been a general of Shaka, the Zulu king, whose empire was expanding in Natal (*see* **Natal** 'History'). The Ndebele carved out their own highveld kingdom, destroying some of the Tswana groups, and by the mid-1830s, parts of the highveld had been depopulated—although the Tswana clans were still active, they had lost their dominance to the Ndebele.

SAR and Gold

Into this confused picture stumbled the Voortrekkers in 1836. After being worsted by Ndebele attacks, the newcomers allied with local Tswana clans and devoted themselves to breaking the Ndebele's power. Following a great battle at Vegkop in the southern highveld, the Boers began pushing the Ndebele north—eventually into modern Zimbabwe—and settled the Witwatersrand in the 1840s as part of their new South African Republic (SAR).

A few towns were founded, including the ramshackle village of Pretoria (which later became the SAR's capital), but as recently as 100 years ago, the area where Johannesburg sprawls today was still open grassland.

In 1886, the area's fortunes changed abruptly. An Australian prospector, George Harrison, discovered signs of gold-bearing rock on the Witwatersrand. He purchased a claim from the SAR, but was not impressed with the quality of the ore he found, and left for the gold rush already happening in the Eastern Transvaal. But other prospectors began trickling in, and by 1888 several hundred were scratching away on the Witwatersrand. More gold was found, and in what promised to be vast reefs, but it was of low quality, and lay in seams too deep for individual miners to reach. To be profitable, the reefs would have to be mined on an industrial scale by a large company with plenty of capital. President Kruger and the SAR government, determined to establish control over the new diggings but lacking the vast funds needed to exploit them, courted the diamond magnates of Kimberley, offering concessions to whoever had sufficient finance to establish large-scale mines.

Meanwhile, in 1886–7, the SAR laid out four small tented villages, selling plots to all-comers at exorbitant rates. Dubbed 'Johannesburg', possibly after Johannes Rissik, the surveyor, or after Paul Kruger, whose first name (which he never used) was also Johannes, within a month the make-shift town was full of speculators intent on the coming boom. Concessions were granted to several mining companies, but the chief investor was Cecil Rhodes' De Beer's Diamond Company, which opened its Witwatersrand office under the name of Consolidated Goldfields.

The one obstacle facing the mining companies was labour. Because the gold ore was of low quality, and the capital investment enormous, only the cheapest possible labour could be employed. Except where specialized machine skills were necessary, white labour was thus out of the question. The mine bosses knew that rural blacks could be persuaded to work for very low wages—as had been proved at Kimberley—but the proposed Witwatersrand project would need far more labourers than Kimberley ever had, more even than were available within the whole SAR. Recruiting officers were sent all over South Africa to persuade rural black men to come and work on 'the Rand', as the area was already known, attracting them with lies about high wages and good living conditions. In fact, the only housing was in primitive compounds near the mines, to which the workers were not allowed to bring their families.

City of Sin

Johannesburg grew up a violent, hard-drinking town servicing tens of thousands of black labourers, skilled white machine operators (mostly imported from Britain) and entrepreneurs. Within three years it was the largest city in South Africa. With so few available females, prostitution soon became the most lucrative industry after mining, and pimps began sending scouts to Europe, tempting working class girls to come to Johannesburg with paid passage and a promise of domestic work, then keeping them as virtual slaves in the brothels that sprang up all over town. By the early 1890s a few genteel suburbs, like Parktown and Houghton, had appeared for mining magnates and their families, but the great, squalid city remained an anarchic place governed by money, greed and raw energy.

Paul Kruger and his government were appalled at the city of sin they helped create. But their mining dividends soon became so large that, although laws were passed to try to curb prostitution and liquor manufacturing, little was done to temper the vice of the brash new city. However, Kruger was shrewd enough to see a potential political threat in the growing fortunes of the *uitlanders* (foreigners) of Johannesburg; the mining bosses, in particular, were known to be very pro-British. Kruger instituted a blanket policy to protect his government: no *uitlander* whether magnate, technician, pimp, or whore was to be granted citizenship of the SAR. And without citizenship, the *uitlanders* could have no vote.

This soon caused great dissent, as the magnates and miners knew that they were fuelling the SAR's now burgeoning economy. Throughout the 1890s Johannesburg's press called on both the Cape and the British government to persuade Kruger to grant them the franchise, by force of arms if necessary. The mining magnates, or 'Randlords' also took up the cause; Cecil Rhodes, of the De Beers Company, was now South Africa's richest man, and from 1890, managed to get himself elected Prime Minister of the Cape Colony. From Cape Town, he began secret negotiations with the British government to provoke a war with the SAR. In 1895, Rhodes financed an attempted coup d'etat on Pretoria. But the raiding party, under one Dr Jameson, was caught by Kruger's *commandos* and promptly thrown in jail.

Strife and Strikes

Such was probably Rhodes' intention; the Jameson Raid excited much ridicule and censure from the European powers, and inspired calls in the British press for the army to redress the embarassment. As much from this pressure as from a desire to grab the gold mines, Britain officially took up the 'plight' of Johannesburg's *uitlanders* in 1896 and began moving towards a serious attempt at annexing the gold-rich SAR. The Second Anglo–Boer War was declared in 1899 (*see* **South African History**). Johannesburg fell silent, as the *uitlanders* fled south of the SAR. The British army occupied Johannesburg in 1900, and the city remained uncharacteristically ordered and quiet until the Boer surrender of 1902, when business opened again with renewed vigour.

By 1904, the shallowest gold reefs had been exhausted. Deeper seams would have to be tapped. But working at deeper levels meant increased costs for the companies and terrible conditions for the black miners. To make sinking the shafts profitable, the mine bosses brought over thousands of Chinese labourers on three-year contracts at pitiful wages. Strikes were attempted by black and white miners, alike, but were quickly put down. The Chinese stayed from 1907–1910, and were repatriated after having sunk the shafts much deeper, and the mining companies gave their employees no choice but to go back to work under worse conditions.

But the Rand's political problems were just beginning. From 1911, the government, pressurized by newly-formed white trade unions, passed laws reserving unskilled mine labour for blacks and skilled jobs for whites. This displeased the mining companies, who knew they could reduce costs by training blacks for skilled work at low wages. For quite different reasons, the job colour bar also displeased the Rand's growing numbers of poor whites, as it excluded them from the unskilled labour market. Finally, it displeased black workers because it denied them any possibilty of an increase in wages. The only group whose future had been secured for the better were the skilled white mineworkers, but even they were unhappy—with the deep working conditions—and began to demand better wages and more flexibility from the mine bosses.

In 1913, some 19,000 white workers went on strike over the sacking of five men who disputed their working hours. Every mine was shut down, riots broke out in Johannesburg and troops were sent in. Alarmed, the government re-instated the five men who had been fired, but passed the Riotous Assemblies bill, which empowered them to use force to stop any meeting that threatened public order. However, between 1914 and 1920, taking advantage of the government's need for increased production to pay for its war effort, strikes and fighting between white mineworkers and police became a regular feature of life in the Witwatersrand, and the mining companies were forced to grant several pay rises.

The success of white strikes inspired the Rand's black workers to organize their own industrial action. In 1918, Johannesburg's 'bucket boys' (human night soil collectors) struck over over low pay and poor conditions, and the revolt spread to mines where tens of thousands of workers also went on strike. Despite being brutally put down, the black strikes caused the mining companies more worry than the white strikes, as the whole industry ultimately relied on black labour. The Randlords told the government that the job colour bar would have to go if gold mining was to be ensured for the future.

This incensed the skilled white workers. In 1922, a general strike was called, with 24,000 white workers in the Witwatersrand downing tools. and taking over the city. Prime Minister Smuts sent in the army and air force, and more than 200 people were killed in street battles before the miners went back to work. However Smuts took the lesson to heart—South Africa's skilled whites represented the bulk of the voting public. Despite the mining companies' protests, the job colour bar remained in place.

The Townships

Meanwhile, the government decided that the best way to control the Rand's black workers would be to physically contain them. From 1923–27 a series of laws were passed confining blacks to specially demarcated residential areas. By the mid-1930s several 'townships' had been built where modern Soweto sprawls today, but the law was too much for Johannesburg's local government to cope with and urban black culture began to flourish in the city, particularly in Sophiatown, just west of the central business district. Literature, dance, and jazz (known collectively as *Kwela* culture) thrived in Sophiatown between the 1930s and '50s, and was strong enough to launch some international careers, notably those of saxophonist Dollar Brand and singer Miriam Makeba.

The *Kwela* movement did much for black morale in Johannesburg—reflected in the appeareance of the first black trade unions. The Council for Non-European Trade Unions (CNETU) was founded in 1936, changing its name to the African Mineworkes' Union (AMU) in 1941. From 1939, the Rand's black workers profited from the government's being distracted by the war effort. By 1943, the AMU had grown to 25,000 members and had won several campaigns for wage increases. A series of successful bus boycotts brought commuter fares down, and blacks began to alleviate the severe overcrowding of the new townships and Sophiatown by setting up squatter camps, in direct defiance of the segregation laws. The South African Communist Party (SACP) also became multi-racial during the late 1930s, and this, combined with the growing powerbase of the ANC, made it look as though Johannesburg's blacks might at last gain some real political prestige.

Apartheid

But once the Second World War was over, Smuts' government decided that the Rand's blacks had gone far enough. In 1946, when 60,000 AMU members struck over pay and working conditions, the police were sent in with guns. Over two days, twelve miners were killed and more than 1000 injured. But Smuts was perceived by many South African whites as having allowed too many concessions. In 1948, the Afrikaner-led, ultra right-wing, National Party won a general election and promised the systematic and strict enforcement of total colour segregation; in short, apartheid, and the advances made by the Johannesburg's blacks were quickly reversed.

In 1950, the SACP was outlawed, and the ANC came under strict surveillance. In 1952, the government announced that the hated pass books that black mine workers had been forced to carry to qualify for work, were to be carried by all blacks at all times. Not being able to produce the book would mean jail, and probably a beating. Thousands of ANC supporters across the country were arrested for flouting the new law. However, this confirmed the determination of the ANC's members to resist. In 1953, in Kliptown, just outside Johannesburg, the organisation drafted a 10-clause **Freedom Charter**, which aimed to introduce non racism at all levels of life, and started to lobby parliament to have it accepted. Forty-one years on, the Charter has finally become ANC government policy, but in 1953, the Afrikaner government was in no mood for such concessions. Instead, legislation was passed to make squatting illegal, giving local authorities the right to use force for eviction. Next, the Rand's mission schools, where the black intelligentsia that had led the pre-War movements had been educated, were shut down, and blacks were barred from the major universities. Johannesburg's University of the Witwatersrand staged a massive protest, and the ANC tried to set up independent schools in Johannesburg, but money for this ran out by 1956. Black children were to be educated only as the government thought fit. Finally, prime minister D. F. Malan ordered the forced removal of Sophiatown's residents to the newly contructed township of Soweto in 1955. Armed police arrived with bulldozers, and in less than a week Sophiatown, the heart of urban black South Africa, had ceased to be.

Having razed the Rand's centre of black resistance, the government turned its attention to the resistance organizations themselves. In December 1956, police arrested about 500 people, black and white, on charges of treason. A series of mass trials (known as the Treason Trials) were held in Johannesburg's Old Drill Hall from 1957 to 1961. Most defendants were eventually acquitted, but the protracted hearings and detention of ANC and SACP members did considerable damage. Resistance merely went underground: in 1959, several ANC leaders met in Soweto, and formed the more militant Pan African Congress, or PAC, pledging to fight apartheid step by step, starting with the Pass Laws.

On March 21, the PAC spearheaded a call for all African men in the Rand to throw away their pass books, and present themselves for arrest. It was an inspired idea: the Rand's industry came to a sudden halt as tens of thousands of black men assembled at police stations in the townships around Johannesburg. The police were baffled, and their jails could not cope with the numbers. But the plan went awry; at **Sharpeville**, south of

Johannesburg, the police, scared by the size of the (unarmed) crowd around them, opened fire without orders. Some 69 protesters were killed and 180 wounded.

Rather than prosecute the murderous policemen, the government took advantage of Sharpeville to call a State of Emergency, ban the ANC and PAC and arrest their leaders. The response of both organizations was to form military wings and set up training camps abroad. But in 1963, a young lawyer named Nelson Mandela, head of the ANC's armed wing Umkhonto we Sizwe (MK), and several colleagues arrested at Rivonia near Johannesburg, were charged with plotting terrorism and given life sentences. In July 1964,, a bomb exploded, at Johannesburg's railway station, injuring 23 people. The saboteur, a white schoolteacher named John Harris, was arrested in Roodepoort, in western Johannesburg. The MK was implicated: John Harris was hanged.

Education and Violence

The resistance movement in the Rand's townships was silenced for over ten years after the Rivonia Trial. But resentment still smouldered, particularly amongst Soweto's schoolchildren, who saw their parents cowed, and themselves moulded by apartheid through compulsory learning of the government's language—Afrikaans. In June 1976, students of Meadowlands Tswana School and Marius Isaacson High School in Soweto vandalized their school buildings, and had minor clashes with local police. Students from all over Soweto planned a mass rally at Orlando Sports Stadium. Hundreds marched; local police fired teargas canisters, and the schoolchildren replied with a hail of stones. The police opened fire. General rioting ensued, and sporadic clashes with police and schoolchildren continued through the next two years, in which several hundred schoolchildren and others died. The government closed most of Soweto's schools and a whole generation of Witwatersrand blacks lost their formal education, a legacy that the present government has now inherited in the form of an unemployable, disaffected and increasingly criminal youth.

Through the late 1970s and '80s the region became increasingly violent. Unfortunately, most incidents of mass violence came from the increasingly factionalised black political parties and degenerated into horrific ethnic fighting, under the banner of the parties themselves or in the form of irrational violence. Many people suspect the government's security forces of incitement, especially for the waves of attacks on black workers travelling on local commuter trains which became endemic in the late 1980s, yet seemed inexplicable at the time. The townships' *tsotsis*, or criminal youth, had a field day, and crime became rampant, even in Johannesburg's city centre, which became a no-go zone after dark.

But despite high crime rates, Johannesburg's city centre and white suburbs saw almost no political violence until early in 1994, when IFP and ANC supporters clashed in central Johannesburg, leaving scores of bodies in their wake. However, this has been the one exception; since the 1994 elections, violence across the whole region has declined remarkably (with the exception of Katlehong). Many of the imbalances and wrongs of apartheid have yet to be redressed, and crime still runs high, but Johannesburg itself is one of the few places in South Africa where the races mix, at all levels of life, as a matter of course—especially in the yuppie/bohemian suburbs of Yeoville and Berea. Houses in the inner neighbourhoods are increasingly being bought by black families—especially east of the city centre in Jeppestown, the Bezuidenhout Valley, and Hillbrow.

In the one, brief century since its birth, Johannesburg has been the dynamo for almost all the events in the country's turbulent political history. The hope is that, after such a difficult childhood, the city will mature into a more mellow centre for South Africa's urban culture, and grow away from its cycle of violence; but meantime there is still no more exciting city in the whole of South Africa.

Getting to and from Johannesburg

by air

Johannesburg's international and domestic **Jan Smuts Airport** (information ✆ 975 9963) receives daily flights from Britain and Europe. The airport is about 25km north-east of the town centre along the R21 highway towards Pretoria. Impala Buses connect the airport with Johannesburg's centre every half-hour from 5am–10pm. Airport buses drop travellers off at the Airport Terminal in the Rotunda Bus Station on the corner of Rissik and Wolmarans Streets in the city centre, from whence buses can be taken to all of South Africa's main towns and cities. **Lanseria Airport**, the other domestic terminal runs no shuttle service to/from the city centre, but most charter companies throw in transport to/from Lanseria as part of the flight package, ✆ 659 2750 for details. For transport to other areas of Johannesburg from the Rotunda it is best to take a taxi, especially at night.

by car

Johannesburg is linked to the Northern Transvaal, the Orange Free State and Cape Town (via the Karoo) by the N1 highway, from the Eastern Transvaal and Mozambique via the N4, from Durban, Natal and the north-eastern Orange Free State by the N3, and with the Northern Cape via the N12.

by bus

Long-distance buses run from the **Rotunda Bus Station** on the corner of Rissik and Wolmarans Streets, at the western end of the city centre. Bus services connecting Johannesburg with most of the country's major towns and points in-between include: **Greyhound** ✆ 333 2136, **Transtate**, and **TransLux**, ✆ 774 3313 for both and **Intercape** ✆ 333 5231. These are the main services for long-distance bus journeys. Unfortunately, the Rotunda has no central information line.

by rail

Johannesburg's central railway station entrance is on Wolmarans Street (information ✆ 773 5878). Trains leave daily for Cape Town, via Bloemfontein and Kimberley (a 24-hour trip). Durban services run at 12.30pm Sun–Fri, and East London/Port Elizabeth services run on Tues, Thurs and Sun. The Blue Train (*see* **Travel**) can also be booked from here. Suburban trains out to Pretoria also run from here. These run about every half-hour and are much used by commuters. In the late 1980s and early '90s, random attacks became common on these services, as well as on the lines connecting Johannesburg with the townships, but armed guards now patrol the trains, and they are safe to travel.

hitch-hiking

A way to get around the problem of hitching out of Johannesburg's dangerous inner-city freeways, is to dial **Share-A-Lift**, ✆ 444 1559. While not completely free, you will only be asked to share minimal petrol costs, and, provided you have a few days to wait for a lift to come through (they go to most areas and cities), this is undoubtably the cheapest way to travel safely.

Getting Around

by bus

Johannesburg's central buses run from Eloff Street in the city centre to all neighbourhoods (information: ✆ 838 2125) about once every 15 minutes. Weekend services to most neighbourhoods can be picked up from Vanderbijl Square, on the corner of Rissik and Main Streets. Weekday and (infrequent) weekend services shut down after 8.30pm, but after dark, it is *always* better to take a taxi, despite the extra cost, as the city centre becomes unsafe, especially if you are weighed down with baggage.

by taxi

You cannot hail a taxi in Johannesburg: either ring for one, or take one from a taxi rank. These can be found at the Rotunda Bus Station and outside the Carlton Centre on Commissioner Street. Telephoning is much easier, and you can get a price before you travel. Consult the *Yellow Pages*.

by black taxis

These pick up from bus stops along all the main routes and go out to most neighbourhoods. Fares average around 1–2 Rand. However, as ever, these minibuses have a high accident rate and mugging is not unknown.

car hire

Although Johannesburg has all the standard, overpriced car hire firms, it also has some good local deals. Try **U-Drive** ✆ 331 3735, **Tempest** ✆ 397 1850, **Dolphin** ✆ 885 1122 or **Imperial** ✆ 337 2300.

Tourist Information

Publicity Association: North State Building on the corner of Market and Kruis Streets, in the southern city centre, ✆ 294 961.

Johannesburg's Neighbourhoods

Most of the city's life goes on in the neighbourhoods immediately surrounding the downtown area, including most accommodation, points of interest, entertainment, nightlife and restaurants. For this reason, it is as well to acquaint yourself with the city's geography before arriving.

Johannesburg City Centre

N

Main nightlife areas

500 metres
500 yards

Yeoville, Berea and **Melville** are the three liveliest suburbs, with the most enjoyable safe streetlife. They all have galleries, restaurants, bars and music venues, particularly Rocky Street, on the Yeoville/Berea border. **Hillbrow**, which used to be safe, has now become dangerous by night, but is still known for the cabaret clubs established there in the late 1950s. **Braamfontein** houses the University of the Witwatersrand (known as 'Wits'), South Africa's most prestigious university after Cape Town, and is a theatre and nightclub distict by night. Just west of the city centre is **Newtown**, which has a lively precinct around the old town market that now includes a large theatre, flea market, galleries and restaurants. East of the city centre is the man-made **Bruma Lake**, on whose southern shore lies the 'largest flea market in Southern Africa'. North of Yeoville is the yuppie area of **Orange Grove**, which also has good bars, and north of here, start the rich residential neighbourhoods known collectively as The Northern Suburbs, including **Houghton** and **Parktown**, where the first Randlords built their mansions, **Rosebank**, known for upmarket galleries and restaurants, and **Sandton**, known for wealth, pure and simple.

The City Centre

Downtown Johannesburg has little to interest the traveller except for its transport centres, a few museums, plush shopping centres and the chance of being mugged. The most central zone—called the CBD (central business district)—becomes a deserted and dangerous urban ghetto after dark. Even by day, an obvious foreigner is likely to become a target for crime. If you are going to explore downtown Johannesburg, only do so during office hours, decide where you are going, and walk purposefully. On no account wander around with a backpack. When arriving at the bus or train station, take a taxi to your destination, even if it is a rip-off, and stow your belongings safely before walking the streets.

Museum Africa, © 833 5624, on the corner of Wolhunter and Bree Streets (*open Tues–Sat 9–5*), is one of South Africa's most comprehensive cultural museums. The emphasis is on African art and craft from all over the continent, including colonial exhibits, displays of ethnic life and belief and exhibits dedicated to modern Africa and its international culture. The museum hosts regular exhibitions specialising in groups of artists and specific crafts. On the fourth floor is an excellent photography museum whose displays include a photographic history of Sophiatown and Soweto. Telephone first to find out what's on.

The older **Geological Museum**, on Market Street (*open Mon–Sat 9–5*), has a breakdown of South Africa's astonishing mineral wealth and varied geological make-up. Apart from the inevitable diamonds and gold nuggets, the museum has a history of the mining industry that brought about the country's present wealth. In the same building is the **Public Library**, which has such useful things as nationwide Yellow Pages, and national and international newspapers and magazines.

Railway enthusiasts will enjoy the **Transnet Museum** (*open Mon–Fri 7.30–3.45*) in the old main hall of the Johannesburg's central railway station. The entrance is on De Villiers Street. Old steam locomotives dominate the displays, but there are also boats, cars and wagons, as well as a small gallery of paintings by Pierneef, one of South Africa's best-known landscape painters, active at the turn of the century.

The **Johannesburg Art Gallery** (*open Tues–Sun 10–5*), founded in 1910, is at the edge of the infamous Joubert Park, on King George Street. It houses a general collection of old and contemporary South African art, combined with some international works, old and new, of varying quality. There are early 20th century works by the better-known South African artists, such as Pierneef and Irma Stern, combined with modern township art. Next door is a shop selling African handcrafts.

The **Carlton Centre**, which occupies almost the whole block between Commissioner and Main Streets, is central Johannesburg's principal landmark and houses a massive shopping centre and landmark, which, above its plush shops has a revolving tower, the **Carlton Panorama**, on the 50th floor. There is a small charge payable before entering the lift that takes you up. From here, the view out over the wide, flat Witwatersrand is unparalleled. The mines, mine dumps, 'townships', and the great sprawl of Johannesburg itself (which now stretches almost all the way to Pretoria) are all laid out before you, and a sense of the sheer scale of the place, and of the human energy that has gone into creating it in such a short time.

The **Standard Bank Centre**, ✆ 636 4231, on Frederick Street (*open Mon–Fri 8.30– 4.30, Sats 8–12.30*), has a gallery that hosts exhibitions of contemporary South African and foreign art, as well as concerts and lectures. Selected works from the Grahamstown Festival usually go on show here.

Shoppers usually flock to the **Smal Street Mall**, linking Bree and Jeppe streets, near their intersection with Von Wielligh Street. This is a pedestrian strip fronted by small but smart shops, with a few outdoor cafés. Worth looking into is the **Operation Hunger Craft Shop**, which sells very good work from all over Africa at far cheaper prices than the Smal Street address would imply. Continue west along Jeppe Street for about nine blocks, and you come to **Diagonal Street**. This used to be one of the most dangerous areas of Johannesburg (and still is after dark), but by day, its old function as the city's financial centre, has re-established itself. The old colonial-style shops have now become rather smart, and, apart from a monstrous skyscraper, the street has a pleasant, old-world feel. Also on Diagonal Street is the magnificent old **Stock Exchange**. Guided tours are offered Mon–Fri at 11am and 2pm. These are quite fun, and the guides have several good anecdotes about the early Randlords and the almost obscene size of some of the deals they struck when the gold reefs first boomed in the 1900s. The Stock Exchange also made the news in 1991, when PAC terrorists planted a bomb there that killed several stockbrokers and money dealers.

Diagonal Street makes a good place from which to walk to the Market theatre complex in Newtown (see below) or due north to Doornfontein, the area just north-east of the city centre. This is both the university and the theatre district. Its **Alhambra Theatre** on Sivewright Street, is the city's most handsome, a turn-of-the-century building with many late Victorian and Art Nouveau elements. Now a national monument, it still stages large productions (*see* 'Entertainment').

Downtown Johannesburg has three small, specialist museums, including the **Chris Lessing Boxing Museum** (*open Mon–Fri 8–1, 2–4.30*), on the corner of Kerk and

Harrison Streets; and the **First National Banking Museum**, on Market Street (*open Mon–Fri 9–4*), which offers a dry history of banking and money-making in South Africa since the early days of 17th-century Cape Town, through the diamond and gold booms, to the uncertain present.

Newtown

This area, just to the west of the city centre, is reached by Bree and Jeppe Streets. The **Market Theatre** and its surrounding restaurants and bars are the main attraction, and the area is lively (and safe) by night. By day, the **Market Galleries** are worth checking out. These are in what is known as the Market Precinct, or AngloVaal Mall, which runs in front of the large theatre entrance. Contemporary art is displayed, mostly painting, sculpture and prints. The **Thupelo Art Gallery** is in the basement underneath the precinct, and displays township art and pottery. The **Institute of Contemporary Art**, near the flea market on Jeppe Street, claims to 'bridge the gap between academic and commercial galleries'. Its displays tend to the avant-garde. The **Newtown Galleries** occupy an old warehouse at the corner of Bree and Wolhuter Streets, also by the Flea Market, and sell modern art, jewellery, and other crafts. If your head is reeling from too much art, visit Newtown on Saturday for the **Flea Market** (*open 9–4*), one of the city's best, selling everything from antiques to T-shirts, puppets, rugs and shoes. The **Mineral Market** on Bree Street, sells semi-precious Southern-African gems (mounted and unmounted) all through the week. Another market, but of totally different character, is the **Oriental Plaza** off the west end of Park Road, an Indian Bazaar selling spices, foods and general goods. You will be expected to haggle.

Braamfontein

This is the northwest part of downtown. The vast central campus of the **University of the Witwatersrand** is here, on Jan Smuts Boulevard, as is the large **Civic Theatre** (opposite the **Civic Centre**), which shows both mainstream and fringe productions. On the corner of Hospital and Stiemens Streets is the **Adler Museum of Medicine** (*open Mon–Fri 9–4*) which, apart from displaying implements and histories (the world's first heart transplant was performed in South Africa), also has a herbarium, with the medicinal properties of each plant explained, and a *sangoma's* (witch-doctor's) hut. These attractions aside, Braamfontein is best visited at night for its plentiful theatre, live-music and nightclub scene (*see* 'Entertainment' and 'Nightlife').

Yeoville and Bellevue

These two neighbourhoods, just northeast of the city centre, comprise Johannesburg's liveliest area. Linked by one long road, called Raleigh Street at the west end of Yeoville, and becoming **Rockey Street** at the beginning of Bellevue, this part of town has the most lively bars, cafés, nightlife and music. Almost all the places worth visiting are on Raleigh and Rockey Streets (in fact the same street) and the residential avenues leading off are home to a large concentration of Johannesburg's bohemians.

The best way to take it in is to walk, by day or night, from the first few blocks of Rockey steadily west onto Raleigh Street, until you reach the sign telling you that you are entering the Berea neighbourhood (approximately 3km) Listings of the cafés, bars, restaurants and music venues appear below under the relevant sections. Suffice to say here that, by day the long strip includes a regular flea market, outside terraces to drink on (the most popular being **Rockerfellas Jazz Bar** and the **Bar Pita** on lower Rockey Street), and a mixed crowd of black and white trendies, students, and others. By night it is just as busy, but with people moving between restaurants, bars and clubs.

The Yeoville end is smarter and fairly yuppified, with cafés being the main attraction. The Rockey Street end is (appropriately) more rocking—a mix of hippies, metalheads, funk and jazz fans and young people just hanging out. Most of the bars and music venues are down here. There are also some interesting shops, including second-hand bookshops, and jewellery and clothing shops, some of which are clustered together just off Rockey Street, in a little enclave called the **Bizarre Centre**. Set out and explore. The tension so pervasive in many parts of Johannesburg is happily absent here.

Hillbrow

This used to be Johannesburg's number one area for nightlife. Situated on the hill just north of downtown, and recognizable from afar for its tall radio tower, Hillbrow is undergoing rapid change. Its original inhabitants, mostly poor Afrikaners, were later joined by European immigrants, who in turn are giving way to blacks moving into the city from the townships. This should be a positive change to an already cosmopolitan district, but so far the inevitable tensions resulting from a mix of these groups has made Hillbrow unsafe for tourists, if only by night. However, the jazz and cabaret clubs, for which Hillbrow became famous in the 1960s and '70s, still thrive and it is worth checking them out, only be sure to take a taxi both to and from the venue. You can wander two main strips by day, which have some good record shops. But even then, stay out of the side streets. The clubs are listed below (*see* 'Nightlife'). Also worth visiting is the **Windybrow Theatre**, a whimsical 1920s mock-Tudor building that has several stages (*see* 'Entertainment').

Mellville

This suburb, west of the city centre (reached via the R55, Empire Street) has been largely colonised by yuppies, and has a safe, relaxed feel. Its Main Street is one of Johannesburg's best areas for entertainment, as several good bars, restaurants and live music venues can be found there (see 'Eating Out' and 'Entertainment'). Melville also has good moderate and cheap accommodation, and makes a good place to stay if you have a car and don't have to rely on buses from the city centre.

Bruma Lake

Bruma Lake has what claims to be the largest covered flea market in Southern Africa on a weekend, you can buy just about anything here, but the emphasis is on jewellery and crafts. Look out for the traders from Zaire, who sell incredible masks, palm-leaf mats, carvings, printed cloths and other artefacts. They will expect you to bargain. If you speak French to them, the prices may drop considerably.

The market sits by a large man-made lake. On the opposite bank to the market, and linked to it by a footbridge, is a development called **Fisherman's Village**, a series of cafés, bars and restaurants designed to resemble a Mediterranean village. This sounds ghastly, but it is one of the few such enterprises in South Africa that actually seems to have worked—if only for weekend pleasure-seeking—a combination of the dry, sunny light, and the crowd. Bruma Lake is great fun to visit at the weekend, but is rather dead through the week.

Orange Grove

This is another yuppie/bohemian area about 2km northeast of Yeoville and Rockey Street. It is mainly composed of houses, but its commercial strip, Louis Botha Avenue, has a very good bar that should not be missed, the **Radium Bar**, which has not changed since the 1940s. On the contrary, the Portuguese-run bar still attracts the same mixed crowd of professionals, drinkers and young pleasure-seekers as it always did. The place gets very busy most nights, but it is a good place to meet people and get local information.

The Northern Suburbs

This is where the money is. The real money, that is. **Houghton** and **Parktown**, the oldest of the northern suburbs (just north-west of the city centre), were built at the end of the 19th century by the Randlords, or mining magnates, who moved their operations from Kimberley to Johannesburg when gold began to pay better than diamonds. Their mansions are mostly still private houses. Tours into some of them can be arranged via **Parktown Heritage** © 482 3349, (mornings only). The tour guides dress in period costume and are ready with anecdotes about the rich eccentrics who built the mansions. Some of them are worth seeing for the gardens alone.

Trendier than Parktown is **Rosebank**, with many upmarket art galleries, restaurants and a repertory cinema along its main strip of Oxford Road. Some of the galleries showcase the most fashionable artists, both black and white. Details are listed below (see 'Art Galleries').

Sandton, the next suburb north, is the wealthiest of all. Sandton housewives are the butt of many Jo'burg jokes, for example;

Q.'How many Sandton housewives does it take to change a lightbulb?'

A. 'Mah dear, we have *people* to take care of those sorts of things.'

Behind their giant, security-fenced walls, the vast homes rival those of Beverly Hills in opulence and ostentation. Other than that, the area is dead, except for the massive **Sandton Centre**, a vast, shopping centre on several floors that sells only the most expensive of everything, and where the traveller can observe the housewives in question at play. For all its being a monument to money, the Sandton Centre does have one or two very good shops, particularly those selling Africana. The **Totem** shop (shop U17) in particular sells very beautiful artefacts from West Africa, some antique, some modern, at prices that, owing to the favourable exchange rate, most travellers can afford.

Gold Reef City

This theme park (comprising a re-constructed pioneer town and funfair) lies just southwest of the city centre along the M2 highway. A squeaky-clean re-creation of Johannesburg during its early prospecting days of the 1880s, the place exists for tourists to spend their money. But a visit can be fun; of particular note are the **Gumboot Dancers**, performing African dances originated by the first of the migrant workers to come to Egoli (the city of gold) in the 1890s. Their loose-fitting rubber boots, part of the standard uniform issued to mineworkers on arrival at the Reef, are incorporated into the dance by slapping and stamping to create a rhythm. Displays are held every day at 1 and 2pm.

Most of Gold Reef City's re-built houses now host small museums of early Johannesburg life, and there are bars and restaurants staffed by people in Edwardian costume. The highlight of the place is an old mine shaft, down which you can ride in an old elevator. The adjoining funfair complex has some good rides, such as the water-ride 'Thunder Mountain' and the 'Runaway Train'. An imitation Victorian funfair, a farmyard, Zulu village and the over-promisingly named 'Night-time Action Bar' are among the other attractions. For those who like theme parks, there is also an expensive hotel.

The ticket you buy at the gate entitles you to all buildings and rides. For information on shows and buses out to Gold Reef City, phone Johannesburg Publicity on © 294 961.

Zoo Lake

Johannesburg's zoo is worth visiting for the museums attached to it, rather than for the animals, which are better seen in the wild. Zoo Lake (the zoo sits next to a large, man-made lake) is about 15km north of the city centre via the R24, or the number 27 Bus to Parkhurst. Inside the zoo is the superb **Museum of Rock Art** (*open daily 10–1, 2–4*), which features reproductions of South Africa's best rock paintings and engravings by San (bushman) artists (at least the best ones that are known about). The art displayed varies in antiquity from thousands of years ago to just the last century (South Africa's last San rock artist was shot in the Drakensberg mountains in the 1850s). Some of the later paintings, which depict settlers' ox-wagons and men on horseback, are of particular interest.

Next door to the zoo is the **National Museum of Military History** (*open Mon–Sat 9–4.30*). This deals with the South African army's 20th century campaigns (with the exception of Boer and British army weaponry, uniforms and photographs from the Second Anglo-Boer War, 1899–1902). Those interested in South African history will find the exhibits interesting, especially those dealing with the country's aggressive bush wars in Angola and Mozambique during the 1970s and '80s, which show just how much money was being spent by the apartheid government in de-stabilising South Africa's neighbouring countries, and inflicting death and destruction on their inhabitants.

The Gold Mines

There are no working mines immediately around the city centre, but tours out to mines on the Reef can be arranged via the Publicity Association, or the Chamber of Mines, ✆ 838 8211. Tours leave from the Carlton Hotel, and are often booked up in advance, especially at weekends, so try for a midweek slot if possible. Although quite expensive, usually between R100 and R150 per person, tours last for almost a full day, include all transport and sometimes lunch, and are very interesting. Some take you down to more than a kilometre below ground, into the surreal, stiflingly hot world of South Africa's underground industry. The sweating workers, incessant noise and wierd, high-tech machinery seem oddly out of keeping with Africa, and provide some insight into the hell lived by those who have made the country rich. Spare a thought for what conditions must have been like in the early days. You will be very glad to get above ground again at the end of the day.

Shopping

 Flea markets selling both African and European crafts can be found at weekends at the Market Theatre Complex, Newtown, west of the city centre, and on Wednesdays, Fridays, Saturdays and Sundays at Bruma Lake, in the Bezuidenhout Valley, east of the city centre.

Galleries and Studios

Apart from the main galleries listed above, Johannesburg has a host of small commercial galleries selling work by South Africa's comtemporary artists, and more general artefacts. Yeoville and Berea have two good galleries, the **Apple Gallery**, 33 High Street, Berea, which sells African and eastern work, and **Congo Joe's Artworks** at 13a Raymond Street, which crosses Rockey Street, selling European hippy-style crafts. In Rosebank, the **Jacana Gallery** on Cradock Street specializes in township art and crafts, the **Everard Read Gallery**, 6 Jellicoe Avenue, is a prestigious gallery dealing in modern South African work. The **Alternatives Gallery**, on the lower level of Rosebank Mall, Oxford Road, sells ceramics and furniture, as well as paintings, as does the **Marialuisa Marino Gallery**, in shop W16, Mutual Square. Sandton also has some prestigious galleries, notably the **Goodman Gallery**, at 3b Hyde Square, Hyde Park, Sandton, the **Natalie Knight Gallery**, 8 Lower Mall, Hyde Park, Sandton (both contemporary art) and the **Mordechei Brodie Gallery of African Magic** (folk and totemic art).

The **Johannesburg Studio Route** opens the studios of several working South African artists on the first Sunday of every month. A map with information on each studio is available from Johannesburg's Publicity Association. **Operation Hunger**, on Smal Street, in the town centre, has a craft shop selling superb work, from both South African and other countries, at cheaper prices than at the more chi-chi galleries listed above.

Johannesburg © (011–)

Where to Stay

expensive

Johannesburg has many large, bland expensive chain establishments, such as the Sun, Holiday Inn and Protea line of hotels. Of these, the best are the luxury ultra-modern **Sandton Sun**, © 780 5000 on the corner of Alice and 5th Streets in Sandton, the **Carlton Hotel** on Main Street, in the city centre, © 331 8911, and the **Garden Court Holiday Inn**, © 297 011 on Smal Street in the city centre. Also worth trying for standard expensive fare are the **Aloe Ridge Hotel** on Muldersdrift Road in Honeydew suburb, © 659 0605, and the **Devonshire Hotel** in Braamfontein, © 339 5611.

However, more interesting places to stay within this price range include: **Joel House**, 61 Joel Road, Berea, © 642 5221, an Edwardian townhouse still furnished with period antiques, with 5 en suite bedrooms (some with fireplaces). B&B or full board is offered. This is at the moderate end of the expensive scale. Berea is a tranquil neighbourhood between the city centre and Yeoville. **The Cottages**, 30 Gill Street, Observatory, © 648 4279 are quiet, secluded and very comfortable. The **Johannesburger Hotel** on Twist Street by Joubert Park in Doornfontein, © 725 3753 has a slightly old-fashioned feel, at the moderate end of the expensive range.

moderate

At the top end of the scale, the **Jacaranda Guest House**, © 708 1542, on Cedar Avenue in Fourways suburb, has had excellent reports from mid-budget travellers for its family run B&B set in beautiful gardens. Also popular is **Irene's Guest House**, © 402 9622, in Catalina Gardens off Hatfield Road in Berea. A little cheaper is **La Rosa**, © 642 7438 on Abel Road, also in Berea. The rather modest but grandly named **Diplomat**, © 292 161, on the corner of Bree and Klein Streets in the city centre (if going out at night from here, always take a cab) and the equally grandly-named **Dorchester**, © 642 4491, on Twist Street in Hillbrow, offer very reasonable rates for B&B. You might also try these three in Berea: the **Chelsea Guest House**, © 642 4541 on the corner of Katherine and Soper roads, the **Coronia**, © 643 7011 on O'Reilly Road and the **Sands Guest House**, © 642 7211 on the corner of O'Reilly and Fife. Given the recent rise in tourism to South Africa, a number of new guest houses and B&Bs were set to open at the time of writing, contact the **Johannesburg Publicity Association**.

The International Travellers' Hostel, a large Victorian house on 1st Street in the Bezuidenhout Valley east of the city centre, ✆ 614 4640/624 2793, is friendly and lively, with dorms, double rooms and a bar. But be warned, the atmosphere can be a little eccentic, following the unpredictable character of the owner. For a quieter stay, try the **Backpacker's Ritz** on Caroline Street, Brixton, west of the city centre, ✆ 839 2068, who offer free lifts from the airport and bus station, a pool, dorms and double rooms. On Regent Street, near funky Rockey Street is the **Backpackers**, ✆ 648 8766 which can organize safaris as well as free airport/bus station pick-ups, single, double and dorms. Also near Rockey Street is the **Pink House Backpackers**, ✆ 487 1991 on Becker Street, Yeoville, again offering droms and doubles and free pick-ups. Johannesburg also has three **official youth hostels** (YHA affiliated), one on Fife Avenue, near Hillbrow/Berea, ✆ 643 1213, another in Fairview suburb, ✆ 618 2048 and the third in the suburb of Kew, ✆ 887 9072, all offer comfortable dorms and 24-hour check-in, but do not provide free pick-ups. Telephone from the bus station/airport for exact bus directions for each.

Johannesburg ✆ *(011–)*

Leipoldt's on Juta Street in Braamfontein, ✆ 339 2765, is named after the South African poet, doctor and gourmet C. Louis Leipoldt, whose books on Cape Cuisine, written in the 1920s, are famous in South Africa (*see* **People and Culture**, 'Cape Cuisine'). The restaurant serves some of the best traditional Cape recipes, such as *bredies*, *sosaties* and *bobotie*, and also specializes in game (through the winter) including buffalo fillets (surprisingly tender) and crocodile's tail, whose delicate meat is reminiscent of crayfish. At the lower end of the expensive scale, it should not be missed. **Harridan's** at the Market Theatre, Bree Street, Newtown, ✆ 883 6729, serves French and spicy Cape dishes in an informal atmosphere. **Gramadoela's**, also at the Market Theatre, ✆ 838 6960, serves Cape, Ethiopian dishes and Southern African specialities (including fried mopane worms and black tripe) in a re-created Cape Dutch interior. **The Dragon Tower** on Twist Street, Hillbrow, ✆ 725 1710, is probably Johannesburg's best-known Chinese restaurant and justifiably so; these dishes have not been made bland for a western palate. **Suki Yama** in the Johannesburg Sun Hotel on Smal Street, ✆ 297 011, serves excellent sushi. In the Northern Suburbs, **Le Canard**, set in a neo-Georgian house on Rivonia Road, Sandton, ✆ 884 4597, serves traditional cordon bleu. Of note are the frog's legs in a pernod mushroom sauce.

In Melville, the relaxed, yuppie neighbourhood just northwest of the city centre, is **Chaplin's**, on 4th Avenue, ✆ 726 5411/2507, a nouvelle cuisine restaurant without the usual pretensions that so often go with such places. Starters include fresh oysters and asparagus (all year). For a main course, try the kingclip provençal with fennel, or the prawn curry. In season, game is offered, including gemsbok fillets with wild mushrooms and impala or kudu sirloin in port wine.

moderate

Yeoville has several very good, moderately priced restarants. **La Lanterna** on Rockey Street, ℗ 648 7201, serves good Italian pasta and seafood in a superbly tasteless dining room. Much favoured by a young crowd, La Lanterna is pleasantly relaxed. **Delfini's** on Hunter Street, ℗ 648 3500, serves traditional Greek food, also to a mainly young crowd. The tiny **Chez Rachel** on Fortescue Street, ℗ 648 4114, serves very spicy North African food. Take your own wine. Again, this is a relaxed place, favoured by young professionals.

In Braamfontein, try **Paolo's Kariba** on Stiemen's Street, ℗ 399 3131, a small place next door to the Alexander Theatre and Civic Centre. The seafood is particularly good. **Linger Longer** on Wierda Street in Sandton, ℗ 884 0465, is at the top end of this price scale, and serves mostly French dishes.

In Melville, **Coco de Mer** on Main Street, ℗ 726 4104, serves unusual French Creole dishes (mostly highly-spiced seafood). Take your own wine. On the same road, is **Freddie's of Melville**, ℗ 726 1908, which specializes in French cooking. Further north, in Rosebank, is **Arlecchino**, ℗ 880 2615, on Oxford Road, a good-value pizzeria and Italian restaurant. There is an outdoor courtyard and imported Italian wine, as well as Cape wine. In Norwood, near Orange Grove, is another Italian restuarant, **La Lampara**, ℗ 728 4715, on Grant Avenue, which also has an outdoor courtyard, and makes its own fresh pasta and bread.

cheap

Rockey Street in Yeoville has the best selection of cheap eateries. The **Bar Pita** serves Middle-Eastern food (*shwarmas* and *falafels*) in a hippy/rock 'n' roll atmosphere. No need to book; take your own wine. On the other side of the street is the **Tandoor**, whose back room is a rock venue. Very cheap Indian food is served here. On the same street is **Café Society**, which is good for light meals; their breakfasts are superb, and their main menu has such delights as fresh crêpes with savoury fillings, and wholesome soups. This is recommended after a heavy night on Rockey Street.

Bars and Cafés

Café Society on Rockey Street serves excellent coffees and light meals, while **Rockerfella's**, further west along the same street, is an open-air bar and café that often has live jazz/fusion, and where a lot of beautiful people hang out, as well as oddities such as the very well-behaved Johannesburg Hell's Angels. The **Bar-Pita** opposite Rockerfella's has a lively bar next door to its restaurant that plays good rock and reggae, and is a good place to meet people and get information on Johannesburg's nightlife.

The **Radium Bar** on Louis Botha Avenue in Orange Grove, is Portuguese-run and has not been redecorated since the early '40s. It gets very busy, but is a good place to meet people among a mixed crowd of yuppies, drunks and young partygoers.

Theatre and cabaret are long-established Johannesburg traditions. Larger productions, both mainstream and fringe, can be found at the Newtown, Braamfontein and City Centre theatres. The **Market Theatre Complex**, ✆ 832 1641, is in Newtown on the corner of Bree Street and Wolhunter Street. The **Civic Centre**, Braamfontein, ✆ 403 3408, carries the largest scale productions, while nearby, the **Alexander Theatre**, on the corner of Stiemans and De Beers Streets, ✆ 339 3461, stages more fringe productions, and acts from the townships. In the northeast city centre, the **Alhambra Theatre**, ✆ 402 6174, on Sivewright Avenue, is one of the city's oldest and specialises in dance. In Hillbrow, the **Windybrow Theatre**, ✆ 720 7094/5, on the corner of Nugget and Pietersen Streets, stages small, often very good productions from the best of the fringe.

Hillbrow is known for cabaret, sometimes risqué, sometimes comedy, sometimes song and dance. Good venues are: the **Cotton Pub**, ✆ 725 3300, on the corner of Twist and Kotze Streets, and the **Ground Level Club**, on the corner of Catherine and Kotze Streets. **Pink Cadillac** is in the basement of the Ambassador's Hotel, on the corner of Banket and Pretoria Streets. The **Talk of the Town** on Pretoria Street, ✆ 648 0248, shows classic cabaret. In town, the **Dungeon** on the corner of Marshall and Goud Streets, ✆ 334 5655, has mostly gay cabaret and a disco. **Hurricane's** in 4-Ways Mall plays Techno and House.

Nightlife

Discos and nightclubs worth going to are **Sneaky Pete's**, ✆ 403 2535, on Juta Street, Braamfontein, which plays rock and dance music, and the **Doors Club** on Marshall Street, ✆ 648 9288, which plays psychedelic, hip-hop, techno and rock music. **Dylan's** on Rockey Street, Yeoville, ✆ 648 0125, is relaxed and plays mostly '60s music. Nightclubs, particularly for rave and techno music, tend to come and go, so it is worth asking in bars and cafés for what's current.

Live Music: Johannesburg has no shortage of good bands. For jazz, try the **252 Tavern** on Jeppe Street, ✆ 337 1944, **Café Nicola**, ✆ 333 0446 on the corner of Klerk and Troye Streets, known for the best of the township jazz outfits, and the **Softown Jazz Club**, ✆ 333 1793, on the corner of De Villiers and Claim Streets.

For rock, reggae and township jive, try the **Tandoor** on Rockey Street, ✆ 487 1569, and **Timewarp**, ✆ 726 8400, on Main Road, Melville. Also on Main Road is the **Roxy Rhythm Bar**, ✆ 726 6019, which has very varied line-ups. For hard rock and metal, go to **Stone Rose**, ✆ 403 2535, on Juta Street, Braamfontein. **Dylan's** on Rockey Street, ✆ 648 0125, also hosts hard rock bands. **Gay clubs** are quite well represented in Johannesburg. Good examples are **Champions**, ✆ 725 2679, on the corner of Rissik and Wolmarans Streets in Braamfontein, the **Club Embassy**, ✆ 788 4708, at the Constantia Centre, Rosebank and **Mrs Hendersons**, ✆ 337 4492, on the corner of Kruis and Commissioner Streets in the city centre.

The South Western Townships (Soweto is an abbreviation of this), sit southwest of Johannesburg along the N1 highway. Home to over two million people, Soweto is the powerhouse from which the Witwatersrand's mines, service industries and general labour are drawn. Of course, Soweto is not the only large 'township' in the region, but it has become the cultural heartland of the black Witwatersrand, and was the centre for most of the resistance to apartheid from the 1950s to the 1990s. Few other 'townships' comprise such a cultural cross-section as Soweto; most of South Africa's black ethnic groups can be found here, there are areas of great wealth, with huge mansions, areas of griding poverty and tin shacks, and large neighbourhoods of ordinary residential houses. In fact, to call Soweto a 'township' is to mis-name it; Soweto is more of a city in its own right, even though it is hardly 40 years old (see 'Johannesburg History').

Unfortunately, in recent years, Soweto has become a no-go area for casual visits by whites, whether South African or foreign travellers. There are two reasons for this; the first is crime. Soweto is generally very poor, despite its few rich neighbourhoods, and unemployment is high. A white skin represents money to many 'township' residents, and Soweto has a high enough crime rate in its own right; simply wandering in is to tempt fate too hard. The second reason is race hatred. Many of Soweto's residents have good cause to dislike white people, and have been subject to the humiliations of apartheid for most of their lives. Although most residents of Soweto are not prone to race hatred, there is a strong enough minority of people, especially male youth, who are. However, it must be said that this has come rather recently; in the late 1970s and early '80s, Soweto's jazz clubs and bars were reasonably safe for whites, and there was greater movement between Johannesburg and Soweto. With the change of government, this may happen again, and it is worth asking around in Johannesburg for the latest word as to whether there are any clubs in Soweto now open to all comers.

For the time being, those who want to see Soweto can only do so safely by taking a guided tour. The Johannesburg Publicity Association has details of the tour companies, which leave from outside the Carlton Hotel, on Commissioner Street in Johannesburg city centre most weekday mornings. Tours usually last for about a half-day and some include tea in private homes.

North of the city, although development stretches along the M1 highway almost as far as Pretoria, there are still some large stretches of open countryside, reached by the R511 and R512 roads north of Randburg and Sandton. This is predominantly horse country, and several riding stables operate in the area (*see* 'Activities'). The most intersting from a travellers point of view, is the **Lipizzaner Riding School**, an imitation of the Spanish Rising School, in Vienna. Displays of highly-skilled Classical dressage are given, just as in Vienna, on white Lipizzaner stallions whose riders wear 18th century costume. Founded by an Austrian emigré in the 1960s, Johannesburg's Lipizzaner Riding School is an incongruous thing to find in the bare highveld grassland that stretches around the great city. The school is reached via the R55 from Sandton (about 15km) and is signposted from the road.

South of the city, along the N3 highway towards the Free State and Natal, then along the R550, following the signposts, is the **Suikerbosrand Nature Reserve**. This is a large, unspoilt area of highveld (almost 14,000ha), with mixed woodland, some marsh, and even one or two pockets of fynbos heath, which is usually found only in the Cape. The reserve's empty silence is a blessed relief after Johannesburg, and makes a superb escape for anyone working in the city, or simply stay there for a few days. Game includes eland, kudu, red hartebeest, black wildebeest, zebra, reedbuck, duiker, oribi and steenbok. A few shy cheetah and brown hyena also inhabit the reserve.

Suikerbosrand has several hiking trails, from one hour to six days in length, with overnight huts supplied with firewood and water. There are also three camp sites with ablution facilities and communal kitchens. Hiking trails of more than one day must be booked in advance, © (0151) 2181/2/3.

..The Volksraad decided to establish in the centre of the territory a new village to be called Pretoria after the late commandant... at the base of a range of mountains which, owing to a petty chief named Magali having been found at its western extremity... has since been called the Magaliesberg.

History of the Boers in South Africa 1887, George McCall Theal

The staid older sister city of noisy Johannesburg sits on the highveld 65km to the north, marking the gateway to the Northern Transvaal. Although handsome, especially in its leafy suburbs, Pretoria is rather dull and conservative. As the country's seat of government, the small city centre is rather sober and business-like, lacking the vibrancy and street culture of neighbouring Johannesburg. Wide streets lined with great jacaranda trees that become clouds of purple blossom in October, a measured pace of life and (apart from the semi-industrial suburb called Pretoria North) a general prosperity among the white inhabitants, give the impression is of a large regional town rather than a city.

By the same token, Pretoria is also much safer than Johannesburg, and is a pleasant place to pass a couple of days in on the way north or south, and there are some surprisingly wild and rugged landscapes and reserves within reach.

History

Named after Andries Pretorius, the Voortrekker leader who defeated the Zulus at Blood River in Natal (*see* **Natal** 'History'), Pretoria was founded on the banks of the Apies River in 1853. It was the second capital of the infant South African Republic (or SAR, one of three statelets founded by the Voortrekkers in the Transvaal—*see* **History**), the first having been Potchefstroom in the Western Transvaal. After 1860, Pretoria became the general capital of all three Transvaal states when they united to form the greater South African Republic. Before the Voortrekkers arrived, the fertile, well-watered grasslands around Pretoria had been farmed by Sotho/Tswana groups whose communities had suffered depredations by the warlike Ndebele who had migrated from Natal in the 1820s. Under the leadership of their king, Mzilikazi, the Ndebele had established dominance over most of the highveld through the 1830s, and fought the Voortrekkers for over twenty years, before finally being pushed up into modern Zimbabwe (*see* **Northwest Province** 'History'). The temporary depopulation caused by the Ndebele/Tswana/Sotho fighting resulted in the myth, propagated by colonial historians, that the Transvaal and Orange Free States were 'empty' when the Voortrekkers arrived.

But if the *burghers* of the new SAR manged to subdue the Ndebele, their own society was riven by family feud and petty rivalry. Even after unification in 1860, leaders of the different Transvaal regions spent most of their time squabbling over the constitution and how the new republic should be run. The first president, Marthinius Pretorius, was unable to raise the necessary revenue to run any kind of administration, and Pretoria was not much more than a show-capital with little real authority. This suited most of the Boers around Pretoria who, through the 1850s and '60s took advantage of returning populations of Sotho, Kgatla, and other clans who had been driven from the area by the Ndebele, and were now drifting back to their former homes. Many local Boer farmers pressed these people into servitude, and even went on kidnapping raids to neighbouring areas to bring back children to work on their farms (a practice that later became common throughout the SAR).

With such help the Boers could run cattle and plant maize over huge tracts of land, as well as freely butchering the local game, especially elephants, whose hides and ivory they sold to agents from the Cape and Natal. By the late 1860s a few individuals had amassed large personal fortunes. Some used their connections to buy land from government officials at low prices, among them Paul Kruger and Piet Joubert—later to lead the SAR to war against the British—who soon had more money than the SAR's creaking government. By 1870, most of the good land in the SAR was in the hands of a select group of Boers, while the rest of the country sunk steadily into poverty. A measure of the republic's disastrous early economy was the failure of its paper money, issued in 1866 by President Pretorius. Not a single *burgher*—not even government officials—would accept it.

The rich Boers (who bought and sold in English pounds) began selling off farms to incoming European settlers at great profit, which incensed the smaller farmers. They felt (quite rightly) that the government was hand-in-glove with the larger landowners, and there was talk of rebellion. This became real during the late 1860s, and Pretoria itself was besieged by angry *burghers*. Pretorius managed to calm them and persuaded them to return to their farms without reprisal (not that there was regular army to cary out such tasks). However, an impoverished class of landless Boers, or *bywoners*, was emerging which was to haunt South Africa into the following century.

The foreign (usually British) settlers were quick to take advantage of the corrupt republic. One Alexander McCorkindale set up the first commercial bank in Pretoria, and started several mining, immigration and farming companies. In return for organizing a loan of £250,000 for Pretorius' government, he secured 200 farms for himself.

Britain, taking advantage of the region's instability, sent troops into the eastern region, supposedly to subdue the Pedi, whom the Boers had been unable to subjugate, regardless of the fact that the SAR government had not asked for British assistance. Then gold was found in the Transvaal Drakensberg and in 1877 Britain, correctly judging that the republic could offer no concerted resistance, occupied Pretoria and the SAR was declared British territory. Only *after* taking the SAR did the British then put down the Pedi, using Swazi mercenaries.

The republic's new president, Thomas Burgers, had power politely wrested from his hands, and the SAR seemed destined to become another British colony. However, faced with the presence of the hated British (from whose authority they had trekked away from in the first place) the SAR's squabbling *burghers* finally managed to leave aside their internal wranglings and organize resistance. Such was the chaotic nature of the SAR that it took four years for this to have any concrete result, but through the late 1870s Paul Kruger (who had himself profited from the lucrative sale of land to foreigners that had led to the British annexation) quietly began to organize armed *commandos* in the Pretoria district and along the SAR's border with Natal. The British were too busy transforming Pretoria into a proper regional capital, regularizing the SAR's tax system and erecting public buildings, to take much notice. They expected little resistance, as the invasion had gone off with hardly a shot fired, and the Boers were generally regarded as too fragmented and short-sighted to come together and fight. But the British were very wrong. In 1881 the small British garrisons of the SAR were attacked. Paul Kruger declared the First Boer War, and defeated the British main force at the battle of Majuba, on the Natal border. The British were forced to retreat, highly embarrassed, and lacking the resources to re-occupy the SAR they restored the republic's full independence in 1884.

Paul Kruger assumed the presidency and set out to unify the disparate republic, and to prevent it from relapsing into the bankruptcy, corruption and disharmony that had allowed his own rise to prominence. His principal policy was to seal off the SAR from outsiders, or at least to contain them in some way and keep the government strictly Boer. In the early 1880s, large reefs of gold were found near Barberton in the east; prospectors and speculators poured in uncontrolled, with little of the revenue going to government.

When gold was discovered on the Witwatersrand south of Pretoria in 1886, Kruger and his government determined to secure the wealth for the SAR by controlling the number of foreigners coming into the goldfields.

They sent one Johannes Rissik down to the newly-discovered mines, who laid out plots for four tent villages, which were then sold at great profit to Boer and foreign speculators. Next, they invited the Randlords of Kimberley to develop the reefs under direct government control.

The project worked up to a point; Kruger managed to control the number of mining magnates, and the hitherto empty coffers of the SAR began to fill. But it was impossible to curb the influx of foreigners. Within three years Johannesburg exceeded any other South African town in size, and became a seething pit of prostitution, gambling and hooch rackets, as the miners, starved of women and flush with money, turned the new city into one of 'unbridled squalor'.

For all their previous corrupt financial practices, Kruger and his ministers looked at their self-created Sodom with pious horror. From their moral eyrie at Pretoria, they decided that as long as these *uitlanders* (foreigners) could be kept as temporary residents, then the SAR would not come to too much moral harm. They refused to grant any foreigner the vote, or citizenship of the SAR.

There was an outcry from Johannesburg. The Randlords, in particular Cecil John Rhodes, the head of the De Beers Company (at that time one of the world's richest men), began to stir up support in the Cape and British press for the *uitlander* cause, with the tacit support of the British government, who favoured the creation of a climate that would justify a future annexation of the SAR. By 1895, Rhodes felt sufficiently confident to fund a private coup d'état on Pretoria. He persuaded a jingoistic associate, one Dr Jameson, to take an irregular force into the SAR from the Cape and seize Pretoria from Kruger and his ministers. The British government knew of the plan unofficially, and stood by. Kruger got wind of it before the force had even left the Cape, and sent *commandos* to meet them. The two forces clashed west of Pretoria, and the Britons ended up in Pretoria jail.

Kruger knew full well that the Randlords were behind the plan, and became even more determined to deny any foreigner the franchise of the SAR. He made vain attempts to contain the immorality of Johannesburg, limiting liquor licences to a few individuals, and trying to close the best-known brothels. But the momentum was unstoppable. Kruger began to use his own mine revenues to buy sophisticated weaponry, mostly from Germany; both artillery (including the massive Schneider seige guns, known as 'Long Toms') and rifles, mostly state-of-the-art repeating Mausers. Naturally this further alarmed Britain. Chamberlain and Milner, the Cape Governor and British Colonial Secretary, began to intrigue with Pretoria's own politicians. In 1898, they began to court the chairman of the SAR's Industrial Commission, one Schalk Burger. They persuaded him to lobby for the franchise, but met with flat refusal from Kruger and his government. Chamberlain and Milner then delivered Pretoria an ultimatum for granting the franchise, and again met with refusal, and in 1899, the SAR and Britain entered the Second Anglo–Boer War (1899–1902).

RIVIERA

SOUTPANSBERG

SOUTPANSBERG

Union
Buildings

GORDON

BECKETT

CHURCH

CHURCH

M2

PRETORIUS

PRETORIUS

R27

ARCADIA

SCHOEMAN

R27

HATFIELD

Pretoria Art
Museum

PARK

PARK

BURNETT

SUNNYSIDE

JORISSEN

JORISSEN

LYNNWOOD

UNIVERSITY

LYNNWOOD

WALKER

BROOKLYN

CHARLES

CAMERON

DUNCAN

BROOKLYN

RUDDEL

CHARLES

QUEEN WILHELMINA

BOSHOFF

Dr Austin Robert's
Bird Sanctuary

RUPERT

M11

MIDDEL

CLARK

Anton von
Wouw Museum

MAIN

N

Fort
Klapperkop

M9

800 metres
800 yards

517

After the initial Boer successes of 1899, the British invaded the Orange Free State and SAR, and occupied Pretoria in 1900, formally dissolving the Republic and renaming it the Transvaal—a British colony. Kruger went into exile, and the war dragged on until 1902, when the Boer generals finally surrendered at the Treaty of Verreegning.

Between 1903 and 1910, Pretoria dropped from centre of the political stage as Milner and his British administrators set about running South Africa (at this stage still divided into four separate colonies; the Cape, Natal, Orange Free State and Transvaal). But after Britain decided to unify the colonies and grant them independence as the new Union of South Africa (1910), Pretoria was made the new country's administrative capital. In 1913, the elegant Union Buildings were built on the hill overlooking the city centre, and Pretoria began its 20th century job of South Africa's quiet capital.

Quiet is the word; for all the controversy and violence that has marked South Africa's 20th-century history, Pretoria itself remained largely aloof from the political events inspired by the presidents who governed from here. Although the ANC bombed the city centre in 1983 (a car bomb that killed 19 people), and several (largely peaceful) mass demonstrations went through the city centre in 1993/4, the political strife of neighbouring Johannesburg and the Vaal triangle towns hardly disturbed the calm surface of day-to-day white life in Pretoria, which as the seat of government, was a heavily protected bastion of apartheid. Despite many pessimistic predictions, this unruffled surface has continued since the government change-over of April 1994.

Getting There

by air

Pretoria is serviced by Jan Smuts International Airport, which lies about 50km south along the R21 to Johannesburg. Buses to and from the airport pick up and set down at the **Tourist Rendezvous Centre** on the corner of Vermeulen Street and Prinsloo Street in the city centre. Services run every hour from 5am–9pm daily (except Saturdays, when the last service runs at 7pm).

by road

Pretoria lies on the N1 about 65km north of Johannesburg. The N4 connects Pretoria with the Eastern Transvaal, while the Western Transvaal is reached by a series of minor tarred roads.

by bus

Long distance buses run between Pretoria and most of the country's main centres, setting down and picking up at the **railway station** on the corner of Sheiding Street and Paul Kruger Street at the south of the city centre. Call Greyhound, ✆ 315 2815, or TransLux, ✆ 315 2333, for details.

by train

Pretoria is linked to Johannesburg and from there to most of South Africa's larger towns. The Blue Train (*see* **Travel**) starts and finishes its Cape–Transvaal route at Pretoria.

Pretoria's city centre is only about 1km by 2km and walking is often the quickest way to get around, especially in the busy middle of the day. The city centre gets so choked with traffic in the middle of the day that driving and parking can be a real problem. The best place to park is around Struben Street and Bloed Street in the northern city centre.

By bus: Buses for the suburbs leave from Church Square. The routes advertised at bus stops or ✆ 283 562.

By train: Commuter services to some of the more remote suburbs between Pretoria and Johannesburg (such as Irene and Verweordburg) leave every half hour from the fine 19th-century railway station on the corner of Kruger and Scheiding Streets, ✆ 315 2401/6.

By black taxi: As in all South African cities, these provide quick transport along the bus routes, but have a worrying accident record. However, within the city and inner suburbs such accidents are rare: most occur along the M1 (N1) highway.

By taxi: As in all South African towns, Pretoria's taxis must either be called via the *Yellow Pages* or picked up from a taxi rank; you cannot hail them on the street. Taxi ranks can be found at the corner of Vermeulen and Andries Streets, and at the corner of Church and Van der Walt Streets.

Pretoria Publicity Association, The Information Bureau, Ground Floor, Munitoria Building. On the corner of Van der Walt and Vermeulen Streets, ✆ 323 1432 or ✆ 313 7980.

The City Centre

Pretoria's small city centre is very busy by day, and all but deserted at night. **Church Square**, a small park, around a large statue of Paul Kruger, is more or less the geographical centre. The city's buses terminate here, among some of the city's oldest buildings, including the Main Post Office. On crisp winter mornings, those waiting for buses sun themselves around the high wall of the south side of the square. In the afternoon, city workers eat their lunch on the lawns. Anywhere in the city centre is within ten minute's walk of Church Square, including most of the city's museums. The **Pierneef Museum** on Vermeulen Street (*open Mon–Fri 8–4*) has an extensive collection of works by this well-known South African landscape painter from the 1900s. His paintings of the Namib are particularly dramatic, and all the works manage to capture something of the deep, indefinable calm that seems to hang over African landscapes. The **Post Office Museum** round the corner on Proes Street (*open Mon–Fri 8–4*), is an uninteresting re-creation of a Victorian post office, while the **Transport Museum** (*open Mon–Sat 8–4*), one block north on Stuben Street displays old wagons, cars and photographs. Also on Struben, about two blocks further east, is the small **Jansen Collection of Africana** (*open Mon–Fri 8–4*), which displays mostly

Cape furniture and silver. The more interesting **National Cultural History Museum**, (*open Mon–Fri 8–4*) on Boom Street covers both black and white interests with a collection than includes exhibits as diverse as Cape Dutch furniture and San (bushman) rock engravings. Particularly good are the scenes of African life painted by a nun, Sister Vorster. Some of her alarmingly life-like sculptures are also on view; especially beautiful are her family groups and the busts of the Nama and San people who lived at her mission station.

South of Church Square, on Paul Kruger Street, is the **Transvaal Museum of Natural History** (*open Mon–Sat 9–5, Sun 11–5*), one of the best in South Africa. Apart from the usual displays of stuffed fauna, there is an emphasis on early man, including some of the fossil remains found in the Eastern Transvaal dating back roughly 1 million years. African hunting cultures are presented clearly with the help of video, and there is a superb collection of South African birds. Map buffs will enjoy the attached **Museum of Geographical Survey** (*open Mon–Sat 9–5, Sun 11–5*) a smaller affair that shows what a huge task the mapping of South Africa has been. There is also an extensive collection of rock and semi-precious stones.

One block north, on the corner of Paul Kruger and Skinner Streets, is the **South African Museum of Science and Technology** (*open Mon–Fri 8–4, Sun 2–5*), which has standard educational displays explaining the workings of various machines. More interesting is **Burgers Park**, two blocks southeast on Andries Street, a formal, square set of lawns and large shade trees covering several hectares. In the centre is an exotic hot house (which seems odd for Africa, but Pretoria winter nights can be very cold), with a luxuriant garden of tropical plants. On Rissik Street, which runs by the south side of the park, is **Melrose House** (*open Tues, Weds, Fri and Sat 10–5, Thurs 10–8, Sun 12–5, closed Mon*), a Victorian mansion where the Boer and British generals met to sign the Treaty of Vereegning in May 1902, following the Boers' surrender at the end of the Anglo–Boer War. There is little in the house to suggest such momentous events, although there is one room full of artefacts made by the Boer prisoners of war who were sent to St Helena between 1899 and 1902, including ships carved from bone, with every piece of equipment made to scale, religious pictures and tools. Works of great beauty and detail testify to the enforced leisure of camp life. You can have tea on the verandah of Melrose House, looking out over the lawns.

On Bosman Street, a few blocks northwest of Melrose House, is the old **City Hall**, a handsome piece of overblown Victoriana overlooking statues of the Andries and Marthinus Pretorius, the Boer father and son who founded the town in the 1850s. Of more direct historical significance is **Paul Kruger's House** (*open Mon–Sat 8.30–4, Sun 11–4*) at the western end of Church Street, lived in by 'Oom Paul' from 1884–1901. As an indication of how personal and classless (as long as you were white) the old Boer republics were, it is true fact that 'Oom Paul' used to sit outside his house on days when he was not busy in any of the government offices, and would converse with anyone who so wished. Apart from the usual personal effects, photographs and furniture, there is a display of presents from European governments expressing their support for the Boer cause during the war with the British. Kruger did not want presents, but foreign troops. These he did not get, and the exhibits of handsome silverware and other trifles make a poignant reminder of the impossibility of the Boers' resistance to British imperialism. At the far west of the city centre, on

Seventh Street, just below Boom Street, is one of Pretoria's few attractions not related to Boer or British nostalgia; the **Miriammen Temple**, a Hindu temple (*open daily, all day*). Built in 1905 and hence as old as anything in Pretoria, this temple is devoted to, of all things, the Hindu goddess of infectious diseases. Its exotic, perfumed interior, full of votive images, is a far cry from the staid, stately atmosphere of most of Pretoria's monuments and museums, and is worth visiting if you have time, if only for the contrast.

Just north of the town centre, fronting Boom and Paul Kruger Streets, are the **National Zoological Gardens** (*open daily, 8–5*). Although it is far more interesting to observe game in the wild (and Pretoria is within reach of several good game reserves) this zoo is still worth visiting for those seriously interested in wildlife. Rare indigenous species, such as giant eland (a great beast of an antelope), cheetah and aardwolf (a nocturnal, ant-eating relative of the hyena) have been raised here, some for re-introduction to the wild. Other rare African species, such as the scimitar-horned oryx (which has been all but shot to extinction in its natural ranges of North Africa and Arabia), Hartmann's mountain zebra and pigmy hippo, as well as completely foreign rarities like the Brazilian maned wolf, and Chinese Pere David's deer, are bred at the zoo's special game farm in the Western Transvaal. The zoo has examples of all its rare species on show. Many of the enclosures can be viewed from above by a special cable-car.

The Older Suburbs

Arcadia, the oldest suburb, is just east of the city centre. Here, on the hilltop park at the eastern end of Church Street, are the **Union Buildings**, South Africa's official seat of power since 1910. Among the most successful neo-classical buildings of British imperial architecture, they were designed by Sir Herbert Baker, who was responsible for many of South Africa's turn-of-the-century public buildings. Built from red sandstone, the Union Buildings have a Italianate feel, and surround a long ornamental lake with good views out over the city. Unfortunately, visitors are not allowed inside. Also in Arcadia, on Schoeman Street, is the **Pretoria Art Museum** (*open Mon–Sat 10–4.30*) whose small collection of South African art by such painters as Pierneef and Frans Oerder, and a few old Dutch Masters (Van Dyck, Frans Hals) are worth taking in on the way down from the Union Buildings.

Sunnyside, the first suburb southeast of the city centre, is something of a centre for nightlife, with a large, multi-storey shopping centre housing a variety of bars and restaurants. Most of Pretoria's nightlife goes on here. East of Sunnyside, along Walker Street, (which becomes Charles Street as you leave the area), is Brooklyn, a handsome suburb of late 19th- and early 20th-century houses, where many of Pretoria's wealthy professionals live. There is a small museum at 299 Clark Street (*open Mon–Fri 9–4.30*), once the home of sculptor **Anton Van Wouw**, whose massive bronze statue of Paul Kruger frowns down on Pretoria's Church Square. Inside the house are various smaller works, mostly in bronze.

South of town two old hilltop forts over-look the city, **Fort Klapperkop** and **Fort Schanskop** (*open Mon–Sat 10–4*). Both these late 19th-century fortifications house small military museums devoted to the Second Anglo–Boer War and the South African soldiers who fought in the Second World War desert campaigns. Nearby is the massive, rather grim **Voortrekker Monument** (*open daily 8–5*) which, like the two forts, is clearly signposted from the R28 south of the city centre. The square stone 1940s edifice, built to commemorate the Great Trek of 1838, is surrounded by giant stone wagons representing the laagers used by the Voortrekkers as a fortress from which to mow down the attacking Zulu at Blood River.

The monument is ponderous but full of solemn presence, like a Boer farmer's beard. If the outside is a little like a giant stone fridge guarded by the statue of a gaunt, fierce Boer woman shaking her fist at the unknown, the inside is rather beautiful; a vast, airy vault with a neo-classical frieze depicting the Great Trek. Although similar in style, the various panels could have been carved by different artists; the uniformity of expression, features and clothing produces a slightly comic effect, especially in the faces of the Boer heroes such as Piet Retief, Louis Trichardt and Andries Pretorius, who are almost indistinguish-able from each other. Most interesting is the battle scene between the Voortrekkers and the Xhosa, which shows Xhosa warriors mounted on oxen trained to charge, surround and maul the enemy, a tactic learned from the Khoi. Riding oxen, whether for racing or warfare, died out in the Eastern Cape by the late 1870s, after the Frontier Wars (*see* **Eastern Cape** 'History'), and today the practice is preserved only in ancient cave paintings or in works of art such as this frieze.

The top of the monument is open to the sky, and has been designed so that at noon on 16 December—the Day of the Covenant, a public holiday commemorating the Voortrekkers' defeat of the Zulu at Blood River—a ray of sunlight falls onto the long stone slab in the centre of the the the building, lighting up the carved words: 'Ons Vir Jou, Suid Afrika' (We are yours, South Africa). For some years, at an accompanying semi-religious ceremony, thanks were given to God for delivering the Voortrekkers from the threat of massacre by the Zulu, and for the foundation of the modern Boer society—a neat illustra-tion of how deeply entwined are the Boer political and religious creeds. Since April 1994 the Day of the Covenant has been abolished, but the public holiday has been kept under a new name, the 'Day of Conciliation'.

Two galleries run around the top of the monument. One inside is terrifyingly vertiginous, as it seems to bend downward towards the parapet and the floor 100ft below. An outside gallery gives excellent views out over the city and over to the lovely Magaliesberg hills. Inside the main hall is a small gift shop which sells among its range of souvenirs what must be one of the most prized items of South African kitsch; scale-model candles in the form of the Voortrekker Monument.

Pretoria ℭ (012–)

Where to Stay

expensive

Pretoria has no lack of expensive chain hotels, but **La Maison**, ℭ 434 341, is without doubt the best. Set in the southern suburb of Hatfield, near most of Pretoria's foreign embassies and consulates, La Maison offers B&B and en suite bedrooms in an opulent Victorian white-stuccoed mansion with beautiful gardens and a pool. In the city centre, on the corner of Vermeulen and Hamilton Streets, is **Orange Court Lodge**, ℭ 326 6346. At the low end of the expensive scale, this old Victorian stone hotel has dark-stained beamed ceilings, fireplaces and a large garden. Self-catering only.

Die Werf, ℭ 991 1809, in Lynnwood, at the far eastern edge of Pretoria, is a charming Cape Dutch country house with private verandahs opening from simple, rustic bedrooms and superb Boer country cooking. Such delights as pumpkin fritters, turmeric rice, Karoo lamb and *bobotie* are served in the little restaurant.

moderate

Battiss Guest House, ℭ 467 318, a 1930s family house at 92 20th Street in the suburb of Menlyn Park, used to be the home of Walter Batiss, a moderately well-known South African artist, some of whose paintings are still in the house. The two en suite rooms open onto coutyards. In Brooklyn, at **59 Brooks Street**, ℭ 436 834, is a larger, Victorian manor house built in a mixed Classical-Gothic style complete with a little turret. **The Malvern Guest House** at 575 Schoeman Street in Arcadia, ℭ 341 7212, is an oldish suburban house offering clean, comfortable rooms and B&B within walking distance of the city centre.

cheap

That's It, 5 Brecher Street, Sunnyside, ℭ 344 3404, offers dormitory accommodation and cheap double rooms for backpackers and budget travellers, and a reputation for fun—the owners organize pub crawls and clubbing forays and have a wealth of information on budget eating out and general activities in the area.

Allegro, ✆ 322 1665, in the State Theatre on Church Street, serves very good Italian and more simple traditional food. It is modern, unpretentious, popular and usually lively. There are two good French restaurants in town: **La Madeleine,** 258 Esselen Street, Sunnyside, ✆ 446 076, offers fine Belgian cooking and a low-key feel. Go for the mussels. **Chez Patrice,** on the corner of Soutpansberg and Wells Streets in Riviera, ✆ 708 916, serves good French food.

Goldfields, ✆ 322 1665, also in the State Theatre on Church Street, serves standard but tasty meat and two veg dishes, with a few French and Italian specials thrown in. Quite informal and relaxed, Goldfields is a good place to start an evening downtown. In the Burgers Park Hotel, by Burgers Park (reached by Park Lane in the south of the city centre), is **Ambassadeurs,** ✆ 322 7500, a French restaurant at the expensive end of the moderate scale. This is particularly good for lunch, as a stroll across the formal lawns of Burger's Park makes for a pleasant afternoon.

In the eastern suburb of Lynnwood there is a very good country restaurant called **Lombardy,** ✆ 871 284, on a smallholding called Tweefontein Farm. As the name suggests, Italian food is the speciality and the semi-rural surroundings make for a very pleasant atmosphere. Best to get there in the early evening, when the scent from the trees is at its strongest, and watch the sun go down over the highveld before dinner.

Apart from take-aways, it is hard to find cheap food in the city centre. However, **Pinnochio's,** a Portuguese restaurant on Paul Kruger Street serves very good value set menus specializing in seafood (try the calamari) and spicy chicken. No need to book. A cheap chain restaurant, **Nando's,** in the Tramshed Centre on Schoeman Street, serves an excellent chicken and chips.

More variety can be found on Esselen Street in Sunnyside, which has a wealth of good, cheap restaurants. The stuffed vine leaves and fish dishes at **Santorini's,** ✆ 448 045, are worth leaving the city centre for, as are the stuffed pancakes a few doors down at the appropriately named **Fillings For Pancakes,** ✆ 343 1683, which sometimes features live jazz. Good pasta and pizza can be found at **Giovanni's,** ✆ 341 0689/0846, and light meals (breakfast and lunch only) at the **Grapevine Café.** In Hatfield, you might try the American burger joints of **Ed's Easy Diner** and the **Hard Rock Café,** on Park Street. In Burnett Street in the centre of Hatfield is **Bachini's,** a small Italian restaurant. No need to book for any of these three eateries.

The **State Theatre Complex** on Church Street, ℂ 322 1665, stages large and small scale productions of drama, ballet, modern dance and music in its five theatres. For movie-going, the **Tramshed**, a converted railway terminus on Schoeman Street, has a good cinema that screens non-mainstream movies. For more Hollywood-style films, the **Sterland Centre** on Beatrix Street has two cinemas, and, of all things, an ice-rink. **Cabaret acts** perform at the **Café Kahlua** on Esselen Street.

Nightlife

In comparison with wild Johannesburg staid Pretoria's nightlife is not exactly humming, despite the city's two universities. However Pretoria has a few places that can offer something more than just Top 40 music and 'smart, casual' punters. **McCoy's** on Schoeman Street is a late-night bar that plays a good mix of rock, reggae and soul. A mix of professionals, students and pleasure seekers make this bar lively later in the evening. Next door is **The Creek**, a small rock/metal club with a lively, sweaty atmosphere featuring live bands. For dancing, try **Caesar's Palace** on Pretorius Street, which plays rock and techno music, or the city's largest disco, **Jaqueline's Danseteria**, also on Pretorius Street, which plays techno and Top 40. **Chaps**, a gay club on Schoeman Street, has more atmosphere than is usual for Pretoria.

Live Music

Again, Johannesburg dominates the area's music scene, but live blues can generally be found at the **Crossroads Bar** in the Tramshed Centre on Schoeman Street. In the same street, rock and metal bands play at **The Creek**, next to McCoy's bar.

Around Pretoria

South of Pretoria on the M1 and on the commuter line is the old village of **Irene**, now fast becoming a suburb of Pretoria. Irene was built on a massive dairy farming estate, most of which still stretches south of the suburb. The tree-shaded lanes, meadows, irrigated pastures and woodlands of the still-active **Irene Farm** make a welcome change from the city and give an idea of what the Witwatersrand looked like before creeping urbanization.

Also in Irene is Prime Minister Jan Smuts' house, **Doornkloof Farm** (*open Mon–Fri 10–5*), a ramshackle tin affair which still contains most of its original furniture, as well as his photographs and letters. Smuts achieved international fame for leading South Africa into the Second World War, but his contribution to South African history, both good and bad, lasted from 1900 to 1948 and included the Second Anglo–Boer War, the violent industrial unrest of the 1920s and the power struggle between imperial government and

Afrikaner nationalism of the 1930s (*see* General and Johannesburg Histories) Smuts' pressed and documented collection of African herbs, can also be seen. Next to the house is a tea-room and camp site. The house seems to embody Pretoria's dull but safe tranquility. A little further south is the **Van Riebeeck Nature Reserve**, reached by the same road from Irene to Doornkloof, but a little further east. This extensive wild area surrounds a dam, and has a network of hiking trails up to two hours in length. Expect to see eland, zebra, oribi and duiker. There is no accommodation.

Wonderboom Nature Reserve, on Voortrekker Road on the outskirts of Pretoria's northern suburbs, was founded to protect a huge wild fig tree, the *Wonderboom* ('wonder tree'). The size of a small building, this magnificent tree is over 1000 years old and 23m high. It was a traditional meeting-place for Ndebele chiefs, and later for Voortrekkers and settlers, who left messages for each other here. The spreading branches cover a huge area, and some have even grown back into the soil to form underground runners which have re-emerged as separate trees around the old parent, creating a wood. The effect is magical: the twisted, randomly-spiralling, smooth branches and the massive bulk of the main tree provide welcome shade from the harsh Transvaal sun. Today, the reserve covers about 90ha, run through with self-guided walking trails.

Roodeplat Nature Reserve surrounds a dam only 16km northeast of the city along the R512 to Cullinan. It can be crowded at weekends, but mid-week there are few visitors. From the walking trails and game-viewing roads you are likely to spot antelope such as sable, kudu, waterbuck, blue wildebeest, red hartebeest, impala, steenbok and duiker. Zebra are also common. The water is safe for swimming and there is a small camp site with ablution blocks. About 100km northeast of Pretoria is the small former 'homeland' of **Kwa-Ndebele**. Now officially re-absorbed into South Africa, the area is still markedly undeveloped compared to the surrounding countryside, and is still marked as separate on most road maps.

Ndebele History and People

The Ndebele are the descendants of a renegade Zulu regiment that fled their homeland in the 1820s under their general Mzilikazi, an opportunist who saw a chance to carve out his own kingdom amid the upheavals of the *Mfecane*. The Ndebele successfully used the Zulu fighting tactic known as known as the 'horns of the bull'; they would encircle the enemy flanks while attacking on a full front then close in for a general slaughter with short, stabbing spears, whose blades were wide to inflict maximum damage. Through the late 1820s and '30s, the Ndebele raided and conquered the Sotho-Tswana clans living in the highveld, being repulsed only by the BaSotho (*see* Lesotho). The Ndebele settled in the Western Transvaal and absorbed the women of conquered clans into their own. Their numbers grew rapidly and, by 1835, Ndebele raiding parties were penetrating far west to the Griqua territory near the Orange River in modern Bushmanland, and to Swaziland and Venda in the northeast Transvaal.

Mzilikazi was as much statesman as warlord, and he established diplomatic relations with Robert Moffat and John Campbell, British missionaries of Griqualand. With his clan's mastery of the highveld undisputed, Mzilikazi might have looked forward to the dubious benefits of becoming a British protectorate and keeping a measure of independence as white settlement penetrated the highveld in the 1830s.

But the first whites to arrive in his territory were the Voortrekkers, in 1836. Armed with muskets, and supported by Griqua and some Tswana auxilliaries, the Boers set about enslaving the Ndebele. After initial skirmishes, Mzilikazi wiped out three Voortrekker parties, then attacked the main Voortrekker *laager* at Vegkop late in 1836. Mzilikazi's frontal tactics failed against the Voortrekker's massed musketry and he lost thousands of warriors in one fell swoop. Mzilikazi withdrew to the Northern Transvaal, pursued by a Voortrekker, Griqua and Rolong Tswana force who again defeated the Ndebele at Mosega in 1837. Mzilikazi escaped with most of his people and livestock, but ran into another combined force under Andries Pretorius near modern-day Pretoria, and suffered a heavier defeat.

In one year, the Ndebele had been reduced from one of the most powerful clans in the Transvaal, to its weakest. Mzilikazi bowed to the inevitable and took his remaining regiments over the Limpopo River into modern-day Zimbabwe, where he subdued the MaShona people and established a dominance that passed to his son Lobengula and lasted until the the British invaded the territory in the 1890s. Now known as the Matabele, Mzilikazi's clan are the modern Zimbabwe's second largest nation, although a few isolated groups still live in South Africa.

After Mzilikazi went north, the Boers experienced little resistance to their new dominance of the highveld, and the Voortrekker leaders Andries Pretorius and Hermanus Potgieter, began to found more permanent towns. However, black military endeavour had not been totally crushed. In 1854 a large Sotho band under chief Makapan went to war with the highveld Voortrekkers and were defeated near modern Potgietersrus, but succeeded in killing a large number of Boers, including Hermanus Potgieter himself. Determined to put an end to the troublesome Makapan, the Boers pushed the chief and his people into a set of deep caves (the Makapansgat, where fossil hominid remains were to be found in the 20th century) and laid siege until all the Sotho had died from hunger, thirst or disease. (*see* **Northern Transvaal**).

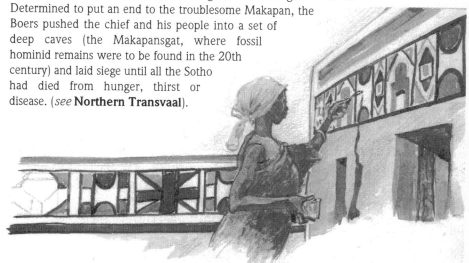

However, the creation of modern Kwa-Ndebele was due to modern Afrikaner rather than to Ndebele history. The former 'homeland' was declared in 1981, the last to be created by the Nationalist government in their attempt to re-settle South Africa's blacks in their own 'independent' areas. Ndebele people were uprooted from their homes and forcibly moved to the present site, an arbitrary location supposed to represent the Ndebele's 'original' range.

Now that the former 'homeland' has been re-absorbed into South Africa, these people face a long fight to reclaim the properties from which they were moved, and which were confiscated from them when the 'homeland' was created.

Like most former 'homelands', Kwa-Ndebele is poor, overcrowded and over-grazed, with a growing rural population struggling to exist on too little land, and with most of its young men seeking work in Johannesburg. However, many traditions survive, in particular the painting of huts in beautifully-executed, exact geometric designs, a series of polygons filled in with vibrant colours. And the Ndebele maidens' practice of wearing beaded neck rings that gradually elongate the neck can still be seen in places. The former 'homeland' draws some income from the **Ndebele Show Village**, where tourists can watch Ndebele customs at work; from dancing and 'witchdoctor' ritual, to the more every-day grinding of millet and maize, and preparing food. Crafts, such as bead-work and woven rugs, are on sale. Although the whole concept of such show villages, let alone tribal 'homelands', is a legacy of apartheid, places such as this are as close as many tourists have time to get to traditional African culture. Bear in mind, too, that visitors inject much-needed money into the local, struggling economy. The village is near **Hammanskraal**, about 80km northeast of Pretoria on an unnumbered road between Pretoria and Marble Hall, south of the Rust De Winter Nature Reserve.

Rust De Winter Nature Reserve is about 65km north along the N1 from Pretoria, at the gateway to the bushveld zone of the northern Transvaal. At weekends it is packed out by water-skiers and fishermen from Pretoria, but it can make a convenient rest-stop on a long drive along the N1. Bird watchers will enjoy the waterfowl species, such as black duck, Egyptian goose, and white stork. There is unlimited walking along the dam's shore but remember that there are crocodile and bilharzia in the water, so don't paddle. Accommodation is in a camp site only, and you must get there before 6pm.

The Magaliesberg Mountains

The Magaliesberg range runs west of Pretoria. Although most of the area belongs to private farms, the hills are surprisingly wild and open to hikers. Two reserves, **Rustenburg Nature Reserve** (about 100km west of Pretoria along the R27 at the western end of the range) and **Mountain Sanctuary Park** (45km west of Pretoria along the R27, then 30km along the R512 after the junction at the Haartebeestpoort Dam) provide immediate access to the Magaliesberg; to get into the rest of the range requires arrangement in advance via the National Hiking Way Board in Pretoria, ℰ (012) 299 2632.

Rustenburg, the larger of the two, has interesting rock formations and strangely mixed vegetation comprising woodland, marshland (whose reedbanks look a shimmering blue when seen from a distance), dry aloe hillsides and thornveld. There are even pockets of fynbos, which is rare outside the Cape, over 1000km away. There is a 2-day trail with overnight huts or a 3-hour self-guided trail, along which hikers can expect to see water-buck, kudu, red haartebeest, klipspringer, duiker and, if lucky, the rare sable antelope. Raptors are common, in particular black and martial eagles and Cape vultures, and the views from the Magaliesberg out to the north are lovely. A few shy leopard and caracal hunt in the hills, and brown hyena are present, but the visitor is unlikely to see these. Apart from hiking huts, accommodation is a camp site with ablution blocks. Mountain Sanctuary Park also has self-guided walks and a variety of plains game, such as zebra, kudu and reedbuck. Again, there are long views out over the Transvaal plains, and accommodation is in chalets or a camp site with ablution blocks.

Due north of Pretoria, a section of what used to be Bophuthatswana 'homeland' (accessible along the trunk road to Mapobane via the town of Brits), is the superb **Borakalalo National Park**, ℰ 0020 and ask for Jericho 0264. About 100km north of Pretoria, Borakalalo stretches over 14,000ha of bushveld, riverine wood-land, dry forested kloofs and grassland and harbours white rhino, giraffe and most large antelope, including sable, kudu, tsessebe, gemsbok, waterbuck and eland. The reserve has excellent guided hiking and riding trails into the bush, from which game spotting is almost inevitable. Accommodation is self-catering in permanent safari tents. Visitors should be aware that the Klipvoor Dam, which the park surrounds, carries bilharzia, so do not swim there.

Activities: Around Pretoria

Walking and hiking: Short, self-guided day-trails can be found at Wonderboom Nature Reserve, Roodeplaat Dam Nature Reserve, Rust De Winter Dam Nature Reserve close to Pretoria, and at Rustenburg Nature Reserve and Mountain Sanctuary Park in the Magaliesberg. Borakalalo National Park also has self-guided trails, but visitors should stay overnight in the permanent tented camp, as the distances to and from the park are long, and driving at night in the former Bophuthatswana is not recommended, owing to the amount of stray stock on the roads. Directions for all the parks and reserves are given above.

Hikes of more than a day can be found at Rustenburg Nature Reserve, ℰ (01421) 31051 (a 2-day trail with overnight hut, bookable in advance), and in the main Magaliesberg chain, with accommodation in tents and caves, bookable in advance from the National Hiking Way Board in Pretoria, ℰ (012) 299 2632.

Guided game-spotting hikes can be arranged at Borakalalo National Park ✆ (0200) and ask for Jericho 1441.

Riding: Borakalalo National Park organizes riding trips into the bushveld to see game, for details ✆ (0200) and ask for Jericho 1441.

Where to Stay

expensive

Mount Grace Country House, ✆ (011) 880 1675, is a luxurious thatched hotel at the foot of the Magaliesberg, just west of the town of Magaliesberg on the R24. Accommodation is in individual stone cottages with gardens, a pool, a tennis court and walking trails into the surrounding hills. Classical music concerts are held once a month in a small theatre attached to the hotel. **Valley Lodge**, ✆ (0142) 771 301, is a Victorian country house set in a nature reserve on the backs of the Magalies River, just a few miles from Mount Grace. The bedrooms have four-poster beds and, in some cases, views of the river. Boating and fishing can be arranged. There is a large pool, three tennis courts and a series of walking trails.

moderate/cheap

Mountain Sanctuary Park, ✆ (014222) 1430, also at the southern foot of the Magaliesberg (about 100km west of Pretoria along the R512, just north of Maanhaarrand), has comfortable self-catering chalets, a camp site, walking trails (with plentiful wildlife) and swimming.

Camp sites can be found at **Rustenburg Nature Reserve**, ✆ (01421) 31050. Those prepared to hike for a few hours can stay in one of the overnight refuge huts further into the mountains. **Rust De Winter Dam Nature Reserve**, ✆ (0121712) 2422, 85km north of Pretoria via the N1, also has a camp site with ablution blocks, as does **Roodeplaat Dam Nature Reserve**, ✆ (012) 808 1164, about 45km north east of Pretoria along the N1 and R513.

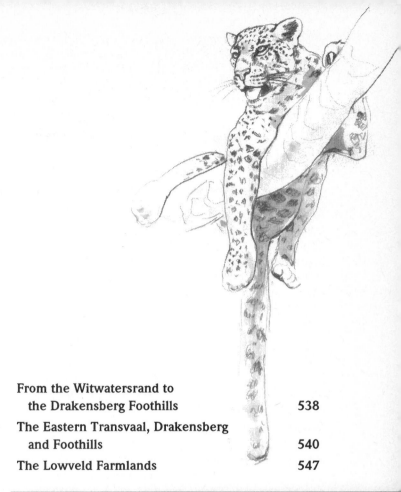

The Eastern Transvaal

> 'On a morning in mid-May I saw the Bushveld for the first time. My
> car breasted the last turn of a mountain pass. The air was startlingly
> clear; a beryl sky overhead... straggling mimosa trees in the fore-
> ground, multiplied by thousands in the middle distance—sandstone,
> or more likely dolomite, tors at infrequent intervals... patches of
> grass in-between—the dust raised by a herd of zebra or wildebeest
> to the right—and the road winding through the scrub to be lost very
> soon in that impenetrable secondary forest.'
>
> *Bushveld Doctor*, Louis Leipoldt

TRAVELLERS SHOULD NOTE THAT EASTERN TRANSVAAL IS MALARIAL

About 200km east of Johannesburg the highveld grasslands begin to flow
into broken hills which soar abruptly into the mountains of the high
Transvaal Drakensberg. An abrupt change from flat grasslands of the
highveld, you climb amid forest, mist and great empty sweeps of
mountain, cut through with fast-flowing rivers. And then the landscape
changes again; east of the Drakensberg the altitude drops severely and
the lowveld, a great expanse of bushveld, stretches away to the low
Lobombo Mountains on the border with Mozambique. Most of this is
wild country. The easternmost strip is dominated by the Kruger National
Park which, to give an idea of scale, is larger than Israel.

With these contrasts the Eastern Transvaal has a huge variety of vegetation and animal life and is one of the few regions where big game is in
general abundance, albeit within fixed reserves.

Many South African game-spotters holiday in the Eastern Transvaal and
there are some overdeveloped spots to be avoided. However, the region
is large enough to make solitude easy to find. For those wanting to see
game there is a confusing variety of private and state-owned reserves. In
general, the large private reserves, most of which border the Kruger
National Park, offer luxury and big game at extortionate prices, but those
with a limited budget can see the same game by spending a few days in
the Kruger itself. To make the choices clearer, the following section
breaks down the parks and reserves in terms of price and game.

The Eastern Transvaal's contrasts extend to its people. The region is
inhabited by Boer, Swazi, Pedi, and a few British South Africans. The
Boers of the region have a reputation for a hard-line right wing attitude,
but the reality is the usual paradoxical hotch-potch of prejudice and
liberalism that characterizes farming communities all over South Africa.
What is true is that under apartheid, more black people have were forced
into 'homelands' here than almost anywhere else in the country. The
former 'homelands' of Lebowa, Gazankulu and KaNgwane were

Kruger National Park

GAME AND NATURE RESERVES

1 HANS MERENSKY NATURE RESERVE
2 CYCAD NATURE RESERVE
3 TSHUKUDU GAME LODGE
4 KLASERIE PRIVATE NATURE RESERVE
5 INGWELALA
6 UMBABAT GAME RESERVE
7 THORNYBUSH GAME LODGE
8 TIMBAVATI PRIVATE NATURE RESERVE
9 BLYDE RIVER CANYON NATURE RESERVE
10 MANYELETI GAME RESERVE
11 INYATI
12 SABI-SAND GAME RESERVE
13 LONDOLOZI GAME RESERVE
14 MALA MALA GAME RESERVE
15 SABI-SABI GAME RESERVE
16 OHRIGSTADT DAM NATURE RESERVE
17 MOUNT SHEBA NATURE RESERVE
18 MTHETHOMUSHA GAME RESERVE
19 MAHUSHE SHONGWE GAME RESERVE
20 SONGIMVELO GAME RESERVE

Waterfalls

A Mac-Mac
B Sabie
C Bridal Veil
D Lone Creek
E Horseshoe

N

Lookout point ☀
Picnic place ✕
Camp ⌂

Land over 1000 metres

30 kms
20 miles

533

fragmented into sections of varying sizes all over the region. Driving through the Eastern Transvaal means continually entering and leaving stretches of former 'homeland', usually marked by a sudden over-crowding of people and cattle after hours of driving through an emptier landscape of huge white-owned cattle and game ranches. Life in these former 'homelands' varies from the westernized to the traditionally rural, or completely wild, and the Lebowa, Gazankulu and KaNgwane parks boards offer cheaper alternatives to the expensive private game reserves of the 'white-owned' lowveld, or the tourist mecca of the Kruger National Park.

The Eastern Transvaal has some of South Africa's best hiking—in the Drakensberg and surrounding forests and foothills, is some of South Africa's most spectacular mountain walking. In the lowveld are some of the best game trails. In particular, the Kruger National Park has some heartstoppingly exciting trails where walkers sleep in bush camps and are guided by armed rangers to within close range of elephant, buffalo and lion.

History

Before the Voortrekkers arrived in the Eastern Transvaal in the early 1840s, the area was inhabited by various Nguni and North Sotho groups (today represented by the Swazi and Pedi) and isolated Tsonga communities, all three of whom had contributed to driving- off the original San (bushmen) hunter/gatherers early in the Middle Ages.

The early Boer settlers had a difficult time; although the temperate mountain regions had good grazing and were not densely inhabited, the lowveld was well populated by people hostile to white settlement. The Boers fought unsuccessfully with the most powerful clan, the Pedi, and in 1845 negotiated land with them on which to build a small town, Ohrigstad. As far as the Pedi were concerned, they were only tolerating the Boers, and for some time the settler's small Ohrigstad Republic was kept from expanding by malaria, tropical fevers, seasonal drought and abundant wild predators.

Boers from the neighbouring South African Republic (or SAR, the first of the three Boer Transvaal republics—the others being Ohrigstad and Zoutpansberg in the north) made repeated raids into the Eastern Transvaal, hunting for ivory and looking for good land, most of which had already been claimed. Having been repeatedly repulsed from the land in the north of the region by the warlike Pedi, the Boers turned their attention to the Swazi in the southeast, who had been ground down by Zulu raids sent north by Shaka and Dingane during the 1820s and '30s (see **Natal** 'History'), and were just beginning to re-establish themselves over their former wide range, despite sporadic raids by the new Zulu king, Mpande. In 1847 the Lydenburg and SAR Boers offered to end the Zulu raids for good, in return for cattle and land grants. The Swazi King Mswati rashly opened up his territory (modern Swaziland) for Boer hunters and granted his allies all the land between the Crocodile and Oliphants rivers, almost the entire eastern lowveld. But, though groups of Swazis lived in the area, most of it was Pedi territory and it was not really his to give away. The Boers turned a blind eye to this, drove Mpande's marauding Zulus south and began settling the lowveld wherever there was water enough for cattle.

Ohrigstad was proving an unhealthy capital for the now large republic, due to its heavy subtropical climate and propensity for malaria. In 1850 the Boers again courted Pedi anger by establishing a new town further north, at a higher, more temperate altitude. Lydenburg is still a regional centre for the Eastern Transvaal Drakensberg.

After 1860, when Lydenburg became part of the SAR (*see* **Gauteng** 'History'), more settlers began arriving in the Eastern Transvaal, and the Pedi, unwilling to lose more land, began to raid white farms, confining settlers to the area around Lydenburg and Swaziland. They further strengthened their position by sending thousands of young men to work on farms in the Cape and Natal and spending the money they sent home on guns.

Frustrated, the Boers began seizing more Swazi territory. King Mswati appealed to the British Governor of the Natal colony, Theophilus Shepstone, for British protection. Shepstone, a passionate believer in the Anglicization of all South Africa, agreed. Nevertheless, over the following twenty years the Boers moved aggressively into Swazi territory, settling where they liked, while Mswati looked on anxiously. It could only be a matter of time before British troops arrived in the Eastern Transvaal.

In 1870, following the discovery of diamonds in Kimberley, over 1000 miles west in Griqualand, the Pedi offered their services as labourers and began to make money and buy arms as never before. Soon afterwards, gold was discovered in the Drakensberg just east of Lydenburg. Although the deposits were patchy and alluvial, with no large underground seams, the mountains were soon crowded with adventurers from all over the world. At the small town of Barberton a stock exchange was opened, and small mining towns, such as Pilgrim's Rest, Sabie and White River began cropping up around the diggings. The resident Boers looked on with some disquiet as the profits from the gold went, not into the state coffers or to local burghers. but to the few miners who struck it rich and the merchants, dealers, gold buyers, black labourers, liquor sellers, prostitutes and thieves who flocked to the little mountain towns.

The discovery of gold refocused unwelcome British attention on the area. In 1877 Theophilus Shepstone persuaded the Colonial Secretary Lord Carnarvon to annex the SAR, take advantage of the gold finds and bring the errant Transvaal Boers back under British rule. The British also sought to contain the Pedi, who were gaining in power to such an extent that farmers in the northern area of the Eastern Transvaal were paying taxes to them rather than to Pretoria.

While the British prepared for invasion, the Boers took an unsuccessful swing at the Pedi in 1876. The following year, British troops entered the SAR, ran up the Union Jack at Pretoria and sent an expedition against the Pedi, partly as a gesture towards the Boers, partly to crush the tribe and thereby ensure a future cheap labour pool.

During the British occupation, the gold diggings in the Eastern Transvaal gradually wound down and the Boers took over the territory of the conquered Pedi. Swaziland remained a British Protectorate and no more settlers were allowed in. From 1882 until the outbreak of the Second Anglo–Boer War in 1899 the Eastern Transvaal was systematically opened up for cattle ranching. However, the obstacles that had confronted the first settlers—tropical disease, drought and wild animals—remained, preventing rapacious settlement and preserving the vast expanses of wilderness for which the region is renowned.

The Eastern Transvaal saw little action during the Second Anglo–Boer War (1899–1902), except for some brief fighting around Pilgrim's Rest in the Drakensberg, which earned one mountain pass the name of Long Tom Pass, after the huge naval guns that the Boers hauled up there to take pot shots at the advancing British. Hunting and farming became the region's main industries and during the early 20th century the Eastern Transvaal settled down into a backwater. There were a few scattered farm strikes by black workers during the 1920s but these were ineffectual, being so isolated from the black political centres of the Witwatersrand and Eastern Cape.

Through the Second World War and the subsequent apartheid years, the Eastern Transvaal developed along two parallel paths, one positive, one negative in the extreme.

The positive movement was that of nature conservation. The Kruger National Park, established in 1898 by Paul Kruger himself (following the pleas of a now forgotten land surveyor and conservationist called Charles Marais) continued to be protected as a showcase for African conservation. During the 1970s and '80s, when massive poaching operations almost wiped out elephant and rhino populations in Africa, the Kruger and its surrounding reserves brought in some of the first shoot-to-kill anti-poaching patrols and the park is now a major breeding centre for repopulating reserves elsewhere in Africa with rare species. For example, the black rhino, threatened with extinction outside South Africa, has retained a sufficient gene pool in the Kruger to make this the only African country where it is increasing its range.

But the Eastern Transvaal reserves did not escape poaching. Today there are almost no large tuskers left and evidence has recently come to light suggesting that high-ranking South African army officers may have been behind some of the intensive 1980s poaching raids (as has proved to be have been the case in Namibia). A full inquiry has yet to be brought, if it ever will; the new South Africa has more pressing problems to deal with than tracking down ex-poachers.

Another negative side of the Eastern Transvaal's recent history was the forced removal of tens of thousands of blacks into 'homelands' in an attempt to strip local Tsonga, Pedi and Swazi of their South African citizenship. These puppet states of Lebowa (for the Pedi), Gazankulu (for the Tsonga) and KaNgwane (for the Swazi) have suffered all the usual poverty and lack of opportunity of South Africa's 'bantustans'. Self-governing, rather than officially independent, Lebowa, Gazankulu and KaNgwane's 'governments' (of South African-paid local chiefs elevated to ministers) have lately been accused of human rights abuses; for example, mass graves found in Lebowa in 1986 contained the bodies of people who had protested against the rule of the 'homeland's' prime minister, Cedric Pathadi. However, as with the poaching in the Kruger, it seems unlikely that any inquiry will be made into these allegations, as the 'homelands' have been re-absorbed back into South Africa since 1994, and the new government now faces problems of a more national scale.

However, the re-absorption of KaNgwane, Gazankulu and Lebowa may bring its own problems, as overpopulation and depleted land resources threaten to spill a huge, unemployable rural population out of confinement and into the pristine veld. To contain this, while at the same time reversing the wrongs of apartheid and continuing the area's excellent record of nature conservation, is the task facing the Eastern Transvaal's new provincial government for the 1990s and beyond.

Getting There

By car: From Johannesburg and Pretoria the N4 heads due east to the Eastern Transvaal's border with Mozambique at Komatipoort, at the southeast corner of the Kruger National Park. From Swaziland the R40 from Bulembu to Barberton, the R570 from Ngonini to the N4, and the R571 from Tjaneni to Komatipoort, all provide access. From Natal, the N11 from Ladysmith to Ermelo joins the R542 which leads straight to Barberton and Nelspruit.

By bus: Greyhound ✆ (011) 333 2136, Transtate and TransLux, ✆ (011) 774 3333 for both, all run regular bus services from Johannesburg to Nelspruit and Tzaneen, jumping off points for the southern and northern sections of the Eastern Transvaal respectively. The same companies also run buses to Komatipoort, convenient for the southern end of the Kruger National Park.

By air: Comair ✆ (011) 973 2911 runs regular flights from Jan Smuts Airport outside Johannesburg to Skukuza in the Kruger National Park. Either pick up local car hire (Comair will arrange this) or arrange a pick-up if you are staying in some of the private reserves. Most private reserves have their own landing-strips and you can arrange flights when booking.

By rail: The Komaati Express runs daily from Johannesburg to Komatipoort (and v.v.) via Nelspruit, telephone Johannesburg railway station ✆ (011) 773 2131.

Getting Around

By car: This is by far the best way, as entry to the game reserves is almost impossible without a vehicle. The cheapest option is to hire from one of the private car hire companies listed in the Johannesburg section of this guide.

By bus: Transtate run services between most of the smaller towns from Nelspruit and Tzaneen.

If you are without a vehicle and cannot afford a safari company, the **Kruger Backpackers and Adventure Centre** in Hazyview, near the Kruger's Numbi Gate, ✆ (01317) 67224, runs a private bus service from Johannesburg and will drive you into the park more cheaply than you can find elsewhere.

By black taxi: All of the region's towns and most of the villages can be reached by black taxi. These are safer here than in cities, but they do have a worrying safety record. They are cheap, but use them at your own risk.

By tour group: **Lawson's**, ℂ (01311) 552147, offer specialised wildlife and bird-watching trips into the lowveld from Nelspruit, as do **Norse Safaris**, ℂ (01311) 53325. Several companies operate tours of Eastern Transvaal from Johannesburg, usually taking in part of the Drakensberg and the Kruger Park. The best value for money is probably **Drifter's**, ℂ (011) 888 1160, which offer weekly packages leaving from and returning to Johannesburg. More expensive is **Ingwe Safaris**, ℂ (011) 464 1758, which offer both Eastern Transvaal and Natal packages. If there are no vacancies call the Johannesburg Publicity Association on ℂ (011) 214 961 for other companies.

From the Witwatersrand to the Drakensberg Foothills

The drive east along the N4 highway from Johannesburg runs through the high, flat golden grasslands of the Witwatersrand plateau. For the first 150km the highveld pasture is dominated by mine towers, chimneys and other industrial sights, until the highway clears the pungent coal mining town of Witbank. If you are not in a hurry it is worth driving into the Eastern Transvaal through the highveld farm country, along the R25, R555, R540 or R36, all of which head northeast from the N4. Away from the highway, the scenery has a wide, empty splendour, without the strip developments that beset big roads. Great, empty horizons—with perhaps an isolated farmhouse surrounded by dark gum trees—stretch away on every side. The roads run straight as arrows and you can drive for miles without seeing another car; the sense of isolation up here on the highveld can be exhilarating.

Along the R35, in the farming country north of **Middelburg**, is **Loskop Dam and Nature Reserve**, ℂ (01202) 4184. The reserve is mostly grassland and has a high density of game, including white rhino, buffalo, sable antelope, eland, kudu, nyala and a host of other antelope species. Waterfowl cluster around the dam's shoreline. But be careful walking close to the water; crocs lurk on the banks, and the shallows carry bilharzia. Leopard, brown hyena and jackal are quite common here, but are very shy and mainly nocturnal. A walking trail and a few roads run through the reserve. The accommodation in self-catering chalets or a camp site is often full at weekends, but often deserted in the week.

A few kilometres south of Loskop along the R35 is the smaller **Botshabelo Nature Reserve**, ℂ (0132) 23897 or 25331, which covers a narrow river valley. Again, game is plentiful, mainly zebra, wildebeest, eland and the smaller antelope. The Oliphants River, which runs through the reserve, has a rare species of cycad growing on its banks. Walking trails and game viewing roads wind through most of the reserve and there is an **Ndebele Village**, with geometrically painted houses, at the edge of the reserve, which welcomes visitors. Accommodation ranges from B&B in an old farmhouse, to a cheap hostel with dormitory bunks.

Still further south along the R35, just 15km from Middelburg, is a sign for **Slaghoek**, ℂ (0132) 23764/8, a farm with thatched huts offering self-catering accommodation and three hiking trails into the surrounding hills.

North of the small towns of **Machasdorp**, about 100km east of Middelburg, is the lovely **Schoemanskloof**, a narrow farming valley with low mountains falling to the swiftly-flowing Crocodile River (which no longer harbours crocodiles). The R539 exits from the N4 between Machasdorp and Waterval-Boven, runs along the valley and rejoins the N4 about 45km west of Nelspruit.

Orchards, pastures and small wheatfields adjoin the road, giving the countryside an almost European look, especially where lines of poplars have been planted as windbreaks, and in autumn, when the wheat is cut by hand and laid in stooks on the stubble. Tributary streams fall from the bare uplands above the river, and several walking trails run up into the hills from a country inn halfway along the valley called **Old Joe's Kaia** (*see* 'Where to Stay'). 'Old Joe' is a rock formation just west of the inn, resembling a gnarled old man. The altitude drops steadily from west to east along Schoemanskloof, and marks a gradual transition from highveld to lowveld. At the far eastern end of the valley the Crocodile River drops falls into a large cascade known as the **Montrose Falls**. These are signposted from the R539, and are reached by a short walking trail.

Activities

Walking and Hiking: Bankfontein Farm, ✆ (0132) 23764/8, near Middelburg offers a choice of 4 trails. The 8km Tarentaal Trail runs between the huts and the Oliphants river. Cycad Trail (about 14km) winds in a circle from the huts, taking in river scenery and cycad vegetation. The Suikerbos Trail (18km) and Baboon Trail (26km) follow the Oliphants River through cliffs and narrow ravines. Accommodation is provided. Trails of more than one day can be found at Elandskrans Holiday Resort, ✆ (013262) 176. The 2-day Elandskrans Trail follows a set of waterfalls along the Eland's River valley and has overnight huts supplied with firewood and water. The trail leads from the Elandskrans Holiday Resort to the small village of Waterval-Boven.

Trout fishing: Beats and tackle can be arranged through the Critchley Hackle Lodge and Walkerson Collection Cottages, near Dullstroom on the R540 between the N4 (Belfast exit) and Lydenburg. (*See* below for details.)

Where to Stay

expensive

Old Joe's Kaia, ✆ (01311) 630456, at the Nelspruit end of Schoemanskloof, fronts the Crocodile River and offers accommodation in private log cabins secluded in indigenous bush around a 19th-century coaching inn. Walking trails and trout fishing can be arranged. **Critchley Hackle Lodge**, outside Dullstroom, ✆ (01325) 40145, is said to offer the best trout fishing in the Eastern Transvaal. Built of stone in the 1920s the lodge resembles, of all things, an English country church. There are 23 rooms, lake and stream fishing, tennis courts, indoor and outdoor pools, walking trails, a golf course and a sauna.

The **Walkerson Collection,** ✆ (01325) 40246, also near Dullstroom (12km along the road to Lydenburg), derives its name from the lodge's 15 thatched stone cottages set amid forest and bare hillside. A small nature reserve harbouring antelope stretches away from the lodge, and trout fishing is offered in the estate's lakes. Furnished with antiques, it is a little pretentious but very comfortable, and the surrounding scenery is beautiful. **Bergwaters Lodge,** ✆ (013262) 103, is signposted north from the N4 near Waterval-Boven. This small, intimate country inn sits in the Eland's River valley, amid a variety of hardwood and bushveld vegetation with 11 rooms, a bar, a pool and a tennis and squash court. Trout fishing can be arranged.

moderate

The **Wayside Inn** at Waterval-Boven, ✆ (013262) 425/12, is an old coaching inn (built 1879) next to a house lived in by Paul Kruger. A little adjoining cemetery contains graves of British soldiers killed during the Second Anglo–Boer War. The large, comfortable en suite double rooms are good value for money. **Bankfontein Farm,** ✆ (0132) 23764/8, offers self-catering accommodation at the bottom end of the moderate scale in comfortable, thatched rondavels. Situated off the Middelburg/Groblersdal Road—turn left at the sign saying 'Slaghoek' and follow the signs for the Cycad hiking trail. **Elandskrans Resort,** just north of Waterval-Boven, ✆ (013262) 176, offers self-catering thatched cottages with shared kitchen and braai facilities. Bring a sleeping bag. Four secluded hiking trails follow the Elands River valley through natural bushveld and woodland.

cheap

Loskop Dam Nature Reserve, ✆ (01202) 4184, along the R35 north of Middelburg, has self-catering chalets with bathrooms, and a camp site with shared ablutions and kitchen. There is superb walking, with rare species such as white rhino and sable antelope roaming free in the bush. **Botshabelo Nature Reserve,** ✆ (0132) 23897/25331, offers B&B in an old farmhouse and very cheap dormitories. Apart from walking trails with game, its Ndebele show village and restored mission station are fun to explore.

The Eastern Transvaal, Drakensberg and Foothills

The Eastern Transvaal Drakensberg run south to north in a narrow 200km chain from White River and Lydenburg to Tzaneen. The most populated section is the southern end, between Sabie, White River and Pilgrim's Rest; north of here the range is split by the spectacular **Blyde River Canyon,** one of South Africa's principal natural marvels, then gives way to a further 100km of all but uninhabited mountain accessible only on foot. **Lydenburg,** the westernmost town of the Drakensberg foothills, is reached from N4 via the R540 and Dullstroom, a very pretty drive through steadily rising farm and forest. Established in 1850 as the centre of its own republic, Lydenburg was in fact the second Voortrekker town to be founded in the Eastern Transvaal—the first, Ohrigstad on the nearby lowveld, having been abandoned after a few years because of its feverish climate. It was from Lydenburg that the early Eastern Transvaal Boers launched their wars against the Pedi and Swazi, as well as their massive ivory hunting expeditions in what is now the Kruger National Park. The town was incorporated into the South African Republic in 1866, becoming the prosperous little farming town of today. Some interesting old buildings remain, their style resembling that of late Cape Dutch vernacular. These include the original **Voortrekker School** (built in 1851), a long, low building with whitewashed mud walls and a thatched roof, the **Voortrekker Church** (1852) and **Kruithuis** (old powder magazine, built later in 1894). Most of the town's few streets have surviving 19th-century houses, and its tranquil air gives it a feel of the past.

East of Lydenburg, the R37 leads up into some of the most spectacular scenery in the country, entering the Drakensberg via the steep **Long Tom Pass**. This was named after the huge naval cannons that the Boers used in the early stages of the Second Anglo–Boer War, christened 'Long Tom's' for their disproportionately long barrels.

At the foot of the pass, about 3km east of town along the R37, is the **Gustav Klingbiel Nature Reserve**. Clinging to the slopes of Mount Anderson, the first tall peak east of Lydenburg, this reserve harbours antelope such as eland, mountain reedbuck, bushbuck and duiker, but is best known for the late Iron Age walled villages found here, archaeological discoveries which suggest how settled Bantu-speaking culture had become over the centuries leading up to the wars and upheavals that had raged across the Transvaal in the early 19th-century. Three walking trails lead to the sites (and also to some old Boer War trenches), and up into the hills. There is accommodation in a trail hut, supplied with firewood and water.

East of the reserve the R37 climbs sharply up over the Long Tom Pass, giving splendid views out over the highveld and along the Drakensberg escarpment. At the top is the **Ceylon State Forest**, where the **Fanie Botha Hiking Trail** begins its winding route north along the escarpment to God's Window, near Pilgrim's Rest. This is a spectacular trail, but you will need a pick-up at the other end. Alternatively, you can hike back to the Ceylon State Forest trailhead via one of two alternative circular routes of three days each. If you do not have time for the long hike, it is worth walking for a couple of hours along the trail just to take in the scenery and good mountain air or you can drive to God's Window along the R532 (*see* below).

On the eastern side of the Pass are the **Bridal Veil Falls**, reached from the R37 by a short trail from the signposted car park. The falls are surrounded by dense yellowwood and assegai bush, but litter and graffiti mar this otherwise lovely and secluded spot. The **Lourie Nature Walk** makes a 13km circle through the mountain grassland and forest near the falls.

From Bridal Veil, the road falls steeply down through forest plantation to the town of **Sabie**. Sabie grew up around the forestry industry pioneered in the Eastern Transvaal back in the 1900s. The result is a pleasant, prosperous rural town that serves as the main tourist centre for the region. The excellent **Sabie Tourism Association** on Ford Street, © (01315) 43492, has information covering all of the Eastern Transvaal.

True to South African tradition, Sabie has a small museum dedicated to its local industry. The **Forestry Museum,** on Ford Street (*open Mon–Fri 9–4 Sat 9–1*), charts the history of South Africa's timber trade and has a section on the conservation of indigenous forests and the ecology of the exotic eucalyptus and pine plantations that cover vast stretches of South Africa's mountains.

The **Lone Creek Falls Trail,** an undemanding walking trail through the mountain plantations near the town, is signposted 13km west of town along the R37. The falls themselves plunge 70m into a narrow kloof filled with dense indigenous montane forest.

About 12km north of Sabie, along the R532, are the **Mac Mac Pools,** a set of natural rock pools below a large waterfall. Swimming here is heaven; the clear water is pure, free from bilharzia, and surrounded by forest. Little rustic changing rooms have even been provided, and the surrounding glades are now popular picnic spots. Anyone sweating through a hot mountain drive should cool off here. A short trail, the **Secretary Bird Walk,** winds through the forest near the pools and joins the 3km **Forest Falls Walk** that leads away though indigenous bush along the Mac Mac River to another set of falls, whose spray has created a miniature rain forest.

The R532 then climbs higher over the **Mac Mac Pass** to a T-junction with the narrow R533. A right (east) turn leads to the small forestry village of **Graskop,** beyond which the road drops sharply down into the lowveld. A left (west) turn leads through mountain heathland to the tiny, perfectly preserved 19th century mining village of **Pilgrim's Rest,** founded in 1873. The village's small stream and surrounding mountains were once the scene of a frenzied gold rush. A few fortunes were made, but by the 1920s most of the gold was gone. One mine stayed open until the early 1970s, but by then Pilgrim's Rest (named in hopeful expectation of wealth) had settled into a comfortable farming village.

Pilgrim's Rest was bought up by the Transvaal provincial government in 1974 for conservation as a living museum. It markets itself accordingly; its narrow street, lined by a single, long row of handsome late 19th-century tin houses, is now mostly given over to curio shops selling olde worlde mock Victoriana. However, some of the residents are genuine locals, and the new lick of paint that probably did not grace the tin houses in pioneer days in no way detracts from their charm. The setting is magnificent, with solemn, mist-shrouded heights looming above the valley and Pilgrim's Rest still has its original **Royal Hotel,** one of the few double-storey tin houses in the village—recently restored to its original order. An old mine at the western end of the village is open to visitors, and panning for gold (a few alluvial deposits still remain) is demonstrated by actors in period costume.

Pilgrim's Rest's three museums are all on the village's one street (*all open Mon–Sat 9–1, 2–4.30*). Most interesting is the **Town Museum,** which gives a photographic history of the town and its eccentric characters. The **Miner's House,** a rough-and-ready recreation of the basic life of pioneer diggers, and the **Old Bank Museum** complete the Victorian picture.

After a couple of hours, the rather forced period atmosphere of Pilgrim's Rest begins to pall. However, a short drive of about 2.5km southwest along the R533 leads to the beautiful **Mount Sheba Nature Reserve**, a small conservation area protecting a stretch of indigenous temperate montane rainforest. Yellowwood and stinkwood, ironwood, mountain cedar (one of the only conifers to occur naturally in Africa) and a bewildering variety of other hardwood species occur, some enormous, some mere saplings. Bushbuck, red duiker, samango and vervet monkeys inhabit the lush undergrowth. Gentle walking trails snake through the forest, but there is no Parks Board accommodation, only the rather expensive **Mount Sheba Hotel**, just outside (*see* 'Where to Stay'). To continue west is to drop steeply back down to the highveld. However, turn back along the R533, back through Pilgrim's Rest to Graskop, and then turn north along the R532, staying on the central mountain spine. A few kilometres north of Graskop a looped detour leads to the area's best known geological features, **Pinnacle Rock** and **God's Window**.

Pinnacle Rock juts like a stone finger from a steep forested mountainside that drops suddenly away for thousands of metres to the eastward expanse of the sub-tropical lowveld. God's Window, about 3km north of Pinnacle Rock, affords the same view, but through a cleft in the mountain wall. North of God's Window the loop detour rejoins the R532, which itself continues almost due north, past two sets of waterfalls, the **Lisbon Falls** and **Berlin Falls**. Both are signposted from the road. Lisbon Falls pour over a horseshoe-shaped cliff into the forest below, and can be reached by a short walking trail from the car park. Berlin Falls are bigger, plummeting 80m into a deep pool surrounded by broken rock. A wooden viewing deck has been built above them to give a safe view of the vertiginous drop.

North of these waterfalls, the R532 continues along the westward escarpment of one of Africa's most spectacular geographical splendours, the breathtaking **Blyde River Canyon**, now a protected nature reserve. The sheer, gagged cliffs rise over 2000m on either side of the Blyde River to form strange, rounded columns of rock clothed in hanging vegetation and cut through with spectacular waterfalls. Because of the dramatic changes in altitude, the 35km canyon contains indigenous hardwood forest, patches of rainforest, protea woodlands, grassland and heath, interspersed with arid stretches of bare rock and scrub similar to the vegetation of the Karoo.

Archeologists have found human remains here dating back to the early Stone Age and, from the density of San (bushman) paintings in the riverside caves, it seems that the canyon was one of their principal hunting grounds until the Voortrekkers hunted them out in the mid 19th century. Certainly, the plentiful water and varied vegetation supported large concentrations of game, and even today mountain reedbuck, grey rhebok, klipspringer, bushbuck and oribi are plentiful enough to feed a large (but shy) leopard, serval and caracal lynx population. Baboons shout from the cliffsides, and the forests echo to the sharp 'yack' of samango monkeys, the low booming of louries and, at night, the eerie scream of bushbabies. Vervet monkeys live in the riverine woodland, and hippo and crocodile still inhabit the deep pools of the Blyde River's dammed sections. Black and martial eagles cruise along the cliff faces, hunting for dassies.

Temperatures vary greatly in the canyon. The floor becomes unbearably hot on summer afternoons, but the whole reserve can be bitterly cold at night, and in winter the upper slopes are often gripped by frost. Summer rainstorms can turn the canyon floor into a careering torrent, and swathe the upper cliffs in dangerously thick mist.

The Blyde River Canyon has several hiking trails running through it, all scenically spectacular, and varying in length from an hour to five days. Overnight huts with water and firewood are provided about every 15km. At the north end of the canyon is an access road to **Blydepoort Resort**, ✆ (01323) 80158, a collection of self-contained cottages and a camp site complete with a supermarket, restaurant, garage and small airstrip. Irritatingly overdeveloped as this is, the only access down into the canyon from the resort is on foot. If you want to enter the canyon by car, you must drive around the head of the nature reserve, over the Abel Erasmus Pass, turn east of the R527 and south on the R531 (which drops down to the lowveld), from where a signposted road leads into a smaller resort of cottages and camp sites called **Swadini Resort**, ✆ (01528) 35172, which sits on the valley floor underneath the towering peaks of Swadini, Marieskop and the humped, free-standing massifs known as the Three Rondavels. An information office and a very small network of game viewing roads surround the camp.

Both resorts get very crowded at weekends and public holidays, but the main expanse of the canyon is accessible only via the hiking trails and there are few people down there at any one time.

About halfway down the canyon are an intruiging set of perfectly round holes set in the rock of the riverbank, known as the **Bourke's Luck Potholes**. The holes, some of which are sunk several metres into the rock, look as though they must be man-made; but are in fact the result of swirling flood waters, giving an idea of the violence of the Blyde River when it becomes swollen with summer rain. On the cliffs above the potholes, reached by a stiff hiking trail or by the R532, is an information centre.

Two day's hike south of Bourke's Luck, the canyon carves its way to the foot of the mountains below God's Window. There are several excellent sets of bushman rock paintings accessible from the hiking trail here.

About 10km west of the Blyde River Canyon, just north of the junction of the R532 and R527, is a smaller, more secretive natural wonder, the **Echo Caves** (*open 7 days, 8–5, tours every half-hour*). Only part of this massive cave system is open to the public: the closed section, called Cannibal Caves, apparantly harbours a bat population of millions. Whether cannibals did inhabit the caves—which is not unlikely, as the Natal Drakensberg certainly harboured cannibals in the 1830s (*see* **Natal** Drakensberg 'History')—groups of bushmen definitely lived here until the mid 19th century. Many of the chamber walls are adorned with their totemic pictures of animals, men and spirits, and it is here that archaeologists have found human remains dating back to the middle Stone Age.

The Echo Caves derive their name from the stalagmites in one of the largest chambers—100m long and over 50m high—which, if tapped with a piece of metal will echo the sound back louder. Outside the public entrance to the caves is the **Museum of Man** (*open Mon–Sat 10–5*), in which the larger Stone Age remains and artefacts are displayed, along with reproductions of some of the cave paintings.

North of the Echo Caves, the Drakensberg chain swings northwest into a wild stretch inaccessible by road. The R532 twists down the northern face of the range to the lowveld via the Abel Erasmus Pass, a descent so difficult that a tunnel has been constructed over part of it, which unfortunately obliterates the view.

On the foothills west of the Blyde River, in a section of the former Lebowa 'homeland', is the massive **Lekgalameetse Nature Reserve**, ✆ (0152302) 1613, reached from the R36 via the Ofcolaco road (signposted from the R36), and then along two short gravel roads. Lekgalameetse's 20,000ha comprise a mixture of indigenous forest and grassland inhabited by small herds of mountain reedbuck, lone bushbuck, duiker, leopard and caracal. Baboons and samango monkeys may appear suddenly on the forest trails. The region is lushly green, benefiting from a high local rainfall, and seldom has more than a few visitors at any one time.

The farthest northern section of the Eastern Transvaal Drakensberg is protected by the vast **Wolkberg Wilderness Area**, reached from Tzaneen (*see* **Northern Transvaal**).

Less rugged but still very beautiful is the small **Ebeneezer Dam Nature Reserve**, reached from the R36 near Tzaneen via the R528. Tall forest plantations provide shaded walks along the dam's shoreline where waterfowl breed in sizeable numbers, although you are unlikely to see any game. The reserve has a small camp site with ablutions.

Activities

Hiking: Several hikes of 1–5 days can be booked in the **Blyde River Canyon**, ✆ (0131512) 196, with overnight huts, firewood and water provided. The 5-day **Fanie Botha Trail**, ✆ (0131512) 307, from Ceylon State Forest Station on Long Tom Pass to God's Window is not a circular trail, but there are two circular options (3 days each), bringing the hiker back to the Station. Overnight trails are provided. Two 5-day trails with shorter options run from **Mac Mac Forest Station**, ✆ (0131512) 307. Again, overnight huts with firewood and water are provided. **Lekgalameetse Reserve** in Lebowa, west of the Blyde River Canyon, ✆ (0152302) 1613, has a 2- and a 3-day trail with overnight huts through some superb indigenous forest. The **Wolkburg Wilderness Area** south of Tzaneen, ✆ (0152222) 53 or (015236) 5633/5755, has a network of hikes ranging all over the wild northern Drakensberg.

Walking: Gentle forest walks of up to 4 hours can be found at Mac Mac Falls, Forest Falls and Bridal Veil Falls near Sabie, and the Blyde River Canyon has some short, circular walking trails in the bush near the two resorts at the northern end. Lekgalameetse Nature Reserve has some short forest walks.

Game Viewing: All the Drakensberg nature reserves listed above harbour game, usually antelope, shy leopard and primates. Blyde River Canyon has the largest density of antelope, as well as hippo and croc in the wider river pools, and large raptors on the heights. Leopard, serval and caracal are present, but seldom show themselves, preferring to hunt the wooded kloofs by night.

Trout Fishing: Stretches of streams can be booked and tackle hired via the Sabie Tourism Association, on Ford Street, Sabie, ✆ (01315) 43492.

Where to Stay
expensive

The **Royal Hotel**, Pilgrim's Rest, ✆ (01315) 81221, has recently been restored. The original two-storey corrugated iron building has been furnished with period antiques, and is comparatively far more expensive now than it would have been in the mining days. However, it is handsome and historically important, the food is good (trout and game are specialities), and its 19th-century ambiance is genuine. There are 8 en suite rooms, a bar and restaurant.

The **Mount Sheba Hotel**, ✆ (01315) 81241, next to the Mount Sheba Nature Reserve, is grand but rather impersonal. The surrounding mountain scenery is among the finest in South Africa, and hiking trails wind off in all directions. The dining room is particularly pleasant, with a stone fireplace and beamed ceiling, and guests stay in individual stone and thatch cottages, each with their own log fire. A swimming pool, tennis and squash courts complete the facilities.

moderate

Fern Tree Park near Sabie ✆ (01315) 42215, have a collection of self-contained cottages nestling in hills near town. There is a pool, and several hiking trails wind off from the site into surrounding forest. The owners will arrange trout fishing for guests. **Lisbon Hideaway** set in the mountains near Graskop ✆ (01315) 71851, offers old stone mining cottages overlooking the Lisbon River. The cottages are self-catering only, while nearby **Summit Lodge** ✆ (01315) 71058, offers thatched rondavels offering full board, half board, or B&B set in gardens with a pool.

Kloofsig Cottages, ✆ (01315) 71489, along the R533 (Kowyn's Pass) east of Graskop, are very comfortable self-catering thatched cottages for up to 5. The Fanie Botha Hiking Trail and two shorter trails, the Hadeda Trail and Treefern Trail, are accessible from here. **Wayfarers B&B**, 92 Malieveld Street, Sabie, ✆ (01315) 41500, has two en suite bedrooms.

Trackers, ✆ (01528) 35033, a private game reserve and wildlife education centre just outside the eastern entrance to the Blyde River Canyon, is signposted from the dirt road heading north from the canyon's access road. Trackers offers chalet and lodge accommodation and a very cheap camp site. Canoeing, hiking, climbing, game-viewing and hunting can be arranged, as well as cheap trips into the Kruger National Park. **Blydepoort Holiday Resort,** ✆ (01323) 80158, and the **Swadini Resort,** ✆ (0528) 35172, at the top of the Blyde River Canyon Nature Reserve, both have stunning settings under the great rock massifs, but have been over-developed South African style, with supermarkets and plastic tack rudely shoved into pristine wilderness. The resorts have good chalets and cottages, restaurants, petrol stations and all amenities, but the only true way to explore the Blyde River Canyon is on foot, hiking from hut to hut.

cheap

Jock of the Bushveld Hostel on Main Street, Sabie, ✆ (01315) 42178, has dormitory accommodation and cheap double rooms. **Themeda Hill** near Pilgrim's Rest, ✆ (01315) 81352 is a quiet mountain retreat of four thatched rondavels (self-catering only) reached via the Robber's Pass Road, then signposted off down a rough forest road (4.5km). **Lekgalameetse Nature Reserve,** ✆ (0152302) 1613, in Lebowa, west of the R36, has self-contained cottages and chalets surrounded by forest. Camping is also allowed, and ablutions are provided.

For those interested in exploring the region's wild interior on foot, the Fanie Botha Trail, Mac Mac Trail and Blyde River Trail have very cheap hiking huts with access to the most beautiful and secluded parts of the Eastern Transvaal Drakensberg.

The Lowveld Farmlands

East of the Drakensberg the land drops away sharply to a low, flat plain of sub-tropical bushveld and savannah that stretches east to Mozambique. Blisteringly hot and humid in the rainy summer, warm and dry in the 'winter', or cooler season, the lowveld is mostly given over to game farming and nature reserves, and is South Africa's best region for viewing big game. The far eastern section, which runs along the Lobombo mountains, is occupied by the massive Kruger National Park. Backing onto the western boundary of the Kruger are a number of private game reserves, adding to the total protected area (*see* Kruger National Park).

South of the Kruger is a prosperous arable farming area centered around the towns of White River and **Nelspruit**, the ugly regional capital. Nelspruit is unappealing, having been given a concrete and glass facelift in the 1970s, but it does have banks, garages, tyre dealerships and supermarkets—the usual amenities needed by people driving to and from the bushveld. Nelspruit also has some private safari companies which take people into the game reserves (*see* 'Activities'). If heading east to Maputo in Mozambique, it is also wise to stock up here on food and possibly a spare tyre or two.

Signposted from the town centre is the elegant, ordered **Lowveld National Botanic Garden**, which covers about 150ha along the banks of the Crocodile River. Small belts of forest, marsh, aloe and voluptuous sub-tropical flowers are linked by a short walking trail. This is a good place for birdlife, particularly the iridescent sunbirds and exotic species such the paradise flycatcher and lilac-breasted roller.

About 26km west of Nelspruit are the **Sudwala Caves**. Travel along the N4 to the Sabie road, then look out for the signposts. These to be claim the oldest caves, in geological terms, in the world. Certainly, they are known to be 200 million years old. Late Stone-Age remains have also been found here. However, the caves are best known for having been a hide-out for dissident Swazi factions during the civil wars that split the nation in the early 19th century. From 1815 to 1840, it was used as a fortress, sometimes housing up to 3,000 people and 500 cattle. During the Anglo–Boer War (1899–1902), the Boers used the caves as an ammunition store for their Long Tom cannon shells (*see* 'Long Tom Pass' above), and their deep, resonant chambers were the inspiration for the caverns in the popular Edwardian adventure stories *King Solomon's Mines* and *She*, by H. Rider Haggard

About 20km north of Nelspruit is **White River**, a forestry town that marks a convenient gateway to the southern lowveld game reserves. The town started life as a British colonial enclave around the turn of the century, but over the past 30 years has become almost completely Afrikaans, to the point that on most maps its name now appears as 'Witrivier'. The tiny town has changed little since the colonial era, but large communities of poor whites have settled in the surrounding forests, forming huge caravan parks that are not unlike black townships in feel. This is one of the few places outside Johannesburg's western suburbs where one is likely to encounter South Africa's poor whites en masse, and it makes an interesting counterpoint to the general impression of white wealth that is the South African norm.

Around White River are several lodges set in their own estates, which offer safaris into the game reserves for people without their own transport (*see* 'Where to Stay'). However, the cost is usually high, and it is probably more economic to hire a vehicle in Johannesburg or Nelspruit. About 150km east of Nelspruit, at a low pass in the Lobombo Mountains, is **Komaatipoort**, a small town with a caravan and camping site, supermarkets and a garage. The bank is only open on Mondays, Wednesdays and Fridays.

There is an amusing story attached to Komatipoort, concerning an English eccentric called Mostyn Owen, or 'Mad Owen', a cashiered officer who lived in the district in the 1870s. Stories about him abound, but this is the best. Riding to the hotel at Komatipoort from the Mozambique side one night, Owen's horse was attacked by a crocodile as he forded the Komaati River. Owen beat the reptile off with his stirrup-iron, rode into town and strode into the hotel, roaring for a gun with which to shoot the offending croc. A German tailor staying at the hotel offered to lend him one, and followed Owen to the ford. Once there, Owen said, 'Now I'm going to stand in the middle of the ford, and when the crocodile comes for me, I want you to shoot him.'

The German protested; he was not a good shot, the night was dark, and he ran the risk, not only of missing, but of hitting Owen.

'All right,' said Owen. 'You go into the river and I'll shoot.'

Owen bullied the unfortunate tailor into the water. Out swam the crocodile, and Owen shot with deadly accuracy. The tailor was relieved, but soon after the incident went completely bald.

Further south, near the border with Swaziland, rise cool mountains, an offshoot of the Drakensberg chain. At their foot is Barberton, the site of South Africa's first gold rush in the 1870s and the gateway to the hiker's paradise of the mountains behind.

The lowveld's 'homelands', KaNgwane, Lebowa and Gazankulu, though generally overcrowded, have some very good game reserves. The best are: **Songimvelo Nature Reserve** in the section of KaNgwane bordering western Swaziland, which protects a huge sweep of pristine uplands in the mountains south of Barberton inhabited by most of the original game; **Mthethomusha Game Reserve** in KaNgwane at the southeast corner of the Kruger Park; and **Manyeleti**, a large bushveld reserve with big game in the section of Gazankulu bordering the western Kruger Park. These reserves are particularly rewarding to visit, as few tourists know of them. See Kruger National Park section for details.

Activities

Safaris: Norse Safaris in Nelspruit, ✆ (01311) 53325, offer game viewing trips into the Kruger National Park and Sabi Sands Private Game Reserve in the early morning, evening and at night. Trips into the Drakensberg and the lowveld countryside are also offered. Trips are quite expensive, but include meals and are a useful option for those without their own transport. Slightly cheaper are Lion Tours, based in Hazyview, ✆ (01317) 67333, who take people into the Kruger in minibuses. Cheaper still are the tours organized by the Hazyview Youth Hostel, ✆ (01317) 67224, which also organize minibus safaris.

Riding: Lowveld Horse Trails, ✆ (01311) 25993/26668, offers rides between one hour and 3 days into the bushveld on good horses. The stables are signposted roughly midway along the R537 between Sabie and White River.

Walking: The Lowveld National Botanic Garden, signposted from Nelspruit's town centre is a large landscaped park on the banks of the Crocodile River. A gentle walking trail of about 2km winds through the varied displays of lowveld vegetation.

Where to Stay

expensive

Frangipani Lodge, ✆ (01311) 33224, is a newly-built mock-period lodge on a working farm between Nelspruit and White River (reached via the R40 then left at the Heidelberg traffic light). The lodge has a verandah-cum-sitting room, and serves lavish meals. Its five en suite rooms are charming in a twee, enthusiastic way. Near White River, 6km along the Plaston Road, is **Kirby Country Lodge**, ✆ (01311) 32645, which has private cottages set among gardens. The food is prepared with home-grown vegetables and herbs. The White River flows through the woods adjoining the gardens, and a thatched great hall doubles as a sitting and dining room. Also near White River, along the road to Hazyview, the luxurious **Hulala Lakeside Lodge**, ✆ (01311) 51710, sits on the wooded spur of a man-made lake offering very comfortable rooms overlooking the water, where ospreys and fish eagles snatch their prey. Sailing, canoeing and fishing are also available.

moderate

Riverside Cottages on the banks of the Sabie River near Hazyview, ✆ (01317) 67103, offer stone-and-thatched comfort (self-catering) in 14 old farm cottages with a pool, fishing rights (tackle is sometimes available) and private walking trails. **Shandon Lodge**, ✆ (01311) 49934, on Saturn Street, Nelspruit, is a large, handsome colonial bungalow with a big verandah overlooking the town. The 4 mock-period en suite bedrooms each have their own verandah. The **Townhouse** at 5 Ferreira Street, Nelspruit, ✆ (01311) 27006/552125, is another handsome colonial suburban house, beautifully decorated with good modern art.

cheap

Hazyview Youth Hostel, ✆ (01317) 67224, offers cheap dormitory accommodation near the Orpen gate to the Kruger. The hostel runs very cheap day-trips into the Park. Nelspruit, Komaatipoort and White River all have camps sites. Otherwise, the nearest cheap accommodation is at the Jock of the Bushveld Hostel, Sabie (*see* above) or at the camp sites inside the Kruger National Park .

The Kruger National Park

History

Larger than any other reserve in South Africa, and one of the largest on the African continent, the Kruger covers a staggering 19,445 square kilometres, bigger than Israel or Wales. Founded in 1898 by Paul Kruger, president of the South African Republic, after urgent prompting by one of his land surveyors, Charles Marais, who realised that, unless conserved, the local game would be completely shot out within another decade. The reserve was first known as the Sabie Game Reserve. Like many other leading Boers of the time, Kruger had made his early fortune through intensive ivory hunting in the Eastern and Northern Transvaal, but had the foresight to see that unless game was actively conserved it would be wiped out in little more than a generation, as was to happen in the Cape during the late 19th century. At the time the reserve was declared, freebooting professional hunters still operated in the area. The best account of this dangerous life is told in the beautifully illustrated book, *Jock of the Bushveld* (*see* **Further Reading**), by Sir Percy Fitzpatrick, who hunted in the area during the 1880s and '90s.

The reserve was re-ratified when the British took over the region in 1902, following the Second Anglo–Boer War, and founded another great reserve next to Sabie—the Shingwedzi Game Reserve. These were later combined to form the present Kruger Park. From 1903, the ranger appointed to look after the enormous territory, Major James Stevenson-Hamilton, found the area largely denuded of game through poaching and immediately established the system of armed patrols that is common practice in most of Southern Africa's game reserves today. This obviously made him unpopular with the lowveld Boers, who still regarded the area as their own hunting ground for hides and ivory, and the local Africans, who killed for meat. A mixture of tough tactics combined with employing local people in the park gradually helped to alleviate the poaching—the park being seen as a source of employment for local blacks. White farmers stopped shooting the game once fences were erected and their crops were no longer in danger from marauding antelope, nor their lives from elephant and lion.

During his 44 years in the Kruger (he retired in 1946), Stevenson-Hamilton managed to re-establish the huge game populations that the Kruger harbours today, and left a legacy of commitment to effective conservation that subsequent governments have retained.

Today's National Park is 350km long and about 65km wide, stretching from the Crocodile River near Komatipoort right up to South Africa's northern border with Zimbabwe. The eastern boundary is marked by the Lebombo Mountains, which form the Transvaal's border with Mozambique and there is talk of South Africa and Mozambique co-operating to extend the protected area far into Mozambique, to the east of the Lebombos, which would make it the largest game reserve in Africa. But as yet, Mozambique lacks funds to implement the project.

Flora and Fauna

The Kruger National Park is mostly flat bushveld and savannah, with pockets of marula and wild fig woodland, and large areas of widely-spaced mopane forest. Several perennial rivers—the Crocodile, Oliphants, Sabie, Timbavati, Letaba, Luvuvhu and Shingwedzi—flow through the park. Game is plentiful. Elephant, black and white rhino, lion, leopard, cheetah, wild dog, spotted and brown hyena, buffalo, and almost all of South Africa's antelope species, from the rare sable and roan, to the tiny suni, are present in large numbers, with herds of impala appearing around almost

wildebeest + zebra.

every bend in the road. Blue wildebeest and tsessebe, zebra, warthog, bushpig, and of course, the nocturnal rarities such as bushbabies, aardwark, aardwolf, genet and civet inhabit the bush, as do large troops of baboons and vervet monkeys, while hippo and crocodile rule the rivers.

The Kruger's range of birdlife is enormous; especially common are the exotic blue and crowned crane, rollers, trogons, storks (including black and marabou), bee-eaters, sunbirds, drongos, grey louries (known as 'go-away birds' because of their weird call), and, of course ostrich. Raptors such as bateleur, martial, black and fish eagles, the pale chanting goshawk and Cape vulture are also regular sights. A host of rarer species, many of them spectacular, also inhabit the park and you should not go in without a field guide.

Getting There

The southern section of the Kruger has several entrance points: **Phalaborwa**, reached from Tzaneen via the R71; **Orpen**, signposted from the R40 from Klaserie; **Paul Kruger**, reached via the R536 from the R40 via **Hazyview**; **Numbi**, reached via the R538 from Nelspruit; Malalane and Crocodile, both reached via the N4 east of Nelspruit.

Getting Around

By car: Unless you have booked one of the superb guided hiking trails, you are confined to your car except within camps and at some picnic sites. For this reason, it is as well to hire a comfortable vehicle with plenty of room, as you will be stuck in it for hours as you drive around the bushveld roads. If you can afford it, hire a bakkie (pick-up), minibus or 4x4, as the raised chassis will afford much better game viewing than an ordinary car, which is too low to see over the first line of bush. For this reason, it can be worth going in with a tour company (*see* 'Getting Around the Eastern Transvaal').

Please be aware that you should not drive faster than 50kph.

On foot: This is by far the best way to see both the game and the bushveld country. Several **guided walking trails** of 1–5 days have been established, taking small groups far off the roads to special camps. Armed rangers accompany the groups as close as possible to big game such as lion, elephant and buffalo. The trails are naturally very popular and are often booked up as much as a year in advance. However, it is possible to get a cancellation, which can be booked in advance and from abroad, via the National Parks Board in Pretoria, ✆ (012) 343 1991.

Bush Camps

The Kruger has a variety of bush camps. The main one, Skukuza, is the size of a small town, complete with an airstrip, bank, post office, petrol station, supermarket, large restaurant and school for the children of the Park's rangers. The majority are smaller, although still well provided with amenities, while some of the more expensive camps are no more than a cluster of cabins built on stilts. Each camp has its own specialities and local game. There is accommodation to suit all budgets (*see* 'Where to Stay'). A good general rule is to book well in advance through the National Parks Board, ✆ (012) 343 1991, and to avoid weekends or holidays if possible, so as not to end up in one of the big camps. All camps close their gates overnight, at times that vary depending on the season, usually between 5.30pm and 6.30pm in the evening. The times are posted on the gates, so make sure you take note as you drive out. Those caught on the roads after the advertised time will be picked up by rangers and tersely escorted in.

Where to Stay
private camps (expensive)

Boulders Camp has room for just 12 people in thatched log cabins built on stilts that the animals pass underneath. Bookings are made from the Letaba Camp, 50km east of the Phalaborwa Gate. The cabins have solar powered electricity and are self-catering only. **Roodewal** and **Nwanetsi** take 19 and 16 people respectively. Accessible from the Orpen Gate, they are booked through Satara and Olifants Camps. Further south is **Jock of the Bushveld Camp**, also self-catering, which also takes 12 people. Bookings are made from Berg-En-Dal Camp, near Malelane Gate in the far south of the park. **Malelane** also has a small private camp of small cottages, bookable from Berg-En-Dal Camp.

general camps (moderate/cheap)

The general camps all have cottages and chalets with their own kitchens and bathrooms, and cheaper camping. All have braaiiing facilities.

Oliphants Camp, east of the Phalaborwa Gate, sits on a high bluff overlooking the Oliphants River. Game viewing is good from here, particularly in the evening, and the camp has a shop, restaurant, petrol station and small museum. The small **Orpen Camp** has a more intimate feel. There is a petrol station and shop, but no restaurant. Even smaller is **Balule Camp**, on the Oliphants River near Letaba Camp. With only a few rondavels, this is one of the quietest public camps in the park. **Lower Sabie Camp** is popular for the large concentrations of game in the vicinity. East of the Paul Kruger Gate, Lower Sabie has a shop, restaurant and petrol station. **Crocodile Bridge Camp** lies on the banks of the Crocodile River in the far southest of the park. Just 20 chalets and a small shop make this a pleasant place to stay, its only disadvantage being the distance to all other points of the park.

Those wishing for greater privacy should try and book into the very small **Talamati Camp** near Orpen Gate, **Mbyamiti Camp**, on the banks of the Crocodile River in the far south, **Sirheni**, in the west, on the banks of the Nwawitsonto River, between the Orpen and Paul Kruger gates.

Travellers should book these camps at the nearest entrance gate, and remember to bring their own food. Three new, small camps have opened far inside the park—**Jakkalbessie**, **Shimaweni**, **Mopani** and **Bateleur**. All have self-contained cottages with their own bathrooms. **Letaba Camp** is a large, well landscaped camp on the Great Letaba River east of Phalaborwa Gate, with a large restaurant, shop, petrol station and garage. **Satara Camp**, east of the Orpen Gate, is set in flat country, hence game viewing from the camp itself is not good. However, this is one of the largest camps, popular with tour groups from Johannesburg, and a good place for young people to meet. Two restaurants, a shop, petrol station, laundry, information centre and garage complete the facilities.

Berg-En-Dal Camp, near the Malelane Gate in the far south of the park, is more attractively landscaped than the other big camps, with the cottages spaced out under large shady trees. The camp has a pool, restaurant, shop, petrol station and laundromat. **Skukuza Camp**, by the Paul Kruger Gate, is the largest in the park. Banks, a post office, a supermarket, several restaurants, car hire, a police station, a doctor, a library and even an airstrip make this a convenient place to stop, but gives little sense of being in the bush. However, it does overlook a hippo pool on the Sabie River. **Pretoriuskop and Shingwedzi**, further inside the park, have a variety of accommodation, including self-contained cottages and chalets, bungalows with share bathrooms, and camping. Both camps have a restuarant and shop. **Maroela Camp**, just east of the Orpen Gate, is the cheapest camp, and is open to campers only. It has a full range of facilities, including a shop, petrol station, restaurant and laundry.

The Private Game Reserves

Tacked onto the western border of the Kruger are a number of private, rather exclusive, game reserves, also harbouring big game. These offer a more intimate look at the bush than is possible in the Kruger (unless you are on one of the National Park's Wilderness Trails). Open-top landrovers allow you to breathe the open air of the bushveld and add a frisson of excitement when approaching a potentially dangerous animal, such as a lion or elephant. Some of the private reserves also offer walking trails similar to those of the Kruger. The bush camps of the private reserves tend to be beautifully laid out, small, and strictly limited in the number of guests allowed at a time, so there is no risk of competing with other vehicles for a sight of game. Most specialize in certain kinds of game,

Hyena

particularly dangerous game, and make a point of bringing their guests as close as possible.

A drawback to the private reserves is the cost, which ranges from the ludicrously expensive to the merely expensive. Hospitality tends to be lavish and the prices include all game drives, food (but not drinks), and facilities such as special hides for photographing animals. But these reserves are generally beyond the reach of anyone travelling on a low budget.

Purist wildlife enthusiasts may also not wish to visit the private reserves, as many conservationists accuse their management of creating false environments out of the need to assure sightings of the 'Big Five'. Practices such as baiting and shining permanent night-time spotlights so as to sight shy species like leopard are commonplace, and opinion is divided as to whether this seriously upsets the natural order of the bushveld. However, tourism is a way of ensuring the wildlife's future (as well as that of its fragile habitat). Make up your own mind.

Johannesburg ✆ (011–)   **Where to Stay**

very expensive

Sabi Sand, ✆ Jo'burg 880 8840/883 5484, is the largest private reserve, a 60,000ha block of bushveld just north of the Paul Kruger Gate into the Kruger (along the R536 from Sabie). Sabi Sand is split into three separate reserves, each offering slightly different game specialities. **Sabi Sabi**, the best known of the three, has the Big Five and is famous for a huge bull elephant called Mandleve, one of the last real tuskers (they reach almost to the ground) left unpoached on the entire continent. Sabi Sabi is also the most expensive and luxurious of Sabi Sand's reserves. **Inyati**, smaller than Sabi Sabi, is known for night drives, and the night-time spotlights near the camp that attract shy animals, such as leopard, to a baited tree. **Ulusaba**, built on a rock outcrop, is surrounded by wild fig forest, and has commanding views of the veld. Slightly cheaper than Sabi Sand's other two reserves, Ulusaba specializes in straightforward safaris looking for the Big Five. **Mala Mala**, ✆ Jo'burg 789 2677, is next to Sabi Sand, and is reached by the same road. It is only half the size, but its game concentration is high, and you can more or less guarantee seeing the Big Five. Again, the bush camps are luxuriously appointed, the food lavish, and the prices very high.

Londolozi, ✆ Jo'burg 726 6701/726 7360, adjoins both Sabi Sand and Mala Mala. Although most big game species are present, Londolozi is famous for its leopards. Guided walks into the bush are a speciality, and, like Sabi Sand and Mala Mala, Londolozi's luxury and prices are both high. **Timbavati**, ✆ Jo'burg 463 1990, is reached via the R53 to the Orpen Gate of the Kruger. Timbavati has long been known for its white lions, a pride that lack certain pigment in their coats, but are not albinos. Thrilling game drives take you to within feet of these unique animals, without the security of metal and glass between you. However, the lions are accustomed to people and there have been no attacks. There are night-time hides from which you can watch lions feeding. The reserve also has particularly large herds of both elephant and buffalo.

Thornybush Game Lodge, ✆ Jo'burg 883 7918/9, near Hoedspruit on the R40 between Nelspruit and Tzaneen, borders Timbavati. Once again, a luxurious lodge and the Big Five are the main attractions, with guided game walks available.

expensive

Klaserie, ✆ Jo'burg, 531 814/538 411, a huge reserve (60,000ha) just northwest of Timbavati, is signposted south of Hoedspruit. Klaserie has no specific game speciality, but the Big Five are all present. Unusually, accommodation is in large safari tents rather than the usual luxury lodge. There are guided game walks during the day and game drives at night. **Tshukudu**, ✆ (01528) 32476, is a family-run reserve without the sometimes oppressive VIP treatment that the more expensive reserves cultivate. Again, although the Big Five are present, the reserve is known for rhino, black and white, and for its animal orphanage, where guests can help feeding baby elephant and lion (which wander freely about the lodge).

moderate

Manyeleti Game Reserve, ✆ 131982 and ask for Manyeleti 2, near the Orpen Gate of the Kruger Park, is signposted from the R536. Run by the Gazankulu government (in whose territory it lies), it lacks the luxury of the above reserves, but the thick, unspoilt bushveld seldom has more than a few tourists at a time and provides a peaceful alternative to the crowded Kruger National Park, at budget prices. There is a small bush camp of self-contained rondavels, a shop, petrol station, restaurant and bar, and the Big Five. Also near the Kruger (at the south-west corner) is **Mthethomusha Game Reserve**, ✆ (01311) 53931, which has all of the Big Five except for lion. Administered by the KaNgwane Parks Board, Mthethomisha has a luxurious lodge, **Bongani**, and the local Swazi people have a share in its profits. You have to book via the KaNgwane Parks Board in Nelspruit (at the above number) to arrange being met at the gate by a Parks Board vehicle—no private cars are allowed in the park.

The **Cheetah Project**, ✆ (015282) 4321, on the R40 between Klaserie and Hoedspruit, has no accommodation, but is worth a visit if you are in the vicinity. Cheetah, which now face extinction in many parts of Africa, are bred here for release into the wild. The very rare, dark-spotted king cheetah, a larger sub-species of the endangered cat, has also been successfully bred. A visit entails handling tame cheetahs (which enjoy being stroked and tickled, and purr like a motorbike engine), and a film on the research and work of the project. The Cheetah Project is closed on Sundays.

South of the Kruger: Barberton, Mountains of the Swaziland Border

The small colonial town of **Barberton** lies at the foot of high, temperate mountains similar in appearance and vegetation to the Drakensberg. Barberton has a special place in South African history as the site of the country's first gold rush, but today there are only one or two national monuments to interest the visitor. The mountain country behind is empty and wild and has some of the Transvaal's best hiking, as well as a game-rich nature reserve.

History

Barberton sprang into existence in the early 1880s as a gold-buying and mining centre. The extensive gold finds in the Eastern Transvaal Drakensberg during the 1870s had sent prospectors hunting through the region's mountains for the elusive metal. The first strike in Barberton (named after one Graham Barber, one of the area's earliest successful prospectors) was made in 1883 by a Frenchman named Auguste Robert. Unlike the Drakensberg finds, those around Barberton were mostly in undergound reefs, rather than alluvial deposits, and so promised greater fortunes. One reef, on the Sheba claim, gave up 50,000 ounces of gold in its first 11,000 tons of ore, making it the richest gold mine in the world at that time. Within weeks of the find, a corrugated iron and tent village called Eureka City had emerged near the site of the present town. Within a few months permanent buildings were going up, some of them grand, like the elegant Stock Exchange, which still stands as testimony to the riches that the surrounding mountains yielded up.

However, it soon became clear that only a few of the reefs ran deep enough to provide long-term yields, and after 1886 most of the prospectors moved north to try their luck on the Witwatersrand.

Barberton soon settled into a small, prosperous regional town with a mostly English speaking population, owing to the large numbers of English prospectors that were attracted to the original Eureka City in the late 19th century. Today, the town still has some working gold mines nearby, and is connected by a cable-way to the asbestos-mining town of Bulembu in Swaziland. The cableway does not take passengers, which is sad, as the views would be magnificent; one unfortunate man tried it a few years ago, but got on too late in the day and was still sitting in the cable-car when the cableway shut down for the night. Owing to the high altitude, he froze to death.

Tourist Information

Barberton Publicity Bureau, Main Street, Barberton, ℂ (01314) 22121 ext 242.

The Town

The **Barberton Museum** (*open Mon–Sat 9–4.30*), on Pilgrim Street, has a good local history of the mining days, with old photographs of characters such as Cockney Liz, a barmaid at the Phoenix Hotel (which still exists) who 'used to put herself up for sale every night and was hopelessly immoral', but who nonetheless would have no bad language in her bar, and who later joined the Salvation Army. The more sedate side of Barberton's early days is preserved in the **Bellhaven House Museum** (*open Mon–Fri 10–5*), a late Victorian set piece. Having experienced such a rapid gold boom, Barberton even sported a **Stock Exchange** during the late 1880s and '90s, and the elegant Cape Dutch-style façade (built 1887) has been preserved. Other surviving historic buildings include the **Masonic Lodge**, the old **Globe Tavern**, which saw more than its share of riots and brawls during the rush, and the Victorian houses of **Stopfoth** and **Fernlea**, both of which now contain the usual collection of old town Victoriana (*open Mon–Sat 9–4.30*). There is also a monument to the Staffordshire bull terrier Jock, the hero of the South African colonial classic *Jock of the Bushveld*—see **Further Reading**.

In Barberton's central park is a **giant fig tree** under which Paul Kruger is supposed to have set up a court to settle cases between miners, on one of his rare visits to the town— as a rule the old Boer president did not like the *uitlanders* that invaded his republic to make money from its minerals, despite the revenues they generated.

Just outside town, on the R38, is the **Barberton Nature Reserve**, which covers a large section of the mountain foothills near town; there is no accommodation, but visitors can walk at will. The hills are mostly grassland, but forested kloofs with fast-flowing streams cut through them. There is little game apart from some shy duiker, baboon, vervet monkeys, and dassies. However, to the south, Barberton borders the enormous (56,000ha) **Songimvelo Nature Reserve** in KaNgwane, ✆ (0134) 830 800, which stretches over the foothills and into the high mountains separating Barberton from Swaziland. White rhino, giraffe, zebra, kudu, bushbuck, reedbuck, and the smaller antelope live here, while hippo wallow in the bilharzia-laden Komati River, which cuts through the reserve.

Songimvelo has a network of beautiful hiking trails through its mixed grassland, heath and woodland, some of which climb up to almost 2000m. The reserve is reached by the R40 from Barberton to Bulembu in Swaziland, with its entrance just before the apex of the Saddleback Pass.

Two other hiking trails into the mountains, the **Pioneer Trail** and **Gold Nugget Trail**, are both 2-day hikes with overnight huts, ✆ (01314) 22121, ext. 242 to book. The flora is particularly good, with forest, grassland and wildflowers such as the large, red Barberton daisy. The trails pass some of the old mines shafts and hikers may enter them, but to go in farther than about 20m is dangerous. The trails begin at the **Dias Reef Base Camp**, about 2km out of town along Crown Street.

Where to Stay

expensive/moderate

The luxurious safari lodge at **Songimvelo Nature Reserve** is very expensive, ✆ (0134) 830 800. Expect to be waited on hand and foot in a superb mountain setting. The surrounding reserve teems with game, and there are guided hikes of one hour to several days, guided riding trails (for guests only) and game drives in the reserve's open-topped vehicles. Drive up the road to Saddleback Pass and Swaziland for about half an hour and look out for the sign (which points to the south).

Just inside the moderate category is the **Phoenix Hotel** on Pilgrim Street, ✆ (01314) 24211, which was one of early Barberton's liveliest liquor joints, but has sadly lost both its outrageousness and the original decor. However, if you are not in a hurry, it is worth crossing the mountains behind Barberton via the R40, which heads over Saddleback Pass into Swaziland. About 30km on the Swaziland side is the delightful **Phopanyane Falls Private Nature Reserve**, ✆ (09268) 71319, reached via the little towns of Bulembu and Pigg's Peak. Phopanyane, set in forest by a long set of waterfalls, has expensive cottages and moderately-priced safari tents hidden from each-other under trees, as well as a small, very good restaurants. Remember to set off before 3pm, as the border post east of Saddleback Pass closes at 4.30pm. See Northwest Swaziland for details of Phophanyane. Closer to town is the **Bougainvillea Hotel**, ✆ (01314) 9684, at the expensive end of the moderate scale, is an old-fashioned South African country hotel, complete with tin roof, extensive gardens, an outside terrace and a pool. There are horses to ride and trails to walk.

cheap

Self-catering chalets and camp sites with ablutions can be found at the **Barberton Caravan Park** in the middle of town, ✆ (01314) 23323, and at the Dias Reef camp site about 2km from town along Crown Street. A few hours' hike from Dias Camp, along the Pioneer Hiking Trail, is an overnight hut with water and firewood.

Far Southeastern Transvaal: between Barberton and Pongola River

If driving down to central Swaziland or northern Zululand from Johannesburg, you will pass through this vast, high, landscape of golden grasslands, dotted with huge blocks of forestry. Although it is mostly composed of large private cattle and timber farms and small farming towns, there are one or two stops worth making.

About 50km southwest of Barberton is the small but overdeveloped town of **Badplaas**, which has a mineral spa—unfortunately built into a frightful leisure complex during the 1970s. However, just north of town on the R38 **Badplaas Nature Reserve** has walking and riding trails through a stretch of rolling hill country where large antelope graze. There are moderately-priced self-contained chalets and a camp site with ablutions. The R541 leads from Badplaas straight into the Swazi capital Mbabane, about 75km to the east, so the reserve makes a good place to break a journey to Swaziland.

Further south, near the town of Ermelo, on the R29 between the N11 and Piet Retief, is the **Ermelo Game Park**, a small reserve surrounding two dams, harbouring large antelope and large populations of waterfowl. A camp site and a group of self-catering chalets make this a convenient spot to break a long drive. About 50km further along the R29 towards Piet Retief is the **Jericho Dam Nature Reserve**, a larger reserve with little game but very good bird life; blue, crowned and wattled cranes in particular have made the dam a regular stop on their ceaseless foraging flights, perhaps because of its isolation. The only accommodation is a camp site.

From Jericho Dam, the R29 leads on to Piet Retief, from which you can either head east into southern Swaziland, or south on the R33 to northern Natal and Zululand.

The Northern Transvaal

... Animal, and bird and beast revealed
The secret of the wilderness that guides
All rebel creatures, singular or spurned
Along safe trails to water-holes and hides

The Lowveld, Charles Eglington

TRAVELLERS SHOULD NOTE THAT NORTHERN TRANSVAAL IS MALARIAL

From Pretoria north to the Zimbabwe border, the Transvaal becomes
progressively wilder and more open. Game abounds, and in the region's
more northerly reaches hunting ranches have almost entirely replaced
stock farms. The landscape consists mainly of flat plains, from which rise
three mountain ranges; the baobab-covered Soutpansberg in the far

north, Waterberg in the west and Strydpoortberg in the Drakensberg foothills of the east. These heights, green from year-round rains, provide cool relief from the relentless heat of the plains. From the high montane forests and waterfalls you can gaze down at the flat bushveld far below and feel yourself a world away from the drought and dust of Africa.

The northern Transvaal has few towns of any size except Pietersburg, Potgietersrus, Louis Trichardt and Messina, all of which are strung out along the 600km section of N1 highway that links Pretoria and Johannesburg with Zimbabwe. Of little interest in themselves, these towns provide access to the region's mountain hiking trails and many game reserves, such as the northern Kruger National Park, the beautiful Lapalala Wilderness Area, and the Leshaba Wilderness.

Under apartheid, vast areas of the Northern Transvaal were set aside as the 'tribal homelands' of Lebowa, Gazankulu and Venda. Although now officially back in the Union, these areas still retain a very different look and feel to the other 'white' areas of the Northern Transvaal, with traditional villages and communal systems of land ownership creating a more obviously African landscape. Most road and tourism maps still show the old 'homeland' borders, and their nature reserves and local administrations are still separate from those of South Africa—though this is set to change in the next two years. Of the three, Venda, stretching north from the Soutpansberg to the Limpopo, is the most unmodernized, a remote territory that was never conquered by the Boers or British, and whose natural landscape has not been obliterated by over-population or over-grazing. In some areas of rural Venda, the people live side by side with game, providing a glimpse of South African life before colonial days.

Northern Transvaal

Climate

Like all eastern parts of South Africa, the Northern Transvaal has a summer rainy season and a dry winter. The low-lying bushveld plains seldom become cold, except on winter nights, and summer days are blisteringly hot. However, up in the mountains a more temperate mini-climate prevails, with rain occuring all year (though mostly in summer) and occasional frosts on winter nights.

Flora and Fauna

The 'Big Five'—lion, leopard, buffalo, elephant and both rhino species—are common in the Kruger National Park, as are large herds of antelope, zebra and wildebeest. Big game such as white rhino, giraffe, buffalo, roan and sable antelope occur in the Waterberg region, especially the Lapalala Wilderness Area, and to the north in the Leshaba Wilderness and Nwadeni National Park in Venda. In the Soutpansberg and Drakensberg forest reserves leopard, caracal lynx, bushbuck, the rare red duiker and samango monkey thrive, but are shy and tend to stay hidden. Crocodile and hippo can be found in the rivers of the Kruger and Waterberg, as well as in the Limpopo, and the region has numerous smaller reserves, most of which support large numbers of indigenous antelope. Game also lives wild on farms, many of which have harnessed the wildlife commercially, becoming game farms and hunting ranches. This is particularly so north of the Soutpansberg, where most of the large game species can be found.

The birdlife on the plains is colourful and diverse; lilac-breasted rollers and bee-eaters are a common sight on the telephone wires along the roads. Bateleur eagles, Cape vultures, pale chanting goshawks, hornbills and other birds associated with the lowveld wilderness are common. Black eagle, green lourie and narina trogon inhabit the mountain forests.

The common thorn tree is not alone on the plains: large stretches of marula forest (their berries a favourite food of elephants), spectacular wild fig trees (usually found near dry river beds), huge baobabs (in the northernmost section around Messina) and large camel-thorn trees (in the west, near Botswana) provide an ever-changing landscape and support large numbers of browsing animals. In the Soutpansberg a huge variety of hardwood trees such as assegai, hard pear, yellowwood, lemonwood (whose fresh scent drifts through the higher reaches of the forest) line the middle slopes, giving way to spectacular aloes on the rocky summits, while in the Drakensberg foothills of eastern Lebowa and near Tzaneen are rare stretches of cycad forest (giant, prehistoric tree-ferns), creating a fantasy landscape that local tribesmen still believe is ruled by a mythical rain queen.

History

The original San (bushman) inhabitants were pushed west from their Northern Transvaal hunting grounds by the southward migration of cattle-owning tribes, who spoke a language similar to that of the Shona in modern Zimbabwe, sometime around the 12th century. By the 16th century these people had emerged into a recognizable nation, the

Venda, and had established themselves in the region's northernmost uplands, in particular the Soutpansberg. Made prosperous by perennial springs and year-round rain, the Venda built walled towns and established an empire that spread over much of the modern province's territory (*see* 'Venda History').

However, in the late 17th century, prolonged civil wars, caused the Venda monarchy to collapse. A loose confederation of chieftdoms continued to thrive in the fortified villages of the northern uplands, but from the late 17th and early 18th centuries, the rest of the territory came under the sway of two other powerful clans, the Pedi and the Swazi, who established strongholds in the northern Drakensberg foothills and hunted bushveld of the Northern Transvaal's hot central plain.

Although these clans fought periodic raiding wars with each other, the territorial balance of power remained stable until the 1820s, when large Zulu raiding parties from Natal began to ravage the north. The Swazi bore the brunt of these depredations and retreated into the most remote mountain valleys of their territory (*see* **Swaziland** 'History'), while the Pedi and Venda managed to beat off the raiders and continue as normal in the years between raids. However, this changed in the late 1820s, when a renegade Zulu clan, the Ndebele, invaded the area and settled the central plain.

The Ndebele confined the Venda, Pedi and Swazi to the uplands and began to raid west into the cattle-rich highveld, while maintaining large villages around the modern towns of Potgietersrus and Pietersburg. Such was the warlike nature of the territory when the Voortrekkers appeared on the scene in the late 1830s. The first party, under Louis Trichardt, passed through peacefully and continued into Mozambique, but in 1840, a second wave, under Andries Potgieter came to stay.

Potgieter's Voortrekkers had come up though the Ndebele country of the Western Transvaal, and had fought Mzilikazi's warriors every step of the way). Although the new Voortrekkers settled at various points along the modern Great North Road (the N1 highway), and founded the Zoutpansberg Republic on the site of the modern town of Louis Trichardt (1848), their aggressive policies of raiding black villages for children to work as farm labourers, and their wholesale slaughter of the local game, especially elephant, won them few friends. War with the Ndebele continued until the 1850s when the last powerful chief in the area was finally besieged with his people in a set of cave near Potgietersrus, and there starved to death (*see* 'Potgietersrus'), but the Pedi and Venda remained hostile, and despite frequent Boer raids, managed to hold their territories against invasion.

From 1860, the Zoutpansberg republic amalgamated with the Transvaal's two other Boer republics, to form the South African Republic (SAR). Although the SAR had to eschew slavery in order to be recognized by the British Cape Colony, the system of kidnapping for forced labour continued to flourish under the innocuous title of 'indentured labour'. Not only the Pedi, Venda and Swazi suffered, but also the Tsonga from the lowveld of neighbouring Mozambique.

But the tide was turning against the Northern Transvaal Boers. By the early 1860s, the region's elephant herds were almost destroyed, and the Zoutpansberg ivory hunters realized that they would have to go east into Mozambique if they wanted to keep their livelihoods. Unwilling to enter that country's fever-ridden lowlands, they taught their 'indentured labourers' to shoot, and sent them into the bush instead, under the supervision of loyal foremen. This was a tactical error; no sooner had the African hunters been armed, than most absconded for the homelands from which they had been snatched as children.

The Tsonga then began demanding payment from the Boers for hunting rights, a tactic which soon caught on with other tribes. Boer rule was further undermined by the Tsonga and Pedi discovering lucrative labour markets away from the harsh Boers, who paid badly and flogged often: by the 1860s these young Tsonga and Pedi were travelling to Natal (and a few years later, to Kimberley), from which they returned with both guns and money.

In 1869 the Northern Transvaal Boers attempted to re-assert their dominance by attacking the Venda. But the *commando* (led by Paul Kruger, the future president of the SAR) was beaten off, and a large Venda force marched south over the mountains, surprised the Boers and burned Schoemansdal (modern Louis Trichardt) to the ground.

The fleeing Boers had retreated south to Pietersburg, then as now the region's largest town, and concentrated on farming the Waterberg and the lush Drakensberg foothills, and attacking the Swazi and Pedi. However, the chaotic nature of events in the SAR was attracting British attention. The Swazi invited the British authorities in Natal to mediate in border disputes with the Boers and the Pedi (*see* **Swaziland** and **Eastern Transvaal** 'History'). Pretending that it was necessary to ensure the Swaziland boundary, Britain sent a force against the Pedi, subdued them, and turned their attention on the Boers. For a few years, they deliberated on whether or not to invade the republic. After gold was found in the Northern Transvaal Drakensberg, the matter was settled. In 1877, British forces invaded the SAR and formally annexed it for the Crown.

Although the Boers did manage to eject the invaders in 1881, they could not re-establish their dominance in the Northern Transvaal away from the central plain. In the late 1890s, both the Venda and the Pedi launched large atacks on Boer settlements near their borders, and before, they could retaliate, the Northern Transvaal Boers found themselves involved in the Second Anglo–Boer War of 1899. All *commandos* were sent on active service against the British in Natal, leaving the Northern Transvaal tribes in peace.

After the war ended in 1902, the territory came back under British rule and steps were taken to open it up. The fertile country around Tzaneen was slowly converted to tea plantations worked by Tsonga labourers in the 1920s, while coal and iron ore mines were opened up in the northeast, and cattle ranching began to creep north towards the Soutpansberg. The Venda were ordered to burn their unregistered rifles, but the law proved impossible to enforce, and the remote Venda country remained more or less independent, with only visiting British administrators and missionaries to represent colonial rule. Venda chiefs were put on the Government payroll as magistrates, a practice that persisted until the 1950s.

Meanwhile, at the southern foot of the Soutpansberg, the new town of Louis Trichardt, built on the ruins of Schoemansdal, developed its farming and forestry interests, eating up large chunks of former Venda territory, and bringing white settlement back to the far north.

Similarly, the farming centres of Pietersburg and Tzaneen prospered. From the 1950s and '60s many northern ranchers changed from cattle to game ranching; cattle were vulnerable to disease and drought, whereas the bushveld could support dense game populations which were disease and drought resistant. The potential revenue from hunting, hides and meat made it more profitable to put the land back under indigenous wildlife. The resulting widespread game ranching has helped to keep much of the region's habitat intact.

However, a far less positive trend from the 1950s–70s was the creation of the region's three tribal 'homelands' of Lebowa (1972) for the Pedi, Gazankulu (1973) for the Tsonga, and Venda (1979). Thousands of people living there were forcibly moved to these infertile, rocky areas, losing both land and livestock, which was never compensated for. Severe overgrazing and overcrowding of this desert land soon forced many to seek work in South Africa, either in the cities, where they had to live without their families, or in the farms and towns bordering the 'homelands', which necessitated long and expensive travelling to low paid jobs. The rulers of these 'states' were usually drawn from the tribe's nobility, but were no longer accountable to the tribe and could be easily bought off by the South African government.

Lebowa and Gazankulu opted for self-government within South Africa, but Venda chose to be a separate country. This nominal 'independence' was never recognized internationally, and served only to strip the residents of their South African citizenship, while still retaining them as cheap labour for the country's industries. However, Venda, perhaps because of its traditional seclusion from the rest of the country and largely unbroken history of self-government, seems to have suffered less than other 'homelands' from overcrowding and the drift to the cities. Water is plentiful and irrigation fairly simple to arrange, so the problems of overgrazing and erosion have largely been avoided.

Since the 1994 election these 'homelands' have officially ceased to exist, but to all intents and purposes they remain; their civil servants are still employed and their police still wear different uniforms from the SA police. And it will be at least two years before they cease to appear as separate territories on the road maps.

Today, the Northern Transvaal remains somewhat isolated from the rest of the country, politically more peaceful, with most of its wild land still intact. The 'homelands' are likely to be re-incorporated into South Africa in the next few years, which will probably result in more development of the tribal areas. This is likely to be agricultural, rather than industrial, with an emphasis on game farming and eco-tourism.

Getting There and Around

By car: The most direct route to Northern Transvaal is via the N1 from Pretoria and Johannesburg, which heads straight through the centre of the region to Messina and the Zimbabwean border. A more beautiful drive is from the Eastern

Transvaal, up the R40 from the Transvaal Drakensberg to Tzaneen, or from the west, along the R510 and R572 through the empty sandveld region bordering Botswana, and the rolling Waterberg. The region is largely remote and not well served by public transport, making a car the simplest way to get around.

Car hire: Cheap car hire can be found in Johannesburg (*see* 'Getting Around'), or from Rassies Car Hire, ✆ (01536) 32556, in Ellisras, in the Waterberg.

By bus: Greyhound, ✆ (011) 333 2136, and TransLux and Transtate, ✆ (011) 774 3333, buses from Johannesburg travel up the N1 and stop at all the main towns. Some continue on into Zimbabwe.

Hitch-hiking: Pick-ups to get into the wild areas can be arranged through private game reserves, or you can hitch to hiking trail-heads without great difficulty. The N1 carries a lot of long-distance traffic, while off the main roads it is easy to get lifts from local traffic. Hitching inside 'homelands' is problematic, and the traffic intermittent.

By rail: Potgietersrus, Pietersburg, Louis Trichardt and Messina are all linked by rail to Johannesburg and Pretoria, with daily services ✆ (011) 773 2131. Trains also run on to Harare in Zimbabwe (*see* **Travel**).

Black taxis: These provide a convenient way into the 'homelands' for those without a car or the money to use a tour company. However, while the people are generally unthreatening, the vehicles have a bad safety record and travellers use them at their own risk.

Tour companies: A number of private companies offer tours to private or public game reserves in the Northern Transvaal. **Clive Walker Trails**, ✆ (011) 453 7645/6, offers expensive but superb guided walks through the big game areas, with transport to and from Johannesburg. **Cat Pardo Safaris**, ✆ (01554) 291, operates in the far north. **Alldays**, ✆ (01536) 71452, runs game and hiking trips, as does **Turn-Key Travel**, ✆ (01524) 4492. **Springbok Atlas**, ✆ (011) 493 0827, offers general safaris. **Lebowa Transport**, ✆ (01521) 913 101, offers direct transport to towns and reserves, as does **Schoonoord Transport and Tourism**, ✆ (0020) 8.

Northwest of Pretoria: The Waterberg and the Tuli Block

The Waterberg are a wild corner of South Africa. The quickest route is 100km along the N1 north from Pretoria to the overdeveloped spa town of **Warmbad** (an unpleasant resort around a mineral pool), or the small agricultural town of **Nylstroom**, from which the R516 or R517 lead into the Waterberg. A slower, more interesting drive is up the R511 or R510 through the former Bophuthatswana to the small town of **Thabazimbi** at the west end of the range.

Whichever route you take, the first place to head for is the superb **Lapalala Wilderness**

Area, ✆ (011) 531 814, signposted from the dirt road connecting the R517 and R518 west of Warmbad and Nylstroom. Lapalala occupies a vast stretch of high hills covered with bush and hardwood forest, above the crocodile infested Palala river. Walking trails lead to close encounters with white (and occasionally black) rhino, kudu, roan and sable antelope, zebra, blue wildebeest. Shy leopard hunt in the cliff caves above the river. Guided canoe trips along the Palala River lead to crocodile-free pools with safe swimming. Be aware that you must have fuel and supplies before you go in. Lapalala has several self-catering bushcamps with ablution and cooking facilities.

Adjoining Lapalala is an even larger private reserve, **Touchstone Game Ranch**, ✆ (01536) 50230/50055, which harbours even larger game, such as elephant, buffalo and giraffe, as well as the wildlife species of Lapalala. More expensive than Lapalala, Touchstone offers superb horse trails of up to ten days, game drives and guided walks. Access is along the R517 60km west of Nylstroom to the village of Vaalwater, then 45km north to Melkrivier. Touchstone's signpost is on the south side of the road a few kilometres east of Marken, which lies about 38km northwest on the R518.

It is worth visiting the small town of **Thabazimbi** (on the R510 at the western edge of the Waterberg), the centre of the local game farming and hunting industry. The town holds an annual Game Festival, which includes a game auction, where private game reserves buy stock. There are many such auctions in the Transvaal, but this is one of the few open to the public. Most of the game is sold in absentia, then tranquilized and collected from its vendor, but some of the smaller antelope species arrive in the auction ring. It is strange to see wild creatures such as impala in these surroundings. If the idea of treating wildlife commercially repels you, rest assured that every care is taken to ensure the animals' safety and comfort. Game farming lies at the heart of South Africa's highly successful game conservation programme, and even the large National Parks sell surplus animals. This not only helps to pay for habitat maintenance, it also saves having to cull excess beasts from land that can only support a certain number of each species. The Game Festival and auction is a movable feast; the **Thabazimbi Tourist Information**, ✆ (01537) 21140, will know the dates.

The land around Thabazimbi is taken up with cattle farms and two small mines (gold and platinum), but wild country soon takes over. South of Thabazimbi, on the far south-west edge of the Waterberg region, is the **Ben Alberts Nature Reserve**, ✆ (01537) 21509, signposted west from the R510 south of town. A small protected area within a greater wild region, this reserve is good for budget travellers, with a secluded, cheap camp site. There are no marked walking trails but there is nothing to stop you wandering the bush or driving the dirt roads in search of white rhino, eland, kudu, giraffe, red hartebeest and other browsers. Also on the southern edge of the Waterberg, just northeast of Thabazimbi, is **Kransberg National Park**, a 27,000ha wilderness area which, except for a walking trail up to a famous vulture colony, is not yet open to tourists. The National Parks Board, ✆ (012) 343 1991, will have the latest details. **Mabula Private Game Reserve**, ✆ (011) 883 7140, is signposted north from the R516 between Thabazimbi and Warmbad. There are guided walks and drives in open-top vehicles among elephant, white rhino and buffalo.

Also at the eastern end of the Waterberg, close to the N1 near Potgietersrus, is **Doorndraai Nature Reserve**, ✆ (015423) 629, an area of bushveld around a large dam. Like most dam reserves, Doorndraai gets crowded with weekend water-skiers and windsurfers but is quiet during the week. Walking trails lead into wooded kloofs where waterfalls tumble down from the Waterberg foothills. Sable antelope and the equally rare tsessebe breed here. Impala, reedbuck, zebra, giraffe and some smaller species are also common. Look out for fish eagles on the dam's wooded shore.

Also on the eastern fringe of the region, just outside Nylstroom, is the **Nylsvlei Nature Reserve**, ✆ (01534) 31074, a large wetland supporting a huge variety of birds, including goliath heron, black stork, fish eagle and jacana. The rare roan antelope, waterbuck, kudu, impala, tsessebe and a few giraffe graze the lush water meadows. There is a camp site, but the reserve is so fragile that only 30 people at a time are allowed in, so be sure to book.

North of the Waterberg the landscape flattens out into dense thornveld used for cattle and game ranching. About 50km south of the area's main town, **Ellisras**, is the **Hans Strijdom Dam Nature Reserve**, ✆ (01536) 33384, signposted east of the R517. The rolling foothill terrain is home to mostly antelope, and the rare roan antelope breeds here. There are crocodiles and bilharzia in the dam, so swimming is discouraged, at least from the banks. This does not stop local farmers bringing their noisy fishing and waterskiing boats here in the belief that there are no crocs in the centre of the dam and you are less likely to contract bilharzia in deep water. So avoid the dam at weekends or public holidays. The **Langjan Nature Reserve**, ✆ (015562) 1211, near the border with Botswana, comprises sandy, Kalahari-type scrub, shaded at intervals by large camel-thorn trees, and patches of lowveld woodland, such as marula and fever trees, near the dry river beds. The reserve is good for birds; look out for bateleur and tawny eagle, kori bustard, ground hornbill and the small barred warbler. Mammals are plentiful, particularly gemsbok (the reserve was set up in the 1930s to protect the Transvaal's last wild herd, though the species now flourishes throughout the province). Giraffe, kudu, eland, red hartebeest and blue wildebeest are also common. At dusk, you should see jackal and bat-eared fox. Leopard and caracal lynx come out after dark. Walking trails have been laid out from the central camp of rondavels.

West of Langjan, across the Limpopo in Botswana, lies the **Tuli Block**. Game from this wild region migrates onto the South African side quite regularly. The larger antelope are common migrants, but even elephant sometimes wander across. If you are in the area, it is well worth making a short side trip into the Tuli Block to **Mashatu Private Game Reserve** (cross the border at Pontdrif on the R521 northwest of Alldays and look out for the signpost). Mashatu occupies a vast (90,000ha) plateau above the meeting of the Sashe and Limpopo Rivers. Staying there is not cheap, but Mashatu offers some of the best game-hiking in Southern Africa; a four day trail that specializes in guiding walkers close to elephant, staying always downwind of them, but with much holding of breath and creeping about so as to remain unseen by the great beasts.

Game Viewing: All the reserves listed above harbour game, in some cases big game such as elephant, white and black rhino, and buffalo.

Walking and Hiking: The Waterberg and Tuli offer some of the most rewarding hiking in South Africa because of the opportunities of getting close to game. Guided trails of 1–5 days with close encounters can be arranged at **Lapalala Wilderness Area, Touchstone Game Ranch** and **Mabula Private Game Reserve** in the Waterberg region. Further north, in the Tuli block of Botswana just over the border, the vast **Mashatu Private Game Reserve** has a 5-day elephant trail that must be booked through **Clive Walker Safaris** in Jo'burg, ✆ (011) 453 7645.

Gentler walks with a good chance of seeing game (mostly antelope) can be found at **Doorndraai Nature Reserve** and at the **Ben Alberts Nature Reserve**.

Riding: The Waterberg is one of the best places for riders to experience wild bush and big game in South Africa. **Equus Trails**, based at the Touchstone Game Ranch, have superbly schooled horses that are a joy to ride. The game is less disturbed by horses than humans and you can get much closer. Trips of 1–10 days are offered, with camping in the bush. Book either in Jo'burg, ✆ (011) 788 3923, or Touchstone Game Ranch ✆ (01536) 50230/50055.

Where to Stay

expensive

In the Waterberg, **Touchstone Game Ranch,** ✆ (01536) 50230/50055, the **Lapalala Wilderness Area,** ✆ Jo'burg (011) 531 814, and **Mabula Private Game Reserve,** ✆ Jo'burg (011) 883 7140 or (015334) 616/717, offer luxurious accommodation. Lapalala has a tented camp, Touchstone private rondavels and Mabula a comfortable lodge. Lapalala is self-catering, except by prior arrangement, but Touchstone and Mabula offer full board.

Welgevonden, ✆ Jo'burg (011) 883 7980 ext 4, is a smaller private reserve, also in the Waterberg, with three bush camps and the option of self-catering or full board. Walking and landrover safaris are offered. Nearby is **Kolobe Lodge,** ✆ Jo'burg (011) 453 7645/6/7, which has four thatched rondavels. Again, guided game walks are a feature, and on some you can visit rock overhangs painted with bushman art. At the cheaper end of the expensive scale, **Shangri-La,** ✆ (01531) 2071/71153/3188, offers full board in a thatched rondavels. Access is via the N1 to Pietersburg, then 10km west along the Kranskop road.

Further north, in the Tuli Block in Botswana, **Mashatu Private Game Lodge** has luxurious bush camps in a vast area of primeval wilderness, with guided hikes and game drives on offer. Bookings must be made in advance through **Clive Walker Safaris** in Jo'burg, ✆ (011) 453 7645/6.

Langjan Nature Reserve, ✆ (015562) 1211, has a moderately-priced camp of self-contained thatched rondavels. In the Waterberg, **Mabula Farm**, ✆ (015335) 730, a few kilometres from Mabula Game Reserve, is a comfortable self-catering farmhouse on the edge of thick woodland. Fishing can be arranged, and walking trails have been laid out.

cheap

Rietbokspruit Farm Cottages, ✆ (01534) 32525, have several self-contained old farm cottages in the Waterberg; each cottage gives onto open bush. Prices are very low for the comfort provided, and Rietbokspruit offers one of the best value-for-money deals in the Transvaal. **Ben Alberts Nature Reserve**, ✆ (01537) 21509, southwest of Thabazimbi, has a cheap, secluded camp site with ablution blocks. Visitors can walk in the reserve, which also has game-viewing roads. **Doorndraai Nature Reserve**, ✆ (015423) 629, southwest of Potgietersrus, has a camp site, as does **Nylsvlei Nature Reserve**, ✆ (01534) 31074, but, owing to the fragile ecosystem of the marsh it protects, the reserve limits the number of visitors. Booking is advised.

The Eastern Section: The Drakensberg Foothills and the Lowveld

East of Pietersburg the long, hot plain of central Northern Transvaal rises in a series of rounded hills where high summer rainfall produces a landscape of lush, sub-tropical vegetation a world away from the harsh bushveld country around Pietersburg. In the dim distance rise the northmost peaks of the Drakensberg mountains. The still, foetid air of the plains becomes cooler as the road climbs between high hills. Tea plantations, orchards and groves of almond and macadamia nut trees announce the quiet country town of **Tzaneen**.

Tzaneen

Tourist Information

Tzaneen Publicity Association: The Town Clerk's Office, Agatha Street, ✆ (01523) 71411.

Tzaneen was a tiny pioneer settlement until the 1920s but experienced a modest boom when the hills around were laid over to tea and fruit growing by the mostly English-speaking settlers. A medical research centre was set up here that managed to eliminate malaria from much of the region. Today's Tzaneen has the usual 'improved' ugliness of so many South African regional towns, but a few elegant colonial buildings survive and the surrounding landscape is so gentle that it is impossible not to be charmed by the place.

West of Tzaneen is one of the region's best scenic drives, through the twisting mountainside of **Magoebaskloof**, whose forested slopes give way to the lowland orchard country at the village of **Haernertsburg**. One of the larger fruit farms, **Cheerio Halt**, is signposted off the R71 between Tzaneen and Haernertsburg. Visitors are welcome, whether to pick their own cherries or to wander in the orchards, which are a delight in the spring. An entrance fee is charged.

Despite its beauty, Magoebaskloof is named after a tragedy; the name Mgoeba is a corruption of Makgoba—after chief Makgoba, who ruled the local Pedi clan in the 1860s and '70s and was a fierce resistor of white rule. He fought numerous raiding wars with the local Boers, who eventually decided to eliminate him aftyer he refused to pay the hut tax to the SAR. In the early 1870s, Makgoba and his followers were hunted to this wild pass and eventually killed by Swazi mercenaries hired by the Boers.

The Letaba river plunges down the steep kloof, forming a man-made lake just west of Hearnetsburg, the Ebeneezer Dam, whose quiet waters are fringed with tall plantations of pine and eucalyptus. The **Ebeneezer Dam Nature Reserve**, ✆ (01523) 5641, is crowded with watersports enthusiasts at weekends, but is a contemplative place through the week. Egyptian geese, storks, herons, blacksmith plovers and other waterfowl feed in the shallows. The reserve has a small camp site. To the south rise the Strydpoortberg, and behind them the northern tip of the Transvaal Drakensberg. This wild mountain interior can be reached via the **Wolkberg Wilderness Area** (*see* Eastern Transvaal) by following the R71 from Tzaneen to the junction with the R529 and looking out for the signs for the New Agatha Forest Station, ✆ (01523) 20347, or ✆ (015222) 53/83. **Grootbosch Nature Reserve**, west of the Ebeneezer Dam along the R71, is accessed from the De Hoek Forest Station. This area of Drakensberg foothills and forestry plantation is crossed by the **Magoebaskloof Hiking Trail**, ✆ (01551) 51152, which is divided into 3-day and 2-day sections. A hiking hut is provided at the forest station, but thereafter, hikers must pitch tent at designated spots along the route. The Grootbosch section of the trail passes through the largest indigenous forest in the Transvaal and passes several waterfalls. One of these, the **Debengeni Falls**, can be visited by car, as can part of the forest via the **Woodbush Forest Drive**, details from Tzaneen Publicity Association.

North of Tzaneen, the R36 leads past the **Fanie Botha Dam Nature Reserve**, known for its coarse angling, up over another pass, the **Duiwelskloof**, on the far side of which is a village of the same name. Another lush area of high rainfall, the Duiwelskloof has several forest hiking trails leading to waterfalls. Permits for the three short day walks and one 2-day hike, the **Leopard Hiking Trail**, are availalbe from the Duiwelskloof Publicity Office on Botha Street, ✆ (015323) 3757.

From Duiwelskloof, the R36 leads north to a signpost for the **Modjadji Cycad Forest** in Lebowa. This strange reserve, filled with thousands of giant cycads (prehistoric tree ferns) is considered sacred by the Lobedu, a clan affiliated to the Venda, and is the traditional home of the **Rain Queen**, a mythical hereditary title held by a real-life woman who lives in seclusion in a royal homestead near the forest. H. Rider Haggard's classic Edwardian adventure story *She* was based on the

Cycad Forest

legend of the local Balobedu people who fled from tribal wars in the Eastern Highlands of Zimbabwe during the 19th century with their queen, who held the power of rain-making. The Rain Queen does exist, having now been absorbed into Pedi culture, and even today she is credited by many to have the power of rain-making. During the region's occasional droughts many farmers, both black and white, have been known to seek her intercession with the rain spirits. You can walk in the forest, but there is no accommodation. Walkers are likely to see nyala crashing into cover, and antelope such as bushbuck and waterbuck are common, while impala browse at the forest fringe.

If you go back to the R71 from Modjadji, and continue east of Tzaneen towards the Phalaborwa Gate into the Kruger National Park, a side road (the R529) turns off northeast after about 30km. This leads into the **Hans Merensky Dam Nature Reserve**, ℂ (015238) 632/3/4/5, in the hills at the southern tip of a great chunk of Lebowa and Gazankulu. The entrance to the reserve has unfortunately been developed by Overvaal Resorts, a company responsible for overpriced and ugly holiday resorts all over the Transvaal. But the reserve itself is wild and beautiful and worth visiting for its 3-day **Giraffe Trail** and its two half-day walks. The plentiful game includes giraffe, sable antelope, blue wildebeest and other antelope. In the Letaba River and the dam itself, crocodile and hippo are common. The terrain varies between lowveld mopane woodland, riverine forest along the Letaba, grassland and bushveld.

Apart from hiking, access to the reserve is only allowed in a resort bus, to prevent overcrowding with cars. A rather kitsch touch is a Tsonga show village where tourists can watch traditional practices like maize-meal grinding and dancing.

Continue further east along the R71, and you come to the small village of **Gravelotte**, near which is a huge boabab tree that once served as an open-air store and bar for the gold miners from the ghost town of **Leydsdorp**, about 12km east of Gravelotte. The town's brief 1890 gold rush collapsed after the opening of main the Witwatersrand gold reefs in the 1890s. Leydsdorp itself is a detour; its abandoned buildings are well preserved and some are being restored.

For a beautiful mountain drive, follow the R36 south to **Ofcolaco** and then the dirt road west into the mountains through the little settlement of **The Downs**. This leads into the spectacular **M'Thalepsi Valley** of indigenous forest and traditional kraals. Much of this area lies within Lebowa, and the huge **Lekgalameetse Nature Reserve**, administered by the 'homeland', provides a chance to walk in the beautiful hills. The forest and grassland supports mountain wildlife such as leopard, caracal, bushbuck, duiker, reedbuck, klipspringer, baboon and both monkey species. There is a variety of accommodation.

West of Lekgalameetse the road eventually joins the tarred R37 at Zeekoegat and heads west and north to Pietersburg; from here the R71 leads back over Magoebaskloof to Tzaneen. Those without time to make the round trip should turn around about 15km after The Downs and head back to Ofcolalo.

East of Gravelotte, the R71 continues to the Phalaborwa Gate into the northern Kruger National Park.

Walking and Hiking: Pleasant day-walks can be found at the Ebeneezer Dam Nature Reserve, the Fanie Botha Dam Nature Reserve, Grootbosch Nature Reserve, Duiwelskloof, the Hans Merensky Dam Nature Reserve, at New Agatha Forest Station, the Lekgalameetse Nature Reserve and the Modjaji Forest Reserve in Lebowa. Hikes of more than one day are the Magoebaskloof Trail (2 or 3 days) at Grootbosch, the 3-day Giraffe Trail at the Hans Merensky Dam Nature Reserve (with overnight huts equipped with firewood, cooking utensils and a shower), the 2-day Leopard Trail at Duiewlskloof, the 2-day Lekgalameetse Nature Reserve, and in the Wolkberg Wilderness Area (up to 5 days). See above for details, except Wolkberg (see **Eastern Transvaal**).

Fishing: Coarse fishing for South African species such as black bass, kurper and yellowfish can be arranged at the dams around Tzaneen, and Fanie Botha Dam Nature Reserve is known as an excellent spot. Tzaneen Publicity, ✆ (01532) 71411, has the details.

Shopping

The **Gallery Tzangeni**, in the Safari Building on Morgan Street in Tzaneen sells local Pedi and Tsonga crafts, including wood carving and woven rugs, Boer pastries and fruit preserves, and curios such as skins and semi-precious stones. Local information can also be gathered here. The **Sasikele Carpet Factory** on Njala Street, also in Tzaneen, sells beautifully woven carpets made from karakul sheep wool (a breed imported from Mesopotamia for their resistance to dry climates and extremes of temperature).

Where to Stay

expensive

Tebula, ✆ (0152302) 44, 40km south of Tzaneen on the R36, is signposted from the Luxembourg turn-off near Ofcolaco. The old colonial country house has a beautiful verandah overlooking the Ngwatsbitsi River. Furnished with colonial antiques, the house sits amongst some of the Transvaal's loveliest farmland and hiking in nearby The Downs can be organized. Accommodation is in six self-contained suites. The **Coach House**, ✆ (0152) 307 3641/2/3/4, is in the small village of Agatha at the foot of the Wolkberg mountains. A coaching inn during the 19th century, it has 45 airy rooms with views out over the hills and log fires in winter. Trails have been marked out in the surrounding woodlands, and the garden has good bird life.

Harmony Game Farm, ✆ Jo'burg (011) 783 4870, near Mica, along the R71 and R40 from Tzaneen, is a private lowveld game reserve. The Blyde and Oliphants Rivers meet here, so hippo and crocodile are plentiful, as are giraffe, kudu, blue wildebeest, zebra and other plains game. Predators include resident spotted hyena and occasional leopard and wild dog, which wander across from the nearby Kruger National Park. Game walks and mountain bike trails are offered, as well as day trips to other reserves. Accommodation is in five comfortable en suite rooms around a huge central living room.

moderate

Wayside Lodge Farm, ✆ (01523) 22366/22813, 8km from Tzaneen on the Wolkberg road, offers self-contained chalets in an eccentric, ramshackle private theme park whose oddities include a castle made of bottles, a Buddhist garden, a Polynesian Village (don't ask me why), a restaurant, pool and jacuzzi. Day visitors are welcomed at a small charge. **The Chalets**, ✆ (0152222) 70, signposted from the R71 between Magoebaskloof and Haernertsberg, is quieter. Built of dark wood and in Swiss style, the chalets do not look out of place in the surrounding hilly country. Fishing, hiking and boating can be arranged, and there is a pool to cool off in. **Magoebaskloof Holiday Resort**, ✆ (01523) 53142/53147, which offers self-contained rondavels in a hillside spur on the R71 between Haernertsburg and Tzaneen. Again, fishing and hiking can be arranged, and there is a pool.

cheap

The **Lekgalameetse Nature Reserve**, ✆ (0152302) 1613, has very low-priced, comfortable rondavels and a camp site. **Grootbosch Nature Reserve**, ✆ (01551) 2202, has a hiking hut with a shower, firewood and all cooking utensils, bookable in advance. Take your own bedding.

The **Ebeneezer Dam Nature Reserve**, ✆ (01523) 5641, has a camp site, as does the **Fanie Botha Dam and Nature Reserve**, ✆ (01523) 5641. Both have ablution blocks and are quiet during the week. Birdwatching for waterfowl is good at both dams.

Gazankulu

Proclaimed a 'homeland' in 1973, but officially re-absorbed into South Africa in 1994, most of Gazankulu lies in a long strip along the western border of the Kruger National Park. Self-governing rather than 'independent', Gazankulu is home to predominantly Tsonga (Shangaan) people, most of whom are the descendents of refugees from the late 19th-century tribal wars in Mozambique.

Most tourists drive through Gazankulu at speed on their way to the Kruger but, although it lacks any tourist infrastructure, the area is rewarding to explore. Here, traditional Tsonga rural life takes its leisurely course, with a mixture of cattle herding and market gardening providing the staple livelihood. The numerous fruit and vegetable markets lining the road testify to the Tsongas' skill at raising crops, and it is worth stopping, not only to buy, but to chat with the women selling their wares, particularly if you know a little Afrikaans, the area's *lingua franca*. Traditional crafts, such as basket weaving, bead-work and rug weaving can usually be bought at roadside kraals.

Although heavily populated along the main R71, large tracts of Gazankulu are wild, inaccessible by car, and home to large wildlife populations. One such area south of the R71 has been designated as **Manyeleti Game Reserve**, where visitors can see elephant, white rhino, lion, cheetah, leopard, spotted hyena, buffalo and all the attendant lowveld game species (*see* **Eastern Transvaal**).

The North: Potgietersrus, Pietersburg and Louis Trichardt

The long, straight N1 highway, and the north/south passenger railway that run up the Northern Transvaal's central plain travels through the region's least spectacular country, but must be travelled to reach the wild sections. Its three large towns, of Potgietersrus, Pietersburg and Louis Trichardt, all lie along the highway in the hot central plain, are of interest only as supply stops and jumping-off points for the nearby mountain ranges, game reserves and tribal areas.

Potgietersrus

Potgietersrus takes its name from the Voortrekker leader Piet Potgieter, who, with his co-leader, Andries Pretorius, settled the local territory in the late 1830s. The Boer farms suffered for want of labour and began raiding the kraals of local Ndebele and Sotho clans, snatching children for 'indentured labour'. Hermanus Potgieter, a cousin of Piet's, was responsible for most of these raids.

The Ndebele had ceased to be a military power in the highveld by this time, having moved north away from the Voortrekkers under Mzilikazi to modern Zimbabwe. But the Sotho, under chief Makapan, retaliated in 1854, attacking Boer farms and finally killing over 40 Boer men from a *commando* sent out to punish them. Hermanus Potgieter was among the dead. Piet Potgieter and Andries Pretorius, worried at this sudden show of teeth and by the fact that the Sotho had begun acquiring firearms, gathered a large *commando* of over 100 Boers and 300 Kgatla warriors (a local clan hired with a promise of a share in the spoils) and attacked Makapan. But he and his people had fled to a set of caves nearby. The Boers and their allies laid siege. After a few skirmishes, during one of which Piet Potgieter was shot dead, the Boers realized the whole clan would eventually perish for want of food and water. Many women and children surrendered, consigning themselves to life as virtual slaves on Boer farms, but after a month the Boer *commando* entered the cave and found the rest of the Sotho dead. The region was now open for unchallenged Boer settlement.

Potgietersrus remains a quiet country town although it primary economy today comes from the ceaseless traffic travelling between Zimbabwe and South Africa.

Should you find yourself with time in Potgietersrus, the **Arend Dieperink Museum** (*open Mon–Sat 9–4*) on Voortrekker Road has an interesting record of early Transvaal life, including pioneer tools, guns, clothes and furniture and some photographs from the late 1800s.

Just north of town is the **Potgietersrus Nature Reserve and Game Breeding Centre**, a reserve belonging to the National Zoological Gardens in Pretoria and devoted to breeding rare species, including cheetah, black and white rhino and the West African pygmy hippo. Plains antelope wander free around the breeding centre and there is also a small camp site. The larger **Percy Fyfe Nature Reserve**, about 30km north of town (look for signposts on the west side of the N1) is also devoted to rare species, specifically roan and sable antelope and tsessebe (also known as topi, which is endangered in Southern Africa, but common in East Africa). Visitors can walk in the reserves bush and rocky outcrops. Again, there is a small camp site with ablution blocks.

Pietersburg

Tourist Information

SATour, corner of Vorster and Landdros Mare Streets, ✆ (01521) 295 3025.

Pietersburg, the largest town in the Northern Transvaal, is the region's administrative centre. It is convenient for both the Waterberg and Tzaneen, but the town is unattractive—mostly modern, hot and noisy with through traffic that has to fight its way across town before rejoining the N1.

A large park, the **Civic Centre**, has been laid out around an ornamental lake in the city centre, and makes for a pleasant stroll if you need a break from driving. At the south end a large conservatory of exotic plants and a little restaurant (Mike's Kitchen) overlook the lake. On Vorster Street, just off Civic Centre Park, is the **Irish House Museum** (*open Mon–Fri 9–4.30*), a collection of Victorian houses in what was a vast late 19th-century trading store. Nearby is a small photographic history of the town is housed in the **Hugh Exton Photographic Museum** (*open Mon–Sat 9–4*), which occupies an old Dutch Reformed Church. On the northern edge of town is the **Exhibition of Historic Memorabilia** (*open Mon–Fri 9–4.30*). This collection of agricultural and industrial machinery, such as tractors, ploughs, a steam engine and a gold-ore crusher are only really of interest to the specialist.

Despite the rather unimaginative name, Pietersburg's small **Municipal Game Reserve**, about 5km south of town along the Molepo road, has a pleasant walking trail leading through bush and grassland where white rhino and large antelope, such as gemsbok, eland and blesbok graze. Red hartebeest and zebra are also present, and there is accommodation in self-contained chalets and a camp site with ablution blocks.

Louis Trichardt

The last of the main towns on the highway north, Louis Trichardt, like Potgietersrus and Pietersburg, is mainly of interest for its surrounding country, in this case the magnificent Soutpansberg mountains and Venda country, a corner of Southern Africa steeped in living folklore that provides the traveller with a rare glimpse of old Africa.

Originally called Zoutpansberg, the town was founded in 1848 by Andries Potgieter, Piet's father, as the capital of a small republic, also called Zoutpansberg. In 1854, the name was changed to Schoemansdal by Stephanus Schoeman, Andries Potgieter's son-in-law. But, as if in punishment for this hubris and for the shameless trade in black slaves that Schoeman allowed to flourish in the town, Schoemansdal was burned to the ground in 1868 after its burghers, under a young man called Paul Kruger, invaded the Venda country to the north of the Soutpansberg mountains with a combined force of Boer, Pedi and Swazi fighters. The Venda beat back the motley army and razed the town, after which the site lay abandoned for a generation.

The town was not revived until the early 1900s, when the British, having annexed the Transvaal after the Second Anglo–Boer War, made it a magistracy. Despite this British influence, the town became a firmly Boer enclave, servicing the local cattle and nut farmers and trading with the Venda, whose territory comes almost to the town limits. It took the name of Louis Trichardt, a Boer leader who passed through the area in the late 1830s and on to Delagoa Bay in Mozambique.

The violence of the southern Transvaal's recent history has hardly touched the north, and Louis Trichardt saw little unrest, even through the height of apartheid. This is probably in part due to the fact that the black population, the Venda, have traditionally been less oppressed than most of South Africa's other black tribes, and have held themselves rather aloof from the country as a whole. In the last 20 years, commercial forestry has extended the wooded regions of the Soutpansberg that rise north of the town. The setting is now one of bushveld giving way abruptly to plantations of pine and eucalyptus, and it is from the forest stations north of town that most travellers begin their exploration of the more interesting indigenous forests of the wild Soutpansberg.

The Soutpansberg

On the first slopes of the Soutpansberg foothills, the marula, thorn and mopane woodland of the bushveld begins to give way to aloe scrub and hardwood trees of the mountain vegetation. This transitional zone is protected in the **Ben Lavin Nature Reserve**, ✆ (01551) 3834, southeast of Louis Trichardt. Visitors can walk several trails and stand a good chance of encountering giraffe, tsessebe, sable antelope, kudu, nyala, waterbuck, wildebeest and a variety of smaller antelope. Birdwatching is good here; rollers, louries (especially cheeky grey louries that scavenge in the main camp), crowned eagle and bishop birds (in the vleis) are worth looking out for. There are rondavels, permanent tents and a camp site with ablution blocks.

North of town begin the Soutpansberg proper, which run east/west for 150km, linking Venda and the Transvaal and marking the last range of uplands before the Limpopo River and the border with Zimbabwe.

The name, which means 'Salt Pan Mountains', could not be less appropriate for this landscape of fresh water, moist forest and fern. The lower slopes are mostly covered in plantations of eucalyptus and pine, but above about 600m this gives way to an indigenous hardwood forest. The air becomes fresh and clear after the heat of the plains, and the lemonwood trees, a species unique to the Soutpansberg, emit a fresh scent of citrus that carries on the breeze. On the peaks above the forest, spectacular aloes cluster on rock outcrops whose caves and buttresses are home to leopard and caracal.

The N1 highway crosses the range north of Louis Trichardt via the low Wylliespoort Pass, on either side of which is a tamed upland landscape of orchards and nut groves, principally almond and macadamia. Apart from this small corridor the range is wild, and the quite hiker can expect to surprise bushbuck, baboon and the rare red duiker.

Much of the Soutpansberg lies in Venda and, although the range is sacred, much of it is open to hikers, with marked trails and overnight huts provided (*see* Venda). Two good hiking trails leave from **De Hoek Forest Station**, signposted from the main road north of Louis Trichardt. One, the 2-day **Hangklip Trail** (with huts, water and firewood provided) can be divided into two sections of one day each.

Longer hikes can be made in **Entebeni State Forest**, which lies partly within Venda, partly within the Transvaal, and is accessible from the R524 east of Louis Trichardt. The 4-day **Entebeni Trail** makes a circle around the whole area of indigenous forest. There are also trails further east into the Venda part of the range, and follow the much longer **Soutpansberg Hiking Trail** (*see* 'Venda').

Activities

Walking and Hiking: All the reserves and state forests listed above have marked walking and hiking trails, with overnight huts where necessary. Short walking trails can be found at the Percy Fyfe Nature Reserve, the Potgietersrus Nature Reserve (both near Potgietersrus), the Pietersburg Game Reserve, and the Ben Lavin Nature Reserve and in Hangklip State Forest near Louis Trichardt. All but the Hangklip trail offer good game-viewing possibilities.

Longer hikes through the southern Soutpansberg can be made from Hangklip Forest Station and Entabeni State Forest, near Louis Trichardt. To book the trails and overnight huts, call the state forester in Louis Trichardt, ✆ (01551) 2201.

Where to Stay
expensive

There is a dearth of good expensive accommodation unless you detour off into the Waterberg, Tzaneen, or far northern areas. One exception, **Shi-awela Lodge**, ✆ (01551) 51220, at the foot of the Soutpansberg near Louis Trichardt, has 4 en suite painted rond-avels in a private game reserve. Guided hiking, climbing and bush drives are offered. Also worth trying are the **Adam's Apple Hotel**, ✆ (01551) 4117, and **Mountain View Hotel**, ✆ (01551) 9631, both up on the Wylliespoort Pass on the N1 north of Louis Trichardt. These are not special hotels, but their situation up in the cool woodlands and their views south over the bushveld plains are superb.

moderate

Ben Lavin Nature Reserve, ✆ (01551) 3834, just south of Louis Trichardt, has self-contained rondavels, permanent safari tents (with bedding) and a camp site. The bushveld setting at the foot of the Soutpansberg is particularly beautiful and the wildlife plentiful. Further south, the **Pietersburg Nature Reserve**, ✆ (01521) 931 114, has self-contained chalets.

Buzzard Mountain Retreat, ✆ (01551) 4196, sits atop the Soutpansberg north of Louis Trichardt and offers secluded self-catering stone cottages or log cabins with sweeping views out over the forests. Recommended for those in search of solitude. Well marked trails wind off into the mountains.

cheap

The **Ben Lavin Game Reserve** and **Percy Fyfe Nature Reserve** both have camp sites with ablution blocks. No need to book.

Venda

Proclaimed 'independent' in 1979, Venda was never conquered or subdued by the Boers or the British (*see* Northern Transvaal History). Now officially re-absorbed into South Africa, Venda is one of the least 'westernized' corners of the country.

Although it is perfectly possible to tour Venda alone, it is far more rewarding to arrange a local guide though the **Tourist Information Office** in Sibasa, ✆ (015581) 4157. In this way, the country's extraordinary web of myth and legend will be opened up to you, particularly the local legends attached to Venda's many sacred sights. Without a guide, you may find it difficult to gain access to sacred areas, and having someone able to interpret from VaVenda, the local language, will enable you to talk to people and to see Venda life at close quarters.

History

By the 16th century, the Venda kings had built a great walled city at Dzata, in the centre of the range, from where trade in ivory and slaves with both the Arabs (who wandered deep into southern Africa during the 16th century), and Portuguese seems to have flourished, judging by the amount of Oriental and European artefacts found in excavations of Dzata and other sites.

A series of civil wars among the Venda nobility in the 17th century eventually caused the monarchy to collapse, and the country to fragment into a loose federation of chiefdoms. Dzata was abandoned, but smaller fortified villages sprang up all over the country, and the

Venda remained militarily powerful. In their remote mountain corner, were hardly touched by the depredations of the great northward Zulu raids of the 1820s and '30s (*see* **South African History**).

Into this self-contained world wandered Conraad De Buys in 1820. Described by contemporary writers as a physical giant, with immense charisma and political ability, De Buys had lived in the court of Ngqika, one of the Xhosa's most powerful chiefs, had been his advisor against the British, and had even had an affair with Ngqika's mother, who was reputed to be the power behind the throne (*see* **Eastern Cape** 'History'). But De Buys had been chased from the Xhosa country by the British after stirring up a joint Boer/Xhosa rebellion. By the time he arrived among the Venda, he had amassed his own clan of African wives and children, and the Venda allowed him to settle. His village, called Mara, remained the home of his descendants (known as the 'Buysvolk') long after Conraad himself had died. However, Buys did not make a huge impact on the Venda people, who only tolerated the presence of his clan as long as they did not interfere with matters of state.

The next Boer settlers did not appear until 1836, when Louis Trichardt and his Voortrekkers stumbled into the region. Trichardt got on well with the Venda, and his men helped the Venda paramount chief, Ramabulana, to regain his ascendancy over the other clans. Trichardt moved on to Mozambique (where he and his party died of fever), but other groups trickled in over the next few years, each intent on annexing the Venda territory. In 1839, an invading Swazi army was beaten off, then an invading Pedi army, as well as a regiment of Zulus under general Manukosi. Meanwhile, civil war in Mozambique resulted in large numbers of Tsonga refugees wandering into Venda. These were allowed to stay and formed a buffer zone between the Venda and the Pedi and Swazi to the south.

1839 saw the arrival of the next batch of Voortrekkers under Andries Potgieter, who carved out the small Zoutpansberg republic south of the Soutpansberg mountains. Although they did not risk an invasion of Venda for 30 years, these Boers soon made themselves unpopular, hunting the local elephant herds almost to extinction and kidnapping and selling Venda, Tsonga and Pedi children. Finally, following the 1860 amalgamation of all the Transvaal Voortrekker republics into one South African Republic (SAR), the burghers of Schoemansdal (as Zoutpansberg was now called) finally decided to invade. A huge *commando* of Boer, Pedi and Swazi soldiers, led by Paul Kruger (the future president of the SAR) crossed the Soutpansberg, only to be chased back to Schoemansdal by an avenging Venda army who burnt the town and forcing the burghers to flee south.

Despite this interference from the white man, the Venda tolerated missionaries, the first of whom had drifted into the country during the 1860s. From about 1872 there was something of a rush for the Vendas' souls, with Dutch Reformed, Swiss and German missions setting up one after the other. These survived the unrest that accompanied the great drought of 1881, which caused famine and civil war all across the Venda country. During this time, a warlord called Makhado emerged as a binding force in the country, subduing the fragmenting clans one by one. It was just as well; by the 1880s, the Boers of the SAR were again looking covetously at Venda and in 1889 established a garrisoned fort on the southern border.

Makhado upheld the borders of Venda country until his death in 1897. The Boers saw this as their chance to re-invade. Continued droughts had resulted in a spate of cross border cattle raids from Venda into the SAR, and this provided sufficient justification for annexing the kingdom, whose throne had just been filled by the inexperienced young king Mphepu. A large Boer force, under Piet Joubert, the commander who later became famous for inflicting a series of humiliating defeats on the British, entered Venda, and forced Mphepu to flee across the Limpopo to Zimbabwe. But the outbreak of the Second Anglo–Boer War in 1899 saved Venda from annexation, as Joubert and his troops were recalled to fight the British in Natal, and Mphepu returned and took back his throne.

In 1902, Venda came under British rule, and the new government, uncomfortable at having such a powerful African kingdom within its boundaries, ordered the Venda to burn all their unregistered firearms. But this was largely avoided, and the Venda wisely kept the peace, giving the British no reason to send troops into the country. Through the first half of the 20th century, white settlement remianed confined to missionaries. Rather than spend money on expensive resident administrators, the British decided to exploit the already able system of tribal government, appointing the various Venda chiefs as magistrates. This lasted until the 1950s, and even under the new Boer apartheid government, partial self-government was allowed in the Venda, largely because of its isolation from the rest of South Africa.

In 1969 Venda's self-government was recognized in Pretoria and in 1973 it was declared a 'homeland', opting for full 'independence' from South Africa in 1979 (as did Ciskei and Transkei in the Eastern Cape). Since then, some attempts have been made at establishing modern industry in Venda, notably with the building of the new capital of Thohoyandou, a hideous eyesore of raw concrete built with South African money. Outside the capital Venda's rural life has remained largely unchanged, with chiefs governing through a democratic council of tribal elders.

However, since the abolition of apartheid, evidence has come to light of government abuse in Venda, in particular of an increase in ritual murder. It appears that government officials, paid from Pretoria and therefore no longer feeling accountable to the nation, secretly sanctioned gathering of human body parts to make *muti* (medicine) for their own political advancement (*see* 'Venda Culture').

Despite this, the Venda remains a safe place for those not involved in the region's internal political struggles. Although relatively prosperous, it is also one of the few places that visitors can see traditional tribal life without having to trek into inaccessible areas.

Venda Culture

Certain aspects of Venda culture, such as building in stone and styles of wood carving, bear closer resemblance to northern Zimbabwean and Malawian culture than to South African. The language, VaVenda, also has its roots north of the country and bear little resemblance to the Northern Sotho and Tsonga languages common in the rest of the Northern Transvaal.

But everyday life in Venda is very similar to other traditional areas of South Africa. Local government is run along the traditional system with a chief, who has nominal control over clan land and resources, but must consult with a council of elders before making any decision that affects the group. To avoid autocratic rule these councils, which happen every two years or so, are compulsory. Failure to attend is punishable by fines.

The rural Venda count their wealth in head of cattle. Their lifestyle is still largely agricultural, with male and female roles clearly defined; men tend the livestock, plough the soil, build and thatch huts and sow crops, while women look after all other phases of crop raising, which involves most of the hard labour, as well as taking care of all domestic duties. Polygamy is still widespread in the countryside, with a division of agricultural and domestic work among the women. Because of the relative prosperity of Venda's farmlands, fewer men leave to work in the mines than in other tribal areas, and traditional life has held together in Venda as a result.

Venda Python Dance

Ritual and belief in the spirit world are still very much a part of rural Vendan life. The 'homelands' forests, lakes and perennial rivers have traditionally been regarded as the homes of spirits that are constantly in need of appeasing. Lake Fundudzi, in the centre of the region and one of the largest natural lakes in South Africa, is still a sacred site—visitors can only approach its shoreline with permission from the lake's priestess. Formed a few hundred years ago by a massive landslide, Fundudzi is the home of the Python God, a central figure of the old Vendan pantheon, after Raluvhimba, the Supreme Being, who is detached from both the human and the spiritual sphere.

The Python God is responsible for the rains and rivers, and is attended by strange beings called *Dituwane*, humanistic creatures with one eye, one arm and one leg. It is said that to see one is to die; fortunately they are so shy as to remain hidden if at all possible, although one legend has it that a party of Boers raiding into Venda in the 19th century were driven off by *Dituwane*, after watering their horses at a sacred pool.

The Python God of Lake Fundudzi is still honoured with a gift of beer poured into the lake once a year, and in the Python Dance, the most famous part of Venda's intricate web of ritual. Also known as the *Domba*, this is performed by Venda's maiden girls as the final stage of their initiation into womanhood, preparatory to being made available for marriage. The young women, naked but for a short beaded skirt, form up in single file and dance solemnly in winding lines, like a snake. The *Domba* can last all night, and its observance is important for securing good rains for the coming year.

Another figure of Venda myth is Sankhabi, a mischievous bird-like spirit who travels between the spirit and human world. A series of moral tales surround Sankhabi, usually involving punishment of human folly or disrespect for the gods and ancestors. Like most South African tribal cultures, ancestors are central to Venda life, and are the spititual mediums through which men must deal with the world.

A more sinister side of Venda culture involves witchcraft and ritual murder. Human body parts are used to prepare special *mutis* or medicines, usually for battle or political intrigue. *Muti* murder, usually of children, has always been relatively common in most of South Africa's traditional areas, but in Venda it appears to have reached epidemic proportions during the 1980s and early '90s. Many Venda blame this on a breakdown in traditional tribal values among government officials aiming to advance their careers, and businessmen wanting to ensure success. This typically South African mix of ancient medical and modern political practice is by no means unique to Venda, but the concentration of incidents here in the last 10 years has been abnormal. A Vendan journalist, Risimathi Mathunzi, stated in a 1991 article in the independent socio-political *Cross Times*:

> *'The people involved in government today are the people who have the businesses and they, the very people who are supposed to be protecting us, are killing us for muti.'*

In the same article a nurse from a rural clinic commented on a local girl who had been murdered:

> *'We heard that her boyfriend picked her up one evening around six. He took her for love, but they went past where they were initially going, off into the woods. Then a group of men came out. Her father was one of them, he was living away from the family. They start cutting you while you are still alive. And they cut the girl at the wrist, the elbow and shoulder. And she said, "please let me go, I won't say anything". But they finished it.'*

In 1991 Edwin Ritchken, a researcher in rural politics at the University of Witwatersrand, and Eddie Kock, a journalist for the *Weekly Mail*, published an article in the *Cross Times* in which they alleged a spate of *muti* murders between 1986 and 1990, implicating cabinet ministers. They reported that a mass stay-away from work in 1988 which resulted in the enforced resignation of the Vendan Minister of Justice, was organized in protest against the ritual killings.

A further problem of these murders are the counter-murders of those accused of being witches, of which 70 were reported in the first six months of 1994 in the Northern Transvaal (*SA Times* June 1994). But despite this side of Venda culture, travellers need not fear *muti*, which is a practice kept firmly inside the local community. Visitors are too far removed from Vendan culture to have any relevance to or involvment in such practices.

Tourist Information

Venda Tourism, Thohoyandou, ✆ (0159) 41577.

Visitors should avoid Venda's ugly new capital, **Thohoyandou**, named after the legendary chief who repulsed Paul Kruger's invading army in 1898. An unpleasant mix of concrete buildings, industrial sites and dust that was quickly erected in 1980, Thohoyandou's main attraction is its brash yet bland Sun Hotel and casino—a standard feature of the 'homelands', where gambling is permitted. Better simply to visit the **Tourist Office** in the Venda Development Corporation building just north of the main through road, arrange your guide and get out as quickly as possible into the farmlands, forests and mountains. Before going, however, visit the **Ditike Craft Centre**, whose woven textiles, wooden carvings and clay pots are among the best available in Venda. South of Thohoyandou, the **Venda Soutpansberg** can be explored by means of the 4-day **Mabudashango Trail**, which links up with the 5-day **Entabeni Forest Trail** in the Transvaal Soutpansberg, or can be walked in a circle by itself (*see* 'Activities').

West of the capital are **Lake Fundudzi** and the surrounding **Thathe Vondo Sacred Forest**, both of which lie at the heart of Venda mythology. Accessible from Louis Trichardt in the Transvaal, Fundudzi is revered as the home of the Python God and permission must be obtained to approach its shores. The forest, however, can be walked via marked trails, and hikers can gaze down on the lake from the surrounding hills. Formed by a landslide that dammed the Mutale River several hundred years ago, Fundudzi's waters must never be mixed with that of other rivers, for fear of angering the Python God. Even the shores are sacred, as these are thought to be the gardens of the dead ancestors of the VaVenda, whose ashes used to be ceremonially scattered over the water in times past.

Like the Soutpansberg's woodlands, the Thathe Vondo forest is a dark green world of waterfalls, cool forest, giant ferns and mountain streams. Venda tradition has it that the Thathe Vondo forest is guarded by a deity called Nethathe, who is half-lion, half-man, and who sleeps in caves under the ground. Certain parts of the forest are out-of-bounds to visitors, as it is thought that their footsteps might disturb his sleep. The existing trails lead through some superb hardwood and cycad stands, to the Mahovhovho and Mutale waterfalls. The forest is one of the few places in southern Africa that is known for mushrooms—in this case giant ones (known as *mwimbi*) which are regarded as the food of the half-lion god Nethane, and so the fungi are not eaten by the Venda.

Southeast of Thohoyandou, at the foot of the Soutpansberg are **Lwamondo Kop** and the nearby **Mpophulo Cycad Reserve**. Lwamondo is famous for its sacred baboons, whose barking used to warn the Lwamondo clan of the approach of strangers, and thus kept the stronghold (there is a ruined stone fort at the top) safe through the endless petty clan wars fought by the VaVenda until the 19th century. About 25km west along the Soutpansberg's foot are the **Tshatshingo Potholes** deep river pools that until the 1900s served as places of execution for those accused of witchcraft.

Game is plentiful in the east of Venda, near the Kruger National Park, but the 'homeland's' only official game reserve is the **Nwadeni National Park**, a mixed terrain of acacia-covered Soutpansberg foothills, and mopane and marula lowveld woodland. White rhino, kudu, eland and a number of antelope roam free, while lion and cheetah can be viewed in enclosures. It seems a pity that the predators should be cooped up, but at least their absence from the main park allows visitors to walk safely along a number of marked trails as well as driving the game-viewing roads.

It is worth visiting Nwadeni for the walking, but anyone who really wants to see the Big Five in the wild should drive east to the new **Makuya Nature Reserve** hard by the Pafuri Gate of the Kruger National Park (near the town of Masisi), where the pristine wilderness has been preserved and the big game roams at will between Makuya and the Kruger. Accommodation within Makuya must be booked through Venda Tourism in Thohoyandou, ✆ (0159) 41577. Venda also has some hot mineral springs. Two are accessible via small resorts—**Sagole Spa** and **Mphephu Hot Springs**. Sagole, in the north of the country, is set among huge baobab trees, one of which, the **Big Tree**, is reached by a short dirt road from the resort, and is reckoned to be over 3000 years old. Mphephu is west of Thohoyandou and can be visited just for the day. Accommodation for both is bookable through the Tourist Office in Thohoyandou.

Finally, visitors to Venda wanting to see the *Domba* **dance** should travel from September to December. Again, this has to be arranged through the Tourist Office, who will organize transport out to the village where it is happening. Thrown in as part of the outing is generally a trip to the village of **Mutale**, just north of the capital, where the sacred rums made to accompany the *Domba* are made. If you ask, the guide will then take you to see a local diviner. This is no piece of tourist kitsch, but the real thing, and if you have questions about the future to ask, you might find them being answered with uncomfortable accuracy. Several travellers have reported Venda diviners' predictions coming to pass after their visit.

Activities

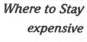

Walking and hiking: Day hikes can be found at Nwadeni National Park, the Thathe Vondo Forest and in the Soutpansberg foothills. The 4-day Mabudashango Trail, ✆ (0159) 31211, follows a wide circle through the Soutpansberg forests and uipland meadows. Huts with firewood and water are provided. Another long hike, also with huts and firewood provided is the Entabeni Trail in the Soutpansberg proper; ✆ (01551) 2201. There are several pleasant day walks in the Mpophulo Cycad Reserve, and in Nwadeni National Park.

Where to Stay

expensive

The overpriced **Venda Sun**, ✆ (0159) 21011, in the new capital of Thohoyandou, should only be a last resort. Its tasteless, suburban interior is indistinguishable from any chain hotel anywhere.

However, its casino, while brash, attracts interestingly dubious 'businessmen' and other characters passing through.

moderate/cheap

The **Nwadeni National Park**, ✆ (015539) 723/753, offers a range of accommodation in central Venda's baobab country. Luxurious rooms in a central lodge fall within the top end of the moderate range, while the self-contained rondavels and camp site with ablution blocks are much cheaper. **Mphephu Resort**, ✆ (01595) 30049, offers self-contained chalets, as does **Acacia Park**, ✆ (0159) 22506/ 23095 in central Thohoyandou. The **Sagole Spa** in the far north of Venda, and Mphephu Resort in the west (booked through Venda Tourism, *see* above) offer slightly more expensive accommodation around their hot mineral springs.

The Far North: Messina and the Baobab Plains

North of the Soutpansberg the country becomes drier, harsher and wilder; the landscape of mopane woodland, thorn and strange rock formations is dominated by the massive, bulbous, utterly African bulk of baobab trees, which jut from the bush every few hundred metres.

The only town to speak of in this area is **Messina**, which sits in the bushveld just 16km south of the border with Zimbabwe. The country around is hardly even farmed; about 30 years ago, most of the cattle ranchers in the area realized it would be more profitable to reintroduce indigenous game and sell hunting licences, meat and hides, rather than steers, which tended to sicken in the sub-tropical heat. As a result, the wild landscape is little changed.

A few of these game ranches run guided walks and photo safaris for guests and day visitors, offering a variety of habitat and game types. **Greater Kuduland Safaris**, ✆ (015539) 720, signposted from the R525 southeast of Messina, comprises typical mopane woodland populated by zebra, giraffe and the larger antelope.

R. du Cow

Sheldrake Game Ranch, ✆ (01553) 2714/2958, in the north near the junction of the Sand and Limpopo Rivers, overlooks the wide Voorburg Dam, and has buffalo and rhino as well as plains game. **Medike Lodge** ✆ (01551) 2481 and **George's Place** ✆ (01554) 641, in the Sand River gorge, in the northern foothills of the Soutpansberg. have shyer game such as leopard, bushbuck and klipspringer, and walking trails through the beautiful Sand River Gorge—where thin belts of hardwood forest, aloe and wild herbs fringe the water margins, and the mountains rise sheer on all sides. Bushman paintings are also a feature.

If you are driving along the R525 towards the Greater Kuduland Safari ranch, it is worth stopping in at the **Tchipies Resort**—a hot springs resort with a large nature reserve at its back, ✆ (015539) 661. Unfortunately, an ugly supermarket, bad restaurant and camp site full of 'Vaalies' in campervans has been built near the entrance, but if you ignore the small complex of buildings, it is bliss to relax in the naturally heated water after a long, dusty drive. The resort's adjacent nature reserve has walking trails into the surrounding bush, which comprises the lower northern foothills of the Soutpansberg, and supports a healthy population of antelope, zebra, wildebeest and giraffe.

The town of **Messina** is a regular stop for truck drivers going between South Africa and the great African interior, and backpackers congregate here in search of long-distance lifts, giving the small town a quietly cosmopolitan feel. It is the only place in the Northern Transvaal with hostel accommodation specifically aimed at backpackers (*see* 'Where to Stay'), and the bar in the town hotel is lively with people passing through.

Just south of town, between the R525 and N1, is the excellent **Messina Nature Reserve,** ✆ (01553) 3235, a large protected area with a high density of enormous baobab trees, some of which are reckoned to be as much as 4000 years old. Unless you see them just after the summer rains, baobabs are usually leafless and seem to support little life. However, they do produce a large, gourd-like fruit, known as monkey bread, and if you are lucky enough to see them in the short bushveld spring (September), their strange, stunted upper branches (which look ludicrously out of proportion to their great bulk of their trunks—like the arms on a tyrannosaurus rex), can be gay with white blossom.

The mopane woodland between the vast baobabs supports a large population of the more spectacular antelope—sable, nyala and kudu—as well as the inevitable impala and other small buck. Giraffe, wildebeest and zebra congregate in the open glades. Leopard and cheetah hunt in the reserve, but are seldom seen by visitors, unless you phone the ranger in advance and ask to be taken to a known lair, which he may or may not do, depending on his mood.

Game-viewing roads criss-cross the reserve, but it is better to walk one of the trails, and stand underneath the baobabs, getting an idea of their outsize scale. The woodland fronting the Sand River, which forms the southeast boundary of reserve, is particularly good for birdlife. Look out for rollers flitting between the trees, and bee-eaters nesting in holes in the river bank.

Activities

Marked nature trails have been laid out among the giant baobab trees, weird rock formations and plentiful game of **Messina Nature Reserve**. **Medike Lodge** in the beautiful Sand River Gorge has walking trails leading along the river to bushman paintings. Longer hikes (up to 5 days) can be booked at **Greater Kuduland Safaris** and **Sheldrake Game Ranch**. These are guided, owing to the presence of buffalo, and must be booked in advance. Short day trails can be found in the mopane woodland of the nature reserve adjoining the **Tchipies Hot Springs Resort**.

Where to Stay

expensive

Medike, ✆ (01551) 2481, lies over the Soutpansberg from Louis Trichardt, in the beautiful Sand River Gorge. There are comfortable permanent safari tents, or a secluded thatched cottage. Also in the gorge is **George's Place**, ✆ (01554) 641, which offers en suite rooms in a lodge, or a more private log cabin. Only 6 guests at a time are allowed, so there are no crowds. Guided bush walks along the river allow a good chance of sighting game.

Sheldrake Game Lodge, ✆ (01553) 2714/2958, is a private reserve and working game ranch overlooking the Voorburg Dam, which sells hunting licenses to cull a percentage of its game every year. It also sells the meat and hides, and organizes photo safaris. There are 3 lodges (each with a pool), white rhino, most of the large antelope species, and good fishing in the dam (tackle can be provided).

moderate

Greater Kuduland Safaris, along the R525 southeast of Messina, ✆ (015539) 720, has a luxurious hutted camp and two more moderately-priced bush camps in the mopane and baobab country just north of the Soutpansberg foothills.

cheap

Messina Backpackers, ✆ (01553) 40160, at 11 Cheynes Street, Messina, offers very cheap double rooms and dormitory accommodation, a kitchen and sitting room.

Northwest Province

We were sitting in Jurie Steyn's voorkamer at Drogevlei, waiting for the government lorry from Bekkersdal to bring us our letters and empty milk-cans. Jurie Steyn's voorkamer had served as the Drogevlei post office for some years, and Jurie Steyn was postmaster. His complaint was that the post office didn't pay. It didn't pay him, he said, to be called away from his lands every time somebody came in for a penny stamp. What was more, Gysbert van Tonder could walk right into his voorkamer whenever he liked, without knocking. Gysbert was Jurie Steyn's neighbour, and Jurie had naturally not been on friendly terms with him since the time that Gysbert van Tonder got a justice of the peace and a land-surveyor and a policeman riding a skimmel horse to explain to Jurie Steyn on what side of the vlei the boundary fence ran.

The Budget, Herman Charles Bosman

A dusty, remote territory of dry grassland and thornveld, the Northwest Province or Western Transvaal is mostly 'platteland'—flat farming country—whose immense mealie and cattle 'camps' stretch to a distant horizon. To the north is the dry wilderness of Central Botswana, to the west the Kalahari, to the south the parched Karoo, and to the east the brown highveld of the Witwatersrand.

There are few nature reserves or national parks, yet the region has a feeling of wildness, of remoteness, that impresses how independent of man the landscape is, though cattle farmers have denuded it of game and, in places, the country has been grazed raw. There is a great and silent beauty here, especially at evening, when the dying light turns the grassland a soft grey-blue, like a dove's plumage, and the heart sighs with pleasure at the sheer space.

The Northwest Province's white population is largely Afrikaans-speaking, although most have some English which can be haltingly started up, like an old, rusty car, if need be. As with the Karoo and the Orange Free State, the traveller who makes it to the Western Transvaal has penetrated the heartland of Afrikanerdom, and the dry, flat heat of the place offers clues to understanding the dour character of many of the Afrikaners themselves. The black population is mostly Tswana-speaking, and until 1994 large sections of the province were administered by the nominally independent former 'homeland' of Bophuthatswana, to which many Tswana people were forcibly removed during the 1970s.

Most tourists know of Bophuthatswana through the casinos of Sun City in Northwest Province's eastern corner, and indeed, from a traveller's point of view, the former 'homeland' has little to offer besides a tapestry of overgrazing and overcrowding on semi-desert scrub. However, the region's only significant game reserves, the Pilanesberg National Park and Madikwe Game Reserve, lie within the former Bophuthatswana. and offer a glimpse of wild Africa, including the 'Big Five' game species. Those that go further into the former 'homeland' are usually only crossing the region at speed on their way to the national parks of the Northern Cape. But should you be passing through, take a litttle time to savour the open emptiness away from the main roads, and lose yourself for a while either in the big game parks or in the dusty, eroded donkey- and goat-grazed waste of the former Bophuthatswana, or the grass-covered emptiness of the white farmlands, your eyes fixed on the far, flat horizon beyond the steering wheel, you mind numb from the heat and space of the endless land around you.

History

The Western Transvaal has been inhabited by hominids since fossil times, proved by the excavation of the remains of a pre-human creature called *Australopithicus*, from caves near Sterkfontein. But while this lends credence to the common anthropological theory of Africa as the 'cradle of mankind', the Sterkforntein discovery sheds little light on who inhabited the region through the millenia preceding our own. All that is known for sure is that, until the early Middle Ages, the Western Transvaal was the hunting ground of numerous San hunter-gatheres whose paintings have been found in caves and rock over-hangs thoughout the province.

These peoples were pushed west to the Kalahari and Bushmanland around 900 years ago by groups of black African-speaking cattle herders working their way down from the north. As usual there is no recorded history of this early period, only an inherited oral tradition, but archaeologists have found evidence of large settled villages whose inhabi-tants were skilled in metal-working and animal husbandry. This presumably was the forerunner of the region's present Tswana culture, the main difference being that settle-ments seem to have been more fragmented in the early period, whereas by the 1800s, when the first white travellers visited the area, the Tswana were living in larger, more centralized groups, or kingdoms, whose leaders ruled after the style of monarchs—with a court of ministers and loyal chiefs to rule the more distant territories. The most powerful of these Tswana clans were the Tlhaping, Taung, Rolong and Tlokwa.

Modern historians believe that this Tswana centralization was part of a more general picture of upheaval among the clans of the highveld clans and Natal, caused by increased trading activity with the Dutch, British and Portuguese. Those clans that became wealthy established standing armies, and began to mount large-scale raids on their neighbours.

The clan whose expansion was best documented was the Zulu of Natal, under Shaka during the 1820s (*see* **Zululand** 'History'). An offshoot of this clan, the Ndebele, raided north and settled in the Western Transvaal around this time, seizing territory from the Tswana clans. Into this arena of Ndebele/Tswana conflict blundered the Voortrekker Boers, during the Great Trek of 1836–8. Alternately trading with, allying with, and fighting with the various Tswana clans, the Boers concentrated their energies on pushing out the Ndebele, who had become the most powerful clan in the highveld. Pitched battles were fought, notably at Vegkop in 1836, where 400 Ndebele were killed in under an hour by musket-fire from a *laager* of wagons. With the help of the Tlokwa and Rolong Tswana, and with Griqua and Koranna fighters from Bushmanland, the Boers managed to push the Ndebele north through the Marico district and into the Northern Transvaal.

The Boers, with the aid of their firepower, began to establish towns in the Western Transvaal (and across the entire highveld), and to subdue the Tswana chiefdoms. Despite increased centralizing of power among these groups, the Tswana were still too fragmented to offer concerted resistance to Boer settlement, and allowed themselves to be played off against each other. By 1838 the Boers had succeeded in establishing a small town at Potchefstroom, which in 1841 became the first capital of the South African Republic (SAR), under the presidency of the trek leader Andries Hendrik Potgieter.

The infant republic's first task was to eliminate the Ndebele, who posed too powerful and organized a threat to the Boers' colonial ambition. Throughout the 1840s and '50s Potgieter and the Boers of the other Transvaal republics of Lydenburg and Soutpansberg, along with considerable Tswana and Griqua help, managed to push most off the Ndebele north of the Limpopo into modern Zimbabwe.

The burghers of the new Republic soon found that, although technically masters of large areas of the Transvaal, they were too few to establish and maintain agricultural colonies, and began trying to coerce the local Tswana into working on Boer farms. This was not easily done and, by the late 1860s, raiding parties of Boers were snatching children from Tswana villages and homesteads to work as 'indentured labour'—virtual slaves.

In 1860 the three Transvaal republics decided to amalgamate, keeping the name South African Republic (SAR), but moving the capital north to Pretoria, a convenient midway point, and the Western Transvaal settled into a peaceful agrarian life (albeit a white-dominated one) that was barely ruffled by the British occupation of the SAR from 1877-84, or by the gold boom on the Witwatersrand in the 1880s, despite the migration of thousands of young Tswana men to the mines.

But conflict returned to the Western Transvaal in 1900, the second year of the Anglo–Boer War, when the British re-occupied the SAR, and the Boer *commandos* retreated to the more remote regions of the Transvaal and Orange Free State, leading the unwieldly British columns a merry dance across the endless veld until the final surrender in 1902. The Western Transvaal was the centre of operations for the Boer general Koos de la Rey, whose effective use of trench warfare around the Modder River area checked the British advance for months, and bought time for the Boer besiegers of the British garrison in Mafeking (modern-day Mafikeng) on the border of West Griqualand, then a British protectorate.

The siege of Mafeking—like those of Ladysmith and Kimberley—was a waste of time for the Boers, as none of these towns were of particular strategic importance. The Mafeking garrison, under Lord Baden-Powell, was held up by the British press as a model of stiff-upper-lipped endurance, but in fact seems to have suffered little; most of the fighting (and starving) was done by the Rolong Tswana living on the outskirts of town, who hoped that a proven loyalty to the British would rid them of Boer (and other white) oppression. Baden-Powell shamelessly used the Rolong, allowing them no credit in his dispatches home, and then abandoned them with the promise of a few land grants once the siege was raised in

1901. The Rolong's ordeal was chronicled by one Sol Plaatje, a member of the clan working as a clerk of the court during the siege, who went on to become a founder member of the South African Native National Congress (SANNC), which later became the ANC.

General de la Rey was a 'bitterender', as those who kept guerilla fighting until the end of the war were called. Following the Boer surrender of 1902, the Western Transvaal and de la Rey remained strongly anti-British, holding to their isolationist stance even after the ex-Boer generals Louis Botha and Jan Smuts assumed the leadership of the new Union of South Africa in 1910. When Botha agreed to send South African troops to France in 1914 (he had little choice—the new Union was still a British Dominion), de la Rey snapped, and called the Western Transvaal to arms again with the intention of leading a full-scale insurrection against Pretoria. But by a weird twist of fortune, he was shot dead in his car before the rebellion could even get off the ground, after running an army roadblock. Without its charismatic leader, the revolt petered out a few weeks later.

From that point on, the Western Transvaal became a rural Boer backwater, staunchly nationalist, but politically inactive compared to the other areas of the Transvaal, perhaps owing to its remoteness. Through the troubled 1930s, when black political organizations and trade unions first began to campaign effectively on the nearby Witwatersrand, through the Second World War and the years of apartheid, the Western Transvaal, while always a stronghold of Afrikaner nationalist support, remained politically inactive, having no large industrial centres or cities—traditionally the centres of political activity.

Not until the creation of the black 'homelands' (or *bantustans*) in the 1970s did the Western Transvaal see direct political action—this time the forced eviction of tens of thousands of Tswana, Ndebele and other black people from landholdings in areas that had been designated 'white'. Large areas of the poorest land were declared part of the 'republic' of Bophuthatswana, and the majority of the region's blacks were moved there, or to other parts of the Transvaal.

As the prospect of a final dismantling of apartheid became a reality in the late 1980s, many fearful Western Transvaalers found a political voice in support of the ultra-right wing AWB under Eugene Terr'Blanche and the region became a core of white resistence. Yet, having pledged to mount a concerted fight against black government, the AWB remained largely inactive through the early 1990s beyond some tragic, random killings and pre-election bombings that failed to seriously impede the country's progress towards democracy. In fact, the Western Transvaal was, ironically, the scene of a major humiliation for the far right just before the 1994 elections, when an AWB 'commando' drove into the former Bophuthatswana to put down demonstrations against its corrupt regime.

However, the regime in question had not called in the AWB, nor had Pretoria asked them to intervene. The organization was acting on its own initiative, to make a public show of upholding the Pretoria-backed Bophuthatswana government. The 'commando' found itself quickly isolated amid an angry mob and a hostile Bophuthatswana police force and was chased out of the 'homeland'. On its way out, three AWB men in a car opened fire on the crowd, and had their fire promptly returned by the police. The driver was hit and the car swerved from the road and stopped. The three occupants were then shot dead by a

Bophuthatswana policeman, while pleading for their lives. The horrific event was captured by a freelance journalist and published around the world. As a grim sequel to the event, the journalist, Kevin Carter, shot himself two weeks after the pictures were published.

Bophuthatswana, like all South Africa's 'homelands', has now officially ceased to exist, .Perhaps the razing of the random borders will allow some inter-racial harmony into this stratified land, as well as some wealth sharing between the two communities.

Getting There

By car: From Johannesburg and the Witwatersrand the most travelled route is through dead flat country to Vryburg via the N14. A more interesting way in is via the R24 or R27 from Pretoria, which run along the south and north foot of the Magaliesberg respectively. From the south, take the N12 up from Kimberley or the R700 from Bloemfontein, via the Bloemhof Dam Nature Reserve. From the west follow the N14.

By bus: Inter-Cape, TransLux, Transtate and Greyhound all run services along the N12 and N14, stopping at the towns along the way. There are also bus services from Johannesburg to Gaberone in Botswana, via the Marico District. If coming from the east, call Johannesburg or Pretoria's Publicity Offices for fares and times. From the south, telephone the Kimberley Publicity Office.

By rail: Services run between Kimberley and Johannesburg most days along the Vaal River, taking in the main towns, and a daily service connects runs through the Marico district on the way between Johannesburg and Gaberone.

The Marico District

> No (Oom Schalk Lourens said) you don't get flowers in the Groot Marico. It is not a bad district for mealies, and I once grew quite good onions in a small garden I made next to the dam. But what you can really call flowers are rare things here. Perhaps it's the heat. Or the drought.

From the short story *Willem Prinsloo's Peach Brandy*
by Herman Charles Bosman

This deeply rural corner of the Western Transvaal is only 100km from Johannesburg. Travellers on their way through to Gaberone in Botswana have to cross the Marico via the towns of Krugersdorp and Zeerust, a landscape of wide, yellow hills, sheep and mealie fields, and lonely farmhouses shaded by dark green eucalyptus trees that was made famous in the short stories of Afrikaner writer Herman Charles Bosman in the 1920s. Each story is narrated by Schalk Lourens, a wily, compassionate, humorous old Boer with a love of the land, its people—black, white and *rooinek*—and its occult soul. Among the best are *The Witchdoctor*, in which a bullying Boer farmer is stripped of his power by a passive witch-doctor, and *Funeral Earth*, in which a group of Boers returned from the Anglo–Boer War learn from their old enemies, the local Tswana clan, how much better it is to farm than to fight.

Krugersdorp, at the far eastern end of the Marico, is reckoned by many to be the most staunchly Afrikaans enclave in the country, partly because of its name, which celebrates 'Oom' Paul Kruger, the Transvaal president who went to war against Britain in 1899. In fact it is mainly a dormitory suburb for those working in the western Witwatersrand area, and so is hardly a Boer (i.e farmer's) town. However, English is not the first language of most of the residents, and the town does serve as a transitional point between the cosmopolitan Witwatersrand and the conservative Western Transvaal.

Apart from its **Railway Society Museum** (*open Mon–Fri 7.30–1, 2–5, weekends 8–1, 2–5*), whose old rolling stock is a delight for steam buffs, Krugersdorp is not a town that caters for tourism. However, just west of town along the R24 is the **Krugersdorp Game Reserve**, ✆ (011) 660 1076, a tract of bushveld country harbouring most plains antelope, including the rare sable and roan antelopes. Two streams run through the reserve with guided walking trails along their banks. Look out for waterbuck and fish eagle. Separate enclosures for lion, white rhino and buffalo can be seen near the reserve's entrance.

North of town towards the Magaliesberg are the spectacular **Sterkfontein Caves** (*open daily 9–5*), famous among anthropologists the world over for their fossils of pre-human primates. It was here in 1896 that Dr Robert Broom, excavator of several caves in the Transvaal, found the fossil skull of a humanoid creature known as *Australopithecus Africanus*, supporting the common view of Africa as the 'cradle of mankind'. The skull, over 1,000,000 years old, is thought to have belonged to an ancestor of *homo erectus*, which preceded *homo sapiens*. There have been several such finds in the area, including those at Taung in Bushmanland and in caves in Swaziland's western mountains. Inside the cave system (which can only be visited by guided tour) are huge stalactite/stalagmite formations, along with a vast, mysterious undergound lake, sacred to the Tswana people.

While waiting for a tour, drop into the small **Robert Broom Museum** next to the cave entrance, where a speculative history of the local humanoids shares space with other fossil finds from the area.

West of Krugersdorp you enter the Marico proper around the appropriately-named town of **Groot Marico**, a back-country farm town as sleepy today as it was when Bosman wrote about it in the 1920s. The Marico's largest town is **Zeerust**, an outwardly conservative place that hosts an annual *mampoer* festival—a mad binge of hard spirit drinking. *Mampoer* is a locally (and legally) brewed hooch similar to peach schnapps that removes your head after a few glasses and replaces it with a turnip. The festival is a moveable feast, but the Brits Publicity Association, ✆ (01211) 589 111, will know the dates. Apart from this annual binge, Zeerust is a straight-down-the-line Boer farming town. However, it connects Johannesburg with the nearest Botswana border crossing and also lies astride the road to Mmabatho, a gambling town and capital of the former Bophuthatswana, reached via the excellently-named village of Slurry.

Bronking Spr

South of Zeerust is **Lichtenburg,** a larger, richer farming town set in a greener landscape. The **Lichtenburg Town Museum** on De La Rey Square (*open Tues–Fri 10–12, 1–5, Sat, 10–1*) is a must for Boer War enthusiasts, as it has a collection of artefacts belonging to the 'bitter-end' Boer General Koos de la Rey, whose trench warfare against the British at Modder River was so effective that the British themselves adopted it for use in the First World War. Also housed in the museum is a small collection of early paintings and sketches of the Transvaal.

Northeast of town and signposted from the R52 is the **Lichtenburg Nature Reserve,** ✆ (01441) 22818, covering a 6000ha stretch of typical bushveld and home to a number of large antelope species. Lichtenburg is also a game-breeding station for the National Zoological Gardens in Pretoria, and its rare species include pygmy hippo (from West Africa), sable and roan antelope, and cheetah (in an enclosed area).

Southwest of Lichtenburg along the R47, just north of the town of Delareyville, is an extraordinary wetland—the last thing you would expect to find in the dry grasslands of the Western Transvaal. **Barberspan Nature Reserve,** ✆ (0144322) 1202, comprises a freshwater lake and surrounding marsh that is home to thousands of waterbirds. Large numbers of flamingoes can usually be seen feeding in the shallows, while storks, ibis, egrets, herons, Egyptian geese, black ducks and a host of other species thrive on the lake's plentiful fish and can be observed from a wooden hide.

Activities

Hiking: Both Krugersdorp and Lichtenburg Nature Reserves have short hiking trails with game viewing opportunities.

Where to Stay
moderate/cheap

Krugersdorp Game Reserve, ✆ (011) 660 1076, has self-contained rondavels and a restaurant. Access is via the R24 west of town. **Lichtenburg Nature Reserve,** ✆ (01441) 22818, signposted from the R52 just north of town, has a camp site, as does **Barberspan Nature Reserve,** ✆ (0144322) 1202. Barberspan is popular, especially at weekends, and it is advisable to book.

'Potch' is the oldest European town in the Transvaal and the original capital of the South African Republic (SAR) founded by the Voortrekker leader Hendrik Potgieter in 1838. The town's capital status was removed to Pretoria in 1860 after which Potchefstroom became what it is now, a conservative Afrikaans-speaking university town—the Potchefstroom Univeristy for Christian National Education.

Despite its age and although not unattractive, Potch has little beyond some good Victorian buildings to distinguish it from many other Western Transvaal towns. It also seems to lack the slightly frivolous atmosphere of a university town—perhaps because the university is a Christian organization and tends to attract a more serious breed of student—whatever the reason, the *joie de vivre* one expects from a university town is not in evidence.

The **Potchefstroom Museum** (*open Mon–Fri 8.30–4.30*) is understandably dedicated to the Voortrekkers. The highlight is one of the wagons used in the *laager* at Blood River, the Boer victory over Zulu *impis* in 1842. Two of the original buildings open to the public are the **Old Fort** (*open Mon–Fri 8.30–4.30*), on the Klerksdorp road opposite the railway station, and the **Powder Magazine**, also on the Klerksdorp road, in Potchefstroom's small industrial area (*open Mon–Fri 8.30–1, 2–4.30*). The Boer general Cronje besieged a small British force in the Old Fort for three months during the First Anglo–Boer War (1880–1), and forcing them to surrender and abandon the post. However, Cronje is not well remembered in Boer History, having earned the unfortunate distinction of being the first Boer general to surrender during the Second Anglo–Boer War (1899–1902) after being heavily shelled by British artillery at the battle of Paardeberg (1900).

Dating from 1868 is **President Pretorius' House** on Van Der Hoff Road (*open Mon–Fri 10–1, 2–5, Sat 9–12.45, Sun 2.30–5*), the residence of the SAR's second president. The interior has been restored and decorated with his paintings and personal effects, and the outbuildings, including an old smithy, set up as a display of early farm life. The **Totius Museum** (*open Mon–Fri 10–1, 2–5, Sat 9–12.45, Sun 2.30–5*) is a lovely red-roofed Victorian bungalow, set in spacious gardens, once the home of the late-19th century writer J. D. Du Toit, a leading light in the Afrikaans language movement whose writings are somewhat religious and sombre. However, the museum is one of the few in the country that charges no admission, and this alone marks it out as special.

In keeping with the town's generally pious atmosphere is the **Hervormde Kerk** (built in 1866, but substantially added to since then) opposite the town hall, is the oldest surviving church north of the Vaal River.

Southwest of Potch along the N12, you pass through the small industrial town of **Klerksdorp**. Apart from its one street of surviving old buildings, **Hendrik Potgieter Road**, the town itself is not much to look at, although its **Town Museum** on the corner of Lombaard and Margeretha Prinsloo Streets (*open Mon–Fri 10–1, 2–5, Sat 9.30–12.30, Sun 2–5*) occupies the original gaol and powder magazine (built 1891) and now houses some interesting early man tools found in the area. The curators can arrange for you to visit a hill 18km north of town along the R30 on a farm called **Bosworth**, which has some very ancient bushman rock engravings, whose occult, animalistic designs seem to have had some ritual purpose, and it is easy to let the imagination go on this lonely rise. Easier to understand are the old gold diggings at **Goudkoppie** (meaning 'gold hill'), on the Silfontein road, where abandoned mine shafts from the 1880s are still to be found, as is some graffiti engraved by British soldiers in the Second Anglo–Boer War (1899–1902).

At the **Faan Meintjies Nature Reserve**, signposted from the R30 north of town. White rhino are the main attraction, with large antelope (including sable), giraffe and black wildebeest as the supporting acts. The reserve has no accommodation.

From Klerksdorp, the N12 crosses the flat grasslands to the small, dusty town of **Wolmaransstad**. In the 1870s and '80s this was a cosmopolitan resting-point midway between the minefields of Kimberley and the Witwatersrand. Today there is nothing to suggest this: the only attractions are the **Makwassie Conservation Area**, 10km east of town, and the old homestead and hotel, **Lindbergh Lodge**. Makwassie Conservation Area covers several thousand hectares of bush, but has only recently been formed and has no tourists facilities as yet. However, plans are afoot for major game restocking. Ask at the Town Clerk's Office, ✆ (01811) 21067, for the current situation. Lindbergh Lodge on the other hand is a vast private estate and game reserve, well stocked with indigenous game, open to residents of the hotel only (*see* 'Where to Stay').

Two reserves front the northern bank of the Vaal River south of Wolmaranastad. **Wolwespruit Nature Reserve**, ✆ (01813) 2026, is close to the small town of Leeudoringstad on the R504. Covering about 2500ha, the reserve supports large antelope, zebra, red hartebeest and wildebeest, and has some short walking trails through riverine woodland. Adjoining Wolwespruit to the west is the much larger **Bloemhof Dam Nature Reserve**, ✆ (018022) 1122, which covers 14,000ha and supports much the same game species as Wolwespruit, only in larger numbers. It is also home to white rhino. The bird life is very good, especially after rains, with a variety of waterfowl contrasting with grassveld species such as korhaans (miniature bustards), weavers and secretary birds. Visitors should telephone before arrival.

Away from the river, about 14km to the east of the small *dorp* of Bloemhof, is the **S. A. Lombard Nature Reserve**, ✆ (018022) 4203. This is a 4000ha block of grass and thorn-veld used as a breeding station for highveld game. Visitors should telephone first; there is no accommodation.

Southwest of Bloemhof along the N12 (also signposted as the R29), is the riverside town of **Christiana**. Site of yet another short-lived diamond rush in the 1870s, Christiana enjoyed a brief Edwardian boom before lapsing into its present torpor. However, because of its proximity to the river, Christiana retains a pleasant old-world charm sadly lacking in many dusty Western Transvaal towns. This makes a good point to break the journey with a stroll along the treed riverbank. Just outside town to the northeast is a less attractive mineral spa with the standard over-priced, rather ugly resort built around it. However, the warm waters (around 40°C) are soothing, and the outdoor pool provides cool relief from the effects of a hot car. The resort has a small (2300ha) game reserve attached to it, where you can walk among large and small antelope (including gemsbok and eland), wildebeest and zebra. Less visited are the **prehistoric rock engravings**, estimated to be tens of thousands of years old, on the Stowlands-on-Vaal farm 6km south of town towards Hertzogville. A short walking trail from the farmhouse leads to the site. For directions, ring the Town Clerk's Office on Robyn Street, ✆ (0534) 2206/7/8.

Activities

Walking: Only Wolwespruit and Bloemhof Nature Reserves offer walking trails, as well as the short one to the bushman rock engravings at Stowlands-on-Vaal near Christiana. Otherwise there are no marked long-distance hiking trails in the region.

Riding: Lindbergh Lodge, ✆ (01811) 22620, hires schooled horses to residents (and to non-residents if arranged in advance) for rides through wild grassland rich in game.

Fishing: The Vaal River teems with indigenous species such as yellow-fish, mud-fish and barbel. To hire tackle, call the Christiana Town Clerk, ✆ (0534) 2206/7/8.

Where to Stay

expensive

Lindbergh Lodge, ✆ (01811) 22620, is a vast private estate in the dry grasslands near Wolmaransstad. Now a game farm, Lindbergh has its original Victorian thatched lodge with a log fire and ancestral portraits in the grand dining room. There are five rooms only. Black wildebeest, sable antelope, giraffe, zebra, gemsbok and other game species wander the reserve. Hiking and riding are offered, and balloon rides over the veld—an unforgettable, silent hour of bliss in the African sky. If you can afford it, Lindbergh is one of the best places to stay in the area.

moderate

The **Rob Ferreira Nature Reserve**, just east of Christiana in the far southwest, has a small, rather ugly resort tacked onto it, run by the Transvaal company Overvaal Resorts. However, the reserve itself, which fronts the Vaal river, is beautiful, and its self-contained chalets moderately priced. There is a shop and fuel. Access is via the R29.

cheap

Bloemhof Dam Nature Reserve, ✆ (018022) 1122, has a camp site with ablution blocks overlooking the Vaal River (access via the R29 or R34). Also on the Vaal is the **Wolwespruit Nature Reserve**, ✆ (01813) 2026, whose large camp site is popular with fishermen. Wolwespruit is south of Wolmaransstad and accessible by dirt road from the R504 south of Leeudoringstad. **Boskop Dam Nature Reserve**, ✆ (0148) 22430, has a camp site overlooking the dam. Boskop is north of Potchefstroom along the R501.

'Fragile and fairy-like was Menyenyane, the little Tswana girl, so named for the dainty, soft short veld grasses that danced their delicate white flowers up and down in the breeze'.

From *Bantu Folk-tales of Southern Africa*
(Timmins, Cape Town, 1974), Elizabeth Mattanyane

Following the elections in early 1994, finds itself in the unusual position of no longer existing officially but continuing to operate in practice while its artificial political structure is dismantled. Bophuthatswana was only created as an 'independent homeland' in 1977 as part of the grand plan of the apartheid government to contain all South Africa's blacks within reserves. Many Tswana people were forced to move thousands of kilometres to their new 'homeland', leaving behind property and jobs. 'Bop' was not even a cohesive space, but was confusingly fragmented into seven different chunks, of which the largest and most commercially viable fall within the Western Transvaal.

The puppet state of Bophuthatswana grew rich from the gambling revenues of Sun City and fortunate discovery of platinum; the capital, Mmabatho, is a kitsch monument to Bophuthatswana's financial success. But only the government leaders and bureaucrats have seen any of this money. The majority of the population remained grindingly poor, living in crowded, semi-urban conditions around the few towns that dot the huge swathes of dry, barren grassveld. However, in parts, the wild veld has been preserved, and game conservation thrives as a secondary means of culling money from the tourist industry. Pilanesberg National Park, near Sun City, now ranks as one of South Africa's best large game reserves.

Tswana History

Bantu-speaking groups, the ancestors of the modern Tswana people, have been present in the region for at least 1000 years. A cattle-owning people, the Tswana's oral tradition is thought to date from around the 12th century. Skilled smiths, their iron tools and weapons established them as powerful warrior-traders when first Arab, then Portuguese, then Dutch trade routes began to penetrate the area from the 15th to the 18th centuries. The principal Tswana clans—the Rolong, Tlokwa, Thlaping and Taung—fought periodically among themselves, but more often with their Sotho-speaking neighbours and with the Griqua and Kora raiders who rode in from the dry country around the Orange River in the early 1800s. In the 1820s the Tswana found themselves fighting for dominance with the mighty Ndebele nation, who took advantage of the Tswana's settled lifestyle to raid for slaves and cattle.

By the time the Voortrekkers arrived in the Western Transvaal in 1836, the Ndebele were the most powerful force in the area. Longing to be rid of the Ndebele menace, the Rolong and Taung allied with the Voortrekkers and together defeated the Ndebele at Vegkop in the Western Transvaal. But it was a Pyrrhic victory for the Tswana—no sooner had the

Voortrekkers ejected the Ndebele than they set about enslaving the Tswana, denying them the right to hold their own land and forcing them to work as farm labourers, or tenant farmers at best.

For a powerful nation who had dominated the region since before the 12th century, this was a bitter pill. But the military superiority of the Boers was hard to challenge. At the outbreak of the Anglo–Boer War in 1899 the Tswana allied with the British where possible. The British garrison then resident at Mafeking (modern Mafikeng) was besieged by a strong Boer force, and the Tswana, particularly the Rolong, turned out in force to help. Among them was a young Rolong man called **Sol. T. Plaatje**, whose mission education and gift for languages had earned him a job as translator in the magistrate court at Mafeking. His account of the siege, *Sol. T. Plaatje's Diary*, is one of the important early texts describing the realities of black life in the colonial era. He makes light of Rolong suffering during the siege—by shelling, skirmishing and starvation—but points an unerring and dispassionate finger at the British commander Lord Baden-Powell, of Boy Scout fame. Baden-Powell promised to give back Rolong land after the War in return for their loyal service, while at the same time denying them food in favour of the town's white residents, and using them as messengers with no thought for those that fell into Boer hands. When the siege was raised in 1901, Baden-Powell conveniently forgot the Rolong and let them suffer at the hands of vengeful Boers.

Plaatje's Mafeking experience left him with no illusions about the realities of white rule, whether Boer or British. He became a lawyer and used the position to become one of the country's first national campaigners for black rights. He is best remembered his work as a founding member of the South African Native National Congress (SANNC), which later became the ANC. He was one of the most vocal opponents of the Natives Land Act of 1912, a bill that proposed the eviction of black 'squatters' (i.e the dependents of black farmworkers) from white farms. Plaatje claimed that this was tantamount to imposing slavery on these dependents by forcing them to labour for no wages if they wanted to avoid eviction. Plaatje and other SANNC members also led two delegations to London in 1913 and 1919 to appeal for a complete rethink of colonial policy towards blacks. Both delegations were unsuccessful, but that did not stop Plaatje from campaigning at home until his death in 1932, during which time he devoted his scant hours of leisure to translating works of English literature into Tswana, including Shakepeare plays.

Later activists have accused him of not being sufficiently militant, but for the time Plaatje's achievements were extraordinary. Not only did he manage to persuade Cape Town and Johannesburg publishers to back his work, but he was one of the first black political activists to attain real credibility in the eyes of the colonial authorities and the British government, which in turn did much to establish the black freedom struggle as a worthwhile cause both in South Africa and abroad.

However, for the majority of Tswana people, the 20th century presented a choice between rural poverty or migrant work in the mines. The permanent water sites in their region of the Transvaal were almost all white-occupied by the 1930s and they were unable to support the livestock that had made them rich in earlier times. By 1950 the Tswana had become one of South Africa's poorest groups, a state that the National Party aimed to perpetuate when they declared the seven regions of Bophuthatswana in 1977. The government set up by Pretoria to administer the fragmented 'homeland', some of whose territories were isolated from each other by as much as 300km, did not reflect any real support from the Tswana people as a whole, and the rulers could only stay in power as long as they co-operated excactly with Pretoria's guidelines.

The plan backfired; Bop's government managed to assert some financial, if not political independence from Pretoria after platinum was found in the 'homeland'. By law, the Bop government could legally keep the mining revenues for this mineral which for its own coffers, not South Africa's. Capitalizing on this good fortune, the new Tswana government took advantage of being technically exempt from South Africa's strictly Calvinist anti-gambling laws to open a huge casino at Sun City. The idea of 'homeland' casinos soon took off but Sun City and its new addition, the Lost City, remain one of South Africa's biggest money-spinning operations; with their gambling and mining revenues, the Tswana look set to become a major influence on South African politics once Bop is fully reabsorbed back into the Republic of South Africa.

Sun City and the Lost City

Situated in the western chunk of the two bits of 'Bop' northwest of Pretoria, Sun City and the Lost City comprise a vast pleasure-house of conspicuous consumption, known to most westerners as the place where a few foreign pop acts, such as Elton John, Queen and Black Sabbath, played in defiance of the 1980s sanctions (remember 'I Ain't Going To Play Sun City', a song that came out in 1986). Sun City is an interesting example of the South African contrast between rich and poor; the gaming rooms and one-armed-bandits operate night and day, while outside the perimeter fence many local Tswana live in terrible poverty. And it is not only the white and the wealthy that come to gamble. A common sight on the gaming machines is a poor black gambler throwing hard-earned money into the great Moloch with the fixed intensity of one who cannot afford to lose.

Sun City itself has now been upstaged by the even larger Lost City—an unimaginably expensive complex that claims to recreate the atmosphere of *King Solomon's Mines*, H. Rider Haggard's turn-of-the-century novel based in Southern Africa. Of course it does nothing of the kind, except perhaps to suggest how the book's heroes might have spent their money when they got home. However, the buildings, covered in intricate carving, wood inlay and mosaic are truly beautiful and transcend the Grand Kitsch of their design (see 'Where to Stay'). Suffice to say here that if money is of no object, then a ridiculously expensive night spent at the Lost City should definitely be included in your itinerary. But if your budget is lower, avoid the blander Sun City—go in for a day, lose some money, and then head out for the nearby **Pilanesberg National Park**, © (01465) 5534/5/6/7. Founded amid hushed-up controversy in 1979 (many Tswana people had to be forcibly removed from the site to make way for the park) today's Pilanesberg is one of the best accessible wild areas in the Transvaal, stretching over more than 50,000ha of bushveld. As well as the Big Five there are cheetah, spotted and brown hyena, hippo and croc, and most of the antelope and plains game species. The bird watching is very rewarding, with large raptors such as bateleur and booted eagle, secretary birds, Cape vulture and smaller species such as sunbirds, grey louries, korhraans, bee-eaters and rollers. Guided game hikes with armed rangers are one of the main attractions. These are similar to those in the Kruger National Park, except they do not need to be booked so far in advance. There is a variety of accommodation to suit all budgets.

The Western Transvaal section of Bophuthatswana has two lesser-known game areas: **Madikwe Game Reserve** (booked through Pilanesberg, ✆ (01465) 55354/5/6/7/8/9) is new, covering a huge area north of Mmabatho, on the Botswana border, and is home to the 'Big Five'—almost all its animals were transported from the Kruger National Park in a massive trans-location known as 'Operation Phoenix'—but the reserve is only for those with big budgets (see 'Where to Stay'). **Botsalano Game Reserve**, ✆ (0140) 895 048, lies about 175km west of Pilanesberg and Sun City, north of the capital Mmabatho and its dirt-poor satellite of shanties, thin donkeys and thinner people. Botsalano, by contrast, stretches over 6,000ha of lovely hill country of grassland and wooded kloofs. White rhino, giraffe, sable and waterbuck antelope, wildebeest and zebra are all common, as are the smaller antelope species. Again, there are guided hikes into the bush and a variety of accommodation.

Lotlamoreng Cultural Reserve is far less wild, covering approximately 200ha on the banks of the Lotlamoreng Dam south of Mafikeng. Although officially known as a nature reserve, Montshiwa, as it is known, supports little game bar waterbirds on the dam's shoreline. Instead, the area has been divided into several African show villages supposed to demonstrate the traditional life of South Africa's main black cultures. The Tswana, Zulu, Ndebele, Pedi, Xhosa, Sotho, and Venda villages are manned by local Tswana in traditional gear. While obviously aimed at tourists, Montshiwa is interesting both because it occupies the site of an old mission station (still standing), and for its sheer incongruity with the nearby squatter camps of Mafikeng and Mmabatho. There is no accommodation.

Far to the south (about 150km) along the R47 via the town of Vryburg is the **Taung Heritage Site**, a small set of caves from which some of the earliest-known pre-human anthropoid fossil remains ever found by archaeologists were excavated earlier this century. Like the fossil remains found at Sterkfontein. These belong to the hominid primate *Australopithecus africanus*, one of the 'immediate' (in evolutionary terms) precursors of ourselves. There is a small museum on the site and a history of both the archaeologists and the early pre-men. There is no accommodation, but nearby is the Taung Sun Hotel, ✆ (01464) 41820.

Activities

Gambling: Sun City and the Lost City have gaming tables and one-armed bandits you can play 24 hours a day for an entry fee of between R5–10. Do not expect the same perks that go with the big casinos in the USA, such as free food and booze. Sun City and the Lost City are strictly here to take your money and nothing is free.

Hiking: To soothe the inevitable financial loss, book a guided game walk at Pilanesberg National Park, ✆ (01465) 2405/2379 or Botsalano Game Reserve, ✆ (0140) 895 048. Hiking huts and food are provided.

Where to Stay

expensive

The Palace at the Lost City, ✆ (014657) 30000, is probably the most luxurious (and the most hyped) hotel in South Africa, and certainly the most interesting of the Sun chain. For once a corporate hotel chain has managed to produce something extraordinary, a creation of such overblown kitsch that it is somehow original. Nothing has been stinted; the marble is real, inlays are of carefully selected hardwoods, and the sculptures, from the life-sized elephant in the entrance hall to the carved wooden foliage in the bedrooms, have been skillfully produced. The effect is of a set from one of Cecil B. de Mille's 1930s Hollywood epics. If only it had been built out in the bush instead of attaching it to the car parks, golf courses and tacky Vegas-style nightlife of Sun City, The Palace would truly be a marvel.

Also at Sun City, the **Cascades Hotel**, with indoor fountains, the **Sun City Hotel**, a bland, uninteresting lump of concrete rising from irrigated lawns, and the **Cabanas**, a smaller place set in beautiful gardens, and which for some reason has its own crocodile park, offer plush comfort, but with nothing like the style of the Palace. However, the tariffs are slightly lower and for those intent on gambling it hardly matters what the bedroom's like, for the casinos stay open all night.

For all of Sun City's hotels, the same central reservation telephone numbers applies, ✆ (011) 780 7800, or (012) 325 1416/7/8.

In the **Pilanesberg National Park**, ✆ (01465) 21621 three luxurious private lodges—offer lavish hospitality and guided game drives. Both have swimming pools and are within reach of Sun City. Pilanesberg also has several luxury tented camps which offer a more tranquil experience of the bush. The new **Madikwe Game Reserve**, north of Mmabatho, also has luxury lodges. Book through Pilanesberg (*see* above).

The **Taung Sun**, hard by the Taung Cultural Site, ✆ (01464) 41820 offers the usual expensive/bland luxuries of the Sun chain.

moderate and cheap

Pilanesberg National Park, ✆ (01465) 55354/5/6/7, has two camps at the upper end of the moderate price range, a basic camp site and some shared log cabins that just fall within the cheap range. At **Botsalano Game Reserve**, ✆ (0140) 895 048, there is a permanent tented camp with ablution blocks and cooking facilities, and a cheaper camp site.

Neighbouring Countries

Many travellers to South Africa make forays into the neighbouring counties to the north. This can often be done without much effort—for example, Johannesburg is only a few hours from the eastern Botswana border, the Eastern Transvaal and Swaziland give convenient access to Mozambique, Zimbabwe lies just over the Limpopo River at the top of the Northern Transvaal, and anyone visiting the Kalahari region is within reach of Namibia and western Botswana.

The following short chapter is not intended as a detailed guide, but merely as a summary of the neighbouring countries, some suggestions for the easiest ways to get around them and the best places to go.

Zimbabwe

This large, roughly circular country immediately north of the Transvaal lies between the Limpopo River in the south and the Zambezi to the north. Landlocked, it borders Mozambique to the east and Bostwana to the west. Zambia sits above it.

Like the Northern and Eastern Transvaal, Zimbawe is a summer rainfall area composed of a semi-temperate highveld plateau in the west, which falls over a high escarpment to an eastern, sub-tropical lowveld plain. At the far eastern edge of this plain, marking the border with Mozambique, rise high, cool, forested mountains cut with fast-flowing rivers and waterfalls. Although the country's agriculture is productive and sometimes intensive, much of the landscape has survived intact, and Zimbabwe is very rich in wildlife. Its capital, Harare, lies in the north/centre of the country (an area whose bushveld is dotted with strange, balancing rock formations), and is the only city of any size, though the large regional town of Bulawayo in the southwest is growing rapidly. Zimbabwe has two main ethnic groups, the **Mashona** and the **Matabele** (in the east, descended from the Ndebele people of South Africa), though smaller groups like the **Tsonga** (Shangaan) are also present. Popular with travellers for its safety, its diverse landscapes and wildlife, and its low cost (foreigners will get a much better exchange rate here than in any other southern African country), Zimbabwe has an established tourist infrastructure, but still offers possibilities for isolation and immersion in primeval landscapes.

Getting There

visas

Visitors from Commonwealth countries or from Norway, Sweden, Switzerland, the USA or Japan do not require a visa, only a passport. All other nationals (including South Africans, though plans are afoot to change this) must obtain a visa before travelling.

health

Sizeable areas of Zimbabwe are malarial, particularly the game-rich Zambezi Valley and lowveld, and on no account should you travel here without anti-malaria tablets. You should also avoid splashing about in the shallows of lakes or rivers, as bilharzia is endemic in Zimbabwe. However, should you contract the disease, a course of antibiotics will put you right. Tsetse-fly can be a problem in the Zambezi valley and parts of the lowveld, but local people will tell you where, and the appropriate clothing (long-sleeved shirts and long trousers) is generally sufficient protection. Tetanus, polio, typhus and cholera shots are worth getting before you travel. Drinking water in towns, farms and national parks/reserves is safe, otherwise use purification tablets. Travellers must also be aware that all across southern Africa HIV and AIDS are rife, and due precautions should be taken.

currency and exchange

Zimbabwe's currency is the Zimbabwe Dollar. Its exchange rate is roughly ZWD$12 to £1, ZWD$6 to US$1 or DM 1. Visitors may import any amount of foreign currency, but are obliged to declare it on a currency form upon arrival; this must be kept and surrendered at departure, complete with details of all currency transactions made. If you lose the form, or do not surrender it, you may only take out foreign currency to the equivalent of ZWD$20. Many people will offer you black market rates of exchange far higher than the official rate. Beware of street dealers, who may be undercover policemen, and if not, are likely to swindle you.

Tourist Information

Zimbabwe Tourist Board in Harare at the corner of Jason Moyo Avenue and Fourth Street, ✆ (14) 706 511. Next door is the **National Parks Board Office**, ✆ (14) 792 786 (useful for for booking accommodation in game reserves, as well as hiking/riding trails).

Getting Around

by car

If you are reading this guide before leaving for Africa, consult **Safari Drive**, a specialist UK-based company, ✆ (071) 622 3891, who offer fully equipped 4x4 vehicles that can cope with the roughest off-road terrain. However, the company will not hire out vehicles casually, and offer a full package, including itineraries (the owners are local experts on the best of remote southern Africa). Knowing the countries so well, Safari Drive can tell you the exact state of roads, difficulty or ease of local terrain etc, and taking one of their vehicles gives you the option of travelling across all the Southern African borders (whereas most vehicles hired in Zimbabwe and Botswana are not allowed across borders). Tariffs are expensive unless shared between a group of 4 or more, which brings the price to within the moderate range.

If you are already in Zimbabwe, reliable car hire is generally expensive, and apart from a private company in Bulawayo called **Transit**, ✆ (19) 76495, you are limited to the three main firms, Avis, Hertz and Europcar. These have offices in all the main towns, but here are their phone numbers in Harare: Avis, ✆ (14) 720 351, Hertz, ✆ (14) 793 701 and Europcar, ✆ (14) 752 559. If on a low budget it is better to take a bus or train to near where you want to explore and either hike (if

in the mountains) or join a safari company and let them take you into the game
reserves—safari companies operate at all budgets (*see* below).

by bus

Several bus companies run north to Harare from Johannesburg, including;
Greyhound, ✆ (011) 333 2136, **TransLux** and **Transtate**, ✆ (011) 774 3313
for both. Within Zimbabwe, most white tourists use the **Express Buses**, ✆ (14)
702 221, and **Blue Arrow Coaches**, ✆ (14) 729 514, which operate between all
the main towns, but nowhere else. For the more adventurous, an extensive and
cheap local bus network connects all the towns, and you can often get to within
striking distances of nature reserves this way. These are friendly, seldom ridiculously crowded and can often be flagged down from the highway. The only
problem is that they tend to pick-up/set-down in the township markets on the
fringes of towns, involving a long walk or a taxi ride (theft can be a problem here
but not mugging). For information, ring the Zimbabwe Tourist Board in Harare,
✆ (14) 706 511.

by train

A daily service leaves Johannesburg for Harare via Masvingo, ✆ (011) 773 5878
for details. Within Zimbabwe, passenger services run from Harare north to Victoria
Falls, west to Bulawayo (and on to Gaborone in Botswana) east to Mutare in
the Eastern highlands and down to Masvingo in the lowveld. Telephone the
Zimbabwe Tourist Board office in Harare for details, ✆ (14) 706 511.

by safari company

For general safaris try **Safari Par Excellence**, ✆ (14) 720 527/736 674, on the
3rd Floor, Travel Centre, Jason Moyo Avenue, Harare, and at Shop 4 in the
Pumula Centre at Victoria Falls, ✆ (13) 4424/4510, and **Shearwater Safaris** in
the Karigamombe Centre on Samora Machel Avenue, Harare, ✆ (14) 735 712/5.
Both companies are well-recognized as being both experienced and reliable. You
can book all kinds of safaris through them, involving simple tours and game drives,
access to remote bush lodges, walking, riding, white-water rafting or canoeing.
Prices vary from upper moderate to expensive. A smaller affair, **Goliath Safaris**, in
Harare, ✆ (14) 708 843, specializes in canoeing safaris down the Zambezi River (4
or 5 days) with superb game and bird-watching, fishing, and accommodation at the
end of each day in tents with mosquito nets. All food is provided and wine is
served with dinner. **Zambezi Wilderness Safaris**, in Victoria Falls, ✆ (13) 4417,
caters for small-group safaris in its own isolated luxury camp in Chizarira National
Park in the Zambezi Valley. Game drives, walks and cultural trips to the villages of
the local Batonka people are offered.

Main Attractions

Victoria Falls, in the extreme northwest of the country, rank as one of the primary natural
wonders of the world. The wide Zambezi plunges over the highveld escarpment in a kilo-
metre-wide horseshoe, a vast rush of spray and thunder. Safaris into the nearby Victoria

Falls National Park and Zambezi, and trips into neighbouring Zambia, Namibia and Botswana (whose borders are all within 60km of this area) are easy to arrange. **Lake Kariba**, in the Zambezi Valley east of Victoria Falls, is a man-made lake about 60km, dotted with wooded islands that are home to large game populations. Safaris in tented camps on Kariba's islands, or island-hopping in a houseboat, are now firmly established on the African tourist itinerary. Fishing for the fearsome-toothed tiger fish, reckoned to be one of the world's best game fish for fighting, is a tradition here. **Mana Pools**, further east along the Zambezi Valley is another game area, equally well-known for its series of freshwater lakes fringed by lush, sub-tropical forest. Walking and canoeing safaris are offered. In the south-eastern lowveld, the ruined city of **Great Zimbabwe** (also known as the Zimbabwe Ruins), sits atop a jutting granite massif near the town of Masvingo. Built in the Middle Ages by the ancestors of the modern Mashona people, Great Zimbabwe thrived on the gold, ivory and slave trade with visiting traders, before falling into decline and being abandoned at some point in the early Modern period.

In Matabeleland, west of Harare, is the massive **Hwange National Park**, renowned for its large concentrations of game and for walking safaris. South of Hwange, are the **Matopas Hills** of Motobo National Park, just southwest of Bulawayo. Another isolated massif, the Matobos have spectacular rock outcrops resembling the human cranium (Matopas means 'bald head' in Ndebele, and the Matabele king Mzilikazi was supposed to have christened the hills with this name when he arrived with his people from the Transvaal in the 1850s). Cecil Rhodes, the mining magnate and empire builder who opened Zimbabwe to British rule in the 1890s, is buried here, and the hills are criss-crossed with walking and riding trails. Finally, the **Eastern Highlands**, as the uplands marking the border with Mozambique are known, provide temperate relief from the hot plains, with good forest and montane heath. Hiking and accommodation in old colonial hotels are available at **Nyanga National Park** in the north, while the south offers more rugged fare at **Chimanimani National Park**, amidst similarly spectacular scenery.

Tourist Traps

Victoria Falls are a terrible tourist trap. Although scenically splendid, the area has lost much of its wild feel due to the vast numbers of foreign visitors, fast-food outlets, illegal money-changers, bars full of drunken backpackers, and general atmosphere of money-making. However, no one should miss seeing the Falls if only for a day, and the town is the place from which to book the superb Zambezi white-water rafting trips, said to be the best in the world (*see* below).

Hidden Delights

The **white-water rafting trips** on the Zambezi below Victoria Falls are a thundering, roaring confusion of speed, adrenaline and soaking spray. Several companies in town offer trips in large inflatable canoes, as well as a couple on the Zambia side (although veterans say that the Zimbabwe companies have more spectacular routes). The best place to book is at the information centre at entrance of the huge camp site on the town's main though-road. The safety record of all the companies is exemplary.

The **Charara Safari Area** and **Matsusadona National Park**, in the Zambezi Valley at the eastern edge of Lake Kariba, and just west of Mana Pools combine the open water and atmospheric ghost forest (dead trees sticking up from the water) of Kariba, with the dense, sub-tropical, game-rich bushveld. Fewer tourists make it to these reserves, and game often wanders freely through the camps. However, you are allowed to walk (at your own risk), and a morning's wander through the rustling, living bush, knowing it to be populated with such beasts as lion, buffalo and elephant, is an intense thrill—always walk in a group so that most game will avoid you. Do not walk at night, when lions are hunting, and beware of crocodiles on the lake shore. **Chizarira National Park** at the western end of the Zambezi valley, offers accompanied walking trails in big game country (with an armed ranger) of 1–10 days. A quieter pleasure is to walk amid the magnificent **Vumba Mountains**, southwest of Mutare in the Eastern Highlands, whose hanging, evergreen forests are cut with marked trails. Just northeast of Mutare is the **M'tarazi Falls National Park**, also part of the eastern Highlands, whose famed waterfall hurtles over a 762m cliff, its spray creating a cloud forest alive with birds and monkeys.

Where to Stay

 The following is just a selection from the many hundreds of lodges, guest houses, hostels etc offered in Zimbabwe. Most are perfectly adequate, and travellers can normally be confident of finding accommodation at all budgets. All the national parks and reserves listed above offer parks board accommodation (again, usually at three budgets), or have hotels nearby.

expensive/moderate

In **Glen Lorne** suburb, 20 minutes from Harare's centre, is the **Imba Matombo Guest House**, ✆ (14) 464201, a large, thatched family mansion with tennis, pool with a hilltop view and a wide verandah looking onto large gardens. Just outside the capital is **Landela Lodge**, ✆ (14) 702 634. Set in semi-wild farmland (with abundant small game), Landela offers riding and walking as well as trips into the city. The lodge is a handsome thatched bungalow surrounded by pleasant gardens. To avoid the crush of people at Victoria Falls, try **Masuwe Lodge**, ✆ (as for Landela), a private wildlife estate bordering the Zambezi National Park, 5 minutes' drive from town, with a waterhole regularly visited by big game. Game drives are also offered, and accommodation is in en suite thatched cabins with teak game-viewing platforms. Also near Victoria Falls is **Camp Mukuni**, ✆ (113) 4424/4510, in the secluded Batoka Gorge, 25km downstream of the Falls. You reach the lodge by raft and eat in the open on a sandy beach by the Zambezi. The camp has hot showers and flush toilets. In the middle of Lake Kariba is **Spurwing Island**, ✆ (161) 2466, whose permanent tented camp surrounds a central gazebo of bamboo and thatch. Game wanders through the camp at night and the daytime game-viewing is offered from shaded rafts that cruise from island to island. A guided 3-day game-hike into the nearby Matusadona Mountains is also offered. Accommodation at expensive and moderate rates.

In the Vumba Mountains near Mutare in the Eastern Highlands, the **Inn on the Vumba**, ✆ (12) 60722/81025 has en suite rooms or thatched cottages at three budgets. Further north, at Nyanga, is the **Pine Tree Inn**, ✆ (129) 25916/388, an old-fashioned hotel with a colonial feel, whose tariffs are at the upper end of the moderate scale. Also upper-moderate is the excellent tented camp known as **The Hide** in Hwange National Park, whose tents surround a thatched boma on a waterhole, where hides give superb opportunities for bird and game photography. Book via the office in Harare, ✆ (14) 797 3814.

cheap

Although budget travellers to Zimbabwe should be prepared to camp (most towns, national parks and game reserves have secure camp sites with ablution blocks), there are many good hostels. The **Pawpaw Lodge** in Harare, ✆ (14) 724 337, offers good, comfortable budget accommodation with a choice of dormitory bunks or double rooms, as does the (often crowded but fun) **Sable Lodge**, ✆ (14) 726 017, on Selous Avenue. Also try the **Backpackers' Con-x-shon**, ✆ (14) 507 4115, **Kopje Lodge**, ✆ (14) 790 637, which has a wood oven for making pizzas, or **Peterborough Lodge**, on Peterborough Street (no phone). In **Bulawayo**, try the **Youth Hostel**, ✆ (19) 76488 on the corner of Twelfth Avenue and Townsend Road, offering dorms. Otherwise, **Shaka's Spear** on Leopold Takawira Avenue (19) 61385, offers cheap and cheerful dorms and rooms.

In the **Eastern Highlands** is the **Heaven Mountain Lodge** at Chimanimani (no phone), which advertises itself as a 'home for the impossibly groovy', and the Cloud Castle at Vumba (no phone). In the town of **Mutare** there is a fair amount of choice: the **Border Home** on Jason Moyo Drive, ✆ (12) 63346, the **Mutare Guest House**, ✆ (12) 60467 on Herbert Chitepe Street, **Drifter's**, on Harare Drive, ✆ (12) 62930, **Peter Mcintyre**, on Livingstone Road, ✆ (12) 63968, or **Ann Bruce** on 4th Street, ✆ (12) 63569. In **Kariba**, the **MOTH** camp site (no phone) also offers permanent tents and cottages and rooms. Down in the lowveld in **Masvingo**, try the **Backpackers' Rest** above the 'Take Away Foods' place in the town centre, ✆ 63960/63282 or **Clovelly Lodge**, who you can phone for a pick-up, ✆ 64751.

Botswana

Landlocked like its neighbour Zimbabawe, Botswana comprises a vast swathe of arid, sandy thornveld (the Kalahari) in the south, and a lusher mixture of bushveld and mopane woodland giving way to the permanent marshland of the Okavango Delta in the north. This wetland is one of the world's great natural wonders—a river (the Kavango) that empties not into the sea, but into the desert, creating a vast underground water reserve for the whole Kalahari, which is why this apparently arid region can support grass and tree cover, and thus fairly dense animal life, despite an almost total lack of surface water.

Away from the area immediately surrounding the capital, Gaborone , the southern part of Botswana is very sparsely populated. Vast herds of game used to move at will across the entire country until about 10 years ago, when large areas of the Kalahari were marked out as cattle ranches and fenced. This has had a disastrous effect on game outside the conserved regions, as animals unable to get across the fences while migrating to permanent water sites wandered back and forth in their tens of thousands until they died. The government even wanted to fence off sections of the Okavango Delta for cattle ranching, and were only blocked by Greenpeace and the resistance of local fishermen.

Fortunately for the wildlife, vast areas of Botswana are still actively conserved and game can move freely between these areas and the surrounding country. Populations of all the indigenous species are still high, and any trip to Botswana will centre almost entirely around visiting wilderness areas and game-viewing, as the country has little to vary its predominantly flat landscapes besides the spectacular fauna that inhabit them. The major drawback from a traveller's point of view is that the country's few roads, and high tariffs within reserves, put it outside the reach of those on a very low budget.

Unless you have a good 4x4 and know how to cope with deep sand (apart from a few immediately around the capital, the country's only tarred roads run between Gaborone, Francistown, Kasane and Maun), travel via an experienced safari company is a must, except for simply crossing the 60km northern strip (a good dirt road) between Namibia and Zimbabwe via Chobe Game Reserve. However, seeing the country by safari company is not as restricting as it sounds, for they have the expertise to get into the remote areas and, once you have committed yourself to being looked after, whether being guided in boats (often *mokoros*, or dugout tree-trunk canoes), on foot, or in a 4x4, you are free to enjoy this wild country without having to deal with the hassles of getting yourself across it.

Getting There

visas

Members of Commonwealth countries do not require a visa to enter Botswana, with the exception of India, Nigeria, Ghana and Mauritius (heaven knows why). No visa is needed for travellers from the EU countries, nor from the USA, Denmark, Austria, Switzerland, Norway, Sweden, Finland, Luxembourg, Lichtenstein or Israel.

currency

Botswana's currency is the Pula, whose exchange rate at the time of writing was roughly 4 Pula to £1, or 2 Pula to $US1, or DM1.

health

The north of Botswana is highly malarial, and should not be entered by those without anti-malaria tablets. Otherwise, health precautions are as for Zimbabwe (*see* above).

by car

As previously stated, Botswana has only two long-distance tarred roads. One starts from Gaborone in the south, heads north to Francistown near the Zimbabwe border and then forks, one branch going to Maun, at the southeastern end of the Okavango Delta, and the other up to Kasane, at the southeast end of Chobe National Park. Other roads within the country vary from reasonable dirt to barely passable sand—which can turn to thick mousse during the summer rains. Those wishing to seriously explore Botswana independently will need a 4x4, and must take their own fuel, as away from the country's few main towns, petrol can be impossible to find.

Before going, you can arrange a fully equipped vehicle and itinerary through the London-based company **Safari-Drive**, ✆ (071) 622 3891 (*see* 'Zimbabwe' for details). Otherwise, private vehicle hire, reckoned to be better than hiring from the main companies (whose vehicles, some travellers report, are sometimes badly serviced) may be found through **Bushlink 4x4 Hire** in Gaborone, ✆ (09267) 371 480. However, bear in mind that small vehicle hire in Botswana is expensive (i.e Avis or Hertz), and that their use is limited to the few good roads. Travelling into any wild area is better done via a safari company—choices for which exist at all budgets (*see* below).

by light aircraft

Air Botswana offers fairly low-priced internal flights (for example P930 Maun/Gaborone rtn), with much cheaper excursion deals for a maximum of 21 days. It is worth considering this rather than hiring a vehicle, if you want to get from, say Johannesburg or Gaborone, up to the points from which safaris leave, such as Maun and Kasane, as the distances are very long, and vehicle hire expensive. The Air Botswana head office is at the airport in Gaborone, ✆ (09267) 314 518.

by bus

Regular buses connect Gaborone with Maun, Serowe, Francistown, Kasane and Victoria Falls, all in the east side of the country. Public transport into the rough roads and empty spaces of the west is non-existent. For details of services, call the knowledgeable **Kudu Travel Agency**, ✆ (09267) 372 224 for details of the various bus companies and their timetables.

by train

Botswana's only rail service is a daily route to/from Johannesburg and Harare via Francistown and Bulawayo (though you can change at Bulawayo and head north to Victoria Falls). This is grindingly slow but quite cheap, and the old railway carriages date from pre-independence days, with green leather and polished wood—a little grubby, but atmospheric. You are bound to get into conversation with the local traders, who appear miraculously from the apparently empty bush every time the train stops (inexplicably) in the middle of nowhere. Again, reservations can be made through **Kudu Travel Agency** (*see* above) rather than trying to phone the station in Gaborone.

by safari company

Pre-booking before you leave home is a good idea. If travelling from England, Europe or North America try **Okavango Tours and Safaris** in London, ✆ (081) 343 3283, who take people into Moremi and Chobe from Maun and cater for all budgets. They have another office in Johannesburg, ✆ (011) 785 5549. Also in Johannesburg, at the top end of the price scale, **Wilderness Safaris**, ✆ (011) 884 1458/4633, take people into Chobe and Moremi and also into the restricted Central Kalahari Game Reserve from Maun, via Makgadikgadi Pan Game Reserve, during April (the end of the rains) when the large game migrations are on. **Penduku Safaris** (also in Johannesburg, ✆ (011) 883 4303 and similarly expensive), take people into the southern part of the Central Kalahari to look for the scattered groups of San hunter/gatherers still living there.

A little cheaper are the guided game-walking trips in the Tuli Block offered by **Clive Walker Safaris**, also in Jo'burg, ✆ (011) 453 7645/6. Lower budget deals can be booked through two other South Africa-based companies, **Drifters**, ✆ (011) 888 1160, **Gametrackers**, ✆ (011) 886 1810 and **Karibu**, ✆ (031) 839 774. Back in Botswana itself, **Sitantunga Safaris** in Maun, ✆ (09267) 660 570 offer a much cheaper, self-catering deal for trips into the Okavango. **Tula Safaris**, also in Maun, ✆ (09267) 660 307, offer trips into most areas at most budgets and **Lloyd Wilmot Safaris**, again in Maun c/o Ensign Agencies, ✆ (09267) 660 351 also has a good reputation, running remote camps in both Chobe and Moremi. The cheapest safaris are also booked via **Ensign Agencies** (*see* above) and comprise a DIY deal whereby you are provided with a *mokoro* and guide, but must supply your own food and equipment. **Oddballs Camp**, on Chief's Island in Moremi, caters for budget travellers (though you have to fly in) and can be booked through **Okavango Tours and Safaris** in Maun, ✆ (09267) 660 220.

Main Attractions

The **Okavango Delta** is undoubtedly Botswana's greatest tourist attraction, and rightly so. Its vast area of wetland (often of the purest, crystal water) supports a large game population, protected by the huge **Moremi Wildlife Reserve**, from whence game can migrate freely to the equally large **Chobe National Park** in the bushveld country further east. The rare sitatunga antelope, a shy, spiral-horned relative of the bushbuck, lives at Moremi. Its extremely wide-splayed hooves and light body weight allow it to walk on the matted reed-beds of the dense swamps without sinking. Other semi-aquatic antelope like lechwe and kob also occur in large numbers, along with the more usual African plains game and large predators. Birdlife is abundant. Moremi has no parks board accommodation (beyond designated camping sites with no facilities), only several permanent camps run by private companies, most of them expensive, with a few cheaper lodges (*see* above). A few 4x4 tracks can be travelled on during the winter dry season, but it is highly unwise to enter the reserve unaccompanied, as it is easy to get lost, and several people have entered and not come back. The best way to see the delta is by *mokoro* canoe, with a game guide, and most lodges and/or safari companies can arrange this. Chobe is easier and safer to get around in independently. The public road running across its northern section (the Namibia/Zimbabwe road) is passable for ordinary vehicles, as is the road between Sedudu and the Ngoma Gate, but the rest of the reserve is only accessible by 4x4. There is parks board accommodation (expensive except for the camp sites, which have ablution facilities). However, Chobe is known for its huge herds of elephants, and for this reason it is recommended that you do not drive at night.

Tourist Traps

Maun, the town at the southeast edge of Moremi, is an unavoidable tourist trap, as almost all travellers to the delta must pass through here in order to book guides, lodges and safaris. However, Maun is still very small, and not unpleasantly developed. In fact, it has something of a pleasant 'edge of civilization' feel, and a generally happy atmosphere of people anticipating going into the beautiful delta, or coming out of it, elated after their adventure. By contrast, many travellers that the author spoke to complained of a less than jovial atmosphere at some of the expensive bush camps in Chobe, especially in the luxury **Chobe Game Lodge**, which is the reserve's most convenient place to stay, being astride the Namibia/Zimbabwe road in the northern section of the park.

Hidden Delights

The **Central Kalahari Game Reserve**, in the central/southwest of the country covers an unimaginably large area (about 52,000 square kilometres) of Kalahari thornveld and grassland with almost no surface water to be found and only a few of the roughest, sandy roads. The general public is not allowed in without the express permission of the government. There is good reason for this: this wild territory is still home to some of the last free-living groups of San (bushman) hunter/gatherers, and if the area was overrun with tourists in search of the 'Lost World of the Kalahari', the San's world would soon be irrevocably changed, as has already happened in South Africa and Namibia. However, a very few companies have the right to take limited numbers of people into the Central Kalahari. Try **Wilderness Safaris**, or **Penduku** in Johannesburg (their trips leave from Maun, *see* above for details).

Also very wild, though available for more general exploration, are **Makgadikgai Pans Game Reserve** and the neighbouring **Nxai Pan National Park**. Both can be accessed from the main Gaborone/Maun road, but require a 4x4 to explore. The time to go is during the rains (October to April) when, although you may have to suffer extreme daytime temperatures, the pans that give the reserves their name become shallow lakes, and game from hundreds of miles around congregates around them. Makgadikgadi is typical Kalahari country—dry grassland with camel-thorn trees, but in Nxai, just to the north, mopane woodland and baobab-studded bushveld creep in, attracting elephant, giraffe and zebra, as well as the more usual Kalahari fauna of eland, gemsbok, springbok and blue wildebeest. You can walk freely in both reserves, but be warned, large predators are fairly common, and you should especially avoid walking at night when lion and spotted hyena are hunting. Makgaikgai has no tourist facilities at all (except for the inevitable man at the gate who takes your entrance fee), but Nxai has two camp sites with ablution blocks, though these are not fenced.

In the far southeast of the country, hard by the border with South Africa's Northern Transvaal and Northwest provinces lies the **Tuli Block**, a game-rich area of mixed Kalahari and bushveld country that supports huge herds of game, both inside and outside the area's reserves. In the **Mashatu Game Reserve**, guided walking trails to look (sometimes uncomfortably closely) at the Tuli Block's large elephant herds operate from a tented camp. Other game species, including large predators, are approached and the bird-watching is, reputedly, excellent—especially for those wanting to see large raptors. The trails have to be booked via **Clive Walker Safaris** in Johannesburg (*see* above).

Where to Stay

Like all southern African countries, Botswana has a confusing array of lodges and tented camps to choose from, and some of the larger reserves like Chobe and Nxai Pan have parks board campsites. However, here are a few samples that were recommended to the author by travellers in Botswana.

expensive

Lloyd's Camp in Savuti (the western end of Chobe National Park) has a carrying capacity of 12 people and lies on the banks of the Savuti River. Travellers have reported excellent game photographing opportunities here, and have made good reports about the bush cuisine. Book via Johannesburg (011) 462 5131, otherwise, you can get details via Ensign Agencies in Maun, ✆ (09267) 660 351. For the delta, **Okavango Wilderness Camps**, also based in Maun, offer two expensive camps, one on Chief's Island, in the middle of Moremi, which offers walks and game drives, and another on the water called **Djebe Camp**, offering *mokoro* and raft trips for game viewing. Both camps offer full board, guides etc.

moderate/cheap

Sitatunga Camp, ✆ (09267) 660 570, is 12km from Maun at the edge of Moremi. Self-catering only, you have a choice of furnished tents, thatched chalets, or you can bring your own tent. There are showers, and the owners can organize trips into the delta. While on the road between Gaborone and Maun/Chobe, a good place to break the journey is **Nata Lodge**, near Francistown, ✆ (09267) 611 210, which offers moderate/cheap accommodation in thatched chalets, permanent tents, campsites for your own tent, ablution blocks, and cooking facilities. There is good birdwatching in the surrounding woodland and trips into the game reserves can be arranged.

Oddballs Camp on Chief's Island in Moremi offers very cheap self-catering accommodation and a *mokoro* and guide for the duration of your stay. Book through **Okavango Tours** in Maun, ✆ (09267) 660 220. **Mokoro Excursions**, booked via Ensign Agencies in Maun, ✆ (09267) 660 351, offer a very cheap DIY method of getting into the delta, whereby you are transported to a point where you pick up a *mokoro* and guide, and from then on pay a very cheap daily rate (about P35 per day) for the guide and the boat. However, you must supply *all* your own equipment—tents, food, sleeping bags, first aid, drinks etc. The cost of the transport to the *mokoro* pick-up is added on top. Public camp sites with ablution blocks can be found at Chobe and Nxai Pan National Parks, Khutse Game Reserve (in the far southwest), and Moremi Game Reserve (usually booked up), but bear in mind that only those by Chobe's entrance gates can be reached without a 4x4, and you must have all your own supplies, including petrol.

Namibia

Four times the size of Germany, but with only 1 million people (most of whom live in the far northern province of Ovamboland), Namibia is southern Africa's most enigmatic country. With only five perennial rivers (the Orange, Kunene, Okavango, Zambezi and Chobe), much of it is semi-desert, rising from rocky, blasted plains in the southern/central region to vast, blood-red sand dunes over 1,000 feet high in the vast **Namib Desert**. The north and east of the country is bushveld—most of it all but empty of people, but teeming with game, both inside and outside the official game reserves. The far northeast, **Caprivi**, is dense, sub-tropical forest and mopane bush, whose wildlife migrates to and from the Okavango Delta in neighbouring Botswana. By contrast, the extreme northwest merges into the mountains and dry bush of **Kaokaland**, where the **Ova-Himba** people—herders and hunters—pursue their traditional life despite years of trading with western tourists. To the west of Kaokaland, the desert takes over once more and the sand dunes march directly into the sea along the aptly-named **Skeleton Coast**, which is so barren that no land plant life can exist except in a few narrow valleys.

The desert areas of Namibia are famous for their unique plant and insect life: except for the Skeleton Coast, the deserts support a surprising density of life, from succulent (water holding) plants such as the kaokoboom (giant aloe tree), halfmens (a bulbous upright plant resembling a human), euphorbias and the strange, 1,000 year-old welwitchias (*see* below) to almost invisible desert lichens that live off coastal fog. Insects like the onymacris beetle, which stands upside-down to catch the morning's few drops of dew on its back legs and trickles them down to its mouth, contrast with large fauna such as the gemsbok, found even in the sand-dune country, which can go without water for weeks and reflects the hot sun with its light, almost white coat. In the northern semi-deserts, scattered, migrant populations of elephant and black rhino, and even a few desert lions wander between the water sites. Antelope (mostly springbok and gemsbok, but sometimes kudu and wildebeest) and Hartmann's mountain zebra are common. The bushveld and mopane regions are as game-rich as anywhere in Zimbabwe and Botswana, and support the full range of southern African wildlife.

From a people point of view too, Namibia is extremely diverse, despite its sparse population. The most numerous group are the **Ovambo**, who live in the lush, well-watered Ovamboland region on the central border with Angola. Next-most numerous are the **Kavango** of the Kavango and Caprivi sub-tropical regions of the northeast Windhoek, but the **Herero** are more widely spread. Their married women often wear a distinctive form of dress inherited from the first German missionaries of the 1890s (Namibia was a German colony from 1890–1914, consisting of wide-hooped skirts and head kerchiefs cut from high quality cloth (though this is very heavy for such a hot climate) and resembling mid-Victorian fashion.

In the south and central northwest regions live the **Nama** and **Damara**, descended from the KhoiSan peoples who once inhabited most of western southern Africa, and who were dispossessed almost everywhere except for Namibia through the 19th century. In Bushmanland, to the east, live large groups of **San** (Bushmen). While few live in the traditional hunter-gatherer way anymore, equally few have fully embraced Western ways, and most inhabit a strange borderland of conflicting cultures. Immediately south of Windhoek, most of the land is owned by a mixed-race people known as the **Bastaards**, who, of mixed Khoi and Dutch blood, trekked into this area in the mid-19th century to escape the oppressive racism of South Africa, and established themselves as farmers and hunters in the good grazing lands around the town of **Reheboth**. Namibia's small but wealthy white population is divided between German-speaking descendants of the first colonists of the 1890s, Afrikaners whose families settled in the country after 1914 (when Namibia became South African territory until 1990), or who came in during the apartheid years to work in the civil service, and a few English-speakers. In Windhoek, a large presence of United Nations workers has given the little capital a cosmopolitan air out of keeping with its size.

Getting Around

visas

Travellers from Commonwealth or EEC countries do not require a visa to travel in Namibia, nor do visitors from the USA, Japan, Russia, South Africa, Finland, Switzerland or Brazil.

currency

Namibia's currency is the Namibian Dollar, the exchange rate for which is roughly NMB$4.5 to £1, or NMB$2.25 to US$1 or DM1. American dollars and Deutschmarks are sometimes accepted at the larger hotels and game lodges.

health

Southern Namibia has a dry, healthy climate, but the north and east are malarial, and must not be travelled without anti-malaria pills. Vaccinations as for Zimbabwe and Botswana are advised, and although the Kavango River is supposedly bilharzia-free, swimming in that region is not recommended unless you are assured otherwise by local lodge-owners (who will also tell you where the crocodile-free spots are). Again, as for anywhere in southern Africa, the HIV risk is fairly high, so due precautions should be taken.

For such an underpopulated country, Namibia's road network is surprisingly good. The tarred B1 highway runs north/south along the geographic centre, connecting with the South African N7 that runs due south to Cape Town, and splits east and west at the town of Otavi in the north. The western section runs via Tsumeb across Ovamboland to Ruacana on the edge of Kaokaland, then turns south again as a good gravel road via the strange frontier town of towns of Opuwo and Kamanjab, from where it loops back, as tar, to Otjiwarongo on the B1 south of Etosha. The eastern section heads through the Kavango country via Grootfontein, past Rundu to near the entrance of the Caprivi Game Park (the tar is being extended further east every year), from where it becomes a reasonable dirt road, with some rough patches (but still passable for an ordinary car), heading straight across the Caprivi strip to Chobe in Botswana and Victoria Falls in Zimbabwe. West of Otjiwarngo, a short stretch of tar leads to Okakarara near the Waterberg Plateau. Other tarred roads connect Windhoek with Swakopmund on the coast, and Otjiwarongo (south of Etosha) with Khorixas, at the edge of Damaraland, while south of Windhoek, tarred stretches connect the B1 with Gobabis in Hereroland, Dordabis and Aranos in the border of Namaland and Hereroland, Malatahohe at the edge of the Namib, Luderitz on the southwest coast (south of which is a vast diamond-mining area out of bounds to travellers), and with Ariamsvlei in southeast Namaland, on the road to Upington in South Africa.

Most of the country's dirt roads between towns are fine for ordinary cars (if you do not travel too fast—it is easy to go into a spin on sandy sections), and the visitor to Namibia will only require a 4x4 if travelling into the unsettled areas such as Kaokaland, northern Damaraland and Bushmanland, or the remoter national parks and nature reserves. As with Botswana and Namibia, if you have yet to make your trip, contact **Safari Drive**, ✆ (071) 622 3891, a London-based company that supplies fully-equipped 4x4s and will help you plan your itinerary. Although quite expensive, for 4 or more people the cost falls to within the moderate range. Another British-based company offering 4x4s and itineraries is **Freshtracks**, ✆ (0822) 840 672. Otherwise, car hire in Namibia is generally expensive, especially if you hire through the large companies such as Avis, Hertz or Budget. The big companies have a better reputation for breakdown back-up and vehicle servicing than the small private companies (about 30 of which now operate in Windhoek). However, try **Kessler Car Hire** (which also hires 4x4s), ✆ (061) 33451, **Adventure 4 Hire**, ✆ (061) 226188 and **Imperial** (a South African company), ✆ (061) 35819. While not cheap, these offer slightly lower prices than the mainstream companies, and are said to have very well-serviced vehicles that can take the dirt roads. For vans, minibuses etc, **Camper Hire**, ✆ (061) 22287/ 229918. For hiring a 4x4 (generally very expensive) try **Namib 4x4 Hire**, in Swakopmund ✆ (0641) 61791 and Windhoek, ✆ (061) 220 604, **East End**

Service Station, ✆ (061) 233 869 or **Oryx Tours,** also in Windhoek, ✆ (061) 217 454. For the really adventurous, **off-road motorbikes** can be hired through **Tours for Africa** in Windhoek, ✆ (061) 224 156.

by bus

InterCape Mainliner run twice-weekly services from Cape Town (direct) and Johannesburg (via Upington) to Windhoek, ✆ (011) 333 5281 for details. The services stop within Namibia at Kamanjab (if from Jo'burg), Keetmanshoop, Mariental and Reheboth. InterCape also run a thrice-weekly service to/from Windhoek and Swakopmund. Also three-times per week is an InterCape service from Windhoek north to Tsumeb via Otjiwarongo and Grootfontein. Apart from this, you are limited to **minibus taxis** which go to most towns with an average price of R10 per 100km), but have a high accident rate. Car hire (including sharing lifts via the Publicity Association office, *see* below) or safari companies are the only way to get into the game reserves.

by train

Passenger services from Cape Town and Jo'burg to Windhoek run weekly (stopping at the above towns), but the trip is very slow (over 24 hours), ✆ (011) 773 5878 for details. Within Namibia, apart from the above service, there is a passenger link to Swakopmund, ✆ (061) 228 160 for details.

by safari company

The following companies can organize trips into most regions. Try **Namibia Adventure Safaris**, ✆ (061) 42388, **Afro-Ventures**, ✆ (061) 36276, **Zebra Tours** (useful for budget travellers), ✆ (061) 221 645, **SWA Safaris**, ✆ (061) 37567, **Skeleton Coast Fly-In Safaris**, ✆ (061) 224 248, **Bushland Safaris**, ✆ (061) 33977/32507, **Southern Cross Safaris**, ✆ (061) 37567/51553, **Africa Adventure Safaris**, ✆ (061) 34720, **Charly's Desert Tours**, ✆ Swakopmund (0641) 4341 and **Desert Adventure Safaris** (expensive, but good for Kaokaland and hiking after desert elephant and rhino), ✆ Swakopmund (0641) 4459/2027.

Ballooning safaris are offered by **Namibrand Game Ranch** in the Namib, near Maltahohe, ✆ (061) 36720 and **Namib Sky Adventure Safaris**, ✆ (066632) 5703 or (061) 36276. These are for high-budget travellers only.

A number of South African companies also offer trips into Namibia, usually beginning from Johannesburg (though you can generally join them while in Namibia). The best, in terms of game knowledge and comfort, is probably **Wilderness Safaris**, ✆ (011) 884 1458/4633. More budget-oriented safaris are offered by **Drifters**, ✆ (011) 888 1160, and **Karibu**, ✆ (031) 839 774.

If confused by the amount of choice, or want to organize a hiking/riding or other specialist trip, Windhoek has some very knowledgeable travel agents who can marry your budget with your desires, try **Trip Travel**, ✆ (061) 36880, the **Namib Travel Shop**, ✆ (061) 226 174 / 225 178, or **WTS**, ✆ (061) 37946.

Those with limited or no funds for car hire or safaris can often hitch up with other travellers and split costs. There is a very useful rides/shared safari noticeboard in the **Windhoek Publicity Association** in the main shopping plaza (Post Street Mall) off Independence Avenue, ✆ (061) 290 2050/2092. At the cheapest end of the tour-company scale is **Easy Tours**, who also organize lifts between Zimbabwe, Botswana and Namibia, ✆ Dean (061) 239 615 (24 hrs).

Main Attractions

Second only to East Africa's Serengeti for game concentrations, **Etosha Pans National Park** is now world-famous for wildlife. However, it must be said that the best of the game-viewing is done at night (owing to the hot daytime temperatures) from the main camp, which has a floodlit waterhole. This makes for a rather public spectacle, and if you want to preserve the feeling of being in a wild place, it is better to head for some of the remoter game reserves (*see* below). The **Namib Desert**, inside the enormous Namib Naukluft National Park (one of the largest national parks in southern Africa) has a major attraction, the red dunes of Sossusvlei, which rear up more than 1,000 feet to form a range of sand mountains, red as blood or wine, in a world of wind and silence. Incredibly, gemsbok and springbok still frequent the area, 60km west of the camp site at Sesreim canyon. You must walk the last 4km to the dunes (slow going, but beautiful) if you do not have a 4x4, and then climb to the top of the highest dune. The exhilaration you feel at the top is indescribable, as is the thrill of surfing down the mountain of sand on your bottom. Remember to take water. **Kaokaland**, the deep wilderness of the northwest, and home to the magnificent Ova-Himba people, can only be penetrated by 4x4, either in a hired vehicle (you must be fully equipped and have good maps) or via a safari company. Although there are no reserves, the area is quite game-rich and Kaokaland offers a chance to see southern Africa as it was before white settlement.

Much lusher is the **Caprivi Strip**, whose lodges and reserves (*see* 'Where to Stay') generally adjoin either Kavango or Zambezi rivers, and whose forests and grasslands seem unbelievably green to anyone who has just come from the dry interior. In the south of the country, amid arid, blasted mountains, is the **Fish River Canyon**, which rivals America's Grand Canyon in scale and beauty, and whose floor has a tough 5-day hiking trail, which crosses and re-crosses the fast-flowing river. The **Brandberg** is a lone massif, or miniature mountain range that shoots up from the plains of western Damaraland, and houses a strange set of San (bushman) paintings known as the White Lady (after the central figure), thought to be around 30,000 years old, depicting San *shamans* communicating with the animal spirits. Also in southwest Damaraland is the Spitskoppe, a picturesque set of jagged, conical mountains at whose feet is a dry gravel plain where grow the famous welwitschia plants, whose grotesque shapes—like overgrown, drunken cabbages—sprawl across the desert floor without any visible evidence of life support, somehow drawing sustenance from the hot sand. A cool, green contrast to this is provided by the **Waterberg Plateau**, a game reserve between Windhoek and Etosha (east of Otjiwarongo), whose heights are covered in a dense forest of wild fig and mopane, and whose flat top is home to a variety of game species, including sable antelope and black rhino. There are a variety of hiking trails in the Waterberg, some guided by an armed ranger (in the rhino and buffalo frequented areas), and the camp site and lodge have access to a restaurant and pool halfway up the mountain along a woodland trail.

Tourist Traps

As mentioned above, **Etosha**, while justly famed for its game, is a terrible tourist trap; you are confined to your vehicle at all times when outside the camp (very hot and stuffy) and have to return to the camp by dusk, just as the game is coming out after the heat of the day. Admittedly the floodlit waterhole at the main camp attracts an exciting array of big game through the night, but you will often share the view with several hundred others. While a trip to Namibia would be incomplete without seeing Etosha, it is better to head for the remoter reserves (*see* below). **Swakopmund** is another tourist trap, but a more pleasant one, as you can move around freely and the sea air is refreshing after the fierce heat of the desert. However, it is hard to see the *point* of Swakopmund. Granted, its turn-of-the-century Bavarian architecture is handsome and intriguingly incongruous amid the surrounding desert coast (dunes going right down to the sea), and there is a slightly romantic post-colonial feel to the place, but it is has little to offer apart from provincial small-town life. Unless resting up after a trip through Damaraland or the Namib (these start immediately to the north and south of 'Swakop', respectively), the town becomes rather boring after a day or two of wandering around and eating German cakes.

Hidden Delights

In a country where landscapes are seldom less than spectacular, **Damaraland** stands out as the most beautiful, particularly its northern section, where the silent, red wall of the **Joubertsberg mountains** rises from a vast rocky plain studded with green euphorbia bush. There is something holy about the silence here. Immediately below the mountains' flat-topped summits runs a wall of sheer cliffs carved by wind and frost into a dancing gallery for unfamiliar, ancient gods. This is the land of the desert elephants, incessantly on the move between the few perrenial springs. Black rhino also move through the area, as do a very few lion and leopard, and despite the apparent lack of vegetation, springbok, kudu and gemsbok thrive here; the odd giraffe herd can even be encountered, bending low to browse the stunted mopane trees that somehow grow from the soiless rock.

West of Damaraland and Kaokoland is the **Skeleton Coast**, so barren that of the many ships' crews who have run aground against its empty sands, none has survived the cruel land where they have been washed ashore. This is where the famous 'roaring sands' are found, dunes that moan as the wind moves through them and disturbs the hot air between the grains. The only safe way in here is by a fly-in safari (*see* above)— very expensive, but worth it if you have the money. Otherwise, those with 4x4s can drive up along the beach from the Skeleton Coast National Park entrance north of Swakopmund (via Henties Bay and the Cape Cross seal colony—worth seeing despite the suffocating stench). The southern coast is also worth visiting, or at least the desert just inland from the fishing town of Luderitz, where the **ghost villages**, abandoned turn-of-the-century mining settlements, may be found, their handsome wooden German-style houses preserved by the dry climate, but slowly sinking under the relentless, westward-marching sands.

The more adventurous should take their 4x4s into the little visited western Kalahari region, home to scattered communities of bushmen, some of whom live traditionally, some of whom have turned to cattle ranching (albeit in a half-hearted manner), and a vast array of wild game. In the north is the **Kaudom Game Reserve** (you are only allowed in if you are in a convoy of at least two vehicles), which though lacking any tourist facilities at all, is full to the brim with big game. Kaudom is just south of another little visited region, the **Kavango**. Most people drive across here in a day on their way to Caprivi or beyond and never explore. Yet the side-road down to the **Mahango Game Reserve** has several superb camp sites in the riverine bush, whose boat trips take you through hippo and elephant country into the reserve, through which you can walk at will.

In contrast to this lush country, the arid heights of the **Naukluft Mountains** of the eastern Namib-Naukluft National Park have a 5-day hiking trail, booked through the Wildlife Department people in Windhoek (*see* above). This trail (of which a day-section can also be walked) follows a valley where several freshwater springs (large enough to swim in) bubble from the ground and support, incredibly amid the surrounding dryness, large wild fig trees, vivid green vegetation, giant tadpoles, and dense bush. As you follow this aptly named **Waterkloof Trail**, you startle herds of zebra, kudu, reedbuck and other herbivores, all of whom live in this narrow valley, which is the only place for miles around that can support such a density of animal life. Look up at the valley walls, and you will spot caves whose entrances, if you scramble up to them, are often strewn with bones, betraying the presence of leopards who prey on the ungulates of the narrow valley.

In the semi-desert plain southeast of the Naukluft, is one of the strangest legacies of the colonial era, a castle called **Duwasib** built by a German aristocrat who retired into this desolate region to breed horses. After his death, the castle fell into disrepair and some of the horses established feral populations in the surrounding veld. Now restored and opened as a museum, the castle's horses still live wild on the plains nearby and are now being protected. If you have a 4x4 it is worth going into the veld to try and find them.

Finally, a feature of Namibia that is often overlooked is the tiny capital, **Windhoek**, whose prosperous streets look out on the bare and empty hills of the **Khomas Hochland**. Because of its diverse human population, Windhoek is extremely lively, and has a nightlife out of keeping with its size, with many excellent local bands playing township and African jive, funk and even rock. Bars come and go, and it is worth asking at the Windhoek Publicity Association (*see* above) for what is new. And the moment you feel jaded, you need only go a short distance from the town to be lost in the wild bush of Khomas Hochland, whose guest farms (*see* below) usually offer riding, hiking and game viewing.

Where to Stay
expensive

Etendika Wilderness Camp (book through the Namib Travel Shop in Windhoek, © (061) 226 174), in the magnificent, silent

Joubertsberg Mountains of Damaraland offers a tented camp (for 16 people), guided walks to find desert elephant and rhino and has a telescope set up though which, by night, you can see the rings of Saturn. Slightly more sociable is the nearby **Palmwag Lodge**, on the Khorixas/Sesriem road (book via Swakopmund, ✆ (0641) 4459/2027), set by a waterhole, where the desert elephants come down to drink. Near the Namib (west of Maltahohe) is **Namibrand Guest Ranch**, ✆ (061) 36720/35853, a vast game farm offering hiking, riding and ballooning. **Ndlhovu Lodge**, by the Kavango River south of the Caprivi road on the Popa Falls road, ✆ (0642351) 436, offers luxurious permanent tents and trips—downriver and into nearby Mahango Game Reserve. At the western edge of Etosha, north of the town of Kamanjab, is **Hobatere Lodge**, ✆ (0020 and ask for 2022). A vast private game reserve housing the 'Big Five', the lodge has en suite bungalows, good food, and game drives/walks. On the eastern side of Etosha, north of the town of Tsumeb, is **Mokuti Lodge**, ✆ (0671) 3084, which offers riding, hiking, luxurious accommodation (chalets or en suite rooms) set around a thatched central lodge with a large pool. The restaurant specializes in game. Smaller and more intimate than Mokuti is **Aoba Lodge** (no phone), just 10km east of Etosha's Namutoni Gate, with game viewing at its own waterhole and thatched bungalows set around a small lodge. Just south of Etosha, signposted from the B1, is the very luxurious **Ongava Lodge**, ✆ (06542) 3413, a new private game reserve offering walking, riding and game drives in a vast mopane country stocked with the Big Five. The cuisine at Ongava is particularly good—especially the gemsbok fillet in cranberry sauce, and the rooms, decorated in polished wood and woven tapestry, have their own balconies over looking the bush.

Just outside Windhoek is the **Hetaku Guest Farm**, ✆ (061) 36674, a game ranch offering hikes, photographic safaris (with hides) and camps in the deep bush. In Windhoek itself try **Villa Verdi**, ✆ (061) 221 9664, a very well-run family house recommended by many expensive/moderate budget travellers. In Swakopmund, the **Hansa Hotel**, ✆ (0641) 311 offers colonial-style comfort, as does the **Hotel Sweizerhaus** (though the building is modern), ✆ (0641) 2419, whose **Cafe Anton** is famous for its German cakes and coffee.

moderate

Okonjima Guest Farm, ✆ (0658) ask for 18212, between Windhoek and Otjiwarongo (look out for the signposts on the west of the B1 about 50km north of Outjo) is one of the most remarkable places to stay in the whole of southern Africa. The headquarters of a big cat conservation charity known as Africat (an ambitious project aimed at re-habilitating big cats into ranchland), Okanjima's surrounding bush is home to several varieties of these predators, as well as plains game. Guided walks are a feature of the farm (during which the flora and fauna are identified and explained), but you can also ride. The two tame cheetahs which live in the lodge will come and allow themselves to be cuddled in the morning; Okonjima also has a tame-ish baboon called Elvis and several domesticated warthogs. There are night-time hides where you can look out for leopard, porcupine, pangolin and aardvark.

The food is superb, and the atmosphere generally so friendly and knowledgeable that it is worth spending a few days exploring if you can.

Touch Africa Safaris offer a lodge in the Caprivi, ✆ (067352) and ask for 453, in the lush country near Katima Mulilo, while **Okosongoro Guest Farm**, ✆ (06532) 1721, halfway between Windhoek and Etosha (just north Omaruru) offers comfortable overnight accommodation with game walks/drives. **Namib Naukluft Lodge**, ✆ (061) 63086/7/8, offers good accommodation at the edge of the Namib with excursions to Sossusveli and a pick-up service from Windhoek. Also near the Namib (west of Maltahohe) is **Burgsdorf Guest Farm**, ✆ (06632) 1330, which offers en suite rooms, good venison and local mutton, trips to Sossusvlei and hiking. If you are driving on the B1 highway and need a break, the **Anib Lodge**, near Mariental in the centre of the country, ✆ (0668) and ask for 12421, has a pool, good cooking, farm walks, and bird-watching. On the coast, near Swakopmund, the **Walvis Bay Lagoon Lodge**, ✆ (0642) 4711 offers B&B in an old thatched fisherman's cottage.

In Windhoek, try the **Hotel Pension Cela**, ✆ (061) 226 295, on Bulowstrasse, which has a very German feel, and if in Swakopmund, try the **Hotel Pension Rapmun**, ✆ (0641) 2035, which has a similarly *mitteleuropean* atmosphere.

cheap

Cheap camping and moderate/cheap self-contained chalets can be found in most of the national parks and nature reserves, and can be booked in advance through a central office—contact the **Ministry of Wildlife, Conservation and Tourism** in Windhoek, ✆ (061) 220 241. Be warned: they will generally tell you the camp sites are full, but don't believe them, just show up and you can almost always be accommodated. In Windhoek, the guesthouse at **1 Ernst Weisker Street**, ✆ (061) 222 793, offers three comfortable double rooms. Offering dorms and rooms is the **Cardboard Box**, ✆ (061) 228 994, which also organizes trips to local game reserves and craft markets and offers very cheap car hire. **Marie's B&B** on Diaz Street, ✆ (061) 51787 and **Martin's Guest House** on Jenner Street, ✆ (061) 230 196, also offer dorms and one double room. You might also try the **Traveller's Lodge**, on Bottle Palm Street, Dorado Park, ✆ (061) 36547.

Out in the old 'coloured' township of Khomasdal, the **Eldorado Youth Hostel**, on the corner of Sterling and Austin Streets, ✆ (061) 212 530 offers an alternative look at life in Windhoek. The area is not 100% safe for walking around at night (though it is very safe by South African 'township' standards), but it is friendly, funky, half poor and run-down, half respectable, and there is great live jazz at the local bars. Dorms and double rooms are offered and there is a pool.

Out of Windhoek, excellent cheap camping is offered at **Twyflfontein Campsite** in Damaraland (no phone), just south of the rock paintings, in wooden A-frames or your own tent, at **Palmwag**, central Damaraland, where the desert elephants come down to drink, ✆ Swakopmund (0641) 4459 to book, and at **Sesreim** in northern Damaraland (no phone), also with a choice of A-frames.

The **Opuwo Guest House** (no phone) in the tiny frontier town of Opuwo at the edge the Kaokoveld provides very cheap rooms or cheaper camping in the garden in this extraordinary, friendly town—go to the large wholesale supermarket and ask for the keys. In Kavango, the excellent **Ngepi Lodge** (no phone), off the main Caprivi road, about 16km down the Popa Falls dirt road towards Mahango Game Reserve, offers riverside camping in A-frames where hippos graze at night and hyenas cackle in the dark. In Caprivi itself, **Hippo Lodge**, ✆ (067352) 684 or 685, offers cheap camping and moderate/cheap bungalows a few kilometres east of Katima Mulilo. In Swakopmund, the **Swakopmund Municipal Bungalows** (no phone), at the southern end of Roon Street, provide very cheap, very basic but comfortable chalets with showers that will seem like heaven after a few dusty weeks on the road. Similar fare is offered at the **Luderitz Rest Camp** on Diaz Street in Luderitz, ✆ (06331) 3351. Near Karibib, in the Swakop River Valley is the **Tsaobis Leopard Nature Park**, ✆ (062252) 1304, with moderate/cheap chalets set amid wild country that is good for hiking.

Mozambique

Since the end of Mozambique's savage civil war in the early 1990s, more and more travellers have been trickling into this rich, beautiful, yet shattered country, which is beginning to get back on its feet after years of bloodshed, disaster and famine. Most of this vast country is still wild and 'undiscovered' in tourist terms, and although various projects are underway to re-open the vast game reserves of the interior, the only existing tourist facilities are in the capital, **Maputo**, and along the coast as far north as the Tanzanian border. A beautiful city despite the ruin and decay caused by the long war, Maputo is a shattered gem of Portuguese colonial architecture, whose rounded turrets and Latin decoration suit the tropical langour of the place. Most people head straight for the tropical islands just offshore which, along with coral reefs, colourful birdlife, dugongs (manatees—one of the world's rarest mammals), dolphins, whales and big-game fishing, also offer well-equipped lodges with restaurants, bars etc.

Apart from this, some travellers visit Beira, further north up the coast from Maputo (but lacking in most tourist facilities except for a few hotels), or use the area of northwest Mozambique known as the **Tete** corridor to pass between Zimbabwe and Malawi. However, this road is sometimes troubled by bandits or guerillas and it is worth getting local information as to the current situation before using this route.

On no account wear any army surplus or camouflage gear while in Mozambique, as mercenaries still operate in some areas and the odd traveller has been shot or arrested for making this mistake in the past.

Recently a good, if necessarily limited guidebook has been published—the *Guide to Mozambique*, by Bernhard Skrodzki, published by Bradt, UK, 1994, and it is worth picking up a copy for its recommended walks around Maputo, restaurants and tips on getting into the interior.

visas

All nationals (except Malawians) require a visa before travelling to Mozambique. You can either do this through an agent (*see* below), or through the Pretoria or Mbabane (Swaziland) embassies, ✆ (012) 343 7840 and (012) 68 42 581 respectively. Visas cost about R35 at the time of writing and take up to 9 working days to process (although agents sometimes procure them more quickly) and you will need to submit two passport photographs with your application form.

currency

The Mozambiquan currency is the **Metical**, and its exchange rate to the rand is roughly M1,500–1,800 to R1. Almost all hotels and lodges demand payment in rands or US dollars, but to buy groceries, souvenirs etc you will need local currency. To avoid bureaucratic hassle, fill in a currency declaration form at the border post when you enter, and keep a record of your transactions to show when you leave.

health

Malaria is the greatest risk here, so visitors to the country must take anti-malaria tablets. Apart from this, vaccinations are recommended as for Zimbabwe and Botswana (*see* above), and some doctors also recommend a yellow fever shot. As everywhere in southern Africa, there is an appreciable risk of HIV, so take due precautions.

Getting Around

by car

This is the only way to get around, although your route is limited to the east/west highway between Komaatipoort in South Africa's Eastern Transvaal or Namaacha in Swaziland and Maputo. The road is in reasonable condition, but you should fill up with petrol as you cross the border (one tank will see you through to Maputo with ease). Otherwise, driving off into the interior is very dangerous, whether from bandits, poor roads and worse drivers, or old mine fields (with the exception of the road across the Tete Corridor and the road from Maputo up to Beira). Travellers wanting to visit the islands off the north coast must book through a Johannesburg agent and fly in (the agents arrange this) from Johannesburg's Lanseria airport. To hire a car in Maputo, ring **Hertz**, ✆ (81) 465534 or 33172/3 or 491 003, or **Avis**, ✆ (83) 465 497 or 465 140. A small car costs around R50/day.

by public transport

Apart from minibuses (black taxis) there is little in the way of public transport, and unless you speak Portuguese you will not get far except on the simplest routes, such as across Tete, or between Maputo and Beira. If you want to explore inland Mozambique, you will have to stay awhile in Maputo and either pick up rides from travelling businessmen (you will meet them in the hotels) or garner sufficient local information and enough Portuguese to set off independently.

Probably the most knowledgeable is the **Mozambique National Tourist Company** in Johannesburg, ✆ (011) 339 7275/7281, who organize trips into Bazaruto, Magaruque and Benguerra Islands near Maputo and up to Pemba Island near the Tanzanian border. They can also arrange car hire and accommodation at all budgets in Maputo or Beira. Also helpful are **Mozambique Hassle-Free** in Maputo itself, ✆ (81) 400 628 or 401 246 or 744 000. **Benguerra Island Lodge** off Maputo has a contact number in Jo'burg that arranges travel, visas and booking, ✆ (011) 483 2734/5.

Where to Stay

expensive

Most of the island lodges booked through the above agencies fall into the expensive category (though this includes the flights in and out). In Maputo, the old colonial **Polana Hotel**, on Julio Nyere Avenue, ✆ (81) 491 001/2/3/4/5/6/7, is ridiculously expensive (over US$200 per person per night) and although you are pampered, it seems silly to pay such prices for something so ordinary as a bed for the night and a smallish breakfast. A little cheaper, but still over $US100 per night is the **Andalucia Hotel** on Patrice Lumuduba Avenue, which also offers luxurious comfort, ✆ (81) 423 051/2/3/4, as does the **Kaya Kwanga Hotel** on Joao de Castro Avenue, ✆ (81) 492 215. Falling within the South African expensive range is the **Mozambiquan Hotel** on Filipe Samuel Magata Avenue, ✆ (81) 429 252 and the **Tourisma Hotel** on 25 de Setembro Avenue, ✆ (81) 426 253.

moderate/cheap

In Maputo, the **Tivoli Hotel**, also on 25 de Setembro Avenue, ✆ (83) 422 005/6/7 is moderately priced, while the **Burger Inn** on Marginal Avenue, ✆ (83) 455211, offers good, cheap B&B. In **Beira**, the **Ambassador Hotel**, ✆ (83) 323 121/3, the **Hotel Mozambique**, ✆ (83) 325 011, and the **Hotel Infante**, ✆ (83) 323 42, fall within the moderate/cheap category. Very low budget travellers can find cheap camping near the lodges of the islands just off Mozambique (you cross by ferry, arranged through any of the hotels), and can negotiate a small tariff from the lodge owners. Cars should be left at the larger Maputo hotels, which have secure parking. Also in Beira is the **Bem Vindo**, known for cheap backpacker accommodation, set in the street just behind the Estroil Hotel, Macuti, just 3 minutes' walk from the beach. Further north in Xai-Xai is a campsite, the **Parque de campismodo**, a reputed paradise for fishing and diving; dormitories should be ready in 1995.

Afrikaans

A word on pronounciation: 'ou' (as in 'Oupa', meaning 'grandfather') is pronounced 'oh'; 'oo' (as in 'kloof') is pronounced 'oo-a'; 'w' is always pronouced as an English 'v', while the Afrikaans 'v' is always pronounced as an English 'f'. If a 'j' is used in a word's spelling (as in 'kopje') it is almost always silent, unless it links to two distinct syllables, when it becomes an English 'y', for example 'bobbejaan' (meaning baboon) is pronounced 'bob-e-yarn'; an 'a' is usually pronounced as a long 'ar' (as in Sara); a 'y' used as a vowel (as in 'Strydpoortberg'— is pronounced as a long 'a' (as in 'hay'); if a word ends in 'dt', you only pronounce the 't'; a 'tj' or 'ty' (as in Embotyi), is usually pronounced as an English 'k', and the preceding 'o' sounds more like 'oy' as in 'boy'.

An irritating habit among South Africans can be that they begin every sentence with 'No'. This does not mean that they are disagreeing with you. Using the the word is merely a formalized slang method for starting a sentence that is completely neutral, and developed from the Afrikaans *ja-nee* ('yes/no')—a traditionally equivocal way of expressing one's objectivity before expressing an opinion.

Herdboys in Bushman shelter — Lesotho

Language

English South Africanisms (mostly from Afrikaans words)

Ach Shame	expression of sympathy, 'oh what a pity.'	*kloof*	narrow, steep valley
Bakkie	a pick-up truck.	*koppie*	hill
blikkiesdorp	mega-hicksville	*kraal*	livestock pen
Boet/ie	little brother	*Location*	a more acceptable word for a black township
bokdrolletjie	(pronounced 'bok-drollocky'), a ball of antelope dung—amazingly, a term of endearment between lovers	*Mealie*	maize, corn-on-the cob
		moere	to kill (usually to beat-up)
		moffie	homosexual (derogatory)
		mysie	(pronounced 'maisy'), miss, specifically, a young Afrikaans woman
braai or *braaivleis*	barbecue		
Brou	brother, as in 'listen my brother'	*O* or *Okie*	a bloke
		overseas	abroad
bundu	bush, as in 'he lives in the bush'	*Poort*	mountain pass
		poytjie	(pronounced 'poyky'), an iron pot or a dish slow-cooked in an iron pot
buttons	mandrax (a powerful narcotic)		
Café	a grocery store or mini market, almost never a place to have coffee.	*Robots*	traffic lights
		sif	horrible
camp	a fenced field	*sis*	'ugh'
China	Mate (cockney rhyming slang, brought over by the sailors)	*stompie*	cigarette butts
		Takkies	gym shoes or trainers
dagga	also marijuana	*tikkiedraai*	a country dance
dop	a drink	*toyi-toyi*	(pronounced 'toy-toy'), the distinctive running warrior dance seen during black political demonstrations
dorp	a small country town—hicksville		
drift	a river ford or crossing of a dry river-bed.		
		Tsotsi	black gangsters
frotte	disgusting or rotting, as in 'my mozzie bites went frotte'	*voetsek*	bugger off (this is the polite interpretation!)
fully	absolutely	*veld*	wild land
Howzit?	How d'you do?	*verlep*	tired, worn out
Izit?	'oh really?'(polite, not ironic, said very often)	*vetkoek*	little dough cakes
		vlel	marsh or swamp, even if dried-out
Just now, or *now-now*	Sometime in the indefinite future	*zol*	(pronounced 'zawl'), marijuana
jol	(pronounced 'jawl'), party		

Africaans Basics

yes	*ja*	Good evening/night	*goeienag*
no	*nee*	please	*asebblif*
Good morning	*goeie More*	thankyou	*dankie*
Good afternoon	*goeie Middag*	nice, lovely,	*lekker*

very	*baie*	station	*stasie*
where?	*weer?*	meat	*vleis*
what?	*wat?*	potatoes	*aardappels*
how?	*hoe?*	cheese	*kaas*
when?	*waneer?*	tree	*boom*
to know	*ken*	thorn	*doorn, or doring*
far	*ver*	a small stream	*spruit*
and	*en*	/pronounced 'sprate')	
from	*van*	game reserve	*wildtuin*
to speak	*praat*	beach	*strand*
Sir	*Meneer*	antelope	*bok*
Madam (also wife)	*Vrou*	little antelope	*bokkie*
I, myself	*Ek*	(term of endearment)	
You	*Jou*	pig	*vaark*
grandfather	*oupah*	horse	*perd*
(often a term of		sheep	*skaap*
address for an old man)		dog	*hond*
grandmother	*oumah*	cow	*koei*
uncle	*oom*	lion	*leeu*
(polite term of		leopard	*luiperd*
address for an older man)		impala	*rooibok*
left	*inks*	rhino	*rhenoster*
right	*regs*	zebra	*quagga*
room	*kamer*	elephant	*olifant*
information	*inligting*	cheetah	*jagtluiperd*
house	*huis*	warthog	*vlakvaark*
shop	*winkel*	vulture	*aasvoael*
town	*stad/dorp*	hippo	*seekoie*
office	*kantoor*	snake	*slang*
chemist	*apteek*	spitting cobra	*rhinkals*

Numbers

one	*een*	nine	*neghe*
two	*twee*	ten	*tien*
three	*drie*	twenty	*twintig*
four	*vier*	thirty	*dertig*
five	*vyf*	forty	*veertig*
six	*ses*	fifty	*vyftig*
seven	*sewe*	hundred	*honderd*
eight	*ag*		

Some Useful Afrikaans Phrases

What is your name?	*Wat is jou naam?*	How far is it to …?	*Hoe ver na?*
How much?	*Hoeveel?*	I cannot speak	*Ek kan nie*
Where is there a	*War is dar 'n petrol*	Afrikaans	*Afrikaans praat nie*
filling station?	*stasie?*		

Xhosa

Note that an 'X' is pronounced as a click.

hello	*molo*	cattle kraal	*ubuhlanti*
How are you?	*usaphila?*	water	*amazi*
I am fine, how are you?	*ndisaphila, uphila njani?*	ox	*inkabi*
		cow	*inkomo*
yes	*yebo*	horse	*ihashe*
no	*xha*	dog	*inja*
Where?	*phi?*	lion	*ngonyama*
Over there	*phaya*	leopard	*ngwe*
Your cattle are beautiful	*Zintle iinkomo zakho*	jackal	*mpungutye*
		rhino	*nkhombe*
sir	*umhlekazi*	wildebeest	*ingu*
madam	*inkhosikazi*	giraffe	*indlulamthi*
woman	*umfazi*	car	*imoto*
person	*umntu*	water	*amazi*
father (polite term of address for an older man)	*bawo*	the sea	*lwandle*
		Grahamstown	*Rini*
		Port Elizabeth	*Bhayi*
circumcised boy (in white clay during the initiation rites)	*umkhwetha*	East London	*Monti*
		Queenstown	*Khomani*
village	*umzi*	Johannesburg	*Rawuti*
hut	*in-dlu*	Cape Town	*Kapa*

Zulu

Note that although spellings vary, the Zulu greetings are also applicable to Siswati.

Hello (meaning 'I see you')	*sawubona*	leopard	*ingwe*
		rhino (white)	*umkhombe*
I'm fine, how are you?	*siyaphila* or *lungili, unjani?* (short for *injani gama lakho*)	rhino (black)	*ubhejane*
		elephant	*indlovu*
		buffalo	*inyathe*
We're fine	*iyaphila nathi*	hippo	*imvubu*
Where are you going?	*uyaphi?*	crocodile	*ingwenya*
		duiker	*impunze*
yes	*yebo*	red duiker	*umsumpe*
no	*cha*	fish eagle	*inkwazi*
Is it far?	*kulude yini?*	green lourie	*igwalagwala*
lion	*ibhubesi*		

South Sotho

(or Sesotho, as spoken in Lesotho by the BaSotho)

Hello father (greeting a man)	*lumela ntate*	I am well	*ke phela hantle*
		mountain	*thaba*
Hello mother (greeting a woman)	*lumela 'me*	water	*meetse*
		flock of sheep	*maku*
How are you?	*o phela joang?*	wild land	*lesoka*

1–3 million years ago	*Australopithecus africanus* present in South Africa (finds at Sterkfontein and Taung caves in Northwest Province).
90,000–1 million years ago	*Homo erectus* present in South Africa (finds at Makapansgat caves in Northwest Province).
30,000 years ago	*Homo sapiens* (possibly San culture) present in South Africa (rock engravings found near the Vaal River in Northwest Province).
2500 years ago	San tribes in Botswana began learning pastoralism from black African tribes, and this practice appeared in the Northern Cape, marking the beginning of Khoi culture.
1300–2000 years ago	Iron-using black peoples first appeared in Northwest province (possible ancestors of the modern Tswana people).
1415	Portuguese sack the Moorish city of Cueta in northwest Africa (near modern Tangier) and begin exploring south along Africa's west coast.
1488	Bartholomieu Dias rounds the Cape and enters Mossel Bay.
1490	Dias names the Cape of Good Hope.
1498	Vasco da Gama rounds the Cape, barters with and fires a cannon at the Khoi at Mossel Bay, then sails on to the East Indies.
1590–1650	English and Dutch sailors begin rounding the Cape and trading with the Khoi on their routes east.
1647	Dutch ship *Haarlem* wrecked off Table Bay. Crew survive by trading and hunting.
1652	Dutch East India Company founds relief station at Table Bay. Jan Van Riebeeck sent out with 100 colonists. Cape Town established.
1660s	Dutch settlement expands into present-day Winelands and West Coast.
1688	Huguenot settlers arrive from France. Beginning of SA wine cultivation. Beginnings of Cape Khoi resistance to white settlement.

Chronology

1690s	Emergence of the trekboer class, who penetrate Namaqualand, the Karoo and modern Garden Route.
1713	Smallpox epidemic devastates Cape Khoi—end of organized Cape Khoi resistance, beginning of their assimilation as a labour class.

1743	Swellendam district established in Overberg.
1750s	Trekboers begin establishing farms in Eastern Cape west of Fish River.
1770s	First clashes with Xhosa and trekboers. Major civil wars among Xhosa east of Fish River.
1795	Britain annexes the Cape Colony for the first time
1803	Britain gives the Cape back to Holland. First Griqua settlements in Northern Cape.
1806	Britain re-occupies Cape. Wars between the African clans in Natal.
1812	Fourth Frontier War of British against Xhosa under John Graham.
1815	Shaka becomes chief of Zulu and begins wars of conquest against other Natal clans, pushing some onto the highveld.
1819	Fifth Frontier War: Ndlambe Xhosa unsuccessfully attack Grahamstown.
1820	Arrival of British settlers in Algoa Bay—Port Elizabeth founded. Emergence of BaSotho leader Moshoeshoe, whose fortress at Thaba Bosiu near modern Maseru protects his people from wars on the highveld. British traders granted concession at Port Natal by Shaka.
1828	Kat River Colony for Eastern Cape Khoi founded on Ngqika Xhosa land. Shaka assassinated by his brother Dingane.
1830–2	Ndebele establish political mastery over highveld clans, except BaSotho.
1834–5	Ngqika Xhosa invade Cape Colony—Sixth Frontier War. British General Sir Harry Smith murders paramount Xhosa chief Hintsa and illegally annexes land between Keiskamma and Kei Rivers for Britain.
1836	Great Trek starts. Voortekkers under Andries Potgieter defeat Ndebele at Vegkop.
1845	Potgieter founds Ohrigstad (later Lydenburg republic) in Eastern Transvaal after treaty with the Pedi people.
1846	Seventh Frontier War (War of the Axe) between Ngqika Xhosa and British. London Missionary Society sends young Xhosa man Tiyo Soga to England for education (graduates from Edinburgh university 10 years later). Boers settle in Swaziland.
1838	Breakaway group of Voortrekkers arrive in Natal under Piet Retief. All but wiped out by Dingane, they rally to defeat the Zulu army at Blood River and drive Dingane north of the Tugela, founding the short lived Boer republic of Natal.
1839	Natal Boers assist Dingane's brother Mpande to usurp Zulu throne.
1843	Britain annexes Natal from Boers.
1848	Natal Boers trek north to highveld. Potgieter founds a new republic of Zoutpansberg at edge of Venda country. Zoutpansberg Boers begin slave raids against peoples of the Transvaal.
1850–53	Eighth Frontier War between Xhosa and British. Kat River Khoi join Xhosa, both suffer loss of independence in aftermath. Moshoshoe prevents Boers from annexing his BaSotho kingdom and sues for peace with British crown. Last San rock artist killed in Natal Drakensberg.

1854	Orange Free State proclaimed.
1856–7	Great Cattle killing among Xhosa. Tens of thousands starve.
1860	The three Boer republics in the Transvaal amalgamate to become the South African Republic (SAR). First Indian labourers arrive in Natal to cut the new sugar-cane plantations of the coast.
1865	Moshoeshoe fights off the Orange Free State Boers.
1867	Hopetown diamond found near Vaal River. Venda sack Schoemansdal and Boers driven from far Northern Transvaal for a generation.
1871	Kimberley diamond strike made. Britain annexes Griqualand West. Start of migrant labour tradition as black Africans travel to Kimberley to work the claims.
1877–8	Britain annexes SAR and defeats the Pedi nation in Eastern Transvaal. Ninth and last Frontier War ends Xhosa military resistance.
1879	Anglo–Zulu War. Britain annexes Zululand and imprison Ceteshwayo, the Zulu king.
1880–1	De Beers mining company founded in Kimberley by Cecil Rhodes. SAR Boers eject British occupation troops at battle of Majuba, beginning and ending the short-lived first Anglo–Boer War. Gun War in Basotholand (modern Lesotho) lost by British. Xhosa intellectual leader J. T. Jabavu founds the first African language newspaper.
1884	Basotholand becomes a British protectorate.
1886	Gold deposits found in the Witwatersrand. Johannesburg founded.
1890	De Beers company gains control of all Kimberley diamond mines. Cecil Rhodes becomes Cape Colony's Prime Minister.
1893	Gandhi arrives in Durban.
1894	*Uitlander* cause taken up by Johannesburg, Cape Press and London.
1895	Jameson Raid against Paul Kruger's government fails.
1899	Outbreak of Second Anglo–Boer War. Venda and Kgatla people of Northern Transvaal defeat Boers and drive them from Soutpansberg and northern lowveld.
1902	Boers surrender at Pretoria. End of Second Anglo–Boer War. Transvaal and Orange Free State recognized as British territory.
1903–7	South Africa's gold output exceeds 30 per cent of world total. Gandhi begins self-help project for poor Indians outside Durban, Natal.
1908	Gandhi organizes passive resistance campaign in protest at Indians being made to carry Pass Books.
1910	Union of South Africa created as a British Dominion. Ex-Boer general Louis Botha becomes its first Prime Minister.
1911	Laws passed to prevent blacks from holding skilled jobs in the mines.
1912	South African National Native Congress (SANNC) formed (the forerunner of the ANC).
1913	Over 20,000 white mineworkers strike in protest against mining companies' threat to overturn skilled labour colour bar. Natives Land Act passed, preventing blacks from becoming large landowners.

1914	South Africa enters the First World War. More mass strikes in Witwatersrand among white workers put down using 70,000 troops. National Party formed in Bloemfontein.Gandhi returns to India.
1916	Battle of Delville Wood in France, tens of thousands of South African troops killed. J. T. Jabavu founds first black university at Fort Hare.
1918	First World War ends. First strike by Africans—Johannesburg's 'bucket boys' (night-soil removers) negotiate a small wage increase. Underground right-wing *Afrikaner broederbond* founded.
1919	Jan Smuts becomes Prime Minister. First black trade union founded.
1920	70,000 blacks in the Witwatersrand strike over wage increases. Protests against Pass Laws across the Transvaal. Put down by police.
1922	General Strike of white workers over threatened mine closures and lifting of the skilled job colour bar brings the whole Witwatersrand to a halt. The army is sent in and over 200 strikers are killed.
1923	SANNC becomes the African National Congress (ANC).
1927	Compulsory racial segregation in cities.
1929	National Party leader Barry Hertzog wins general election.
1934	Hertzog and Smuts form joint United South National Party government—too liberal for hardline Afrikaners, who break away under D. F. Malan to form new National Party (NP).
1936	Cape black Africans lose their franchise.
1939	Outbreak of Second World War. Hertzog resigns, Smuts becomes new Prime Minister. Many right-wing Boers oppose British war effort.
1940–6	Blacks in the Witwatersrand organize a series of successful bus boycotts, pay strikes and squatter camp movements. Soon after the armistice, a black mineworkers' strike is broken by police.
1948	Right-wing, Afrikaner-led National Party wins general election. Era of official *apartheid* begins.
1949	Mixed marriages made illegal.
1950	Group Areas Act passed: blacks no longer to live in 'white' areas but in separate 'locations' townships).
1952	Reference Books (new pass books) to be carried by all non-whites.
1953	Education Act passed; blacks denied access to white universities.
1955	Sophiatown in Johannesburg razed. Black residents forcibly removed to new township of Soweto.
1956	Cape 'coloureds' disenfranchised. Government crackdown on all 'subversive' groups (including ANC and South African Communist Party) leads to mass 'Treason Trials', which last until 1960, effectively immoblizing resistance leadership.
1959	PAC formed.
1960	PAC leads massive anti-reference book protests in Witwatersrand. During demonstrations at Sharpeville, police open fire on unarmed protesters, killing over 200. Government declares State of Emergency

1960 cont'd	and bans ANC and PAC, whose leaders go into exile and form armed wings. Nelson Mandela becomes head of MK, military wing of the ANC and goes to Ethiopia for training.
1962–3	Mandela returns to South Africa and is arrested. MK leadership arrested at Rivonia near Johannesburg. Government witch-hunt nets most ANC and PAC leaders, who are imprisoned (including Mandela). Beginning of 'Silent Decade' for South African resistance to white rule.
1966	District Six in Cape Town razed. 'Coloured' inhabitants forcibly removed to new township of Mitchell's Plain on Cape Flats.
1969	Start of Steve Biko's 'Black Consciousness' movement.
1974	South African troops sent into Angola to destabilize revolutionary government there. Namibia occupied.
1976	Soweto uprising of black schoolchildren protests the forced learning of Afrikaans. Pitched battles with police and army. Government begins 'Tribal Homelands' policy to form 11 'bantustans' (lasts until 1981). Tens of thousands of blacks across the country forcibly removed from their farms and resettled in the 'homelands', losing their property.
1977	Steve Biko dies while in police detention in Port Elizabeth.
1982–3	Mass factional violence breaks out in Soweto, between supporters of PAC and Biko's 'Black Consciousness', continuing throughout 1980s.
1984	United Democratic Front (UDF) formed as an above-ground wing of banned ANC.
1985	National Union of Mineworkers (a black union) founded. Township violence intensifies. Government calls State of Emergency. Anyone suspected of subversive activity detained without trial, including many white UDF members.
1986	International Sanctions hit South African economy. Half-hearted reforms made by apartheid government include abolition of Pass Laws.
1988	F. W. de Klerk becomes Prime Minister. Pledges further reforms. Far-right breaks away to form Conservative Party. Militant Afrikaner military wing, the AWB, formed.
1990	Nelson Mandela freed from 27 years' detention.
1990–3	F. W. de Klerk pledges commitment to a democratic government. Political vigilante forces claim thousands of lives in townships and mineworkers' hostels—many people suspect involvement of government security forces (referred to as 'Third Force'). Political battling between ANC and Zulu-based Inkatha Freedom Party (IFP) reaches fever pitch in Natal Midlands. AWB pledge to go to war against any black-led government. Massive private disinvestment of whites as those who can leave the country, leave.
1994	Democratic elections held with almost no violence. IFP decides to support the elections at the last minute. ANC voted in by huge majority. 'Homelands' abolished and re-absorbed into South Africa. MK absorbed into South African army. Nelson Mandela becomes state president.

History/Early Accounts

Portuguese Voyages, Everyman Library 1960. Contains the journal of Vasco da Gama, who rounded the Cape and bartered with the Khoi people in 1497/8.

South African Journal 1834–1836, by Andrew Smith, edited by W.F. Lye, published for the South African Museum by A. A. Balkema, 1975. An epic, if understated, eye-witness journal from one of the first English-speakers to penetrate the highveld regions. Smith met and talked with such legendary figures as Moshoshoe, Mzilikazi, Waterboer.

Baines' Journal of Residence in Africa 1842–1853, Van Riebeeck Society 1964. Pictures and travelling diary by a remarkable adventurer who witnessed the last Frontier Wars of the Eastern Cape.

Travels in South Africa by Anthony Trollope (written (1877), Allan Sutton 1987. An objective travelogue dealing with social, political, geographical and economic issues in late 19th-century South Africa, humourously written, with a great eye for landscape and blessedly free from colonial racism.

The Shaping of South African Society 1652–1820, edited by R. Elphick and H. Giliomme. Clear commentary on the early white settlers and their effect on the Cape Khoi, San and Xhosa peoples.

A History of Natal, University of Natal Press, Brookes and Webb 1965. A straightforward, if rather colonial, account from the 1490s onwards.

Thank God We Kept the Flag Flying, Heinemann, 1974. An irreverent, deadly accurate look at the Siege of Ladysmith in 1900.

The Boer War Diary of Sol. T. Plaatje, Sphere Books, 1976. An insightful eye-witness account of the siege of Mafeking during the Second Anglo–Boer War (1899–1902). A dispassionate tale of British arrogance and double-dealing.

To the Bitter End by Emmanuel Lee, Penguin 1985. Informative pictorial history of the Second Anglo-Boer War.

The Boer War, by Thomas Packenham, Abacus 1979. Solid and informative.

The Scramble for Africa, by Thomas Packenham, Abacus 1991. Puts the 19th-century colonial confusion into its European perspective.

The Old Transvaal 1834–1899 by Cartwright and Cowan, Purnall 1978. Good photographic record, including the early towns andmain personalities, both black and white.

Reader's Digest History of South Africa—the Real Story, edited by Dougie Oakes and Chris Saunders PhD (Cape Town). A superbly readable, comprehensive history from the earliest pre-human remains to 1990, with different chapters by specific academic experts.

Further Reading

A New Illustrated History of South Africa, edited by Trewella Cameron and S. B. Spies, Human and Rousseau 1991.Very useful for those interested in the fate of the Cape Khoi.

George Grey and the Xhosa, by G. Weldon, Heinemann-Centaur 1993, a well-researched school text on the Xhosa people before, during and after the Frontier Wars, and the colonial policies affecting them.

People and Power, by Andrew Proctor, Academic Books (Harare) 1994. A good, straightforward and up-to-date account of the complex political and social upheavals that have shaped South Africa. Particularly good for understanding the rise of the Zulu empire.

Frontiers, by Noel Mostert, Pimlico Press, 1991. The history of the Xhosa people and the tragedy of the Frontier Wars; South African history traced with academic precision, and a master's pen, from prehistory to the present..An impassionedaccount, beautifully written.

Black Consciousness in South Africa by Steve Biko, Vintage Books 1979. The last writings before his death.

Wildlife and Natural History

Field Guide to the Mammals of Southern Africa by Chris and Tilde Stuart, New Holland 1992. Detailed treatment of characteristics and behaviour from the largest to the smallest. Good photographic identification guide. Handbook size.

Field Guide to the Snakes of Southern Africa by Bill Branch, New Holland 1993. Same format as above. Handbook size.

Field Guide to the Butterflies of Southern Africa by Ivor Migdoll, New Holland 1993. If you intend spending time in the southern Cape forests, pack this book. Handbook size.

Roberts Birds of Southern Africa by Gordon Maclean. The well-acknowledged twitcher's bible. Recommended by the Ornithological Society of Southern Africa. A large handbook.

The Plains of the Camdeboo, by Eve Palmer, Collins 1966—a beautifully written account of the natural history of the Eastern Karoo's rich semi-desert environment, centred around a farm near Graaff-Reinet. Fauna from fossils to *trekbokke* to the recolonization of the farmlands by wild animals. Entomologists and botanists will also find much here.

The Soul of the White Ant and *My Friends the Baboons* by Eugene Marais. Beautifully if a little whimisicially written in the 1930s by the poet, natural historian (and opium addict). For a sense of South Africa's fierce but gentle natural rhythms they are hard to beat.

Veld Plants of Southern Africa by Hobson, Jessop, Ginn and Kelly, Macmillan 1975. Everything you need to know, including medicinal/other uses. Coffee Table size.

Field Guide to the Trees of Southern Africa, by Eve Palmer, Collins 1977. Handbook size.

Landscapes and Geography

A Guide to the Rocks and Minerals and Gems of Southern Africa, by E. K. Macintosh, Struik 1976. Good colour pictures.

Land of Beauty and Splendour, by T. V. Bulpin, Reader's Digest 1976. Despite the corny title, a photographic coffee-table book that does justice to the southern African landscape.

The National Parks of Southern Africa, by Gordon and Bannister, New Holland 1992. Spectacular photographic record of the landscape, flora and fauna of most of the country's national parks (the latest ones, such as the Richtersveld and Vaalbos, are sadly absent) with an informative text. Coffee-table size.

The Living Deserts of Southern Africa by Barry Lovegrove, Fernwood Press 1993. A beautiful book, with a rare focus on the Namaqualand and Karoo semi-deserts, as well as the better-known Kalahari and Namib. Coffee-table size.

The Mountains of Southern Africa by Briston and Ward, Struik 1988. Not all the ranges are treated, but geological histories are accurate and photographs good. Coffee-table size.

This is South Africa by Peter Borchett, New Holland 1993. Despite the twee title, a good general introduction to the people, landscapes and wildlife. Coffee-table size.

Culture, Myth and Legend

Myths and Legends of Southern Africa, Penny Miller, T. V. Bulpin Publications 1979. A beautifully illustrated (by the author) guide to the rich mythology of the sub-continent, from Cape Malay and Afrikaans legends to Swazi, Zulu, Xhosa, Sotho, Venda and even up to the Herero of Namibia and the Mashona of Zimbabwe. Pure delight.

The Lost World of the Kalahari, by Laurens Van der Post, Penguin 1962. A moving account of the San people's besieged primeval culture.

Nisa, by Marjorie Shostak, Earthscan Publications Ltd 1990. A laudably straightforward record of the life-story of a San woman of the Kalahari, from childhood, through adolescence and sexual exploration to motherhood and maturity.

The White-Faced Huts, H. F. Sampson, 1979. Cases of witchcraft killings in the Transkei 1930–55 by an advocate of the supreme court. A strange read.

The Griquas of Griqualand by S. J. Halford, Juta and Co. Ltd, (no date printed)— a dispassionate, colonial account of the people of TransOrangia's wild past.

White Tribe Dreaming, by Marq De Villiers, Macmillan Canada, 1987. A look at the Afrikaner myth of might and right.

Soweto by Peter Magubane, Struik 1990. Everything from coal merchants and football teams to glue sniffing by one of South Africa's best photographers. Coffee-table size

Dorps, by Roger Ballen, Clifton Publications 1986. Photographs of modern poor white life in the *platteland* towns. Coffee-table size.

Language

Lumko—Self-Instruction Course in Xhosa, Rhodes University Press 1969. An all-purpose primer with some useful phrases.

A Southern Sotho/English Dictionary by P. A. Paroz, Morija Sesotho 1950.

Handbook of the Northern Sotho Language, J. C. Van Schaik, 1969.

Tsonga Proverbs, Junod and Jaques, Central Mission Press 1957. A sensitive collection of wise (and often humerous) sayings from the Tsonga people in both Tsonga and English.

Transvaal Ndebele Texts, N. J. Warmelo, 1930. Poems in Ndebele and translation.

Zulu Proverbs, by C. L. S. Nyembezi, Witswatersrand University Press 1954. Also much poetry here, with the Zulu texts translated and explained.

A Grammar of Afrikaans, by Bruce C. Donaldson, Mouton and Greyer 1980.

Art and Architecture

Major Rock Paintings of Southern Africa, edited by Tim Maggs. Indiana University Press 1979. Superb pictures and interpretive text as well as where to find the featured pictures.

Rock Engravings of Southern Africa, by Thomas A. Dowson, Witwatersrand University Press 1992. Similar to the above, plus some good sections on mythology.

South African Graphic Art and its Techniques by F. L. Alexander, 1974. Colonial to township art; all the big names plus some you've never heard of. Good reproductions.

The Life and Sculptures of Sister Joe Vorster by Naka Pitman, Hugh Keartland Publishing 1976. Remarkable photographic record of the artist's life-like sculptures of San people, some of which can be found in the Pretoria Art Museum.

The South African Mural, by Changuion and Mathews, Struik 1989. Mostly South Sotho and Ndebele house painting, with a good interpretive text.

The African Dream—the art of John Muafengo, by Orde Levinson (forward by Nelson Mandela, Thames and Hudson 1992. Mostly lino cuts by the well-known township artist, depicting scenes from rural life and wilderness to the spirit world and township life.

Cape Wine Homesteads, Hoefsloot and Parma, A. D. Donker 1980. All you need to know about Cape Dutch styles.

Historical Buildings in South Africa, by Desiree Picton-Seymour, Struik, 1988. Cape Dutch to Art Deco, plus where to find the best buildings.

Food and Wine

Leipoldt's Cape Cookery, by C. Louis Leipoldt, W. J. Flesch and Partners, 1976. Brief, but an acknowledged masterpiece on Cape Cuisine and *veldkos* by the famous poet, doctor and gourmet (who died in 1947 and is buried on the Pakhuis Pass in the Cape's Cedarberg Mountains). Recipes from ultra-traditional *boboties* to lion steak and tortoise in jelly.

Food from the Veld, by Fox and Young, Delta Books 1982. The complete veldkos.

The South Africa Wine Buyer's Guide by Dave Hughes, Struik Timmins 1993. Essential handbook for those really interested in what is produced where.

South African Literature, Prose

A Century of South African Short Stories, Marquard Ed., A.D. Donker 1978. All the big names and some of the little ones.

The Story of an African Farm, by Olive Schreiner, Penguin London 1981. First published in 1883, an authentic, if overly tortured tale of life and love on an isolated white farm in the arid, Biblical landscape of the Great Karoo.

Mafeking Road, by Herman Charles Bosman, Human and Rousseau. Short stories by the Afrikaans writer dealing with Boer life in the Western Transvaal.

From the Pit of Hell to the Spring of Life, by Daniel Kunene, Ravan Press 1986. Stories of apartheid in the mid 1960s and '70s seen through the black middle-class eye.

A Walk in the Night, by Alex La Guma, Heinemann 1967. An exceptional picture of poor 'coloured' life in Cape Town—a culture that usually goes unseen by white tourists, yet is responsible for Cape Town's whole atmosphere of fatalistic *joie de vivre.*

The Lying Days by Nadine Gordimer, Penguin 1980. Her first novel, set in the early 1950s in bohemian Johannesburg..Written before Sharpeville, this was one of the first books to set out the injustices of apartheid,

A Dry White Season, by Andre Brink, W. H. Allen 1969. A young Afrikaner tries to investigate the circumstances of a black friend's death while in police detention, and finds himself in the dark, confused world of Soweto at the height of apartheid oppression.

Cry the Beloved Country, by Alan Paton, Scribner and Sons 1948. Written the year the first apartheid government came to power—the story of a Zulu minister from Natal coming to Johannesburg to look for his lost son.

I Write What I Like, by Steve Biko, Penguin 1988. A burningly perceptive look at black endeavour and white obstruction by the man who gave his life for his beliefs.

Waiting For the Barbarians, by J. M. Coetzee, Penguin 1988. Allegorical tale of the impending end of apartheid written as if on an imperial outpost of the ancient world.

All One Horse, by Breyton Breytonbach, Faber and Faber 1990. Surreal stories by the man regarded by many as South Africa's best white writer.

You Can't Get Lost in Cape Town, by Zoe Wicomb, Virago 1987. A 'coloured' girl student from Namaqualand's tragic involvement with a white boyfriend.

My Traitor's Heart, by Rian Malan, Bodley Head 1990. Powerfully written, nothing in here is fiction. Those who wish to understand modern South Africa must read this book.

South African Literature, Poetry

The Penguin Book of South African Verse, edited by Jack Cope and Uys Krige, Penguin 1968. From early San and Khoi songs, to 19th-century Zulu, Sotho and Xhosa praise poems, to more contemporary black and white poetry.

Lithoko—Sotho Praise Poems, by Damane and Saunders, Clarendon Press 1974. Stirring warrior poems from the old oral tradition.

Musho!, Zulu Popular Praises, by Gunner and Gwala, Michigan University Press 1991. More stirring stuff.

South Africa in Poetry, edited by Johan Wyk and Pieter Conradie, Owen Burgess Publishing 1988. Comprehensive anthology from prehistoric oral traditions to the present.

Black Mamba Rising, an anthology, Worker Resistance and Culture Publications, University of Natal, for Cosatu Workers' Cultural Local, 1986. South African worker poets in struggle. Powerful, bitter poems of black humiliation and anger under apartheid.

Prey, by Dennis Brutus, published in the anthology *Voices of 20th-Century Africa,* Faber and Faber 1988, is more considered. A 'coloured' English teacher born in Zimbabwe, Brutus was interned, shot and beaten, but survived to write some superb poetry

Travel Literature, Narrative

Jock of the Bushveld by Sir Percy Fitzpatrick, Longmann Green 1909. A beautifully illus-trated account of the life of a freebooting hunter in the lowvveld of the late 19th century.

Forty Years in Africa by Major Tudor Trevor, Hurst and Blackett 1932. A very colonial view, but engagingly written and providing an eye-witness account of the adventurous life of a young Englishman on the Transvaal frontier back in the 'earlies'.

Bushveld Doctor, by the doctor, poet and gourmet C. Louis Leipolt, Lowry 1989. Written in 1989. This is Leipoldt's account of his time as inspector of schools in the Eastern Transvaal lowveld in the 1920s and 30s. Combines an unromantic journal of the poverty and sickliness of the lowveld Afrikaner families of the time with chapters on birds, beasts and magic. A must for travellers in the Eastern Transvaal.

The Electronic Elephant by Dan Jacobsen, Hamish Hamilton 1994. Engaging look at the dry regions of Northern Cape and Northwest Province in footsteps of early missionaries.

Travel Literature, Practical

Discovering Southern Africa by T. V. Bulpin, T. V. Bulpin Publications 1992. An enter-taining, informative introduction to almost every town and region in the sub-continent No places to stay or eat, but excellent background information. Large handbook size.

Field Guide to the National Parks and Nature Reserves of Southern Africa by Chris and Tilde Stuart, Struik 1993. Useful list of every single protected wildlife area, with maps, access information, fauna and some flora, hiking trails , accommodation. Handbook size.

Mike Lundy's Best Walks in the Cape Peninsula, Struik 1991. Superb, detailed informa-tion on foot forays in the mountains and on the beaches. Small handbook.

Day Walks in and around Cape Town by Tim Anderson, Struik 1990. Well laid out and informative set of walks in old Cape Town and the Winelands. Small handbook size.

The Complete Guide to Walks and Trails in Southern Africa, by Jaynee Levy, Struik 1993. A must for anyone who wants to get out into the veld, the trails for foot, horse and canoe are described in detail. Heavy for a backpack, but worth consulting before setting off.

A Backer's Guide to Lesotho, by Russell Suchet, Sani Lodge Publications 1993. An in-depth and sensitive guide for the budget traveller and hiker—the author has spent many years travelling the 'kingdom of the clouds'. Small handbook size.

The Swaziland Jumbo Guide by Hazel Hussey, Hussey and Co. Publications 1992. A good all-round guide to what's available at all budgets, with some very well informed cultural background. Handbook size.

A Guide to the Guest Farms and Country Lodges of Southern Africa, Struik 1994. Very useful for mid-budget travellers. Covers all areas.

Index

chronology 638–43
Ciskei 282, 290, 300, 312–22, 583
cities, safety 25
Citrusdal 197–8
Clanwilliam 195–6
Clanwilliam Dam 196
Clanwilliam Wildflower Garden 196
Clarens 448
Clifton 88, 122
climate 14
    see also under individual places
climbing 29
Clocolan 449
Club Mykonos 188
coasts, landscapes 85–6
Cockscomb Conservation Area 233
Coetzee, J.M. 72
Coffee Bay 343, 345
Cold Bokkeveld 140, 163
Coleford Nature Reserve 388
Colenso, John 379, 394
Colesberg 64, 254–5
Colesberg Kopjie 40, 270, 271
coloureds *see* Cape coloureds
Compassberg 254
conservation 82–4
Constantia **114–15**
    Buitenverwachting 115
    Groot Constantia 63, 96, 114–15, 136,
        141
    Klein Constantia 115
Constantia Nek Forest 116
Constantiaberg 114
consulates 15–16
Coon Carnival 13, 121, 125
copper mining 259
Council for Non-European Trade Unions
    (CNETU) 493
Cradock 251, 255
Cradock, Sir John 255, 268
credit cards 23
creed 53–4
crime 25
Croc World 371
Crocodile River 539
Cronje, General 600
Crossroads (shanty town) 90
Cruikshank, George 104
culture 55–63
Cumming, Gordon 82
currency 22–3, 611, 616, 622, 631
customs formalities 4
Cwebe Nature Reserve 342–3
cycling, mountain 30

Da Gama, Vasco 36, 71, 204, 206,
    352
dagga (marijuana) 15
Damara 622
Damaraland 625, 626
Danger Point 176
Daniell, Samuel 66
Danielskuil 276
Dargle 387
Darling 188, **202–3**

Day of Reconciliation (Conciliation) 382,
    405, 553
Day of the Vow (Covenant) 54, 382,
    405, 522–3
De Beers 40, 270–1, 491, 492, 515
De Buys, Conraad 249–50, 286, 582
De Doorns Wine Estate 167
De Hoek Forest Station 580
De Hoop Nature Reserve 172, **178**, 179
de Klerk, F.W. 48
De la Rey, General Koos 272, 595, 596,
    599
De Mond Lagoon 176
De Mond Nature Reserve 177
De Overberger 181
De Rust 231–2
De Vasselot Nature Reserve 217
De Wet, General Christian 445–6, 456
Debengeni Falls 573
deep sea diving 366
Degas, Edgar 381
Delaire Wine Estate 146
Delheim Wine Estate 145
Denorben 310
Devil's Peak 88, 110, 111, 113, 127
Devon Valley 146
diamond mining 40–1, 260, **270–1**,
    444, 535
Dias, Bartholomieu 35, 206, 305
Dias Reef Base Camp 558
Diepwalle State Forest 213, 214, 220
Dingaan 467
Dingane 39, 159, 354–5, 359, 372–3,
    378, 389, 404–5, 410, 534
Dingane's Kraal 410
Dinigswayo 353–4
divining 74, 469
Dlinza State Forest 410
Domba Dance 13, 584, 587
Donkin, Sir Rufane 291
Doorndraai Nature Reserve 570, 571,
    572
Doornkloof Farm 525–6
Doornkloof Nature Reserve 255, 256
Dordrecht 311
Dordrecht's Kloof 311
Doringbaai 192
Double Drift Game Reserve 305, 317
The Downs 574
drag-hunting 28
Drakensberg 249, 282, 308–12, 349
    Eastern Transvaal 540–7
    foothills 567, **572–7**
    Natal 391–400
Drakensberg Escarpment 439
Drakenstein Valley 152–3
drinks 19–21
drugs, dagga (marijuana) 15
Du Toit, Jakob D. (Totius) 69, 600
Du Toit's Kloof 165–6
Du Wenaar, Renier 452–3
Dube, John 42
Duiker Island 126
Duiwelskloof 573, 575
Dukuduku State Forest 412

Dundee 419, 420
Dunn, John 405, 411
Durban **358–70**, *360*
    activities 366
    beaches 358, 362–3
    Beachwood Mangroves Nature
        Reserve 365
    Bluff Nature Reserve 364
    Botanic Gardens 364
    City Centre 363–4
    Colonial 363-4
    eating out 367–8
    entertainment 368–9
    getting around 359, 361
    Golden Mile 358, **362–3**
    Grey Street Mosque 363
    history 355, **359–61**
    hospitals 362
    Kenneth Stainbank Nature
        Reserve 364–5
    markets 358–9, 365–6
    nightlife 369–70
    Old Fort 364
    Oriental Durban 358, 363
    Phoenix Park Settlement (Peace
        Commune) 361, 363
    Pigeon Valley Nature Reserve 365
    rickshas 363
    shopping 365
    Silverglen Nature Reserve 365
    tourist information 362
    townships 366
    Victoria Street Market 363
    where to stay 366–7
D'Urban, Sir Benjamin 355, 359
Durnford, Major (later Colonel)
    Anthony 394, 406
Dutch 36–8, 92–4, 206, 250, 353, 402
Dutch East India Company 36–8, 92–4,
    105, 142, 173, 201, 249, 283, 286,
    353, 359
Duwasib 627
Dwars River 162
Dwesa Nature Reserve 342, 346
Dzata 63, 581

East Griqualand 376–7
East London 327–9
Eastern Cape 281–346, *284–5*
Eastern Transvaal 531–60
Ebeneezer Dam Nature Reserve 545,
    573, 575, 576
Ecca Nature Reserve 305
Echo Caves 544–5
Edendale 377
Eglington, Charles 562
Eland's Bay 191
Eland's Post 318
Elandskloof Pass 180
Elandslaagter battlefield 420
Elandsvlei 243
electricity 15
Elim **177**, 181
Elliot 311
Ellisras 570

Wildlife Guide

Antelopes

Eland

H: Bushveld, mopane, Karoo scrub, savannah and mountain fynbos.

D: All regions.

Largest member of the antelope family, up to 160cm at the shoulder, eland are adapted to most habitats and occur in large or small groups or pairs. Only males have horns.

Greater Kudu

H: Bushveld and Karoo scrub.

D: Common everywhere but W Cape. Not present around Cape Town.

The country's second largest antelope. Occurs in small family and bachelor herds or as lone male. Only males have horns.

Waterbuck

H: Water margins in bushveld, mopane and savannah.

D: Natal, Transvaal, Swaziland and E Cape.

Large, easily recognized by white band at thoat and rump. Only males have horns.

Sable

H: Bushveld and mopane woodland.

D: Natal, Transvaal and Swaziland.

The most regal of antelopes, sable are aggressive and have been known to kill lions. Occur in small family herds.

Roan

H: Bushveld and mopane woodland.

D: Natal, Swaziland, N & E Transvaal.

Closely related to the sable, this large browsing antelope is one of Africa's rarest. Now making a comeback after intensive conservation programmes.

Bushbuck

H: Hardwood forest and wooded kloofs.

D: W&E Cape, Natal, Swazi, E&N Trans. Shy, but aggressive if cornered. Only males have horns.

Blesbok

H: Montane and highveld grassland.

D: All regions except E Cape.

Common grazer occurring singly or in groups. Large herds on highveld.

Bontebok

H: Lowland fynbos.

D: W Cape.

Distinguished from blesbok by unbroken blaze. Once rare, now recovering.

Rhebok

H: Fynbos and montane grassland.

D: W & E Cape, Natal, E Transvaal.

Shy mountain antelope recognized by its grey coat and straight horns.

Duiker

H: All habitats.
D: All regions.
Largest of the small antelope. An adaptable creature that can live close to man. Has two sub-species, the red and blue duiker.

Oribi

H: Grassland and woodland.
D: Natal, Swaziland, E & N Transvaal.
Not often sighted. Distinguished from the duiker by its lighter build and pale colouring.

Nyala

H: Bushveld and mopane.
D: Natal, Swaziland, E & N Transvaal.
Often mistaken for kudu, nyala males are darker brown with a long neck ruff; females are smaller and more delicate. Only males have horns.

Gemsbok

H: Bushveld, savannah, grassland, desert.
D: All regions, except mountains.
One of the largest antelope, gemsbok (or Cape oryx) are aggressive and tough, able to withstand extremes of temperature and to go without water for long periods.

Grysbok

H: Fynbos and Karoo scrub.
D: W Cape.
Smaller, and shyer than the common duiker, the grysbok is rarely sighted.

Steenbok

H: Bushveld, grassland and savannah
D: All regions. Rare in W Cape.
This elegant little grazer is similar to the grysbok, but is a richer brown in colour.

Today's large herds hardly compare with the millions that roamed the country before hunting severely reduced their numbers. Some species, such as the bluebuck, were even made extinct. However, game farming and conservation have resulted in a major recovery.

Klipspringer

H: Montane fynbos.
D: All regions, but only in upland areas.
Compact mountain-dweller, known for its agility on steep gradients.

...edbuck

Marshland and fynbos.
All regions.
varieties: mountain and swamp.
males have horns. Small herds.

Impala

H: Bushveld and mopane.
D: E Cape, Natal, Swaziland, Transvaal.
Occur singly or in groups; only males have horns.

Springbok

H: Bushveld, Karoo scrub, mopane and fynbos.
D: All regions.
South Africa's national emblem. Thrives in arid conditions.

Suni

H: Lowland forest.
D: E Transvaal and Natal.
South Africa's smallest antelope, about 30cm at the shoulder, the suni is a tiny, nocturnal forest-dweller.

Smaller Predators

Bat-Eared Fox

H: All habitats bar mountains.

D: All regions.

Usually spotted in pairs at dawn or dusk, the bat-eared fox is an inquisitive creature, and will often allow you to approach quite near. Often seen with or near jackals, especially in the Kalahari.

Brown Hyena

H: All habitats—a very adaptable creature.

D: All regions. Most common in N Cape.

A shy, nocturnal hunter and scavenger. Smaller than the spotted hyena. Seen singly or in pairs. Not dangerous to m Much persecuted, but currently making a comeback.

Honey Badger

H: All habitats except mountains, but prefers bushveld.

D: All regions. Rare in W Cape.

Closely related but not a true badger, the honey badger or ratel is nocturnal but can sometimes be seen digging for termites at dusk. Larger than a true badger, this creature is about a metre long.

Varying in size from the cheetah (smallest of Africa's big cats) to the diminutive genet, the country has numerous smaller predators. Species absent from these pages include the small Cape fox, the blackfooted wildcat, the Cape clawless otter, and the dwarf, grey and water mongoose.

Genet

H: All habitats.

D: All regions.

Strictly nocturnal, the genet is a member of the cat family. Hunts small rodents and birds.

African Civet

H: All habitats except desert and high uplands.

D: All regions where habitat is suitable.

Roughly the size of a hunting dog, the civet is a nocturna hunter and scavenger, usually seen singly.

Cape Wild Dog

H: Bushveld and Kalahari.

D: A few reserves in Natal, Transvaal and N Cape.

Recovering from intense persecution, the populations of the Cape wild dog (or hunting dog) have now stabilized and large packs can be seen in the Kruger National Park, the Umfolozi and the Kalahari Gemsbok National Park. Somewhere between a hyena and a jackal in size, hunting dogs are highly social and work out elaborate techniques for tackling large prey such as buffalo.

Spotted Hyena
H: Kalahari thornveld, bushveld, savannah.
D: Natal, Transvaal, Kalahari.
Scavenges by day, hunts in packs by night. Will tackle
large prey and drive lions off a kill. Dangerous to man.

Jackal
H: All habitats except mountains.
D: All regions; densest in Transvaal, Natal
and Kalahari reserves.
A small scavenger seen singly or in pairs.

Cheetah
H: Bushveld, savannah and grassland.
D: Natal, Transvaal, N Cape and some E Cape reserves.
Ruthlessly shot by stock farmers, cheetah are making a slow comeback through
conservation and re-introduction, though still officially endangered.

Caracal or African Lynx
H: All habitats.
D: All regions.
One of South Africa's most common predators, it is shy and
seldom spotted by the casual observer. Over a metre from head
to tail, the caracal has been much persecuted by farmers—
especially the sheep farmers of the Karoo—but still thrives.

Serval
H: Kalahari thornveld, bushveld and Drakensberg.
D: Natal, Transvaal, Swaziland.
About the same size as the caracal, the serval
is equally shy and difficult to spot.

Plains Game & Large Herbivores

'Plains game' is an old hunting term for all African herbivores. Here, it deals with the non-antelope ungulates (though the cow-like wildebeests, hartebeests and tsessebes are related to antelopes), and takes in South Africa's two species of wild pig.

Sneaked in at the bottom of the page are hippo and crocodile— though not officially plains game, their ranges do overlap.

Tsessebe
H: Bushveld and savannah.
D: Natal, E & N Transvaal, Swaziland.
Known in East Africa as the topi, the tsessebe is endangered in South Africa. Occurs in small groups.

Red Hartebeest
H: Bushveld, savannah, grassland and Kalahari.
D: E & N Cape, Natal, Transvaal, OFS, Swaziland.
A highly territorial animal that thrives in both wet arid climates. Occurs singly or in small groups.

Black or Whitetailed Wildebeest
H: Grassland and fynbos.
D: W, N & E Cape, OFS, Natal Drakensberg.
Very handsome, with horse-like movement, the black wildebeest usually occurs in small groups or as a lone male.

Warthog
H: Bushveld, savannah and grassland.
D: All regions except W Cape.
Often seen in small groups by day, warthogs are shy, despite their large tusks, and are a favourite prey of leopards. When alarmed, they hold their tails erect like radio aerials.

Blue Wildebeest
H: Bushveld, savannah, grassland and mopane woodland.
D: All regions except W Cape.
One of Africa's most ecologically successful ungulates, the blue wildebeest occurs in small family groups in wooded country, and in vast herds on grassland.

Bushpig
H: Forest and woodland.
D: All forested regions.
A secretive, nocturnal feeder, the bushpig's shy habits belie its aggressive nature, as many hunters will testify. Rarely seen by casual observers.

Nile Crocodile
H: Lowland, subtropical rivers and lakes.
D: E & N Transvaal, Natal, some reserves in E Cape.
Once endemic to all but the coldest rivers, crocodiles are now confined to certain reserves. Very dangerous to man, Nile crocodiles can grow to over 3 metres.

Giraffe

H: Bushveld and mopane woodland.

D: Natal, N & E Transvaal, E Cape, Swaziland.

The largest (up to 18 feet high) and most elegant of African mammals, giraffe occur singly or in small herds. Sometimes preyed on by lions, the giraffe can deliver a powerful kick and runs fast, despite the slow-motion effect produced by its long limbs.

Cape Mountain Zebra

H: Montane fynbos and grassland.

D: Mountain ranges in W Cape and Great Karoo.

Unique to South Africa, the Cape mountain zebra can be identified by its long, slightly ass-like ears. Once hunted almost to extinction, populations are now stable.

Burchell's Zebra

H: Bushveld, savannah and grassland.

D: E Cape, Natal, OFS, Swaziland, Transvaal.

More elegant, and with smaller ears than the Cape mountain zebra, Burchell's zebra occurs in family groups and large herds, often in company with blue wildebeest.

Hippopotamus

H: Rivers, lakes and swamps.

D: E Cape, Natal, E & N Transvaal.

Once common in all lowland rivers, now confined to reserves. Very dangerous to man, especially if disturbed while grazing on the river bank at night.

Miscellaneous

Aardvark

H: All habitats.
D: All regions.

A bizarre-looking insectivore the size of a small pig ('aardvark' means 'earth pig'), this nocturnal animal is very common, but almost never seen. Its large holes are easier to spot, however, and are often shared with warthog, hyena and porcupine.

South Africa's wealth of fauna makes it impossible to include every mammal species. Missing from these pages are the samango monkey, which lives in the hardwood forests of the Eastern Cape and Natal, the several species of hare (Africa has no rabbits) and the huge variety of rodents, as well as the large bat family. However, shown here are those most commonly sighted, and the most singular smaller mammals of the veld and forest.

Aardwolf

H: All habitats.
D: Most common in Karoo, N Cape and OFS; rare in W Cape.

Related to the hyena, the aardwolf is a nocturnal insectivore, unjustly persecuted by farmers; now rare, making a come-back in Northern Cape reserves.

Pangolin

H: All habitats.
D: All regions.

Almost never seen, this rare, secretive nocturnal insectivore is related to the ant-eaters and armadilloes of the Americas.

Yellow Mongoose

H: Throughout.
D: All regions.

Often spotted hunting close to roadsides in daylight, this is the most common of South Africa's mongoose species. Hunts mainly small reptiles and insects. Sometimes kills snakes, including Cape cobra.

Porcupine

H: All habitats.
D: All regions.

Far larger than its European and N American counterparts, the African porcupine is a nocturnal insectivore whose spines can easily pierce flesh and hide. With such protection, porcupine often share holes with brown hyena and warthog.

Meerkat or Suricate

H: Dry grassland, bushveld, savannah.

D: All arid regions, but most common in N Cape.

The smallest of the mongoose family, meerkats are predominantly insectivores. Highly social and inquisitive, these animals are easily tamed if caught young.

Ground Squirrel

H: Grassland and savannah.

D: N Cape, OFS, W Transvaal.

Alert, quick-moving creatures, ground squirrels often catch the eye with their mad chasing games. Particularly common in the Kalahari.

Vervet Monkey

H: Woodland, forest and bushveld.

D: All regions where even partially wooded.

Occurs singly or in groups. Often quite bold, despite being preyed on by both mammal and bird predators. A regular thief of stray objects at campsites.

Bushbaby

H: Forest and sub-tropical woodland.

D: N Natal, E Transvaal, Swaziland lowveld.

Tiny nocturnal primates, bushbabies are usually heard rather than seen, as their night-scream is piercingly loud.

Chacma Baboon

H: Uplands, forest, woodland and bushveld.

D: All regions.

One of South Africa's commonest large mammals, baboons are highly intelligent and can be aggressive if used to people. In the wild, they are shy.
Their loud barking and human shouts are often heard by hikers. Usually occur in large family groups headed by a chief male. Old males sometimes live alone.

Water Birds

Cattle Egret
H: Near wetlands.
D: All regions.
Rather unspectacularly named considering its beauty, the cattl egret is a sub-species of heron an may often be seen i farmlands, hunting for grubs near livestock—hence its name.

Jackass Penguin
H: Rock promontories and coves.
D: W Cape Coast.
A small bird. The name derives from its harsh cry.

Cape Gannet
H: Promontories and islands.
D: W Cape Coast.
Lives in large colonies.

Darter
H: All wetlands.
D: All regions.
Also known as River Cormorant.

Malachite Kingfisher
H: Lakes and rivers.
D: All regions.
Smallest of S. Africa's kingfishers.

Hammerkop
H: Lakes and rivers. **D:** All regions.
A distinctively southern African bird, the hammerkop is related to the stork family and preys on fish and amphibians.

Egyptian Goose
H: Lakes and rivers.
D: All regions.
Occurs in pairs or small flocks.

Sacred Ibis
H: Lakes and rivers.
D: All regions except N Cape.
Sacred ibis live in large colonies close to water, though they sometimes fly far afield to feed.

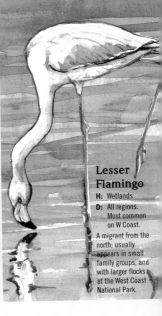

Lesser Flamingo
H: Wetlands
D: All regions. Most common on W Coast.
A migrant from the north; usually appears in small family groups, and with larger flocks at the West Coast National Park.

Smaller Birds

Bishop Bird
H: Reeds.
D: Wetlands in all regions.
A distinctive, brightly coloured little bird that lives in colonies and is highly territorial.

Whydah
H: Bushveld and grassland.
D: Natal, Transvaal, Swaziland.
Although a small bird, the male's tail grows to about half a metre. Often spotted on telegraph wires.

Little Bee-Eater
H: Sandy cliffs & riverbanks.
D: Natal, E & N Trans, Swazi.
One of several South African species of bee-eater, these birds inhabit small colonies and are usually seen in pairs hunting flying insects.

Lilac-Breasted Roller
H: Sub-tropical bushveld.
D: E & N Trans, Swaziland.
Usually seen singly on telegraph poles or roadside trees.

Yellow Hornbill
H: Forest, woodland and bushveld.
D: E Cape, Natal, Swazi, Transvaal.
Largest of the smaller birds. Usually occurs in small groups. Swooping flight.

Martial Eagle
H: Bushveld and savannah.
D: Transvaal, Natal, Swaziland, E Cape.
Preys mostly on other birds, especially guinea fowl.

Fish Eagle
H: All wetlands.
D: All regions.
Takes fish from the water.
Known for its piercing cry.
Quite commonly seen.

Crowned Eagle
H: Hardwood forest.
D: E Cape, Natal, E & N Trans.
A rare raptor. Mostly preys on monkeys and snakes.

Black Eagle
H: Upland regions.
D: All regions.
Common in Cape ranges. Preys mostly on rock hyrax.

ale Chanting Goshawk
Thornveld and bushveld.
Transvaal, Natal and Bushmanland.
e of the largest small raptors.
te the red eyes.

Cape Eagle Owl
H: Rocks, cliffs and forests.
D: All, but commonest in eastern regions.
Main prey: spring hares.

Secretary Bird
H: Bushveld, grassland and savannah.
D: All except W Cape.
Standing over a metre tall, the secretary bird mainly preys on snakes.

Bateleur Eagle
H: Kalahari thornveld and bushveld.
D: Transvaal and Bushmanland.
Easy to spot as it flies low over bush. Can take prey up to small antelope calves.

Crimson Shrike
H: Bushveld
D: Natal, E & N Trans, Swazi.
Brightest-coloured of the shrike family, the crimson shrike shares the gruesome family habit of impaling large insects and small reptiles on sharp thorns, to be eaten at leisure.

Paradise Flycatcher
H: Subtropical forest and woodland.
D: Natal, E Transvaal, Swaziland.
A rare, distinctive forest bird.

Crested Hoepoe
H: Bushveld and savannah.
D: All regions. A migrant from Europe.

Orange-breasted Sunbird.
H: Fynbos.
D: W Cape, E Cape & Natal Drakensberg.
Most spectacular of the iridescent sunbirds.

Grey Lourie
H: Bushveld. **D:** E & N Transvaal.
A regular sight at bush camps.

Large Birds

Lammergeier

D: E Cape, Natal, E Trans Drakensberg.

A rare vulture. Drops bones onto rocks to extract the marrow.

Cape Vulture

H: Rocky outcrops.

D: E Cape, Natal, Transvaal, Swaziland. Isolated colonies in OFS and W Cape.

Cape vultures have been shot out of most areas except nature reserves. However farmers, realizing their 'clean-up' value, are persecuting them less and numbers are rising.

Kori Bustard

H: Kalahari thornveld and grassland.

D: Cape and Northwest Province.

A very large bird, and a common sight in the nature reserves of its range.

Saddlebill Stork

H: Wetlands, lake and rivers.

D: N & E Trans, Zululand.

A spectacular but rare resident. Most common in St Lucia Nature Reserve and the Kruger.

Crowned Crane

H: Wetlands, well-watered grasslands.

D: All regions, but most common in the east.

Known for its beautiful courtship dance and easily identified by its distinctive crest.

White Stork

H: Grasslands near water.

D: W & E Cape, summers only.

This European migrant congregates in large flocks, especially in the Garden Route region.

Blue Crane

H: Congregates by lakes and dams.

D: All regions—nomadic migrant.

South Africa's national bird, the blue crane turns up everywhere, but never for long.

Wattled Crane

H: Wetlands.

D: E & N Transvaal.

One of South Africa's rarest (and largest) birds, the wattled crane is confined to a few lowveld reserves.